Cultural Studies and Communications

Edited by

James Curran
David Morley
Valerie Walkerdine

A member of the Hodder Headline Group
LONDON • NEW YORK • SYDNEY • AUCKLAND

First published in Great Britain in 1996 by
Arnold, a member of the Hodder Headline Group
338 Euston Road, London NW1 3BH
175 Fifth Avenue, New York, NY 10010

Distributed exclusively in the USA by
St Martin's Press Inc.,
175 Fifth Avenue, New York, NY 10010

British Library Cataloguing in Publication Data
A catalogue entry for this book is available from the British Library

Library of Congress Cataloging-in-Publication Data
Cultural studies and communications/edited by James Curran,
Valerie Walkerdine and David Morley.
p. cm.
Includes bibliographical references and index.
ISBN 0-340-65268-3 (hardcover): $59.95
ISBN 0-340-61417-X (pbk.): $16.95
1. Culture. 2. Communication. 3. Postmodernism. 4. Popular culture. 5. Mass media. I. Curran, James. II. Walkerdine, Valerie. III. Morley, David.
HM101.C8925 1996
306—dc20 95-36959

ISBN 0 340 61417 X (Pb)
ISBN 0 340 65268 3 (Hb)

Composition in 10/11 Times by York House Typographic Ltd, London
Printed and bound in Great Britain by J. W. Arrowsmith Ltd, Bristol

Contents

List of Contributors

James Curran, Professor of Communications, Goldsmiths' College, University of London.

Christine Geraghty, Lecturer in Communications, Goldsmiths' College, University of London.

Paul Gilroy, Reader in Sociology, Department of Sociology, Goldsmiths' College, University of London.

Stuart Hall, Professor of Sociology, Open University.

Dick Hebdige, Dean of Critical Studies at the California Institute of the Arts, Los Angeles.

David Hesmondhalgh, Lecturer in Communications, Goldsmiths' College, University of London.

Sarah Kember, Lecturer in Communications, Goldsmiths' College, University of London.

Angela McRobbie, Reader in Sociology, University of Loughborough.

David Morley, Reader in Communications, Goldsmiths' College, University of London.

Gareth Stanton, Temporary Lecturer in Communications, Goldsmiths' College, University of London.

Yvonne Tasker, Senior Lecturer in Media Studies, Chichester Institute of Higher Education.

Valerie Walkerdine, Professor of the Psychology of Communication, Goldsmiths' College, University of London.

Acknowledgements

Thanks are due to the following for permission to reproduce material from copyright sources:

Elsevier Science B.V., Amsterdam, The Netherlands, for David Morley, 'Populism, Revisionism and the "New" Audience Research', *Poetics*, **21**(4): pp. 329–44, 1992.

Dick Hebdige for 'The Impossible Object: Towards a Sociology of the Sublime', *New Formations*, **1**: pp. 47–76, spring 1987.

Speech Communication Association for Stuart Hall, 'Signification, Representation, Ideology: Althusser and the Post-Structuralist Debates', *Critical Studies in Mass Communication*, **2**: pp. 91–114, 1985. Used by permission.

Sage Publications for James Curran, 'The New Revisionism in Mass Communication Research: A Reappraisal', *European Journal of Communication*, **5**: pp. 130–64, June 1990.

Note on cover illustration

R. B. Kitaj's work has often taken its inspiration from books (and their covers). Here we return the compliment, in so far as the painting chosen echoes many of the themes of this book.

From the bottom right-hand corner, the face of Walter Lipmann (author of the classic early work on journalism and the media, *Public Opinion*, 1922) looks out across a complex, nightmare landscape of traps, escape ladders, stairways and double perspectives. In the centre, figures taken from two different popular films of the 1930s (Margaret Kennedy/Basil Dean's *The Constant Nymph* and Alfred Hitchcock's version of John Buchan's thriller, *The Thirty-nine Steps*) confront (or escape) from each other across an uncertain space. Kitaj himself has said that ‘the picture augurs the arriving storm in Europe, preceded by refugee movie people in Hollywood’. Here we are offered a rich criss-crossing of themes and elements from both popular and avant-garde cultures: an admixture which this volume of essays explores.

General Introduction

This book is avowedly multivocal, and multi- if not interdisciplinary by definition, containing, as it does, a body of work produced at the interface of cultural studies and media/communications studies. The authors all either work in, or have close connections with, the Department of Media and Communication Studies at Goldsmiths' College. However, while we share many things, we also have our differences, of intellectual background, inclination and belief. People working in communications and cultural studies at Goldsmiths' do not belong to a single, identifiable tradition. There is no canonical text which hovers as an unspoken presence in the department, no author who is accepted as a unique source of inspiration. Instead, what characterizes the department and thus contributors to this book as a whole, is an unusual degree of catholicism, an ecumenical orientation that finds virtue in different modes of analysis and different intellectual traditions. Thus, the book's three editors, James Curran, David Morley and Valerie Walkerdine, have each come to this field of study via quite different intellectual routes (being initially trained in the disciplines of history, sociology and psychology, respectively) and those differences continue both to inflect our contemporary work, and to inform our debates with one another. Indeed, our department, as a whole, can usefully be defined by reference to the plurality of perspectives represented within it, including staff variously drawn from backgrounds in English, Film Studies and Anthropology. All bring valuable perspectives into play, which enrich our work and enliven our internal arguments.

We can, and do, disagree, sometimes passionately: theoretically, empirically, politically. During the course of this book, the reader will become familiar with debates, among other things, about whether audiences and consumers of popular culture are active or passive, whether the media work 'top-down' or 'bottom-up' and whether psychoanalysis has something interesting to offer to cultural theory, or whether its presence always betokens determinism, or psychic essentialism. These differences play out some of the key debates in the field today. But not only that: the reader will find in the volume the inclusion of topics which have moved far beyond the founding issues of cultural studies in its inception. While Gilroy's arguments about the Black presence in cultural studies have justifiably become internationally famous, the introduction here of concerns around new technologies and around childhood, for example, serves to put right other, thus far notable absences, while many of the chapters introduce, into existing fields, debates that would have been unthinkable 20 years ago. What, then, does cultural studies look like now? What significance does it have in an age which is no longer so concerned with grand theorizations and totalizing categorizations of 'ideology', of 'the subject', or of 'woman', for example? And now? Do the differences assembled here reveal only a fashionable postmodern fragmentation and 'anything goes' of cultural studies? We like to think not, but that the debates which have come to destabilize the older, heady certainties of Grand Theory signify the raising of new political concerns which have now become pressing. Shifting identities, cyborg subjectivities, women's magazines staffed by graduates of cultural studies – these phenomena turn us away from our previous certainties and debates and signal the search for new ways of understanding our cultural and political futures.

If we are committed to maintaining a plurality of perspectives within the department, there are also distinctive areas of overlap and clusterings of background and interest, which are equally apparent in the book. While we would be opposed, in principle, to the kind of originary narrative which would position the Centre for Contemporary Cultural Studies at the University of Birmingham as the sole authenticating source of what is now the highly diversified international field of cultural studies, it is none the less significant that, besides a contribution from CCCS's ex-Director, Stuart Hall, the book also contains work by four ex-Birmingham graduates: Paul Gilroy, Dick Hebdige, Angela McRobbie and David Morley. To be sure, each of these authors now has a distinctive trajectory in their own work, but they deal differently with what is none the less, to some extent, a common inheritance.

Among the book's other authors there are a further series of convergences, parallels and dialogues around issues of mutual concern. Thus, over and above the scaffolding of the book's principal divisions into sections on cultural theory, production and consumption, a number of cross-cutting thematics can also be identified. Valerie Walkerdine's considerations of issues of subjectivity, psychoanalysis and gender are closely linked, at different points, with the contributions made by Angela McRobbie, in relation to the role of young women's magazines in the acquisition of gender identities and with Sarah Kember's address to questions of feminism, science, technology and representation. At the same time, feminist film theory is also the shared informing background to Christine Geraghty's essay on the different theorizations of the 'female audience' in film and television studies.

Another point of convergence for a number of the authors, in all three sections, concerns the question of postmodernism and/or postmodernity. The contributions by David Hesmondhalgh and Yvonne Tasker both address not simply the question of postmodernism as a cultural matrix, but also the material issue of the extent to which the industrial structures of post-Fordism can be seen to have transformed patterns of production (especially 'independent production') in the cultural industries. From a different perspective, David Morley's essay, in Section I, attempts to open up a series of conceptual and definitional issues concerning what is at stake in discussions of the postmodern, while James Curran offers an overview of how these perspectives have been developed within mass communications research in recent years. Dick Hebdige and Gareth Stanton are both concerned with debates about postmodern sensibilities. In Hebdige's case this is achieved by articulating to these debates a detailed contemporary case-study; in Stanton's, by means of a complex historical tracing of the long-buried anthropological roots of recent methodological debates in cultural studies, concerning postmodern ethnography.

Cultural studies can perhaps claim to have made its most significant contributions to the study of the realm of consumption (if, on the whole, at the price of neglect of the field of cultural production). However, the last few years have also seen an important set of debates concerning the question of whether, under the influence of cultural studies, an older fetishization of institutions (and then of texts) has latterly been replaced by an overly populist and romanticized model of media consumption within the wider terrain of media studies at large. These are crucial themes in James Curran's essay in Section I and in his 'debate' with David Morley in Section III.

The politics of identity have been a notable focus of concern and interest over the last few years. Alongside the contributions to those debates from a range of feminist perspectives already noted here, the essays by Stuart Hall and Paul Gilroy are linked by their common address both to issues of identity, at a broad theoretical level and, more specifically, by their focus on questions of race and ethnicity in contemporary cultural theory and politics. In this connection, it is true to say that despite the presence of Hall and Gilroy's essays, overall, the book perhaps remains still more locked up in a British-based, national (and to that extent ethnocentric) perspective than we, as editors, might ideally have wished to achieve. But then, there are also many other limits to the book, as there are, inevitably, to any collection. One could reasonably regret the absence of more material on both class and gay politics, on the State, on globalization – the list would be a long one!

Having offered an internal commentary on the themes and threads from which the tapestry of this book has been woven, it perhaps remains to say a little, by way of a theoretical placing of the book, about the broader external field of contemporary debates concerning cultural studies and cultural politics. Putting matters schematically, it would seem that debates in this field, in the 1990s, have been characterized by a significant backlash against what is often now argued to be a regrettable slide, by many cultural studies scholars, into some kind of uncritical populism. Clearly this is the backdrop to the 'debate' between James Curran and David Morley, in Section III of this book, concerning the strengths and weaknesses of what Curran calls the 'new revisionism' in cultural studies. On a broader canvas, this kind of criticism of cultural studies, for uncritically celebrating supposed 'rituals of resistance' (which, on closer inspection, turn out to be no more than over-romanticized celebrations of an illusory form of consumer sovereignty) has been advanced, most notably by McGuigan (1992), Harris (1992) and Tester (1995). Usually the work of John Fiske is used as the prime evidence of the overall inanity of cultural studies' (supposed) 'pointless populism' (Seaman 1992). Behind this style of criticism, there often lurks (to resort to a 'depth' model of analysis, thus discrediting ourselves with many postmodernists!) a larger, longer and most peculiar teleology, latterly also deployed in attacks on cultural studies' supposed populism by Frith (1991) and Frith and Savage (1992). In astonishing *post hoc ergo propter hoc* style, these critics note that John Fiske's work came after the early work of CCCS; that then came the work of the *New Times* theorists, clustered around *Marxism Today*; and that this was followed by a great deal of postmodern theory, much of it of a culturally relativist kind. It is then often noted that this, in turn, was followed by the work of such luminaries as Toby Young and Julie Burchill, in the pages of their *Modern Review*. Notwithstanding the scorn which Young and Burchill themselves express towards academic cultural studies, the critics listed above then (characteristically) tend to reverse the chain of associations. Thus, postmodern cultural relativism, à la *Modern Review*, is held to have been an inevitable consequence of the *New Times* work; which itself is held to have followed ineluctably from the 'uncritical populism', to which, apparently, work at CCCS was (somehow) bound to lead (with added hindsight). Thus, as McLennan (1994: 128) puts it, according to this perspective, 'once Gramscianism took off, postmodernism was a logical consequence'. To which we (some of us at least) might reasonably reply: tosh!

Not surprisingly, this is a teleology we would reject, as it bowdlerizes the complex and many-branched history of work in this field, in order to shoehorn the facts into the footwear of the critics' choice. We do not see work in cultural studies as usefully (or reasonably) reduced to this kind of singular (and unrepresentative) strand of narrative; nor do we see cultural studies as arriving at some singular (and logically inescapable) conclusion. It is the variety, and the open-endedness of work in this field (and in this book) that we value most highly.

That said, it is also worth indicating what, in its editors' view, at least, this book is (and is not) trying to do. It is not an attempt to produce an authoritative definition (or 'canon') of either cultural studies or media/communication studies. There are, in our opinion, quite enough texts already in existence attempting to do that – in the case of cultural studies, there are already collections of this type, edited by Barker and Beezer (1992), Blundell et al. (1993), During (1993), Gray and McGuigan (1993) and, most tombstone-like of all, Grossberg et al. (1992). In the case of media/communications studies, the field is also already well supplied by the collections edited by Allen (1987), Alvarado and Thompson (1990), Corner and Hawthorn (1994), Curran and Gurevitch (1991), Mellencamp (1990) and Newcomb (1995). Our own ambition has been both more limited – in so far as we have attempted to produce a genuinely introductory text – and more hybrid – in so far as we have aimed to produce a collection that indicates how a *range* of cultural studies perspectives might be applied in the study of issues in the field of media and communications. It is for our readers to now judge how far we have (or have not!) succeeded in that endeavour.

References

ALLEN, R. (ed.), 1987: *Channels of Discourse*. London: Methuen.

ALVARADO, M. and THOMPSON, J. (eds.), 1990: *The Media Reader*. London: British Film Institute.

BARKER, M. and BEEZER, A. (eds.), 1992: *Reading into Cultural Studies*. London: Routledge.

BLUNDELL, V., SHEPHERD, J. and TAYLOR, I. (eds.), 1993: *Relocating Cultural Studies*. London: Routledge.

CORNER, J. and HAWTHORNE, J. (eds.), 1994: *Communication Studies*. London: Edward Arnold.

CURRAN, J. and GUREVITCH, M. (eds.), 1991: *Mass Media and Society*. London: Edward Arnold.

DURING, S. (ed.), 1993: *The Cultural Studies Reader*. London: Routledge.

FRITH, S., 1991: 'The Good, the Bad and the Indifferent: Defending Popular Culture from the Populists', *Diacritics*, 21 (4).

FRITH, S. and SAVAGE, J., 1992: 'Pearls and Swine: Intellectuals and the Mass Media', *New Left Review*, 198.

GRAY, A. and MCGUIGAN, J. (eds.), 1993: *Studying Culture*. London: Edward Arnold.

GROSSBERG, L., NELSON, C. and TREICHLER, P. (eds.), 1992: *Cultural Studies*. London: Routledge.

HARRIS, D., 1992: *From Class Struggle to the Politics of Pleasure*. London: Routledge.

MCGUIGAN, J., 1992: *Cultural Populism*. London: Routledge.

MCLELLAN, G., 1994: 'Margins and Centres', *Sites*, 28.

MELLENCAMP, P. (ed.), 1990: *The Logics of Television*. Bloomington, IN: Indiana University Press.

NEWCOMB, H. (ed.), 1995: *Television: The Critical View*. Oxford: Oxford University Press.

SEAMAN, W., 1992: 'Active Audience Theory: Pointless Populism', *Media, Culture and Society*, 14.

TESTER, K., 1995: *Media, Culture and Morality*. London: Routledge.

SECTION I

Cultural Theory

Introduction

It is impossible to say that the diverse pieces in this section have come to stand for what has become of cultural studies, in its transformation from a small centre in an English department of an English university to a phenomenon spread across the English-speaking world. However all of the authors in their different ways map important contemporary debates for understanding the field of cultural theory and practice.

Stuart Hall engages with a debate which became central from the 1970s onwards, that is, the place of the subject in theories of ideology. This essay sets out clearly the important developments in the way in which the French Marxist philosopher, Louis Althusser, proposed a study of ideological processes as modes of signification and representation which work on unconscious processes, producing the very depths of our subjective experience, even those which we like to imagine are most unique and original. Hall takes us carefully through Althusser's famous 'Ideological State Apparatuses' essay and discusses both parts, the relation of ideology to the economy and the latter part on subjectivity, in an important way. But he does more than this. In a move characteristic of much of the writing in this section he exemplifies his argument with details from the story of his own formation as 'Negro', 'immigrant', 'Coolie' and 'black', and demonstrates the complexity of the practices in which those designations are produced and have their effects.

This is a move further extended by Paul Gilroy's discussion of the place of theories of identity in cultural studies. For Gilroy it was the struggles of the early cultural theorists – Thompson, Hoggart, Williams – which so featured these authors' attempts to engage with class. What was Gilroy, a black British man, to make of these concerns with their slight and shady references to questions of the diaspora and a black presence in Britain? For Gilroy these concerns unsettle an easy account of identity and put him at odds with a simple American-style identity politics, in which identity is presented as such an unproblematic political concept, assuming that it is easy to know who you are. If identity formation is what Gilroy calls a 'chaotic process', it does not seem like the stable foundation upon which to build a political practice; yet any political practice which ignores this chaos will not succeed in the present uncertainty.

It is David Morley who presents for us a reading of the complexity of the present political conjuncture, as signalled by debates about the postmodern. What is it? When did it happen, in what fields, or are the theorists of the postmodern simply mistaking certain features of modernity? If, as Baudrillard suggests, the simulacrum has taken over from the real, then all is postmodern play, excess: we are in a global village in which anything is possible. We try to make some sense in all of this about just how to understand the real effects of Reagan's timing of the bombing of Libya to coincide with the early evening news. The complex construction of such events as media events, argues Morley, does not imply the evacuation of a sense of reality but certainly renders it far more complex than has been suggested by previous theorizations.

Dick Hebdige's beautiful and lyrical essay, 'The Impossible Object: Towards a Sociology of the Sublime' takes examples of the cultural practices and products prized by neighbours in his street in North London – an old Thunderbird car for example – and places his readings of and feelings for these objects and practices against a nihilistic postmodernity which would argue for the end of everything. The complex longing to be and to have something different, unique, a sublime, desired, object is set against a too easy certainty that mass production and consumption has changed all that. What does the longing signify and what can it tell us about the condition of being a subject in the late twentieth century? A man's loving restoration of and devotion to this nostalgic object cannot easily be dismissed as a fashionable retro. After all the owner of the car is a Turkish Cypriot mechanic, not a wealthy young yuppie. It is to explore the place of this longing, a homesickness for something else, something which cannot easily be defined or spoken, which Hebdige explores so eloquently.

So what of subjectivity in all of this? It is psychology which has claimed to have the measure of the subject, but which has had little place in the theorization of subjectivities within cultural studies. Taking us through the debates about psychology, psychoanalysis and ideology, Valerie Walkerdine interweaves a narrative about the formation of the mind of the masses and the necessity for its transformation as central to debates about political transformation. Exploring the idea of 'the working class' as both a historical creation and fictional object, she examines what it might mean to take the psychic consequences of oppression seriously.

The idea of the masses lies at the heart of mass communications research and it is this which James Curran surveys in detail. While Hebdige points to the detail of his neighbour's fetishization of an old car, Curran argues for the need to move out from that level of analysis to one which can explore the social relation of the media and audiences in the wider relations of power. Neither a top-down nor bottom-up approach to the media can adequately grasp the complexity of the relation that Curran argues needs to be addressed. Thus, cultural theorists continue to link the complexity of the formation of political and media cultures to the theorization of the lives of people themselves.

1

Signification, Representation, Ideology: Althusser and the Post-Structuralist Debates

Stuart Hall

Althusser persuaded me, and I remain persuaded, that Marx conceptualizes the ensemble of relations which make up a whole society – Marx's 'totality' – as essentially a complex structure, not a simple one. Hence, the relationship within that totality between its different levels – say, the economic, the political, and the ideological (as Althusser would have it) – cannot be a simple or immediate one. Thus, the notion of simply reading off the different kinds of social contradiction at different levels of social practice in terms of one governing principle of social and economic organization (in classical Marxist terms, the 'mode of production'), or of reading the different levels of a social formation in terms of a one-to-one correspondence between practices, are neither useful nor are they the ways in which Marx, in the end, conceptualized the social totality. Of course a social formation is not complexly structured simply because everything interacts with everything else – that is the traditional, sociological, multifactoral approach which has no determining priorities in it. A social formation is a 'structure in dominance'. It has certain distinct tendencies; it has a certain configuration; it has a definite structuration. This is why the term 'structure' remains important. But, nevertheless, it is a complex structure in which it is impossible to reduce one level of practice to another in some easy way. The reaction against both these tendencies to reductionism in the classical versions of the Marxist theory of ideology has been in progress for a very long time – in fact, it was Marx and Engels themselves who set this work of revisionism in motion. But Althusser was the key figure in modern theorizing on this question who clearly broke with some of the old protocols and provided a persuasive alternative which remains broadly within the terms of the Marxist problematic. This was a major theoretical achievement, however much we may now, in turn, wish to criticize and modify the terms of Althusser's breakthrough. I think Althusser is also correct to argue that this is the way the social formation is in fact theorized in Marx's '1857 Introduction' to the *Grundrisse* (1953/1973), his most elaborated methodological text.

Another general advance which Althusser offers is that he enabled me to live in and with *difference*. Althusser's break with a monistic conception of

Marxism demanded the theorization of difference – the recognition that there are different social contradictions with different origins; that the contradictions which drive the historical process forward do not always appear in the same place, and will not always have the same historical effects. We have to think about the articulation between different contradictions; about the different specificities and temporal durations through which they operate, about the different modalities through which they function. I think Althusser is right to point to a stubbornly monistic habit in the practice of many very distinguished Marxists who are willing, for the sake of complexity, to play with difference so long as there is the guarantee of unity further on up the road. But the significant advances over this delayed teleology are already to be found in the '1857 Introduction' to the *Grundrisse*. There, Marx says, for example, of course all languages have some elements in common. Otherwise we wouldn't be able to identify them as belonging to the same phenomenon. But when we have said that we have only said something about language at a *very* general level of abstraction: the level of 'language-in-general'. We have only begun our investigation. The more important theoretical problem is to think the specificity and difference of different languages, to examine the many determinations, in concrete analysis, of particular linguistic or cultural formations and the particular aspects which differentiate them from one another. Marx's insight that critical thought moves away from abstraction to the concrete-in-thought which is the result of many determinations, is one of his most profound, most neglected epistemological propositions, which even Althusser himself somewhat misinterprets (cf. 'Notes on the "1857 Introduction" ', Hall 1974).

I have to add right away, however, that Althusser allows me to think 'difference' in a particular way, which is rather different from the subsequent traditions which sometimes acknowledge him as their originator. If you look at discourse theory,[1] for example – at post-structuralism or at Foucault – you will see there, not only the shift from practice to discourse, but also how the emphasis on difference – the plurality of discourses, the perpetual slippage of meaning, the endless sliding of the signifier – is sometimes pushed *beyond* the point where it is capable of theorizing the necessary unevenness of a formation, or even the 'unity in difference' of a complex structure. I think that is why, whenever Foucault seems to be in danger of bringing things together (such as the many epistemic shifts he charts, which all fortuitously coincide with the shift from *ancien régime* to modern in France), he has to hasten to assure us that nothing ever fits with anything else. The emphasis always falls on the continuous slippage away from any conceivable conjuncture. I think there is no other way to understand Foucault's eloquent silence on the subject of the state. Of course, he will say, he knows that the state exists; what French intellectual does not? Yet, he tends to posit it as an abstract, empty space – the state as gulag – or as the other of an equally abstract notion of resistance. His protocol says: 'not only the state but also the dispersed microphysics of power', his practice often privileges the latter and ignores the former.

Foucault is, however, quite correct, of course, to say that there are many Marxists who conceive the state as a kind of single object; that is, as simply the unified will of the committee of the ruling class, wherever it is currently meeting today. From this conception flows the necessary 'yoking together' of everything. I agree that one can no longer think of the state in that way. The state is a contradictory formation which means that it has different modes of action, is active in many different sites: it is pluricentred and multidimensional. It has very distinct and dominant tendencies but it does not have a singly inscribed class character. On the other hand, the state remains one of the crucial sites in a modern capitalist social formation where political practices of different kinds are *condensed*. The function of the state is, in part, precisely to bring together or articulate into a complexly structured instance, a range of political discourses and social practices which are concerned at different sites with the transmission and transformation of power – some of those practices having little to do with the political domain as such, being concerned with other domains which are nevertheless articulated to the state, for example, familial life, civil society, gender and economic relations. The state is the instance of the performance of a condensation which allows that site of intersection between different practices to be transformed into a systematic practice of regulation, of rule and norm, of normalization, within society. The state condenses very different social practices and transforms them into the operation of rule and domination over particular classes and other social groups. The way to reach such a conceptualization is not to substitute difference for its mirror opposite, unity, but to rethink both in terms of a new concept – articulation.[2]

Hence we have to characterize Althusser's advance, not in terms of his insistence on 'difference' alone – the rallying cry of Derridean deconstruction – but instead in terms of the necessity of thinking unity *and* difference; difference *in* complex unity, without this becoming a hostage to the privileging of difference as such. If Derrida (1977) is correct in arguing that there is always a perpetual slippage of the signifier, a continuous 'deference', it is also correct to argue that without some arbitrary 'fixing', or what I am calling 'articulation', there would be no signification or meaning at all. What is ideology but, precisely, this work of fixing meaning through establishing, by selection and combination, a chain of equivalences? That is why, despite all of its faults, I want to bring forward to you, not the proto-Lacanian, neo-Foucauldian, pre-Derridean, Althusserean text – 'Ideological State Apparatuses' (Althusser 1970/1971), but rather, the less theoretically elaborated but in my view more generative, more original, perhaps because more tentative text, *For Marx* (Althusser, 1965/1969): and especially the essay 'On Contradiction and Overdetermination' (pp. 87–128), which begins precisely to think about complex kinds of determinacy without reductionism to a simple unity. (I have consistently preferred *For Marx* to the more finished, more structuralist *Reading Capital* (Althusser and Balibar 1968/1970): a preference founded not only on my suspicion of the whole Spinozean, structuralist-casuality machinery which grinds through the latter text but also on my prejudice against the modish intellectual assumption that the 'latest' is necessarily 'the best'.) I am not concerned here with the absolute theoretical rigour of *For Marx*: at the risk of theoretical eclecticism, I am inclined to prefer being 'right but not rigorous' to being 'rigorous but wrong'. By enabling us to think about different levels and different kinds of determination, *For Marx* gave us what *Reading Capital* did not: the ability to theorize about real historical events, or particular texts (*The German Ideology*, Marx and Engels 1970), or particular discursive formations (humanism) as determined by more than one structure (i.e. to think the process of overdetermination). I think 'contradiction' and 'overdetermination' are very *rich* theoretical concepts – one of Althusser's happier 'loans' from Freud and Marx; it is not the case, in my view, that their richness has been exhausted by the ways in which they were applied by Althusser himself.

The articulation of difference and unity involves a different way of trying to conceptualize the key Marxist concept of determination. Some of the classical formulations of base/superstructure, which have dominated Marxist theories of ideology, represent ways of thinking about determination which are essentially based on the idea of a necessary correspondence between one level of a social formation and another. With or without immediate identity, sooner or later, political, legal, and ideological practices – they suppose – *will* conform to and therefore be brought into a necessary correspondence with what is – mistakenly – called 'the economic'. Now, as is by now *de rigueur* in advanced post-structuralist theorizing, in the retreat from 'necessary correspondence' there has been the usual unstoppable philosophical slide all the way over to the opposite side; that is to say, the slippage into what sounds almost the same but is in substance radically different – the declaration that there is 'necessarily no correspondence'. Paul Hirst, one of the most sophisticated of the post-Marxist theorists, lent his considerable weight and authority to that damaging slippage. 'Necessarily no correspondence' expresses exactly the notion prevalent in discourse theory – that nothing really connects with anything else. Even when the analysis of particular discursive formations constantly reveals the overlay or the sliding of one set of discourses over another, everything seems to hang on the polemical reiteration of the principle that there is, of necessity, no correspondence.

I do not accept that simple inversion. I think what we have discovered is that there is *no necessary correspondence*, which is different; and this formulation represents a third position. This means that there is no law which guarantees that the ideology of a group is already and unequivocally given in or corresponds to the position which that group holds in the economic relations of capitalist production. The claim of 'no guarantee' – which breaks with teleology – also implies that there is no necessary *non*-correspondence. That is, there is no guarantee that, under all circumstances, ideology and class can never be articulated together in any way or produce a social force capable for a time of self-conscious 'unity in action' in a class struggle. A theoretical position founded on the open-endedness of practice and struggle must have, as one of its possible results, an articulation in terms of *effects* which does not necessarily correspond to its origins. To put that more concretely: an effective intervention by particular social forces in, say, events in Russia in 1917, does not require us to say either that the Russian revolution was the product of the whole Russian proletariat, united behind a single revolutionary ideology (it clearly was not); nor that the decisive character of the alliance (articulation together) of workers, peasants, soldiers and intellectuals who did constitute the social basis of that intervention was guaranteed by their ascribed place and position in the Russian social structure and the necessary forms of revolutionary consciousness attached to them. Nevertheless 1917 did happen – and, as Lenin surprisingly observed, when 'as a result of an extremely unique historical situation, *absolutely dissimilar* currents, *absolutely heterogeneous* class interests, *absolutely contrary* political and social strivings ... merged ... in a strikingly "harmonious" manner.' This points, as Althusser's comments on this passage in *For Marx* reminds us, to the fact that, if a contradiction is to become 'active in the strongest sense, to become a ruptural principle, there must be an accumulation of circumstances and currents so that whatever their origin and sense ... they "fuse" into a ruptural unity' (Althusser 1965/1969: 99). The aim of a theoretically informed political practice must surely be to bring about or construct the articulation between social or economic forces and those forms of politics and ideology which might lead them in practice to intervene in history in a progressive way – an articulation which has to be *constructed* through practice precisely because it is not guaranteed by how those forces are constituted in the first place.

That leaves the model much more indeterminate, open-ended and contingent than the classical position. It suggests that you cannot read off the ideology of a class (or even sectors of a class) from its original position in the structure of socio-economic relations. But it refuses to say that it is impossible to bring classes or fractions of classes, or indeed other kinds of social movements, through a developing practice of struggle, into articulation with those forms of politics and ideology which allow them to become historically effective as collective social agents. The principal theoretical reversal accomplished by 'no necessary correspondence' is that determinacy is transferred from the genetic origins of class or other social forces in a structure to the effects or results of a practice. So I would want to stand with those parts of Althusser that I read as retaining the double articulation between 'structure' and 'practice', rather than the full structuralist causality of *Reading Capital* or of the opening sections of Poulantzas' *Political Power and Social Classes* (1968/1975). By 'double articulation' I mean that the structure – the given conditions of existence, the structure of determinations in any situation – can also be understood, from another point of view, as simply the result of previous practices. We may say that a structure is what previously structured practices have produced as a result. These then constitute the 'given conditions', the necessary starting point, for new generations of practice. In neither case should 'practice' be treated as transparently intentional: we make history, but on the basis of anterior conditions which are not of our making. Practice is how a structure is actively reproduced. Nevertheless, we need both terms if we are to avoid the trap of treating history as nothing but the outcome of an internally self-propelling structuralist machine. The structuralist dichotomy between 'structure' and 'practice' – like the related one between 'synchrony' and 'diachrony' – serves a useful analytic purpose but should not be fetishized into a rigid, mutually exclusive distinction.

Let us try to think a little further the question, not of the necessity, but of the possibility of the articulations between social groups, political practices and ideological formations which *could* create, as a result, those historical breaks or shifts which we no longer find already inscribed and guaranteed in the very structures and laws of the capitalist mode of production. This must not be read as arguing that there are no tendencies which arise from our positioning within the structures of social relations. We must not allow ourselves to slip from an acknowledgement of the relative autonomy of practice (in terms of its effects), to fetishizing Practice – the slip which made many post-structuralists Maoists for a brief moment before they became subscribers to the 'New Philosophy' of the fashionable French Right. Structures exhibit tendencies – lines of force, openings and closures which constrain, shape, channel and in that sense, 'determine'. But they cannot determine in the harder sense of fix absolutely, guarantee. People are not irrevocably and indelibly inscribed with the ideas that they *ought* to think; the politics that they *ought* to have are not, as it were, already imprinted in their sociological genes. The question is not the unfolding of some inevitable law but rather the *linkages* which, although they can be made, need not necessarily be. There is no guarantee that classes will appear in their appointed political places, as Poulantzas so vividly described it, with their number plates on their backs. By developing practices which articulate differences into a collective will, or by generating discourses which condense a range of different connotations, the dispersed conditions of practice of different social groups *can* be effectively drawn together in ways which make those social forces not simply a class 'in itself', positioned by some other relations over which it has no control, *but also* capable of intervening as a historical force, a new kind of social subject, capable of establishing new collective projects.

These now appear to me to be the generative advances which Althusser's work set in motion. I regard this reversal of basic concepts as of much greater value than many of the other features of his work which, at the time of their appearance, so riveted Althusserian discipleship: for example, the question of whether the implicit traces of structuralist thought in Marx could be systematically transformed into a full-blown structuralism by means of the skilful application to it of a structuralist combinatory of the Levi-Straussean variety – the problematic of *Reading Capital*; or the clearly idealist attempt to isolate a so-called autonomous 'theoretical practice'; or the disastrous conflation of historicism with 'the historical' which licensed a deluge of anti-historical theoreticist speculation by his *epigoni*; or even the ill-fated enterprise of substituting Spinoza for the ghost of Hegel in the Marxist machine. The principal flaw in E.P. Thompson's (1978) anti-Althusserean diatribe, *The Poverty of Theory*, is not the cataloguing of these and other fundamental errors of direction in Althusser's project – which Thompson was by no means the first to do – but rather the inability to recognize, *at the same time*, what real advances were, nevertheless, being generated by Althusser's work. This yielded an undialectical assessment of Althusser, and incidentally, of theoretical work in general. Hence the necessity, here, of stating simply again what, despite his many weaknesses, Althusser accomplished which establishes a threshold behind which we cannot allow ourselves to fall. After 'Contradiction and Overdetermination', the debate about the social formation and determinacy will never again be the same. That in itself constitutes 'an immense theoretical revolution'.

Ideology

Let me turn now to the specific question of ideology. Althusser's critique of ideology follows many of the lines of his critique of general positions in the classical Marxist problematic sketched above. That is to say, he is opposed to class reductionism in ideology – the notion that there is some guarantee that the ideological position of a social class will always correspond to its position in the social relations of production. Althusser here is criticizing a very important insight which people have taken from *The German Ideology* (Marx and Engels 1970) – the founding text of the classical Marxist theory of ideology: namely, that ruling ideas always correspond to ruling class positions; that the ruling class as a whole has a mind of its own which is located in a particular ideology. The difficulty is that this does not enable us to understand why all the ruling classes we actually know have actually advanced in real historical situations by a variety of different ideologies or by now playing one ideology and then another. Nor why there are internal struggles, within *all* the major political formations, over the appropriate 'ideas' through which the interests of the dominant class are to be secured. Nor why, to a significant degree in many different historical social formations, the dominated classes have used 'ruling ideas' to interpret and define their interests. To simply describe all of that as *the* dominant ideology, which unproblematically reproduces itself and which has gone on marching ahead ever since the free market first appeared, is an unwarrantable forcing of the notion of an empirical identity between class and ideology which concrete historical analysis denies.

The second target of Althusser's criticism is the notion of 'false consciousness' which, he argues, assumes that there is one true ascribed ideology per class, and then explains its failure to manifest itself in terms of a screen which falls between subjects and the real relations in which subjects are placed, preventing them from recognizing the ideas which they ought to have. That notion of 'false consciousness', Althusser says quite rightly, is founded on an empiricist relationship to knowledge. It assumes that social relations give their own, unambiguous knowledge to perceiving, thinking subjects; that there is a transparent relationship between the situations in which subjects are placed and how subjects come to recognize and know about them. Consequently, true knowledge must be subject to a sort of masking, the source of which is very difficult to identify, but which prevents people from 'recognizing the real'. In this conception, it is always other people, never ourselves, who are in false consciousness, who are bewitched by the dominant ideology, who are the dupes of history.

Althusser's third critique develops out of his notions about theory. He insists that knowledge has to be produced as the consequence of a particular practice. Knowledge, whether ideological or scientific, is the production of a practice. It is not the reflection of the real in discourse, in language. Social relations have to be 'represented in speech and language' to acquire meaning. Meaning is produced as a result of discursive or theoretical work. It is not simply a result of an empiricist epistemology.

As a result, Althusser wants to think the specificity of ideological practices, to think their difference from other social practices. He also wants to think 'the complex unity' which articulates the level of ideological practice to other instances of a social formation. And so, using the critique of the traditional conceptions of ideology which he found in front of him, he set to work to offer some alternatives. Let me look briefly at what these alternatives are, for Althusser.

'Ideological State Apparatuses'

The one with which everybody is familiar is presented in the 'Ideological State Apparatuses' essay. Some of his propositions in that essay have had a very strong influence or resonance in the subsequent debate. First of all Althusser tries to think the relationship between ideology and other social practices in terms of the concept of reproduction. What is the function of ideology? It is to reproduce the social relations of production. The social relations of production are necessary to the material existence of any social formation or any mode of production. But the elements or the agents of a mode of production, especially with respect to the critical factor of their labour, has itself to be continually produced and reproduced. Althusser argues that, increasingly in capitalist social formations, labour is not reproduced inside the social relations of production themselves but outside of them. Of course, he does not mean biologically or technically reproduced only, he means socially and culturally as well. It is produced in the domain of the superstructures: in institutions like the family and church. It requires cultural institutions such as the media, trade unions, political parties, etc., which are not directly linked with production as such but which have the crucial function of 'cultivating' labour of a certain moral and cultural kind – that which the modern capitalist mode of production requires. Schools, universities, training boards and research centres reproduce the technical competence of the labour required by advanced systems of capitalist production. But Althusser reminds us that a technically competent but politically insubordinate labour force is no labour force at all for capital. Therefore, the more important task is cultivating that kind of labour which is able and willing, morally and politically, to be subordinated to the discipline, the logic, the culture and compulsions of the economic mode of production of capitalist development, at whatever stage it has arrived; that is, labour which can be subjected to the dominant system *ad infinitum*. Consequently, what ideology does, through the various ideological apparatuses, is to reproduce the social relations of production in this larger sense. That is Althusser's first formulation.

Reproduction in that sense is, of course, a classic term to be found in Marx. Althusser doesn't have to go any further than *Capital* (Marx 1970) to discover it; although it should be said that he gives it a very restrictive definition. He refers only to the reproduction of labour power, whereas reproduction in Marx is a much wider concept, including the reproduction of the social relations of possession and of exploitation, and indeed of the mode of production itself. This is quite typical of Althusser – when he dives into the Marxist bag and comes out with a term or concept which has wide Marxist resonances, he quite often gives it a particular limiting twist which is specifically his own. In this way, he continually 'firms up' Marx's structuralist cast of thought.

There is a problem with this position. Ideology in this essay seems to be, substantially, that of the dominant class. If there is an ideology of the dominated classes, it seems to be one which is perfectly adapted to the functions and interests of the dominant class within the capitalist mode of production. At this point, Althusserean structuralism is open to the charge, which has been made against it, of a creeping Marxist functionalism. Ideology seems to perform the function required of it (i.e. to reproduce the dominance of the dominant ideology), to perform it effectively, and to go on performing it, without encountering any counter-tendencies (a second concept always to be found in Marx wherever he discusses reproduction and precisely the concept which distinguishes the analysis in *Capital* from functionalism). When you ask about the contradictory field of ideology, about how the ideology of the dominated classes gets produced and reproduced, about the ideologies of resistance, of exclusion, of deviation, etc., there are no answers in this essay. Nor is there an account of why it is that ideology, which is so effectively stitched into the social formation in Althusser's account, would ever produce its opposite or its contradiction. But a notion of reproduction which is only functionally adjusted to capital and which has no countervailing tendencies, encounters no contradictions, is not the site of class struggle, and is utterly foreign to Marx's conception of reproduction.

The second influential proposition in the 'Ideological State Apparatuses' essay is the insistence that ideology is a practice. That is, it appears in practices located within the rituals of specific apparatuses or social institutions and organizations. Althusser makes the distinction here between repressive state apparatuses, like the police and the army, and ideological state apparatuses, like churches, trade unions, and media which are not directly organized by the state. The emphasis on 'practices and rituals' is wholly welcome, especially if not interpreted too narrowly or polemically. Ideologies are the frameworks of thinking and calculation about the world – the 'ideas' which people use to figure out how the social world works, what their place is in it and what they *ought* to do. But the problem for a materialist or non-idealist theory is how to deal with ideas, which are mental events, and therefore, as Marx says, can only occur 'in thought, in the head' (where else?), in a non-idealist, non-vulgar materialist manner. Althusser's emphasis is helpful, here – helping us out of the philosophical dilemma, as well as having the additional virtue, in my view, of being right. He places the emphasis on where ideas appear, where mental events register or are realized, as social phenomena. That is principally, of course, in language (understood in the sense of signifying practices involving the use of signs; in the semiotic domain, the domain of meaning and representation). Equally important, in the rituals and practices of social action or behaviour, in which ideologies imprint or inscribe themselves. Language and behaviour are the media, so to speak, of the material registration of ideology, the modality of its functioning. These rituals and practices always occur in social sites, linked with social apparatuses. That is why we have to analyse or deconstruct language and practice in order to decipher the patterns of ideological thinking which are inscribed in them.

This important advance in our thinking about ideology has sometimes been obscured by theorists who claim that ideologies are not 'ideas' at all but practices, and it is this which guarantees that the theory of ideology is materialist. I do not agree with this emphasis. I think it suffers from a 'misplaced concreteness'. The materialism of Marxism cannot rest on the claim that it abolishes the mental character – let alone the real effects – of mental events (i.e., thought), for that is, precisely, the error of what Marx called a one-sided or mechanical materialism (in the *Theses on Feuerbach*, Marx 1963). It must rest on the material forms in which thought appears and on the fact that it has real, material effects. That is, at any rate, the manner in which I have learned from Althusser's much-quoted assertion that the existence of ideology is material 'because it is inscribed in practices'. Some damage has been done by Althusser's over-dramatic and too-condensed formulation, at the close of this part of his argument, that – as he quaintly puts it: 'Disappear: the term ideas.' Althusser has accomplished much but he has not, to my way of thinking, actually abolished the existence of ideas and thought, however convenient and reassuring that would be. What he has shown is that ideas have a material existence. As he says himself, 'the "ideas" of a human subject exist in his [or her] actions' and actions are 'inserted into practices governed by the rituals in which those practices are inscribed within the material existence of an ideological apparatus', which is different (Althusser 1970/1971: 158).

Nevertheless, serious problems remain with Althusser's nomenclature. The 'Ideological State Apparatuses' essay, again, unproblematically assumes an identity between the many 'autonomous' parts of civil society and the state. In contrast, this articulation is at the centre of Gramsci's (1971) problem of hegemony. Gramsci has difficulties in formulating the state/civil society boundary precisely because where it falls is neither a simple nor uncontradictory matter. A critical question in developed liberal democracies is precisely how ideology is reproduced in the so-called *private* institutions of civil society – the theatre of consent – apparently outside of the direct sphere of play of the state itself. If everything is, more or less, under the supervision of the state, it is quite easy to see why the only ideology that gets reproduced is the dominant one. But the far more pertinent, but difficult, question is how a society *allows* the relative freedom of civil institutions to operate in the ideological field, day after day, without direction or compulsion by the state; and why the consequence of that 'free play' of civil society, through a very complex reproductive process, nevertheless consistently reconstitutes ideology as a 'structure in dominance'. That is a much tougher problem to explain, and the notion of 'ideological state apparatuses' precisely forecloses the issue. Again, it is a closure of a broadly 'functionalist' type which presupposes a necessary functional correspondence between the requirements of the mode of production and the functions of ideology.

After all, in democratic societies, it is not an illusion of freedom to say that we cannot adequately explain the structured biases of the media in terms of their being instructed by the state precisely what to print or allow on television. But precisely how is it that such large numbers of journalists, consulting only their 'freedom' to publish and be damned, do tend to reproduce, quite spontaneously, without compulsion, again and again, accounts of the world constructed within fundamentally the same ideological categories? How is it that they are driven, again and again, to such a limited repertoire within the ideological field? Even journalists who write within the muck-raking tradition often seem to be inscribed by an ideology to which they do not consciously commit themselves, and which, instead, 'writes them'.

This is the aspect of ideology under liberal capitalism which most needs explaining. And that is why, when people say 'Of course this is a free society; the media operate freely', there is no point in responding 'No, they operate only through compulsion by the state.' Would that they did! Then all that would be required would be to pull out the four or five of their key controllers and put in a few controllers of our own. In fact ideological reproduction can no more be explained by the inclinations of individuals or by overt coercion (social control) than economic reproduction can be explained by direct force. Both explanations – and they are analogous – have to begin where *Capital* begins: with analysing how the 'spontaneous freedom' of the circuits actually work. This is a problem which the 'ideological state apparatus' nomenclature simply forecloses. Althusser refuses to distinguish between State and civil society (on the same grounds which Poulantzas also later spuriously supported – i.e. that the distinction belonged only within 'bourgeois ideology'). His nomenclature does not give sufficient weight to what Gramsci would call the immense complexities of society in modern social formations – 'the trenches and fortifications of civil society'. It does not begin to make sense of how complex are the processes by which capitalism must work to order and organize a civil society which is not, technically, under its immediate control. These are important problems in the field of ideology and culture which the formulation, 'ideological state apparatuses', encourages us to evade.

The third of Althusser's propositions is his affirmation that ideology only exists by virtue of the constituting category of the 'subject'. There is a long and complicated story here, only part of which I have time to rehearse. *Reading Capital* is very similar in its mode of argumentation to Levi-Strauss and other non-Marxist structuralists. Like Levi-Strauss (1958/1972), Althusser also talks about social relations as processes without a subject. Similarly, when Althusser insists that classes are simply 'bearers and supports' of economic social relations, he, like Levi-Strauss, is using a Saussurean conception of language, applied to the domain of practice in general, to displace the traditional agent/subject of classical Western epistemology. Althusser's position here is very much in line with the notion that language speaks us, as the myth 'speaks' the myth-maker. This abolishes the problem of subjective identification and of how individuals or groups become the enunciators of ideology. But, as Althusser develops his theory of ideology, he moves away from the notion that ideology is simply a process without a subject. He seems to take on board the critique that this domain of the subject and subjectivity cannot be simply left as an empty space. The 'decentring of the subject', which is one of structuralism's main projects, still leaves unsettled the problem of the subjectification and subjectivizing of ideology. There are still processes of subjective effect to be accounted for. How do concrete individuals fall into place within particular ideologies if we have no notion of the subject or of subjectivity? On the other hand, we have to rethink this question in a way different from the tradition of empiricist philosophy. This is the beginning of a very long development, which begins in the 'Ideological State Apparatuses' essay, with Althusser's insistence that all ideology functions through the category of the subject, and it is only in and for ideology that subjects exist and culminates in Foucault.

This 'subject' is not to be confused with lived historical individuals. It is the category, the position where the subject – the I of ideological statements – is constituted. Ideological discourses themselves constitute us as subjects for discourse. Althusser explains how this works through the concept, borrowed from Lacan (1966/1977), of 'interpellation'. This suggests that we are hailed or summoned by the ideologies which recruit us as their 'authors', their essential subject. We are constituted by the unconscious processes of ideology, in that position of recognition or suture between ourselves and the signifying chain without which no signification of ideological meaning would be possible. It is precisely from this turn in the argument that the long trail into psychoanalysis and post-structuralism (and finally out of the Marxist problematic) unwinds.

There is something both profoundly important and seriously regrettable about the shape of this 'Ideological State Apparatuses' essay. It has to do exactly with its two-part structure: Part I is about ideology and the reproduction of the social relations of production. Part II is about the constitution of subjects and how ideologies interpellate us in the realm of the Imaginary. As a result of treating those two aspects in two separate compartments, a fatal dislocation occurred. What was originally conceived as one critical element in the general theory of ideology – the theory of the subject – came to be sustained, metonymically, for the whole of the theory itself. The enormously sophisticated theories which have subsequently developed have therefore all been theories about the second question: how are subjects constituted in relation to different discourses? What is the role of unconscious processes in creating these positionalities? That is the object of discourse theory and linguistically influenced psychoanalysis. Or one can inquire into the conditions of enunciation in a particular discursive formation. That is the problematic of Foucault. Or one can inquire into the unconscious process by which subjects and subjectivity as such are constituted. That is the problematic of Lacan. There has thus been considerable theorizing on the site of the second part of the 'Ideological State Apparatuses' essay. But on the site of the first part – nothing. Finito! The inquiry simply halted with Althusser's inadequate formulations about the reproduction of the social relations of production. The two sides of the difficult problem of ideology were fractured in that essay and, ever since, have been assigned to different poles. The question of reproduction has been assigned to the Marxist (male) pole, and the question of subjectivity has been assigned to the psychoanalytic (feminist) pole. Since then, never have the twain met. The latter is constituted as a question about the 'insides' of people, about psychoanalysis, subjectivity and sexuality, and is understood to be 'about' that. It is in this way and on this site that the link to feminism has been increasingly theorized. The former is 'about' social relations, production and the 'hard edge' of productive systems, and that is what Marxism and the reductive discourses of class are 'about'. This bifurcation of the theoretical project has had the most disastrous consequences for the unevenness of the subsequent development of the problematic of ideology, not to speak of its damaging political effects.

Ideology in *For Marx*

Instead of following either of these paths, I want to break from that impasse for a moment and look at some alternative starting points in Althusser, from which I think, useful advances can still be made. Long before he had arrived at the 'advanced' position of the 'Ideological State Apparatuses' essay, Althusser said, in a short section in *For Marx* (1965/1969: 231–6), some simple things about ideology which bear repeating and thinking about. This is where he defined ideologies as, to paraphrase, systems of representation – composed of concepts, ideas, myths, or images – in which men and women (my addition) live their imaginary relations to the real conditions of existence. That statement is worth examining bit by bit.

The designation of ideologies as 'systems of representation' acknowledges their essentially discursive and semiotic character. Systems of representation are the systems of meaning through which we represent the world to ourselves and one another. It acknowledges that ideological knowledge is the result of specific practices – the practices involved in the production of meaning. But since there are no social practices which take place outside the domain of meaning (semiotic), are *all* practices simply discourses?

Here we have to tread very carefully. We are in the presence of yet another suppressed term or excluded middle. Althusser reminds us that ideas don't just float around in empty space. We know they are there because they are materialized in, they inform, social practices. In that sense, the social is never outside of the semiotic. Every social practice is constituted within the interplay of meaning and representation and can itself be represented. In other words, there is no social practice outside of discourse. However, this does not mean that, because all social practices are within the discursive, there is nothing to social practice *but* discourse. I know what is vested in describing processes that we usually talk about in terms of ideas as practices; 'practices' feel concrete. They occur in particular sites and apparatuses – like classrooms, churches, lecture theatres, factories, schools and families. And that concreteness allows us to claim that they are 'material'. Yet differences must be remarked between different kinds of practice. Let me suggest one. If you are engaged in a part of the modern capitalist labour process, you are using, in combination with certain means of production, labour power – purchased at a certain price – to transform raw materials into a product, a commodity. That is the definition of a practice – the practice of labour. Is it *outside* of meaning and discourse? Certainly not. How could large numbers of people either learn that practice or combine their labour power in the division of labour with others, day after day, unless labour was within the domain of representation and meaning? Is this practice of transformation, then, nothing but a discourse? Of course not. It does not follow that because all practices are *in* ideology, or inscribed by ideology, all practices are *nothing but* ideology. There is a specificity to those practices whose principal object is to produce ideological representations. They are different from those practices which – meaningfully, intelligibly – produce other commodities. Those people who work in the media are producing, reproducing and transforming the field of ideological representation itself. They stand in a different relationship to ideology in general from others who are producing and reproducing the world of material commodities – which are, nevertheless, also discursively inscribed. Barthes observed long ago that all things are also significations. The latter forms of practice operate in ideology but they are not ideological in terms of the specificity of their object.

I want to retain the notion that ideologies are systems of representation materialized in practices, but I don't want to fetishize 'practice'. Too often, at this level of theorizing, the argument has tended to identify social practice with social discourse. While the emphasis on discourse is correct in pointing to the importance of meaning and representation, it has been taken right through to its absolute opposite and this allows us to talk about all practice as if there were nothing but ideology. This is simply an inversion.

Note that Althusser says 'systems', not 'system'. The important thing about systems of representation is that they are not singular. There are numbers of them in any social formation. They are plural. Ideologies do not operate through single ideas; they operate, in discursive chains, in clusters, in semantic fields, in discursive formations. As you enter an ideological field and pick out any one nodal representation or idea, you immediately trigger off a whole chain of connotative associations. Ideological representations connote – summon – one another. So a variety of different ideological systems or logics are available in any social formation. The notion of *the* dominant ideology and *the* subordinated ideology is an inadequate way of representing the complex interplay of different ideological discourses and formations in any modern developed society. Nor is the terrain of ideology constituted as a field of mutually exclusive and internally self-sustaining discursive chains. They contest one another, often drawing on a common, shared repertoire of concepts, rearticulating and disarticulating them within different systems of difference or equivalence.

Let me turn to the next part of Althusser's definition of ideology – the systems of representation in which men and women *live*. Althusser puts inverted commas around 'live', because he means not blind biological or genetic life, but the life of experiencing, within culture, meaning and representation. It is not possible to bring ideology to an end and simply live the real. We always need systems through which we represent what the real is to ourselves and to others. The second important point about 'live' is that we ought to understand it broadly. By 'live' he means that men and women use a variety of systems of representation to experience, interpret and 'make sense of' the conditions of their existence. It follows that ideology can always define the same so-called object or objective condition in the real world differently. There is 'no necessary correspondence' between the conditions of a social relation or practice and the number of different ways in which it can be represented. It does not follow that, as some neo-Kantians in discourse theory have assumed, because we cannot know or experience a social relation except 'within ideology', therefore it has no existence independent of the machinery of representation: a point already well clarified by Marx in the '1857 Introduction' but woefully misinterpreted by Althusser himself.

Perhaps the most subversive implication of the term 'live' is that it connotes the domain of experience. It is in and through the systems of representation of culture that we 'experience' the world: experience is the product of our codes of intelligibility, our schemas of interpretation. Consequently, there is no experiencing *outside* of the categories of representation or discourse. The notion that our heads are full of false ideas which can, however, be totally dispersed when we throw ourselves open to 'the real' as a moment of absolute authentication, is probably the most ideological conception of all. This is exactly that moment of 'recognition' when the fact that meaning depends on the intervention of systems of representation disappears and we seem secure within the naturalistic attitude. It is a moment of extreme ideological closure. Here we are most under the sway of the highly ideological structures of all – common sense, the regime of the 'taken-for-granted'. The point at which we lose sight of the fact that sense is a production of our systems of representation is the point at which we fall, not into Nature but into the naturalistic illusion:

the height (or depth) of ideology. Consequently, when we contrast ideology to experience, or illusion to authentic truth, we are failing to recognize that there is no way of experiencing the 'real relations' of a particular society outside of its cultural and ideological categories. That is not to say that all knowledge is simply the product of our will-to-power; there may be some ideological categories which give us a more adequate or more profound knowledge of particular relations than others.

Because there is no one-to-one relationship between the conditions of social existence we are living and how we experience them, it is necessary for Althusser to call these relationships 'imaginary'. That is, they must on no account be confused with the real. It is only later in his work that this domain becomes the 'Imaginary' in a proper Lacanian[3] sense. It may be that he already had Lacan in mind in this earlier essay, but he is not yet concerned to affirm that knowing and experiencing are only possible through the particular psychoanalytic process which Lacan has posited. Ideology is described as imaginary simply to distinguish it from the notion that 'real relations' declare their own meanings unambiguously.

Finally, let us consider Althusser's use of this phrase, 'the real conditions of existence' – scandalous (within contemporary cultural theory) because here Althusser commits himself to the notion that social relations actually exist apart from their ideological representations or experiences. Social relations do exist. We are born into them. They exist independent of our will. They are real in their structure and tendency. We cannot develop a social practice without representing those conditions to ourselves in one way or another; but the representations do not exhaust their effect. Social relations exist, independent of mind, independent of thought. And yet they can only be conceptualized in thought, in the head. That is how Marx (1953/1973) put it in the '1857 Introduction' to the *Grundrisse*. It is important that Althusser affirms the objective character of the real relations that constitute modes of production in social formations, though his later work provided the warrant for a quite different theorization. Althusser here is closer to a 'realist' philosophical position than his later Kantian or Spinozean manifestations.

Now I want to go beyond the particular phrase I have been explicating to expand on two or three more general things associated with this formulation. Althusser says these systems of representation are essentially founded on unconscious structures. Again, in the earlier essay, he seems to be thinking the unconscious nature of ideology in ways similar to those which Levi-Strauss used when he defined the codes of a myth as unconscious – in terms of its rules and categories. We are not ourselves aware of the rules and systems of classification of an ideology when we enunciate any ideological statement. Nevertheless, like the rules of language, they are open to rational inspection and analysis by modes of interruption and deconstruction, which can open up a discourse to its foundations and allow us to inspect the categories which generate it. We know the words to the song, 'Rule Britannia' but we are 'unconscious' of the deep structure – the notions of nation, the great slabs and slices of imperialist history, the assumptions about global domination and supremacy, the necessary Other of other peoples' subordination – which are richly impacted in its simple celebratory resonances. These connotational chains are not open nor easily amenable to change and reformulation at the conscious level. Does it therefore follow that they are the product of specific unconscious processes and mechanisms in the psychoanalytic sense?

This returns us to the question of how it is that subjects recognize themselves in ideology: how is the relationship between individual subjects and the positionalities of a particular ideological discourse constructed? It seems likely that some of the basic positionings of individuals in language, as well as certain primary positions in the ideological field, are constituted through unconscious processes in the psychoanalytic sense, at the early stages of formation. Those processes can then have a profound, orienting impact on the ways in which we situate ourselves in later life in subsequent ideological discourses. It is quite clear that such processes *do* operate in early infancy, making possible the formation of relations with others and the outside world. They are inextricably bound up – for one thing – with the nature and development of, above all, sexual identities. On the other hand, it is by no means adequately proven that these positionings *alone* constitute the mechanisms whereby all individuals locate themselves in ideology. We are not entirely stitched into place in our relation to the complex field of historically situated ideological discourses exclusively at the moment alone, when we enter the 'transition from biological existence to human existence' (Althusser, 'Freud and Lacan', 1970/1971: 93). We remain open to be positioned and 'subjected' in different ways, at different moments throughout our existence.

Some argue that those later positionings simply recapitulate the primary positions which are established in the resolution of the Oedipus complex. It seems more accurate to say that subjects are not positioned in relation to the field of ideologies *exclusively by* the resolution of unconscious processes in infancy. They are also positioned by the discursive formations of specific social formations. They are situated differently in relation to a different range of social sites. It seems to me wrong to assume that the process which allows the individual to speak or enunciate *at all* – language as such – is the same as that which allows the individual to enunciate him- or herself as a particular gendered, raced, socially sexed, etc. individual in a variety of specific representational systems in definite societies. The universal mechanisms of interpellation may provide the necessary general conditions for identification but it is mere speculation and assertion which so far suggests that they provide the sufficient concrete conditions for the enunciation of historically specific and differentiated identities. Discourse theory one-sidedly insists that an account of subjectivity in terms of Lacan's unconscious processes is itself *the* whole theory of ideology. Certainly, a theory of ideology has to develop, as earlier Marxist theories did not, a theory of subjects and subjectivity. It must account for the recognition of the self within ideological discourse, what it is that allows subjects to identify themselves in the discourse and to speak it spontaneously as its author. But that is not the same as taking the Freudian schema, reread in a linguistic way by Lacan, as an adequate theory of ideology in social formations.

Althusser himself appeared, earlier (in his 'Freud and Lacan' essay, first written in 1964 and published in Althusser 1970/1971), to recognize the necessarily provisional and speculative nature of Lacan's propositions. He repeated the succession of 'identities' through which Lacan's argument is sustained – the transition from biological to human existence paralleling the

Law of the Father, which is the same as the Law of Culture, which 'is confounded in its formal essence with the order of language' (p. 193). But he does then pick up the purely *formal* nature of these homologies in a footnote:

> Formally: for the Law of Culture which is first introduced as language ... is not exhausted by language; its content is the real kinship structures and the determinate ideological formations in which the persons inscribed in these structures live their function. It is not enough too know that the Western family is patriarchal and exogamic ... we must also work out the ideological formations that govern paternity, maternity, conjugality and childhood ... A mass of research remains to be done on these ideological formations. This is a task for historical materialism.
>
> (p. 211)

But in the later formulations, (and even more so in the Lacanian deluge which has subsequently followed) this kind of caution has been thrown to the wind in a veritable riot of affirmation. In the familiar slippage, 'the unconscious is structured like a language' has become 'the unconscious *is* the same as the entry into language, culture, sexual identity, ideology, and so on.'

What I have tried to do is to go back to a much simpler and more productive way of beginning to think about ideology, which I also find in Althusser's work though not at the fashionable end of it. Recognizing that, in these matters – though our conceptual apparatus is extremely sophisticated and 'advanced', in terms of real understanding, substantive research, and progress to knowledge in a genuinely 'open' (i.e. scientific) way – we are very much at the beginning of a long and difficult road. In terms of this 'long march', *For Marx* is earlier than the flights of fancy, and occasionally of fantasy, which overtake the 'Ideological State Apparatuses' essay. It ought not, however, be left behind for that reason alone. 'Contradiction and Overdetermination' contains a richer notion of determination than *Reading Capital*, though not so rigorously theorized. *For Marx* has a fuller notion of ideology than does 'Ideological State Apparatuses', though it is not as comprehensive.

Reading an Ideological Field

Let me take a brief, personal example as an indication of how some of the things I have said about Althusser's general concept of ideology allow us to think about particular ideological formations. I want to think about that particular complex of discourses that implicates the ideologies of identity, place, ethnicity and social formation generated around the term 'black'. Such a term 'functions like a language', indeed it does. The language of race and colour, as deployed in the Caribbean and British situations, both vary in meaning from one another, and from the way these languages function in the American context. It is only at the 'chaotic' level of language in general that all these different terminologies mean the same. In fact what we find are differences, specificities, within different, even if related, histories.

At different times in my 30 years in England, I have been 'hailed' or interpellated as 'coloured', 'West Indian', 'Negro', 'black', 'immigrant'. Sometimes in the street; sometimes at street corners; sometimes abusively; sometimes in a friendly manner; sometimes ambiguously. (A black friend of mine was disciplined by his political organization for 'racism' because, in order to scandalize the white neighbourhood in which we both lived as students, he would ride up to my window late at night and, from the middle of the street, shout 'Negro!' very loudly to attract my attention!) All of them inscribe me 'in place' in a signifying chain which constructs identity through the categories of colour, ethnicity, race.

In Jamaica, where I spent my youth and adolescence, I was constantly hailed as 'coloured'. The way that term was articulated with other terms in the syntaxes of race and ethnicity was such as to produce the meaning, in effect: 'not black'. The 'blacks' were the rest – the vast majority of the people, the ordinary folk. To be 'coloured' was to belong to the 'mixed' ranks of the brown middle class, a cut above the rest – in aspiration if not in reality. My family attached great weight to these finely-graded classificatory distinctions and, because of what it signified in terms of distinctions of class, status, race, colour, insisted on the inscription. Indeed, they clung to it through thick and thin, like the ultimate ideological lifeline it was. You can imagine how mortified they were to discover that, when I came to England, I was hailed as 'coloured' by the natives there precisely because, as far as they could see, I *was* 'black', for all practical purposes! The same term, in short, carried quite different connotations because it operated within different 'systems of differences and equivalences'. It is the position within the different signifying chains which 'means', not the literal, fixed correspondence between an isolated term and some denotated position in the colour spectrum.

The Caribbean system was organized through the finely graded classification systems of the colonial discourses of race, arranged on an ascending scale up to the ultimate 'white' term – the latter always out of reach, the impossible, 'absent' term, whose absent-presence structured the whole chain. In the bitter struggle for place and position which characterizes dependent societies, every notch on the scale mattered profoundly. The English system, by contrast, was organized around a simpler binary dichotomy, more appropriate to the colonizing order: 'white/not white'. Meaning is not a transparent reflection of the world in language but arises through the differences between the terms and categories, the systems of reference, which classify out of the world and allow it to be in this way appropriated into social thought, common sense.

As a concrete lived individual, am I indeed any one of these interpellations? Does any one of them exhaust me? In fact, I 'am' not one or another of these ways of representing me, though I have been positioned as all of them at different times and still am some of them to some degree. But, there is no essential, unitary 'I' – only the fragmentary, contradictory subject I become. Long after, I encountered 'coloured' again, now as it were from the other side, beyond it. I tried to teach my son he was 'black' at the same time as he was learning the colours of the spectrum and he kept saying to me that he was 'brown'. Of course, he was *both*.

Certainly I am from the West Indies – though I've lived my adult life in England. Actually, the relationship between 'West Indian' and 'immigrant' is very complex for me. In the 1950s, the two terms were equivalents. Now, the term 'West Indian' is very romantic. It connotes reggae, rum and coke, shades, mangoes, and all that canned tropical fruit salad falling out of the coconut trees. This is an idealized 'I'. (I wish I felt more like that more of the time.)

'Immigrant' I also know well. There is nothing remotely romantic about that. It places one so equivocally as *really* belonging *somewhere else*. 'And when are you going back home?' Part of Mrs Thatcher's 'alien wedge'. Actually I only understood the way this term positioned me relatively late in life – and the 'hailing' on that occasion came from an unexpected direction. It was when my mother said to me, on a brief visit home: 'I hope they don't mistake you over there for one of those immigrants!' The shock of recognition. I was also on many occasions 'spoken' by that other, absent, unspoken term, the one that is never there, the 'American' one, undignified even by a capital 'N'. The 'silence' around this term was probably the most eloquent of them all. Positively marked terms 'signify' because of their position in relation to what is absent, unmarked, the unspoken, the unsayable. Meaning is relational within an ideological system of presences and absences. 'Fort, da.'

Althusser, in a controversial passage in the 'Ideological State Apparatuses' essay says that we are 'always-ready' subjects. Actually Hirst and others contest this. If we are 'always-ready' subjects, we would have to be born with the structure of recognitions and the means to positioning ourselves with language already formed. Whereas Lacan, from whom Althusser and others draw, uses Freud and Saussure to provide an account of how that structure of recognition is formed (through the mirror phase and the resolutions of the Oedipus complex, etc.). However, let us leave that objection aside for a moment, since a larger truth about ideology is implied in what Althusser says. We experience ideology as if it emanates freely and spontaneously from within us, as if we were its free subjects, 'working by ourselves'. Actually, we are spoken by and spoken for, in the ideological discourses which await us even at our birth, into which we are born and find our place. The new-born child who still, according to Althusser's reading of Lacan, has to acquire the means of being placed within the law of Culture, is already expected, named, positioned in advance 'by the forms of ideology (paternal/maternal/conjugal/fraternal)'.

The observation puts me in mind of a related early experience. It is a story frequently retold in my family – with great humour all round, though I never saw the joke; part of our family lore – that when my mother first brought me home from the hospital at my birth, my sister looked into my crib and said, 'Where did you get this Coolie baby from?' 'Coolies' in Jamaica are East Indians, deriving from the indentured labourers brought into the country after Abolition to replace the slaves in plantation labour. 'Coolie' is, if possible, one rung lower in the discourse of race than 'black'. This was my sister's way of remarking that, as often happens in the best of mixed families, I had come out a good deal darker-skinned than was average in my family. I hardly know any more whether this really happened or was a manufactured story by my family or even perhaps whether I made it up and have now forgotten when and why. But I felt, then and now, summoned to my 'place' by it. From that moment onwards, my place within this system of reference has been problematic. It may help to explain why and how I eventually became what I was first nominated: the 'Coolie' of my family, the one who did not fit, the outsider, the one who hung around the street with all the wrong people, and grew up with all those funny ideas. The Other one.

What is *the contradiction* that generates an ideological field of this kind? Is it 'the principal contradiction between capital and labour'? This signifying chain was clearly inaugurated at a specific historical moment – the moment of slavery. It is not eternal, or universal. It was the way in which sense was made of the insertion of the enslaved peoples of the coastal kingdoms of West Africa into the social relations of forced labour production in the New World. Leave aside for a moment the vexed question of whether the mode of production in slave societies was 'capitalist' or 'pre-capitalist' or an articulation of both within the global market. In the early stages of development, for all practical purposes, the racial and the class systems overlapped. They were 'systems of equivalence'. Racial and ethnic categories continue today to be the forms in which the structures of domination and exploitation are 'lived'. In that sense, these discourses do have the function of 'reproducing the social relations of production'. And yet, in contemporary Caribbean societies, the two systems do *not* perfectly correspond. There are 'blacks' at the top of the ladder too, some of them exploiters of other black labour, and some firm friends of Washington's. The world neither divides neatly into its social/natural categories, nor do ideological categories necessarily produce their own 'appropriate' modes of consciousness. We are therefore obliged to say that there is a complicated set of articulations between the two systems of discourse. The relationship of equivalences between them is not fixed but has changed historically. Nor is it 'determined' by a single cause but is, rather, the result of an 'over-determination'.

These discourses therefore clearly construct Jamaican society as a field of social difference organized around the categories of race, colour and ethnicity. Ideology here has the function of assigning a population into particular classifications organized around these categories. In the articulation between the discourses of class and race-colour-ethnicity (and the displacement effected between them which this makes possible), the latter is constituted as the 'dominant' discourse, the categories through which the prevailing forms of consciousness are generated, the terrain within which men and women 'move, acquire consciousness of their position, struggle, etc.' (Gramsci 1971: 377), the systems of representation through which the people 'live the imaginary relation to their real conditions of existence; (Althusser 1965/1969: 233). This analysis is not an academic one, valuable only for its theoretical and analytic distinctions. The over-determination of class and race has the most profound consequences – some of them highly contradictory – for the *politics* of Jamaica, and of Jamaican blacks everywhere.

It is possible, then, to examine the field of social relations, in Jamaica and in Britain, in terms of an interdiscursive field generated by at least three different contradictions (class, race, gender), each of which has a different history, a different mode of operation; each divides and classifies the world in different ways. Then it would be necessary, in any specific social formation, to analyse the way in which class, race and gender are articulated with one another to establish particular condensed social positions. Social identities, we may say, are here subject to a 'double-articulation'. They are by definition over-determined. To look at the overlap or 'unity' (fusion) between them, that is to say, the ways in which they connote or summon up one another in articulating differences in the ideological field, does not obviate *the particular effects* which each structure has. We can think of political situations in which alliances could be drawn in very different ways, depending on which of the different articulations in play became at that time dominant ones.

Now let us think about this term, 'black' within a particular semantic field or ideological formation rather than as a single term: within its chain of connotations. I give just two examples. The first is the chain – black-lazy, spiteful, artful, etc. – which flows from the identification of 'black' at a very specific historical moment: the era of slavery. This reminds us that, though the distinction 'black/white' that is articulated by this particular chain, is not given simply by the capital-labour contradiction, the social relations characteristic of that specific historical moment are its referent in this particular discursive formation. In the West Indian case, 'black', with this connotative resonance, is a way of representing how the peoples of a distinctive ethnic character were first inserted into the social relations of production. But of course, that chain of connotations is not the only one. An entirely different one is generated within the powerful religious discourses which have so marked the Caribbean: the association of Light with God and the spirit, and of Dark or 'blackness' with Hell, the Devil, sin and damnation. When I was a child and I was taken to church by one of my grandmothers, I thought the black minister's appeal to the Almighty, 'Lord, lighten our darkness', was a quite specific request for a bit of personal divine assistance.

Ideological Struggle

It is important to look at the semantic field within which any particular ideological chain signifies. Marx reminds us that the ideas of the past weigh like a nightmare on the brains of the living. The moment of historical formation is critical for any semantic field. These semantic zones take shape at particular historical periods: for example, the formation of bourgeois individualism in the seventeenth and eighteenth centuries in England. They leave the traces of their connections, long after the social relations to which they referred have disappeared. These traces can be reactivated at a later stage, even when the discourses have fragmented as coherent or organic ideologies. Common-sense thinking contains what Gramsci called the traces of ideology 'without an inventory'. Consider, for example, the trace of religious thinking in a world which believes itself to be secular and which, therefore, invests 'the sacred' in secular ideas. Although the logic of the religious interpretation of terms has been broken, the religious repertoire continues to trail through history, usable in a variety of new historical contexts, reinforcing and underpinning more apparently 'modern' ideas.

In this context, we can locate the possibility for ideological struggle. A particular ideological chain becomes a site of struggle, not only when people try to displace, rupture or contest it by supplanting it with some wholly new alternative set of terms, but also when they interrupt the ideological field and try to transform its meaning by changing or rearticulating its associations, for example, from the negative to the positive. Often, ideological struggle actually consists of attempting to win some new set of meanings for an existing term or category, of disarticulating it from its place in a signifying structure. For example, it is precisely because 'black' is the term which connotes the most despised, the dispossessed, the unenlightened, the uncivilized, the uncultivated, the scheming, the incompetent, that it can be contested, transformed and invested with a positive ideological value. The concept 'black' is not the exclusive property of any particular social group or any single discourse. To use the terminology of Laclau (1977) and Laclau and Mouffe (1985), the term, despite its powerful resonances, has no necessary 'class belongingness'. It has been deeply inserted in the past into the discourses of racial distinction and abuse. It was, for long, apparently chained into place in the discourses and practices of social and economic exploitation. In the period of Jamaican history when the national bourgeoisie wished to make common cause with the masses in the fight for formal political independence from the colonizing power – a fight in which the local bourgeoisie, not the masses, emerged as the leading social force – 'black' was a sort of disguise. In the cultural revolution which swept Jamaica in the later 1960s and 1970s, when for the first time the people acknowledged and accepted their African-slave-black heritage, and the fulcrum or centre of gravity of the society shifted to 'the roots', to the life and common experience of the black urban and rural underclasses as representing the cultural essence of 'Jamaican-ness' (this is the moment of political radicalization, of mass mobilization, of solidarity with black struggles for liberation elsewhere, of 'soul brothers' and 'Soul', as well as of reggae, Bob Marley and Rastafarianism), 'black' became reconstituted as its opposite. It became the site for the construction of 'unity', of the positive recognition of 'the black experience': the moment of the constitution of a *new* collective subject – the 'struggling black masses'. This transformation in the meaning, position and reference of 'black' did not follow and reflect the black cultural revolution in Jamaica in that period. It was one of the ways in which those new subjects were *constituted*. The people – the concrete individuals – had always been there. But as subjects-in-struggle for a new epoch in history, they appeared for the first time. Ideology, through an ancient category, was constitutive of their oppositional formation.

So the word itself has no specific social connotation, though it does have a long and not easily dismantled history. As social movements develop a struggle around a particular programme, meanings which appear to have been fixed in place forever begin to loose their moorings. In short, the meaning of the concept has shifted as a result of the *struggle* around the chains of connotations and the social practices which made racism possible through the negative construction of 'blacks'. By invading the heartland of the negative definition, the black movement has attempted to snatch the fire of the term itself. Because 'black' once signified everything that was least to be respected, it can now be affirmed as 'beautiful', the basis of a positive social identity, which requires and engenders respect amongst us. 'Black', then, exists ideologically only in relation to the contestation around those chains of meaning, and the social forces involved in that contestation.

I could have taken any key concept, category or image around which groups have organized and mobilized, around which emergent social practices have developed. But I wanted to take a term which has a profound resonance for a whole society, one around which the whole direction of social struggle and political movement has changed in the history of our own lifetimes. I wanted thereby to suggest that thinking that term in a non-reductionist way within the theory of ideology opens the field to more than an idealistic exchange of 'good' or 'bad' meanings; or a struggle which takes place only in discourse; and one which is fixed permanently and forever by the way in which particular unconscious processes are resolved in infancy. The field of the ideological has its own mechanisms; it is a 'relatively autonomous' field of constitution, regulation and social struggle. It is not free or independent of determinations. But it is not *reducible* to the simple determinacy of any of the other levels of the social formations in which the distinction between black and white has become politically pertinent and through which that whole 'unconsciousness' of race has been articulated. This process has real consequences and effects on how the whole social formation reproduces itself, ideologically. The effect of the struggle over 'black', if it becomes strong enough, is that it stops the society reproducing itself functionally, in *that* old way. Social reproduction itself becomes a contested process.

Contrary to the emphasis of Althusser's argument, ideology does not therefore only have the function of 'reproducing the social relations of production'. Ideology also *sets limits* to the degree to which a society-in-dominance can easily, smoothly and functionally reproduce itself. The notion that the ideologies are always-ready inscribed does not allow us to think adequately about the shifts of accentuation in language and ideology, which is a constant, unending process – what Volosinov (1930/1973) called the 'multiaccentuality of the ideological sign' or the 'class struggle in language'.

Notes

1 The general term, 'discourse theory', refers to a number of related, recent, theoretical developments in linguistics and semiotics, and psychoanalytic theory, which followed the 'break' made by structuralist theory in the 1970s, with the work of Barthes and Althusser. Some examples in Britain would be recent work on film and discourse in *Screen*, critical and theoretical writing influenced by Lacan and Foucault, and post-Derrida deconstructionism. In the US, many of these trends would now be referred to under the title of 'postmodernism'.

2 By the term, 'articulation', I mean a connection or link which is not necessarily given in all cases, as a law or a fact of life, but which requires particular conditions of existence to appear at all, which has to be positively sustained by specific processes, which is not 'eternal' but has constantly to be renewed, which can under some circumstances disappear or be overthrown, leading to the old linkages being dissolved and new connections – rearticulations – being forged. It is also important that an articulation between different practices does not mean that they become identical or that the one is dissolved into the other. Each retains its distinct determinations and conditions of existence. However, once an articulation is made, the two practices can function together, not as an 'immediate identity' (in the language of Marx's '1857 Introduction') but as 'distinctions within a unity'.

3 In Lacan (1966/1977), the 'Imaginary' signals a relationship of plenitude to the image. It is opposed to the 'Real' and the 'Symbolic'.

References

Althusser, L. 1969: *For Marx* (B. Brewster, trans.). London: Penguin Press. (Original work published 1965).

ALTHUSSER, L. 1971: *Lenin and Philosophy and Other Essays* (B. Brewster, trans.). London: New Left Books. (Original work published 1970).
ALTHUSSER, L. and BALIBAR, E., 1970: *Reading Capital* (B. Brewster, trans.). London: New Left Books. (Original work published 1968).
DERRIDA, J. 1977: *Of Grammatology* (G.C. Spivak, trans.). Baltimore, MD: Johns Hopkins University Press.
FOUCAULT, M. 1980: *Power/Knowledge: Selected Interviews and Other Writings 1972–1977* (C. Gordon, ed.), (C. Gordon, L. Marshall, J. Mepham and K. Soper, trans.). New York: Pantheon. (Original work published 1972).
GRAMSCI, A. 1971: *Selections from the Prison Notebooks* (Q. Hoare and G. Nowell-Smith, trans.). New York: International.
HALL, S. with SLACK, J. and GROSSBERG, L. (forthcoming): *Cultural Studies*. London: Macmillan.
HALL, S. 1974: 'Marx's Notes on Method: A "reading" of the "1857 Introduction"', *Working Papers in Cultural Studies*, 6: pp. 132–70.
LACAN, J. 1977: *Ecrits: A Selection* (A. Sheridan, trans.). New York: International. (Original work published 1966).
LACLAU, E. 1977: *Politics and Ideology in Marxist Theory*. London: New Left Books.
LACLAU, E. and MOUFFE, C. 1985: *Hegemony and Socialist Strategy*. London: New Left Books.
LEVI-STRAUSS, C. 1972: *Structural Anthropology* (C. Jacobson and B.G. Schoepf, trans.). London: Penguin. (Original work published 1958).
MARX, K. 1963: *Early Writings* (T.B. Bottomore, trans.). London: C.A. Watts.
MARX, K. 1970: *Capital*, vol. 3. London: Lawrence and Wishart.
MARX, K. 1973: *Grundrisse* (M. Nicholaus, trans.). London: Penguin. (Original work published 1953).
MARX, K. and ENGELS, F. 1970: *The German Ideology*. London: Lawrence & Wishart.
POULANTZAS, N. 1975: *Political Power and Social Classes* (T. O'Hagan, trans.). London: New Left Books. (Original work published 1968).
THOMPSON, E.P. 1978: *The Poverty of Theory and Other Essays*. New York: Monthly Review Press.
VOLOSINOV, V.N. 1973: *Marxism and the Philosophy of Language* (L. Matejka and I.R. Tutunik, trans.). New York: Seminar. (Original work published 1930).

2

British Cultural Studies and the Pitfalls of Identity

Paul Gilroy

> It is only in the last phase of British imperialism that the labouring classes of the satellites and the labouring classes of the metropolis have confronted one another directly 'on native ground'. But their fates have long been indelibly intertwined. The very definition of 'what it is to be British' – the centrepiece of that culture now to be preserved from racial dilution – has been articulated around this absent/present centre. If their blood has not mingled extensively with yours, their labour power has long since entered your economic blood-stream. It is in the sugar you stir: it is in the sinews of the infamous British 'sweet tooth': it *is* the tea leaves at the bottom of the 'British cuppa'.
>
> (Stuart Hall)

> Whenever I felt an inclination to national enthusiasm I strove to suppress it as being harmful and wrong, alarmed by the warning examples of the peoples among whom we Jews live. But plenty of other things remained over to make the attraction of Jewry and Jews irresistible – many obscure emotional forces, which were the more powerful the less they could be expressed in words, as well as clear consciousness of inner identity, the safe privacy of a common mental construction. And beyond this there was a perception that it was to my Jewish nature alone that I owed two characteristics that had become indispensable to me in the difficult course of my life. Because I was a Jew I found myself free from many prejudices which restricted others in the use of their intellect; and as a Jew I was prepared to join the Opposition and to do without agreement with the 'compact majority'.
>
> (Freud)

This short piece cannot hope to provide a comprehensive exposition of the concept of identity, its surrogates and kin terms in the diverse writings of cultural studies. Indeed, if the discrepant practices that take place under the tattered banners of British cultural studies can be unified at all, and that must remain in doubt, exploring the concept of identity and its changing resonance in critical scholarship is not the best way to approach the prospect of their unity. Reflecting upon identity seems to unleash a power capable of dissolving those tentative projects back into the contradictory components from which they were first assembled. Highlighting the theme of identity readily flushes out disagreements over profound political and intellectual problems. It can send the aspirant practitioners of cultural studies scuttling back towards the quieter sanctuaries of their old disciplinary affiliations, where the problems and the potential pleasures of thinking through identity are less formidable and engaging. Anthropologists utter sighs of relief, psychologists rub their hands with glee, philosophers relax confident that their trials are over, sociologists mutter discontentedly about the illegitimate encroachments of postmodernism while literary critics look blank and perplexed. Historians remain silent. These characteristic reactions from the more secure positions of closed disciplines underline that few words in the conceptual vocabulary of contemporary cultural analysis have been more flagrantly contested and more thoroughly abused than 'identity'.

The history of the term, which has a lengthy presence in social thought, and a truly complex philosophical lineage that goes back to the pre-Socratics, is gradually becoming better known (Gleason 1983; Hall 1992a; Calhoun 1994). However, though it has received some attention in debates over modernity and its anxieties, little critical attention has been directed towards the specific puzzle involved in accounting for identity's contemporary popularity. Though the philosophical pedigree of the term is usually appreciated by today's users, identity is invoked more often in arguments that are primarily political rather than philosophical. The popular currency of the term may itself be a symptom of important political conflicts and a signal of the altered character of postmodern politics especially in the overdeveloped countries. Another clue to this change is provided by the frequency with which the noun 'identity' appears coupled with the adjective 'cultural'. This timely pairing is only the most obvious way in which the concept 'identity' directs attention towards a more elaborate sense of the power of culture and the relationship of culture to power. It introduces a sense of *cultural* politics as something more substantial than a feeble echo of the *political* politics of days gone by. This cultural politics applies both to the increased salience of identity as a problem played out in everyday life, and to identity as it is managed and administered in the cultural industries of mass communication that have transformed understanding of the world and the place of individual possessors of identity within it.

The stability and coherence of the self has been placed in jeopardy in these overlapping settings. This may help to explain why identity has become a popular, valuable and useful concept. Though the currency of identity circulates far outside the walls of the academy, much of its appeal derives from a capacity to make supply connections between scholarly and political concerns. These days, especially when an unsavoury climate created by the unanswerable accusation of 'political correctness' makes too many critical scholars, political thinkers and cultural activists hyper-sensitive about professional standards and the disciplinary integrity of their embattled work, identity has become an important idea precisely because of these bridging qualities. It is a junction or hinge concept that can help to maintain the connective tissue that articulates political and cultural concerns. It has also provided an important means to both rediscover and preserve an explicitly political dynamic in serious interdisciplinary scholarship.

It would be wrong, however, to imagine that the concept of identity belongs exclusively to *critical* thought, let alone to the emancipatory intellectual and political projects involved in enhancing democracy and extending tolerance. Identity's passage into vogue has also been mirrored in conservative, authoritarian and right-wing thought, which has regularly attempted to use both enquiries into identity and spurious certainty about its proper boundaries to enhance their own interests, to improve their capacity to explain the world and to legitimate the austere social patterns that they favour. The crisis involved in acquiring and maintaining an appropriate form of *national* identity has appeared repeatedly as the principal focus of this activity. It too makes a special investment in the idea of culture, for nations are presented as entirely homogeneous cultural units staffed by people whose hyper-similarity renders them interchangeable.

Apart from these obviously political claims on identity, the concept has also provided an important site for the erasure and abandonment of *any* political aspirations. Clarion calls to comprehend identity and set it to work often suggest that mere politics has been exhausted and should now be left behind in favour of more authentic and powerful forms of self-knowledge and consciousness that are coming into focus. Thus, if the idea of identity has been comprehensively politicized it has also become an important intellectual resource for those who have sought an emergency exit from what they see as the barren world of politics. Identity becomes a means to open up those realms of being and acting in the world which are prior to and somehow more fundamental than political concerns. Any lingering enthusiasm for the supposedly trivial world of politics is misguided, untimely and therefore doomed to be frustrating. It also corrodes identity and can profitably be replaced by the open-ended processes of self-exploration and reconstruction that take shape where politics gives way to more glamorous and avowedly therapeutic alternatives.

This type of reorientation has occurred most readily where reflection on individual identity has been debased by simply being equated with the stark question 'who am I?' This deceptively simple question has been used to promote an inward turn away from the profane chaos of an imperfect world. It is a problematic gesture that all too often culminates in the substitution of an implosive and therefore anti-social form of *self*-scrutiny for the discomfort and the promise of public political work which does not assume either solidarity or community but works instead to bring them into being and then to make them democratic. That memorable question ends with a fateful and emphatically disembodied 'I'. It refers to an entity, that is represented as both the subject of knowing and a privileged location of being. When it sets out in pursuit of truth, this 'I' can be made to speak authoritatively from everywhere while being nowhere if only the right methods are brought to bear upon its deployment. This fateful fiction has a long and important history in the modern world, its thinking and its thinking about thinking (Taylor 1989; Haraway 1991). This 'I' can readily become a signature and cipher for numerous other problems to which the sign 'identity' can help to supply the answers. For example, if we are committed to changing and hopefully improving the world rather than simply analysing it, will political agency be possible if the certainty and integrity of that 'I' have been compromised by its unconscious components, by tricks played upon it by the effects of the language through which it comes to know itself or by the persistent claims of the body that will not easily accept being devalued in relation to the mind and the resulting banishment to the domain of unreason? Is the 'I' and the decidedly modern subjects and subjectives to which it points, a product or symptom of some underlying history, an effect of individual insertion into and constitution by society and culture? At what point or under what conditions might that 'I' bring forth a collective counterpart, a 'we'? These are some of the troubling questions that spring to mind in a period when the previously rather contradictory idea of 'identity politics' has suddenly begun to make sense.

This is a time in which *what* (no longer even *who*) you are can count for a great deal more than anything that you might do, for yourself and for others. The slippage from 'who' to 'what' is absolutely crucial. It expresses a reification (thingification) and fetishization of self that might once have been captured by the term 'alienation', which was itself a significant attempt to account for the relationship between the subject and the world outside it upon which it relied. Today, social processes have assumed more extreme and complex forms. They construct a radical estrangement that draws its energy from the reification of culture and the fetishization of absolute cultural difference. In other words, identity is inescapably political, especially where its social workings – patterns of identification – precipitate the retreat and contraction of politics.

No inventory currently exists – either inside or outside the flimsy fortifications of existing cultural studies – of the ways in which identity operates politically and how it can change political culture, stretching political thinking so that modern secular distinctions between private and public become blurred and the boundaries formed by and through the exercise of power on both sides of that line are shown to be permeable. Before the preparation of that precious inventory can proceed, we must face how the concept of identity tangles together three overlapping but basically different concerns. This suggestion involves a degree of over-simplification, but it is instructive to try and separate out these tangled strands before we set about making their symptomatic interlinkage a productive feature of our own thinking and writing. Each cluster of issues under the larger constellation of identity has an interesting place in the chequered history of the scholarly and political movement that has come to be known as cultural studies.

The concept of identity points initially towards the question of the self. This is an issue that has usually been approached in the emergent canon of cultural studies via histories of the subject and subjectivity.[1] We should note, however, that it has not been the exclusive property of cultural studies' more theoretically inclined affiliates. These ideas and the characteristic language of inwardness in which they have been expressed are extremely complex and immediately require us to enter the wild frontier between psychological and sociological domains. On this contested terrain we must concede immediately that human agents are made and make themselves rather than being born in some already finished form. The force of this observation has had a special significance in the development of modernity's oppositional movements. Their moral and political claims have arisen from a desire to estrange social life from natural processes and indeed from quarrels over the status of nature and its power to determine history.

Feminist thought and critical analyses of racism have made extensive use of the concept of identity in exploring how 'subjects' bearing gender and racial characteristics are constituted in social processes that are amenable to historical explanation and political struggle. The production of the figures 'woman' and 'Negro' has been extensively examined from this point of view (de Beauvoir 1960; Fanon 1986; Schiebinger 1993). The emergence of these durable but fictive creations has been understood in relation to the associated development of categories of humanity from which women and blacks have been routinely excluded. This kind of critical investigation has endowed strength in contemporary political thinking about the modern self and its contingencies. This is not solely a matter of concern to the 'minorities' who have not so far enjoyed the dubious privileges of inclusion in this official humanism.

The obligation to operate historically and thereby to undermine the idea of an invariant human nature that determines social life has been readily combined with psychological insights. This blend provided not only a means to trace something of the patterned processes of individual becoming but to grasp, through detailed accounts of that variable process, the kind of protean entity that a human agent might be (Geertz 1985). The endlessly mutable nature of unnatural humanity can be revealed in conspicuous contrast between different historically and culturally specific versions of the boundedness of the human person. Labour, language and lived interactive culture have been identified as the principal media for evaluating this social becoming.

Each of these options stages the dramas of identity in a contrasting manner. Each, for example, materializes the production and reproduction of gender differences and resolves the antagonistic relationship between men and women differently. All raise the question of hierarchy and the status of visible differences, whether they are based on signs like age and generation, or the modern, secular semiotics of 'race' and ethnicity. The ideal of universal humanity certainly appears in a less attractive light once the unsavoury exclusionary practices that have surrounded its coronation at the centre of bourgeois political culture are placed on display. Nietzsche showed long ago how an archaeological investigation of the modern self could lead towards this goal.

Identity can be used to query the quality of relations established between superficial and underlying similarities in human beings, between their similar insides and dissimilar outsides. By criticizing the compromised authority invested in that suspect, transcendant humanity, identity – understood here as subjectivity – presents another issue: the agent's reflexive qualities and unreliable consciousness of its own operations and limits. Posed in this way, the theoretical coherence of identity unravels almost immediately. The concept is revealed to be little more than a name given to one important element in the interminable struggle to impose order on the flux of painful social life.

The impossible modern quest for stable and integral selfhood points towards the second theme that has been (con)fused in the compound inner logic of identity. This is the equally complicated question of sameness. It too has psychological and psychoanalytic aspects. In this second incarnation, identity becomes visible as the point where a concern with individual subjectivity opens out into an expansive engagement with the dynamics of identification: how one subject or agent may come to see itself in others, to be itself through its mediated relationships with others and to see others in itself. Dealing with an agent's consciousness of sameness unavoidably raises the fact of otherness and the phenomenon of difference. Politics enters here as well. Difference should not be confined exclusively to the gaps we imagine between whole, stable subjects. One lesson yielded up by the initial approach to identity as subjectivity is that difference exists within identities – within selves – as well as between them. This means that the longed-for integrity and unity of subjects is always fragile.

In many of the political movements where the idea of a common identity has become a principle of organization and mobilization, there is an idea of interplay between 'inner' and 'outer' differences that must be systematically orchestrated if their goals are to be achieved. For example, differences within a group can be minimized so that differences between that group and others appear greater. Identity can emerge from the very operations it is assumed to precede and facilitate. The investment in ideas of essential difference that emerges from several different kinds of feminist thinking, as well as from many movements of the racially oppressed and immiserated, confirms that deeper connections have been supposed to reside unseen, hidden beneath or beyond the superficial, non-essential differences that they may or may not regulate.

Identity as sameness can be distinguished from identity as subjectivity because it moves on from dealing with the formation and location of subjects and their historical individuality into thinking about collective or communal identities: nations, genders, classes, generational, 'racial' and ethnic groups. Identity can be traced back towards its sources in the institutional patterning of identification. Spoken and written languages, memory, ritual and governance have all been shown to be important identity-producing mechanisms in the formation and reproduction of imagined community. The technological and technical processes that create and reproduce mentalities of belonging in which sameness features have also come under critical scrutiny. Exploring the link between these novel forms of identification and the unfolding of modernity has also provided a significant stimulus to politically engaged interdisciplinary research (Gillis 1994). So far, Benedict Anderson's ground-breaking discussion of the role of print cultures in establishing new ways of relating to the power of the nation-state and experiencing nationality has not acquired a postmodern equivalent. The mediation and reproduction of national and postnational identities in cyberspace and on virtual paper await a definitive interpretation. The changing resonance of nationality and the intermittent allure of subnational and supranational identities demand that we note how theorizing identity as sameness unfolds in turn into a concern with identifications and the technologies that mediate and circulate them. We must acknowledge the difficult work involved in thinking about how understanding identification might transform and enrich political thought and action.

Analysis of communal and collective identity thus leads into the third issue encompassed by identity: the question of solidarity. This aspect of identity concerns how both connectedness and difference become bases on which social action can be produced. This third element moves decisively away from the subject-centred approach that goes with the first approach and the intersubjective dynamic that takes shape when the focus is on the second. Instead, where the relationship between identity and solidarity moves to the centre-stage, another issue, that of the social constraints upon the agency of individuals and groups, must also be addressed. To what extent can we be thought of as making ourselves? How do we balance a desire to affirm the responsibility that goes with accepting self-creation as a process and the altogether different obligation to recognize the historical limits within which individual and collective subjects materialize and act? This reconciliation usually proceeds through an appeal to supra-individual identity-making structures. These may be material, discursive or some heuristic and unstable combination of them both. Attention to identity as a principle of solidarity asks us to comprehend identity as an effect mediated by historical and economic structures, instantiated in the signifying practices through which they operate and arising in contingent institutional settings that both regulate and express the coming together of individuals in patterned social processes.

Apart from its extensive contributions to the analysis of nationality, 'race' and ethnicity, the term 'identity' has been used to discern and evaluate the institution of gender difference and of differences constituted around sexualities. These unsynchronized critical projects have sometimes coexisted under the ramshackle protection that cultural studies has been able to construct. Conflicts between them exist in latent and manifest forms and have been identified by several authoritative commentators as a key source of the intellectual energy (and perversely as a sign of the seriousness) in some cultural studies writing (Hall 1992b). These tensions have also been presented as part of a corrective counternarrative that has been pitched against some inappropriately heroic accounts of political scholarship and pedagogy in the institutional wellspring of cultural studies: the Centre for Contemporary Cultural Studies at Birmingham University. Undermining those overly pastoral accounts of the Birmingham experience that might obstruct the development of today's cultural studies by mystifying it and sanitizing its embattled origins may be useful. However, those conflicts – which are usually presented as phenomena that arose where the unity of class-oriented work supposedly crumbled under the impact of feminisms and anti-racist scholarship – are only half the story.

In assessing the importance of the concept of identity to the development of cultural studies, it is important to ponder whether that concept – and the agenda of difficulties for which it supplies a valuable shorthand – might have played a role in establishing the parameters within which those conflicts were contained and sometimes made useful. I am not suggesting that the term 'identity' was used from the start in a consistent, rigorous or self-conscious way to resolve disagreements or to synchronize common problems and problematics. But rather that, with the benefit of hindsight, it is possible to imagine a version of the broken evolution of cultural studies in which thinking about identity – as subjectivity and sameness – can be shown to have been a significant factor in the continuity and integrity of the project as a whole. It may be that an interest in identity and its political workings in a variety of different social and historical sites provided a point of intersection between the divergent intellectual interests from which a self-conscious cultural studies was gradually born. I will suggest below that a tacit intellectual convergence around problems of identity and identification was indeed an important catalyst for cultural studies, and by implication, that identity's capacity to synthesize and connect various enquiries into political cultures and cultural politics is something that makes it a valuable asset even now – something worth struggling with and struggling over.

There is an elaborate literature surrounding all three aspects of identity sketched above. It includes work in and around the Marxist traditions that contributed so much to the vision, verve and ethical commitments demonstrated in British cultural studies' early interventionist ambitions. Much feminist writing has also made use of the concept of identity and generated a rich discussion of the political consequences of its deployment (Fuss 1990; Haraway 1990; Riley 1990). But before that generation of feminist scholar-activists was allowed to find its voice, the themes of identity as sameness and solidarity emerged in the political testing ground provided by the urgent commentary on the changing nature of class relations: conflict, solidarity and what we would now call identity. A new understanding of these questions was being produced as new social and cultural movements appeared to eclipse the labour movement, and old political certainties evaporated under pressure from the manifest barbarity of classless societies, a technological revolution and a transformed understanding of the relationship between the overdeveloped and underdeveloped parts of the planet that had been underlined by decolonization and mass migration. These half-forgotten debates over class are a good place to consider subjectivity, sameness and solidarity because they took place beyond the grasp of body-coded difference in a happy interlude when biology was not supposed, mechanically, to be destiny and classes were not understood to be discrete bio-social units. No one dreamed back then of genes that could predispose people to homelessness or drug abuse.

If a deceptive oblique stroke was sometimes placed between the words 'culture' and 'identity', this was done to emphasize that the latter was a product of the former – a consequence of anthropological variation. This literature on class encompassed research into both historical and contemporary social relations. It was governed by political impulses that were not born from complacent application of anachronistic Marxist formulae but rather from an acute comprehension of the political limits and historical specificity of Marxist theory. This stance suggested that class relations were an integral part of capitalist societies but that they were not, in themselves, sufficient to generate a complete explanation of any political situation. Insights drawn from other sources were needed to illuminate the process in which the English working class had been born and in order to comprehend the more recent circumstances in which it might be supposed to be undergoing a protracted death. The subtle and thoughtful concern with class and its dynamics yielded slowly and only partially to different agendas set by interpretation of countercultural movements and oppositional practices that had constituted new social actors and consequently new politicized identities. Women, youth, 'races' and sexualities: under each of these headings interest in subjectivity, sameness and solidarity developed the order of priorities that had taken shape as a result of exploring class. Partly, this was because an important divergence existed between political movements and consciousness in which the body was an immediate and inescapable issue and those where the relationship to phenotypical variation, though certainly present, was more attenuated, arising, as it were, at one remove.

Historical materialism as a political and philosophical doctrine was strongest where the politicization of the body and the consequent grasp of embodiment as the guarantor of shared identity were weakest. The reluctance to engage biology or the semiotics of the body produced a heavy theoretical investment in the idea of labour as a universal category that could transcend particularity and dissolve differences. Willingness to accept the exclusion of the body from the domains of rational cognition and scientific inquiry was thought to establish the hallmark of intellectual enterprise. The abstraction 'labour power' was offered as a means to connect the actions and experiences of different people in ways that made the kind of body in which they found themselves a secondary and often superficial issue. Marx's cryptic observation that there is a 'historical and moral element' that affects the differential price paid for the labour power of different social groups suggests otherwise and is an important clue to comprehending how these superficial differences could resist the embrace of a higher unity. This unity was situational. Consciousness of solidarity and sameness as well as collective class-based subjectivity grew from common submission to the regime of production and its distinctive conceptions of time, right and property.

Edward Thompson's 1963 *Making of the English Working Class* broke with the complacent moods of mechanical materialism and productivism and reformulated class analysis in an English idiom that supplied later cultural studies with vital political energy and a distinctive ethical style. Recognizing the strongly masculinist flavour of this important intervention should take nothing away from contemporary attempts to comprehend how it could have grown as much from the context supplied by CND, the New Left and 'practical political activity of several kinds, [that] undoubtedly prompted me [Thompson] to see the problems of political consciousness and organisation in certain ways.' (Thompson 1980: 14). Thompson's famous statement of the dynamics of class formation is relevant here:

> We cannot have love without lovers, nor deference without squires and labourers. And class happens when some men, as a result of common experiences (inherited or shared), feel and articulate the identity of their interests as between themselves, and against other men whose interests are different from (and usually opposed to) theirs.
>
> (pp. 8–9)

This is not the place to attempt some hasty resolution of the difficult issues implicit in this formulation, such as the base and superstructure relationship, the tension between different forms of consciousness and the epistemological valency of immediate experience. Nor is this an appropriate moment in which to try and chart the convoluted debates arising from the need to conceptualize the material effects of ideology and the materializing capacities of discourse (Butler 1993). Thompson's celebrated formulation links identity to selfhood, self-interests and political agency. To say that his politicized notion of identity derived from an engagement with powers which operate outside of and sometimes in opposition to those rooted in production, for example, in the residential community, would be too simple. An interest in identity was not injected into the thinking of the labour movement and its scholarly advocates by an alternative feminist historiography. An explicit and implicit concern with the political mechanisms of identity emerged directly if not spontaneously from complex analyses of past class relations. This work by Thompson and others was produced in a continuous dialogue with the urgent obligation to understand the present by seeking its historical precedents. Almost without being aware of the fact, these analyses reached beyond themselves, not towards an all-encompassing holy totality but, in the name of discomforting complexity, towards deeply textured accounts of bounded and conflictual consciousness that could illuminate contemporary antagonisms.

Though he makes use of the idea of identification rather than the concept of identity, something of the same political and imaginative enterprise can be detected in the closing pages of Raymond Williams's *The Long Revolution* (1961: 354). Grasping for the 'new creative definitions' through which that oppositional process might be maintained if not completed, Williams wrote of 'structures of feeling – the meanings and values which are lived in world and relationships' and 'the essential language – the created and creative meanings – which our inherited reality teaches and through which new reality forms and is negotiated (p. 293). Williams's conclusion seeks to make the individualization effect of contemporary society into a problem. It is not therefore surprising that he avoids the ambiguities of identity – a term which has a strongly individualistic undertone. However the theme of political identity as an outcome of conflictual social and cultural processes rather than some fixed invariant condition is clearly present:

> the reasonable man ... who is he exactly? And then who is left for that broad empty margin, the 'public opinion of the day'?
>
> I think we are all in this margin: it is what we have learned and where we live. But unevenly, tentatively, we get a sense of movement, and the meanings and values extend.
>
> (p. 354–5)

It took me a long time to appreciate how the founding texts of my own encounter with English cultural studies could be seen to converge around the thematics of identity. The key to appreciating this architecture lay in the ideas of nationality and national identity and the related issues of ethnicity and local and regional identity. Structures of feeling and the forms of consciousness that they fostered were nationally bounded. Similarly, for Thompson, the magical happening of class was something that could only be apprehended on a national basis. Along with Thompson's *Making of the English Working Class* and Williams's *The Long Revolution*, Richard Hoggart's *The Uses of Literacy* (1957) can be positioned so that it triangulates the rather ethnocentric space in which cultural development and cultural politics came to be configured as exclusively English national phenomena. Though each of these critical thinkers had his own subnational, regional and local sensitivities and obligations, culture and its political forms were comprehended by all of them on the basis that nationality supplied. To be sure, the nation was often recognized as riven with the antagonist relations that characterized the struggle to create and maintain the domination of one group by others. But the boundaries of the nation formed the essential parameters in which these conflicts took shape.

Though by no means always celebratory in tone, none of these important texts conveyed a sense of Britain and British identity being formed by forces, processes that overflowed from the imperial crucible of the nation-state. Williams's fleeting mentions of jazz or Hoggart's scarcely disguised apprehension about the catastrophic consequences of uniform 'faceless' internationalism (his code for the levelling effects of American culture) suggest other conclusions and reveal their authors' direct interest in what might be worth protecting and maintaining amidst the turmoil of the post-war reconstruction of British social life.

Each of these founding texts in the cultural studies canon can be read as a study of becoming: as an examination of class-based identity in process – transformed by historical forces that exceed their inscription in individual lives or consciousness and, at the same time, resisting that inevitable transformation.

This often unspoken fascination with the workings of identity has several additional facets. It does not always initiate the tacit collusion with Englishness that has been the festive site of cultural studies' reconciliation to a bunting-bedecked structure of feeling that its democratic, libertarian and reconstructive aspirations once threatened to contextualize if not exactly overturn.

The significantly different political alignments and hopes of these writers, as well as their contrasting stances within the generative political context that the New Left supplied for their attempts to grapple with class, popular culture and communications (Thompson 1981), should not be played down. That the direction of Hoggart's investigations was parallel to those of Thompson and Williams was signalled in the force of his opening question 'Who are the working classes?'. His thoughtful and stimulating book elaborated the distinguishing features of working-class English cultural identity. They were apprehended with special clarity even as they were assailed by the insidious forces of Americanism and commercialism: as they yielded 'place to new' in a process he understood exclusively in terms of diminution and loss: 'the debilitating mass trends of the day'. The diseased organs of a vanishing working-class culture were anatomized in a sympathetic conservationist spirit. This mournful operation captured the pathological character of their extraordinary post-1945 transformation.

Hoggart's interest in the class-based division of the social world into 'them' and 'us' and his enthusiasm for the 'live and let live' vernacular tolerance that thrived there could not be sustained once the insertion of post-colonial settler-citizens was recognized as a fundamental element in the transformation of Britain that alarmed and excited him. Immigration would become something that tested out the integrity and character of national and class identities in ways that he was not able to imagine. Hoggart's interesting speculations about the lack of patriotism in the working class, their spontaneous anti-authoritarianism and 'rudimentary internationalism' sounded hollow. This was not only because complications introduced into the analysis of class and nationalism by the existence of a 'domestic' fascism (Mosley 1946) were somewhat brushed over but, more importantly, because he was entirely silent about the social and political problems that mass black settlement was thought to be introducing into the previously calm and peaceable urban districts of England and Wales. It is not illegitimate to point to the narrowness of

Hoggart's concerns or, in the light of the subsequent patterning of British racial politics, to remind ourselves that his enigmatic silences on that subject could be used to undermine the authority of his pronouncements overall.

This is not just a question of hindsight. Before Hoggart's great book was published, Kenneth Little's *Negroes in Britain* (1947) had included a section entitled 'the coloured man through modern English eyes' (pp. 240–68). Michael Banton's *The Coloured Quarter* (1955) – which had preceded Hoggart into print by some two years – had drawn explicit attention to the problems precipitated by large-scale 'Negro immigration' into 'the large industrial cities of the North and the Midlands, in particular Leeds, Sheffield and Birmingham' (p. 69). By this time, the morality and injustices of the British colour bar had been extensively discussed in a wide range of publications including the *Picture Post* (Kee 1949). The moral and physical health status of 'colonial coloured people' had been given a good public airing by this time and associated panics over the proliferation of half-caste children, Negro criminality and vice were all established media themes when Hoggart's book was published[2].

Learie Constantine (1955) attempted to sum up the situation when, as Harold Macmillan has revealed, the Conservative government discussed the possibility of using 'keep Britain white' as its electoral slogan (Macmillan 1973: 73–4). Constantine's insightful view of the class and gender topology of English racism in the same period that produced *The Uses of Literacy* is worth quoting at length. It is a valuable reminder to anyone who would suggest that a sensitivity to the destructive effects of racism did not arise until after the 1958 'race riots' in London's Notting Hill and Nottingham (see Pilkington 1988):

> After practically twenty-five years' residence in England, where I have made innumerable white friends, I still think it would be just to say that almost the entire population of Britain really expect the coloured man to live in an inferior area devoted to coloured people, and not to have free and open choice of a living place. Most British people would be quite unwilling for a black man to enter their home, nor would they wish to work with one as a colleague, nor to stand shoulder to shoulder with one at a factory bench. This intolerance is far more marked in lower grades of English society than in higher, and perhaps it disfigures the lower middle classes most of all, possibly because respectability is so dear to them. Hardly any Englishwomen and not more than a small proportion of Englishmen would sit at a restaurant table with a coloured man or woman, and inter-racial marriage is considered almost universally to be out of the question.
>
> (Constantine 1955: 67)

Repositioned against the backdrop of this minoritarian history, it seems impossible to deny that Hoggart's comprehensive exclusion of 'race' from his discussion of postwar class and culture represented clear political choices. His work certainly exemplifies a wider tendency to render those uncomfortable political issues invisible. The same fate awaited the unwanted 'coloured immigrants' to whose lives the problems of 'race' in Britain became perversely attached. It may be too harsh to judge his inability to perceive the interrelation of 'race', nationality and class as a form of myopia induced by an indifferent ethnocentrism and complacent crypto-nationalism, but that is exactly how it seemed to me as a student of cultural studies on the twentieth anniversary of the publication of *The Uses of Literacy*.

What is more important to me now, almost twenty years later still, is the possibility that the distinctive sense of cultural politics created by those precious New Left initiatives supplied critical resources to the investigation of identity. And further, that mingled with insights drawn from other standpoints, these very resources encouraged us to see and to transcend the limits of the quietly nationalistic vision advanced by British cultural studies' imaginary founding fathers.

Thankfully these days, the writing of contemporary cultural history has become a less self-consciously ethnocentric affair than it was in the 1950s. Stuart Hall uncompromisingly insisted that, contrary to appearances, 'race' was an integral and absolutely internal feature of British political culture and national consciousness; Hall made a solid bridge not so much from scholarly nationalism to internationalism but towards a more open, global understanding of where Britain might be located in a decolonized and post-imperial world order defined by the cold war. Hall's consistent political engagements with the identity-(re)producing actions of Britain's mass media allocated substantial space to the issue of racism and used it as a magnifying glass through which to consider the unfolding of authoritarian forms that masked their grim and joyless character with a variety of populist motifs.

Particularly when appreciated in concert with the interventions of Edward Said, whose study of the Orient as an object of European knowledge and power endowed cultural studies with new heart in the late 1970s, Hall's work has supplied an invigorating corrective to the morbidity and implosiveness of figures like Williams, Thompson and Hoggart. Said and Hall are both thinkers whose critiques of power and grasp of modern history have been enriched by their own experiences of migration and some ambivalent personal intimacies with the distinctive patterns of colonial social life in Palestine and Jamaica. Both draw explicitly upon the work of Antonio Gramsci and implicitly on the legacy of the itinerant anglophile Trinidadian Marxist C.L.R. James. With the supplementary input of these intellectual but non-academic figures, cultural studies' evaluations of identity were comprehensively complicated by colonialism as well as the enduring power of a different, non-European or marginal modernity that had been forged amidst the cultures of terror that operate at the limits of a belligerent imperial system.

The nation-state could not remain the central legitimizing principle brought to bear upon the analysis of the cultural relations and forms that subsumed identity. It was not only that core units of modern government and production had been constituted from their external activities and in opposition to forces and flows acting upon them from the outside. Henceforth, identities deriving from the nation could be shown to be competing with subnational (local or regional) and supranational (diaspora) structures of belonging and kinship.

The main purpose of this inevitably cursory and oversimplified genealogy of identity is not to rake over the fading embers of the 'Birmingham School' or to endorse a specific canon for cultural studies' institutional expansion. It has been to prompt enquiries into what cultural studies' committed scholarship might have to offer to contemporary discussions, not of culture, but of multiculture and muliticultural*ism*. Today, the volatile concept of identity belongs above all to the important debate in which multicultural*ism* is being redefined outside the outmoded conventions that governed its earlier incarnations, especially in the educational system. The obvious reply to this demand – for a new theory of multicultural society that can yield a timely strategy for enhancing tolerance and respect – renounces innocent varieties of orthodox pluralism and starts afresh by rethinking cultural difference through notions of hierarchy and hegemony. This is surely valuable but can only be a beginning. Multiculturalism in both Britain and the United States has retreated from re-examining the concept of culture in any thoroughgoing manner and drifted towards a view of 'separate but equal' cultures. These parcels of incompatible activity may need to be rearranged in some new compensatory hierarchy or better still, positioned in wholesome relations of reciprocal recognition and mutual equivalence that have been denied hitherto by the unjust operations of power which is not itself comprehended in cultural terms. In this approach, power exists outside of cultures and is therefore able to distort the proper relationship between them. The best remedy for this unhappy state of affairs is supposedly to be found in strengthening political processes and modernity's neutral civic identities so that cultural particularity can be confined and regulated in appropriately private places from which the spores of destructive incommensurability cannot contaminate the smooth functioning of always imperfect democracy. A political understanding of identity and identification – emphatically not a reified identity politics – points to other more radical possibilities in which we can begin to imagine ways for reconciling the particular and the general. We can build upon the contributions of cultural studies to dispose of the idea that identity is an absolute and to find the courage necessary to argue that identity formation – even body-coded ethnic and gender identity – is a chaotic process that can have no end. In this way, we may be able to make cultural identity a premise of political action rather than a substitute for it.

Notes

1 This was a strong component of the early analyses of subculture produced by Paul Willis, Iain Chambers, Dick Hebdige and Angela McRobbie. See also Probyn (1994).

2 For a preliminary survey of the English political discussion of race during this period, see Carter et al. (1987). See also Smith (1986) and Rich (1986).

References

Banton, M., 1955: *The Coloured Quarter*. London: Jonathan Cape.

Butler, J., 1993: *Bodies that Matter*. New York: Routledge.

Calhoun, C. (ed.), 1994: *Social Theory and the Politics of Identity*. Oxford: Basil Blackwell.

Carter, B., Harris, C. and Joshi, S., 1987: 'The 1951–55 Conservative Government and the Racialization of Black Immigration', *Immigrants and Minorities*, 6(3).

Constantine, L., 1955: *Colour Bar*. London: Stanley Paul.

De Beauvoir, S., 1960: *The Second Sex*. London: Four Square Books.

Fanon, F., 1986: *Black Skin, White Masks*. London: Pluto Press.

Fuss, D., 1990: *Essentially Speaking*. New York: Routledge.

Geertz, C., 1985: 'The Uses of Diversity', *Michigan Quarterly Review*.

GILLIS, J.R. (ed.), 1994: *Commemorations: The Politics of National Identity*. Princeton, NJ: Princeton University Press.

GLEASON, P., 1983: 'Identifying Identity: A Semantic History', *Journal of American History*, 69.

HALL, S., 1992a. In L. Grossberg, et al. (eds.) *Cultural Studies*. New York: Routledge.

HALL, S., 1992b: 'The Question of Cultural Identity', in S. Hall, C. Nelson and P. Treichler (eds.) *Modernity and Its Futures*. Oxford: Polity Press.

HARAWAY, D., 1990: *Simians, Cyborgs and Women*. London: Free Association Books.

HARAWAY, D., 1991: 'Situated Knowledges'.

HOGGART, R., 1957: *The Uses of Literacy*. London: Chatto & Windus.

KEE, R., 1949: 'Is There a British Colour Bar?', *Picture Post*, 2 July.

LITTLE, K., 1947: *Negroes in Britain*. London: Routledge & Kegan Paul.

MACMILLAN, H., 1973: *At the End of the Day, 1961– 63*. Basingstoke: Macmillan.

MOSLEY, O., 1946: *My Answer*. Horley: Mosley Publications/Invicta Press.

PILKINGTON, E., 1988: *Beyond the Mother Country*. London: I.B. Tauris.

PROBYN, E., 1994: *Sexing the Self*. Routledge.

RICH, P.B., 1986: 'Blacks in Britain: Response and Reaction, 1945–62', *History Today*, 36(January).

RILEY, D., 1990: *Am I That Name?*. Basingstoke: Macmillan.

SCHIEBINGER, L., 1993: *Nature's Body*. Boston, MA: Beacon Press.

SMITH, G., 1986: *When Jim Crow Met John Bull: Black American Soldiers in World War II Britain*. London: I.B. Tauris.

TAYLOR, C., 1989: *Sources of the Self*. Cambridge: Cambridge University Press.

THOMPSON, E.P., 1980: *The Making of the English Working Class*. Harmondsworth: Penguin.

THOMPSON, E.P., 1981: 'Culturalism', in R. Samuel (ed.) *People's History and Socialist Theory*. London: Routledge.

WILLIAMS, R., 1961: *The Long Revolution*. London: Chatto & Windus.

3

Postmodernism: The Rough Guide

David Morley

Introduction

Postmodernism has been the subject of intense debate in recent years and yet it remains unclear, to many people, what the phenomenon actually amounts to. Those writing about postmodernism exhibit no central consensus as to what it actually refers, in concrete terms, and those who have criticized the whole postmodern project aim their barbs at quite disparate parties. We can usefully begin by outlining four different possibilities, four different ways of considering the phenomenon:

- we might start by suggesting that postmodernity represents a period of social life, a period that postdates something called modernity
- we might consider postmodernism as a form of cultural sensibility, characteristic of this period
- it might be viewed as an aesthetic style, expressive of the ethos of the period
- or it could be viewed as a mode of thought, particularly appropriate to analysing the period.

These are the parameters in which I shall operate, in order to try and offer a better appreciation of all the debate and controversy surrounding postmodernism.

All discussion of postmodernism implies an attempt to suggest some kind of watershed or transition from an earlier period, or way of understanding, or acting in, or on, the world. This concerns chronology and ideas about historical development and historical processes. To say post- is to say past; some kind of shift is signalled in the term itself. It is usually implied, in discussions of postmodernism, that what is being moved beyond or surpassed is 'modernity' or modernism. Not unnaturally, there are various definitions of what we are talking about here. Some versions of postmodernism seem to rest on the notion of a visual style or aesthetic, one which has developed in reaction against the artistic and critical avant-gardes of modernist art and artistic practice – those ways of thinking about art which came to prominence in the metropolitan centres of Europe, and then America, in the late nineteenth and twentieth centuries. At other times 'modernity' is used to refer to the development of particular forms of industrial, metropolitan and urban organization, most notably Fordism and its precursors such as Taylorism. Even more confusingly, modernity is also used to refer to the development in the sixteenth and seventeenth centuries of mercantile capitalism, the northern European nation-states, the founding of colonial empires and the development, around the same time, of particular ideas about science, progress and reason, in the European Enlightenment. We can think here of the French Revolution and the ideas encapsulated there or the notions of citizenship that developed out of the American War of Independence. One other remaining theme deserves mention. Postmodern theory also often expresses a strong sense of disillusionment (if we think in terms of Raymond Williams's notion of a 'structure of feeling' of an age). Perhaps disillusionment is too strong; it might be better to talk of the growing awareness of 'limits' of various kinds – for example, the discovery of ecological limits to industrialization (pollution specialists in Europe are talking in terms of sums of as high as £500 billion pounds to clear up the mess left in Europe by a few centuries of industrial progress), or perhaps of the end of certain dreams of 'progress' in the west.

The term 'modern' derives from the fifth-century Latin term *modernus*, which was used to distinguish an officially Christian present from a Roman, pagan past. Thereafter, the term is used to situate the present in relation to the past of antiquity, appearing and reappearing exactly during those periods in Europe when the consciousness of a new epoch formed itself. However, in the eighteenth century, with the emergence of the French Enlightenment, we see a different conception of modernity – as a distinctive and superior period in the history of humanity. In relation to reason, religion, and aesthetic appreciation, it was argued that the 'moderns' were more advanced, more refined, and in possession of more profound truths than the ancients. The quarrel over the respective merits of old and new effectively ended the blind veneration of classical antiquity, and prepared the way for the eighteenth-century Enlightenment philosophical project, of developing the spheres of science, morality and law, in order to achieve what the German philosopher Jürgen Habermas (1987) terms a 'rational organisation of everyday social life'.

It is worth noting, specifically, that there is something decidedly 'new' about modernity, as a category of historical periodization: unlike other forms of epochal periodization (mythic, Christian or dynastic, for example) it is defined in terms of temporal attributes. This stress is apparent in the German term *neuzeit*, literally 'new time', a term which appeared in Germany in the 1820s. Much of the debate about modernity hinges on the fate of the concept of Enlightenment, or more specifically, the Enlightenment concept of autonomous reason. For it is through this idea that modernity first came to be conceived philosophically, not just as a new historical period, or a new form of historical time, but, more substantively, as a world historical project; or, in the terms of Immanuel Kant (see his 'What is Enlightenment?', and responses by Nietzsche and Foucault, in Waugh 1992), as a conception of a universal history, which would represent a decisive break with the past, and thus mark the beginning of 'rational history'. In this connection, a social theorist such as Max

Weber is perhaps best considered as a theorist of modernization – of which the key concept is 'rationalization'. Modernity is, then, from this perspective, the consequence of a process of rationalization, by which the social world comes under the domination of asceticism, secularization and the universalistic claims of instrumental rationality. Modernity arises with the spread of western imperialism in the sixteenth century; the dominance of capitalism in northern Europe (especially in England, Holland and Flanders) in the early seventeenth century and the widespread acceptance of scientific procedures, with the publication of the work of Francis Bacon, Isaac Newton and such thinkers. Modernity is a term for the massive social and cultural changes which took place in northern Europe from the middle of the sixteenth century, and it is consequently (and necessarily) bound up with the analysis of industrial capitalist society – as a revolutionary break with tradition and with forms of social stability founded upon a relatively stagnant agrarian civilization. 'Modernity' is centrally about conquest – the imperial regulation of land, the discipline of the soul, the creation of truth and the conquest of nature by man.

In short, we have a set of interrelated notions here: modernization, rationalization and progress, and an implicit vision of the gradual perfectibility of society, to be achieved by rational planning and social reform. However, as we know, things don't always go to plan. Nowadays, in philosophy and social theory, a concept of postmodernism has been invoked to signify that the limits of the modern have been reached. It has been argued that the promises of modernity – to achieve the emancipation of humanity from poverty, ignorance, prejudice, and the absence of enjoyment – are no longer considered feasible. Such grand hopes, associated with globalizing or totalizing forms of social theory have been diminished. Thus Lyotard (1986) has suggested that the grand narratives of modern social theory and philosophy have been rendered inoperative, have lost their credibility.

According to the conservative historian Arnold Toynbee, the events which first disrupted the cosy complacency of western bourgeois notions of modernity and of the onward march of progress were the two 'World Wars' of the early twentieth century. These were described by Toynbee as having brought into focus a series of problems associated with the rapidity of technological change and the persistence of political and economic inequalities which, in so far as they threatened prevailing forms of life, raised the spectre of the mortality of Western civilization. Toynbee argued that western technological advance had precipitated a crisis in human affairs, through the imposition of a rate of change beyond the adaptional capacity of a single life, a problem subsequently described by Alvin Toffler (1970) as 'future shock'. That, however, is the point about modernity: modernization was always economically driven by capitalism and, as Marx observed, capitalism, by its very nature, is driven by the constant need to transform and revolutionize the means of production. The logic of capitalism dictates the constant necessity of the search for a better mousetrap – constant technological innovation. But, of course, technological innovation is always disruptive of existing social relations. The factory destroys the social foundations of agrarian society; the microchip, arguably, destroys the social foundations of industrial society. This is, therefore, a system in which, as Marx (and Marshall Berman (1983) after him) put it: 'All that is solid melts into air'. This happens not occasionally, not sometimes, as an incidental problem, but as an intrinsic principle of the system – which is, by definition, a system of constant change.

However, all of this is still premised on the assumption that it is the history of Europe, since the fifteenth century, which is the key to world events. Perhaps that is so, but only in so far as the history of imperialism shows us that, during that period, those Western European societies have largely dominated the world stage. But perhaps now that period is over. Modernity has always been associated with an idea of the West, but perhaps the period of post-modernity will have its axis in the Pacific, not the Atlantic (see Morley and Robins 1995). Certainly another way of understanding the West's present predicament is in terms of the realization that the goals and values which have been central to Western European civilization can no longer be considered universal, and that the associated project of modernity is *necessarily* unfinished – because its completion is inconceivable and its value in question. It is possible that the preoccupation with the distinction modernity/postmodernity reflects the growth of a concern over the possible emergence of a post-European era, if not a post-Western era. That is then to pose the problem another way, and to suggest that the current preoccupation with the postmodern may be symptomatic not so much of the demise or exhaustion of the modern, as a belated recognition of its geopolitical relocation, the shift of its creative, innovatory momentum and influence from the Atlantic to the Pacific Rim, and to the developing societies of the East.

In this introduction, I have attempted to set up some of the key themes and issues at stake in discussions of postmodernism and postmodernity. Let us now attempt to be rather more precise about these questions.

Postmodernism/Postmodernity

According to some commentators, postmodernism is a particular cultural experience, a 'structure of feeling' or 'cultural logic' which is itself the product of a particular shift in social and economic structures. Thus, according to Frederic Jameson (1984), postmodernism is the cultural logic of late capitalism. Other commentators categorize the social form differently: some refer to the post-industrial society; others to the information society; others to post-Fordism, rather than late capitalism, to describe the societies which are characterized, it is claimed, by this periodization. Whatever term is used, we are dealing, necessarily, with the question of periodization. The claim is usually made that 'society' (which society, you may well ask – none of these theories are very good at distinguishing between different societies) is characterized by a 'new type' of cultural experience. The central claim is that there has been a fundamental transformation in the economic structure of postmodern societies, which has caused these cultural changes. Thus, despite their disavowal of Marxism (which is one of the things that many of these theories of postmodernism have in common) curiously enough, many theories of postmodernity actually rest on a very old-fashioned Marxist base-superstructure model, in which the transformation of cultural experience is ultimately explained by a set of economic transformations, in the modes of production and consumption. At which point we might wish to begin to be a little more specific, and understand all this as a set of theories about the experience of postmodernity in the advanced capitalist societies of the Western world, rather than a global theory of universal social experience. That would be to argue that postmodern times have perhaps only occurred in certain places, while other kinds of times – pre-industrial or perhaps even modern – are still the dominant experience, in many other places.

Specifically, postmodernism has been argued to be the culture of a post-Fordist, post-industrial, economy or society (see Piore and Sabel 1984), in which case the first question has to be what was 'Fordism', as a mode of production, if that is what has been superseded, and if that is what the contemporary period is being defined by contrast to. Certainly in the West, at present, one set of debates concerns the notion of whether we can reasonably talk of a transition to a post-Fordist economy. This transition involves, as key dimensions, the ideas of the end of mass production, the end of mass markets and the corresponding emergence of 'flexible specialization' in production (shorter runs of a more varied set of product lines, such as those offered by a company like Benetton, and only made possible by computer technology) for a differentiated set of segmented markets. Similarly, in broadcasting, the debate is about the end of *broad*casting as such, and the emergence of *narrow*casting – a proliferation of channels and the segmentation of output for differentiated 'niche' markets or audiences. This, it is argued, is the shape of the post-Fordist (aka postmodern, post-industrial/information) society (see Robins 1989).

However, we clearly cannot really debate *post*-Fordism without an adequate understanding of what Fordism is, or was. The phenomenon which goes under the name of 'Fordism' has given us an image of a whole era of western capitalist society, based on the name of one man who owned a motor car factory: what does it signify? Perhaps two aspects are important: first, mechanized forms of standardized factory/industrial production (whether of car parts or other objects) which reduce costs through economies of scale. In this system there is little scope for consumer choice: as Ford himself said of his first Model Ts: 'You can have any colour you like, as long as it's black.' Second, a high-wage economy, where the workers' relatively high wages form the basis of large consumer markets on the part of the working classes.

In summary, we can view Fordism as a combination of mass production techniques in manufacturing industry, plus mass consumption, plus Keynesianism in State policy (a commitment to full employment, etc.). Of course, in the contemporary period, in Western Europe and America, all of this has collapsed. We have witnessed a transformation of government policy from Keynesianism and support of the welfare state towards monetarism; we have seen the collapse of the corporate State (as incorporating the government, CBI and trade unions, in Britain for example); the end of a commitment to Keynesianism in economic policy; and the drawing back of the frontiers of the State's responsibilities for the public framework of society: in short, a return to classic nineteenth-century forms of capitalism, abandoning social democratic ideas of a managed, welfare society.

Nowadays in the western economies we also see, increasingly, the collapse of manufacturing industry, the end of mass production, the move to the service sector, the return of the sweatshop, the disintegration of trade unions. We also see changes in the sphere of consumption (for some, the reduction of mass consumption possibilities) and the transformation of the workforce, under the threat of unemployment. We see a move to a key distinction between the 'core' workforce (still in full-time employment) and an increasingly large number of peripheral workers in short-term, or part-time, employment – with periods of unemployment in between – i.e. a 'flexible' or 'casualized' workforce. On the outer fringes of the economy we see a growing sector of non-employable, disenfranchised, second-class citizens, without the economic power to partake in consumption.

In effect, Henry Ford's name has been used as a shorthand way to describe a system of mass production which sought to exploit economies of scale in assembly-line factories, making standardized goods for homogeneous mass markets, by means of specialized machinery and unskilled or semi-skilled labour. It was only when it was coupled with suitable macro-economic government policies that it could exploit its full potential, so that the mass purchasing power to sustain mass production was assured. Fordism and Keynesianism, together, were responsible for the great post-World War II boom in the West. Fordism was also the basis of the political strength of a relatively homogeneous male, white, and full-time manual working class. Correspondingly, one of the points about the shift to post-Fordism is that what we see happening is also a fundamental shift in the gender of the workforce: a massive drop in male, full-time employment and a massive increase in female part-time employment – a process which has been described by some as the 'feminization' of the labour force. However, this complication aside, what we see is a general picture in which the old industrial world pioneered by Henry Ford, built on a large-scale production and uniform mass consumption, has had its day. In its place, new small-batch flexible production systems, based on robotics and information technology, combined with increasingly segmented markets, are prefiguring an altogether more pluralistic and innovative social order, the post-Fordist age. In consumption terms, this has been described as involving a key shift in sensibilities – involving a shift from 'keeping up with the Joneses' to 'keeping away from them', as consumers attempt to develop their individual identities through the adoption of a particular 'lifestyle' – a particular, individual 'style' or 'identity'.

Some argue that Fordism was the heyday of capitalism, when there was a happy marriage between particular technologies, labour processes and consumption patterns. Fordism – characterized by mass production and consumption, semi-skilled labour and easy credit – was an example of such a regime of accumulation, but it has broken down. Capitalism can only emerge from its difficulties, it is now sometimes argued, if it embarks on a new era of neo- or post-Fordism, based on advanced technologies, flexible specialization and subcontracting. The basic argument, then, is that in this postmodern, post-Fordist era our world is being remade. Mass production, the mass consumer, the big city, and the big-brother State are in decline: conversely flexibility, diversity, differentiation, mobility, communication, decentralization and internationalization are in the ascendant.

From Modernism to Postmodernism

As noted earlier, the postmodern can only be defined in relation to the modern. So what was the experience and structure of modernity? Berman (1983) defines the three processes of industrialization, urbanization and mechanization as the key social transformations at the heart of the condition of modernity, and gives as its key institutions the factory, the city and the nation. In which case, it is not hard to deduce that postmodernity might be characterized by de-industrialization: the transition to the information society, in which the service sector replaces manufacturing industry, the computer replaces the lathe, and trade in information replaces the production of goods. Simultaneously, according to this model, mechanization is superseded by automation, and the factory is disaggregated into the home-based, dispersed, computerized workforce. The industrial city is broken up and itself dispersed into the continuous suburb; urbanization goes into reverse, as employment leaves the city for regional locations. At the same time, the nation disintegrates from two directions at once. On one hand, we see the rise of regional cultures across Europe (a process of localization and fragmentation) and, on the other, we see a contradictory process of globalization, in which the geographical boundaries of the nation are transcended by advertising, marketing and satellite television, with its transnational flows of information and culture – which, according to McLuhan (1964) were going to create the global village. Thus we see forces of fragmentation and homogenization in play, at the same time.

All of that, of course, refers to the notion of postmodernity as a period – we have also to consider the notion of postmodernism as a cultural style or aesthetic. In this case, it must be defined in relation to the modernism which itself was the key aesthetic of nineteenth-century and early twentieth-century Europe. So again, as it is a relational definition, first we have to define modernism as an aesthetic before we can then understand what postmodernism might be. By modernism is, in fact, meant many things, but as a descriptive term for an aesthetic, it would include things such as the novels of James Joyce, the poems of Ezra Pound, the plays of Samuel Beckett, the architecture of the Bauhaus and Le Corbusier, the paintings of Matisse and Picasso, the music of Stockhausen and John Cage and the films of Eisenstein and Godard. Stephen Spender once described modernism neatly (if circularly) as a movement of modern art in which artists reflect their awareness of their unprecedented 'modern' situation in new forms and new values. In such movements as Futurism, Cubism and Constructivism, artists attempted to create new languages of representation in which to express the bewildering (if exciting) complexity of their rapidly changing world. The point, it was argued, was that the old forms of classical, realist, conventional, art were inadequate to represent the conditions of the modern world.

These are the forms of artistic expression that also correspond to the modern 'consciousness' – the famously 'decentred subject'. This is the subject who lives in a world in which things look quite different, after the interventions of Marx, Freud and de Saussure. Why? Because Marx tells us that consciousness, in any society, will tend not to represent the truth, but rather to be an ideologically distorted reflection of the 'hidden truths' of the economy; Freud tells us that our conscious thoughts are, anyway, merely the tip of the iceberg of unconscious mental activity, where our desires are formed and driven in ways quite inaccessible, ordinarily, to our conscious minds; and de Saussure tells us that far from being a question of us formulating our thoughts and then putting them into language – to communicate to others – rather, our very thoughts themselves are structured, unconsciously, by the rules and concepts of the language and the culture in which we have been socialized since childhood. All of which, of course, decentres the traditional idea of the individual consciousness (Descartes's '*Cogito, ergo sum*') as the source of meaning. The modern subject, it is argued, must now be recognized as decentred, and only new forms of art are able to adequately express that condition or predicament.

The connecting thread among all these modernist styles and approaches is a particular sensibility – the works are all difficult in a certain sense, the object being represented is problematized – and the emphasis shifts to the exploration of the mechanisms and the processes of representation and communication itself. In many cases the works can be seen, in one way, as the high point of a particular European tradition of art. These are works, still, of 'serious culture' – of the kind of which art historians approve, for example, when they talk about the proper, critical function of art. One part of the argument about modernism concerns the fact that, while all of these modernist art works *were* seen as revolutionary (and in many cases scandalous) in their time, they have now become accepted as part of the classical canon – they define the syllabus of university English courses, they are hung in the most prestigious galleries, and perhaps more significantly, the boundaries between them and popular culture are no longer as hermetically sealed as they once were. What for the surrealists of the 1930s was a controversial joke, thrown in the face of the art establishment of the time, is now a commonplace of TV ads. In short, these works themselves, it is argued, have now both been absorbed into the conservative art world of the establishment, and, increasingly, into popular culture. Thus, advocates of a postmodern aesthetic would argue that modernist culture no longer has a critical or progressive function. From their point of view, modernism is criticized for being, in its difficulty, both snobbish and exclusive; for being (especially in its architecture, for example) grandiose (and, in a way, totalitarian – of which more later) and for being imperialist and improperly universalist in its abstraction (note the apogee of this tendency – Abstract Expressionism (in the paintings of Rothko, etc.) – which has been criticized as the art of American imperialism – see Guibault 1983).

Against all this, postmodernist art tends to be figurative, rather than abstract, local rather than grandiose or universalist and, its practitioners claim, popular and accessible, rather than snobbish or exclusive. At which point we might want to distinguish between postmodernism and anti-modernism – because a lot of, for example, postmodern architecture is explicitly anti-modern, in its rejection of anything new and its insistence on a return to classical form and classical materials and shapes. Which, of course, has a profound popular (if not populist) emphasis. Thus Prince Charles's campaign against the awfulness of modern British architecture touches a deep chord with many people, when it focuses, for example, on the tower block as the hate symbol of modern architecture. Similarly, when he insists that architecture should respect local conditions, rather than impose universalist solutions, and that architects should consult local people and respect their views, rather than play the role of the 'expert' who knows best and has the power to impose their solution on everybody else, this too 'rings true' for many. This brings us to another dimension of the debate; the sense in which modernity is often now equated with a particular set of themes – progress, reason, rationality, social engineering and planning – which themselves, while growing, in Habermas's argument, directly out of the European tradition of the Enlightenment, are now seen as having a deeply problematic and inherently totalitarian edge. To give one example, the main motive for postmodern architecture is seen as the social failure of modernist architecture. Indeed modern architecture has been repeatedly declared to be dead in recent decades, one of the first little 'deaths' being the 1968 collapse of an English tower block, Ronan Point, through cumulative structural faults, as its floors gave way after an explosion. Even more symbolic was the deliberate destruction of tower blocks on the Pruitt-Igoe housing project in St Louis in the USA in 1973, when they were declared unfit for human habitation. Such events drew attention to the fundamental failures of modern architecture and modernist building methods: cheap pre-fabrication, lack of personal/defensible space and the alienating housing estate – in essence, housing not properly built to an 'appropriate' human scale, but rather designed with reference to inhumane models of abstract 'efficiency'.

According to the postmodernists, the forces of modernity, progress and rationality can now be seen to have led up a historical cul-de-sac. The great metanarratives of the modern period – the beliefs in rationality, science and planning, in the cause of human emancipation and progress – all these, according to writers such as Lyotard (1986) have been shown to have blood on their hands. These beliefs are now seen to have also functioned as ideologies, legitimating everything from nuclear weapons to racism and the bureaucratic use of the Gulag camps in the service of totalitarian communism. As a result of all this, says Lyotard, we see a widespread collapse of faith in these meta-narratives which 'leaders' and 'experts' have used to justify their actions – by claiming that they alone had access to the truth of our social existence and that, on this basis, we should accept their authority.

Negations of Modernism

Hebdige (1988) proposes that we consider the postmodern project as centrally composed of a series of negations of modernism. He identifies three negations as central to the postmodern ethos; the rejection of (1) totalization, (2) teleology, (3) Utopianism. Let us take each in turn:

1 Against totalization ('no total solutions')

By this, Hebdige refers to the widespread rejection of all the generalizing aspirations of the Enlightenment – all those discourses which set out to define an essential human nature, to prescribe a particular destiny to human history and to define collective human goals. Thus, postmodernists reject the universalist claims of modernist discourses – to know the truth of the human condition, or to speak in the name of abstract concepts of justice or society. Any such large claims are, according to the postmodernists, to be properly treated with suspicion, as is any political party claiming the right to lead the masses towards such predestined goals, in the abstract. The only possibility left to us, according to Foucault (1980) is micro-politics: local struggles, around particular issues – anything more is suspected of leading to improper 'totalizations', and thus to totalitarianism.

2 Against teleology ('you can't know anything for certain')

By this, Hebdige means the increasing scepticism in postmodern circles, regarding the idea of decidable origins and causes in human affairs, as evinced by any form of 'depth model' of the universe (which unites all modernist discourses, such as Marxism, psychoanalysis and structuralism). All these discourses claim to be able to discover a 'hidden truth' behind the surface of appearances: Marxism claims to discover the hidden/real economic relations behind the surface forms of ideological appearances; psychoanalysis claims to discover the truth of unconscious motives lying behind everyday, seemingly simple, actions and statements; structuralism claims to discover, beyond our individualities, in a similar way, the unconscious foundations of language and culture, which structure our very consciousness. Against all of this, postmodernism asserts the collapse of any such possibility – the argument is that the 'experts' who claim to discover these truths are mere charlatans. As, according to the postmodernists, we can never, finally, know these hidden truths with full confidence, better to accept that we live in a world of appearances (a world without depth) or 'simulacra' (in Baudrillard's terminology). This is a universe where bits of information, images and television close-ups float about in a 'hyperreal' space (see Eco 1986). In this postmodern culture, it is sometimes claimed that the schizophrenic experience of dissociation may now be the psychic norm of the postmodern condition (according to Jameson). If so, this simply is the condition with which we have to come to terms, without resorting to discredited depth models of analysis, in attempting to discover any 'hidden truths' lying behind this realm of images and appearances. All of this may perhaps be related to the question of why the postmodern period is characterized by such an emphasis on image, design and style, but, of course, that is already to use a discredited depth model of analysis, i.e. to try to explain why the period *really* has had such a distinctive emphasis on style. Perhaps we should rest content with 1980s style guru Peter York's credo (after Oscar Wilde): 'only a fool doesn't judge by appearances'. But then again, of course, it is not clear what is being judged here. If appearances are being judged to give us clues as to hidden truths, then we are in fact, right back with a form of depth model. The 'hidden depths' of Peter York, perhaps.

3 Against Utopia ('don't go mistaking paradise for that home across the road')

The third negation, according to Dick Hebdige, is that of any notion (or model) of a Utopia, against which present societies might be judged and found wanting. The problem, it is argued, is that once you set out on this road, fortified by notions like having 'God' or 'history' on your side, convinced that you have a mission to lead people towards some promised land, what actually happens is that you turn into Robespierre or Pol Pot and that, in your conviction of your revolutionary rightness, you end up instigating a terroristic process, justifying the elimination of your enemies by reference to the ultimate justice of your goal and the rightness of your cause. This way lies '1984' say the postmodernists, even if, despite the date, we haven't quite got there yet. Thus, it is argued, we cannot believe in totalities, hidden truths or Utopias, as we stumble around in this 'society of the spectacle', where the real has been replaced by its image, and the image supplanted by the 'simulacrum' which is, of course, itself hyperreal . . .

There is a problem. All these theorists of the postmodern condition, whose fundamental claim is that one can no longer speak with any credibility of what is 'real' or 'true' in any generalized sense, do themselves in fact seem to be in the business of making statements of precisely this kind – offering us abstracted, generalized models of the 'truth' of the postmodern condition – which raises a fascinating set of epistemological problems. I shall return to this issue. In a moment we will try another tack, and ask how it feels, out there in the postmodern world. However, before that, let's just be reductionist for a few moments. Postmodern theory is offered as a general analysis of the postmodern world: one question would concern how it applies in relation to the majority of the world's population – are they simply further behind in a linear narrative of world history, struggling still to enter the modern era, and able to look forward, in the longer term, to their own final arrival in postmodernity? In parallel with older modernization theorists such as Rostow (1960) do we simply have here yet another unilinear vision of world history, leading to only one conclusion: America? (For a more contemporary version of this unilinear vision, see Fukuyama 1992.)

We could also try a cheap version of the sociology of knowledge, and ask who is it who advances the theory of postmodernism? The theory is advanced as a set of claims about how the world is, but from whose point of view is it being seen? The theory claims to speak of a cultural crisis, in a general sense, but perhaps we could locate it more particularly as the expression of a more particular crisis – the crisis of the downwardly socially mobile white intellectuals of Western Europe and America, working in a decaying set of public sector institutions, under the specific conditions of monetarist policies. As West acidly comments of Lyotard's theories: 'who is he talking about? Him and his friends hanging about on the Left Bank?' (West 1991: 5).

We could also, perhaps, put some crude dates and names to events which mark some of the parameters of this rather vaguely defined 'postmodern' period. Among these we might, for instance, include explicitly political markers – including perhaps the failed Hungarian revolution of 1956, out of which emerged the 'Socialism or Barbarism' and 'Situationist' groups in France. It was, after all, out of these groups that Baudrillard, Lyotard and Virilio finally emerged, many years later, via their detour round the 'failure' of the 1968 revolt in France and Solzhenitsyn's visit to Paris in 1974, when the French intellectuals finally 'learnt' about the gulags in the USSR, and a number of them moved from Left to Right, to emerge as the 'new philosophers' of the era.

Or we could start in another place, and look for cultural markers. We might begin with 'pop art' in Britain in the 1950s and the emergence of Andy Warhol in the USA as the postmodern artist of the consumer society. This would be to link the concerns of postmodernism more directly to debates about popular art and consumer culture. Or, more prosaically, as an economic watershed, we could perhaps take the oil crisis of 1973, the point at which the dollar ceased to be the world's key currency. That was the point at which the long post-World War II boom in the West finally went into reverse and the conditions (recession and unemployment) began to emerge which led finally to the installation of monetarist conservative governments throughout the West in the 1980s and to the gradual collapse of the social democratic model of society. This would certainly be to speak of a 'new' era but perhaps a more localized and specific one than the postmodernists would have in mind. None of this is in any way conclusive, but is offered, in postmodern spirit, as a way of questioning the grandiose and totalizing claims of variants of postmodern theory and by way of trying to situate these claims and themes themselves in their local conditions, as it were.

Postmodernism: How Does it Feel?

To return to the experiential question, we could simply ask, what is the experience of postmodernism? How does it feel? What is the 'structure of feeling' of the period? Ignatieff (1989) claims that it can be characterized as the '3-minute culture' – the culture of the short attention span, where politicians no longer address us in speeches, but in 30-second 'sound bites' and through 'photo opportunities'; a world in which the news comes to us in 90-second bits, each disconnected from the last, in a plethora of little stories and images; where we are all so used to the fast editing of the adverts and the pop promos that the traditional Hollywood film seems so slow as to be almost quaint. It is, says Ingatieff, a culture which induces us to graze the TV channels, zapping back and forth whenever our boredom threshold is triggered, rather than watching a programme. It is, he says, a culture where very rarely does anyone do just one thing at a time, in a concentrated way for an extended period; it is, he says, increasingly a culture catering for people with the attention span of a flea. So, he says, look at the media: narrative is replaced by flow; connection replaced by disconnection; sequence replaced by randomness. The cost, he says, is memory. He claims that we are, increasingly, an 'amnesiac culture', where everything is jumbled up together in an over-polluted swamp of images and sensations – a kind of fast food culture for the mind, served up in easy to chew, bite-sized sections, where everyone snacks all the time, but no one (hardly) ever consumes the intellectual equivalent of a square meal.

Ignatieff argues that it is, of course, the adverts which are the 'masterpieces' of this '3-minute culture', the 'best things on TV', and no wonder many of the people who are now the most successful film directors learnt their trade directing adverts. Everything is new, of course (except that which is deliberately marketed as 'traditional') and the speed of change (the rate of cultural obsolescence) is accordingly rapid. But curiously enough, says Ignatieff, that also means that everything is, increasingly, the same everywhere. Thus he observes that a shopping centre in one place increasingly looks exactly the same as one in another, and every High Street in the UK looks exactly the same – Body Shop, Tie Rack, Next, etc. Every time someone has a new retail idea, everybody else copies it, so the new urban environment is both uniform geographically (and, indeed, internationally) at any one time, while also changing more rapidly than ever before, from year to year, or season to season. Ignatieff offers us a vision of a world of rapidly changing images, governed by a logic of impermanence – a culture of amnesia, in which everything is forgotten or thrown away almost immediately, only to reappear a little later as 'nostalgia' or 'retro-chic.' So where does that leave us?

The Society of the Spectacle?

In fact, many postmodernists take their lead from an early group of French theorists, the Situationists. These theorists of 'the society of the spectacle', such as Guy Debord (1970) argued that

> the entire life of societies in which modern conditions of production prevail, announces itself as an immense accumulation of spectacles. Everything that was directly lived has moved away into a representation . . . reality becomes a spectacle ... the spectacle becomes real ... and the spectacle is the image of capitalist production.

Or, as Baudrillard (1988) puts it, we are seduced into the hyperreal, post-modern world of 'pure floating images', behind which there is nothing. The object has become a commodity; use-value has been totally eclipsed by exchange value; goods no longer have anything to do with the satisfaction of material needs; they principally (exclusively, perhaps) function as signs without referents: we principally consume them as signs. First, Baudrillard says, the image reflected reality; then it masked reality; then it marked the absence of reality. Now, in the final phase, the image bears no relationship to any reality, but has become its own 'simulacrum'. That which is real has become that which can be simulated. And you only really know that it's real when you see it on TV. This, of course, sounds very postmodern. But consider the following quotation: 'Without doubt our epoch ... prefers the image to the thing, the copy to the original, the representation to the reality, appearance to being.' The problem is that this is Feuerbach, writing about mid-nineteenth-century Germany, quoted in Debord (1970), which leaves us with something of a problem about the specificity of the postmodern period.

Baudrillard follows Eco ('Towards a Semiological Guerilla Warfare', in his *Travels in Hyperreality*, 1986) in arguing that we live in a media universe, where there is more and more information and less and less meaning. The very production of this 'excess' of information precludes response by the recipient, according to Baudrillard. Indeed, he argues, this excess of high-speed information is destructive of the possibility of meaning. The 'superfluidity' of information devours its own contents, as it goes along, in an amnesic spiral. The result, according to Baudrillard, is a 'hyperreality' of communication and meaning, 'more real than the real', where, in the end, the 'real' is abolished, in favour of the continuous presentation of a meaningless spectacle of images. This is rather like a Velvet Underground version of Marshall McLuhan, where you end up simply with noise, rather than meaning. A 'global village' indeed, but one where all the inhabitants have become terminally passive, as they sit in front of their flickering TV screens. In an odd way, Baudrillard claims that the very passivity of the 'masses' is also their salvation, in that, by becoming passive, they somehow nullify the effects of the media. This, he claims, creates an 'implosion' of meaning which, he argues, short-circuits the system. Thus, in Baudrillard's vision, the 'masses' victoriously 'resist' the media by absorbing its messages without responding to them, in a 'refusal of meaning' (a rather narrow and unproductive form of resistance, you might think, but it is the only one Baudrillard allows for). So, with the gradual, uniform bombardment of information, all differences of content are cancelled: all that is left is the Spectacle, without meaning. In this world of surfaces, television takes over from the real as the place where 'real' things happen only if they are screened. In a thoroughly 'imaged' universe, politics becomes largely an adjunct of PR and showbiz. Rational critique is replaced by the 'ecstasy of communication' – a state characterized by 'banal seduction' and mindless fascination. In this world any kind of rational judgement (Is that true? Did this really happen? Is this only a story?) becomes not only impossible, but even irrelevant. In this vision of the 'information revolution' the sheer volume and variety of information finally overwhelms everything, and the hype creates its own reality (in Britain, the activities of a PR agent such as Max Clifford are a good example). This is the reality of the *Sunday Sport* ('Aliens turned my son into an olive') offered as a kind of joke, in which the reader is (knowingly, with a wink and a smile) invited to participate, with a kind of suspension of disbelief.

The problem, of course, is that while all this might be fairly amusing, to misquote Neal Postman (1986) we might finally be in danger of 'amusing ourselves to death'. While the postmodern media might offer a certain kind of pleasure, the implicit premiss – that we give up any notion of a realm of verifiable public truths, as Baudrillard suggests – is deeply problematic; today aliens from Mars kidnap joggers, yesterday Auschwitz didn't happen, tomorrow who knows or cares what actually happens . . . ? You detect a tone of frustration. Quite true. But perhaps there are ways in which some of what Baudrillard says is 'true' – even if he would regard the very statement as nonsensical.

Television and the Real

Over the last 30 years or so, one of the staples of media analysis has been work considering the coverage of real events (elections, strikes, etc.) by television, asking questions about the degree of objectivity or bias in the coverage, etc. The problem with work of this type is, of course, that it presupposes that there is, first of all, a thing such as 'a general election', for example, and *then* a representation, the coverage of it on TV. Now that is a distinction that is, in some ways, rather difficult to sustain. Contemporary elections in the West are *principally* 'TV events'. They have their principal existence in and through the medium of TV. Indeed, in so far as political campaigns are still fought outside the TV studios at all, they are planned with a view to how they will look on TV. In a similar way, when President Reagan bombed Libya, he didn't do it at the most effective time of day, from a military point of view. The timing of the raid was principally determined by the timing of the American TV news; it was planned in such a way as to maximize its televisual impact. It was timed to enable Reagan to announce on the main evening news that it had 'just happened' – it was planned *as* a TV event.

That, argue a number of people (e.g. Hall and Jacques, in Hall 1988) who take a different view of postmodernism from Baudrillard et al., is also what was interesting about 1980s 'media events' such as Band Aid and the Mandela concerts; these were not pre-existing events which happened to be televised – they were designed as televisual events in the first place. The 'communities of the airwaves' that they produced were themselves perfectly real and had quite definite political and cultural effects. We can then begin to speak of 'community' in such a way that does not necessarily imply physical contiguity. We can begin to speak of 'communities' of electronic (rather than geographical) space, and of new forms of politics, conducted through these electronic media. Which brings us again to the question of the masses in their electronic dimension, the so-called 'silent majorities', in whose shadow, according to Baudrillard, we exist. Perhaps we should just end by reminding ourselves of what Raymond Williams had to say on the question. Williams, of course, argued that there are no masses, only ways of thinking about other people as masses, postmodern or otherwise.

Note

I would like to thank Gareth Stanton for his contributions to this chapter. For a further development of this analysis, concentrating on the ethnocentricity of many of the debates about postmodernism, see my essay 'The End of What', in Morley and Robins (1995) or my essay 'EurAm, Modernity, Reason and Alterity', in Morley and Chen (1995).

References

Baudrillard, J., 1988: *Selected Writings* (edited by M. Poster). Oxford: Polity Press.
Berman, M., 1983: *All That is Solid Melts into Air*. London: Verso.
Debord, G., 1970: *The Society of the Spectacle*. Detroit: Black and Red Books.
Eco, U., 1986: *Travels in Hyperreality*. London: Picador.
Foucault, M., 1980: *Power/Knowledge*, Brighton: Harvester Press.
Guibault, S., 1983: *How New York State Stole the Idea of Modern Art: Abstract Expressionism, Freedom and the Cold War*, Chicago: Chicago University Press.
Fukuyama, F., 1992: *The End of History and the Last Man*, Harmondsworth: Penguin Books.
Habermas, J., 1987: *The Philosophical Discourse of Modernity*, Oxford: Polity Press.
Hall, S., 1988: *The Hard Road to Renewal: Thatcherism and the Crisis of the Left*, London: Verso.
Hebdige, D., 1988: *Hiding in the Light*, London: Comedia/Routledge.
Ignatieff, M., 1989: 'Cleverness is All', *The Independent*, 7 January.
Jameson, F., 1984: 'Postmodernism, or the Cultural Logic of Late Capitalism', *New Left Review*, 146.
Lyotard, F., 1986: *The Postmodern Condition: A Report on Knowledge*, Manchester: Manchester University Press.

McLuhan, M., 1964: *Understanding Media*, London: Routledge & Kegan Paul.

Morley, D. and Chen, K.H. (eds.), 1985: *Stuart Hall: Critical Dialogues in Cultural Studies*, London: Routledge.

Morley, D. and Robins, K., 1995: *Spaces of Identity: Global Media, Electronic Landscapes and Cultural Boundaries*, London: Routledge.

Piore, M. and Sabel, C., 1984: *The Second Industrial Divide*, New York: Basic Books.

Postman, N., 1986: *Amusing Ourselves to Death*, London: Methuen.

Robins, K., 1989: 'Reimagined Communities: European Image Spaces – Beyond Fordism', *Cultural Studies*, 3(2).

Rostow, W., 1960: *The Stages of Economic Growth*, Cambridge: Cambridge University Press.

Toffler, A., 1970: *Future Shock*, New York: Praeger.

Waugh, P., 1992: *Postmodernism: A Reader*, London: Edward Arnold.

West, C., 1991: 'Decentring Europe', *Critical Quarterly*, 33(1).

4

The Impossible Object: Towards a Sociology of the Sublime

Dick Hebdige

> A Klee painting named *Angelus Novus* shows an angel looking as though he is about to move away from something he is fixedly contemplating. His eyes are staring, his mouth is open, his wings are spread. This is how one pictures the angel of history. His face is turned towards the past. Where we perceive a chain of events, he sees one single catastrophe which keeps piling wreckage upon wreckage and hurls it in front of his feet. The angel would like to stay, awaken the dead, and make whole what has been smashed. But a storm is blowing from Paradise; it has got caught in his wings with such violence that the angel can no longer close them. This storm irresistibly propels him into the future to which his back is turned while the pile of debris before him grows skyward. This storm is what we call progress.
>
> (Walter Benjamin, 'The 9th Thesis on the Philosophy on History')

> *Cosmogony Legends*. Like almost all Indians, the Algonquin tribes believe in the Thunder Bird, a powerful spirit whose eyes flash lightning, while the beating of his wings is the rolling of thunder. He it is who prevents the earth from drying up and vegetation from dying.
>
> (Robert Graves (ed.), *New Larousse Encyclopaedia of Mythology*)

1

In recent years, the reappraisal of political and intellectual priorities which has been forced upon us by a whole series of cultural, political and epistemological crises has led to a renewal of interest in the genealogy and origins of contemporary modes of thought, ways of seeing and saying. As part of this process of critical, reflexive practice – a movement back which can involve either a painful but necessary return to primary questions or a wilful retreat from the challenge of the present – there has been a renewal of interest in the origin and meaning of the aesthetic experience. Attention has been concentrated on two founding moments: the origin of western philosophy in ancient Greece and the birth of formal aesthetics in the Enlightenment when the categories of the Sublime and the Beautiful were first used to differentiate the varieties of aesthetic experience.

At the same, the rhetoric of postmodernism has helped to induce and articulate a generalized 'sense of an ending' which is focused around a refusal of totalities, explanatory systems, older certainties of all kinds. Often, and paradoxically, the genealogical impulse has here been combined with a tendency to engage in what Jean Baudrillard calls 'science fiction': a sense of play and prophecy, along with forms of parable and allegory, has entered 'serious' critical discourse, sometimes in the shape of highly schematic diagnoses of our present 'condition'. In this spirit, some commentators have deconstructed the 'aesthetic', and in a Derridean flourish turned it inside out, presenting in its place a critical postmodern 'anti-aesthetic'.[1]

Taking advantage in what follows of the critical licence opened up within the Post (post-structuralism, postmodernism) I shall move back and forth across this landscape mobilizing different kinds of knowledge, different voices, different kinds of writing, to reflect upon the provenance in the modern period of the idea of aesthetics and aesthetic judgement and to summarize two different but related critiques of the 'aesthetic': on one hand, Pierre Bourdieu's work on the social origin and functions of aesthetic taste and, on the other, the postmodernist promotion, following Nietzsche, of an 'anti-aesthetic' based on a rejection of the Enlightenment idea(l) of beauty. At the same time, by cutting back at regular intervals to more grounded 'ecological' descriptions of the street in London where I live, by concentrating in particular on the heterogeneous (sub)cultural-ethnic mix that constitutes the local demographic, I hope to 'bring home' – in both the literal and figurative senses of the phrase – the implications of issues raised in these larger debates on taste, aesthetics, postmodernism. This weaving together of incommensurable levels, tones, objects represents an attempt to engage *suggestively* in those debates, to alternate between, on one hand the personal, the confessional, the particular, the concrete, and on the other the public, the expository, the general, the abstract: to walk the flickering line between vertigo and ground.

The ghost of a totality hangs in the air like the shadow of Klee's Angel over the discourse(s) of the Post but the Angel also has another side and a different name. (In other places it answers to the name of Thunder Bird.) This article, centred as it is on the reverie of the impossible object (a sociology of the Sublime is, after all, impossible) is also intended as an invocation of the Thunder Bird: as a tracking of the Angel's brighter aspect. The invocation ends with a question: if sociology is concerned with the discovery and examination of invisible, impalpable structures which cannot be directly apprehended in experience but which none the less condition everything that passes as *social* experience, then what can sociology do with the unconscious, what can it do with those invisible, impossible, imaginary structures we inhabit every night as we sleep? What kind of sociology would take dreams as 'data'?

2

There is a paradox in the historical development of the word 'taste'. Originally denoting physiological sensations, the word was generalized from meaning essentially passive physiological responses (primarily palatal) to given stimuli, to a sense either of the active attribution of value to aesthetic objects or of the more or less codified rules of polite society – so called 'good taste'. By the eighteenth century, according to Raymond Williams,[2] the word had been, as it were, etherialized so that it no longer referred to the physical senses but rather to the underlying principles which are taken to govern the laws of conduct and aesthetics alike. From that time onwards, taste can be taken to refer to the judgement of either social or formal values, while the 'laws' or 'rules' which are invoked to legitimate and authorize those judgements are in both cases typically seen as God-given, universal, timeless.

It is that confusion surrounding the term – a term which can designate at once physical sensations of attraction and repulsion and the elaboration of both social and formal codes – which provides the starting-point from which subsequent debates on taste proceed. The entire fragile edifice of modern aesthetics could be said to rest upon the founding set of contradictions and oppositions traced out during the eighteenth century around the word 'taste'. A struggle over the meaning of the term begins in earnest in the latter part of the century. The romantic poets, for example, as part of their resistance to the commercialization and commodification of literature – itself linked to the decline of aristocratic patronage and the rise of the literate mercantile and industrial middle classes – begin to articulate a mythology of artistic production around the solitary figure of the alienated and marginalized poet-prophet. This romantic archetype of the isolated creative genius, estranged from urban 'polite society', temperamentally aligned with Nature and the Folk (as opposed to the Public), develops in explicit opposition to the cultural aspirations of those sections of the emergent bourgeoisie which are seeking to emulate aristocratic models, to gatecrash 'high society', to codify and generalize the rules of taste and manners so that they can consolidate their economic ascendancy in the cultural field. The conflict arises, then, between those who resist any attempt to submit or reduce literature and the arts to the laws of the market, and those fractions of the emergent elites who seek to conceal and euphemize the 'vulgar' sources of their wealth in industry and commerce and to raise themselves and their offspring to a 'higher', more spiritual level. For Wordsworth, who in the preface to the *Lyrical Ballads* had referred contemptuously to those 'who will converse with us as gravely about a *taste* for Poetry, as they express it, as it if were a thing as indifferent as a taste for rope-dancing, or Frontiniac or Sherry',[3] only the poets, men (*sic*) of principle and insight, in tune with Nature and the eternal verities, pledged to defend and renew the living language through their poetry, should be entrusted with the sacerdotal role of distinguishing the good from the bad, the beautiful from the ugly, the enduring from the transitory. And these oppositions develop, in the succeeding decades, alongside other ideologically weighted distinctions between, for instance, 'art' and 'industry', 'individual' and 'mass', 'organic' and 'mechanical', 'high' and 'low' culture. In other words, they develop alongside and in parallel with all those structured oppositions which form around the superordinate polarity between culture and society which Raymond Williams shows to have dominated literary-critical and aesthetic discourse in England from the latter part of the eighteenth century until the middle of the twentieth.[4]

But the question of taste, of discrimination, of the generalizability or otherwise of aesthetic judgements, is posed much further back, at the root of the western philosophical tradition, in the Platonic concept of ideal forms, where the objects which we encounter in sensory experience are held to be mere tokens: imperfect, mortal echoes of the absolute forms of the Good, the True and the Beautiful which are said to exist beyond the reach of our senses, 'on the other side' of sensory experience, beyond time and change. In a famous series of metaphors, of which the fable of the cave is the most developed and concise, Plato argued that the phenomenal forms of perception were mere shadows of the Real, of the absolute and timeless Forms which lay beyond sensory perception. Implicit in this distinction between the ideal and the actual, reality and appearance, soul and body – the distinctions upon which western conceptual dualism, monotheism and metaphysics are generally assumed to have been founded – is the assumption that there can be an ideal knowledge of what is and is not beautiful, that the Beautiful, the Good and the Just can be ascertained through the dialectics of rational argument and enquiry.

In Plato's ideal Republic, it is the philosophers who sit at the top of the societal pyramid. Only they can be entrusted with the exalted role of discriminating between the good and the bad, the beautiful and the ugly. The prominent social role proposed by Wordsworth for the poet is a variation on this Platonic theme of the philosopher-as-arbiter-of-value. It is this figure which is reinvoked by literary intellectuals throughout the modern period in the form of Coleridge's clerisy, Matthew Arnold's priesthood, Leavis's enlightened army of critics capable of 'unprompted first-hand judgement', who are presented as the redeemers of a fallen industrialized world – as the defenders of properly authentic values.

3

European aesthetics proper – as the systematic elaboration of a rational approach to the questions posed around the term 'taste' – is a product of the Enlightenment. It is generally held to have its origins in the eighteenth century, in a text called *Aesthetica Acromantica* (1750) by Alexander Baumgarten. Immanuel Kant's *Critique of the Judgement of Taste* was in part a response and a riposte to this book and to Edmund Burke's *Philosophical Enquiry into the Origin of Our Ideas of the Sublime and the Beautiful.*[5] Kant argues against Burke's empiricism and his physiologism – his insistence on referring aesthetic experience back to bodily sensations – because such an orientation effectively invalidates the possibility of any higher ordering principle or Reason. Kant argues against both Burke's physiologism and Baumgarten's notion that aesthetic pleasure is based in a conceptually determined relationship to the work of art. If Burke is too coarse, too physical for Kant, then Baumgarten is too pedantic and mentalist.

Kant rejects Baumgarten's theory as mechanical and narrow because it proposes that the exercise of taste involves categorical judgements rather than reflective ones. Reflective judgements, Kant argues, move from the particular to the universal, from the work of art to the judgement of it, whereas categorical judgements proceed in the opposite direction, from the universal, the rule, to the particular case. Reflective judgements are to do with the contemplation of an indeterminate, relatively open and free relationship among the internal properties and overall order of a work of art or of a pleasing natural phenomenon; but that pleasure is not a 'mere' corporeal, bodily or carnal pleasure such as we derive, for instance, from eating or sex. It is of a more refined order, kindled by a free harmony or interplay between the function of images and the function of concepts; and beauty itself is a symbol of the morally good in so far as it consists in the transposition of aesthetic and moral terms which is reckoned to be immediately and intrinsically pleasing.

Kant introduced a number of influential distinctions and axioms:

1. that aesthetic judgement is predicted upon the detachment of form from any purposes. The proper object and goal of all authentic high art is 'purposiveness without purposes' – the work of art has that effect of intentionality, that compelling sense of destination, of going somewhere but it doesn't actually *do* anything; it serves no external or ulterior purpose or interest. The sense of beauty is 'without any interest whatsoever'
2. that a work of art is like an organism – a unity surrounding a manifold of perception: a totality which is more than the sum of its parts
3. that, following Burke, a distinction can be made between the sublime and the beautiful. Whereas the form of the beautiful is said to consist in limitation (contemplation of a framed picture, a bounded narrative, etc.), the sublime challenges the act of judgement itself by suggesting the possibility of limitlessness. The sublime mixes pleasure and pain, joy and terror, and confronts us with the threat of the absolute Other – the limitations of our language and our capacity to think and judge, the fact of our mortality. In Burke's and Kant's category of the sublime, reason is forced to confront its incapacity to deal rationally with the infinite.

More crucial still for the present argument, Kant claimed that a judgement of aesthetic taste may either express a mere liking (or aversion) which remains an individual preference, or may in addition claim universal validity. Whereas to say a picture seems beautiful to me does not imply a general assertion of its aesthetic value, to say a picture *is* beautiful is to claim that those who disagree are wrong.

These categories and distinctions have recently received a great deal of critical attention. For example, Peter Fuller has attempted to retrieve the idea of the universal validity of 'legitimate' aesthetic judgements.[6] Confronted by what is for him the disastrous collapse of a common visual aesthetic beneath a welter of competing styles – a collapse which has been facilitated by the profane intrusion of advertising motifs and values into fine art and the manic neophilia of the art market – Fuller combines anthropological and psychoanalytic approaches to argue the aesthetic sense back to its 'natural' source and point of origin in the perception of the human body. In his fundamentalist quest for universal aesthetic values, Fuller goes even further than his Enlightenment forebears, claiming that Kant was wrong to discount the possibility that even preferences for particular foods or for 'good' wine over 'plonk' are rationally verifiable and generalizable.

Fuller claims, further, that the hegemony of a modernist design aesthetic like Bauhaus functionalism – what he calls the inhuman 'taste of the machine' – has been superseded by an even more debilitating and wrongheaded dogma, an untenable and anti-human ideology of arbitrariness and 'anything goes' (what, I think, other people call postmodernism). Fuller has also called for the restoration of reason and order through the establishment of independent institutional bodies (commissions) staffed by accredited experts equipped with the necessary refinement, taste and knowledge to legislate on what is and is not good art and design, to decide what should and should not be manufactured, exhibited, worn. In other words, Fuller proposes a return to the *Republic* with the art critic replacing the philosopher at the apex of the social hierarchy. Although Fuller's Utopianism – his prophetic and denunciatory tone – have drawn fire from both Left and Right, the patent absurdity of some of his arguments should not be allowed to obscure the force, consistency and strategic value of his overall position at a time when the New Right is intent on giving such ideas an explicitly authoritarian inflection; at a time, too, when attacks on the arts in general and on art education in particular are being justified in terms of the narrowest and crudest kinds of market-oriented logic.

The influence of Kant's critique of aesthetic judgement, however, stretches far beyond such local controversies and debates. Kant's distinctions and axioms were fundamental in the formation both of European aesthetics as an academic discipline and of *aestheticism* – that structure of feeling that might be more accurately termed a 'feeling for structure': a sensibility which systematically privileges form over content or function, style over substance, abstraction over representation, and means of representation over thing represented. It is this sensibility, this set of preferences for form, style, abstraction, means over content, function, substance, matter, which recurs again and again from the 1840s onwards, to animate a long line of metropolitan European literary and aesthetic avant-gardes from Baudelaire and the cubists to the abstract expressionists and Jean-Luc Godard. Such a sensibility, such a set of preferences, might be said to inform much of what gets defined as today's 'post-avant-garde': the collage writing of Kathy Acker, for instance; the flat post-Pop representational style and knowing parody of Biff cartoons; the found sounds and quotation aesthetics of Talking Heads, Brian Eno, Malcolm McLaren. It might also be said to animate the academic and critical equivalents of those avant-gardes – those intellectual tendencies from Russian formalism to Swiss and French structuralism, Barthesian and Kristevan post-structuralism, Derridean deconstructionism. All these tendencies focus attention on form, pattern, style, structure or on the other side of what is, after all, the same coin: polysemy and *signifiance* – the escape from structure, the unrestricted play of signifiers unconstrained by external referents.

While many of these terms and the tendencies they designate would seem to cut right against the grain of Kant's project (explicitly so, in the case of Derrida and the post-structuralists), they none the less share many of the features of what Althusser might have called the Kantian 'problematic'. They are all based on the assumption that aesthetic pleasure should be dispassionate, disinterested, detached ('critical') and rooted in a relationship defined by distance, by the refusal of identification or merger with the object. The favoured aesthetic response is a 'pure gaze' cleansed of any involvement with or immersion in the subject-matter, in the fictional or imaginary worlds that art makes possible. The only surrender which is permissible is the surrender to the 'text', to the radical 'undoing' of the subject in a 'pure' play of language. Such facile pleasures as identification should be blocked, refused, deconstructed. The properly aesthetic experience has to be bracketed off from those forms and practices which are merely decorative, distracting, recreational or straightforwardly enjoyable and therefore 'vulgar', in the original sense of the word: i.e. 'in common use, ordinary, popular'. This aversion to a relation of ease between the spectator and the art work may itself be rooted in a more general mistrust of the visible and of visual representations which in turn has been traced back to the Talmudic prohibition on graven images.

There is a further connection with Kant, in so far as all these critical and terroristic avant-gardes concur in the assumption that art should be addressed to the 'higher faculties', to the spirit, or its modern equivalent, the intellect. Even when the body figures prominently, as in Barthes, it is in a highly abstracted, intellectualized though eroticized (eroticized *because* intellectualized) form. Art should be serious. Art should be improving – even if the improvement now has no moral pretensions beyond the destruction of the notion of morality as such; even where the intention is to dismantle or destroy the *doxa* (Barthes) or to deconstruct the metaphysics of Presence (Derrida).

Most importantly, all these avant-gardes share with Kant a refusal of the popular, the vulgar. They share, too, his repugnance for the body and the body politic, the common herd – even when this repugnance presents itself in critical, Marxist or anarchistic guise as a critique of the 'culture industry'; a repudiation of 'mass society', a hostility towards the ideological or metaphysical residues lurking at the heart of *common* sense. In other words, all these avant-gardes could be said to share with Kant a literal *elitism*. This elitism, furthermore, is not incidental. On the contrary, it is essential.

4

> In his essay of 1954, 'Building, dwelling, thinking', Martin Heidegger provides us with a critical vantage point from which to behold this (modern) phenomenon of universal placelessness. Against the Latin or, rather, the antique *abstract* concept of space as a more or less endless continuum of evenly subdivided spatial components or integers – what he terms the *spatium* and *extensio* – Heidegger opposes the German word for space (or rather, place), which is the term *Raum*. Heidegger argues that the phenomenological essence of such a space/place depends upon the *concrete*, clearly defined nature of its boundary, for as he puts it, '*A boundary is not that at which something stops, but, as the Greeks recognised, the boundary is that from which something begins its presencing*' [my emphasis]. Apart from confirming that western abstract reason has its origins in the Mediterranean, Heidegger shows that etymologically the German gerund *building* is closely linked with the archaic forms of *being, cultivating*, and hence *dwelling*, and goes on to state that the condition of dwelling and hence ultimately of being can only take place in a domain that is clearly bounded.
>
> (Kenneth Frampton, 'Towards a Critical Regionalism', in Hal Foster (ed.) *Postmodern Culture*)

When I moved two years ago into the house where I now live, I had to go through the usual process of acclimatization, of boundary marking and boundary acknowledgement. Moving house involves far more than the mere transplantation of oneself and one's possessions from one blank site to another. The move requires quite specific social and cognitive skills if it is to be accomplished successfully. In order to find out where you really *are – as opposed to where you are geographically (to use Heidegger's terms, to 'find yourself' in relation to* Raum *rather than* spatium) *– you have to develop the kind of fortitude, resourcefulness and map-reading skills needed in orienteering – that sport in which one gets dropped in an unfamiliar location with a fragment of a map and has to match the symbolic to the real in order to 'get home' to the prescribed destination. When it comes to socio-cultural orienteering, to borrow a phrase from London cab drivers' slang, you have to 'do the knowledge': learning how the place fits together as a social space through experience on the ground. You have to actively interpret and internalize significant features of the local environment through a process of osmosis, to learn how to gauge and judge the terrain, to develop a working topography before you can act effectively within that environment and upon it. You have to become sensitive to the finely drawn boundaries and distinctions in social and physical space (and to the relations between them) before you can even attempt to establish your own boundaries: to impose your own presence, to be properly 'at home' in the neighbourhood.*

I had to compare and contrast the suitability of particular places, – e.g. shops, pubs – for my needs. The alternatives had to be weighed in the balance, this shop is cheaper than that shop, this pub is nearer than that one. As I acquired more information, it became possible to qualify these purely quantitative assessments: the cheap shop sells old vegetables; this pub is nearer but the clientele is disproportionately white given the ethnic composition of the locale (a rumour circulates that it's used as a meeting place for the racist National Front party). To 'fit in' I had to be able, in other words, to decipher the signs and memorize the relations between them, to marry forms to contents. To borrow Clifford Geertz's term, I had to internalize increasingly 'thick descriptions'[7] of the local cultural scene. Crucially, I had to try to surmise with a fair degree of accuracy the intentions *– conscious or otherwise – behind the communications of my neighbours.*

In some cases, form, content and intention seemed to fit together neatly: there was a perceptible 'homology' between these different communicative levels or 'moments'. I soon learned there was a homology between the form of the house two doors down – rubbish in the front garden, unwashed windows, peeling paint, an absence of (the statutory respectable working-class) net curtains, and a gaunt, forbidding stencilled face on the front door – and the occupants of the house – the group of anarcho post-punk musicians who lived there and who were given to playing loud discordant 'Dark Wave' music every night (except Fridays and Saturdays) between three and seven o'clock in the morning. In this case, there seemed to be a direct or transparent connection between the form, content and manifest intention, i.e. to destroy the 'straight world' by demoralizing what remains of the local workforce (one in five local people are currently (early 1986) out of work) by keeping it awake every night of the working week. Put less facetiously, the probable intention behind this particular organization of visual and audible signifiers – the dishevelled façade, the deafening anti-music – is to mark out territory. The absence of curtains and the presence of noise are the recto and verso of the same sheets of paper upon which is scrawled the message: WE ARE NOT YOU. (It is an ambiguous message, i.e. 'We are not (the same) as you', or in a more aggressive inflection, one which is foregrounded whenever I've been round to complain, 'We are. (But) you aren't.') The decayed frontage of the house and the 'decadent' noise produced by its occupants function to signal the difference the post-punks perceive between their bohemian freedom and our bourgeois confinement within the norm; to signal the distance between the wilderness, the nature, the libertarian chaos of a short-life squatted tenancy and our culture, the constriction and order of the straight world of the owner-occupiers and permanent council tenants who make up the rest of the street's population. Their visual and aural 'noise' serves to mark off this household – symbolically and actually – from all the other households in the street – the more-or-less respectable, more-or-less working-class families of Asians, West Indians, Africans and Irish who dominate the street numerically. (There is a slight majority of Sikh households in our section of the street at the moment; slightly fewer households of people of West Indian descent, together with a scattering of London Irish, African and white working-class families and single people.) It is also used to mark the difference between themselves and people like myself – the upwardly mobile gentrifiers who represent one potential future for the locality in general – a future they intend to resist with all the wattage they can muster.

The public space of the street itself is perhaps the single most important focus of attention for the newcomer anxious to fit in and feel at home on the local 'manor'. I soon noticed that access to the public space of the street where I live is unevenly divided between the Asian boys and girls. Whereas during the day the air is filled with the boys' cries and their footballs, the pavements blocked by their BMX bikes, the Asian girls are only visible to me as faces glimpsed between the curtains and the window panes staring down – one hand underneath the chin – watching their brothers staking out the domain from which they themselves have already been excluded.

But to 'thicken' the description a little: a number of factors intervene to complicate or obscure my 'readings' of the street. Whereas I felt I could assume the legibility and transparency of my interactions with my (white) post-punk neighbours and their 'obvious', 'anti-social' 'refusals' of order, the interactions which took place between the various ethnic social and familial groups on the street itself proved relatively impenetrable. The street is the stage on which regular dramas of cross-cultural contact and subcultural conflict are enacted. Within the patriarchally ordered territory of the street, cars function as the major currency and medium of these exchanges. The maintenance of cars, their finish, their make and their performance are relentlessly monitored by the males and made to signify within a more-or-less common but none the less unstable system of codes, values and strictly ranked preferences. There is, as is to be expected, a pecking order and a status game. Number plates are highly 'expressive' counters in this game indicating as they do the age of the vehicle and hence the likely resale value. There is nothing unique in this either. Cars function universally in this way in the industrial, semi-industrial and post-industrial worlds as loaded signifiers of masculinity representing – at least in relatively 'unsophisticated' communities – a crude phallic mastery of space and time. (Amongst 'sophisticated', design- or ecology-conscious middle-class communities and those aristocratic groupings which define their superior taste against 'vulgar ostentation', it is possible for this to be inverted with the maxim 'Less is more'.) As Barthes,[8] *Wolfe,*[9]*Packard,*[10] *and others have indicated, highly structured sets of rules govern the uses and meanings of cars and they function as much as means of communication as modes of transport, conveying 'messages' as well as passengers.*

On the street in which I live, the rules of the car game have mutated in a particular way in response to local circumstances. The amount of time and energy expended on competitive display (car cleaning, customizing, repairing and respraying bodywork, fine-tuning, general maintenance) increases in line with the rising unemployment rate. The high proportion of unemployed or casually employed young car owners who live in the vicinity have relatively more time *to spend working on the stationary object than they have* money *to spend on petrol to make it move.*

Another factor complicating the car game in my street is the heterogeneous cultural-ethnic mix (the clash of different cultural-ethnic codes contributes to the relative instability of the system). Amongst the more affluent and street-wise West Indian and black British youths, the car tends to function as an extension of the body: as a kind of phallic carapace. Highly polished and often with the protective plastic covers still adhering to the seats, the car can be a mobile alternative to the parental home: a complete living space equipped with a hi-fi tape deck or a radio tuned to one of the local pirate radio stations and often a rack of drycleaned clothes in plastic bags on hangers in the back. The formerly popular Ford Cortina which for the last ten years or so has been associated with working-class youth culture particularly in North London,[11] *is losing favour as the prime symbol of a solvent and cool bachelorhood. There are fewer signs of Cortina culture nowadays (e.g. furry lucky dice hanging over a windscreen on which the owner's Nickname – MIKEY, EXTRA CLASSIC, LEE VAN CLEEF, etc. – has been stencilled in white letters). Now the more self-consciously stylish West Indian and black British young men (who tend to be the style leaders throughout North London) seem to prefer Triumphs, old Rovers, foreign cars and Japanese 'Range Rover' replicants. (The replicants form part of an 'English County look' ensemble, other elements of which include deerstalker hats, Burberry raincoats, 'classic' tweed and expensive umbrellas. The entire ensemble has been ironically appropriated by some black British youths as a signifier of 'class' (i.e. quality) and 'traditional Englishness'.) With the windows wound down and the bodywork gleaming, the street filled with the pulsing rhythms of reggae or (more commonly these days) the stuttering beat of rap, electro funk and jazz, the car serves as an assertion of the owner's physical presence, or corporeal pleasure against the work ethic and as a provocation to the police who in my neighbourhood still insist on regarding cars driven by young black men as stolen property.*[12] *Here – amongst the young single men, both black and white – the car can be used to perpetuate the fantasy of the male as a self-sufficient, possibly dangerous predator, the 'Wanderer' (Dion) out to get what's his.*

On the other hand, among the adult population – particularly among Muslims (Pakistanis and Turkish Cypriots, for instance) – the car tends to be seen first and foremost as a reflection of the status of the family headed by its owner. In this context, the car may signify within the Islamic code of Izzat *– a term which corresponds in some ways to the Chinese concept of 'face' and which combines the ideas of masculine pride, family honour, dignity and proper bearing in* *public. As for myself, as a non-driver I fail to figure in either system. Instead I am perhaps consigned to a no-man's land beyond or beneath gender and the order of things. As a lecturer-writer-researcher, I occupy, to use Pierre Bourdieu's terminology, a different class* habitus *– a different constellation of moral and aesthetic dispositions, of institutionalized pressures and 'background expectancies' which, according to Bourdieu, can determine everything from my physical posture and 'body hexis' to the way I classify the social world and am in turn classified within it.*

5

Bourdieu has argued that it is only by understanding the social function of bourgeois *and* ostensibly anti-bourgeois, 'radical', avant-garde tastes that we can properly grasp the significance and the long-term effects of Kant's work on aesthetics.[13] For according to Bourdieu, the pure aesthetic taste constitutes itself precisely in the refusal of impure taste and sensation, in the refusal of the 'vulgar' 'taste of the tongue, the palate and the throat'. Bourdieu traces the origin of the pure, detached aesthetic gaze historically to the emergence of an autonomous field of artistic production in the late nineteenth century – a development which reaches its apogee in the production first by poets, then by painters, of 'open works' which are intrinsically and deliberately polysemic.

The implication of Bourdieu's argument is that there is nothing particularly novel, still less 'revolutionary', in the post-structuralist privileging of the signifier over the signified. Post-structuralism is seen merely as an especially explicit and elaborated moment in a long-term tendency to formalism which by definition characterizes all aesthetic discourse. Bourdieu suggests, then, that the trajectory from the neo-Kantian fascination with form which typifies the 'classic' Levi-Straussian phase of structuralism to the demolition of the signified undertaken in different ways at a later moment by Derrida, Barthes and the *Tel Quel* group is not a movement 'beyond' Kant at all but rather a natural or logical progression from Kant's initial propositions and premisses.

From the point when artists in Europe deliberately set out to explore polysemy, Bourdieu argues, art no longer requires an outside (a referent or a public). It revolves increasingly around a concern with its own histories, codes and materials and it addresses an audience equipped with the philosophical, art historical, critical and/or literary competences which the viewer or reader needs to get something out of such an art work. Bourdieu suggests that this audience is as concerned in the final analysis as the artists themselves are to distance itself both from the 'vulgar' mob or mass and the 'commercial' bourgeoisie. The avant-garde and the marginals, intellectuals and dilettantes which it services are defined by Bourdieu as the 'dominated fractions of the dominant class' (i.e. the petit bourgeoisie, the déclassés, the shabby gentry, etc.) who are high on cultural capital (education, qualifications, [high] cultural expertise, 'sensibility', etc.) but low on economic capital and political power.

Through a massive empirical survey in which Parisians of all classes, occupations and ages were interviewed and tested on their cultural knowledge and taste preferences, Bourdieu sets out to provide a quasi-positivist sociological answer to and refutation of Kant's critique of the judgement of taste. He demonstrates that all cultural pursuits are conditioned by, first, the level, duration and quality of the education of those engaging in such pursuits and second, by their social origin and class *habitus*. Bourdieu distinguishes four basic taste formations: legitimate, middlebrow, popular, pure. Legitimate taste – the preference for and knowledge of the accredited 'classics' and the 'most legitimate of those arts that are still in the process of legitimation (e.g. cinema, jazz)' increases 'with educational level and is highest in those fractions of the dominant class that are richest in educational capital'. Middlebrow taste which brings together 'the minor works of the major arts' and the 'major works of the minor arts . . . is more common in the middle classes than in the working classes or in the "intellectual" fractions of the dominant class'. Popular taste, signalled by the choice, for instance, 'of so-called "light" music or classical music devalued by popularization . . . and especially songs totally devoid of artistic ambition or pretension . . . is most frequent among the working classes and varies in inverse ratio to educational capital (which explains why it is slightly more common among industrial and commercial employers or even senior executives than among primary school teachers and cultural intermediaries)'. Finally the 'pure' aesthetic disposition which is most clearly dependent on the acquisition of a specific 'aesthetic' competence is capable of 'applying to *any* object the pure intention of an artistic effort which is an end in itself'. The pure gaze perceives as art that which it nominates as art and involves the categorical assertion of the primacy of form over function.

Using these categories as broad guidelines in his interpretation of the empirical data, Bourdieu sets out to demonstrate how taste 'classified the classifier' and he finds systematic correlations between social class, occupation, education and cultural and aesthetic preferences in food, music, photography, fiction, etc. When confronted with an unidentified photograph of the Lacq gas refinery taken at night, manual workers indicated bewilderment ('I can't make head or tail of it'); small employers were hostile because they saw it as 'experimental' ('That stuff leaves me cold'); junior executives were disconcerted but sought to disguise their discomfort by being non-committal and confined their remarks to technical rather than aesthetic matters ('It's just light captured by the camera'). Only members of the highly educated dominant class (professors, senior civil servants, etc.), often recognizing the object represented, accepted such photographs as 'art' ('It's aesthetically pleasing'). In the same way, a photograph of an old peasant woman's hands elicited an empathetic and/or ethical response from manual workers ('The poor old girl') but never an aesthetic judgement. Lower-middle-class clerical and technical workers oscillated between sympathy, populist sentimentality and a concern for aesthetic properties ('The sort of hands you see in early Van Goghs'). At higher levels in the social hierarchy the remarks became more abstract 'with [other people's] hands, labour and old age functioning as allegories or symbols which serve as pretexts for general reflections on general problems ("It's the very symbol of toil")'. Thus Bourdieu claims that taste, far from being purely personal – a mysterious unclassifiable faculty exercised by freely choosing sovereign subjects – is a quintessentially social phenomenon, that social differences are reinforced, perpetuated, reproduced by antagonistic judgements of taste – that taste always operates as a differentiating agent in the social field.

While the contents of the categories – legitimate, middlebrow, popular, pure – may change over time (Bourdieu cites jazz, 1940s' *film noir*, American pop kitsch and science fiction passing up from the popular via the pure to the legitimate, while certain styles of painting, etc., drop down in the same period from the legitimate via the middlebrow to the popular), none the less the relations between these taste formations remain constant. Invariably those relations are antagonistic and antithetical. Taste is a purely negative category in Bourdieu. Each taste formation is constituted in the refusal of other tastes, particularly in the refusal of adjacent formations. Popular taste, for instance, is defined as 'the refusal of the refusal of pure taste'.

Against the rigours and austerity of the avant-garde, popular taste is marked by a Rabelaisian mood of insolence, carnival and category inversion. It celebrates the body, the emotional and sentimental properties of life and art, seeking out the moment not of distanced contemplation but of the loss of individuality in the collective, the suspension of disbelief as the self is dissolved not in the 'play of signifiers' – far from it – but rather in the remorseless narrativity that characterizes much popular art. Furthermore, Bourdieu suggests that these differences and antagonisms are far from innocent. Popular taste is predicated on a knowledge that it is both plundered and despised by its 'betters' and that the difficulty of avant-garde art and legitimate taste (despite the protestations of their adherents that they long to 'educate' and 'elevate' the public and to 'popularize' the classics) derives, on the contrary, *precisely from the will to keep the masses out*.

The distinctions and antagonisms penetrate as far as the dining table and the kitchen. The working-class man as represented in Bourdieu's survey favours substance over style of presentation, is encouraged by the female (mother/wife), who prepares his food, to eat with gusto, to get silently lost in his plate, is often licensed to make appreciative smacking sounds with his lips, is inclined to relish good, simple French food taken in the prescribed Gallic sequence – hors-d'oeuvre (charcuterie for the men, crudités for the women and children!), main dish and dessert – and rejects fish as too delicate and insubstantial. (One is reminded of Richard Hoggart's description of the 'traditional' working-class dietary emphasis on strong taste, bulk and meat whenever possible.[14] The bourgeois French person, on the other hand, focuses attention on the style of presentation, on the cutlery, the tablecloth, the glasses, flowers, etc., on the look of the food not its quantity (think of *nouvelle cuisine*), will often skip a course electing to 'taste' (but not consume) one or two 'specialities' – refined, rare or exotic (even foreign!) dishes – and claims to relish the conversation as much as if not more than the food. The differences – when presented in this way – are virtually symmetrical: they are 'structured in dominance' around those social class distinctions which they serve to duplicate and dramatize. The oppositions are right underneath our noses. In fact they even extend to the way in which we clear that organ:

> It would be easy to show … that Kleenex tissues, which have to be used delicately, with a little sniff from the tip of the nose, are to the big cotton handkerchief, which is blown into sharply and loudly, with the eyes closed and the nose held tightly, as repressed laughter is to a belly laugh, with wrinkled nose, wide-open mouth and deep breathing ('doubled up with laughter') as if to amplify to the utmost an experience which will not suffer containment, not least

> because it has to be shared, and therefore clearly manifested for the benefit of others.[15]

Bourdieu sums up the system of distinctions by resorting to a paradox – suggesting that those at the lower end of the social ladder are compelled to 'choose the necessary' in the form of 'simple pleasures' – the straightforward satisfaction of primary needs – whereas those who lay claim to the 'aesthetic disposition' can literally *afford* to sublimate primary needs in such a way that the detachment of the pure gaze could be said to be conditioned by negative economic necessities – a life of ease – that tends to induce an active distance from the principle of necessity itself. He concludes that the classificatory boundaries between culture and nature, higher and lower, body and soul serve to reproduce and legitimate social inequalities, to naturalize the idea that hierarchically ranked social distinctions are simply *there* – are not subject to modification – and that systems of social stratification are in themselves nothing more than the natural order of things transposed to the social domain. He concludes:

> The opposition between the tastes of nature and the tastes of freedom introduces a relationship which is that of the body and the soul, between those who are 'only natural' and those whose capacity to dominate their own biological nature (through sublimation, the search for 'higher truths') affirms their legitimate claim to dominate social nature . . . the theory of pure taste (then) has its basis in a social relation: the antithesis between culture and corporeal pleasure (or nature if you will) and is rooted in the opposition between a cultivated bourgeoisie and the people.[16]

Or put another way, the 'pure aesthetic' – the apparently disinterested contemplation and appreciation of 'purposiveness without purposes' – itself serves a 'higher' (baser) purpose: the perpetuation of social distinctions, the justification of the very principle of inequality.

Although his work on taste has had a very uneven impact in Britain and has generally, perhaps predictably, been less enthusiastically received by those professionally engaged in textual criticism (literature, art, film studies) than the work produced by other more Kantian and text-fixated French intellectuals, none the less Bourdieu's scepticism concerning the adequacy of non-reflexive non-sociological accounts and critiques of the aesthetic field has been welcomed by those working within cultural studies who seek to move beyond the formal and philosophical preoccupations of post-structuralism and deconstructionism and to rethink popular culture in more positive, less proscriptive ways. Like Bakhtin,[17] Bourdieu is often invoked to puncture the pretensions of more ascetic or solipsistic Parisian *philosophes*, and both writers have often been recruited by those (myself included) who have set out to question the dominant paradigms of what taste is and how it functions, and to describe instead a more dynamic, heterogeneous and socially variegated cultural field – one in which, for instance, social groups are seen to establish public identities through shared commodity and 'lifestyle' preferences.[18]

Perhaps the myth of the inert masses is in danger of being replaced by a countermyth of the robustly iconoclastic, healthily corporeal and debunking culture of the popular classes. A kind of inverted snobbery is sometimes operative here. Just how applicable Bourdieu's analysis is to the very different field of British culture is in any case hard to establish in the absence of an equivalent empirical survey of indigenous tastes. The generalizability of his thesis is further thrown into question by the time-lag. Although appearing in translation for the first time in 1984, Bourdieu's *Distinction* is based on research conducted in Paris in the early 1970s. The confidence with which he links class, culture and occupation would perhaps be misplaced in the 1980s with the recomposition of social classes, the restructuring of work, the decline of the manual sector and the growth of the service industries. It would be less easy now than it was even 10 years ago to give centre stage to the manual worker in any definition of either popular culture or the popular classes. Still less would it seem appropriate to present the working class as essentially male, as Bourdieu tends to do, or to proffer the working-class male as the wholesome touchstone of immutable good sense, as a kind of bucolic embodiment of tough unsentimental folk wisdom.

None the less, Bourdieu's project provides a healthy counter to the more formalist and text-centred approaches which till now have tended to dominate discussions of the aesthetic response. However, if Bourdieu's work is easily distinguishable in its tone, intentions and objectives from the positions of other prominent French intellectuals, it inevitably shares a certain amount of common ground with them. Despite the hostility to structuralism which, here as elsewhere,[19] forms one persistent strand of Bourdieu's polemic, the stress in *Distinction* on system, pattern, symmetry and difference is likely to strike the English reader as being pre-eminently structuralist. In the same way, while the concept of class *habitus* opens up a limited space for social subjects as reflexive agents capable of formulating strategies of self-enhancement, calculating the probable outcomes of specific lines of action and shaping their own lives accordingly, it still places a great deal of emphasis – for those trained in more strictly Anglo-American traditions of enquiry, perhaps an inordinate degree of emphasis – on the *systematic* overdetermination of people's life options by institutional factors.

However, it is the way in which Bourdieu places himself in relation to the great continental traditions of social theory and philosophy which distinguishes him most clearly from British sociologists with more positivist, straightforwardly empiricist or culturalist leanings and which draws him closer to those intellectual figures whose positions his book sets out expressly to critique.

6

When I first moved into my present home, I was intrigued by one car in the street – a great spotless Thunderbird, its maroon bodywork and sculptured chromium accessories glistening all the year round, irrespective of the weather. This Thunderbird is the single most conspicuous anomaly in the Victorian terraced street in which I live. It is a cathedral among hovels. It is out of scale, out of place (its real home is Detroit or Dallas), out of time (its real time is pre-1974, pre the Oil Crisis). I immediately assumed – drawing on my stock of Hollywood-derived cultural stereotypes – that the car belonged to a pimp, a gangster or a 'big shot' of some kind, that it should be referred to the young man's code of phallic braggadocio, *that it was a boast in three dimensions. These assumptions turned out to be unfounded. The car is owned by one of the gentlest, most gracious and modest men I know. Mr H. is a slight, mild-mannered Turkish Cypriot who lives with his wife in a run-down, sparsely furnished ground-floor flat in the house opposite. He rents the apartment from the Hindu family who own it and who occupy the rest of the house. Mr H. is in his 50s, short and thin, speaks broken English very softly and is usually dressed in (unfashionable) flares and a pullover. There is nothing remotely 'flash' or ostentatious about his appearance and demeanour. His car is his only conspicuous luxury. He is a believer in Allah but is not dogmatic and smoked Bensons all the way through Ramadan explaining: 'Some pretend not eat, not smoke, not drink – just for show. It's what is in the heart that matters.' He has given us a vine and a jasmine plant as a gift from his garden to ours, has sent us a card and a plateful of honey-drenched, almond-speckled cakes baked by his wife at Christmas.*

Mr H. is the local car doctor. A semi-pro mechanic, he sits by the window behind the net curtains in his front room and in his own words he 'listens to the street' – to the rush and whirr of cars as they sweep past, to the cough of ignition keys being turned and engines being revved. He can diagnose a sick motor just by the sound. In reasonable weather he spends as much time on his car (though not in it) as he does inside his flat. At least three times a day – more if there are showers – he washes and polishes his beloved Thunderbird, tunes and tunes and retunes the engine.

From his vantage point beside or underneath the car, Mr H. can socialize with neighbours as they pass by on their way to the shops or to work and he can keep an eye on neighbours' houses to make sure that there are no break-ins. Once a week or so – usually on a Sunday – he emerges from the house followed by his wife who as a conventional Muslim keeps a few paces behind him. They get into his car and Mr H. sinks into the white leather upholstery of the driver's seat, grasps the enormous wheel and takes her (the car/his wife) for a short and what I suspect is a quite nerve-wracking drive – nerve-wracking because of the Thunderbird's loose, wide-open steering and its size in relation to the narrow London streets.

7

There is something curiously Derridean in Bourdieu's 'sociological' deconstruction of Kant. Bourdieu's work is clearly linked to the projects of Marx, Durkheim and Weber; but it can also be seen – though this is not explicitly acknowledged by Bourdieu himself – as an extension of Nietzsche's corrosive anti-metaphysical attack on the fundamental premisses of post-Socratic philosophy. His insistence on the health and vitality of popular culture may not be very Nietzschian, but his physiologism certainly is. For Nietzsche, the difference between the beautiful and the ugly is entirely dependent on and derivative from primary phylogenetic drives. It is determined by the imperative of species preservation. The sense of the beautiful, the intuition of the good in Nietzsche's account have nothing whatsoever to do with other-worldly forces or values, with a transcendental 'above' or 'beyond', with imperfect, ghostly memories of the Ideal or the Divine. They simply serve to valorize all that is life-enhancing, beneficial, species-preserving. Ugliness for Nietzsche is merely all that which is harmful, dangerous, worthy of suspicion: the decadent, the demeaning, the rotten. Aesthetics is, to use his own words, 'nothing but applied physiology' and his objections to Wagner after he turned against his former friend and mentor in 1876 were, he claimed, not ideological or aesthetic, political or ethical, but simply physiological: 'My objections to Wagner's music are physiological objections: why conceal them under aesthetic formulas? My "fact" is that I no longer breathe easily as soon as this music begins to affect me.'[20]

Nietzsche's physiologism, his contempt for euphemism, pretension and cant, his refusal of the transcendental and Utopian claims of art, his insistence on the ineluctable pressures of necessity and the power of sublimation – all these are strongly recalled in Bourdieu's tone and thesis (though Bourdieu declines, unlike many French literary intellectuals, to adopt Nietzsche's enigmatic aphoristic style, arguing instead that glib 'smart' literary effects would actively subvert the scientific, anti-aesthetic ambition which motivates his project).[21]

The Nietzschian legacy is felt not only here. The debt to Nietzsche has been acknowledged by those writers from Foucault to Derrida, from Deleuze to Baudrillard, who together – though not in unison and from quite different directions – have opened up and occupied the discursive spaces of the Post. To take just one example – an untypically demonstrative moment is that trajectory from Marx to Nietzsche – Barthes writing in 1969 recommended a move from 'mythoclasm' (ideology of revelation) to 'semioclasm' (destruction of the sign, the symbolic order and the subjectivities it allegedly supports and 'positions'), thereby sketching out a kind of abbreviated manifesto for the Post (at least for its reformed (i.e. 'post-Marxist') libertarian wing):

> In an initial moment, the aim was the destruction of the (ideological) signified; in a second, it is that of the destruction of the sign: 'mythoclasm' is succeeded by 'semioclasm' which is much more far-reaching and pitched at a different level. The historical field of action is thus widened: no longer the (narrow) sphere of French society but far beyond that, historically and geographically, the whole of Western civilisation (Graeco-Judaeo-Islamic-Christian), unified under the one theology (Essence, monotheism) and identified by the regime of meaning it practises – from Plato to *France-Dimanche*.[22]

Widened indeed . . . The Nietzschian disposition, so clearly in evidence here, is central to the cultural, political and existential 'decentring' which constitutes – an ideal goal – the project of the Post and which in the years after 1968 forms – as socio-political 'fact' – the object of its multiple enquiries and de-scriptions. The Nietzschian problematic is inscribed in the very prefix 'post' and the elements of that problematic shape the characteristic concerns of Post discourse: the preference for questions of genealogy and origin over those of prediction and agency; the emphasis on *agon* and process; the suspicion of all models of historical causality and progress. Some have argued that the distinction between post-structuralism and postmodernism is crucial[23] and definitive, and it is clear that not all the strands that are woven round the Post are made of the same thread. Similarly, the moment of supersession (of structuralism, of modernism) can be differently periodized depending on which particular history, movement or historic aspiration is being defined as finished or on the point of exhaustion. However, the apocalyptic tone is unmistakable throughout the literature. The founding proposition of the Post – shouted Zarathustra-style from the various disciplinary peaks from which Post intellectuals gain access to their exalted 'overviews' – is that God is dead, though different gods are decreed dead from different mountain-tops. God can be (i.e. 'has been') Marx, the Logos, Hegel's World Spirit, Brecht, Breton, Freud, the Enlightenment project, European rationalism, the Party, the Law of the Father, the Transcendental Signified. But whoever or whatever He or It was, the fact of His/Its passing – the proclaimed sense of an ending – and the programmatic tone in which the announcement is made tend to be quite similar.

It is around the term 'postmodernism' that debates about the visual arts, about the general theory of aesthetics and the broader issues raised in the deployment and critique of culture as an anthropological and analytic category, have most clearly and consistently revolved. Most notably Jean-François Lyotard has been engaged in a lengthy meditation on these issues within the domain of art theory and philosophy, and it is he who has been most influential in focusing critical attention in recent years on the question of the sublime. As part of his critique of the Utopian impetus within the Enlightenment project – a project defined here as a twofold aspiration towards universalization (Reason) and social engineering (Revolution) – Lyotard defines the European modernist achievement as a series of gestures motivated by the intention to 'present the unpresentable'.[24] This elevation of the sublime as the originary impulse within modernism involves an explicit rejection of the relatively facile pleasures of the beautiful – that which can be represented, framed, assimilated. More importantly, Lyotard also uses it to question the viability of the project of modernity and the accompanying ideologies of 'historical necessity' and 'guaranteed progress'. For Lyotard uses the notion of the sublime as a kind of metaphor for the *absolute* nature of those limitations placed on what can be said, seen, shown, presented, demonstrated, put into play, put into practice and he implies that each encounter with the sublime in art provides us with the single salutary lesson that complexity, difficulty, opacity are always there in the same place: *beyond our grasp*. The inference here in the insistence on the palpability of human limitation is politically nuanced at those points when Lyotard talks about the disastrous consequences which have flowed from all attempts to implement the 'perfect (rational) system' or to create the 'perfect society' during what he calls the 'last two sanguinary centuries'.[25]

These arguments have been developed in the context of the French philosopher's protracted debate with Jürgen Habermas who, whilst distinguishing his own position from Marcuse's, has none the less stressed the emancipatory dimensions of art favouring an aesthetics of the beautiful. From this latter position, the fact that the harmonious integration of formal elements in an art work gives us pleasure indicates that we are all drawn ineluctably by some internal *logos* (reason reflexively unfolding/folding back upon itself through the dispassionate contemplation of form), that we are, in other words, drawn towards the ideal resolution of conflict in the perfection of good form. Here our capacity both to produce and to appreciate the beautiful stands as a kind of 'promissory note' for the eventual emancipation of humanity. Lyotard, on the other hand, in a move which is reminiscent of the deconstructive strategies exemplified by Derrida, takes the relatively subordinate, residual term, the 'sublime' in the binary coupling upon which Enlightenment aesthetics is based – the beautiful: the sublime, where the sublime functions as that-which-is-aesthetic-but-not-beautiful – and privileges it to such an extend that the whole edifice of Enlightenment thought and achievement is (supposedly) threatened. For whereas the idea of the beautiful contains within it the promise of an ideal, as yet unrealized, community (to say 'This is beautiful' is to assert the generalizability of aesthetic judgements and hence the possibility/ideal of consensus), the sublime in contrast atomizes the community by confronting each individual with the prospect of his or her imminent and solitary demise. In Lyotard's words, with the sublime 'everyone is alone when it comes to judging'.[26]

The sublime functions in Lyotard's work as a means of corroding the two 'materialist' faiths (positivism and Marxism) which characterize the superseded modern epoch.[27] Embracing paradox, computational logics and simulations, he identifies himself (and the 'postmodern condition') with the production of *les immatériaux*,[28] and speculates upon those abstract structures and invisible forces which shape and constitute human experience whilst remaining inaccessible to that experience. Lyotard associates the revolutionary animus of the modern period with that litany of abominations which Adorno called simply 'Auschwitz' and argues that, from the time of Robespierre on, disaster has followed in the wake of the succession of revolutionary vanguards and tribunals which have set themselves up as the subject and agents of historical destiny. In that sublime presumption to 'speak for' (i.e. 'make') history, these vanguards and 'people's courts' have sought to place themselves outside the normative framework provided by the web of 'first order narratives' in which popular thought, morality and social life are properly grounded.[29] Those moments when men and women believed themselves to *be* Benjamin's Angel of History who 'would like to stay, awaken the dead, and make whole what has been smashed',[30] moments of illusory omnipotence and certainty, are, for Lyotard, the dangerous moments of supposedly full knowledge, when people feel fully present to themselves and to their 'destiny' (the moment, say, when the class in itself becomes a class for itself). The sublime remains the prerogative of art alone: the *socio-political aspiration* to 'present the unpresentable', to embody in the here and now the that-which-is-to-be, is deemed untenable: 'paranoid'.[31] The sublime by definition is *das Unform*[32] – that which is without form, hence that which is monstrous and unthinkable – and rather than seeking to embody universal values of truth, justice and right, finding the licence for such pretensions in the great metanarratives ('the pursuit of freedom or happiness'[33]), Lyotard recommends that we should instead think of the human project in terms of the 'infinite task of complexification ... complexifying the complexity we are in charge of'.[34]

8

Lying in bed at 4 a.m. on one occasion unable to sleep because of the racket emanating from the squatters' house I decided to 'have it out' with them 'once and for all'. I got dressed and walked into the night air which was filled with the whine and screech of feedback and guitar. Having failed to rouse them by knocking on the door and shouting through the letter-box, I picked up an empty beer can and threw it at the first-floor window. The noise died off suddenly as the window was thrown open and a line of faces appeared. In the course of the ensuing argument I yelled (and I could hear the old man in my voice)'Can't you turn the amplifiers down?' this seemed to strike a note of discord. There was a brief hiatus (was 'amplifier' an obsolete term? didn't musicians use amplifiers any more?) and then the response came loud and clear: 'You don't understand.' Opting like an irate father for a well-worn strategy – one that had been used on myself by older 'authority figures' many times in the past – I shouted back: 'I don't care whether I understand or not! Just keep the —— noise down! There are families with young babies in this street.' The absurdity (and the irony) of this exchange between the members of 'an anarchic youth subculture' and a 'former expert on subcultural resistance' was lost on me at the time but walking back towards my house five minutes later, I felt strangely elated, lighter on my feet: I was turning my back not only on a quieter scene, but also on an earlier incarnation. Released from the obligation to 'understand', I was free to sleep – at last! – the dreamless sleep of the senex or the fool.

9

Lyotard ends by dissolving dialectics into paralogy and language games but there are within the debates in France on post-structuralism, postmodernism and postmodernity other variations on the Nietzschian theme of the end of the Western philosophical tradition. In some ways, those discourses from Foucault to Derrida, from the Barthes of the *Tel Quel* phase to the Jacques Lacan of *Ecrits* might be said to be posited following Nietzsche on the no-man's land (the gender here *is* marked!) staked out between the two meanings of the word 'subject': first, 'I' the self-present subject of the sentence; secondly, the subjected subject of the symbolic order: the subject of ideology. This no-man's land is just that – a land owned by nobody in the space between the *énoncé* and the *énonciation* where questions of agency, cause, intention, authorship, history become irrelevant. All those questions dissolve into a sublime, asocial Now which is differently dimensionalized in different accounts. For Derrida in grammatology, that space is called *aporia* – the unpassable path – the moment when the self-contradictory nature of human discourse stands exposed. For Foucault, it is the endless recursive spirals of power and knowledge: the total, timeless space he creates around the hellish figure of the Panopticon: the viewing tower at the centre of the prison yard – the *voir* in *savoir/pouvoir*, the looking in knowing. For *Tel Quel* it is the moment of what Julia Kristeva calls *signifiance*: the unravelling of the subject in the pleasure of the text, the point where the subject disintegrates, moved beyond words by the materiality, productivity and slippage of the signifier over the signified. And for Lacan, it is the Real – that which remains unsayable and hence unbearable – the boundless, inconceivable space outside language and the Law beyond the binaries of the Imaginary register: the Real being the promise/threat of our eventual (unthinkable) disintegration, our absorption into flux. The sublime is here installed in each case as the place of epiphany and terror, the place of the ineffable which stands over and against all human endeavour, including the project of intellectual totalization itself. Lacan's Real, Foucault's power-knowledge spirals, Kristeva's *signifiance*, Derrida's *aporia*, Barthes's text of bliss: all are equivalent, in some senses reducible to Lyotard's category of the sublime.

The elevation of the sublime (which has its more literal, or crass, quasi-empirical corollary in the cult of schizophrenia – the cult, that is, of dread, of the sublime mode of being in the world) could be interpreted as an extension of the aspiration towards the ineffable which has impelled the European avant-gardes at least since the symbolists and the decadents and probably since the inception in the 1840s of metropolitan literary and artistic modernism with the 'anti-bourgeois' refusals of Baudelaire. It implies a withdrawal from the immediately given ground of sociality by problematizing language as tool and language as communicative medium, by substituting models of signification, discourse and decentred subjectivity for these older humanist paradigms and by emphasizing the *im*possibility of 'communication', transcendence, dialectic, the final determination of origins and outcomes, the fixing or stabilization of values and meanings. The moment which is privileged is the solitary confrontation with the irreducible fact of limitation, Otherness, 'difference' (Derrida), with the question variously of the loss of mastery, 'death in life' (Lyotard), of the 'frequent little deaths' or 'picknoleptic interruptions' of consciousness by the unconscious (Virilio).

The conversion of asociality into an absolute value can accommodate a variety of more or less resigned postures: scepticism (Derrida), stoicism (Lyotard, Lacan, Foucault), libertarian anarchism/mysticism (Kristeva), hedonism (Barthes), cynicism/nihilism (Baudrillard). However, such a privileging of the sublime tends to militate against the identification of larger (collective) interests (the isms of the modern epoch e.g. Marxism, liberalism, etc.). It does this by undermining or dismissing as simplistic or 'barbaric'[35] what Richard Rorty has recently called 'our untheoretical sense of social solidarity[36] and by bankrupting the liberal investment in the belief in the capacity of human beings to empathize with each other, to reconcile opposing 'viewpoints', to seek the fight-free integration of conflicting interests. There is no room in the split opened up in the subject by the Post for the cultivation of 'consensus' or for the development of a 'communicative community', no feasible invocation of a possible progress towards an 'ideal speech situation' (Habermas). The stress on the asocial sublime further erodes the sense of destination and purposive struggle supplied by the 'optimistic will' (Gramsci) and the theoretical means to recover (that is, to emancipate) a 'reality' outside discourse obscured by 'something called "ideology" (created by power) in the name of something called "validity" (not created by power)'[37] (Habermas again). The stress on the impossible tends, in other words, to limit seriously the scope and definition of the political (where politics is defined as the 'art of the possible'). A series of elisions tends to prescribe a definite route here (though it is a route taken by more disciples than master-mistresses). First there is the absolute conflation of a number of relatively distinct structures, paradigms, tendencies: the emergence of industrial-military complexes, the Enlightenment aspiration to liberate humanity, the rise of the bourgeoisie and the modern 'scientific' episteme, the bureaucratic nation-state, the 'Auschwitz'. Next these discrete and non-synchronous historical developments are traced back to the model of the subject secreted at the origin of western thought and culture in transcendental philosophy. Finally an ending is declared to the 'tradition' thus established and the equation is made between this ending (the end of philosophy) and the ending of history itself.

10

One day someone ran a key along one side of the Thunderbird, scratching a line across the paintwork of one of the panels. Mr H. sent off to Detroit and had a replacement for the damaged section crated up and sent over at a cost somewhere in excess of £600. Another time the mentally retarded son of Mr H.'s landlord accidentally threw a stone which made a minute hole in the centre of the windscreen. Mr H. sent off to the States for another replacement, though he claimed the next day that the windscreen had miraculously healed itself – he surmised that it contained a special fluid what had set overnight across the tiny aperture.

Mr H. demanded satisfaction: a confession from the boy, an apology from the father. There were threats of court action. (Honour was at stake here, Mr H. explained, not just property. He didn't want the boy to be punished. He knew he wasn't really responsible for what he'd done. But he couldn't bear to hear the father denying what had really happened.) One day the boy appeared at our door. He seemed distraught. He looked across the street towards his father's house. (Was someone watching from the window? Had he been sent by his family to enlist our support in the battle with Mr H.?) The boy seemed confused, close to tears (under normal circumstances he's more prone to song and to sudden gusts of laughter). Now his shoulders were stooped. His long thin arms hung listlessly at his sides. He stood on the doorstep glancing back from time to time towards the net curtains in the windows of the house opposite. Could he come here? he asked. Could he go up there? He pointed up the stairs behind me. He said he wanted to go home. 'You know where you live, J.,' I said, pointing to his house. 'You live over there.' The boy refused to turn around. He said he could get home by going through our house and climbing over the garden wall at the back. The garden wall borders a railway line (did he know this?). It faces in a direction which is diametrically opposed to his parents' house.

11

Schizophrenia is often identified as the psychic state which most clearly embodies the subjective response to the 'postmodern condition'. The word 'subjective' is problematic in this context: schizophrenia is the ghost that rises from the corpse of 'authentic' subjectivity. It is the only (valid?) 'life' that's left after the 'death of the subject' (see Deleuze and Guattari, Baudrillard, Jameson). The binary structures on which post-Socratic thought, and hence western civilization and culture, are reckoned to be based – reality v. appearance, real relations v. phenomenal forms, science v. false consciousness, consciousness v. the unconscious, inside v. outside, subject v. object, etc. – are systematically dismantled as the 'depth model' disappears along with the exalted vantage point and the 'penetrating insights' of the totalizing intellectual-as-seer. The implication is that we are left stranded in a world of meaningless surfaces: 'lured' this way and that by the 'fatal' fascination exercised upon us by mirrors, icons, images. As the production economy of an earlier epoch with its 'technocratic' or 'instrumental' rationality, its purposive strategies, its regulated sexuality folds into the consumption economy of the Post, we move into an unbounded space of unconstrained imaginaries, licensed promiscuity, drift and dreamwork where subjects and objects, mainstreams and margins are inextricably merged. In an economy geared towards the spinning of endlessly accelerating spirals of desire, consumption allegedly imposes its own 'ecstatic' or pluralist (dis)order (Jameson's 'heterogeneity without norms'[38]). Baudrillard's 'obscene' 'ecstasy of communication' involves an 'implosion of meaning' such that all distinctions are flattened out in the 'hyperreal' where the precession of image-bloated simulacra work to substitute the model for the real.[39] For Jameson, there is the schizophrenic consumer disintegrating into a succession of unassimilable instants, condemned through the ubiquity and instantaneousness of commodified images and instants to live forever in *chronos* (this then this then this) without having access to the (centring) sanctuary of *kairos* (cyclical, mythical, meaningful time). And for Deleuze and Guattari there is the homeless wandering 'nomad' drawn 'like a schizophrenic taking a walk' across *milles plateaux* from one arbitrary point of intensity to the next.[40]

Postmodernity is presented in each case as positively schizogenic: a grotesque attenuation – possibly monstrous, occasionally joyous – of our capacity to feel and to respond. Within this grim scenario, as psychosis replaces neurosis as the emergent psychic norm, the dominant subjective modality of our current 'condition', postmodernity becomes nothing more than modernity without the hopes and dreams which made modernity bearable.

The tendency within such accounts to flatten the temporal-sequential dimension beneath spatial metaphors, to outlaw progressive models of history, to engage in general arguments, to adopt postures of cultural and political pessimism can all be read back to the Nietzschian problematic in which the discourse(s) of the Post remain embedded. From such a perspective it is impossible to countenance the prospect of any historically constituted collective (any putative 'We') changing anything for the better. A 'constant (postmodern) condition'[41] has to be confronted, negotiated, come to terms with. By definition, it will not be modified, changed, still less 'transcended' or 'resolved'. Alternatively, within the diagnosis of postmodernism as a condition peculiar to 'late capitalism', in the absence of any identifiable sources of renewal or resistance there can be no 'elsewhere' – no 'better place' – to move towards. The word 'post' suggests that the clock has stopped and without a clock it is difficult to estimate just how 'late' it is in 'late capitalism'.

And yet, however dramatic the changes in the deployment and accumulation of capital in the postwar period; however dramatic the changes in the production and the uses of new technologies, in the organization of the work process or in the level of investment in communications, data banks, information, image; however prevalent pastiche and parody in the arts, in critique, in film, TV and advertising it is surely palpably misguided to expect to find these shifts automatically re-enacted in (the dissolution of) the individual human psyche, or in the total transformation of the cultural sphere. We might look to a less general crisis afflicting particular academic institutions to understand the broader historical significance of such a 'sense of an ending'. For the varieties of postmodernist critique which abjure all hope might be said to presage the historic decline not of politics, or meaning in general, but rather of a specific professional intellectual formation. What is perhaps most clearly intimated in such accounts is the impotence of negative critique. Rather than surrender mastery of the field, the critics who promulgate the line that we are living at the end of everything (and are *all* these critics men?) make one last leap and resolve to take it all – judgement, history, politics, aesthetics, value – out of the window with them. In a gesture redolent of Nietzsche's own decline into insanity and silence, they propose that we live the penultimate negation.[42] The implication seems to be that if they cannot sit at the top of Plato's pyramid, then there shall be no pyramid at all. And in the final analysis, in our appraisal of the claims made on behalf of the 'anti-aesthetic', do we honestly believe in the schizophrenic as the contemporary answer to the Cartesian monad? Is the widespread 'waning of affect'[43] a historical reality?

None of this is to deny the pertinence of postmodernism *per se*. These postmodernist accounts offer in an extraordinarily compact and vivid way a description of what it *feels* like to be alive in Western Europe in the late 1980s. The issues raised within the discourse(s) of the Post – about the collapse of Marxism as a total explanatory system, about representation and sexual identity, about who has the right to speak for whom – are crucial ones. They have to be addressed, confronted, lived through. It is vital, for instance, that we – all of us, but most especially us men – strive to open ourselves up to that which is just beginning, that we become more flexible, more sensitive to difference, that we become alert to the dangers of speaking from a position of unacknowledged mastery, or 'speaking for' a universal subject, for history and unchallengeable truth, that we become in other words, and most especially, alert to the possibilities inscribed on the other, hidden side of crisis and decay.

12

Mr H. is not a rich man, he owns very little. His one indulgence is the Thunderbird. It is an indulgence he can ill afford in material terms. The car is the object of a devotion which whilst not being in the least idolatrous (Mr H. is no worshipper of Baal) none the less does have a religious, transcendental component. The car is a love object: the literal embodiment of an ideal. The attention he lavishes upon it is a public declaration of his commitment to the quality of life and to the ideal of quality as something that is not given, that cannot just be bought with money but that has to be striven for, worked for, achieved through dint of effort, saving, self-denial.

How would Baudrillard or Bourdieu deal with such an excessive relation to such an ostentatious object? In an essay which predates his immersion in the Post Baudrillard set out to investigate how objects function to externalize social values, to objectify social distinctions and to embody aspirations and fantasies, how they act, to use his own words, as 'carriers of indexed social significations of a social and cultural hierarchy'.[44] He looks at the contents of a room or a house and notes that all the objects do not share the same symbolic space, that there are different degrees of intensity – of emotional and aspirational investment – surrounding different objects. (Possessions, in other words, are not arranged within an abstract spatium.*) He remarks that all objects of one class (e.g. chairs) do not necessarily fulfil the same purposes (e.g. if a chair is an heirloom it is not just for sitting on but also serves to guarantee the continuity of family traditions, to conserve a living* sense *of family across the generations). He suggests that:*

> *In apartments one often notices that from the point of view of status, the configuration of the ensemble is not homogeneous – rarely are all objects of a single interior on the same wavelength. Do not certain objects connote a social membership, a factual status, while others a presumed status, a level of aspirations? Are there 'unrealistic objects', that is to say those which falsely register a contradiction of the real status, desperately testifying to an inaccessible standing (all else remaining equal, they are analogous to 'escapist' behaviour or to the utopian behaviours characteristic of critical phases of acculturation)? Conversely, are there 'witness objects' that, despite a socially mobile status, attest a fidelity to the original class and a tenacious acculturation?*[45]

If Baudrillard's analysis of the apartment is transposed to my street and to Mr H.'s Thunderbird, where does it fit in Baudrillard's suggested scheme? It does not fit Baudrillard's category of the 'witness object' testifying against the owner's intentions to an earlier, occluded or suppressed social origin – unless we accept that Mr H. is downwardly mobile which in a limited, literal sense he probably is. He was once a small landowner in Cyprus and first arrived in London in the 1960s as a chauffeur before going on to work the nightshift for twenty years in a local bakery. But he has never been rich enough to properly afford the car he now owns and he was not brought up to expect ever to own such a car (although it is likely that in the culture into which he was born, the public display of material possessions was taken as a direct index to the owner's wealth and status). The Thunderbird perhaps corresponds more closely to Baudrillard's 'unrealistic object' testifying in a desperate fashion to a social standing which remains forever unattainable in 'real life'. It is 'escapist' and 'Utopian'. However, these terms seem scarcely adequate either, because they suggest a flight from the real conditions of existence, a false consciousness – and the Thunderbird is real enough. It sits there, blinding passers-by as the sunlight bounces off its polished surfaces. 'Escapist', 'Utopian': these terms are, in the context in which Baudrillard places them, purely negative and their negativity is predicated in Baudrillard's implicit conviction that the paramount realities are social class, occupational status, ownership of capital: that secular relations of power are all that matters. (This latter conviction survives Baudrillard's shift into nihilism, cynicism and 'fatalism'.) But is that really the case socially, existentially? Is that all *life appears to be about?*

I think it is better, then, to introduce another category and to call Mr H.'s car an 'impossible object'. It is impossible not because it encapsulates an unattainable dream of opulence – I don't really think that Mr H. craves to join the international jet set or to live inside an episode of Dallas. *It is impossible because it serves so many different (symbolic) functions, supplies so many diverse needs – the need for recognition and respect, yes, but also the need for something to care for and to care about, to bring up, cultivate, stand in awe of. It is impossible because it is a screen on to which so much inchoate yearning and desire are projected that putting them into words is impossible. That investment of energy, that projection of desire exceeds rational description – in a word, it is sublime. The car is also impossible because it is impossible to own, to use, or to protect properly given the circumstances in which Mr H. lives. It is impossible simply because he doesn't own a garage; impossible ultimately because he has to rely on faith in God – faith in people's good will – to protect the cherished possession from the carelessness, indifference and violence which threaten order of whatever kind wherever it's imposed. This is what makes it an impossible object.*

When I asked Mr H. how he felt about being kept awake by the post-punk musicians opposite, he said he felt unable to complain because they once threw a beer can at his car from one of the upstairs windows. If he complained he feared they would retaliate. Mr H. is frail and is not a fighter but he is no coward. He once threatened to kill a young man twice his size and less than half his age for allegedly 'bothering' his 13-year-old niece. It wasn't physical fear – fear for his person – which prevented his complaining. At least it wasn't only that. It is just that his love is too exposed. He couldn't afford to take the risk.

Mr H.'s relationship to his car is distinguished by a love as unreasonable, as inflated, as impractical as the love of Romeo and Juliet. It aspires to bring too much beauty into an imperfect world. The Thunderbird is an impossible object because it elicits an excess of feeling, an undecidable mix of proprietorial, paternal and filial emotions, of pleasure and fear. While no doubt rooted in the sensuous, in the erotic or quasi-erotic drives (the car, she: the beautiful madonna, inviolable, ever-virginal object – her hymen restored (magically like the hole in the windscreen) with every coat of wax), the exaggerated love Mr H. bears towards the Thunderbird involves a transubstantiation of the erotic, the libidinal into the spiritual. I don't think this is folly – either Mr H.'s exaggerated attachment to his car or my exaggerated description of that attachment. It is just that what we are talking about here is an act *of love and an act of love is always impossible, it is always made against the odds. After all, what is an act of love but the attribution of ideal values to actual objects?*

In his famous essay on the work of art in the age of mechanical reproduction, Walter Benjamin suggested that the democratization of the media and of image-making would lead to the politicization of the aesthetic at the point when the desacralizing potential of the technologies of mass reproduction – film, photography, printing – was realized and the aura of the work of art – its uniqueness, authenticity, single authorship – was finally destroyed. How curious, then, that what I see in Mr H.'s agonized investments in an American car goes precisely against the secular grain of Benjamin's prediction. What Mr H. seems to have done is to confer upon an object the sacred aura denied it by the conditions and mode under which it was produced. There is no 'waning of affect' here but rather an amplification, an intensification, an excess of affect: a caring which is virtually palpable. Mr H. is humanizing and aestheticizing what is essentially blank, flat and given – an object which requires no creative expenditure on his part – a car made in a factory and sold on the market (though it does require technical mastery and driving skills to be used as *a car). Through this humanization, this aestheticization, this act of love, he is giving value back, giving value (back) for money, turning a sign into an icon, a mass-produced into a beautiful one-off. The words 'commodity fetishism' do not in my opinion do justice to the heroic transcendence of alienation, juvenile (post-punk) nihilism and virtual poverty which is encapsulated in Mr H.'s strange, hyperbolic,* impossible *relation to his beloved Thunderbird.*

13

I have tried in this chapter to pose the question of aesthetics from a slightly different angle, challenging both the traditional Platonic and Kantian formulations and the bleaker aspects of the critical vision represented by some versions of postmodernism. I have none the less retained some characteristically 'Post' emphases, perceptions, foci, but I have attempted to move back against the Nietzschian grain which is built into that critical discourse. For it may be the case *intellectually* that, for certain kinds of cosmopolitan intellectual, the old explanatory and interpretive frameworks have collapsed, that the age-old need for a metaphysic, an ideal, an aesthetic which is capable of conferring value, meaning and direction on our experience has been thrown (again!) into question. But it is not the case ontologically, culturally, politically, existentially. So I have ended by returning home to the particular, to the concrete, to the culturalist, the ethnographic mode, in order to stress the primacy of that vital point where the individual and the biographical meet the collective and the historical, the point where lived culture – the experience of actual women and men – can intervene against the bleak perspectivism of certain currently fashionable kinds of crystal-ball gazing.

To those who would represent what is, after all, a welcome loosening of the old ties and constraints, a welcome opening-up to speech of different voices, different genders, different races as a global end-of-everything or a decentring 'anti-expressive' 'anti-aesthetic', I would say that 'anywhere' – the abstract 'anywhere' addressed in some postmodern descriptions – is quite simply nowhere. It does not exist because people do not occupy space in that way unless they are unfortunate enough to live in psychiatric hospitals. I would say, remember that no general tendency (no tendency to generalize) should be allowed to obscure the sense of the particular and the local – of *place* and *boundary* in the Heideggerian sense – which is the essential ground of a *sane* existence and which provides the lived and living ground upon which culture and politics are always made and remade. By starting from this universally felt need for place and boundary, from this nostalgia (in its most literal sense of 'homesickness') for the ideal made actual, we may perhaps be able to relocate and reassemble the components of a more open, more joyful and productive – that is more egalitarian – sense of what the aesthetic is and what it means. We may become sensitive once more to the liberatory potentials residing in that yearning for perfection and the possible which seems to be intrinsic, which seems to constitute what we might call the aesthetic imperative: that drive to go beyond the existent, beyond that which is 'already', to that which is ready to be brought forward into being. For in the end, *this* is the 'house of being' and all of us – intellectuals and non-intellectuals alike – will have to learn to live inside it because, as Nietzsche himself took such pains to point out, there is simply nowhere else to go.

14

One night I dreamt that Mr H.'s face appeared weeping at my window. His lips moved as if he were trying to speak but I couldn't hear the words. He lifted his arms as if to open the window but I saw he had no hands. The cuffs of his shirt were soaked in blood. His eyes were shining, blazing out against me and the darkness that threatened to engulf him. I knew – though I could scarcely acknowledge the fact – that it was I who had inflicted this injury upon him. To shut him out, I tugged at the curtains so sharply that I pulled them off the rail. I closed my eyes but when I'd opened them, Mr H. had flown and as soon as I had said this to myself, I heard a noise behind me: a feathery commotion as if a flock of birds were trapped inside the chimney. I turned round to see Mr H. suspended in the air hovering above the bed. Two huge red wings were spread out behind him like an oriental fan. They were twitching gently, brushing lightly against the ceiling and floor. (He had the measure of my house.) The air was filled with the sweet smell of honey, the thick musty odour of almonds. Without looking up into his face, I knew that Mr H.'s eyes were on me and I felt ashamed.

What was it I had taken from this man?

I saw that Mr H.'s feet were naked and I wanted to apologize for stealing his new shoes but as I looked up towards him, he threw his head back and laughed a booming laugh which reverberated off the walls, like thunder in a cave. The wings opened and closed in an arc over him and underneath him. Slowly, still laughing with his head thrown back, Mr H. flew across the room and through the wall. With the laughter still ringing in my ears, I followed him. I must explain. I must apologize. I tried in vain to find his face in the window and in the darkness beyond the window. In the space in the street reserved for Mr H.'s Thunderbird I saw a charred, deserted hulk, a mass of rust and tangled metal. The darkness grew suddenly deeper, heavier, and then as the lightning came to crack the darkness open, the rain began to fall and as it fell the rust formed bloody rivulets which gushed and churned and eddied round the metal shell. Somehow I knew the rain would never stop. The rivulets would form a stream, the stream would become a torrent, then a ruddy lake, at last a raging sea. This sea would swallow everything: these bits of twisted metal, this street, these houses, these words.

I looked up and saw the outline of a rose traced like a letter in the sky.

The rose was the promise in the wake of flight.

The bird had flown. The bird had found its wings.

Notes

1 See Hal Foster (ed.), *Postmodern Culture* (London: Pluto, 1895), published in the USA as *The Anti-Aesthetic* (Port Townsend, Washington: Bay Press, 1983).

2 Raymond Williams, *Keywords* (London: Fontana, 1973).

3 William Wordsworth, quoted in ibid.

4 Raymond Williams, *Culture and Society 1780–1950* (Harmondsworth: Penguin 1959).

5 See Jean-François Lyotard, 'The sublime and the avant-garde', *Artforum* (April, 1984).

6 Peter Fuller, 'Taste - you can't opt out', *Design 423* (March, 1984). See also Peter Fuller, *Aesthetics after Modernism* (London: Writers & Readers, 1983): Peter Fuller,

Art and Psychoanalysis (London: Writers & Readers, 1980): Peter Fuller, *Beyond the Crisis in Art* (London: Writers & Readers, 1980).

7 Clifford Geertz, 'Thick description', in *The Interpretation of Culture* (Basic Books, 1973).

8 Roland Barthes, 'The goddess: the new Citroen', in his *Mythologies* (London: Cape, 1972).

9 Tom Wolfe, *The Kandy-Kolored Tangerine-Flake Streamline Baby* (London: Bantam, 1964); Tom Wolfe, *The Pump House Gang* (London: Bantam, 1969).

10 Vance Packard, *The Wastemakers* (Harmondsworth: Penguin, 1963); Vance Packard *The Status Seekers* (Harmondsworth: Penguin, 1961). See also P. Willis, *Profane Culture* (London: Routledge & Kegan Paul, 1978).

11 See 'The Private Life of the Ford Cortina' (directed by Nigel Finch), a TV documentary for the BBC arts series, *Arena*.

12 For corroboration of this point, listen to 'Police officer', a satirical reggae lament by the young black British talk-over artist Smiley Culture. In the song, Smiley Culture enacts an imaginary dialogue between himself as a young black reggae star and a (white cockney) police officer who has stopped his car but who eventually agrees to let him go without a body search in return for an autograph. The song is peppered with Smiley's pleas delivered in a strong West Indian accent: 'Police officer, don't touch me ganja!', 'Police officer, don't give me no producer' (i.e. a demand to produce his driving licence for inspection at a specified police station within a specified period). The song points up the extent to which young black drivers are subject to routine harassment by the Metropolitan Police.

13 Pierre Bourdieu, *Distinction: A Social Critique of the Judgement of Taste*, translated by Richard Nice (Cambridge, Mass.: Harvard University Press, and London: Routledge & Kegan Paul, 1984); originally published by Les Editions de Minuit (Paris, 1979). All Bourdieu quotes in this article are from this book unless otherwise indicated in a separate footnote.

14 Richard Hoggart, *The Uses of Literacy* (Harmondsworth: Penguin, 1958).

15 Bourdieu, op. cit.

16 ibid.

17 Mikhail Bakhtin, *Rabelais and his World* (Cambridge, Mass.: MIT Press, 1968), published in Russian (1965).

18 See, for instance, Dick Hebdige, *Subculture: The Meaning of Style* (London: Methuen, 1979); Dick Hebdige, *Hiding in the Light: On Images and Things* (London: Routledge, 1988); Willis, op. cit. 1978. For the use of Bakhtin see, for instance, Peter Wollen's introductory essay to the Komar and Melamid exhibition catalogue (MOMA) (Oxford, 1985); also Dick Hebdige, 'Some sons and their fathers', in *Ten. 8: Men in Camera*, 17 (1985).

19 See, for instance, Pierre Bourdieu, *Outline of a Theory of Practice* (Cambridge: Cambridge University Press, 1977).

20 Friedrich Nietzsche, 'Nietzsche contra Wagner', in Walter Kaufmann (ed.), *The Portable Nietzsche* (Chatto & Windus, 1971).

21 'The style of the book, whose long, complex sentences may offend – constructed as they are with a view to reconstituting the complexity of the social world in a language capable of holding together the most diverse things while setting them in rigorous perspective – stems partly from the endeavour to . . . prevent the reading from slipping back into the simplicities of the smart essay or the political polemic': P. Bourdieu, preface to the English language edition of *Distinction*, op. cit.

22 Roland Barthes, 'Change the object itself', in his *Image, Music, Text*, edited and translated by Stephen Heath (London: Fontana, 1977).

23 See Wollen, op. cit. 1985.

24 See Jean-François Lyotard, *The Postmodern Condition: A Report on Knowledge* (Minneapolis: University of Minnesota Press, and Manchester: Manchester University Press, 1984) especially the essay 'What is postmodernism?'. Also Lyotard, 'The sublime and the avant-garde' (April, 1984).
25 Jean-François Lyotard, 'Defining the postmodern' in Lisa Appignanesi (ed.), *Postmodernism: ICA Documents 4* (London: Institute of Contemporary Arts, 1986).
26 Jean-François Lyotard, 'Complexity and the sublime', in ibid.
27 A more developed version of the argument presented in this section is available in an article entitled 'Postmodernism and "the other side"' in Hebdige, *Hiding in the Light* (Routledge, 1988) and in *Journal of Communication Inquiry*, summer 1985.
28 *Les Immatériaux* was the title of an exhibition mounted by Jean-François Lyotard at the Pompidou Centre in 1984. The exhibition was designed to explore the new postmodern *sensorium* made available through simulation-technologies. See Jean-François Lyotard, 'Les Immateriaux', in *Art & Text 17: Expositionism* (1984).
29 See Lyotard, *The Postmodern Condition.*
30 Walter Benjamin, 'Theses on the philosophy of history', in his *Illuminations* (London: Fontana, 1973).
31 Lyotard, 'Complexity and the sublime'.
32 Kant cited ibid.
33 ibid.
34 ibid.
35 Lyotard, 'Defining the postmodern'.
36 Richard Rorty, 'Habermas and Lyotard on postmodernity', in Richard J. Bernstein (ed.), *Habermas and Modernity* (Oxford: Polity Press, Basil Blackwell, 1985).
37 ibid.
38 Fredric Jameson, 'Postmodernism or the cultural logic of late capitalism', *New Left Review*, 146 (July–August, 1984).
39 See Jean Baudrillard, *Simulations* and *In the Shadow of the Silent Majorities*, edited by Jim Fleming and Sylvere Lotringer, translated by Paul Foss, Paul Patton, Philip Beitchman, John Johnston (New York: Semiotext(e) Foreign Agents Series, 1983). Also Baudrillard, 'The ecstasy of communication', in Foster (ed.), op. cit.
40 Gilles Deleuze and Felix Guattari, *Anti-Oedipus* (New York: Viking Press, 1977).
41 See Lyotard, *The Postmodern Condition.* The postmodern condition is defined here as an impossible tense – the 'future anterior' – post meaning 'after', modo meaning 'now'.
42 For Nietzsche the final negation was the negation of negation: the (heroic) affirmation of what is.
43 Jameson, op. cit.
44 Jean Baudrillard, 'Sign function and class logic', in *For a Critique of the Political Economy of the Sign* (New York: Telos, 1981).
45 ibid.

5

Subject to Change without Notice: Psychology, Postmodernity and the Popular[1]

Valerie Walkerdine

It could you know, it could have started here.[2] Memory's a tricky thing. She remembers El Cid *well enough though. Charlton Heston and Sophia Loren were not, according to Mr Holl, the headteacher and the one who took A level French classes, the kind of stars that one should encourage children to go and see. They were reading Corneille's* Le Cid *and, after all, it was the same story, so she had argued that it would constitute an educational visit. The fact that Mr Holl did not share the same opinion did not totally baffle her. After all, by the sixth form she was used to the utter disdain accorded to popular culture. Mr Holl thought it was a travesty of a fine French classic, but all you got at school was Geoffrey Stapley who couldn't say* tu *and it was, frankly, boring. While* El Cid, *playing at the Derby Gaumont had the big screen, stars. But, perhaps it was also that she had never really wanted to learn French for the literature: it was for the excitement, the romance, the glamour, the Other: after all she had seen* Gigi *and the advertisements for French cigarettes showing those young men with earrings in their ears who suggested a wildness quite out of step with the nice boys with shiny shoes that her mother seemed to favour.[3] No, it wasn't the finer points of literature that excited her imagination, but the thought of travel (an air hostess, a bilingual secretary perhaps), of glamour, of making it. But somehow, somewhere there, French theory and popular pleasures got mixed up together.*

Phil Cohen (1992: 2) writes that 'most theories have a strong, if disavowed, autobiographical element in them' and 'most of the general theories have rested on a very slender and sometimes non-existent, empirical base'. But what if the autobiographical element is made to stand in a clearer light and the general seen to be very particular indeed, what then? Sherry Turkle (1992) argued about the mixing of personal and theoretical in the psychoanalyst, that the idea that the analyst who is revealed to have particular problems in a specific area (the most notable example being Melanie Klein's relationship with her daughter, highlighted by the play about her) must be said to be biased, her vision clouded by pathology. Instead, Turkle argues that, indeed, her very difficulties in this area made her especially sensitive to the issues involved. Of course, aspects of her personal biography drove her obsessions, but this should be understood as quite opposite to the idea that this perverted and distorted an objective search for scientific truth. It was precisely what she knew, was sensitive to, had problems with, that gave her work strength in a particular direction.

We all have trajectories which implicitly or explicitly fuel our research, but mine – which covers a working-class provincial childhood to primary teacher training (a good job for a woman: 'you can always go back to it ... '), to teaching, psychology, PhD in developmental psychology, teaching in education departments, researching cognitive development, gender, mathematics, subjectivity, making art and films, moving to an art department and then media studies – must at least rank as one of the more unusual! There are some issues that I want to draw out of this trajectory to make some links between the past and the present.

It was the popular imagination that fuelled my growing up and has a special place for me in attempting to explore the issues at stake for me in the present. There has long been, and I want so much to talk about it, a sense of the relation between the masses, the working class, the popular, mass consumption, communication, media, as bad. The masses are seen as bad and the markets and media make them even worse. So, we have an endless stream of psychological research aiming to examine the 'effects' and 'uses' of television and other media. There has been, in both psychology and media and cultural theory, a constant seesawing dynamic of good/bad, reactionary/progressive between the mass and the media. But if I was formed as a woman who grew up as one of the postwar mass, the grammar school-educated proletariat, the working-class girl who was shown only the pathologizing romance, how come I have the job I do? And how can we examine the place of the popular in the making of the subject? The popular, understood as low, working class, feminine: how do we view its place, a place where fact and fiction blend? This chapter is about me because I am one of its subjects. It is about the possibility of a recognition that the traditional boundaries between subject and object have broken down and that this means that our own subjectivity is formed like that of those we research. The implications of that alone for social science are vast.

Just like the place that France and the French had in the awakening of my longing, the longing for the Other, to be Other, someone else, somewhere else, exotic foreign, was important to the adolescent Valerie. French theory had its place in that other imaginary space, the space of the British Left and emerging 1970s feminism (Walkerdine 1996). France was the place where 1968 had happened. OK, so there was no revolution, but at least it seemed to the eager English imagination that they had been near to one. After all, there had been barricades, riot police, endless attempts to account for the failure of the moment. But that moment was especially important to a group of young academics who felt trapped, as did many others at the time, by the empiricism and positivism of British psychology, by the failure to take on board the lessons of European social theory. This put theory on the agenda because we wanted to explain the constitution of the subject and its intertwining with the social. It refused the idea of a pregiven subject who is made social through a process of socialization which left the dualism of individual and society intact. It is this work, which refused the split between individual and society, and thus between psychology and sociology, which helped to inaugurate particular forms of media and cultural theory and which rehabilitated psychoanalysis to a place in the British academy, and which has been so important to me personally and to many others.

Subject to Change

James Donald (1991) recalls the politics of the time well when he remembers that, in the wake of 1968, the failure of the Left to have a theory of the subject seemed very important: in understanding why the workers had not joined the students in great force, why a revolution had not happened. One of the central issues here that I will return to later is the place of the (never-quite-delivering-the-goods) working class.

Meanwhile, economistic models failed to engage adequately with the production of subjectivity and the place of this is both the production of the social and social change. In Britain, this was played out in critiques of the old New Left, especially the empiricism of notions of shared experience producing working-class identity, as in the work of E.P. Thompson, for example. Thompson had argued that working-class consciousness was produced out of shared experience of oppression. Instead of the idea of shared experience constituting identity, Althusser posited an entirely different relation between ideology and consciousness. While class consciousness had always been central to Marxist thinking, Althusser argued that the traditional models of true or false consciousness linked to accounts of ideology – as a process of distortion of perception, an inability to see the true state of oppression and exploitation – was too crude and that much thinking on the Left was too economically determinist. He argued that the realm of ideology was relatively autonomous from the level of the economy and, indeed, went as far as proposing that it was only determined by the economy in a 'last instance', an instance that he argued never comes. Althusser's theory was not supported by a Cartesian account of experience, cognition or perception but with the work of the French psychoanalyst, Jacques Lacan, the man who had been responsible for a structuralist and semiotic reading of Freud. It is his work that became especially important for the argument that I am going to develop. In using Lacanian psychoanalysis, Althusser presented the necessity of a theory of a psychologically complex subject as a central aspect of the analysis of the social world and, moreover, an account of the subject taken from psychoanalysis and not from psychology. The particular version of psychoanalysis that Althusser chose also had its own complex version of the social produced in fantasy through the motor of desire. This got over the problem of individual/social dualism and hence the split between psychology and sociology (and accounts of a pregiven individual to be made social), but it helped to point up the serious study of ideology in its own right. This was enormously important to British film studies, which did much to promote psychoanalytic work in this country by publishing, in the journal *Screen*, a hugh body of psychoanalytically inspired film theory. In addition, cultural and media analysis was much influenced by this work, the work that developed from it and the work of Italian Communist Antonio Gramsci, which interpreted ideology through his work on hegemony. In all of these ways studies of the relation between ideology and consciousness in Britain, central to social and cultural theory, took off. Feminists were arguing for the importance of psychoanalysis as well, especially after Juliet Mitchell's influential *Psychoanalysis and Feminism* (1984). Psychoanalysis began to enter the stage of serious academic debate, but it was not any old psychoanalysis, but as Donald (1991: 2) put it 'a feminist rereading of a Lacanian rereading of Freud'. This version began to flourish in sociology, media and cultural studies, literature: anywhere, it may be said, except psychology!

It is at this point, then, that a group of young psychologists and sociologists begin to publish a journal aimed at psychologists and social theorists, called *Ideology and Consciousness*. Later, when we were more enamoured of Foucault than Althusser, we changed the name to its initials, *I and C*. In Britain this formed part of the development of new kinds of work in the realm of the psychological, work on subjects and subjectivity, inspired by structuralism, post-structuralism and psychoanalysis. We saw it as a profound critique of the positivism and empiricism of Anglo-American psychology and it has taken until the 1990s for a greater body of work to begin to be established in both countries in traditions that have become variously known as post-structuralist, deconstructive, discursive and postmodern psychologies. One of the first books in this wave was *Changing the Subject* (Henriques et al.) in 1984.

This work attempted to go further than Althusserian structuralism in producing a theory of the subject using the work of Michel Foucault, who went beyond the split between science and ideology retained by Althusser to examine the place of the human and social sciences (in my case, especially psychology). For Foucault, psychological stories were not false or pseudo science but fictions which function in truth, scientific stories whose truth value had a central place in the government and regulation of the modern and postmodern order. To cut a very long story short, Foucault argued that the individual was not the same thing as the person or the subject of psychology, but a historically specific form of the subject. In this account, the individual was understood as *produced* by means of a set of apparatuses of social regulation or management of populations in which scientific knowledges about the social and subjective were fictions central in the production of a management which sought to regulate through self-regulation, by producing discourses and practices (in education, law, medicine, social work, etc.), creating the subject which was claimed to be described.

This work had a number of consequences which, put briefly, were about a subject who was not a pregiven entity or essence, but who was produced in the signs, narratives, fictions and fantasies which make up the social world. For Foucault, 'the child', 'the woman', were fictions created in the practices of regulation. And our 'fit' with those stories, how we came to embody them, was what was at stake here. His work had a profound impact upon the social sciences and upon literary theory, though its impact on psychology was much slower to take hold. It is an irony that this kind of work on the subject and subjectivity was far more widely known and respected outside psychology. However, it is also the case that, to this day, media cultural and social theorists are apt all too easily to dismiss psychological work in their field as reductionist (see Morley 1993), thereby ignoring the psychological completely, while maintaining an apparent ignorance of the growing body of critical psychological work.

I do not have time here to discuss the particular ways I used this body of work to intervene in debates about developmental psychology (especially cognitive development and language) nor in debates about gender, rationality and education. But, briefly, I argued that subjects are produced within discursive practices and that this is strongly critical of accounts of universalist models of development, for example, or work which understands 'the child' or 'femininity' outside specifically historically and culturally located practices in which subject positions are produced through the interchange of signs (see Walkerdine 1988, 1989 and 1991 for example).

Subject to Change: Who Notices?

One of the major issues with this approach was how to understand the relationship of the subject in Foucault's terms and how subjectivity is lived, both in relation to historicity and materiality, and how a non-unitary, non-rationalist subjectivity is held together. This subjectivity cannot be reduced to Thompson's 'lived experience', but the problems of how to understand it were forcibly brought back to me when I came to the recognition that there was something that both I and the theory and politics needed to come back to: the popular and what the French call the popular classes.

While I started to work on popular culture, returning to issues that had been important to me as a child (children's literature, girls' comics, for example) something else was happening. *Class* came back to me with a jolt, not as a theoretical issue, even (and, perhaps as we shall see, especially through the Left), but as a profoundly personal one. Psychoanalysis was bringing back my childhood, or at least my fantasies and memories of it, and with that, a lot of pain. It was a fertile period in my work but also a time in which I was dealing with a deep depression, a terrible anger, which came out in some of my writing, most notably 'Dreams from an Ordinary Childhood' (Walkerdine 1985) and *Democracy in the Kitchen* (Walkerdine and Lucey 1989). But the depression and anger allowed to come to the surface issues around class and the popular which I now want to explore.

She was always such a good girl, a goody-goody, even. Good at school. But, the longing, the desire to get out, to travel, glamour, all the things that girls in her position were set up for. Her mother did her best, but the ambition to be an artist never really took off, even though she loved art more than anything else. Art for her signified the capture on paper of that fantasy space (she drew scenes and glamorous women, while Brenda Orton made copies of the blue ladies they sold in Boots department store in Derby, the exoticized blue-tinted blue oriental women). But the artist and art college? All those paint-splattered wild-looking girls in duffle coats: no, a primary school teacher. This was, after all, the respectable working class, that group that come to be so dismissed by the new New Left. But she insisted on London. Why did nobody tell her that you could go and study a subject because you liked it? It meant nothing to her or to her friends, like the time when she and Carolyn Hales decided that it was better to do art at training college because it only took three years, whereas going to art school and then teacher training would take five, so you would be able to be adult, work for a living more quickly if you went to training college. And somehow, the little rebellions were never much, and wouldn't have been understood as rebellions by those intellectuals. The highs and lows, the isolation, the ignorance, with the romance of poverty and dirt locked firmly inside the fantasies of the Left itself. When she first wrote about the dreams of her ordinary childhood one reviewer called her life stultified. It hurt and brought once again to the surface that immense well of hate.

But there was that entry into the longed-for space, the glamorous intellectual Left where she felt as though in a masquerade – the splitting, the not belonging, the fear of being found out to be stupid – the parties where people talked of being in the Young Communists at fourteen, when what she remembered was South Pacific, *Radio Luxemburg and the Methodist Youth Club.*

She felt stupid, frightened, like the time when granny said that Mum had shown her up on a coach trip by eating her fish skin during a fish-and-chip supper. Or when, having learnt to put the peas on the back of her fork, later as a PhD student, she watched a professor's daughter in her twenties stick her finger in a chocolate mousse or others lick plates (licking tea in saucers, dipping biscuits in tea, were definitely practices to hide – to like but to be ashamed of). This shame didn't start when she joined the intellectual Left, but long before. To be respectable was not to be like the rough children or the families with a dad in prison. It was to wear clean underwear in case you were knocked down and taken to hospital or to polish the silver in case the Queen might call. A vigilant self-regulation was always necessary to avoid being the object of external regulation or pity or charity, and you hadn't to want too much either:
everything in moderation
much wants more
manage
cope
don't break down
don't get into debt

Of course. And we can find all of those forms of population management which formed my family in that way. But just then, at that moment when I looked for it, for some place in which that history of which I was trying to speak was being spoken about, I found nothing. And perhaps because of psychoanalysis I could no longer split and keep one thing in one place, another in another. The best, the cleverest, beat the post-structuralists at their own game so that they couldn't throw me out, back to the provinces, babies, depression, sinks, coping, moderation and yet the overwhelming need to make a Left and a feminism which refused to look in this direction, take some notice.

Working-class Subjects: Who's Noticing?

For feminism, class was often presented in a debate about capitalism versus patriarchy, class versus gender as though it were possible to be either one or the other and always, as usual, as though class only referred to one class:

the pathologized Other, not the normalized middle class. In addition, it was often taken to be the case that working-class girls and women were too feminine or less feminist. For the Left, increasingly in the 1970s and 1980s, the respectable white working class had become the source of the problem, not the hope for the revolution. It was positioned as a problem in all popular Left movements, like the politics of the GLC or Left councils, where the respectable white working class was also viewed as the biggest problem in the implementation of anti-racist and anti-sexist policies. As Franco Bianchini admitted (1987), the politics of the GLC did nothing for the white working class. I couldn't, it seemed, have chosen a worse moment to want to talk about the respectable white working class, precisely the moment when not only was the issue completely out of favour but had come to be associated with the epitome of reaction.

But, I want to argue that while in one way the Left appeared to have abandoned the white working class, class having seemed to disappear from the agenda, the proletariat, the mass, has been an obsession, a central if sometimes silent figure during all the debates from modernity through to postmodernity. Indeed, we might say, following Foucault, that stories about the masses circulate endlessly. The issue is not so much that they have disappeared, but where and how they are talked about, what kind of object they become. And, in all of this, the popular has a particular place.

Noticing the Masses

Let us go back again to that Althusserian moment, when for the British Left, the thing to be explained was not the possibility of class consciousness, but the failure. Theories of ideology were to explain not a subject whose vision was clouded, but a subject produced in ideologies, in media and other texts. For Althusser, the working class was constructed not in the real relations of production but in a set of imaginary relations in which bourgeois fantasies, especially those in the mass media, had produced the very mirrors in which the workers' identity was formed. By referring to Lacan's psychoanalysis, the way this work was taken up clearly implied an account in which working-class identity was an ideological product down to the very unconscious meanings of the original fantasies. Lacan's Imaginary built on Freud's idea of imaginary wish fulfilment. The infant, argued Freud, deals with the terror that it feels when food and warmth and human comfort are inevitably not on tap twenty-four hours a day by 'hallucinating the absent breast'. Freud later saw this as the origin of fantasies of wish fulfilment and the organizer of psychic life. The fantasy space, the unconscious, was the one to be filled with fantasies of plenty and presence. For Lacan, then, the imaginary order is the order of wish-fulfilment fantasies, fantasies of an impossible reunion with the lost mother. This eventually Oedipal fantasy could only be solved for Freud by the castration complex, and for Lacan, by the move to the symbolic order in which the desire to be the object of the mother's desire is cross-cut by a deeply competitive patriarchy, one which is no less a fantasy but a fantasy of control through which the social world is organized. For this, Lacan made reference to the structural anthropology of Levi-Strauss. In analyses that followed, much work in film theory using this model concentrated fruitfully upon Oedipal analysis of Hollywood movies and, following a very important 1974 paper by Laura Mulvey (1992), on the place of Hollywood in constructing a patriarchal fantasy of woman, a woman who was not a distorted stereotype, but who did not exist except as symptom and myth of a male fantasy, a fantasy constructed in the Dream Factory itself.

This meant that the working class increasingly came to be identified as being totally formed in ideologies, in mass media, trapped in a Hollywood which played upon its most infantile fantasies, constructing a patriarchal fetishization of women: a sexist and infantilized working class, the very working class constructed in the fantasy of the new New Left. I want to argue that this paved the way for not only the dropping of class from cultural analysis but also the idea that by the 1980s the working class no longer existed as a viable entity.

But to explain this I want to go back, to at least the beginnings of social science, to the modern period of grand metanarratives, the grand stories of psychology and sociology, the stories which claimed to tell the truth about the human condition, the stories of, among other, Darwin, Freud and Marx. Darwin's story of evolution charted civilization as a narrative of survival and adaptation, taken up as social Darwinism in which capitalism, industrial competition and the rise of the bourgeoisie were explained using an evolutionary discourse, with the white bourgeois male placed at the highest point, the most civilized, with a series of others underneath, those closer to the animals, less evolved: children, women, colonial peoples, the proletariat. The proletariat: the crowd, the mass, the mob. Marx took it one way, Le Bon – the French originator of mass or crowd psychology – another. A civilized proletariat, one better evolved, was understood as central to the emergence of the possibility of effective government. In these accounts the state of the proletarian mind was thought of as central to their transformation from a mass or a mob into either docile bodies, law-abiding, well-regulated subjects or to that entity 'the working class' that would recognize its true mission through the production of the appropriate form of revolutionary consciousness. What Le Bon feared in mob rule, dark anti-democratic forces, threatening the bourgeois order, a threat only lessened by individuation, (a theme which was to be central to accounts of the mass from media to football fans) was countered by Marx's modernist proletariat, who had to be able to see the world as it really was and understand the state of its alienation and exploitation in order to make the revolution. The working-class mind seems to have become a heavily contested space.

But what if this proletariat, this white, rough and respectable working class is not a fact of modernity, but a fiction, a fantasy, one created in the imagination of the bourgeoisie (a point echoed by Raymond Williams, see Chapter 3, p. 64)? What if it is a fiction, in Foucault's terms, functioning in truths, very powerful truths that constitute and regulate modern forms of government? In this scenario, the working class always exists as a problem, to be transformed one way or another. It begins to be endlessly described and monitored in every detail. When I say that it is a fiction, I do not mean that poverty, oppression and exploitation do not exist or that class does not become an important designation through which we recognize ourselves, but that the way that the working class is created as an object of knowledge is central to the strategies which are used for its creation as a mode of classification and regulation. These strategies tell us about the fears and fantasies of the regulators, the bourgeoisie for whom the proletariat forms an Other, to be feared, desired, directed, manipulated. In this sense I am arguing that this truth is constructed inside the fertile bourgeois imagination, an imagination that sees threat and annihilation around every corner because of its shaky position in between the aristocracy and the proletariat. The truth about the working class then is the mirror of the fears and hopes of the bourgeoisie. In these fantasy stories the proletariat becomes everything which Darwin described as lower, more animal, less civilized, less rational. The mass has to be tamed. It is mapped and classified and found wanting. It is pathological to the bourgeoisie's normal. But it can be made normal: managed, policed to become normal like the bourgeoisie. It can be educated, tested, its intelligence monitored, its mental health, its mothering, fathering, cleanliness, work habits and on and on. This class is endlessly described. And that other class? Only in so far as it is presented as the norm. As Helen Lucey and I described in *Democracy in the Kitchen* (1989), the bourgeoisie is no less regulated, the women no less oppressed, but their oppression inheres in the very normality of which they are presented as guardians.

These stories of course have their heroes and villains, the good and the bad. There are the salt-of-the-earth working class, the hard workers as well as the feckless drunken poor, the bad mothers. Is bourgeois desire enshrined in those fantasies? A desire for a more equitable world in Marx, versus a smooth-working capital in liberalism? But are they any less fantasies for that? Just as Edward Said argued in *Orientalism* (1985) that those Western stories of the Orient told us more about the fantasies of the West than anything about the East, might not those stories of the working class, endlessly recirculated and enshrined in the everyday regulation of the population as if to make them true, might not they too tell us more about their creators than those so ardently described, so liberally, nay humanistically, regulated?

Yes, from the solidarity of the Welsh pit village to C4 and Essex Man, might they not all be fictions imbued with fantasy? Shouldn't we be looking at whose stories there are, how they came to be told and what effect they have in the constitution of actual working-class subjects – subjects designated by that very classification?

In fact, if we look back to that moment of the constitution of the mass, I want to argue that it paved the way for modernity's look at the media. In *The Future of an Illusion* (1927: 7) Freud writes that the 'masses are lazy and unintelligent: they have no love for instinctual renunciation and they are not to be convinced by argument of its inevitability'. For Freud, then, it would be impossible to dispense with control of the mass by the minority. What, in his view, had to happen was the provision of good leadership, which would induce the masses 'to perform work and undergo the renunciations upon which the existence of civilization depends' (p. 7). In Freud's view, therefore, civilization is against the mass. It is the mass which is closer to the body, to pleasure, to animality. Bad leadership, stressing deprivation and leading potentially to fascism with an easily swayed mass, who are closer to their emotions than to rationality, is understood as one side of the coin of which the mass media and consumption are the other. Precisely by catering to the easy pleasures and not the necessary privations, the mass media and markets, in this view, work against civilization.

Creating the Postwar Working Class

I want to move to the 1950s with its idea of the meritocracy, of social mobility, through the tripartite system of education designed to find the bright among the working class, but also a period when the newly consuming working class appears to be deviating from its historic mission: it is taken to be becoming bourgeois. It is the beginning of the mass market and mass media. Indeed, the problem of the mass as proto-fascist reasserts itself in the discourse of the Frankfurt School, which locates the causes of fascism in authoritarian child-rearing. In empirical analyses of authoritarianism using empiricist variants of psychoanalysis which were to have a profound effect on social psychology, authoritarianism is charted by means of projective tests, Likert attitude scales, Rorschach blots. It is precisely this position that is taken up by the Frankfurt School in the postwar period. It is important to me that at this moment, the moment of my childhood, a number of issues come together in the regulation of the masses: the tripartite system of secondary schooling, leading to the expansion of higher education, the mass market, media and communication. So, Adorno, Horkheimer and others place easily together prejudice, proto-fascism, authoritarianism and the uncivilized pleasures of the mass. The mass, then, is both becoming more educated and threatening to swamp the civilized world with its easy consumption, its authoritarian parenting, its passive television viewing, its escapism. It is my view that social and psychological research has a particular place at this point in the surveillance and regulation of the masses, a point which becomes clear in relation to psychological research on media audiences.

Perhaps the love/hate fantasy about the working class always said more about the desire of an intellectual Left for the masses to do the transforming, the dirty work as usual, while they could write, think, lead. In whose fantasies were we constituted and how did we grow up inside those different fantasy scenarios?

The monitoring of the working-class family takes a new turn. The danger of the consuming working class is the threat of a turn to reaction, a reaction understood as being central to the mass media, with their propagandizing appeal. The pathological family is joined by the pathologizing media. And the way that the one is watched by the other becomes a test of proto-fascism, of abnormality in the social psychology of family viewing. Social theorists begin too to assert that the working class with its penchant for consumer goods and its wage settlements has lost its way. It is being caught by the mass and enticed away from its revolutionary goal. Already its decline as a class is mapped: the fantasy is in danger. Simultaneously, then, working-class people are being presented with home ownership, consumer goods, holidays, education; the possibility that, for the first time, their sons and daughters may not have to face the same tiring, poor, soul-destroying jobs as them. The class becomes a place to leave. And why on earth would you not want to leave it for the life that is being offered? Why should anyone see a romanticism in back-breaking work or poverty? Why, having faced so many defeats, would you want to try again? But the injunction to be 'true' and the urge to consume, to better oneself, to move out, constitute the working-class subject as the object of hopelessly contradictory discourses. To want to move out is to sell out and not to sell out is to remain stupid, animal, reactionary, pathological, anti-democratic. Take your pick. I don't like the choice very much.

You can after all, succeed in education. Here from that period is *My Fair Lady*, in which a flower girl living in poverty can be educated to pass for a princess. To be educated, however, is first of all to be maligned as a dirty animal.[4]

The violence of this inauguration into being a lady never struck me when I first saw it as a child. I remember only the songs and the transformation of Audrey Hepburn into a princess. What she was, what I was, was presented as so very sordid, so very worthless compared with what was on offer: rags to riches, pauper to princess. Glamour, excitement, exotic Otherness. New worlds of wealth and glamour and plenty.

So, you too can get out, but beware, authoritarian families lurk – families who bear the responsibility for the success and failure of grammar-school boys; fathers who are too strict for child-centredness, who are so anti-democratic and not progressive; mothers who deprive, fail, don't talk or stimulate their offspring – who produce delinquents, criminals. Progress is now taken to be in the hands of the liberal middle classes, who allow their children to grow up towards autonomy. The mass is one of the problems: the market, manufacturing and the media. Ah yes, the media.

It is the 1950s which sees the Frankfurt School and other social psychologists such as Henri Tajfel begin to look at the mass media, at groups and inter-group conflict. The early research on media effects begins here. But significantly it is at this time too that these early researchers comment on the power of the new mass markets and media to produce new forms of social and psychic life. C. Wright Mills (1956) argued that mass communications created a pseudo-world of products and services, but also the lifestyles inherent in buying those products and services. Two American anthropologists, Horton and Wohl talk about the way in which television brings simulated communication into the living room. Interestingly these sentiments are ones that we associate more with the 1980s than the 1950s, with postmodernity rather than modernity. However, what is visible here already is a version of the mass subject with an identity defined by mass consumption. The fear, the danger understood as lurking inside is the production of a proto-fascist mass of consumers, living in a bubble. But who is in the bubble? By the 1950s, are these endlessly-to-be-watched consumers the ones who have lost their way? Of course, we should have known. As usual, the normal middle classes are all right because they see through mass consumption, they talk to their children about television, they buy healthier foods, and of course – but nobody seems to remember this – they have more money and they have access to a culture which they regard as infinitely superior to the one that the poor unfortunates are dragged into. The avant-garde in relation to the popular, but that's another story.

Well, here we are again then back in the 1950s with me and my dreams. Not a grammar-school boy or angry young man. Descriptions of me fade. But wait.

I had thought that the stories of that time were all about boys and that girls were left silenced as usual. But I was wrong. Quite wrong. What I have discovered while researching this chapter is that there is a whole postwar narrative about girls growing up into upward mobility, the very narratives which so fired my imagination.

These narratives, found in *My Fair Lady*, *Gigi*, Walt Disney's *Cinderella*, build upon prewar narratives also featuring girls: Shirley Temple movies, Orphan Annie comic strips, Judy Garland in *The Wizard of Oz*. I am not going to discuss these (though I do explore certain aspects in more detail in Chapter 15), except to point to the central place of girls in movies about poverty, wealth and the Depression. Here the girls are poor and often orphaned; and like Judy Garland they dream of a place where wishes are granted through the intervention of good fairy godmothers, thwarted by bad witches, to reach a place where men can grant ultimate wishes which are about turning poverty to wealth and poor men into fine ones.

But by the 1950s, the story of the girl is a story of rags to riches transformation through education. Here, the girl does not just intercede for others, she may actually be shown to move out of the horror that is herself towards a transformation both to adult womanhood and to wealth, glamour and romance. While these movies certainly present wish fulfilment and have strong Oedipal elements, to describe them only in these terms is to miss a central point. The girls in these movies are not constituted only in a sexual wish fulfilment. That narrative only makes sense in relation to a historically specific story about upward mobility, a move to be a lady, through an education leading to the possibility of betterment through a marriage to a person from a higher class. This story also relates to and builds upon others told in other places for girls, like girls' comics that I have analysed elsewhere. But I think that the story is not simply about Althusser's version of Lacan's Imaginary, nor is it Gramscian hegemony. The unspoken and unanalysed elements are poverty, class exploitation and oppression, and how women get out of these at a moment of history when the film stories show the way as the glamorous – perhaps the only – way. I would say, then, that these films constitute a certain truth about class and mobility at a conjuncture when certain paths and fantasies are open to poor women. Nor do I think that the films are, in any simple sense, bad. As I have tried to show, they – far more than the culture of school – helped to get me to the place in which I am today. Without the possibility of those dreams, higher education would have meant nothing to me at the age of fourteen. Contradictory as that message was, it cannot simply be condemned out of hand. It has to be understood in terms of the conditions of my subjectification and as resistance to the life that was accorded to my mother. Why would I want to be a housewife when I thought that I might become a princess?

But there is something else here too. I think that the glamorous option has to be seen as a defence, a defence against the Other that it hides. Neither the mother nor the father is shown as adequate; rather in the stories I have talked about they are poor, exploited, uncouth, animal, dirty, reactionary, depriving, nasty and sometimes exploiting. What is presented as the feared place, to be defended against at all costs, is a return here. But it is the bourgeois fantasy which constitutes this inadequacy and which places itself as a grid for the girl to read her own history against. That those mothers and fathers struggle to do what they can in the circumstances they find themselves cannot be contemplated in this scenario. While the working class is endlessly described, very particular stories are being told and some issues do not even get a mention, as I shall demonstrate later. But of course, those working class women are spoken about everywhere from the 1950s to the present. They stare out of every developmental psychology, education, social work textbook. They are the bad or potentially bad mothers. So while social democracy struggles to reform our mothers, a door opens and a few of us are let in (ashamed, afraid ever to be like that again, defiant).

No material for a revolution here. Only a story about how come they (I can't say 'we' now, having escaped the fate worse than death) came to be like this. Failed again.

But, come to think about it, it is not very surprising that the erstwhile middle-class students of 1968 should have missed the class narratives inside Hollywood and opted only for a world of Oedipus. For it was those students, the sons and daughters of the bourgeoisie who, in their own revolt, reacted against the conformist privilege of their parents. Such young people must have found it virtually impossible to identify with a respectable aspirant working class. The young women who so desperately wanted to get out of the despised place and into glamour could hardly claim to be or want to be part of the romanticized and fetishized working class that the rebellious bourgeois youth imagined. That bourgeois resistance simultaneously created a desirable working class that contained everything that it wanted, as opposed to its despised parents. This working class was not respectable. It, like the new communes, had dirty kitchens, away from bourgeois housework, a far cry from the incessant cleaning, in case the Queen might call, like the respectable and tidy houses that I knew. No, if that working class did not live up to the romantic expectations it would have to be cast aside in the Left's dreams to find a truly revolutionary constituency, one in which it could be imagined that there were no anti-revolutionary deviants: blacks and women were the next on the fantasy list. And again I am suggesting that what was being created here too was an impossible object, one that like the white working class could never live up to all the expectations and fantasies placed upon it. And the respectable white working class got dropped while the new theorists of mass consumption went shopping.

Postmodernity and the Popular

During this time, psychological studies of the mass media tended to be concentrated in two paradigms: so-called 'effects' and 'uses and gratifications' research. The theoretical development of both may be seen in relation to the historical and theoretical trajectory of which I have spoken. This is particularly true of postwar American research and later British work. While the idea of a hypodermic injection of media into the person was abandoned as too simplistic, nevertheless researchers' main concerns, in one way or another, depended upon the early psychoanalytic work, even if transformed out of all recognition by empirical social psychology. How the media gratified the mass, the effects on the mass, its uses in their lives, how it related to psychological needs, all played upon this underlying fear of the inherent dangers of mass communication, linked to the already 'dangerous classes'.

While the Frankfurt School was understanding the mass as caught inside mass consumption in a pessimism that prefigured Baudrillard, Screen theory looked to Lacan. This theory had the masses even more tightly caught than the social psychologists, who had left a certain room for voluntarism. Here, the subjectivity of the masses was formed, right down to the unconscious, in the media (an unconscious not gratified by easy pleasures, but actually formed in the signifiers that make up ideological signs). In Screen theory the grip appeared so tight that there appeared to be little escape, except to move beyond the imaginary fulfilment of an impossible desire to the symbolic order. And it was this which was later resisted in some sociological work, and which led to a rejection of psychological and psychoanalytic paradigms in cultural studies. At the time, certain theorists of subculture and the popular, especially using Gramsci, were apparently defending the working class. I say 'apparently' because work which proceeded from Resistance through Rituals in the 1970s' CCCS understood subculture as arising out of alienation and being a mark of resistance and therefore of proto-revolutionary activity. It has been well documented that such work was mostly about young men and that it presented only certain groups as working class. There was no place here for the respectable or older or female working class.

Later, Fiske (1986) argued that popular culture and especially television was not a medium which created the identities of the working class, because it as audience was able to raid it for progressive meanings and even to make resistant readings. There are some important insights in this work, which I do not have the time nor the space to go into here. However, I wonder if there is not a defensive optimism in the way in which these authors see a working class that can make 'progressive' readings, that has not wholly been taken in.

In following Fiske and others down this road, there has been a general opposition to the over-determinist and pessimist psychoanalytic readings in which total identity is produced in the media.

Judith Williamson (1986a) argued that her media studies class managed to deconstruct an advert at five paces, but insisted that they liked the fantasies presented. They resisted her attempt to take away their pleasure. She later added about Fiske, that it is all very well to defend working-class raiding and progressive moments taken out of more reactionary narratives but this is insufficient as a theory of popular culture. In a sense that could be one view of what I took out of *Gigi* and *My Fair Lady*. But I think that would be wrong. Elsewhere, Williamson (1986b) asserts that redemptive readings of what the masses make with the popular are a problem when they have access to only one code. This attempt to suggest that audiences make active meanings in their consumption and are neither passive consumers nor have their identities totally determined by the text invokes an American discourse of empowerment, of voicing and authentic creation. But I think that it is not only wrong but patronizing. It is a defence (again) of the working class as equal but different. Look folks, they are not taken in and they are actually bright enough to make their own meanings! But neither they nor the readings are equal but different. It makes working-class readings seem like the consumption of pick-and-mix sweets in a postmodern shopping mall. But while I think that it is correct to assert that people make what they can of what is available, we seem to move from determinism to voluntarism with no idea how to produce an understanding of subjectivity which is not at either end of these poles. Watching *Gigi* and *My Fair Lady* certainly helped fuel my dreams, but these were dreams that were already being produced in the complex relations set up in the practices of upward mobility, of family, class and sexuality, into which I was inscribed. They were also centrally about oppression, exploitation, poverty, something which appears on neither the determinist or voluntarist agendas.

If I feel patronized by all the 'equal but different' arguments it is because I do not think that the difference is equal at all. A reading of oppression as pathology leads to particular practices through which that pathological subject is to be formed only to be corrected. Of course in that process we make what we can of what we can find, but that does not mean that there is not a complex psychodynamic at work, nor that the only discussion to be had is about a push-me, pull-you, will they, won't they reactionary/progressive seesaw. I want to change the agenda.

In none of the above analyses can I find any reference to how oppressed peoples are formed and live under oppression. I cannot find it precisely because the agenda has been set elsewhere. If the masses have been the central pivot of analysis the aim has been to account for their place in the making of revolution, democracy, totalitarianism. So busy have some of the intellectuals been in creating the stories of the working class to fit their fears and their desires that they do not seem to have been at all interested in addressing questions about the constitution and survival of oppressed peoples. Indeed, by the 1980s, some cultural theorists in the endless missionary position had come out from socialist puritanism and discovered that if the working class (which no longer existed anyway) liked to go shopping then it was OK to admit you liked it too. So writers in the magazine *Marxism Today* variously waxed lyrical about shopping in Camden Sainsbury's and went ecstatic over the food court at Euston Station. Comments in the same magazine suggested that if young blacks liked to buy expensive suits then this was a signal that it was OK for the Left middle classes to admit to liking this too, all the time failing to see that the two were not the same thing.

Meanwhile, Baudrillard had caught a sharp dose of Frankfurt School pessimism. Repeating and extending ideas from the 1950s, he envisaged a scenario in which media simulation had created an atomized and silent mass, a mass reduced to a physical entity. The mass here is indeed off the streets and in its homes, watching television or playing video games, but the threat of the eruption of violence is still blamed upon them – as in the Bulger case, for example. Now, I think that some of Baudrillard's pronouncements about the masses, while they certainly build upon fantasies of which I have already spoken, are not as wacky as they have been presented. And he does try to document the subjectification of a mass which no longer is understood as having an authentic voice, since it is no longer the true revolutionary class. And he does recognize that the class is both endlessly defined and resisting definition, endlessly asked to be autonomous while endlessly asked to conform. And he refused to read them using those grand metanarratives. He believes that the modernist democratic project of calculation, education, policing, definition of the masses is finished, because the masses refuse it: an optimism about regulation if ever there was one.

Subjectivity and Oppression

The project which I want to signal here is critical of those grand metanarratives that have endlessly described and defined away the respectable white working class. While it might be said that the atomized and individualized poor now have no place to turn except the imaginary communities created on the screens in their living rooms, the communities and organizations which were their strength having been crushed, I wonder if that too does not hark back to a romantic reading which was certainly not true in my own childhood. No, I want to try to construct a different story about what media fantasies mean in the lives of oppressed peoples. Here I want to draw on work on oppression and psychodynamics which has helped me and then to go on to look briefly at one example. I do not think that we can explore the constitution of this subjectivity without examining how poverty, pain, oppression, exploitation are made to signify. The popular as escape, indeed: the longing, the hope.

I am trying to construct a way of analysing the production of subjects in practices as a way of getting beyond the dualism of the media effects work and the over-simplification of the text-based work. My aim, then, is to account for subjectivity and the place of the popular in making oppressed subjects now, not audience research *per se*. I cannot go into all the details of how I am approaching the idea of subjectivity in practices, but just let me suggest a few pointers. The practices in which subjects are produced are both material and discursive, but the relation is not one of representation, but signification. Indeed, if fictions can function in truth then fictions themselves can have real effects. Subjects are created in multiple positionings in material and discursive practices, in specific historical conditions in which certain apparatuses of social regulation become techniques of self-production. These are imbued with fantasy. We cannot therefore separate something called 'working-class experiences' from the fictions and fantasies in which I hope I have demonstrated that life is produced and read. What is the relation between those fictions and fantasies and the psychic life of the oppressed? What gaps and silences are there in the fictional discourses, like the fact that they may speak of pathology, of difference, of poverty even, but rarely oppression? How then is oppression lived and is it spoken? If so, how? And how is the absent material a relation in this subjective constitution?

I made a documentary called 'Didn't She Do Well' (Metro Pictures 1991), about a group of working-class women all of whom have gone through higher education at some time in their lives. In the Women's Therapy Centre in London, these women talk about their lives. The toll of pain, suffering, survival and courage is almost overwhelming. But they begin to speak about the specific historical constitution that I have referred to. I found little help in understanding this discourse from a traditional psychoanalysis that cannot handle materiality, nor from a Lacanian reading. Oppression simply does not enter discussions about the psychopathology of working-class women, who appear on the scene not as upwardly mobile girls, but as pathological mothers.

What I am talking about here are patterns of defences produced in family practices which are about avoiding anxiety and living in a very dangerous world. Work on the holocaust and torture in Latin America (see, for example, Puget 1988) has made if perfectly clear that certain defences may be necessary to survive danger and that one cannot assess those defences on a scale of normal to pathological. But it is possible to examine the place of those defences in constituting the very practices in which subjectivity is produced, just as I suggested that there was something to be defended against in the fantasy of upward mobility, notably the oppressed, poor animal working class. I want to suggest that such defences are part and parcel of the constitution of the lives of the oppressed and that we can look at the popular in this postmodern order as part of that defensive organization, as something that makes life possible, bearable, hopeful, but cannot be understood as either good or bad, without locating its place in the conditions and survival of oppression.

Gail Pheterson (1993) points out that the defensive structure incorporates all subjects embodied in relations of domination, complex as they are. Class domination, then, does not just touch the working class, as I have tried to show, but is central to the fantasy structures and defences of the bourgeoisie.

Witnessing humiliation and exploitation acts differently for those who have a cleaner than for a women who works as one. Middle-class people often only see the working class in relations of service or as frightening others in areas of town that they do not want to enter. Their defences are cross-cut by the way in which the Other is made to signify and the fictions in which they are inscribed. When Ronald Fraser (1984) let a beggar into the manor house in which he lived as a child, he learned painfully that his parents were not pleased, that there are some people who are not to be welcomed into one's home. When the four-year-old Sarah (Walkerdine and Lucey 1989) looks out and asks her mother why the man cleaning their windows has to be paid for his work, she understands a different relation to work and service and money than the young working-class girl who is told that she cannot have new slippers because money is scarce, that her father earns the money at a factory he cannot leave until he is allowed to do so and, again, from the young child who watches her mother being humiliated in a Social Security office. Psychodynamic forces: wishes, drives, emotions, defences are produced in conflicting relations, in a context in which materiality, domination and oppression are central, not peripheral. But accounts of psychodynamics rarely include these issues and as we have seen, they have disappeared entirely from the post-Althusserian debates. So the working class, the gradually disappearing class, locked inside ideologies in infantile wish fulfilment because of a refusal to engage with the psychodynamics of oppression. In addition, as Pheterson argues, there has been a reluctance, even a refusal, to call into question 'normal' or 'normative' relations of domination, the 'normal' everyday designations of Otherness, the defences. The consequences of this are enormous and make all accounts very one-sided. Indeed, she goes further and argues that perpetrators of abuse, for example racism, are understood sociologically; and their victims psychologically, as in need of therapy. This is overwhelmingly the case with the distress witnessed in the upwardly mobile working-class women in my film. I made the film precisely because I wanted to contest the view that this pain is an individual pathology that needs to be corrected, the result of inadequacy or inadequate families. Rather I wanted to make public the psychic effects of living in and under oppression. Oppressed groups, such as the working class have to survive, but survive in a way which means that they must come to recognize themselves as lacking, deficient, deviant; as being where they are because that is who they are, that is how they are made – an insidious self-regulation – while individual effort is allowed those clever enough to plan an escape, an escape only to be pathologized by those others who romanticize the oppression in the first place.

As Pheterson (1993: 110) remarks, 'genocidal persecution is not required to elicit psychic defence; daily mundane humiliation will do'. What, then, are the consequences of living that daily humilation and for children to grow up watching their parents face it? How do they live watching parents do without, face hardship, be hurt or killed at work, never stop working, become drudges, old before their time and so forth. As one doctor put it to Christine's father, 'I'm sorry Ernest, there's nothing I can do for you, you're worn out.' Or Diane Reay's mother, with eight children, who she never remembers seeing sitting down. Why are not these the questions that are being asked? Bergmann and Jucovy (1982) report that responses to natural disasters have less lasting psychic effect than continuous systematic and organized assault on a people singled out as less than human. It becomes clear that if we look at the effectivity of the media in the constitution of subjectivity in this way, what is at stake changes dramatically. For indeed, the five women in the film tell us clearly and courageously what that continuous systematic and organized assault is like, what is means to witness routine humilation in one's parents and to long to leave, to not be like them, but to feel the terrible guilt of leaving, of survival. A survival which defensively may have to be many hundreds of miles away in another place, which cannot bear to see the pain, the humilation that has been escaped and to feel the shame both of having been like that and also of getting out when others are still there, and have no obvious means of escape. That is what I want to talk about and it makes 'equal but different' and the trite stories of finding progressive elements in the mass media trivially offensive.

The film shows the five women's stories and identifications: the defences become clear in the film, clear that they are means of survival. Fiona McLeod tells about her fears that she might not survive all the pain she has gone through even though she is now a well-paid social worker and lives 500 miles from her family on an Edinburgh housing estate.[5]

Diane Reay tells us of the time she went to a union dance when she first went to university. I have chosen it because the dance is so redolent of all those balls, the balls in the films in which one had to learn to pass as a lady. Diane is afraid that her masquerade has not worked well enough.[6] Diane took the protective step of marrying the middle-class man who first befriended her, saving her from the men who wanted to constitute her as Other, as oversexed and easy. This could be interpreted as a defence against something unbearable, not an ideological failing, an over-femininity of a working-class woman who cannot see beyond patriarchy, as has often been suggested.

That Diane wants to be able to be sexual, but is to have that sexuality read as animal, dirty and deviant is likely to produce complex conflicts and defences. I am trying to begin to tell a story, one which I cannot elaborate here, about the practices of survival in which such defences are not only produced but are necessary. Necessary, but not without contradictions. Seen in this light, wishes for a glamorous upward mobility – a new happy bourgeois family as presented in the media portrayals – take on a different light. They tell us about what is being guarded against and how practices are stories told to make that survival, escape, hopeful, bearable. These practices must in fact be passed into family practices themselves, and down generations, as complex cultural resources, ways of being and belonging.

How does all this relate to working-class families watching television, families who are the object of all that regulation? Eliana, aged six, is the middle of three sisters. Her father is Maltese, her mother from Yorkshire. The sisters decide to put on the video of the musical *Annie* that Daddy has bought for them. They play in front of it, their mother in the kitchen, their father out. I want to share with you one tiny little bit of a much longer analysis. *Annie* presents us with a dispossessed and unworking proletariat. Annie is an orphan. She is adopted by the rich and self-made armaments manufacturer, Daddy Warbucks. The only way out for the little orphan is to charm her way into the rich family. Here the working-class family and community is not deficient, it is non-existent. There is only one solution: escape. This version of going to the ball gives not a prince but a family, happiness, servants, plenty; oppression is taken away, defended against. Pain is removed. This magical solution could be especially appealing to Eliana and her sisters. They make reference to only one part of the film and they address their remarks to me, sitting recording in the living room. The remarks are about a sequence in the film in which Miss Hannigan, the drunken woman in charge of the orphanage is swaying in front of the camera, with a bottle in her hand, apparently drunk.[7] Eliana tells me that Miss Hannigan is only acting: 'She's supposed to be drunk, but she ain't . . . cos it's water.'

Two minutes later the little sister Karen emerges from the kitchen to tell me 'Mummy's drunk', which prompts the mother to deny it to me. So in the film there is a woman who looks drunk but is in fact acting, but at home there is a mother who does not look drunk but is proclaimed to be, all for my benefit.

Eliana's mother is systematically being beaten by her husband, a husband who, according to her, is having a relationship with another woman, a woman he takes the children to visit. Eliana is apparently coping, but is displaying distressing symptoms at school, from docility to the point of apparent stupidity to fits of hidden rage where she breaks the heads off dolls.

I want to argue, to cut a long analysis short, that *Annie* provides her with a narrative framework into which she can envisage an escape from the daily misery which she watches her mother endure. The drunken Miss Hannigan is the bad working-class mother, in fact the nearest to a mother that the orphans get. She is contrasted with the beautiful secretary to Daddy Warbucks, Grace, and to Daddy Warbucks himself, who is so charmed by Annie that his hard surface softens to reveal a soft father. So, the happy family can be found by dint of the efforts of the resourceful orphan. Daddy is the one with the money, the home, the happiness, to be contrasted with the drunken mummy. In Eliana's life I am presented with a drunken mummy who is responsible for her own oppression and who comes off badly when compared with the escape offered by Daddy and the other woman. Indeed, there is a metonymic relation, since Eliana's daddy bought the video of *Annie*. He is the one who offers the fantasy of escape. But *Annie* offers no narrative of the oppression suffered by the mother, nor of her possible escape. Neither is there any model for the father's cruelty except that which can be tamed by an alluring little girl. But the mother does use the film to provide the girls with her account of what is happening. She addresses her remarks to me in front of them. She talks of the difficulties of her life, her suffering and why she gets angry with the eldest sister's siding with her father. The conversation and the film therefore act as a vehicle through which she can refute the *Annie* version of events. The video offers dreams of escape, but its presence cannot be judged outside some understanding of the conditions under which the family lives and the practices that it has produced to cope with these. Fantasy and escape then have to be understood as part of a whole ensemble of defences against the pain of that routine oppression and humiliation of which I spoke earlier.

Subject to Change . . .

So how is it possible to produce a new kind of psychological work on the masses and the popular? The issues which fuelled the debates of modernity have not disappeared or dissipated, now that the fragmented poor watch the television behind the net curtains on the fifteenth floor of a crumbling tower block, while these 'new poor' are being turned into a non-working class. Indeed, in some ways, the fears grow more desperate, the concerns as potent. Is it possible to work in another way on the relation of the subject to the popular? I have turned to work on myself, precisely because I have been remade as a professor out of the feared mass. Is the process of my civilization then, the move to bourgeois culture, also one which allows me to work as both insider and outsider? Is there a new kind of knowledge that can be constituted in this way?

Surely we must be able to tell some new stories. Sometimes the cultural theorists miss the wood for the trees, because they are so busy charting resistance or raiding that they seem to miss the way that routine humiliation, the present forms of management, constitute the subjectivity, defences and coping practices of most of the population. So busy looking at a progressive/reactionary dichotomy and working with, not taking apart, this fiction which functions in truth, they seem not to see the ways in which subjects cope and produce defences against extreme conditions that frankly sometimes are not very nice. How some cultural theorists long for things that never seem to enter the intellectual imagination because they seem not only unable to know how to look but because they are so busy talking about working-class fantasies they never analyse their own. Yes, intellectual work and personal histories do come together. And I do not think it is simply about objectivity or bias, but about how certain stories get told and how they too can fulfil fantasies, be defences. I want to address the questions which seem to be left out of the constant descriptions of the majority of the population. Such descriptions help to build a fortress simulacrum to keep them out because the romantic fantasies have failed, to construct only a defence against its opposite – the nightmare. Puget's (1992) work on psychoanalysis in Argentina during the dictatorship documents that defence well. The feeling that it will always happen to somebody else defends against the terror that it will indeed happen to oneself.

So I want a happy ending, you know. Like those happy-ever-after stories of my childhood or my mother's soothing 'it'll be all right chicken'. But, neither that nor Gramsci's optimistic will seem appropriate. We need to look in a new way at our daily lives and to recognize that the end of grand metanarratives of 'the working class' is not the end of oppression. Indeed, quite the reverse.

But the professor has an injunction to speak, to profess, tell certain kinds of stories with an authority vested in her position. The little girl was so quiet, trying so hard to say the right thing, to be loved. To the schoolgirl, the goody-goody, the teacher, the silent student. But there was always a rage underneath all that goodness, the nurturant loving of the children in the progressive classroom, always the deep fear of being thrown out for her ideas, for opening her mouth to spit out all that anger, the anger that she found lurking even beneath the engaging feminine smile of her childhood.[8] The dilemma of the angry powerful woman is enacted at both conscious and unconscious levels, but it is also lived historically and socially.[9]

It has long been women who have had an injunction to speak about the personal, to tell their secrets, just as it has always been those of the working class who have been asked to tell of their lives, to explain their pathology. The fact that it takes two classes to tango appears to have escaped the notice of those who constantly ask us to tell it like it is. It does not seem surprising, then, that the injunction to speak about it has become one of the modes of regulation of the modern age: to bare all, to allow the natural to emerge, only to be better regulated. In our understanding of the regulation of the postmodern order, we need to examine the place of that voicing and where it appears, on television, films, the radio, the popular, who is being made to speak what, to and for whom? No, we have to create some other stories, which face the present and confront it, write new songs and begin to sing them.[10]

Notes

1 This paper was given as an inaugural lecture and included a mixed-media presentation. It has not been possible to preserve the entire flavour of the visuals and sound in the text. I note where visuals were shown and what they were. A video tape of the lecture including the visual material is available from the author.

2 The lecture began with the final moments of the film *El Cid*, starring Charlton Heston and Sophia Loren, in which the dead El Cid, strapped to his horse leads his troops in the final victory against the Moors. His wife and young daughters look on from the ramparts. This was accompanied by stirring music and the words 'THE END'. The clip was shown as the lights dimmed and the opening words of the lecture were spoken as the clip faded.

3 A clip from *Gigi* at this point shows a sequence towards the end of the film in which Gaston, the wealthy playboy, asks Gigi's grandmother for Gigi's hand in marriage. This is followed by a still from a 1960s Gitane cigarette advertisement showing a young man, earring in one ear, smoking a Gitane.

4 At this point in the lecture I showed a clip from *My Fair Lady*, with Audrey Hepburn and Rex Harrison. The clips shows Hepburn and Eliza being inaugurated into the regime by which Professor Higgins is to change her speech patterns to make her pass for a lady. Higgins tells Eliza that she is very dirty and the whole scene is quite violent.

5 Fiona McLeod talks in the clip about her feelings about her father, who died in a fire in their flat. She felt that he wanted to be a giant but feared that in reality he was a dwarf. She sees herself as like him now and finds it hard to believe in herself. Like him, she fears that she might not survive.

6 Diane tells the group that she went to a union dance and was pursued by a man who said that he thought he'd seen her in Woolworths. She interprets this as meaning that he thought that she was a girl from town, who had just happened to get into the dance. She did not want to be seen as this because the male students treated such women badly, seeing them as having 'easier virtue'. She concluded that her masquerade was not working well enough and that she felt that she had to try harder.

7 I showed the clip of this on video at this point.

8 This has been documented in my installation, *Behind the Painted Smile* and discussed in the piece of the same name in *Schoolgirl Fictions* Walkerdine (1991), where my period as a primary school teacher is also written about.

9 The tightrope walked by many women in the academy, who have been patronized and envied, rejected and passed over, made to work harder and for less reward than their male colleagues, continues to be a testimony both to the courage of women and to their continued oppression.

10 The lecture ended with the song 'Coming' from Sally Potter's film *Orlando*. On the screen were end credits, thanking the Department of Media and Communications for support and technical assistance with the lecture, especially Colin Aggett, June Melody, Joanne Donovan and Helen Pendlebury.

The lecture was dedicated to the memory of Jo Spence, 1926–1992.

References

Bergmann, M.S. and Jucovy, M.E. (eds.), 1982: *Generations of the Holocaust*. New York: Basic Books.

Bianchini, F., 1987: GLC R.I.P. Cultural Policies in London, 1981–1986. *New Formations*, pp. 103–17.

Cohen, P., 1992: 'Playgrounds of prejudice' Occasional papers, University of East London.

Donald, J., 1991: 'On the Threshold: Psychoanalysis and Cultural Studies', in J. Donald (ed.) *Psychoanalysis and Cultural Theory: Thresholds*. London: Macmillan.

Fiske, J., 1986: *Understanding popular culture*. London: Routledge.

Fraser, R., 1984: *In search of a past*, Verso. London.

Freud, S., 1927: *The Future of an Illusion*, Standard Edition of the Complete Psychological Works of Sigmund Freud, Volume XXI. Hogarth Press, London.

Henriques, H., Holloway, W., Urwin, C., Venn, C. and Walkerdine, V., 1984: *Changing the Subject: psychology, social regulation and subjectivity*, Methuen, London.

Mitchell, J., 1984: *Psychoanalysis and Feminism*. Harmondsworth: Penguin.

Morley, D., 1993: *Television audiences and Cultural Studies*, Routledge, London.

Mulvey, L., 1992: 'Visual and Other Pleasures', in *Screen* (ed.) *The Sexual Subject: A* Screen *Reader in Sexuality*. London: Routledge.

PHETERSON, G., 1993: Historical and material determinants of psychodynamic development in J. Adleman and G. Enguidanos (eds.) *Racism in the lives of women*, Haworth Press, New York.

PUGET, J., 1992: Social violence and psychoanalysis: the unthinkable and the unthought, *Free Associations 13*, pp. 84–140.

SAID, E., 1985: *Orientalism*. New York: Plenum Press.

TURKLE, S., 1992: '*Psychoanalysis and the Public Sphere*', keynote address to conference. University of East London.

WALKERDINE, V., 1985: 'Dreams from an ordinary childhood', in L. Heron (ed.) *Truth, dare or promise: girls growing up in the 50s*, Virago, London.

WALKERDINE, V., 1988: *The mastery of reason*, Routledge, London.

WALKERDINE, V., 1989: *Counting Girls Out*, Virago, London.

WALKERDINE, V., 1991: *Schoolgirl Fictions*, Verso, London.

WALKERDINE, V., 1996: *Daddy's Girl: Young girls and popular culture*, Macmillan, London.

WALKERDINE, V. and LUCEY, H., 1989: *Democracy in the kitchen: regulating mothers and socialising daughters*, Virago, London.

WILLIAMSON, J., 1986a: *Consuming Passions*. London: Marion Boyars.

WILLIAMSON, J., 1986b: 'The Problems of Being Popular', *New Socialist*, September.

WRIGHT-MILLS, C., 1956: *The Sociological Imagination*. London: Routledge & Kegan Paul.

6

Rethinking Mass Communications

James Curran

Introduction

At one level, this chapter provides a textbook, guided tour of media sociology over a forty-year period.[1] It describes the liberal and radical traditions, and indicates in summary form how they have evolved over time.[2]

At another level, it contributes to the debate in the field. At the heart of much media sociology are two contrasting functionalist perspectives. One sees the media as operating on behalf of the power structure of society, the other as serving the public. These different approaches are linked to alternative conceptions of media power, with one side holding that the media dominate the audience, and the other side arguing that the audience dominates the media. In this essay, we shall explore a third position situated between these polarities, while seeking also to avoid the rigidities of functionalist analysis.

Liberal Reflection Theories

Exponents of the liberal-pluralist tradition tend to see the media as a reflection of society. But what precisely is being reflected is hotly contested. One view still popular among journalists is to see the media as a mirror of reality. It is a view eloquently expressed in Neil Simon's *The Odd Couple* by the lifting of an eyebrow:

> *Cecily*: What field of endeavour are you engaged in?
> *Felix*: I write the news for CBS.
> *Cecily*: Oh. Fascinating.
> *Gwendolyn*: Where do you get your ideas from?
> *Felix*: (*He looks at her as though she is a Martian*): From the news.
> *Gwendolyn*: Oh yes, of course. Silly me . . .
>
> (cit. Golding 1981: 64)

For Felix, and other like-minded journalists, the media are merely messengers: the message is reality. Good journalists have a 'nose' for news, an instinct partly innate and partly trained for distinguishing what is important from what is unimportant. This ensures allegedly that the news is a record of everything that is fit to be published. 'True professionals' also check the accuracy of what is reported and are painstakingly neutral in the way in which they balance contending opinion. They have standards and procedures that are a guarantee of good faith in reporting the world 'as it is'.

This celebration of the craft of journalism is not entirely fanciful. The conventions of professionalism do constrain the way in which personal biases and subjective experiences shape news output. This is why a view that news reporting is *merely* the expression of the personal views and backgrounds of journalists[3] – whether they be conceived as being biased as a consequence of being mainly left-wing or right-wing, men or middle class – is partly misleading. People with different views and experiences can in fact produce surprisingly similar news reports, providing they work within the same news conventions (Epstein 1973, 1975).

This said, the canons of professionalism are not sufficient to sustain the claim that the media reflect objective reality. The news we receive, as numerous critics have pointed out, is the product of organizational processes and human interaction. It is shaped by the methods used by journalists in gathering the news, the sources they draw on, and the organizational requirements, resources and policies of the institutions they work for (Fishman 1980; Sigal 1987; Tiffen 1989). To take but one example, the need of news organizations to secure regular, predictable and usable copy results in some journalists being assigned to particular 'beats' – such as the town hall, law courts or legislatures. This pre-cues the news, encouraging activity in these areas to be reported more fully (Tuchman 1978a; Hess 1984). It also locks journalists into a complex pattern of interaction with key sources in which information is traded for publicity (Gandy 1982; Ericson et al. 1989). And it encourages group conformity in which journalists on the same beat form collective news judgements (Tunstall 1971). In short, a prior decision about the allocation of personnel within a news organization can influence what news is reported, and how it is reported.

Some liberal critics also point out that information is selected and presented as news within socially constructed frameworks of meaning (Hallin and Mancini 1984; Schudson 1991). The news is signified through the 'symbolic system' of society. It draws upon assumptions and premises, images and chains of association, that are embedded in cultural tradition. The news is also structured by the formats and genre conventions of news reporting, which vary in different societies and evolve over time (Schudson 1982, 1994). News in this view is thus the product of the culture of society, and of the industry, in which it is processed.

This kind of cautious reasoning has prompted some people to see the output of the media not as a reflection of raw, unmediated reality but rather as a social index of attitudes and feelings. As Virginia Woolf elegantly put it, 'newspapers are thin sheets of gelatine pressed nightly on the brain and heart of the world' (Woolf 1965: 93). An eloquent presentation of this view is provided by Kjell Nowak (1984) who shows that there was a marked decrease in prestige appeals and overt class coding in advertisements in the Swedish press between the mid-1960s and mid-1970s. This was accompanied by a decline in the formal pronoun of address, and an increase in positive invocations of equality in press editorials. All these changes in the press, carefully quantified, were a reflection, he argues, of the rise of egalitarianism in Swedish society, which experienced a shift towards a more equal distribution of incomes during approximately the same period.

A somewhat similar argument, though from a different perspective, is advanced by Leo Lowenthal (1961), who showed that there was a shift of attention from business leaders to sports and entertainment stars in selected American publications in the first half of the twentieth century. This reflected, in his view, a shift in the 'dream world' of American society from the 'idols of consumption' to the 'idols of production'. Likewise, analysts of American television regularly attribute changes in programme content to wider changes in society. For example, the rise of socially relevant TV drama in the early 1970s is often explained in terms of the growth of social commitment during this period (D'Acci 1994; Gitlin 1994).

These accounts usually see the media as responding to generalized changes in society, conceived as a single social entity. This approach is implicitly problematized by other accounts which portray the media as a variegated system relating to different groups in society. For example, some programmes, films, magazines and books are directed primarily towards women, and relate specifically to their experiences and concerns as distinct from those of men. However, some women's media address different subgroups within the general female population, ranging from traditionalist magazines celebrating conventional definitions of femininity to campaigning feminist publications (Ferguson 1983; Winship 1987). Some of these media also relate to different (and sometimes contradictory) identities and structures of feeling within the same individual (Winship 1987; Ang and Hermes 1991). The media are thus portrayed as reflecting not a common culture and unified society but a plurality of social groups and the hybridity of individual personalities.

A further complication is introduced by those analysts who distinguish between values and normative attitudes, or between consensus and contended opinion (Alexander 1981; Blumler and Gurevitch 1986). Here, the argument is that the media both express the values and beliefs that most people in society hold in common, and also give voice to those differences of opinion and orientation that characterize a pluralist democracy. One way in which the media may reflect change, it is argued, is to register a shift in the boundaries between these two things over time (Hallin 1994).

Independent Media

While there is disagreement about what aspect of society the media reflect, there is a broad agreement within the liberal tradition that the media have a high degree of autonomy in advanced liberal democracies. This is the cornerstone, almost the sacred oath of allegiance, of the liberal approach. In its most thoroughbred version, in Parsonian sociology, the media in the United States are portrayed as independent both of the state, and also of social 'subsystems' comprised by political, economic or solidary groups. This confers on the media the essential freedom it needs to respond to the totality of society. As the

Parsonian sociologist, Jeffery Alexander (1981: 35) claims of the American media, 'its peculiar social position [as an independent institution] means that it "reflects" the conditions around it'.

However, changes in the ownership and structure of the media pose a problem for analysts in this tradition. Ownership of the media has become more concentrated, increasingly on a global not merely a national scale. In some sectors (notably the press) it has become more monopolistic; and, above all, control of the commercial media has passed into the hands of big business corporations. The argument that the media are independent institutions, controlled ultimately by the public, would seem to fly in the face of trends indicating the opposite: namely, that the media are controlled by corporate businesses in market conditions which allow them to manage public demand.

One part of the refutation of this argument advanced by liberal academics is that staff, with a commitment to professional goals, have achieved a high degree of autonomy within media organizations. This is viewed as the culmination of a historical process in which media staff acquired a stronger sense of their own worth, gained increasing personal decision-making power as a consequence of the growing division of labour and specialization within media organizations, and developed a commitment to a professional set of values that embodied a public interest culture. The building-up of this professional power has ensured that the media continue to be independent even if most commercial media have come to be owned by big business (Gans 1980; Alexander 1981; Hetherington 1985).

The second part of the liberal refutation is that media controllers have changed. The dispersal of shareholdings in large media conglomerates and the increase in the scale of their operation have weakened and diluted 'proprietorial' control. More power has been ceded to professional managers concerned with market performance rather than the pursuit of ideological goals. In contrast to previous epochs characterized by a party-controlled press, or media moguls in the mould of Hearst who sought to exercise personal and unaccountable power, the new generation of media controllers are more inclined to be market-oriented pragmatists (Emery 1972; Hyer et al. 1975; Whale 1977; Koss 1984).

Certain inferences are derived from this conception of a market-oriented but professionally staffed media system. One is that media staff are integrated into the consensus of society, and articulate unconsciously its collective aims and values, albeit sometimes in an inflected form (Gans 1980). Another claim is that good journalists develop an instinctive rapport with their particular audiences by identifying with them and subjectively experiencing life from their viewpoint (King 1967; Smith 1975). A third argument is that the professional orientations of journalists ensure, or should ensure, that all important points of view are represented in the media (O'Neill 1990). All three contentions offer an explanation of how the media reflect the different elements of society.

However, the argument most often proposed in liberal accounts is that competition within a market system compels the media to respond to the wants, needs and views of the public. The ratings antennae of commercial television are on constant alert to pick up the first perceptible tremor of a change in public preference. Audience figures are anxiously scanned because they are the TV equivalent of gold. Much of the effort, energy and creativity of television corporations and other commercial enterprises goes into pleasing the audience in a fiercely competitive environment. Media corporations have developed strategies for doing this: researching and pre-testing products; building creative teams; repeating or recombining formulae that have been successful in the past; scanning the boundaries of the market for new talent and trends; creating stars, promoting heavily and over-producing as a way of managing demand; integrating businesses horizontally (i.e. across media) or vertically (from production to sales outlets) in order to gain economies of consolidation and increased market control; and developing ways of selling the same or spin-off product in different media packages (Hirsch 1972; Frith 1987; Turow 1991; Cantor and Cantor 1992; Gitlin 1994). Yet, despite their best efforts, goes the argument, media corporations even in market-dominant positions are constantly wrongfooted by rivals, back losers, get it wrong (Collins 1990). The vagaries of the market keep media controllers on their toes, and firmly under the sovereignty of the consumer.

This necessarily simplified and condensed summary edits out a number of important debates within the liberal tradition, which need to be mentioned briefly. One area of discussion is concerned with the degree to which the public interest claims of media professionalism are justified. Some are sceptical, echoing Bernard Shaw's (1979: 496) complaint that 'all professions are conspiracies against the laity' (Tuchman 1972; Schudson 1978). Others are relatively uncritical, arguing that professionalism should be reinforced through professional leadership and the benign offices of university-based, media education (Peterson 1956; Stepp 1990).

Another line of criticism within the liberal tradition challenges the notion that journalists, and media staff more generally, are ventriloquists of their audience's thoughts. Some participant observation studies or surveys portray media workers as unrepresentative, out of touch or even downright hostile towards their publics (Tunstall 1971; Elliott 1977; Gans 1980). Media staff are also featured as belonging to a self-enclosed world in which colleagues and friends – or, in the case of independent Hollywood TV producers, network executives – become surrogates for the real audience (Cantor 1971; Burns 1977; Gans 1980). But while all these studies cast doubt on the assumption that media staff have a natural rapport with their audience, they are balanced in a sense by portrayals of media managers as the people who provide the driving force behind the media's commitment to pleasing the public (D'Acci 1994; Gitlin 1994).

A third line of criticism attacks the over-commercialization of the media – in particular, its increasing blurring of the distinction between news and entertainment, and its over-reliance on tired formulae in TV fiction (Gitlin 1994; McManus 1994). This is responded to by others in the liberal tradition in three ways. One reaction rejects such complaints out of hand, arguing that they merely reflect elitist disdain for the values and preferences of the general public. Another similar response argues that the market-based drive to please audiences ensures that the media are answerable to the public rather than to the state and self-appointed, cultural vigilantes (Murdoch 1989). A third response sees the professional commitments of media staff as a restraint on market-induced excess (Hallin 1994).

The study of media processes is an area where radical and liberal traditions overlap, and where some of the most interesting analysts have one foot inside and one foot outside the liberal tradition. There are critical debates about the implications of professionalization, the representative character of journalists, and the ethics and performance of the media. But this should not obscure the central assumption of the liberal tradition that the mass media in free societies are independent institutions, regulated by the market and the professional concerns of communicators, that serve ultimately the public.

Limited Media Influence

Whereas the classical radical tradition sees the media as agencies of mystification that 'bend reality' and engender false consciousness, the liberal tradition assumes a much greater degree of affinity between media, reality and the public. The media are assumed to reflect rather than to shape society.

Scepticism about the power of the media to 'determine' society was powerfully reinforced within the liberal tradition by effects research. From the 1930s onwards, liberal researchers demonstrated through survey and experimental research that media audiences have minds of their own.[4] How people respond to the media – not merely what they will accept but even, sometimes, what they understand or remember – is powerfully influenced by what they think already. This results in dissimilar groups of people responding to the same communication in different ways.

Underlying this 'obstinacy', argue liberal researchers, is the fact that audiences are not empty vessels waiting to be filled by the media. Audience members have prior values, opinions and cognitions formed by early socialization, membership of social networks and personal experience. Even in relation to issues reported by the media about which they know absolutely nothing, people still have simplifying maps of meaning – 'interpretive schema' – which enable them to assimilate information in a selective way.[5]

The autonomy of the audience was cited by liberal researchers to confound those who believe that the media are top-down channels of influence and control in a dominated society. The 'popular imagery' of *vertical* control, argued Katz and Lazarsfeld in a landmark study, is refuted by their evidence of '*horizontal* opinion leadership, that is, leadership which emerges on each rung of the socio-economic ladder, and all through the community' (Katz and Lazarsfeld 1955: 325, original emphasis). Networks of personal influence filtered, they concluded, the rays of media power. They also acted as a check on elite flows of influence since 'some individuals of high social status apparently wield little independent influence, and some of low status have considerable personal influence'. In short, the interaction between families, friends and work colleagues constituted, in their view, a self-regulating space in which people framed their own ideas and preferences in ways that were significantly independent.

These sceptical accounts which emphasized the autonomy of active audiences and the social mediation of communications gave rise to the view that the media are a subsidiary source of influence. 'Mass communications', concluded

Joseph Klapper in an influential survey, 'ordinarily do not serve as a necessary and sufficient cause of audience effects' (Klapper 1960: 8).

However, this minimal effects consensus was challenged within the liberal camp by a new generation of effects researchers from the early 1970s onwards. They argue that the world has changed in ways that make the media more influential. The rise of television, with its bipartisan tradition of reporting, has reduced selective avoidance of communications that challenge cherished ideas and beliefs (Blumler and Gurevitch 1982). The decline of mass political partisanship during the last three decades has made more people accessible to media influence (Miller 1991). Accelerated social change, it is also claimed more speculatively, has increased the number of people seeking guidance and orientation from the media in a world of flux and uncertainty (DeFleur and Ball-Rokeach 1989).

The other key theme of this reappraisal is that the media's influence is contingent on the characteristics of the audience and the wider context of reception. Studies suggest that certain sorts of people – such as those who are nonpartisan, with a low interest in politics, with no tacit theory of the topic under review or who are uncertain – can be more influenced by the media than others (Blumler and McQuail 1968; McLeod et al. 1974; Blumer and McLeod 1983; Iyengar and Kinder 1987; McCombs 1994). Media influence is also shown to increase if its 'message' resonates with personal experience, is supported by interpersonal influences or is consistent with social norms and behaviour (Rogers and Shoemaker 1971; Gerbner et al. 1986; Perloff 1993).

The effects research tradition is not without problems. It is generally confined to a short-term measurement of what is generally a long-term process of influence. While attempts have also been made to measure the cumulative influence of the media on the basis of longitudinal data, this merely confounds the problem central to effects research of distinguishing between media and non-media influences on audiences. But leaving aside problems of interpretation, what the 'new look' effects research actually suggests is that, generally, only minorities of people – and often only tiny minorities – are influenced by the media in a measurable way in terms of their attitudes and behaviour, after non-media influences have been taken into account. However, the media have a greater impact in changing cognitions (i.e. perceptions). They can have a pronounced short-term effect on what issues people think are important. (Iyengar and Kinder 1987; Rogers and Dearing 1988; McCombs 1994).[6] They can also affect how people make evaluations – for example, the issues on which the performance of political leaders are judged (Iyengar and Kinder 1987). More interestingly, the media can also affect some people's terms of reference in making sense of the news, influencing whether they attribute responsibility to the individual, society or the government (Iyengar 1992). However, audience research which argues that the media provide a symbolic environment that structures heavy TV viewers' understanding of the world (Buerkel-Rothfus and Mayes 1981; Morgan 1982; Gerbner et al. 1986, 1994) is more open to question, its conclusions being explicable in terms of other factors.[7]

The new wave of effects research thus revised upwards but did not dislodge the basic conclusions of pioneer audience research about the limited influence of the media.

Liberal Functionalism

If the mass media have so little effect, why study them? This was the central problem posed by effects research for the liberal tradition. The answer advanced by liberal functionalists was that the media may have small effects on the audience but they have big consequences for society – an argument which has been developed in a particularly interesting way during the last decade.

But before we consider liberal functionalist arguments, brief reference should be made to two other interesting lines of thought. There is a mainly historical tradition which argues that the mass media have changed society by modifying dimensions of time and place (Innis 1950; McLuhan 1964; Eisenstein 1978; Ferguson 1990). There is also a political studies tradition which argues that even if the media do not change the minds of most voters, they have changed the political process. Modern media have transformed the conduct of elections, influenced the selection of political leaders (who have now to be good on television), encouraged centralization within political parties, diminished the symbolic role of national legislative assemblies, and, more contentiously,[8] promoted the evocation of images and values at the expense of rational policy debate (Ranney 1983; Cockerell 1988; Seymour-Ure 1989; Allen 1993; Hallin 1994; McQuail 1994; Newman 1994; McManus 1994).

However, the main way in which the media are said to 'matter' in liberal analysis is by facilitating the functioning of society. This was conceived initially in terms of the political system, and took a rather predictable form. The media inform the sovereign electorate; act as a two-way channel of communication and influence between government and governed; and provide a check on the abuse of state power through the disclosure of information (McQuail 1992a; Kelley and Donway 1990). To these three core functions of liberal democratic theory have been added others, such as: assisting the aggregation of interests within the political process; providing a channel of communication between elites; facilitating the revision of the aims and policies of society through collective debate; and helping society to identify social problems and strains and to adopt appropriate political remedies (Rose 1965; Coleman 1973; Alexander 1981; McQuail 1994).

The core themes of this functionalist analysis were scripted in the eighteenth and early nineteenth centuries when the principal media of communication were small circulation, highly politicized newspapers and periodicals. Since then most media have become entertainment-based, and liberal democratic theory is in need of a major overhaul that takes account of this transformation (Curran 1991).

By contrast with time-worn discussion of the media's functioning for the political system, a 'sociological' functionalist perspective remained for some time rather undeveloped. A classic early version was advanced by Harold Lasswell in 1948, when he argued that the media have three important social functions: they enable people to monitor what is happening in ways that disclose 'threats to the value position of the community and of component parts within it' (Lasswell 1971: 98); they facilitate the co-ordination of society by providing channels of communication between different social groups, enabling a concerted response; and they assist the transmission of values from one generation to the next.

The development of social functionalism was encrusted during the 1950s and 1960s in systems theory, now largely and rightly forgotten.[9] It was later derailed – or at least diverted – by the revival of uses and gratifications research in the 1970s and early 1980s. Informing this revival was the largely unspoken assumption that, even if the media do not shape people's thinking, they occupy a lot of their time. What was needed therefore was a better understanding of what people got out of the media.

Using focus groups and survey research methods, researchers discovered an enormous variety of media functions (i.e. uses), reflecting differences in the goals, psychological needs and social experiences of individual audience members. These included promoting a sense of belonging, providing companionship, facilitating personal interaction, acquiring insight into self and others, forging a sense of identity, gaining a feeling of being in control, experiencing emotional release, escaping from unwanted reality, providing a source of relaxation, to mention only some of the gratifications derived from the media (Blumler and Katz 1974; Rosengren et al. 1985; Rubin 1986; Zillman and Bryant 1986). The implication of this research is that the media offer a cafeteria service from which people take what they want (Dayan and Katz 1992). The conventional categories of 'inform, educate and entertain' have no necessary relationship to how people use the media in practice, and are merely inadequate formulations derived from the media's manifest content.

Uses and gratifications research generally focuses on the individual. However, the resurgence of Durkheimian sociology and borrowing from social anthropology prompted a return during the last decade to a discussion of the social functioning of the media in relation to society as a whole. In an elegantly written book, James Carey (1992) argues that much mass communication has a ritual meaning which draws people together and affirms the underlying continuity of things. This is similar to Alexander's argument that mass communications help people to visualize society, feel connected to it, and make sense of its processes through a shared set of understandings (Alexander 1981). Media representations provide, in his view, a 'functional substitute for concrete group contact, for the now impossible meeting-of-the-whole' of modern differentiated societies. This 'contact', this sense of belonging (with its accompanying sense of place) is fostered by 'the symbolic images of national unity and identity' – such as the royal family – featured in the media (Cardiff and Scannell 1987). The media not only promote a 'we-feeling' but also foster integration into society's normative order of moral values, its sense of what is right and wrong. Thus the media regularly mark out the boundaries of what is acceptable and unacceptable through the expression of collective disapproval (Ericson et al. 1987), directed not only at law-breakers but also at those who transgress social norms (such as 'runaway mums') who are sometimes stigmatized in the British tabloid press.

Some of these general arguments are illustrated by Dayan and Katz (1992), who show how 'media events' – such as set-piece occasions of state, rites of passage of the great and sporting contests – can function as unifying experiences. Through the power of television, the private home is transformed into a shared public space in which individuals are linked to each other, and to society, in a collective celebration of something they hold in common. Typically, these media events affirm a common identity. They can also enable society to see itself in an idealized way, or involve the celebration of a shared value, memory or experience.

Dayan and Katz give as an example the televised wedding of Prince Charles and Lady Diana Spencer, which was watched by millions in Britain after an advance fanfare of mounting anticipation and excitement. The broadcast event celebrated the universal experience of love, courtship and betrothal, and ritually affirmed a consensual commitment to the institution of marriage, in an occasion of national rejoicing that induced a liminal sense of togetherness, an 'overflowing of communitas'. While Dayan and Katz tease out other meanings from the event as well, it is the collective and socially integrative aspects of the royal wedding that, as liberal functionalists, they focus attention on (Dayan and Katz 1987, 1992).

In short, it is not necessary to think of the media as a powerful generator of influence in discrete behavioural terms (whether it be inducing violence or changing votes) in order to conceive of it as playing a central role in society. That role, according to liberal functionalists, is to assist the functioning of society in terms of aiding its collective self-realization, co-ordination, self-management, social integration, stability and adaptation.

Radical Critique of Liberal Functionalism

The liberal functionalist approach has been lambasted by radical critics on the grounds that it is rooted in two false premisses. The first is the belief that there is an underlying unity of interest in society (Chaney 1986). Strengthening the bonds of society through the integrative functioning of the media is assumed therefore to be in everyone's interests. However, in reality, winners and losers do not have the same investment in the social order. The media's projection of an idealized social cohesion may serve to conceal fundamental differences of interest. Its effect can be to repress latent conflict, and weaken progressive forces for social change, not least by promoting national solidarity at the expense of class solidarity. Nor should empirical evidence of a consensus in society which the media 'reflect' be interpreted uncritically. All that this reveals, according to radical critics, is that dominant social forces have successfully won consent for social arrangements that consistently favour their interests.

Second, the liberal functionalist approach is based generally on the false assumption that the media are independent and socially neutral agencies in society. This ignores the close ties that can exist between the media and the twin peaks of the state and big business. It also ignores the unequal division of power in society, which can result in the media being co-opted to serve the interests of dominant institutions and social groups. Thus, the civic rituals mediated by press and television are often performative rites whose real purpose is to legitimate institutions of authority (Elliott 1980). Take, for example, the royal wedding anatomized by Dayan and Katz. At one level, its function was to draw people together in a unifying event that celebrated the 'universal' experience of love and marriage. But its more important function, according to radical funcitonalists, was to consolidate the popular association between the monarchy and the family, and in this way renew loyalty to the crown. Its main consequence was therefore to reinforce an institution which is the symbolic apex of the British class system, to legitimate a highly centralized and, in certain important respects, undemocratic State, and to sustain a 'culture of backwardness' that stands in the way of modernizing British society (Nairn 1988).

Radical Functionalist Alternative

The difference between liberal and radical functionalism is perhaps most easily understood in terms of a series of oppositions. First, whereas liberal functionalists emphasize the autonomy of the media system, radical functionalists stress its subordination. One strand of radical functionalism holds that the political economy of the media – its ownership by corporate business, its links to the state, the socialization of media staff into organizational norms, and the constraints imposed by market distortions, advertising and the pursuit of profit more generally – all predispose the media to serve dominant interests (Murdock and Golding 1977; Curran 1977). Another, structural-culturalist strand of radical functionalism sees the media as shaped by the dominant culture and power structures of society (Hall 1986; Hall et al. 1978). A third, more mainstream tradition argues that the structures of control within media organizations intermesh with those in society (Herman and Chomsky 1988). But common to all three positions is the conviction that the media tend to sustain dominant social forces in society.

Second, whereas liberal functionalists generally portray the media as reflecting a consensus, their radical counterparts argue that the media produce 'consent' for the social order. The media, according to this argument, disguise the nature and dynamics of power in society. For example, the powerful influence of business elites, and the ways in which the capitalist system structures political choices, tend to be played down as a consequence of the news media's focus on government and the political process as the locus of power in electoral democracies. Much TV fiction and many press human interest stories revolve around the individual, explain the world in terms of human motivation rather than social processes, and tacitly offer solutions in terms of individual rather than collective action (Curran et al. 1980; D'Acci 1994). The media also tend to report the news as discrete events, divorced from their wider contexts. In this way, they encourage a view of the social order as natural and inevitable, 'the way things are' (Golding and Elliott 1979).

This mystification supposedly arises from the way in which some things are included and other things are excluded in media 'constructions' of the world. It is also nurtured by overt explanations of the workings of society. Class conflict is often concealed through a signifying process of fragmenting, recreating and uniting social entities around an imaginary point of unity (Hall 1977). In the first place, opposed social classes are dissolved and reconstituted as non-antagonistic entities by being conceptualized as the electorate, the public or 'public opinion'. These are then presented as having an equal interest in the 'public good' or the 'national interest'. Similarly, conflicts of interest between employers and employees are submerged by focusing on the world of consumption where all are presented as having a shared identity as consumers.

More generally, it is argued, the media function to unite dominant forces in society, and to disunite their opponents (Hall 1977). Dissent is stigmatized and rendered unacceptable by eliding categories of moral and political deviance, by criminalizing symbolically expressions of opposition (Hall 1974). Disunity among subordinate groups is also furthered by making protests (such as industrial strikes) appear inexplicable or threatening, and their consequences harmful to the public (Morley 1981; Glasgow University Media Group 1976). While the media allow some degree of debate, this is allegedly within defined bounds that stop short of challenging the social order (Downing 1980). This 'variety-within-bounds' pluralism can facilitate the maintenance of the social system by encouraging the 'incorporation' of main sections of the working class within reformist movements.

This analysis of media content focuses on the media's role in maintaining class domination. However, there is also a feminist-functionalist tradition which focuses on the media's support for patriarchy (Sharpe 1978). The media, claimed Gaye Tuchman (1978b) in an influential essay, sustain male domination through 'the symbolic annihilation' and 'trivialization' of women as sex objects and domestic consumers, and through teaching women to direct their hearts to hearth and home. There is also a further strand of radical functionalism which sees class, gender and ethnic domination as merely different aspects of the same system of control sustained by the media (Parenti 1993; Downing 1980). However, what all these different strands of radical functionalism have in common is their relative lack of ambiguity, their emphasis on what they see as recurring and systematic features of media manipulation.

Third, while liberal functionalists stress the limits of media influence on the audience, radical functionalists emphasize the power of the media. Effects research tends to be dismissed by the latter as being both methodologically and conceptually flawed (Hall 1982). The power of the media is conceived in terms not of discrete effects but as a central source of information and signification. The media, according to this argument, not only help us to know more about the world but also to make sense of it. It structures our understanding by 'actively ruling in and ruling out certain realities, offering the maps and codes which mark out territories and assign problematic events and relations to explanatory contexts' (Hall 1977: 341). Indeed, in a strong version of this argument, the dominant system of ideas and representations relayed by the media provide the means by which people ordinarily 'live' (i.e. selectively experience) an imaginary relationship to their real conditions of existence (Althusser 1984).

Radical Misgivings

Underlying radical functionalist perspectives is, generally, a domination theory of society. 'The objection', wrote Herbert Marcuse (1972: 21), 'that we overrate the indoctrinating power of the "media" ... misses the point. The preconditioning does not start with the mass production of radio and television and the centralisation of their control. The people entered this stage as preconditioned receptacles of long standing'.

It was precisely this conception of people that was the first of a number of assumptions underpinning radical functionalism to be challenged in a fundamental reassessment. The stimulus for this came not so much from liberal pluralists – the two sides in the debate tended then, as now, not to read attentively each other's work (suggesting that there is something in cognitive dissonance theory after all) – but from self-criticism within the radical tradition.

A key break occurred when some brilliant and imaginative studies of youth cultures challenged the assumption that economically dominant forces are culturally dominant. These studies portrayed a variety of subcultures – from sometimes racist 'skinheads' who accentuated the core values and style of 'lumpen' working-class life, through to Rastas who rejected their parents' desire for respectability in a celebration of blackness – as the expressions of a submerged form of dissent (Cohen 1972; Clarke 1976; Willis 1977; Hebdige 1979). These subcultures were revealed to be highly complex and sometimes contradictory responses to the experience of being (among other things) young and working class, with low status, income and expectations, and often involved a purely symbolic and imagined 'solution' to real-life problems. But they were hailed as 'rituals of resistance' in which youth groups 'won space' and kept in play 'contrary cultural definitions' to those that were dominant (Clarke et al. 1976). While these studies have been criticized subsequently for their focus on young men to the exclusion of women (McRobbie 1981), their selective concentration on non-conformist culture (Clarke 1990), and their inherent romanticism (Gitlin 1991; Skeggs 1992), they did demonstrate very effectively the inadequacy of the conception of a preconditioned, dominated society.[10]

A similar reassessment occurred also within the radical feminist tradition. Its initial conception of patriarchal control – in which most women are assumed to be socialized into acceptance of subordination, their true nature repressed through the cultural control of men within the capitalist system – implies two things, both of which were increasingly rejected. One is that capitalism and patriarchy are but two facets of an indivisible system of control. The other is that women have an essential being, rooted in their gender, which is denied through patriarchal domination. Indeed, this essentialist approach gave way to the argument that women have different natures and identities which contain an element of volition, and which are the outcome of complex social processes that cannot be adequately understood only in terms of male control (Zoonen 1994, 1991).

These twin conceptions of subcultural resistance and the self-determining woman undercut simple domination theories of society to which radical functionalism had generally been tied. The next domino to fall was the notion of a 'dominant ideology', which forms the consensus of society and legitimates the dominance of ruling social forces. This was attacked on several counts (Abercrombie et al. 1984; Hall 1985). The notion implied, it was argued, a cultural and ideational domination that did not exist. It was 'reductionist' in the sense that it sought to reduce the meaning and provenance of ideas to a single set of economic interests, whereas ideas are partly shaped by argument and dialogue, and have a relative autonomy of their own. And, in actual practice, there was not in any case a coherent, ruling 'ideology', a single system of thought, but rather clusters of ideas – 'a field of discourses' – which were incommensurate and contradictory. These sensible qualifications were transformed, in some forms of postmodernist analysis, into a total repudiation of the notion that there is any kind of link between mental activity and the play of economic self-interest. In effect, all forms of 'materialist' analysis – whether Marxist, social democratic or, for that matter, conservative – were rejected in favour of a conception of 'culture' as wholly autonomous.[11]

The drift away from a stress on economic determination was paralleled by a revival of pluralism. Marxist functionalism is usually based on the assumption that there is a high degree of concentration of economic, political and cultural power in 'monopoly capitalism'. This came to be challenged by other views which emphasized the multiple ways in which power is manifested, the contradictory and multi-centred character of state institutions, the complex articulation of economic, political and cultural realms, the resourcefulness and self-determination of subordinate groups, the playful movement of subjectivity in an era of relativism and change, mobility and reflexivity (McRobbie 1992; Ang and Hermes 1991; Fiske 1989a, 1989b; Lyotard 1984; Foucault 1980, 1982). Liberal pluralism was reborn as postmodernist pluralism in which power, to adapt David Morley (1992a), was conceived as being defused or diffused (or both).[12]

Gramscian Rearguard Action

In the face of this self-immolation of the radical tradition, an attempt was made to 'hold the line' by adopting and developing the ideas of the Italian Marxist, Antonio Gramsci (1985, 1981, 1971). Society was reconceived in terms of a contest between broad-based and shifting social coalitions which seek to gain control of the strategic institutions of society, and to win the hearts and minds of people by interpreting society within its horizon of thought. Even in contexts where the dominant coalition appeared to be dominant, its hegemony was still held to be both incomplete and something that had to be constantly striven for. Viewed from this perspective, the media came to be seen as a battleground fought over by opposed social forces rather than as, in radical functionalism, an agency of domination. In the new jargon that was to become familiar, the media are a 'contested space'.

This position made a number of accommodations to revisionist analysis. It emphasized the existence of 'resistance' and dissent generally missing in radical (and also liberal) functionalist analysis. It conceived conflict in broad, inclusive terms as being rooted not only in the social relations of production but also in multiple forms of oppression – including those linked to gender and ethnicity – which could give rise to broad-based 'national-popular' movements of opposition to the social order (Simon 1982; Mouffe 1981). It brought 'culture' more fully into the frame so that not only the political and economic realms but also the 'politics of everyday life' – even subcultural styles – could be viewed as inextricably linked 'sites' of contest. It offered a penetrating understanding of cultural processes as the outcome of history in which different 'traces', derived from past struggles, lay like layers in the subsoil of popular culture. And it offered a flexible analysis in which the notion that ideas and economic interests are linked was retained but in a complex and contingent form which acknowledged that ideas have a partly independent trajectory.

However, the sandbags of this defence soon began to leak. The conception of class conflict that was in fact central to Gramsci's own analysis came to be de-emphasized in favour of other forms of social cleavage. Cultural dissent was increasingly analysed in discrete terms without reference to how it related, concretely, to other forms of struggle. The notion of the economic determinacy of ideas, in a qualified form, became still more attenuated. Indeed, the rise of Gramscianism – at its height in the mid-1980s – can be seen retrospectively as part of a process of reappraisal that helped to discredit radical functionalism without replacing it with an established radical alternative.

The Gramscian tradition also became something of a blank cheque. Its themes were repressed through extremely partial incorporation by some traditional Marxists (Parenti 1993), stretched by others to fit 'the feminist ticket' (Holub 1992) and absorbed selectively by others, still, in eloquent postmodernism (Hebdige 1988). The attempt to rally behind 'liberal' Marxism became for many radical critics an exit out of Marxism, the occasion for a general diaspora. However, the Gramscian legacy still has something to offer – a theme to which we shall return when we consider how media research might be reoriented in the future.

Reinterpreting Media Processes

The way in which Gramscianism proved to be a staging post in a process of disenchantment with traditional radical positions is perhaps best illustrated by how Stuart Hall, the leading exponent of Gramscianism in mass communication research, came under a fusillade of fire. Hall had always been unconvinced by traditional radical political economy arguments, which explained the media's output primarily in terms of their political and economic organization. Media staff, he insisted, enjoyed a significant degree of autonomy from overt control. So why was it, he asked, that the media 'freely orchestrated themselves around definitions of the situation which favoured the hegemony of the powerful?' (Hall 1982: 86; cf. Hall 1985). The main answer given by Hall and his colleagues was that the structure of power in society is reproduced as a structure of access to the media, and this is converted into an indirect form of editorial control due to the routines and self-effacing conventions of news reporting. News media, argued Hall and his associates (1978; cf. Hall 1986), accord accredited status to the 'powerful' as news sources, and allow them to dictate the 'primary' interpretation of an event or topic. This interpretation then '"commands the field" in subsequent treatment and sets the terms of reference within which all further coverage of debate takes place' (Hall et al. 1978: 58). This then exerts pressure on subordinate groups to situate themselves within this interpretive framework in order to obtain a media hearing. In this way, the dominant field of discourses tends to be reproduced 'spontaneously and without compulsion' by journalists even though they enjoy significant autonomy.

A rising volume of criticism greeted this analysis.[13] The principal argument advanced by critics is that sources with privileged access to the media should not be conceived as one bloc ('the powerful') who advance a single definition of events, but rather as a shoal of sources which have different degrees of access and different degrees of news status, and which part of the time advance different definitions of the news. For example, Schlesinger and Tumber revealed that opposition political parties and accredited pressure groups in the crime and criminal justice field had less access to the media than state agencies, yet were able to gain space, especially in elite media, for arguments which accused the police of illegitimate violence, racial discrimination and involvement in miscarriages of justice, as well as the need for prison reform and rethinking penal policy (Schlesinger and Tumber 1994). A broadly similar argument was advanced by Daniel Hallin, though not in the context of this debate, in relation to the American news media. He showed that growing differences among key sources gave rise to a more multiperspectival and less uncritical television coverage of the Vietnam War, and later of American involvement in Central America (Hallin 1986, 1994; cf. Williams 1993). Similarly Lang and Lang (1983) argue that it was divisions within the American establishment (and not, incidently, heroic investigative journalism) that provided the main driving force behind media exposure of the Watergate scandal, and the forced resignation of President Nixon.

All these case studies illustrate the importance of source disagreement in generating a degree of media diversity. However, there is a difference of emphasis in the presentation of this argument. The American literature tends to portray interaction between elites as the key environmental influence on American news media, in a context where non-elite voices are marginalized (Sigal 1987; Lang and Lang 1983; Hess 1984; Nacos 1990; Hallin 1986, 1994). However, some British case studies argue that non-elite groups – Protestant workers in Ulster mounting a political strike, and the Labour left with roots in local government – can in certain circumstances gain the upper hand in shaping definitions of the news in broadcast media (Miller 1993; Curran 1990). A further complication is added by studies that draw attention to the organizational mediation of sources. Which sources are used, and how they are used, is influenced sometimes by the partisan editorial policies of the news media that journalists work for (Nacos 1990; Curran 1987).

Yet despite these differences, two things in this reassessment became clear. It is wrong to imagine that the media are equally accessible to all points of view, as in the liberal functionalist model, because different social groups have unequal access to the media. However, it is also misleading to suppose that the media systematically favour, in Hall's phrase, 'the hegemony of the powerful' because 'the powerful' are not all of one mind, and the rest are not always excluded. Even a structural-culturalist version of the radical project proved, in the event, not to be weatherproof.

Reinterpreting Media Content

Revisionist interpretations of media processes were echoed by different accounts of media content. Whereas radical functionalists tended to offer unambiguous 'readings', revisionists tended, by contrast, to detect complexity and ambiguity. Their recurrent refrain was that media 'texts' have contradictions or tensions, offer up discursive spaces that encourage divergent or subversive interpretations, are in important ways different, and are changing (generally for the better).

In particular, this line of argument was deployed with considerable effect by feminists who challenged early indictments of the media as unambiguous agencies of patriarchy. Thus, Tania Modleski (1984) claimed that the portrayal of the archetypal villainess in American TV soap opera, who transforms traditional feminine weaknesses into the source of her strength, provides potentially an object of ambivalent identification and an outlet for feminine anger. Radway (1987) showed how some romantic fiction offers a proto-feminist fantasy in which men are transformed through the love of a woman into warm, nurturant, even decent human beings. In this book, Angela McRobbie argues persuasively that women's and girls' magazines in Britain have changed, and some now offer more egalitarian, liberated or diverse understandings of what it is to be a woman, by comparison with their more conventional and prescriptive predecessors. Breakthroughs of a sort have also occurred in American (and, therefore, global) television. For example, the long-running American TV series, *Cagney and Lacey* featured in the lead roles two female detectives who are 'in control', good at their jobs, personally sympathetic, with a warm, supportive friendship that helps them to withstand discrimination at work (D'Acci 1994). While the radicalism of its early episodes became muted due to network and market pressure, it still continued to draw upon the ideas and humour of the American liberal feminist movement. Something of its flavour comes through in this exchange:

> *Lieutenant Samuels* (male boss): Cagney, will you get on with your job and let me talk to my men?
> [*Cagney elaborately turns to Lacey and with great interest begins a new tack.*]
> *Cagney*: That certainly was a delicious stew you made last night, Mary Beth. Could you give me the recipe?
> *Lacey*: Well, first you buy a pig.
> [*Samuels glares at them.*]
> *Cagney*: Buy a pig? I didn't know that you could buy a pig in this town.
> *Lacey*: Oh, you can buy a pig almost anyplace in this town. You don't want an old pig, or a fat pig, you just want a nice succulent . . .
>
> (cit. D'Acci 1994: 149)

These studies do not contest that the media, in general, still tend to support partriarchal values but present this argument in a more nuanced, qualified and complex form. Much the same is true of accounts of media representations of ethnic minorities. A considerable body of evidence suggests that ethnic minorities are liable to be presented in the media as a problem or threat; they often feature in association with crime or conflict; and that racial conflicts and disadvantage tend not to be contextualized in terms of their causes.[14] But some accounts stress that media representations are slowly changing. African Americans are more visible in American media (Martindale 1986), more often portrayed in high-status roles in American TV fiction (Jhally and Lewis 1992), and are projected as less threatening in the US media by comparison with the past (Wilson and Gutierrez 1985), though racist constructions do not seem to have diminished significantly in the British press during the last 25 years (Dijk 1991; Troyna 1981; Hartmann and Husband 1974).

More generally, revisionist accounts point to the diversity of the media with the implication that the 'media' cannot be discussed usefully as a single generic category (Beharrell 1993; Curran 1990). Many television programmes, it is also argued, are ambivalent and accessible to alternative interpretation partly as a market-oriented strategy designed to offer something for everyone in a mass audience (Fiske 1987).

Reinterpreting the Audience

Revisionist misgivings about the extent to which society is controlled encouraged a new orientation towards the audience. This argument is outlined and debated later in this book,[15] and need not be rehearsed in detail here. It is sufficient merely to note that critics from the radical tradition discovered that audiences are active and selective in their responses to the media. This insight unleashed – and continues to sustain – a succession of studies illustrating this central insight. For example, Brown and Schultze (1990) found that black and white university students in the United States tended to make sense of two Madonna videos differently because they brought to their viewing different frameworks of understanding and cultural references. Corner et al. (1990) found that Conservative and Labour activists, Friends of the Earth campaigners and nuclear industry workers, the unemployed and Rotarians (local business people) responded differently to programmes about nuclear energy. John Fiske (1991) describes how homeless native Americans physically manipulated the meaning of classic westerns by celebrating early sequences when their fictional forebears took a homestead or wagon, and then turned off in order to forestall the inevitable white settler victory. His account has almost an allegoric quality in the way in which it celebrates the central theme of revisionist audience research: the power and autonomy of the audience.

This research tradition is different from effects research in that it tends to use different methods, and derives from different ideological and disciplinary roots. It has broken new ground in illuminating the dialogue that takes place between media and audiences. As a body of research it is not homogeneous.

This said, the difference in the technical language used by radical revisionist and liberal effects researchers should not conceal the underlying similarity of their argument: namely, that audiences respond to the media in active and selective ways. The inferences derived from this insight by eloquent radical revisionists like John Fiske (1989a, 1989b and 1989c) are similar to those of liberal effects researchers like Katz and Lazarsfeld, and their successors, in that both celebrate in an appealing way the self-willed independence of people.

Wind of Fashion

Liberal researchers walk with a new spring in their step. The wind of fashion is behind them. Recent trends in radical research – the reconceptualization of society in more pluralistic terms, the waning of radical political economy, the stress on source competition, the emphasis on ambiguity and 'tension' in media texts, the celebration of audience power – have all wrenched the radical tradition closer to the territory of liberal research. Indeed, some of these revisionist themes have been drawn upon skilfully in a way that has re-invigorated a liberal functionalist understanding of the media. This is perhaps best illustrated by reference to a clever essay by Horace Newcomb and Paul Hirsch (1984).

Newcomb and Hirsch argue that just in the way that traditional societies examine themselves through the experience of ritual, so contemporary societies do the same through their arts, foremost of which is television art.[16] Television

> presents a multiplicity of meanings rather than a monolithic point of view. It often focuses on our most prevalent concerns, our deepest dilemmas. Our most traditional views, those that are repressive and reactionary, as well as those that are subversive and emancipatory, are upheld, examined, maintained, and transformed. The emphasis is on process rather than product, on discussion rather than indoctrination, on contradiction and confusion rather than coherence.
> (Newcomb and Hirsch 1984: 62)

The fictional world of television, in their view, constitutes a forum of normative debate influencing our understanding of who we are, how we should relate to others, and how society might be improved. The world of television fiction offers, in their useful phrase, 'the dramatic logic of public thought' (Newcomb and Hirsch 1984: 63).

They intriguingly take as an example *Father Knows Best*, a 1960s American TV series which some critics refer to dismissively as a hegemonic hosanna to middle-class values and cosy domesticity, divorced from social conflict. They focus on a seemingly unpromising episode in which the eldest daughter of the household tries to become an engineer, walks off a job-experience scheme on the first day after taunts from a young man, with whom she then forms a flirtatious relationship when he comes to her house to apologize. Newcomb and Hirsch offer an initial reading of this episode, in traditional radical style, as a typical example of mystification in which conflict is 'defused, contained, and redirected'. But the key point about it, they argue, is that our emotional sympathy is with the daughter throughout the episode. Nowhere in the programme is the viewer encouraged to think that her ambition to be an engineer is unnatural. The episode, therefore, poses a question about appropriate sex roles: it functions as an ideological commentary rather than as a conclusion. In this respect, it is exemplary since 'conflicting viewpoints of social issues are, in fact, the elements that structure most television programmes' (Newcomb and Hirsch 1984: 65).

This familiar theme of textual ambiguity is yoked to another revisionist theme, that of audience autonomy. The diversity of television meanings, Newcomb and Hirsch argue, is amplified still further by the diversity of audience responses. The wide range of 'interpretive variance' of TV programmes is a cue for still more diverse interpretations in which viewers generate their own meanings and make sense of programmes in terms of their varied personal experiences and interpretive frameworks. Television, in short, is an open-ended cultural forum, the means by which a pluralistic society communes with itself.

This is a rightly celebrated essay which has important things to say about the way in which TV fiction potentially informs the collective dialogue of society. But it is anchored to the fallacy, central to the liberal tradition, that television reflects the full diversity of society. As Newcomb and Hirsch put it, 'While each of these [programme] units can and does present its audience with incredibly mixed ideas, it is television as a whole system that presents a mass audience with the range of ideas and ideologies inherent in American culture' (Newcomb and Hirsch 1984: 64).

Yet, it is precisely this conception of the media as a faithful reflection of society – in this instance, as an open cultural forum which enables society to debate with itself – that the radical tradition sought originally to challenge. However, revisionist themes need not necessarily be routed to a liberal terminus. They can also be deployed in a way that sustains a more convincing radical, alternative analysis of the media. How this might be attempted is explored below in relation to just two issues: how the media connect to society, and the debate over media influence.

Rethinking the Links Between Media and Society

As we have seen, mainstream liberal and radical traditions in media studies offer us two contrasting views of the media's relationship to society. One portrays the media as bottom-up agencies of communication and influence, as independent institutions which give voice to the people and reproduce the collective conversation of society. It emphasizes popular control of the media through the market, stresses the importance of 'professional' mediation, and tends to see the media as organizations autonomous from the power structure of society.

The other portrays the media as top-down agencies of control, as institutions which are subordinated to established power and serve its interests. The media are perceived to be subject to influences that are one-directional and mutually reinforcing. As Ralph Miliband argued, for example, 'there are a number of influences [on the media] – and they all work in the same conservative and conformist direction'. He went on to claim that capitalist ownership of the media, the 'official climate' in which public service broadcasting is 'steeped', advertising censorship, the consensual values of media staffs, in addition to other factors, all merge together in a single irresistible force which makes the media 'weapons in the arsenal of class domination' (Miliband 1973: 203–13).

Herman and Chomsky offer an American equivalent of this analysis which, while not Marxist, follows essentially the same logic. The American news media, they argue, are subject to five news filters ranging from advertising censorship to '"flak" as a means of disciplining the media'. These, they maintain,

> interact with and reinforce one another. The raw material of news must pass through successive filters, leaving only the cleansed residue fit to print. They fix the premises of discourse and interpretation, and the definition of what is newsworthy in the first place . . . The elite domination of the media and marginalization of dissent . . . results from the operation of these filters.
>
> (Herman and Chomsky 1988: 2)

The full-blooded versions of the radical and liberal approach could not, seemingly, be more different. Yet, they tend to have in common a reluctance to think of the media as responding to cross-pressures, to influences from both above and below. The Gramscian reappraisal broke with this by highlighting usefully the ways in which the media can be caught in a crossfire between dominant and subordinate social forces. But while this is a significant advance, it has tended to be articulated in a rather mechanical form, as a universal proposition. The Gramscian reappraisal also grew out of the culturalist tradition in radical media studies, and is inclined to view the media as literally a 'contested space', an unconstrained vacuum, determined by the wider relations of power in society. This conception oversimplifies. What is needed is a more systematic analysis of the influences shaping the media that takes account of the insights of radical political economy.

Top-down Pressures

There are at least ten different weights which pull the media towards the orbit of powerful groups in society. That is to say, the media are subject to systematic influences that undermine – or potentially undermine – their claim to independence and neutrality, their disinterested mediation of the collective discourses of society. The fact that some of these influences are invisible or are not 'intended' (in the sense of being consciously sought or desired) has tended to result in their existence being overlooked.

These are also counterbalanced by weights pulling in the other direction so that the media are ordinarily exposed to contrary influences. But, first, let us consider top-down pressures, which are presented for the sake of brevity in note form.

1 Restrictions on market entry

The high cost of entry into most media markets constitutes an invisible ideological barrier, a means of limiting competition in the 'market-place of ideas' by excluding those who lack large sums of money or lines of credit. For example, in the United Kingdom it costs at least £20 million to establish a new national daily, and many times this to establish a new satellite TV channel.[17]

2 Corporate ownership

Ownership of private media has passed largely into the hands of big business (Chadwick 1989; Lorrimer and McNulty 1991; Bagdikian 1992; Golding and Murdock 1991). The power conferred by ownership to influence the ethos, editorial direction and market definition of commercial media – principally through the hiring and firing of staff, the setting of organizational policy and the allocation of rewards within media organizations – is now largely vested in one corporate sector. This is in contrast to the past when the ownership of private media was more widely distributed within society.

As we shall see, the power of media controllers is constrained in significant ways. The connection between their broadly defined material interests and the output of the media has also been reduced as a consequence of the greater market and entertainment orientation of media organizations. However, this is not the same as saying that the current pattern of private media ownership is entirely neutral in its consequences – an extreme liberal position that is clearly unsustainable. Media controllers have imposed, at times, changes from above in ways that have furthered policies and agendas favouring big business, as is illustrated by the transformation of *The Sunday Times* and *the Jerusalem Post* by Rupert Murdoch's News Corporation and Conrad Black's Hollinger Group respectively, both in the teeth of strong staff opposition (Frenkel 1994; Curran and Seaton 1991; Giles 1986).

3 *Media concentration*

In most Western countries, 'mono-media' concentration (that is, concentration within particular media sectors) has become more advanced. The one major exception to this is broadcasting, where concentration has diminished.[18] However, this has been offset by another trend; the growth of *multi-media* concentration in both a national and international context, facilitated by privatization, deregulation and the accelerated development of global media markets (Sanchez-Tabernero et al. 1993; European Commission 1992; Murdock 1990).

Media groups vary in terms of the degree to which internal control is centralized or devolved (McCombs 1988; Franklin and Murphy 1991; McQuail 1992a; Shawcross 1992). But growing concentration has increased the potential for centralized control over the media. Its dangers were dramatically affirmed in Italy's 1994 election when the Fininvest TV channel (with a 40 per cent market share) gave thinly veiled support to its controller and right-wing businessman, Silvio Berlusconi, who was catapulted into the premiership without ever having held public office before. However Berlusconi's rise, though facilitated by his concentration of media power, was primarily the consequence of the crisis of Italy's political system, and was followed by his ousting as prime minister.

4 *Mass market pressures*

The mass media are rather like political parties in that they tend to gravitate towards the centre in response to competitive pressures. These are particularly acute in the media industries because of the advantages of economies of scale arising from high fixed costs. In general, the larger the audience reached by the media, the more unit costs are decreased and the marginal rate of profit increased since high 'first copy' costs can be spread over a larger volume of sales. For example, commercial TV channels can increase spectacularly their revenue without necessarily incurring any extra cost simply by achieving higher ratings. Similarly, the return on cinema sales rises sharply with higher audiences since the cost of making additional film copies is extremely small in relation to the initial investment cost. Economic pressures thus generate a powerful pressure on media organizations to gravitate towards the consensual and conventional in order to reach a mass public.

This said, market majoritarian pressures on the media can favour the forces for progressive change when the tide is flowing strongly in their favour.

However, mass-market pressures can also cause radical perspectives to be softened or muted in order not to alienate a significant section of a mass, undifferentiated audience. And when the left is weak, mass-market pressures tend to encourage its further marginalization.

5 *Economic weighting of consumer demand*

The media tend to over-represent the ideological interests and concerns of the affluent because they have more consumer power than low-income groups. In the first place, the affluent have higher disposable incomes to spend on additional media services (Golding 1990), which causes them to have a disproportionate influence on left-over, niche markets. Secondly, they generate higher advertising expenditures than low-income groups. This can cause mass media to drift upscale in order to attract audiences that advertisers will pay more to reach (Baker 1995; D'Acci 1994; Curran and Seaton 1991). It can also distort the provision of minority media services which are powerfully influenced by the unequal advertising value of high- and low-income audiences (Curran 1986).

6 *Advertising censorship*

Advertising is the major source of revenue for many media. This can generate pressure to avoid giving offence to advertisers, their products and political agendas, and to create an editorial environment conducive to selling products – though these pressures are often strongly resisted by media staff.[19]

7 *News routines and values*

These tend to function against the weak and unorganized. They have low prestige as sources; they tend not to be included on regular news beats (save as law-breakers); and they generally lack resources and expertise in news management. However, wider changes in society can mitigate unequal access to the media.

8 *Aesthetic conventions*

In particular, the narrative conventions of television fiction and newspaper human interest journalism promote an individual-centred view of the world, and tend to frame 'solutions' to problems in individual-moral rather than collective-political terms. This works against bottom-up pressures for structural changes in society.

9 *Unequal division of power and resources*

The systems of thought, chains of association and images which occur spontaneously to media staff, working under pressure of time, tend to be those that are most widely circulated in society. These are strongly influenced by dominant groups which have generally superior discursive, institutional and material resources at their command.

10 Ambivalence of state power

The power of the state can be used, as we shall see, on behalf of different groups. However, traditional elites tend to have privileged access to state institutions, and can use this to control or influence the media. This can take the form of coercive laws restricting freedom of media expression; the abuse of the regulatory system through the lifting of monopoly controls to aid media allies or the manipulation of broadcasting regulations to intimidate state-linked broadcasters; and the deployment of the resources of the state (including its large public relations apparatus) to influence the climate of opinion and political agenda.

Bottom-up Pressures

All these pressures tend, all other things being equal, to propel the media towards the sphere of influence of dominant groups in society. However, the media are also subject to countervailing pressures which can potentially pull in the other direction. There are at least six different ways in which popular forces can influence the media in liberal democracies. Since the general thrust of this argument is contentious, at least within some strands of the radical tradition, it needs to be outlined in more than note form.

1 Countervailing cultural power

Subordinate social forces can develop alternative understandings of society, engender a strong sense of collective identity, and transmit collective allegiances and radical commitments from one generation to the next, through personal interaction, social rituals and the institutions under their control or influence. Through collective action in the workplace and civil society, and through participation in the collective dialogue of society, they can seek to modify or change prevailing opinions and attitudes. Above all, their numerical strength means that potentially they can secure, through the electoral process, political influence over the state and use its power and resources to change the organization and culture of society.

Recent trends have weakened the position of the working class in Western industrial societies. The latest phase of capitalist development has caused the number of industrial workers, generally the core group of radical political coalitions, to decline. The rise of the transnational economy and the new international division of labour has eroded the strength of trade unions. It has also diminished the effectiveness of the nation-state as an instrument of economic management and reduced the ability of social democratic parties to serve their social constituencies. A number of economic and social changes have also weakened class identity.[20]

Against this background of potential but shrinking strength, there is a significant variation in the achieved position of the organized working class and its allies. In Scandinavia, the working class is still organized into strong trade unions, sustains effective political parties, and shares control of the state through liberal corporatist arrangements. Its collectivist and egalitarian values have penetrated deep into the culture of Scandinavian society, and act as a powerful environmental influence on its mass media.

In contrast, there is no mass working-class party in the United States. Its unions are weak, and sometimes also conservative. There is currently no powerful, organized and stable social bloc in a position to radicalize the culture of American society which is more individualistic and inegalitarian than the culture even of a conservative European country like Britain (Davis 1986), and still more so by comparison with social democratic Scandinavia. The contrast between American and Nordic societies thus illustrates the ways in which differences in their internal disposition of power affect the distribution of meanings to which the media are exposed.

2 *Countervailing political power*

Another way in which subordinate groups can have an effect is to shape the goals, policies and organization of the mass media. In the United States, 'citizen' power takes the form primarily of interest groups seeking to influence the editorial direction of media organizations by, for example, campaigning against negative images of ethnic or sexual minorities. TV networks are lobbied almost as if they are branches of government. This is in a context where the media are overwhelmingly market-based, and where state involvement in the media, following a cumulative process of deregulation, has been minimalized (Hoynes 1994; Kellner 1990; Entman 1989).

In contrast, subordinate and other groups in Western Europe have turned to the state in order to influence who controls the media, how it is run and for what purpose. This has given rise to public service broadcasting systems whose defining characteristics are some form of representative control, a commitment to programme quality and diversity, and an obligation to reflect different views in society and/or maintain a bipartisan approach in reporting contentious issues.

European public service broadcasting systems conform to three main models: the *social devolutionary* approach (as in The Netherlands) where different sectional groups are given control over part of the broadcasting system (McQuail 1992b; Browne 1989); the *liberal corporatist* approach (as in Germany) where representative social and political groups have strategic influence over broadcasting in what are, in effect, power-sharing arrangements (Hoffman-Riem 1992; Porter and Hasselbach 1991; Etzioni-Halevy 1987); and the *civil service* model (as in Britain) where public trustees exercise nominal control within a system that devolves power to professional broadcasters and administrators (Curran and Seaton 1991; McNair 1994; Tunstall 1993). In addition, a *social market strategy* has been developed in the northern European social democracies in relation to the privately owned, market-based media of press and film. This can involve financial assistance to resource-poor groups to enter the market; public intervention to facilitate market access (for example, municipal ownership of cinemas in Norway); and economic support for minority media (as in the Swedish press) (Solum 1994; Picard 1988). More radical blueprints, building on existing features of European media systems, have also been proposed (Williams 1966; Curran 1991; Keane 1991).

The efficacy of different public media systems has varied greatly. Some state-linked broadcasting systems, as in Greece, have remained under the shadow of government (Dmitras 1992), while others, as in Britain, have achieved a considerable (though still threatened) degree of autonomy (Barnett and Curry 1994; Negrine 1994). However, such empirical distinctions are rejected almost as a matter of principle by some commentators. These fall into three broad categories: economic liberals like Rupert Murdoch (1989), who believe that public broadcasting systems are always beholden to governments, and that the true wishes of the people can only be registered through market democracy; traditional Marxists who believe that media freedoms will always be abused by a state that is controlled ultimately by the bourgeoisie (Sparks 1985);[21] and, implicitly, Marxist culturalists who see all media, however organized, as being equally regulated by structures of domination in society (Connell 1980). The objection to the first two positions is that they have a flawed understanding of the state.[22] The objection to the last is that it pays insufficient attention to the effect of different organizational structures on media output. And the counter to all three positions is that some state-linked media systems offer a greater degree of pluralism than their deregulated capitalist counterparts (McQuail 1992a; Blumler 1991; Curran 1990).

3 *Source power*

Subordinate groups can also influence the media by effecting changes in the composition and orientation of the news sources used regularly by journalists. The single most effective way of doing this is to secure the election of a government that will represent their perspectives, since governments are a key strategic source for all Western news media. Thus, the election of the Carter administration in the United States, with a concern for human rights, encouraged the American TV networks to revise their Cold War perspective of the world by making prominent a new criterion of judgement (Hallin 1994). Governments can also have a sacerdotal role conferring news status on interest groups that receive their benediction (Anderson 1991).

Success or failure in the democratic process, more generally, can also affect the authority of news sources. Thus, campaigners against the Vietnam War in the United States ceased to be consigned to 'the sphere of deviancy' as extremists and subversives by the TV networks when their candidate won the 1968 New Hampshire primary, and they demonstrated their 'mainstream' political support in the 1968 National Democrat Convention (Hallin 1986). Similarly, Sinn Fein's status as a news source rose sharply in the estimation of British news journalists when it demonstrated that it had a popular base by winning elections in Northern Ireland (Miller 1994).

The rise of new social movements can also change the source environment of news media. For example, trade unions emerged from a quasi-criminalized position in early nineteenth-century Britain to gain an accredited status as news sources about industrial relations and – for a time – about the economic and social management of Britain, before being demoted in the British media. Their demotion seems to have been linked to their loss of power and exclusion by the state in the 1980s and early 1990s. By contrast, the rise of the environmental movement during the same period led to its cadet accreditation as a news source. Its arguments were more frequently reported in the media, though often referred to the fora of 'formal politics', 'public authorities' and 'science' for validation or refutation (Hansen 1991).

However, radical news sources tend to have 'legitimacy problems'. Thus while British trade unions, Irish republican militants and American peace campaigners all gained access to the airwaves, this was often within a framework that was hostile to them (Glasgow University Media Group 1976; Hallin 1986; Miller 1994). This said, changes in the balance of power and popular support in society do influence source inputs to news media and this can affect how the news is reported.

4 *Staff power*

Subordinate groups can also be 'represented' by media staff whose professional self-definition rests on the claim that they serve the wider public. However, this argument needs to be viewed critically, and raises a number of issues that cannot be dealt with easily in a brief space.

The first issue is the degree to which journalists are autonomous in their work environment, as they often claim to be in surveys (e.g. Weaver and Wilhoit 1986). To some degree, their sense of independence may stem from their internalization of the norms of their employing organization: they do what is expected without being told.

The second issue is the extent to which journalists are independent of the hierarchy of power in society as a consequence of their commitment to professional goals. A blistering assault on the professionalization of journalism has been mounted by critics who argue that it is based on a stunted version of objectivity as a 'strategic ritual' designed to avoid the effort of evaluating what is true, avert the danger of giving offence to the powerful and keep at bay the terror of deadlines (Tuchman 1978a); that it legitimates reliance on a narrow oligarchy of sources (Sigal 1987); and results in pro-establishment and trivializing forms of journalism (Gitlin 1990).

However, these criticisms arise out of specific studies. They cannot be framed in general terms without taking into account differences in the conception and practice of journalism. One definition of journalism, strongly entrenched in the United States, sees the role of the journalist as representing a unified and passive public (and tends to be both anti-government and relatively conservative). Another tradition, more entrenched in Western Europe, views the role of the journalist as facilitating a dialogue in society (and tends to take its political bearings from the leaders of the main parliamentary parties). Among other significant traditions, there is also a radical paternalist strand which holds that the journalist should, in the words of Malcolm Maclean Jnr, 'communicate what it means to be poor among the rich, to be hungry among the well-fed, to be sick among the healthy ... to be unheard, unheard, unheard

... in a society noisy with messages' (cit. Manca 1989: 170). Implicit in these different definitions are divergent conceptions of the public that journalists serve, and how it should be served.

Yet, after all necessary qualifications have been made, there is an important sense in which media staff can act as a check on state and corporate influence over the media. This claim can be briefly supported by three examples, relating to different sectors of the British media. In 1984, the editor and staff of the *Observer* opposed successfully an attempt by Tiny Rowland, chief executive of its parent company, Lonrho, to suppress a report of a government atrocity in Zimbabwe which jeopardized the company's large and highly profitable investments in that country (Curran and Seaton 1991). In 1985, the staff of the BBC went on strike opposing the suppression of an illuminating *Real Lives* documentary about Northern Ireland in response to government pressure, and succeeded in getting it broadcast with only minor changes (Barnett and Curry 1994). In 1988, Thames TV and the Independent Broadcasting Authority refused the government's request to withdraw *Death on the Rock*, a programme that suggested that British troops had murdered an unarmed IRA unit in Gibraltar. It was subsequently repeated, and awarded a top industry (BAFTA) award in a symbolic affirmation of the broadcasting community's determination to maintain its independence (Curran 1991). All three examples show how professional aspirations to independence are not entirely mythical, and can sustain the functioning of the media in terms of a wider public interest.

5 *Consumer power*

People can influence the media by how they spend their time and money. This is in fact one of the most effective means of exerting leverage. It is also one that is extensively mythologized, so it is important to establish the extent of this influence. There are three key limitations. First, consumer power is limited by the range of choice available. The more restricted the choice, the more consumer power is curtailed. Second, consumer preferences are responded to in a market context where all consumers are not equal. As mentioned before, the logic of the market tends to privilege majorities at the expense of minorities, and the affluent at the expense of low-income groups. Third, the maximization of profit is not, contrary to conventional neo-liberal analysis, the exclusive organizational goal pursued by all commercial media organizations.

The sometimes complex ways in which consumer power percolates upwards can be illustrated with reference to the British national press. It does not reflect its readers' opinions in a simple sense. In every single general election during the last half century, it has been more Conservative than the electorate (Seymour-Ure 1991). In 1992, for example, 64 per cent of national daily sales supported the Conservative Party, compared with 42 per cent of the electorate. This consistent difference between editorial and public opinion is due to a number of things. The British press is dominated by Conservative controllers with strong ideological commitments. Consumer choice is restricted by oligopoly and high entry costs. Popular newspapers are entertainment-based, and many readers choose newspapers primarily in terms of their entertainment content (Curran and Seaton 1991). The result is that intensely Conservative, hierarchically controlled newspapers reach deep into the heartland of working-class, Labour support (Negrine 1994). Yet, this reveals only part of the complex relationship between press and public. Because there is intense competition between titles controlled by a small number of groups, newspapers do not simply impose a view of the world on their readers, but start from their readers' experiences and interests and work them into a pleasurable form. This generates tensions and contradictions in the pages of the popular press, most notably between the political sections that tend to register the influence of controllers, and other content that more closely connects to the outlooks and interests of readers.

6 *Market power*

Subordinate groups can gain a voice through owning their own media. This is despite the fact that they have multiple disadvantages compared with established media enterprise. They tend to have less money; less cultural capital (in the sense of relevant knowledge and expertise); they encounter various market obstacles, most notably in distribution; and they are generally less well adapted to the market system because market success is often not their main objective.

Yet, outsiders have succeeded sometimes in breaking into the market. Historically, organized labour launched mass-circulation newspapers by pooling working-class resources in order to meet the price of market admission. Some of these flourished, though most have since been eclipsed by the rise of entertainment-centred, market-oriented papers. For a time, radical musical labels also had a considerable mass market impact, before being rolled back by the music majors and in some cases being incorporated by them in tie-in arrangements (Burnett 1990). In some countries, there are also significant 'alternative' media. However, these tend to be confined to niche markets where entry costs are still low. They tend also to be short-lived, and to attract relatively small audiences. Most of the radical radio stations, for example, that were launched in Italy and France subsequently closed down (Lewis and Booth 1989), while alternative film, newspaper, magazine, book and cable TV/video companies have generally had a chequered history (Downing 1985). There remain, however, some outstanding successes like the Radio Pacifica network in the United States (Barlow 1993).

Media in Liberal Democracies

The media do not occupy, in reality, the no-man's land of the liberal imagination. They are rarely autonomous institutions in the idealized way in which they are often presented. On the contrary, they tend to be predisposed in favour of dominant social forces in multiple ways: through unrepresentative and concentrated forms of ownership, through the dynamics of the market that limit competition by resource-poor groups and are skewed towards affluent consumers, through the news values and aesthetic conventions of routine media operations, and through the cultural and political pressures that arise from the unequal division of power in society.

However, the media can also be exposed to countervailing tendencies in society. Not all pressures flow in one direction, as they are assumed to do in radical functionalist analysis. To adapt the terminology of Herman and Chomsky, there are also 'counter-filters' – channels of influence or potential influence that can pull the media in the other direction. Subordinate groups can gain increased access by securing the institutional reform of the media through the agency of the democratic state. Through collective organization in civil society, they can renew and strengthen the collectivist and egalitarian traditions that are part of the culture of many liberal democracies. They can also influence the character of privately owned media via source competition, consumer power, market challenges and the desire of some media professional staff, central to their self-concept, to serve a wider public.

The media are generally neither the 'voice of the people' nor agencies of domination. Rather, they are often institutions which have close links to established forms of power but which are also exposed to countervailing pressures. This accounts for the often ambiguous position of media systems in liberal democracies. They are frequently neither fully independent of, nor fully subordinated to, the structure of power in society.

Yet, how the media function in society depends upon the way in which pressures and counter-pressures are played out in the wider social and political context. One only has to consider media systems in individual countries to be alert to the widely different ways in which the media relate to society, reflecting differences in the organization of the media and in the configuration of power in those countries. In the United States, where class-based opposition to existing social arrangements is extremely weak, the media are powerfully shaped both by competing elites and populist market pressures (Gitlin 1994; Hallin 1994). In Italy, the media were – until the recent crisis of its political system – partly balkanized into enclaves controlled by class-based social blocs (Mazzoleni 1992; Mancini 1991; Wagner-Pacifici 1986). In Britain, the broadcasting media approximate to the metaphor of a contested space fought over by opposed, class-based social coalitions. Yet, in Norway, the media function primarily as agencies of a liberal corporatist consensus based on an agreed social settlement between organized labour and corporate business (and other social interests) mediated through the social democratic state (Syvertsen 1992, 1994; Host 1990). In Singapore's authoritarian 'liberal democracy', by contrast, the domestic media would seem to be more uncompromisingly agencies supporting the ascendancy of a relatively cohesive, dominant power bloc (Kuo et al. 1993; Hachten 1989; Ramaprasad and Ong 1990).

In short, the media in liberal democracies are often exposed to pressures from above and below. But how these pressures are manifested – and even whether counter-pressures are present in a significant form – depends upon the specific context in which the media operate.

Reassessing Media Influence

So far we have only considered media processes and how they affect the media's relationship to society. However, it is difficult to assess the media's position in society without also assessing their influence on audiences. As we have seen, there are two contrasting views. One sees the media as dominating the audience, the other sees the audience as dominating the media. Yet, there is a grey area between these two polarized positions which needs to be explored more fully. In order to do this, it is worth drawing eclectically upon all traditions of audience research – effects research, ethnographic audience research ('reception studies') and 'moral panic' studies – to see what they can tell us.

Power of Reinforcement

Studies in all three audience research traditions make one key point: the media are powerful agencies of reinforcement.

Ironically, the tradition that documents this most extensively makes the least of it. Thus, when Lazarsfeld and his associates (1944) found that the main effect of the media in the 1940 American presidential campaign was to activate people to vote in the way in which they intended, they concluded that the media's influence had been minimal. The media's role was likened by them to providing signposts guiding people to a predetermined destination. This denial of reinforcement as a significant influence has persisted, despite some dissenters, throughout the history of effects research. For example, Perloff (1993) classifies any media effect that does not involve a change consciously sought as a non-effect.

Yet, Lazarsfeld and associates' core finding of media reinforcement in election campaigns has been repeatedly replicated, though with significant modifications due to increased voter volatility. Summarizing a large body of research into the influence of the media in election campaigns, the following conclusions emerge: the media can cause a small number of people to switch votes or stay at home as a protest; they can influence a larger number of people to revise their perceptions of key issues, leaders and party performance; but their main impact is to galvanize people to vote in ways which are consistent with their 'predispositional characteristics' (Miller 1991; Harrop 1987; Blumler and Gurevitch 1982; Blumler and McQuail 1968). The heat generated by mass-mediated political debate tends to activate latent partisanship. This power of reinforcement (which is not as easy to measure as change) is further borne out by research which shows that the amount of attention given by television to election campaigns significantly affects the level of turn-out (Blumler 1977).

In general, effects research reveals that people tend to derive reinforcement from elements of communication which accord with what they think. How they assess the quality of communications (such as party political broadcasts in Britain), or who they think won the argument (as in the famous Kennedy-Nixon televised debates) is powerfully influenced by their prior opinions (Katz and Feldman 1962; Blumler and McQuail 1968; cf. Vidmar and Rokeach 1974). Consequently, successful information campaigns tend to make a personal connection with audiences in the sense of linking up to their needs or beliefs (Perloff 1993; Harris 1989). Media persuasion often takes the form of canalization, that is to say channelling attitudes and behaviour in different but similar directions. For example, a widely viewed 1969 TV programme, *The Royal Family*, which portrayed the Queen in informal settings, did not convert republicans into monarchists but increased the number of monarchists who perceived the Queen to be 'in touch', 'relaxed' and 'modern' (BBC cit. Curran 1996).

Selective Reinforcement

Effects research is generally conceived within a 'transportation' model in which the media are the starting point and audiences are the terminus. However, the reinforcing power of the media takes on a different meaning if it is considered in terms of a radical framework in which the media are assumed to be linked, in some way, to the power structure of society.

This is the framework in which most moral panic studies are situated. The best of these argue that the media are able to mobilize a moral panic around a particular issue, perceived to be symptomatic of a wider malaise in society, because they are reinforcing existing attitudes and providing a focus for current frustrations and discontents. Thus, Stuart Hall and his colleagues (1978) show how the press generated growing public indignation against muggers partly in response to a public relations initiative by the police. This succeeded, they argued, because it drew upon well-established images of deviance, hostility towards black immigrants, fears and resentments arising from social change and a set of well-embedded social values. Similarly, Golding and Middleton (1982) argue that a tabloid offensive against welfare cheats succeeded in mobilizing public anger partly because it drew upon a deeply entrenched animosity towards the 'undeserving poor' that can be traced back over four centuries, and because it fanned the resentments of those in work who were suffering a fall in living standards during a recession. Similarly, again, Simon Watney (1987) argues that the way in which the outbreak of AIDS was reported in the British press mobilized increased hostility towards gays because it drew upon homophobic attitudes, still enshrined in legal and theological proscriptions.

The other, important part of the moral panics thesis is that they involve *selective* processes. First, they are triggered by selective media definitions of reality. The media moral panic about mugging, argue Hall et al. (1978), was based on a misleading claim that there was an unprecedented increase in a new strain of crime when the crime was not new and its increase was not unprecedented. The tabloid press's focus on welfare payments to the poor, Golding and Middleton (1982) point out, chose to concentrate on its abuse by the 'work-shy' rather than the fact that large numbers of the poor were not claiming the welfare payments to which they were entitled. Similarly, Watney (1987) and Kitzinger (1993) point out that the initial British press spotlight on AIDS greatly exaggerated the risk of casual contagion, and portrayed gays, drug addicts and prostitutes as 'threats' to the 'innocent' community.

Second, these media definitions reinforce or orchestrate selectively within a field of competing public discourses. They support some discourses, and withhold support from or actively undermine others, in a context where public attitudes are not monistic. Punitive attitudes towards criminals can coexist with negative images of the police. Anger directed at welfare cheats can go hand in hand with collectivist support for the welfare state. Hostility towards gays can be accompanied by sympathy for those dying in discomfort. What moral panics do, it is claimed, is to define reality in a way that supports some attitudes and weakens others.

This process of selective reinforcement did have significant consequences in the three cases that we have considered. The moral panic about muggers led more people to demand tougher punishments, and seemingly fuelled support for a time for the creation of a more authoritarian state (Hall et al. 1978). The moral panic about 'scroungers' resulted in increased public criticism of welfare payments, and weakened welfarist attitudes (Golding and Middleton 1982).[23] And the moral panic about AIDS gave rise to more widespread hostility towards homosexuals, as well as unrealistic fears about the threat posed by the 'killer plague'.[24]

The stress on the selective processes involved in moral panics is important because it differentiates this tradition (at least in its refined form) from a leading strand of effects research. Reinforcement can be conceived as a closed circuit in which the media (or elements of media communications) and audiences are locked in a cycle of mutual reinforcement, the outcome of which is merely the fortification of existing beliefs and patterns of behaviour. What the best of moral panic studies argue, by contrast, is that the media selectively reinforce elements of popular consciousness in ways that produce a shift or realignment of attitudes. This argument is usually presented in terms of the media's buttressing of 'dominant' social norms or political perspectives in the context of a right-wing mobilization of the public. However, subordinate groups can reverse this process by winning media support for counter-definitions that strengthen progressive elements in popular culture.

This is the theme of a study of a failed moral panic in the early 1980s. Initially, a tabloid campaign against the left-wing Greater London Council (GLC) weakened support for it in the local community by projecting it as a profligate sponsor of 'loony left' causes, and contributed to a decision by the government to close it down as an unnecessary expense. However, the GLC succeeded in redefining the central issue posed by its closure as that of local democracy, and was able to draw upon deeply rooted democratic values, local patriotism, and anti-authoritarianism. The large majority of Londoners sided with the GLC, and in the process support for left-wing policies and an active interventionist role for local government also strengthened (Curran 1996).

Both this study and moral panic research in general invoke 'weak' notions of media influence. They assume that the media are influential only if they work with the grain of existing audience predispositions. The media can selectively reinforce some attitudes but not others by making salient a particular definition of a topic or event. Support for the view that the media can have this definitional influence is to be found in research into the cognitive influence of the media, already referred to,[25] which shows that the media can influence popular agendas and frameworks of understanding.

Audience Activity

The general thrust of this argument might seem to run counter to the tenor of ethnographic audience research. This emphasizes that there are no fixed meanings in media texts; that these are created through the interplay of text and audience; and that this interplay is powerfully influenced by the discourses that audiences bring to their media consumption (Fiske 1989c; Corner et al. 1990; Neuman et al. 1992; Schlesinger et al. 1992).

But while audiences are active and selective, this does not necessarily mean that they are 'in control' (Morley 1992b). Audience responses are generally not entirely random and wilful. As a useful ethnographic study demonstrates, audiences are also influenced by signifying mechanisms in texts. 'Viewers rarely invent meanings', concludes Birgitta Hoijer (1990), 'that have no support in the programme.'

Furthermore, *how* audiences are active is influenced by the backgrounds, experiences and outlooks of audience members, and the wider distribution of meanings in society. The first point is well documented in David Morley's seminal study of audience reactions to the former television news magazine programme, *Nationwide*. This showed that groups of viewers (such as bank managers and working-class apprentices) who broadly shared the perspective of the programme were much less critical in their responses than others (like trade union officials and students in higher education) who came from more radical milieux (Morley 1980).

This general point needs to be understood in terms of a wider social context. If large numbers of people are oppositional or alienated, this produces a general pattern of adversarial audience responses to 'mainstream' media. This would seem to have been the case in Iran in the period leading up to the well-supported, popular uprising that led to the deposition of the Shah in 1979. The broadcasting media were controlled by the elite centred around the upstart Pahlavi dynasty, and reflected official policy. They reached a population increasingly alienated by the regime's policy of westernization and secularization, accompanied by rising inflation, deepening inequalities between rich and poor, and growing repression. This disaffection was fanned by an active, broad-based opposition, and sustained by a well-developed social network based on the bazaars and mosques as well as by an alternative media system (Hobsbawm 1994; Mohammadi 1990). Television's lack of influence (before it was silenced by a lengthy strike) is, thus, to be explained partly by the fact that it encountered a strong culture and social network of opposition.

However, the pattern of audience responses is less adversarial in consensual societies. Audiences do not cease to be active and selective. But the pattern of selectivity is more inclined to take the form of selective reinforcement rather than of outright rejection. This comes through in a key ethnographic study of American audience responses to the *Cosby Show*, a long-running situation comedy series featuring a well-to-do black doctor and his family (Jhally and Lewis 1992).

Jhally and Lewis found that the series had a skilful ambiguity which enabled dissimilar groups of viewers to identify with the family in the series. They also show that different viewers responded to the *Cosby Show* in divergent ways. For many black viewers, its positive portrayal of a successful black family was a feature of its appeal since it contrasted with the often negative ways in which African Americans were portrayed on television. However, many white viewers found in the series reassuring confirmation that racism had become a thing of the past, making it possible for anyone to prosper and succeed in American society.

But these different reactions took place in a society where many African Americans have not prospered, primarily because of their class position and racial disadvantage in a society where vertical mobility is, in fact, rather restricted. This wider context tended to be excluded in the series. Indeed, in celebrating the success of a talented, black family, the series tacitly affirmed the American Dream.

The *Cosby Show* had the effect, argue Jhally and Lewis, of reinforcing a complex set of attitudes among many white viewers – what they call 'enlightened racism'. This took the form of positive acceptance of middle-class families like the one featured in the series, combined with a view of blacks as a whole as culturally inferior since they had 'failed' in American society. Among black viewers, it produced more differentiated and perplexed responses about what the series revealed about reality. But underlying both sets of responses was a widely shared acceptance of the meritocratic mythology of the American society (at least in terms of its denial of class) which the series upheld.

The influence of the programme series (which has spawned a number of imitations) is thus presented as being oblique but potent. It sustained among white viewers discriminatory attitudes indirectly – and indeed, unexpectedly, since a positive image of African Americans was being presented – by reinforcing a perception of the United States as an open-opportunity society in the context of public awareness of the relative lack of material 'success' among blacks. What the study revealed, in other words, was a pattern of selective reinforcement as well as of active audience response.

Retrospective

A wave of revisionist criticism has undermined the radical functionalist tradition that was once at the heart of radical media studies. The key assumptions of that tradition – its conception of the concentration of power in monopoly capitalism, its portrayal of the media as being integrated into the power structure of society, and its conviction that the media are powerful agencies indoctrinating an already dominated public – have fallen like dominoes before the relentless pressure of revisionist argument.

Yet, this revisionist movement has been strangely one-sided. It has been directed at the fundamentalist Left positions of an older generation of radical academics without addressing the liberal pluralist tradition that this generation once confronted. The result has been a lopsided development of media and cultural studies in which revisionist criticism has destabilized one tradition without weakening its adversary (which has remained dominant in many parts of the world). Indeed, some radical revisionist critics have moved towards positions that are, in fact, rather close to classic liberal perspectives or have generated arguments that fit readily within the liberal-pluralist tradition. This tradition has also been reinvigorated during the last ten years by the development of liberal functionalist arguments derived from Durkheimian sociology and borrowings from social anthropology.

However, the liberal canon is also vulnerable to attack, and this essay has pointed to some of its weaknesses. In particular, it overstates in general the autonomy of the media from the hierarchy of power; it is often blind to conflicts of interest in society; and it tends, even in its 'new wave' form, to understate the media's ideological influence.

What is needed, it has been argued, is a reappraisal that responds to the weaknesses of *both* the liberal and radical paradigms. The radical conception of the media as a top-down agency of control and its antithesis, that of the media as a bottom-up agency of empowerment, need to be revised in favour of the view that the media are more often institutions which are exposed to cross-pressures both from above and below. Similarly, the conception of the dominated or obstinate audience that is associated with the two traditions needs to take account of the way in which audiences can be both self-willed and also subject to significant media influence. The main way in which this influence tends to work is through selective media reinforcement of existing cognitions and attitudes.

However, this argument is presented in a contingent form. The media can be exposed to both elite and popular pressures, and can selectively reinforce within a field of contending discourses. But what actually happens depends upon the particular configurations of society at a given point in time. There is no acceptable, universally valid model of the media despite the siren calls of functionalists of all denominations.

Notes

1 An attempt has been made to differentiate this description from that in Chapter 11 by taking a longer timespan, paying more attention to liberal-pluralist arguments, and by being more explicitly prescriptive. I have also sought to minimize overlap by shrinking the description of certain arguments in this chapter. This said, this chapter can be usefully read in conjunction with Chapters 11, 12 and 13.

2 The word 'liberal' means different things in American and English. In American it means radical, whereas in English it means centrist. In a political context, this latter meaning is associated with support for individual rights and market competition, as well as democracy and social improvement.

3 This view is often expressed by right-wing politicians, and in my experience by radical and feminist students. A considered academic presentation of it from a conservative perspective is presented by Noelle-Neumann (1981).

4 This is outlined more fully in Chapter 11.

5 Hoijer (1992) argues rightly that I understated the importance of the cognitive psychological tradition in the review, reprinted as Chapter 11, and supplies a useful account. For an alternative and more detailed survey of this tradition, see Harris (1989). A well-known and accessible study is Graber (1988).

6 The review by McCombs (1994), though good, should be treated with caution since he only highlights those studies which support the media agenda-setting hypothesis.

7 For an exchange which illustrates some of the methodological difficulties of distinguishing between media and non-media influences, see the acrimonious debate between Hirsch (1980, 1981a and 1981b) and Gerbner et al. (1981).

8 See Schudson (1993) for a useful antidote to the romanticization of rational political discourse in the pre-television era.

9 Part 1 of Schramm and Roberts (1971) provides a guide to how early liberal functionalist theory developed in relation to the media.

10 In retrospect, they can be seen as part of a wider intellectual movement in which radical revisionist historians, using rather similar arguments, challenged the notion of 'bourgeois domination' in Victorian Britain.
11 For further discussion of these arguments, see Stuart Hall in Chapter 1 of this book.
12 For useful surveys of the evolution of the cultural studies tradition in Britain, see in particular Turner (1990) and McGuigan (1992).
13 Schlesinger's key essay (1990) launched what seems set to be a small cottage industry of researchers investigating news sources. While he cites excerpts from Stuart Hall's writing on the subject that certainly sustain his accusation of ahistorical functionalism, the wider framework of Hall's more general and evolving argument points by implication to a different and more complex analysis of the operation of news sources.
14 A useful overview of the literature is provided by Dijk (1991).
15 See Chapter 11.
16 For an excellent development of this theme, see the lengthy introduction in Mukerji and Schudson (1991).
17 One problem with all such estimates is that they need to take properly into account run-in costs before a new enterprise can be expected to make a profit. On this basis, the figures given are probably underestimates.
18 However, the physical limitation of the number of channels was sometimes offset by a public service commitment to pluralism.
19 For sceptical accounts of the 'censorship' powers of advertisers, see Curran (1978, 1980 and 1986). For an alternative view, see an excellent study by Baker (1994).
20 However, a number of commentators in the cultural studies tradition exaggerate the extent of the change that has taken place. For evidence of the continuity of class-based voting since 1964, see Heath et al. (1991), and for the continued importance of class in shaping attitudes and identities, see Marshall et al. (1989).
21 However, this consistently interesting writer seems to have shifted – or be shifting – positions. See Sparks (1993).
22 For a useful discussion of theories of the state from a European perspective, see Dunleavy and O'Leary (1987); from an American perspective, see Alford and Friedland (1985).
23 Golding and Middleton show, on the basis of a local survey, the way in which welfarist attitudes were weakened. Further evidence supporting the conclusion that the tabloid campaign against 'scroungers' influenced public attitudes is to be found in Crewe (1988: 34 (Table 1)) who reports that the proportion of people who said that welfare benefits available to people had gone 'much to far' rose from 34 to 50 per cent between 1974 and 1979.
24 Watney fails to provide concrete evidence that press reporting did have an influence. However, this is supported by Kitzinger's ethnographic audience study (1993). It is also consistent with survey evidence presented by Brook (1988), who shows that in 1987, no less than 60 per cent thought that AIDS would kill more people than any other disease in the next five years, while those saying that homosexual relations were always or mostly wrong increased from 62 to 74 per cent between 1983 and 1987.
25 See page 125.

References

ABERCROMBIE, N., HILL, S. and TURNER, B., 1984: *The Dominant Ideology Thesis.* London: Allen & Unwin.

ALEXANDER, J., 1981: 'The Mass Media in Systematic, Historical and Comparative Perspective', in E. Katz and T. Szecsko (eds.) *Mass Media and Social Change*. Beverly Hills, CA: Sage.

ALFORD, R. and FRIEDLAND, R., 1985: *Powers of Theory: Capitalism, the State, and Democracy*. Cambridge: Cambridge University Press.

ALLEN, C., 1993: *Eisenhower and the Mass Media*. Chapel Hill, NC: University of North Carolina Press.

ALTHUSSER, L., 1984: *Essays on Ideology*. London: Verso.

ANDERSON, A., 1991: 'Source Strategies and the Communication of Environmental Affairs', *Media, Culture and Society*, 13 (4).

ANG, I. and HERMES, J., 1991: 'Gender and/in Media Consumption', in J. Curran and M. Gurevitch (eds.) *Mass Media and Democracy*. London: Edward Arnold.

BAGDIKIAN, B., 1992: *Media Monopoly*, 4th edition. Boston, MA: Beacon Press.

BAKER, C.E., 1994: *Advertising and a Democratic Press*. Princeton, NJ: Princeton University Press.

BARLOW, W., 1993: 'Democratic Praxis and Pacifica Radio', in O. Manaev and Y. Pryliuk (eds.) *Media in Transition*. Kyiv: Abris.

BARNETT, S. and CURRY, A., 1994: *The Battle for the BBC*. London: Arium.

BEHARRELL, P., 1993: 'AIDS and the British Press', in J. Eldridge (ed.) *Getting the Message*. London: Routledge.

BLUMLER, J. (ed.), 1977: *Communicating to Voters*. London: Sage.

BLUMLER, J., 1991: 'The New Television Marketplace: Imperatives, Implications, Issues', in J. Curran and M. Gurevitch (eds.) *Mass Media and Society*. London: Edward Arnold.

BLUMLER, J. and GUREVITCH, M., 1982: 'The Political Effects of Mass Communication', in M. Gurevitch, T. Bennett, J. Curran and J. Woollacott (eds.) *Culture, Society and the Media*. London: Methuen.

BLUMLER, J. and GUREVITCH, M., 1986: 'Journalists' Orientations to Political Institutions: The Case of Parliamentary Broadcasting', in P. Golding, G. Murdock, and P. Schlesinger (eds.) *Communicating Politics*. Leicester: Leicester University Press.

BLUMLER, J. and KATZ, E., 1974: *The Uses of Mass Communications*. Beverly Hills, CA: Sage.

BLUMLER, J. and MCLEOD, J., 1983: 'Communication and Voter Turn-out in Britain', in T. Leggatt (ed.) *Sociological Theory and Survey Research*. Beverly Hills, CA: Sage.

BLUMLER, J. and MCQUAIL, D., 1968: *Television in Politics*. London: Faber & Faber.

BROOK, L., 1988: 'The Public's Response to AIDS', in R. Jowell, S. Witherspoon and L. Brook (eds.) *British Social Attitudes: The 1986 Report*, 5th report. Aldershot: Gower.

BROWN, J. and SCHULTZE, L., 1990: 'The Effects of Race, Gender and Fandom on Audience Interpretations of Madonna's Music Videos', *Journal of Communication*, 40 (2).

BROWNE, D., 1989: *Comparing Broadcasting Systems*. Ames, IA: Iowa State University Press.

BUERKEL-ROTHFUSS, N. with MAYES, S., 1981: 'Soap Opera Viewing: The Cultivation Effect', *Journal of Communication*, 31.

BURNETT, R., 1990: *Concentration and Diversity in the International Phonogram Industry*. Gothenburg: University of Gothenburg.

BURNS, T., 1977: *The BBC: Public Institution and Private World*. London: Macmillan.

CANTOR, M., 1971: *The Hollywood TV Producer*. New York: Basic Books.

CANTOR, M. and CANTOR, J., 1992: *Prime Time Television*, 2nd edition. Newbury Park, CA: Sage.

Cardiff, D. and Scannell, P., 1987: 'Broadcasting and National Unity', in J. Curran, A. Smith and P. Wingate (eds.) *Impacts and Influences*. London: Methuen.
Carey, J., 1992: *Communication as Culture*. London: Routledge.
Chadwick, P., 1989: *Media Mates*. Melbourne: Macmillan.
Chaney, D., 1986: 'The Symbolic Form of Ritual in Mass Communication', in P. Golding, J. Murdock, and P. Schlesinger (eds.) *Communicating Politics*. Leicester: Leicester University Press.
Clarke, G., 1990: 'Defending Ski-Jumpers: A Critique of Theories of Youth Sub-Cultures', in S. Frith and A. Goodwin (eds.) *On Record*. London: Routledge.
Clarke, J., 1976: 'The Skinheads and the Magical Recovery of Working Class Community', in S. Hall and T. Jefferson (eds.) *Resistance through Rituals*. London: Hutchinson.
Clarke, J., Hall, S., Jefferson, T., and Roberts, B., 1976: 'Subcultures, Cultures and Class', in S. Hall and T. Jefferson (eds.) *Resistance Through Rituals*. London: Hutchinson.
Cockerell, M., 1988: *Live From No. 10*, 2nd edition. London: Faber & Faber.
Cohen, P., 1972: 'Sub-Cultural Conflict and Working Class Community', *Working Papers in Cultural Studies*, 2.
Coleman, J., 1973: *Power and the Structure of Society*. New York: Norton.
Collins, R., 1990: *Television: Policy and Culture*. London: Unwin Hyman.
Connell, I., 1980: 'Television News and the Social Contract', in S. Hall, D. Hobson, A. Lowe and P. Willis (eds.) *Culture, Media, Language*. London: Hutchinson.
Corner, J., Richardson, K. and Fenton, N., 1990: *Nuclear Reactions*. London: Libbey.
Crewe, I., 1988: 'Has the Electorate Become Thatcherite?', in R. Skidelsky (ed.) *Thatcherism*. London: Chatto & Windus.
Curran, J., 1977: 'Capitalism and Control of the Press, 1800–1975', in J. Curran, M. Gurevitch and J. Woollacott (eds.) *Mass Communication and Society*. London: Edward Arnold.
Curran, J., 1978: 'Advertising and the Press', in J. Curran (ed.) *The British Press*. London: Macmillan.
Curran, J., 1980: 'Advertising as a Patronage System', in H. Christian (ed.) *The Sociology of Journalism and the Press*. Sociological Review Monograph 29. Keele: University of Keele Press.
Curran, J., 1986: 'The Impact of Advertising on the British Mass Media', in R. Collins, J. Curran, N. Garnham, P. Scannell, P. Schlesinger and C. Sparks (eds.) *Media, Culture and Society: A Critical Reader*. London: Sage.
Curran, J., 1987: 'The Boomerang Effect: The Press and the Battle for London, 1981–6', in J. Curran, A. Smith and P. Wingate (eds.) *Impacts and Influences*. London: Methuen.
Curran, J., 1990: 'Culturalist Perspectives of News Organisations: A Reappraisal and Case Study', in M. Ferguson (ed.) *Public Communication*. London: Sage.
Curran, J., 1991: 'Mass Media and Democracy: A Reappraisal', in J. Curran and M. Gurevitch (eds.) *Mass Media and Society*. London: Edward Arnold.
Curran, J., 1996: *Media and Power*. London: Routledge.
Curran, J., Douglas, A. and Whannel, G., 1980: 'The Political Economy of the Human-Interest Story', in A. Smith (ed.) *Newspapers and Democracy*. Cambridge, MA: MIT Press.
Curran, J. and Seaton, J., 1991: *Power Without Responsibility*, 4th edition. London: Routledge.
D'Acci, J., 1994: *Defining Women*. Chapel Hill, NC: University of North Carolina Press.

DAVIS, J., 1986: 'British and American Attitudes: Similarities and Contrasts', in R. Jowell, S. Witherspoon and L. Brook (eds.) *British Social Attitudes*. Aldershot: Gower.

DAYAN, D. and KATZ, E., 1987: 'Performing Media Events', in J. Curran, A. Smith and P. Wingate (eds.) *Impacts and Influences*. London: Methuen.

DAYAN, D. and KATZ, E., 1992: *Media Events*. Cambridge, MA: Harvard University Press.

DEFLEUR, M. and BALL-ROKEACH, S., 1989: *Theories of Mass Communication*, 5th edition. New York: Longman.

DIJK, T.A. VAN, 1991: *Racism and the Press*. London: Routledge.

DMITRAS, P., 1992: 'Greece', in E. Ostergaard (ed.) *The Media in Western Europe*. London: Sage.

DOWNING, J., 1980: *The Media Machine*. London: Pluto.

DOWNING, J., 1985: *Radical Media*. Boston, MA: South End Press.

DUNLEAVY, P. and O'LEARY, B., 1987: *Theories of the State*. London: Macmillan.

EISENSTEIN, E., 1978: *The Printing Press as an Agent of Change*, 2 vols. Cambridge: Cambridge University Press.

ELLIOTT, P., 1977: 'Media Organisations and Occupations: An Overview', in J. Curran, M. Gurevitch and J. Woollacott (eds.) *Mass Communication and Society*. London: Edward Arnold.

ELLIOTT, P., 1980: 'Press Performance as a Political Ritual', in H. Christian (ed.) *The Sociology of Journalism and the Press*. Sociological Review Monograph 29. Keele: University of Keele Press.

EMERY, E., 1972: *The Press in America*, 3rd edition. Englewood Cliffs, NJ: Prentice-Hall.

ENTMAN, R., 1989: *Democracy Without Citizens*. New York: Oxford University Press.

EPSTEIN, E., 1973: *News from Nowhere*. New York: Random.

EPSTEIN, E., 1975: *Between Fact and Fiction*. New York: Vintage.

ERICSON, R., BARANEC, P. and CHAN, J., 1987: *Visualizing Deviance*. Milton Keynes: Open University Press.

ERICSON, R., BARANEC, P., and CHAN, J., 1989: *Negotiating Control*. Milton Keynes: Open University Press.

ETZIONI-HALEVY, E., 1987: *National Broadcasting Under Siege*. London: Macmillan.

EUROPEAN COMMISSION, 1992: *Pluralism and Media Concentration in the Internal Market*. Brussels: EC.

FERGUSON, M., 1983: *Forever Feminine*. London: Heinemann.

FERGUSON, M., 1990: 'Electronic Media and the Redefining of Time and Space', in M. Ferguson (ed.) *Public Communication*. London: Sage.

FISHMAN, M., 1980: *Manufacturing the News*. Austin, TX: University of Texas.

FISKE, J., 1987: *Television Culture*. London: Methuen.

FISKE, J., 1989a: *Reading the Popular*. Boston, MA: Unwin Hyman.

FISKE, J., 1989b: *Understanding Popular Culture*. Boston, MA: Unwin Hyman.

FISKE, J., 1989c: 'Moments of Television: Neither the Text nor the Audience', in E. Seiter, H. Borchers, G. Kreutzner and E-M. Warth (eds.) *Remote Control*. London: Routledge.

FISKE, J., 1991: 'Postmodernism and Television', in J. Curran and M. Gurevitch (eds.) *Mass Media and Society*. London: Edward Arnold.

FOUCAULT, M., 1980: *Power/Knowledge*. Brighton: Harvester.

FOUCAULT, M., 1982: 'Afterword: The Subject and Power', in H. Dreyfus and P. Rabinow (eds.) *Michel Foucault: Beyond Structuralism and Hermeneutics*. Chicago: University of Chicago Press.

FRANKLIN, B. and MURPHY, D., 1991: *What News? The Market, Politics and the Local Press*. London: Routledge.

FRENKEL, E., 1994: *The Press and Politics in Israel*. Westport, CT: Greenwood.

FRITH, S., 1987: 'The Industrialisation of Popular Music', in J. Lull (ed.) *Popular Music and Communication*. Beverly Hills, CA: Sage.

GANDY, O., 1982: *Beyond Agenda Setting*. Norwood, NJ: Ablex.

GANS, H., 1980: *Deciding What's News*. London: Constable.

GERBNER, G., GROSS, L., MORGAN, M. and SIGNORIELLI, N., 1981: 'Final Reply to Hirsch', *Communication Research*, 8 (3).

GERBNER, G., GROSS, L., MORGAN, M., and SIGNORIELLI, N., 1986: 'Living with Television: The Dynamics of the Cultivation Process', in J. Bryant and D. Zillmann (eds.) *Perspectives on Media Effects*. Hillsdale, NJ: Erlbaum.

GERBNER, G., GROSS, L., MORGAN, M. and SIGNORIELLI, N., 1994: 'Growing Up with Television: The Cultivation Perspective', in J. Bryant and D. Zillman (eds.) *Media Effects*. Hillsdale, NJ: Erlbaum.

GILES, F., 1986: *Sundry Times*. London: Murray.

GITLIN, T., 1990: 'Bites and Blips: Chunk News, Savvy Talk and the Bifurcation of American Politics' in P. Dahlgren and C. Sparks (eds.) *Communication and Citizenship*. London: Routledge.

GITLIN, T., 1991: 'The Politics of Communication and the Communication of Politics', in J. Curran and M. Gurevitch (eds.) *Mass Media and Society*. London: Edward Arnold.

GITLIN, T., 1994: *Inside Prime Time*, revised edition. London: Routledge.

GLASGOW UNIVERSITY MEDIA GROUP, 1976: *Bad News*. London: Routledge & Kegan Paul.

GOLDING, P., 1981: 'The Missing Dimensions – News Media and the Management of Social Change', in E. Katz and T. Szescho (eds.) *Mass Media and Social Change*. Beverly Hills, CA: Sage.

GOLDING, P., 1990: 'Political Communication and Citizenship: The Media and Democracy in an Inegalitarian Order', in M. Ferguson (ed.) *Public Communication*. London: Sage.

GOLDING, P. and ELLIOTT, P., 1979: *Making the News*. London: Longman.

GOLDING, P. and MIDDLETON, S., 1982: *Images of Welfare*. Oxford: Martin Robertson.

GOLDING, P. and MURDOCK, M., 1991: 'Culture, Communications, and Political Economy', in J. Curran and M. Gurevitch (eds.) *Mass Media and Society*. London: Edward Arnold.

GRABER, D., 1988: *Processing the News*, 2nd edition, White Plains, NY: Longman.

GRAMSCI, A., 1971: *Selections from Prison Notebooks*. London: Lawrence & Wishart.

GRAMSCI, A., 1981: 'Gramsci', in T. Bennett, G. Martin, C. Mercer and J. Wollacott (eds.) *Culture, Ideology and Social Process*. Milton Keynes: Open University Press.

GRAMSCI, A., 1985: *Selections from Cultural Writings*. London: Lawrence & Wishart.

HACHTEN, W., 1989: 'Media Development Without Press Freedom: Lee Kuan Yew's Singapore', *Journalism Quarterly*, 66.

HALL, S., 1974: 'Deviancy, Politics and the Media', in M. McIntosh and P. Rock (eds.) *Deviancy and Social Control*. London: Tavistock.

HALL, S., 1977: 'Culture, the Media and the "Ideological Effect" ', in J. Curran, M. Gurevitch and J. Woollacott (eds.) *Mass Communication and Society*. London: Edward Arnold.

HALL, S., 1982: 'The Rediscovery of "Ideology": Return of the Repressed in Media Studies', in M. Gurevitch, T. Bennett, J. Curran and J. Woollacott (eds.) *Culture, Society and the Media*. London: Methuen.

HALL, S., 1985: 'Signification, Representation, Ideology: Althusser and the Post-Structuralist Debates', *Critical Studies in Mass Communication*, 2 (2). (Reprinted in this book).

HALL, S., 1986: 'Media Power and Class Power', in J. Curran, J. Ecclestone, G. Oakley and R. Richardson (eds.) *Bending Reality*. London: Pluto.

HALL, S., CRITCHER, C., JEFFERSON, T., CLARKE, J. and ROBERTS, B., 1978: *Policing the Crisis*. London: Macmillan.

HALLIN, D., 1986: *The 'Uncensored War'*. Berkeley and Los Angeles: University of California Press.

HALLIN, D., 1994: *We Keep America on Top of the World*. London: Routledge.

HALLIN, D., and MANCINI, P. 1984: 'Speaking of the President: Political Structure and Representational Form in US and Italian Television News', *Theory and Society*, 13.

HANSEN, A., 1991: 'The Media and the Social Construction of the Environment', *Media, Culture and Society*, 13 (4).

HARRIS, R., 1989: *A Cognitive Psychology of Mass Communication*. Hillsdale, NJ: Erlbaum.

HARROP, M., 1987: 'Voters', in J. Seaton and B. Pimlott (eds.) *The Media in British Politics*. Aldershot: Avebury.

HARTMANN, P. and HUSBAND, C., 1974: *Racism and the Mass Media*. London: Davis-Poynter.

HEATH, A., CURTICE, J., JOWELL, R., EVANS, G., FIELD, J. and WITHERSPOON, S., 1991: *Understanding Political Change*. Oxford: Pergamon.

HEBDIGE, D., 1979: *Subculture*. London: Methuen.

HEBDIGE, D., 1988: *Hiding in the Light*. London: Routledge.

HERMAN, E. and CHOMSKY, N., 1988: *Manufacturing Consent*. New York: Pantheon.

HESS, S., 1984: *The Government/Press Connection*. Washington DC: Brookings Institution.

HETHERINGTON, A., 1985: *News, Newspapers and Television*. London: Macmillan.

HIRSCH, P., 1972: 'Processing Fads and Fashions', *American Journal of Sociology*, 77.

HIRSCH, P., 1980: 'The "Scary World" of the Non-Viewer and Other Anomalies: A Reanalysis of Gerbner et al.'s Findings on Cultivation Analysis Part 1', *Communication Research*, 7.

HIRSCH, P., 1981a: 'On Not Learning from One's Own Mistakes: A Reanalysis of Gerbner et al.'s Findings on Cultivation Analysis Part 2', *Communication Research*, 8.

HIRSCH, P., 1981b: 'Distinguishing Good Speculation from Bad Theory: Rejoinder to Gerbner et al.', *Communication Research*, 8.

HOBSBAWM, E., 1994: *Age of Extremes*. London: Michael Joseph.

HOFFMANN-RIEM, W., 1992: 'Protecting Vulnerable Values in the German Broadcasting Order', in J. Blumler (ed.) *Television and the Public Interest*. London: Sage.

HOIJER, B., 1990: 'Studying Viewers' Reception of Television Programmes: Theoretical and Methodological Considerations', *European Journal of Communications*, 5 (1).

HOIJER, B., 1992: 'Socio-Cognitive Structures and Television Reception', *Media, Culture and Society*, 14 (4).

HOLUB, R., 1992: *Antonio Gramsci: Beyond Marxism and Postmodernism*. London: Routledge.

HØST, S., 1990: 'The Norwegian Newspaper System: Structure and Development', in H. Ronning and K. Lundby (eds.) *Media and Communication*. Oslo: Norwegian University Press.

HØYER, S., HADENIUS, S. and WEIBULL, L., 1975: *The Politics and Economics of the Press*. London: Sage.

HOYNES, W., 1994: *Public Television for Sale*. Boulder, CO: Westview.

INNIS, H., 1950: *Empire and Communication*. Oxford: Clarendon Press.

IYENGAR, S., 1992: *Is Anyone Responsible? How Television Frames Political Issues*. Chicago: University of Chicago Press.

IYENGAR, S. and KINDER, D., 1987: *News That Matters*. Chicago: University of Chicago Press.

JHALLY, S. and LEWIS, J., 1992: *Enlightened Racism*. Boulder, CO: Westview.

KATZ, E. and FELDMAN, S., 1962: 'The Kennedy-Nixon Debates: A Survey of Surveys', in S. Kraus (ed.) *The Great Debates*. Bloomington, IN: Indiana University Press.

KATZ, E. and LAZARSFELD, P., 1955: *Personal Influence*. Glencoe, IL: Free Press.

KEANE, J., 1991: *The Media and Democracy*. Cambridge: Polity Press.

KELLEY, D. and DONWAY, R., 1990: 'Liberalism and Free Speech', in J. Lichtenberg (ed.) *Democracy and the Mass Media*. New York: Cambridge University Press.

KELLNER, D., 1990: *Television and the Crisis of Democracy*. Boulder, CO: Westview.

KING, C., 1967: *The Future of the Press*. London: MacGibbon & Kee.

KITZINGER, J., 1993: 'Understanding AIDS: Researching Audience Perceptions of Acquired Immune Deficiency Syndrome', in J. Eldridge (ed.) *Getting the Message*. London: Routledge.

KLAPPER, J., 1960: *The Effects of Mass Communication*. New York: Free Press.

KOSS, S., 1984: *The Rise and Fall of the Political Press in Britain*, vol. 2. London: Hamish Hamilton.

KUO, E., HOLADAY, D. and PECK, E., 1993: *Mirror on the Wall*. Singapore: Asian Mass Communication Research and Information Centre.

LANG, G. and LANG, K., 1983: *The Battle for Public Opinion*. New York: Columbia University Press.

LASSWELL, H., 1971: 'The Structure and Function of Communication in Society', in W. Schramm and D. Roberts (eds.) *The Processes and Effects of Mass Communication*. Urbana, IL: University of Illinois Press.

LAZARSFELD, P., BERELSON, B. and GAUDET, H., 1944: *The People's Choice*. New York: Columbia University Press.

LEWIS, P. and BOOTH, J., 1989: *The Invisible Medium*. London: Macmillan.

LORIMER, R. and MCNULTY, J., 1991: *Mass Communication in Canada*. Toronto: McClelland & Stewart.

LOWENTHAL, L., 1961: *Literature, Popular Culture and Society*. Englewood Cliffs, NJ: Prentice-Hall.

LYOTARD, J-F., 1984: *Postmodern Condition*. Manchester: Manchester University Press.

MCCOMBS, M., 1988: 'Concentration, Monopoly and Content', in R. Picard, M. McCombs, J. Winter and S. Lacey (eds.) *Press Concentration and Monopoly*. Norwood, NJ: Ablex.

MCCOMBS, M., 1994: 'News Influence on our Pictures of the World', in J. Bryant and D. Zillman (eds.) *Media Effects*. Hillsdale, NJ: Erlbaum.

MCGUIGAN, J., 1992: *Cultural Populism*. London: Routledge.

MCLEOD, J., BECKER, L. and BYRNES, J., 1974: 'Another Look at the Agenda-Setting Function of the Press', *Communication Research*, 1.

MCLUHAN, M., 1964: *Understanding Media*. London: Routledge & Kegan Paul.

MCMANUS, J., 1994: *Market Driven Journalism*. London: Sage.

MCNAIR, B., 1994: *News and Journalism in the UK*. London: Routledge.

MCQUAIL, D., 1992a: *Media Performance*. London: Sage.

MCQUAIL, D., 1992b: 'The Netherlands: Safeguarding Freedom and Diversity Under Multichannel Conditions', in J. Blumler (ed.) *Television and the Public Interest*. London: Sage.

MCQUAIL, D., 1994: *Mass Communication Theory*, 3rd edition. London: Sage.

McRobbie, A., 1981: 'Settling Accounts with Subculture: A Feminist Critique', in T. Bennett, G. Martin, C. Mercer and J. Woollacott (eds.) *Culture, Ideology and Social Process*. Milton Keynes: Open University Press.

McRobbie, A., 1992: 'Postmarxism and Cultural Studies: A Post-script', in L. Grossberg, C. Nelson and P. Treichler (eds.) *Cultural Studies*. New York: Routledge.

Manca, L., 1989: 'Journalism, Advocacy and a Communication Model for Democracy', in M. Raboy and P. Bruck (eds.) *Communication For and Against Democracy*. Montreal: Black Rose Books.

Mancini, P., 1991: 'The Public Sphere and the Use of News in a "Coalition" System of Government', in P. Dahlgren and C. Sparks (eds.) *Communication and Citizenship*. London: Routledge.

Marcuse, H., 1972: *One Dimensional Man*. London: Sphere.

Marshall, G., Rose, D., Newby, H. and Vogler, C., 1989: *Social Class in Modern Britain*. London: Unwin Hyman.

Martindale, C., 1986: *The White Press and Black America*. New York: Greenwood.

Mazzoleni, G., 1992: 'Is There a Question of Vulnerable Values in Italy?', in J. Blumler (ed.) *Television and the Public Interest*. London: Sage.

Miliband, R., 1973: *The State in Capitalist Society*. London: Quartet.

Miller, D., 1993: 'Official Sources and "Primary Definition": The Case of Northern Ireland', *Media, Culture and Society*, 15 (3).

Miller, D., 1994: 'The Struggle over and Impact of Media Portrayals of Northern Ireland', PhD thesis, University of Glasgow.

Miller, W., 1991: *Media and Voters*. Oxford: Clarendon.

Modleski, T., 1984: *Loving With a Vengeance*. New York: Methuen.

Mohammadi, A., 1990: 'Cultural Imperialism and Cultural Identity', in J. Downing, A. Mohammadi and A. Sreberny-Mohammadi (eds.) *Questioning the Media*. London: Sage.

Morgan, M., 1982: 'Television and Adolescents' Sex-Role Stereotypes: A Longitudinal Study', *Journal of Personality and Social Psychology*, 43.

Morley, D., 1980: *The 'Nationwide' Audience*. London: British Film Institute.

Morley, D., 1981: 'Industrial Conflict and the Mass Media', in S. Cohen and J. Young (eds.) *Manufacture of News*, 2nd edition. London: Constable.

Morley, D., 1992a: 'Populism, Revisionism and the "New" Audience Research', *Journal of Poetics*, 21: pp. 329–44. (Reprinted in this book).

Morley, D., 1992b: *Television, Audiences and Cultural Studies*. London: Routledge.

Mouffe, C., 1981: 'Hegemony and Ideology in Gramsci', in T. Bennett, G. Martin, C. Mercer and J. Woollacott (eds.) *Culture, Ideology and Social Process*. Milton Keynes: Open University Press.

Mukerji, C., and Schudson, M. (eds.), 1991: *Rethinking Popular Culture*. Berkeley, CA: University of California Press.

Murdoch, R., 1989: *Freedom in Broadcasting*. London: News International.

Murdock, G. (1990) 'Redrawing the Map of the Communication Industries: Concentration and Ownership in the Era of Privatization', in M. Ferguson (ed.) *Public Communication*. London: Sage.

Murdock, G. and Golding, P. (1977) 'Capitalism, Communication and Class Relations', in J. Curran, M. Gurevitch and J. Woollacott (eds.) *Mass Communication and Society*. London: Edward Arnold.

Nacos, B., 1990: *The Press, Presidents and Crises*. New York: Columbia University Press.

Nairn, T., 1988: *Enchanted Glass*. London: Century Hutchinson.

Negrine, R., 1994: *Politics and the Mass Media in Britain*, 2nd edition. London: Routledge.

NEUMAN, W., JUST, M. and Crigler, A., 1992: *Common Knowledge*. Chicago: University of Chicago Press.
NEWCOMB, H. and HIRSCH, P., 1984: 'Television as a Cultural Forum: Implications for Research', in W. Rowland and B. Watkins (eds.) *Interpreting Television*. Beverly Hills, CA: Sage.
NEWMAN, B., 1994: *The Marketing of the President*. London: Sage.
NOELLE-NEUMANN, E., 1981: 'Mass Media and Social Change in Developed Societies', in E. Katz and T. Szesko (eds.) *Mass Media and Social Change*. Beverly Hills, CA: Sage.
NOWAK, K., 1984: 'Cultural Indicators in Swedish Advertising 1950–1975', in G. Melischek, K. Rosengren and J. Stappers (eds.) *Cultural Indicators: An International Symposium*. Vienna: Verlag der Osterriechischen Akademie der Wissenschaften.
O'NEILL, O., 1990: 'Practices of Toleration', in J. Lichtenberg (ed.) *Democracy and the Mass Media*. Cambridge: Cambridge University Press.
PARENTI, M., 1993: *Inventing Reality*, 2nd edition. New York: St Martin's Press.
PERLOFF, R., 1993: *The Dynamics of Persuasion*. Hillsdale, NJ: Erlbaum.
PETERSON, T., 1956: 'The Social Responsibility Theory', in F. Siebert, T. Peterson and W. Schramm (eds.) *Four Theories of the Press*. Urbana, IL: University of Illinois Press.
PICARD, R., 1988: *The Ravens of Odin*. Ames, IA: Iowa State University Press.
PORTER, V. and HASSELBACH, S., 1991: *Pluralism, Politics and the Market Place: The Regulation of German Broadcasting*. London: Routledge.
RADWAY, J., 1987: *Reading the Romance*. London: Verso.
RAMAPRASAD, J. and ONG, J., 1990: 'Singapore's Guided Press Policy and its Practice on the Forum Page of the *Straits Times*', *Gazette*, 46.
RANNEY, A., 1983: *Channels of Power*. New York: Basic Books.
ROGERS, E. and DEARING, J., 1988: 'Agenda-Setting Research: Where has it Been and Where is it Going?', in J. Anderson (ed.) *Communication Year Book*, vol. 11. Beverly Hills, CA: Sage.
ROGERS, E. and SHOEMAKER, F., 1971: *Communication of Innovations*, 2nd edition. New York: Free Press.
ROSE, R., 1965: *Politics in England*. London: Faber & Faber.
ROSENGREN, K., WENNER, K. and PALMGREEN, P. (eds.), 1985: *Media Gratifications Research*. Beverly Hills, CA: Sage.
RUBIN, A., 1986: 'Uses, Gratifications, and Media Effects Research', in J. Bryant and D. Zillmann (eds.) *Perspectives on Media Effects*. Hillsdale, NJ: Erlbaum.
SANCHEZ-TABERNERO, A. et al., 1993: *Media Concentration in Europe*. Manchester: European Institute for the Media.
SCHLESINGER, P., 1990: 'Rethinking the Sociology of Journalism: Source Strategies and the Limits of Media-Centrism', in M. Ferguson (ed.) *Public Communication*. London: Sage.
SCHLESINGER, P., DOBASH, R.E., DOBASH, R.B. and WEAVER, C., 1992: *Women Viewing Violence*. London: British Film Institute.
SCHLESINGER, P. and TUMBER, H., 1994: *Reporting Crime*. Oxford: Clarendon.
SCHRAMM, W. and ROBERTS, D. (eds.), 1971: *The Process and Effects of Mass Communication*, revised edition, Urbana, IL: University of Illinois Press.
SCHUDSON, M., 1978: *Discovering the News*. New York: Basic Books.
SCHUDSON, M., 1982: 'The Politics of Narrative Form: The Emergence of News Conventions in Print and Television', *Daedalus*, 111.
SCHUDSON, M., 1991: 'The Sociology of News Production Revisited', in J. Curran and M. Gurevitch (eds.) *Mass Media and Society*. London: Edward Arnold.

SCHUDSON, M., 1993: 'Was There Ever a Public Sphere? If So, When? Reflections on the American Case', in C. Calhoun (ed.) *Habermas and the Public Sphere*. Cambridge, MA: MIT Press.

SCHUDSON, M., 1994: 'Question Authority: A History of the News Interview in American Journalism, 1860s–1930s', *Media, Culture and Society*, 16 (4).

SEYMOUR-URE, C., 1989: 'Prime Ministers' Reactions to Television: Britain, Australia and Canada', *Media, Culture and Society*, 11 (3).

SEYMOURE-URE, C., 1991: *The British Press and Broadcasting since 1945*. Oxford: Blackwell.

SHARPE, S., 1978: *Just Like a Girl*. Harmondsworth: Penguin.

SHAW, B., 1979: cited in *Oxford Dictionary of Quotations*. Oxford: Oxford University Press.

SHAWCROSS, W., 1992: *Murdoch*. London: Pan.

SIEBERT, F., PETERSON, T. and SCHRAMM, W., 1956: *Four Theories of the Press*. Urbana, IL: University of Illinois Press.

SIGAL, L., 1987: 'Sources Make the News', in R. Manoff and M. Schudson (eds.) *Reading the News*. New York: Pantheon.

SIMON, R., 1982: *Gramsci's Political Thought*. London: Lawrence & Wishart.

SKEGGS, B., 1992: 'Paul Willis, *Learning to Labour*', in M. Barker and A. Beezer (eds.) *Reading into Cultural Studies*. London: Routledge.

SMITH, A.C.H., 1975: *Newspaper Voices*. London: Chatto & Windus.

SOLUM, O., 1994: 'Film Production in Norway and the Municipal Cinema System', Unpublished paper. Oslo: University of Oslo.

SPARKS, C., 1985: 'The Working-Class Press: Radical and Revolutionary Alternatives', *Media, Culture and Society*, 7 (2).

SPARKS, C., 1993: 'State, Market, Media and Democracy', in O. Manaev and Y. Pryliuk (eds.) *Media in Transition*. Kyiv: Abris.

STEPP, C., 1990: 'Access in a Post-Social Responsibility Age', in J. Lichtenberg (ed.) *Democracy and the Mass Media*. Cambridge: Cambridge University Press.

SYVERTSEN, T., 1992: 'Serving the Public: Public Television in Norway in a New Media Age', *Media, Culture and Society*, 14 (2).

SYVERTSEN, T., 1994: *Public Television in Transition*. Oslo: Levende Bilder.

TIFFEN, R., 1989: *News and Power*. Sydney: Allen & Unwin.

TROYNA, B., 1981: *Public Awareness and the Media: A Study of Reporting on Race*. London: Commission for Racial Equality.

TUCHMAN, G., 1972: 'Objectivity as Strategic Ritual: An Examination of Newsmen's Notions of Objectivity', *American Journal of Sociology*, 77.

TUCHMAN, G., 1978a: *Making News*. New York: Free Press.

TUCHMAN, G., 1978b: 'Introduction: The Symbolic Annihilation of Women by the Mass Media', in G. Tuchman, A. Kaplan and J. Benet (eds.) *Hearth and Home*. New York: Oxford University Press.

TUNSTALL, J., 1971: *Journalists at Work*. London: Constable.

TUNSTALL, J., 1993: *Television Producers*. London: Routledge.

TUNSTALL, G., 1990: *British Cultural Studies*. London: Unwin Hyman.

TUROW, J., 1991: 'A Mass Communication Perspective on Entertainment Industries', in J. Curran and M. Gurevitch (eds.) *Mass Media and Society*. London: Edward Arnold.

VIDMAR, N. and ROKEACH, M., 1974: 'Archie Bunker's Bigotry': A Study in Selective Perception and Exposure', *Journal of Communication*, 24 (2).

WAGNER-PACIFICI, R., 1986: *The Moro Morality Play*. Chicago: University of Chicago Press.

WATNEY, S., 1987: *Policing Desire*. London: Methuen.

WEAVER, D. and WILHOIT, G., 1986: *The American Journalist*. Bloomington, IN: University of Indiana Press.

WHALE, J., 1977: *The Politics of the Media*. London: Fontana.

WILLIAMS, K., 1993: 'The Light at the End of the Tunnel: The Mass Media, Public Opinion and the Vietnam War', in J. Eldridge (ed.) *Getting the Message*. London: Routledge.

WILSON, C. and GUTIERREZ, F., 1985: *Minorities and the Media*. Beverly Hills, CA: Sage.

WILLIS, P., 1977: *Learning to Labour*. London: Saxon House.

WILLIAMS, R., 1966: *Communications*, revised edition. London: Chatto & Windus.

WINSHIP, J., 1987: *Inside Women's Magazines*. London: Pandora Press.

WOOLF, V., 1965: *Jacob's Room*. Harmondsworth: Penguin.

ZILLMANN, D. and BRYANT, J., 1986: 'Exploring the Entertainment Experience', in J. Bryant and D. Zillman (eds.) *Perspectives on Media Effects*. Hillsdale, NJ: Erlbaum.

ZOONEN, L. VAN, 1991: 'Feminist Perspectives on the Media', in J. Curran and M. Gurevitch (eds.) *Mass Media and Society*. London: Edward Arnold.

ZOONEN, L. VAN, 1994: *Feminist Media Studies*. London: Sage.

SECTION II

Cultural Production

Introduction

Mainstream cultural studies has given surprisingly little attention to the institutional contexts in which mass communications are produced. This has had two harmful consequences. It has encouraged a simplistic view of media representations as the expression or reflection of some aspect of society without reference to organizational mediation. It has also encouraged a Panglossian conception of the audience as autonomous and sovereign, without regard to the ways in which audience responses can be constrained by the political economy of the media.

This section thus seeks to rectify cultural studies' relative neglect of the organizational processes of the media. It considers how the context of production – whether this be conceived as an occupational milieu, a specific organization, an industry or the wider social relations of power in society – influences what is produced. For example, has a generalized shift towards independent production and freelance employment encouraged a more open, diverse and innovatory set of cultural practices? Or has the simultaneous trend towards the rise of media empires, global production, and the multimedia packaging of cultural goods had the opposite effect? More generally, is it possible to differentiate between contexts of production in terms of whether they promote social empowerment or subordination, foster aesthetic innovation or traditionalism, enhance or detract from the quality of what is produced?

The opening essay by Angela McRobbie, describing work in progress on women's magazines, offers an original analysis that is, in a sense, a logical culmination of a particular line of argument in cultural studies. Early feminist work presented a ringing indictment of women's magazines as both failing the women they claimed to represent, and actively damaging them by constructing conventional, subordinate subjectivities that reinforced patriarchal domination. However, this uncompromising appraisal was followed subsequently by qualifications and reservations which emphasized the complexity of female representations in the media, the multiple subjectivities and identities of many women, and the active, playful and subversive ways in which female readers could subvert meanings in publications seemingly steeped in traditional gender values. The revisionist thrust of this argument is further extended by McRobbie's reconceptualization of what she significantly calls the 'interdiscursive space' of production. She points out that new, successful women's and girls' magazines have come into being whose irony, exaggeration and hyperbole, and transgression of previous taboos, produce a kind of openness about what it is to be a woman in contrast to the narrow, prescriptive and traditional definitions of femininity to be found in former bestselling magazines like *Honey*. These new magazines are the product not of a traditional patriarchal culture but of a postmodern economic environment, characterized by flexibility and openness. Many of their journalists have been influenced by feminism, in some cases reinforced by the media studies degree courses they attended; they see themselves as part of the community they write for, and strive to achieve a relationship of real communion with their readers. Above all, intense competition has fostered an adjustment to new times in which readers are more liberated, sophisticated and reflexive. While the women's magazine press is constrained in certain important ways by advertising funding and genre conventions, an important part of it is both reflecting and reinforcing women's liberation by promoting definitions of sexual identity that are 'more complex, more knowing and "equal" in their relationships with men'.

This optimistic account, characteristic of a certain strand of feminist postmodernism, is in marked contrast to the more sceptical trend in the study of popular music charted by David Hesmondhalgh. He shows how the supposed dichotomy between the artifice of pop music for the mass market produced by the music majors, and the creative art, expressive of a genuine community, produced by small record companies – so central to the legend of rock – has been systematically debunked by academic iconoclasts. In this critical account or rather accounts, rock musicians belong to an exclusive community removed from that of their publics; protest and innovation are only intermittent rather than defining features of their work; independent record companies are merely unsuccessful and exploitative capitalist enterprises, or the low-cost satellites of the record majors to which they are linked through partnership deals; and the record majors appear, ironically, to be less 'corporate' and bureaucratic than they were. For a time, the romantic rock thesis of protest and rebellion had an afterlife in studies of youth subcultures which portrayed some music styles as part of a 'ritual of resistance'. But this, too, was deflated by sceptical accounts which viewed music consumption as markers of group membership, as a way of establishing a social identity that excluded others, rather than as an expression of social dissent. Yet lurking in the wings, Hesmondhalgh suggests, is potentially an analysis which can reclaim the significance of the music fringe. The component elements of this alternative assessment include a new stress on the aesthetic politics of music and recognition of some independents as sites of innovation – and a cautious recognition of the potential of new music technology, and of the power of music's polycentrism, to forge alliances between different marginal groups.

Yvonne Tasker considers the question of whether there is a 'new Hollywood', characterized by a shift from the studio system, manufacturing standardized, genre movies in a streamlined production process, to a postmodern economy of independent producers, who are flexible and responsive to change, employ new filmic techniques, defy genre conventions and combine irony, ambiguity, pastiche and parody in a new film style. Her conclusion is that the seeming contrast between the old and the new in fact conceals some underlying continuities: perhaps most significantly, the retention of economic control by a slightly enlarged oligopoly in which 'independent productions' are largely funded by major producer-distributors. However, new opportunities have been created, most notably for the bigger-budget production and distribution of the work of African-American film-makers. There have also been significant style changes in part of Hollywood's output, which seems to have been engendered in part by the decline of the Hollywood factory system, the rise of independent producers and freelance employment, and perhaps also the multimedia marketing and packaging of films.

The last essay in this section is concerned not with music, magazines or film but with the production of science and technology, and knowledge about it. This is an important topic that cultural studies, with its roots in the humanities and social sciences, has tended to ignore. Yet as Sarah Kember's chapter reveals, it has long been an area of intense feminist debate that in certain respects parallels feminist anlysis of the media. Early, radical feminist critiques of science tended to see capitalism and patriarchy as a joint system of domination, and to adopt a homogenizing perspective of women as the victims of oppression or as the possessors of shared characteristics as a consequence of their biological or psychological differences from men. A subsequent postmodernist analysis incorporated notions of difference in relation to feminine experience and identity in an alternative conception of what the world of science might become. One version of this 'successor' science celebrates the end of male domination and feminist socialism alike, while another adopts a more pluralist and also radical approach in which science is conceived not as an autonomous area, but one embedded in the hierarchy of power which can only be transformed through collective human agency. But in either case, argues Kember, the 'virtual power of metaphor' – the ability to conceive and articulate an alternative way of organizing things – provides the seeds of change.

Each of these essays thus seeks in different ways to understand the processes that structure culture. McRobbie describes the 'space' of women's magazine production as an environment of flux and mobility, which is responding to profound changes in women's consciousness. Kember, by contrast, invokes an image of a male-dominated world of science securely lodged within the power structure of society, touched but not transformed by the transfigurative power of feminist imagination. Between these two polarities are accounts of film and music production that stress continuity in the context of change, and express the collective disappointment of many commentators that marginal forces have not had a more transformative impact.

7

More!: New Sexualities in Girls' and Women's Magazines

Angela McRobbie

Feminists Looking at Women's and Girls' Magazines

Magazine scholarship has been a constant presence in media and gender studies for almost twenty years. Given this sustained attention to the magazine as a cultural phenomenon, it is not surprising, perhaps, that we can read in this body of work the history of a field of enquiry as it progressively moves through a series of questions provoked both by the constancy of the magazine form itself and also by changes in this distinctive mass medium.

In the first instance, it is a feminist body of work which emerges as a direct response to the popularity and indeed the centrality of the women's magazine as possibly the most concentrated and uninterrupted media-scape for the construction of normative femininity. This is also a multiple site of representation where a whole range of concerns intersect with each other across the pages. For feminist writers turning their attention to the magazine from the mid-1970s onwards, virtually everything in the women's magazine connects with oppression. In advertising, the female body is consistently the reference point for the persuasion to consume; in romance, women and girls are subjected to the dubious pleasures of sexual submission; in features, what it is to be a woman is relentlessly debated but with numbing repetition within limited horizons; and fashion, too, is found here prominently displayed in the centrefold of the women's magazine, which is also the point where feminine consumerism comes into its own, with the fashion pages issuing an endless series of imperatives to buy.

What can be seen in early magazine scholarship is a sharply focused feminist critique emerging in response to these commercial femininities. As Brunsdon (1991) and Stuart (1990) have both pointed out, the significance of the two terms 'feminism' and 'femininity' as counterpoints to each other should not be underestimated in relation to this early work. They provided the kind of strong framing devices required to get a new area of study off the ground, giving it also a legitimacy inside the academy through the study of a distinctive type of medium, and also outside the academy within the field of feminist politics.

While magazines have since occupied a marginal status, perhaps in contrast to the rapid growth of television and film studies, the scholarship which has been produced remains a valuable resource. It tells the story of the complex, repetitive but also changing social construction of femininity, and also of the emergence and development of feminist media and cultural studies itself. In the first instance, the magazine embodies the stereotype of objectified femininity, unachievable and unreal. This immediate response becomes more theoretically sophisticated under the influence of Althusser's (1971) theory of ideology. This, together with the impact of semiology, structuralism and post-structuralism, means that the question is no longer that of searching for a more realistic or truthful rendition of womanhood in magazines, but rather one of understanding the range of interconnected meanings constructed around the category of women. From this emerges, particularly through the concept of ideology, a preferred or a dominant cluster of meanings. In my own early work on *Jackie* magazine this entailed a strongly repetitive code of 'love' being confirmed through the centrality of romance in the magazine and the sameness of the narrative structures which carried this code week after week (McRobbie 1991). In Winship's work it was domesticity in women's magazines which not just signalled but installed women in the home (Winship 1987). Rosalind Coward showed how, against early feminist objections, it was not simply that images of women in fashion or advertising were fragmented and fetishized – after all, most representations in visual culture entail fragmentation or distortion of a larger image – and so the point cannot be that images fail to show 'whole' women (Coward 1987). The question instead must be how images of women in magazines are made to mean; the answer being that the meanings typically make a number of connections which continue to position women in a relation of subordination, passivity and sexual availability. Thus whether it is legs, or breasts, or eyes, the meanings drawn out from these bodily parts are that these women either seek or have already gained the approval of the male gaze. Alongside this important work must also be set Judith Williamson's seminal *Decoding Advertisements*. Here extensive use is made of both feminist-influenced psychoanalysis and structuralism to demonstrate how advertising occupies a critical place in the production of femininity (Williamson 1978). From this point on, psychoanalysis looks more to film than to the magazine form. However, from the language of psychoanalytical feminism found in film studies the question of female pleasure then provided one of the watersheds in the study of magazines. Up until that point, the tone had been that of rebuke. Women's and girls' magazines not only failed the women they claimed to represent, they actively damaged them, constructing injured and subordinate subjectivities.

The turning point also comes when the theory of ideology – with its power to interpellate the subjects of femininity through directly addressing them, giving them a name (Girls! You May Not Know This But Boys Like . . .') – is recognized as both important and also problematic. First, there is an admission by feminist writers of the pleasure of these texts, the glossy pages, the visual images, the fantasies of the perfect face, body and wardrobe, in short the pleasures of conventional femininity. This admission is legitimated through the psychoanalytical work emerging in the early 1980s on sexual difference and on the difficulty of psychic change and the complicity of feminists with their own subordinate femininity even where that is recognized as harmful or dangerous. The fact that reason and political analysis tells us that this is bad, while the unconscious continues to produce guilty pleasures and fascinations, evokes at the very least a complexity in the process of consuming these images. This actually has an equalizing effect in that feminists can no longer occupy the high moral ground. The enjoyment of magazines breaks the barrier which divides feminists from 'ordinary' women and girls. This comes with a shift away from the assumed success of ideology. Perhaps it was not so effective after all, and at any rate, to dismiss so many millions of women as victims of ideology and therefore as on the other side of feminism was both simplistic and demeaning to those ordinary women. The emphasis on ideology also presupposed some state of purity, knowledge and truth outside ideology, a space which in those early days feminism felt itself to occupy.

One of the great values of psychoanalysis was that it insisted on the difficulty of sexuality and identity, showing how neither are fully achieved. It also allowed feminists to confess to the pleasures which they otherwise felt obliged to repress or which they assumed they had overcome or transcended (this repressed material erupting only in dreams or in fantasy). Jacqueline Rose's work also showed how femininity as a normative structure of gender identity was never as assured as culture would want it to be (Rose 1987). Hence the repetitive anxiety in cultural forms to keep on trying to tie it down, to secure this otherwise more meandering sexual identity to its correct place in the symbolic order. This indicated both a tension and an urgency in the invoking of femininity on such a regularized basis as found in women's magazines. Femininity could not be relied upon to exist as required without such strenuous symbolic activity. The insecurity upon which this hard cultural work was based also allowed feminists to prise open contradictory dynamics within a field which otherwise had been seen as a unity, a world of women's magazines.

While it is quite wrong to see this recognition of pleasure in magazines as a full-blown celebration of mainstream commercial femininity, the revision of femininity posed something of a threat to that aspect of feminism which remained censorious. By the early eighties it was quite clear that a movement as potentially wide as the women's movement would inevitably fragment. Those who at this moment wanted to bring distinctly feminine pleasures into the embrace of feminism often did so as a way of rescuing a kind of essential femininity which, if explored in depth, could be shown also to be the site of both complexity and also resistance. It was a way of showing that ordinary women did indeed have the resources and the will to produce quasi-feminist responses. Such an optimistic position (in sharp contrast to the pessimism of the ideology thesis) finds its fullest expression in Radway's work on romance, where she finds that avid romance readers evade the demands of their domestic role by escaping into the world of romance and sexual fantasy (Radway 1984). More generally there is a suggestion that 'womanly' pleasures, including cooking, childcare, domesticity, fashion and soap opera, are as legitimate and important as any other human pleasures. Far from representing that which has got to be left behind when feminism takes over, this sphere of activity deserves full approval and recognition. Nor need it signify a dependence on men: it can exist as a much more autonomous set of activities.

As will become apparent later, there are quite profound problems in the essentialism of this reappraisal of the pleasures of femininity, not least of which is the heterosexual assumptions upon which many of these pleasures are uncritically based, particularly romance. Butler and others have more recently argued that the assumption of universally experienced female pleasures is itself a feminist violation, an example of feminists invoking a normativity. (Butler 1990). Can black women, historically excluded from the joys of romantic narratives (as found in *Gone with the Wind*) find enjoyment in the same kind of pleasurable abandon as Helen Taylor reports her respondents to indulge in (Taylor 1989)? When all the female characters in the picture or photo love stories are white, can Asian girls also concur with these fantasies? Even the pleasures of maternity reconsidered by feminists can be exclusive to women, not all of whom, for example, are, can be, or want to be mothers. To invoke motherhood as a universal female experience is to reinforce an already existing hierarchy of feminine activities and expectations. Moreover, the sense of universalism invoked in these appeals to shared womanly pleasures resists the possibility of these being historically specific, and consequently transcended and rejected by younger women for whom they are no longer appropriate.

Thus we have an emergent set of perspectives which, by the early 1980s at least, acknowledge the diversity both of systems of representations, and those whom they appear to represent. Female readers are granted more power in relation to the ideological effect of the text. Frazer, for example, (and also Beezer et al.) show how my own early work on *Jackie* was based on an assumption that the ideology of adolescent femininity actually worked in a mechanistic kind of way (Beezer et al. 1986; Frazer 1987). There is, they argue, a too-direct assumption of the interpellation reaching its addressees direct, unmediated and uncomplicated by other intervening factors. This critique also coincides with more attention being paid in feminism to aspects of personal memory and autobiography. If magazines like these give rise to fond memories on the part of adult feminists, even in their oppressive guise, then how can they be blamed for reproducing sexual inequality? If we feminists turned out not so badly, on what basis can we assume that magazines have such a damaging and dangerous effect on all their other readers? Not all feminist critics are willing to reconsider magazines in this way, however. Walkerdine usefully reminds readers of the endless, repetitive emphasis in young girls' comics on the rewards of being a good girl, which means, in effect, tolerating pain, injury and injustice without so much a flicker of anger (Walkerdine 1990). In this respect Walkerdine's analysis is quite at odds with my own, which attributed to these pre-teenage magazines the power to ascribe to young girls, in the format of the picture story, skills, talents, confidence and abilities (on stage, on the ice-rink, hockey pitch or tennis court) which adolescence soon forced them to relinquish in favour of boys (McRobbie 1991). It would probably be more accurate to see these two dimensions coexisting as conflicting desires; in Walkerdine's case to suffer, be good and win eventual praise and even the 'prince'; and in my own work, to be ruthless, bold, competitive and to enjoy the rewards of power, leadership and recognition.

This debate then leaves off at a moment of dissolution. The poles of feminism and femininity no longer exist as fiercely opposed alternatives. There is a call for the presence in feminist media studies of the voices or experiences of those who are otherwise assumed to be the subjects of ideology or discourse. Reader ethnographies represent one possible way of moving away from the overwhelming emphasis on the texts and their various readings. This focus, it was hoped, would contribute an additional level of analysis in the otherwise assumed cycle of production and consumption of meaning. And, as ordinary readers are granted more power over the meaning of the text, so also do feminists acknowledge the ambivalence of their own responses. This also coincides with questions being asked of feminism in terms of its representational claims. Who are its women? What right does feminism have to speak on behalf of all women? Has the universalism of feminism rested, indeed, on the marginalization or even exclusion of many other women, revealing it to be in fact more narrowly Eurocentric and heterosexual than is apparent in its language of a global sisterhood?

By the mid-1980s it is also quite clear that magazines themselves have suddenly undergone a quite rapid transformation. They no longer possess such predictability, some might say they have changed beyond recognition. The more solid version of femininity – with its romantic narratives, its lessons on the art of seduction and its advice about how to hold on to your man – have faded away. When romance reappears it is within the knowing, ironic, self-mocking language of postmodernism. When *Just Seventeen* decided in 1994 to revive the love story, it did so with the quotation marks fully on display. No reader could be so naïve as to swallow it straight. In the following section we will return to the absence of naïvety and the assumption of sophistication and knowingness in magazines. We will also ask how popular feminism, as Andrea Stuart has described it, has become a password for the diverse, uneven and contradictory femininities now advocated in magazines.

Reconceptualizing the Space of Production and Consumption in the World of Magazines

To understand how change has been effected in the pages of some of the best-selling magazines, and also to understand the popularity of new publications like *More!* as well as the rapidly increasing circulation of *Marie Claire* it is necessary to develop a mode of analysis which moves beyond the emphasis on ideology and textuality which characterized so much of the early work. Cultural studies has been concerned with representational forms and their meanings, leaving the terrain of lived experience completely to the side. Likewise social institutions and their practices have also been disregarded except in their discursive and regulative modes. Both post-structuralist cultural studies and more recent postmodern cultural theorizing have lost sight of the space of experience, social interaction, the space of cognition and, indeed, opposition.

It is of course possible to recast experience into the language of post-structuralism and discourse. Butler, for example, extends Foucault to argue that change can be pursued and perceived at the heart of power through the process of re-signification (Butler 1993). This entails making new meanings, not afresh, but through a process of twisting and cathecting existing meanings from within the possibilities opened up by meanings never being fixed and stable in the first place. Instead meanings have been forced into a false stability through the violences and violations of the language of dominant culture. Butler's work develops further the politics which is inscribed within post-structuralism by doing the work of prising open that which seems fixed, immutable and natural and by asking what it excludes, how it got to be there, and on what sort of foundational basis. To get back, through this model of re-signification, to social experience would not require access only to speech (as in an ethnographic study of magazine readers) as the source of individual truth; indeed it would totally debunk this as a humanist assumption, which posits an original 'I' which can be got to through speech and ethnography and which can therefore be relied upon to speak the truth of 'its' own experience in an ethnographic situation. A Butler-influenced ethnography would look very different, and would presumably see the 'I' who speaks as a temporary fixing of identity within the structures of the discursive situation in which he or she is located. He or she then activates, performs or acts a more coherent identity within the normative expectation of the observed interview or researched environment.

Alternatively, Butler's work would legitimate an altogether more partial use of ethnography, rejecting from the start the idea that the spoken response connects with or belongs to some prior history of personal experience as if this was a coherent totality. 'Experience' described or observed would instead be seen as temporal and situational. We would not then be looking for the whole person who speaks his or her truth in the interview and is therefore a more legitimate 'primary resource' than other textual material. Returning to the terrain of magazine scholarship, this post-structuralist emphasis could indeed be usefully applied to *both* the question of meaning production through the activities of magazine professionals and also to meaning consumption by conceptualizing an ethnography of fragmented female identity through processes of looking and reading.

The emphasis here, however, is to show how in the field of magazines, by taking into account the activities of their producers and by positing some questions about their consumers, it is possible to pinpoint a series of quite dramatic shifts, most notably an intensification of interest in sexuality. More than ever before sex now fills the space of the magazines' pages. It provides the frame for women's magazines in the 1990s. Proclaimed on the covers ('Oral Sex? Pussy Power?') sex sets the tone, defines the pace, and shapes the whole environment of the magazine. Everything in this new world of magazines is simultaneously inflated, exaggerated and also presented with a hint of self-parody. Superlatives and imperatives ('The Hottest Summer Yet! Essentials for the Beach, You Can't Be Seen in Anything Else!') have long been the way in which magazines speak to their readers: a teasing, coaxing, but also urgent language. But now it is the stakes of sexuality rather than fashion and beauty which are the highest.

What is the meaning of this new sexuality? First, the high sexual content sells. Circulation figures rocket when the magazines announce features on oral sex on the cover. *More!* is now by far the largest-selling fortnightly magazine in existence. Second, this sexual material marks a new moment in the construction of female sexual identities. It suggests new forms of sexual conduct, it proposes boldness (even brazenness) in behaviour. The girl who knows what to expect is in a better position to make the right choices. Her sexual confidence makes her more able to insist on using a condom and she is therefore able to protect herself against HIV. Third, the widespread sense of parody and irony in the presentation of this sexual material in the magazines also implies a certain detachment or ironic distance from the old stakes of sexuality for girls. They are far removed from romantic abandon and there is instead a determination to meet their male counterparts on equal grounds. The editors and writers speak to their readers in arch, ironic tones. This suggests both detachment from the objects of their desire and also from the actual practices of sex, so minutely described. I will argue later that in this space of irony there is something more than the usual attempts at intimate address between the magazine and its readership. This space offers a degree of critical reflection on the normative practices of both femininity and sexuality endlessly incited, invoked and otherwise presented as imperative. In some ways the magazines, within the constraints of their own codifications, have (recently) extended 'the possibilities of what it is to be a woman' (Butler 1993).

Of course Foucault has taught us to beware new freedoms (Foucault 1983). In the pleasures and the possibilities they promise, power is most active in setting and defining new boundaries, producing new exclusions. Magazine discourse brings into being new female subjects through these incitations, but it is also more nervous and uncertain than it seems. Let me therefore problematize both the amplification of sexual discourse and the 'knowing' tone through which this sex is spoken. Let us consider what it might mean that the editors and writers of magazine like *Elle, Marie Claire* and *More!* appear to visibly play with the codes of magazine production as much as they assume their readers play with the style and identity. Sex has long been primary material of women's magazines. It has been that privileged site where, with the full blessing of consumer culture, a recognizable female self, a self, fully female in her appearance, in her gestures, in the way she styles her body and in the disposition of her feminine sexuality towards an assumed appreciative male viewer, has been endlessly produced. The changes which can be seen in these magazines in the 1990s articulate a commitment to tradition in this respect, and also in the reproduction of the norms of female beauty through the invocation of an assumed, universalistic feminine culture devoted to fashion and the body. But they also speak of a crisis, or at least a tension, in what it is to be a woman now.

I want to suggest that the language of production and consumption, most often deployed in recent cultural studies work, is too broad, too general, and for this reason unable to generate a more rigorous account of the complex and multilayered relation between the production of meaning in the magazine and the diverse ways in which these meanings are consumed by readers. Although this is how the question has been posed in the past, it is actually too premature, too inattentive to the various levels of activity which comprise how magazines are actually created. We cannot explore new sexual representations through concentrating exclusively on the complex structuring of textual meaning in magazine production, but neither can we legitimately move, in one great leap, from this level to some real world out there where girls and women can be tapped into as though these were simply the product of magazine culture. As I suggested earlier, what is needed is an altogether more particular approach.

Let us consider, for example, the young women who get jobs on magazines, or those who are at college doing media studies courses and on work placement in a magazine studio. Or perhaps we might look more closely, casting a sociological eye over the groups of readers who the editors use over a period of time to test out new developments or ideas in the magazine. We have to abandon the idea that production and consumption can be neatly understood as mechanical and parallel activities. Nixon, Du Gay, and Negus have recently insisted not only on a return to more detailed study of the culture industries, but also to a more nuanced and less monolithic approach (Nixon 1993; Du Gay and Negus 1994).

Readers exist as both consumers of magazines and of the products they advertise, and for this reason they represent a key point of reference for magazine professionals at every level. Nixon argues that it is imperative that we reconsider the precise way in which the economics of magazine production (typically considered as the bottom line, the moment of 'determination') is actually coded and conducted in cultural terms. Economics does not, he suggests, exist as some pure activity outside the everyday practices of producing magazines. It is neither the base, nor the 'boss', neither the bottom line of sales and circulation figures, nor the commands from the upstairs offices of the editor-in-chief. Instead the processes of launching a magazine and finding a new market of readers are discursively constructed through often competing cultural values. These are debated within the editorial departments and in the boardroom in and through the more general language of taste, style and innovation rather than in terms of sales, prices or profits (Nixon 1993). Nixon's study points to the importance of examining the multiple and uneven practices which together constitute magazine production. This would entail looking both beyond and behind the text right into the offices and the design studios. Nixon shows the magazine to represent a site of intersecting but also often conflicting interests between publishers, advertisers and design professionals. In the case of *The Face* the publishers considered themselves the same as the projected readership. Initially this shared identity met with suspicion if not disbelief on the part of the advertisers, who had to be gradually convinced. This positioning of the editor, entrepreneur or journalist as ideal reader encourages us to reconsider the category of the reader as a space of projection. This suggests that cultural producers consider themselves to be creating a product for themselves and their friends, which in turn indicates a world of strongly articulated cultural values, tastes and commitments – in Bourdieu's terms, a 'habitus' – that is a regulated and controlled social space within which distinctive practices are pursued by social agents (Bourdieu 1984).

Significantly, this is exactly what emerges from recent interviews I have carried out as part of a study of fashion in magazines.[1] All the journalists have described themselves as magazine addicts and as having read them avidly as girls, long before they thought of a career in this field. They define themselves as creative individuals, interested from an early age in taste, style, pop music, the arts and of course fashion. Drawing on this strong sense of personal taste and style, the editors attribute the success of their magazine to the instinct that what they and their friends want to read or look at, proves to be equally appealing to readers. They not only identify with their readers, making decisions and arguing their case by casting themselves as readers, they also see themselves as actively assisting and thereby producing readers as fashionable young women (a process symbolized in the familiar 'make-over' features). This process is not, however, uncontested and frequently brings the editors into conflict with the advertisers on whose revenue the overall success (and the image) of the magazine also depends. Between the editors and the advertisers the vexed question of what a woman, or girl is today is constantly debated.

This, drawing again on Nixon's innovative work on men's magazines, suggests the resolved, but also unstable image of the magazine (the *Elle* girl, the *Cosmo* woman) existing as an interdiscursive space. Readers provide an input here in circulation figures and also, through market research, as data-banks for the advertisers. But they are also produced as female subjects who can, in Althusserian terms, recognize themselves in the magazine's repeated interpellations (Althusser 1971). It is this recognition that creates the magazine as popular, representative, a success story, 'award winning', etc., and it also produces for its readers a field of pleasure and enjoyment. In high fashion magazines like *Elle* there is a field of fashionable femininity. What the editors and writers on *More!* and *19* describe as their magazine's image is 'sexy, adventurous, fun'; while Glenda Bailey of *Marie Claire* describes its image as 'sophisticated, modern, intelligent'. A more detailed analysis than I am able to present here would of course disentangle these statements, showing them to be part of the professional ideologies of women's magazine producers, part of the distinctive styles of the magazines as they compete on the market-place, and also part of the corporate 'mission statements' representative of the magazine as a whole.

Sally Brampton (who I interviewed in September 1994) was the first editor of British *Elle*, launched in 1981. She summarized her role as follows:

> Editors and writers continually say 'Would I want to read this/wear this/do that/go there?' or 'Is this the kind of fashion me and my friends would have wanted to look at and buy when we were at college? Before I put the dummy issue together I did my own market research by testing out my ideas with approximately thirty friends, all women of more or less the same age and outlook as myself. I then presented my findings and got the job.

In this way the readers come to represent an extended community of the producer's own circle of friends and acquaintances; they are constructed and imagined in this intimate kind of way. This closeness to the reader is maintained and carefully nurtured when the magazine is being produced for mass circulation. This points to a different set of relations existing between media professionals and media consumers than is typically conceptualized within the political economy of media. It also points to the role of market research in defending the editorial style of the magazine not just for, but often against, cynical or disbelieving advertisers. Du Gay as well as Nixon has pointed to how new sectors, for example, new retail outlets, invest in studying consumers and producing huge banks of information (Du Gray 1993). Once in business this is developed further in EPOS (electronic point of sales) systems which can instantly provide precise figures on customer tastes and preferences, on strong and weak lines, etc. Magazine culture over the last ten years, in a highly competitive environment, has adopted similar tactics, investing heavily in market research, as an ongoing source of information and confirmation that they are doing it right. This information allows the readers to be further 'shaped' so that they can also be delivered to the advertisers as part of a more manageable consumer group. In retail, Du Gay argues that this means creating for customers a highly coded field of representation (i.e. a shopping environment) where potential consumers are produced by being directed around a carefully designed space which is highly conducive to sales. The magazine could be seen in similar terms as an environment of images and meanings which deliver the reader to themselves as 'shaped up' individuals (Du Gay 1993) and also as consumers into the hands of the cosmetics companies without whose advertising revenue the magazines could not exist.

This relationship of proximity is also coded into the magazines, not just through reader 'make-overs', special offers and 'road shows'; it also informs staff recruitment policies which require that the prospective employee should also embody the typical *Just Seventeen* 'girl', or the ideal *Cosmopolitan* woman. In this way an 'imagined community' of producers and consumers is constructed in the pages of the magazine. Editors, design professionals and advertising departments are continually describing and defining their ideal girl or woman through a language of consumer choices, career choices, lifestyle and outlook. For example, 'She shops in Jigsaw, works in the City, likes to listen to Courtney Pine, and her ideal night out is at the Jazz Café.' or 'She is vegetarian, fancies Johnny Depp, is studying graphic design and wants to own her own studio.'

These feminine typologies, again drawing on Du Gay, could be seen as cognitive (and consumerist) maps of desirable feminine subjectivities. The reader is expected to identify herself here and then literally put herself together through this range of connected social practices. The assumption in these lists of social distinction and differentiation is that they are temporary, lifecycle interests or even obsessions. What will remain is the fashion-conscious girl or woman. The contents of these lists will inevitably be altered by time. This has been one of the the standard ways in which magazines have created their readerships over the years, as Barthes' early work on *The Fashion System* reminds us. Here Barthes quotes directly from a 1950s French women's magazine: 'She likes studying and surprise parties, Pascal, Mozart and cool jazz. She wears flat heels, collects little scarves, adores her big brother's plain sweaters, and those bouffant, rustling petticoats' (Barthes 1983: 225).

Clearly these marks of female distinction conform closely to Butler's argument about femininity being produced as a power nexus of exclusion through inciting and invoking on a repetitive basis what it means to be female. The question is what is excluded, and whether or not, as I have argued above, the net of femininity is now cast wider allowing new possibilities to emerge. Since the women's magazine is by definition devoted to a recognizable category of women (which it simultaneously produces), it would be generically impossible to imagine it departing from this commitment (i.e. to speak to and for 'women'). So, in a straightforward way, magazines inevitably draw up the boundaries of a fixed gender identity, which in turn is assumed to be the natural sign of an original sexual demarcation as female. The 'women' of women's magazines could be different or even change dramatically over time but they will still, naturally, be women! This, argues Butler, is where an invisible process of exclusion is practised, in that women who veer from the path of normative, recognizable femininity – in particular lesbian women – are not actually fully recognized as sexual, desiring women in this easy, automatic, natural way. Instead they exist, like black women, as a category in the magazines, as a sign that we now live in a more open, multicultural, sexually diverse society.

From this perspective it is hard to argue that the magazine form has done anything for women who previously did not 'fit in', more than attempt latterly to shape them up as beautiful, chic or glamorous. What remains normative across the board is the pleasure of consumption, the enjoyment of being a girl or woman and the assumption that this state of femininity is natural, the simple and unproblematic meeting point of sex and gender. Failed femininity is urgently addressed in the language of self-improvement. The magazine, as adviser or agony aunt, can come to the rescue of any unfortunate reader who is counselled in a way which assumes a fundamental shared commitment to dominant femininity. These strategies appear to fix or stabilize feminine identities, since the troubled reader can only be helped within certain normative constraints.

What is not stable or reliable, however, is the response to this normativity among readers themselves, who are, as we know, shaped and produced by other competing discourses: those of education, family, community, social class, ethnicity, and other media forms. So what produces the anxiety and the uncertainty is not only the female subject of the magazine, but rather 'her' in competition or even conflict with other girls, or other women produced elsewhere. Knowledge gained from reader profiles ('Write in and tell us about yourself!') is anxiously put to work in creating more fixed subjectivities. But the reader is more recalcitrant, it seems. She often slips the net of the market research and confounds the professionals by her unpredictable and even unknowable desires. Her brand loyalty is therefore less certain than it once was and she less directly progresses from one magazine to the next. Instead she cruises the space of the magazine, tempted this month by *19*, the next by *Marie Claire*. Often she stops buying them altogether and watches more television instead. Magazines are required therefore to take the lead from the market leaders while at the same time carving out a distinctive and strong identity for themselves. They have to shout loudly and provocatively to readers from the shelf of WH Smith.

To show how this affects editorial practice, it would be necessary to examine relationships between magazines, to look at how editors and assistants describe the competition, how they attempt to persuade advertisers that markets for new products can be created in their pages. This tension, ever-present about 'getting it right' for every issue, is also what produces the frantic atmosphere of the magazine offices. The magazine must not look too much like its competitors. The cover picture must fit with the season, the new colours, the new look and so on. Working relations are always pressured and time is always running out. As in the fashion industry, there are always disasters at the last minute. Personnel move from one magazine to the next, bringing precious expertise and knowledge of the other magazines with them. Magazines increasingly rely on part-time or freelance editors, writers and stylists. They are by definition less loyal than full-timers and might even take a *Marie Claire* story to one of its competitors. Many freelancers come from the quality press and they frequently have a stronger feminist voice in features (Suzanne Moore writes regularly for *Elle*, as does Melanie McFadyean; Bea Campbell has written regularly for *Cosmopolitan*). More attention would need to be paid to all of these questions, in particular, we would need to ask, who are the media producers, the editors, stylists and journalists and what exactly do they bring to their specific practice on the magazines?

Once again my own research shows not only that young employees on *Elle*, *Marie Claire* and *More!* define themselves as avid magazine readers, they have also completed media studies courses or degrees, which in many cases have involved carrying out detailed studies of the magazine industry.[2] In addition these young women also represent Stuart's category of popular feminism through having studied aspects of feminism or women's issues as part of their education. The point is that they also bring this with them and attempt to integrate at least aspects of these political or feminist discourses into their place of work. In my recent research on magazine personnel, it has been helpful to have written on this subject in the past since employees, from assistants to editors seem to be familiar at some level with this work.[3] This connection has given me access to a research field which might otherwise be difficult to get into. All of this gives substance to Jameson's category of postmodern knowingness (Jameson 1984). Far from this being a tired and weary sense of cultural overdose, an overaccumulation of knowledge for which there is no useful function, giving rise to the waning of effect manifest in so much postmodern culture, this can be re-deflected to transform knowingness in women's and girls' magazines from a dead category into one which is very much alive. Many young women working in magazine journalism know about feminist criticism of the magazine form and also about research on magazines in cultural studies.

If the new generation of editors, writers and design professionals know well the language of sexual politics, by talking about pop stars, male pin-ups and heart-throbs in language which is mocking and ironic, the writers are providing a space for critical reflection on the part of their readers. 'Isn't he hunky, girls?' contains a hint of cynicism, a suggestion of enjoyment in turning the tables on boys and men and subjecting them to the same scrutiny that women have been expected to accept as natural. These new magazine professionals refuse, they claim, to talk down to readers as they felt they were sometimes talked down to by magazines in the past. They do not want to portray readers as boy mad in the way they know magazines used to. At the same time they want to retain the pleasure and the fantasy of the magazine form.

The success of new magazines is now more predicated on this willingness to signal clearly that most girls and women understand for example that being a fan of Take That or East 17 is ridiculous, but that this does not mean they cannot have fun and also otherwise function as intelligent human beings. Thus the magazines poke fun at the fans, the stars and themselves. In magazines teenybopper stars now come out as gay, and as a result become even more popular with their female fans, because everyone now knows that the love between star and fan was always one of fantasy. At the same time this openness also marks something of a watershed, where gay and lesbian identities now move more freely across the field of popular women's and girls' magazines. These exist as sexual possibilities where in the past they were permitted only a shadowy stigmatized existence. This new sexualized presence, also apparent in other media sites – most notably soap operas – raises the question of the conditions of existence, the rules which permit such a presence. Is this a matter of producing more normative images of 'gay' or 'lesbian' identities and, in so doing, negating other more disruptive definitions? Is this homosexual identity the binary opposite of heterosexuality, and is it thereby secured into a less dangerous position? Against the pessimism of Butler's analysis, which registers only new more sophisticated grids of exclusion within a broadened spectrum of still normative femininities, I am suggesting here that there are sources of disruption to the fixed and stable idea of girlhood or womanhood upon which the magazines appear to depend. These are found in other institutional sites (work, education, family, state, etc.) and they exist as external but intrusive gender discourses which run alongside and potentially contradict the concerns of the magazine. Likewise they are brought right into the editorial offices of the magazines by the new magazine professionals, well-qualified young women, often self-proclaimed feminists, by no means all exclusively white, middle class and heterosexual.

More!, *Marie Claire*, *Elle* and the Others: New Sexual Subjectivities

What we can see is a sharp sense of transition and fluidity in these magazines as to what it is to be a young woman today. This is addressed almost entirely through sexuality. Kobena Mercer has suggested that 'Contrary to the impression given by academic deconstructionists, the moment of indeterminacy, undecidability and ambivalence is never a neutral or a purely textual affair – it is when politics is experienced at its most intense.' (Mercer 1990: 62). I also want to draw on Mercer's recognition that 'The new movements (in this case feminism and gay politics) have had significant impact on personal relations and lived experience in the commodified forms of the cultural marketplace.' (p. 67). The suggestion that feminist impact can be seen in the heartland of consumerism has since become something that cultural studies has paid dearly for. In seeing 'resistance in shopping' as some of its most virulent (and mean-spirited) critics have put it, cultural studies becomes an apologist for capitalism. (See Frith and Savage's (1993) suggestion is that cultural studies now merely advertises 'sales and styles'.) It is not my intention to get involved in this debate here, merely to point to the magazine as *the* privileged space for discourses of normative commercial femininity to be played out, explored and actively promoted and to consider the spaces, the openings and the possibilities for the rearticulation of meaning inside and outside this inarguably consumer-led space.

Already I have suggested the importance of considering the employment and recruitment patterns in the magazines. This is necessary if we are indeed to consider the slippages and openings which destabilize the normative femininity which the magazine supports. Who works in these magazines? What sort of agendas do they bring to the magazine and how do they pursue these agendas? My own current research shows a much more open forum for debate within magazine structures than might be imagined. One interview showed a young editor invoking market forces to persuade her senior male colleagues that readers had changed and that they now wanted more realistic and adventurous material. As *Just Seventeen* editor, Morag Purdy, said in a 1990 interview:

> We commissioned a huge market research survey and we got thousands of girls to fill in the questionnaires and we were then able to deliver this material into the hands of the cynics and show them that we could create a more up-to-the-moment magazine by getting rid of all the slushy romantic stuff.

In addition, slight though it might be, the choice to buy or not to buy a magazine – the development of brand loyalty – represents a significant power on the part of the purchaser. For example, the slipping sales of *Cosmopolitan* since 1992 from its position of absolute dominance in the women's magazine sector has caused a flurry of anxiety within the editorial team. However, since the message put out by the editor remains intransigently that of success through 'keeping your man happy' and having a hugely successful career in corporate management, this more American mode of femininity now seems insufficiently complex and nuanced in comparison with its competitors, i.e. *Marie Claire*, whose sales figures have climbed consistently over the last five years, reaching 430,000 a month in 1995, with *Cosmopolitan* barely holding on to its lead at 460,000.

Circulation wars bring into play a range of strategies. Clearly the question of sales marks that point at which the most commercial of pressures exerts itself, and yet even here at the cutting edge of capitalist economics, we find cultural questions playing a significant role in how the editors try to win back the readers. Most clearly the editors are forced to study the readership, to find out what they want, and this produces a looseness as well as a tension, since what they find is precisely the diversity of contemporary femininities, the competing needs and desires of women, and the difficulty of reducing this down to one winning formula. At the same time the editors are forced to look closely at their competitors to see what they are doing, but since the whole identity of magazine culture hinges round the distinctiveness of each of the titles, this too produces a tension and a nervousness since they cannot afford to look as though they are taking the lead from the competition. Thus in a field which is overflowing with titles, new possibilities are continually being explored. As we shall see in the next section, one theme which has emerged comprises sexual representations which breach the boundaries of what in the past has been considered appropriate for girls or young women. So prominent are these strong themes (oral sex in particular) that they overshadow the stylistic differences between the different titles, creating a whole field of sex which is significant in its distance from the old world of boyfriends, orgasms, and living together.

Where does this new sexuality come from? Does it reflect the fact that sex always sells? Or does it tell us something more significant about what girls and women want to know about sex? Alternatively, does it mark out a new transgressive field of social regulation, the production of ever more free sexual practices and fantasy material as a way of fixing and stabilizing wayward sexual identities? Following Foucault, power is most effective where it is productive, generative and apparently generous, tolerant and expansive rather than repressive. And sexuality, the 'fictive unity' *par excellence*, is thus the key modality by which we know ourselves. Sexuality in magazines in this ample, intensive, and visually expansive form provides a guide for how we might be expected to be, for how we might expect to feel. In this way it also produces and brings into being new frank, fearless and therefore free female sexual subjectivities.

The findings of the market research, and the information and data then applied in the production processes of the magazine, could therefore be understood entirely within a Foucault grid, where surveillance of, and market research on girls and women, allows new categorizations to be drawn up and translated into social typologies or subjectivities which, in their newness and their radical and even feminist dispositions, confirm the magazine to be at the cutting edge of fashion and social change while still speaking of a social order which requires normative femininities in the interests of what Butler calls reproductive heterosexuality.

I want to argue that it is possible to recognize the regulative work done by the magazines and the role they play in defining and producing the norms of cultural intelligibility through which a girl or woman is permitted to understand herself and through which others also recognize her as acceptably female. But the magazines also do other things within their regulative remit which are not entirely reducible to what Butler sees as a zone of exclusion. Notwithstanding the heterosexual assumption, there is also some work of denaturalization going on. For example, sex is now recognized as something which has to be learnt. There is no longer the assumption that, like romance, it all comes naturally if you are with the man you love. Both romance and sexual expertise have been revealed as myths and they have been replaced by a much more frank, even mechanical approach to sex, but one which is without the cold, clinical or moralistic language associated with sex education. Alongside this there is a huge expansion of sexual fantasy material for girls and women, not just in the form of male pin-ups, but also in terms of written features, and also in the guise of 'information'.

We could see all of this as sexual control recast to fit with the pleasure zone of the magazine. But the impact of popular feminism cannot so easily be dismissed or discarded as so flawed by its heterosexism as to have nothing to say and no role to play in the politics of magazine production. The emphasis on female sexual pleasure; the demystification of romance and the idea that sexual technique has to be learnt and that it is not some magical or mystical effect; the wide availability of information; the assumption that knowledge is power; the attention to sexual health and to equality in sexual relationships, even the question of sometimes liking what is bad for us; all of these were issues endlessly debated in feminism from the mid-1970s onwards. The way in which figures like Gloria Steinem, Erica Jong and Germaine Greer have become the elder stateswomen of women's magazines, in terms of being quoted, interviewed and referenced also tells us something significant about how feminism has become popularized inside these pages. This is not to suggest that feminism is a monolith, nor is it to suggest that figures like Greer and Steinem were wholly representative of femininism then or now. The point is that a feminist history and tradition, including a set of debates and a series of figureheads, has entered into general discussions in the mainstream of popular culture.

Of equal significance in this new field of representations is the impact of AIDS. It is the language of safe sex which provides a new licence for magazines to carry very explicit material which ten or fifteen years ago would have been unthinkable. HIV prevention programmes, sponsored by agencies like the Health Education Council, have found that magazines offer one of the most effective vehicles for promoting information about safe sex. They can plug into the intimate tone which characterizes this particular medium, and as a result magazines have been targeted for getting the safe-sex message across to their millions of readers. This has produced contradictory and unstable effects, most vividly in the magazine *More!* – now the biggest-selling young women's magazine. In 1993 it carried with one of its issues a 'good sex handbook' which contained detailed information, graphically illustrated, about all methods of safe sex including 'rimming', 'sex toys', mutual masturbation, game playing and even sado-masochism. Each page of the supplement carried the logo of the HEC and a well-known brand of condoms. Given that all girls' magazines are read by a younger readership than the magazines themselves actually like to acknowledge, it was surprising that this special issue caused only a ripple of concern among the moral guardians. *More!* (whose readers are, on average, between 15 and 17 years old) now carries a feature titled 'Position of the Month'. It is not, therefore, that AIDS awareness produces one stable and identifiable set of effects in the realm of popular representations of sexuality, but rather that it warrants a new agenda in which knowledge, fantasy and autoeroticism play a more central role for girls and women than it has done in the past. This is what a recent issue of *19* had to say about female masturbation. 'Masturbation is true loving – it's a way of making yourself feel loved . . . Many girls find it easier to orgasm through masturbation because they're not worried about their boyfriend seeing their cellulite/bum/hairy legs.' The article concludes: 'And by satisfying yourself regularly, you'll be less tempted to have sex for the sake of it, thus reducing your chance of catching STDs' (*19*, January 1995, p. 7).

Once again this discourse of health and safety can be understood as constraining sexual exploration, risk and fantasy through endlessly describing it, by recording in detail the terms of its existence, what it looks like, how it is done. By pushing back the limits of what can be shown in the hitherto innocent space of the girls' magazine, the new sexual discourse can present itself as bold, adventurous and controversial where in fact it is limiting and controlling. It is laying down the law by appearing to say 'now you *can* do this or that, which in the past you thought "nice girls" never did'.

However I would still argue that this destabilizes the more singular femininity which the magazines once endorsed and, in blurring the line between good and bad girls, some of the tighter constraints of normative femininity are broken up; new alliances are also made possible, between girls no longer strictly defined according to the older grid of sexual behaviour and conduct. Slut, tramp, slapper: all undergo ironic reversals. They are, in Butler's terms, made to re-signify. They become joky, ironic terms of self-definition and endearment between girls ('God! I'm such a tart', or 'She's such a slapper') and they lose their punitive and pejorative meanings. And although the terms of sexual practice are largely, though not exclusively, set within a heterosexual frame, where there is a constant incitement to transgress sexual boundaries there is no reason to believe that heterosexuality remains unquestionable, certainly not where gay and lesbian sexualities are so frequently invoked as they now are in these pages.

Another frame of reference which needs to be taken into account in understanding new sexualities could be described as the 'Madonna effect'. Magazines depend on stars and the whole world of popular culture for an increasing amount of their copy. There is much more intertextual material than used to be the case in magazines. Stars, films, new records, new TV series, even new books now provide all the popular girls' and women's magazines with a tremendous amount of promotional (and therefore cheap) copy, both visual and written. Indeed in a magazine like *More!* a good deal of the sexual material is relayed through the gossip sections about who is 'shagging' or 'snogging' who. Madonna has played a key role in transforming the sexual subjectivities of young women over the last ten years. Notwithstanding the failure of her *Sex* book to register with a female readership, Madonna's sexual presence, her endorsement of safe sex, her masturbation sequences on stage and on video, her SM wardrobe, and her constant jokes about oral sex in *In Bed With Madonna*, and finally her own sexual ambivalence and her long association with gay and lesbian sexuality, place her at the absolute forefront of this new 'knowing' sexual subjectivity. She herself personifies this proliferation of female sexualities embodied as possibilities in one female self. She is the slut who poses for pornographic photographs, the lesbian girlfriend, the heterosexual dominatrix, the material girl, the feminist heroine for a generation of young female fans.

Cruising the Pages

In this final section I am going to take a cruise through a sample of girls' and women's magazines, providing a more vivid sense of what these new sexual subjectivities look like. What differentiates the dicourses in which these subjectivities are produced from their predecessors is their heavily ironic tone. The magazines speak in a voice of slightly mocking humour. This tone is one that actively stretches out and embraces the readers, it is the language of a shared knowingness, it signals a willingness to dispel the illusion that magazines speak the truth. Instead it suggests openly that they trade in dreams, fantasies and the pursuit of unattainable goals. This is also a sophisticated discourse which declares the death of naïvety. Girls and women need to be forewarned. With this acknowledged, the magazines can then more freely explore fantasy, fun and pleasure. The irony, the touch of parody, and the refusal of feminine naïvety produces, I would argue, a space for greater reflexivity and critique on the part of the reader. She is given a distance from what in the past was presented as a feminine destiny, to find the man of one's dreams. The social consequences of this reflective and ironic mode of address, now visible across a wide range of cultural forms, has prompted social theorists like Giddens (1994) and Lash and Urry (1993) to posit a new and more intelligent population of cultural consumers. Giddens explains his notion of reflexivity through the rather glib idea of 'clever people'. Certainly girls are achieving better educational qualifications and they have higher career expectations than ever before. They constitute a formidable and important group of young consumers. Most significantly, they now possess an awareness of sexual politics. Popular feminism has permeated every sector of the female population. It has been most staunchly supported and advocated by the female professionals who work in the media and the culture industries which produce magazines and other female media.

The result is by no means a monolithic or homogeneous femininity, or a single 'feminist' female sexuality. Instead what can be seen is the coexistence of a series of different, sometimes complementary and sometimes contradictory, female subjectivities. The dialogue in magazine culture comprises, then, of a new generation of female cultural intermediaries (including TV celebrities and comedians like Ruby Wax – also a regular contributor to *Marie Claire* – and Jennifer Saunders and Dawn French) talking to their readers, viewers or consumers in a different kind of language. As they speak, they make fun of the conventions which, in this context, they are part of. Magazines which show no willingness to enjoy irony in this way, and which subscribe instead to the old language of sexual prescription with penalties for failing to make the grade, are losing their hold over their readers. They are being replaced by a more open-ended, less judgemental world of femininities. And while the norm is still white and heterosexual, lesbian sexuality now finds a glamorous place within this open field of sexual possibilities. Likewise the new black women's glossy magazine *Pride* covers similar issues with the same humorous interest in sexual detail.

Sexuality is, then, the modality for the construction of contemporary femininity in women's magazines. It provides a frame for identity, into which are placed all the features which conventionally make up the space of the magazine. Fashion shots give the strongest visual imaging to female sexuality while beauty features make the body into something which can be endlessly and lovingly made over, worked on and improved. In both cases there is no naïvety about nature or the natural, there is no requirement that women hide the labour of body-work. Nor is there the assumption that this is done for men. Instead fashion and beauty are presented as sensual, autoerotic activities in and of themselves. Magazines heighten the visual pleasure of looking at the female body. Readers do not look at the endless shots of Claudia Schiffer or Naomi Campbell only from the viewpoint of envy. While these looks are not those of desire (lesbian desire is carefully and studiously avoided), they are certainly about enjoyment. This is not to suggest there is no power being exercised in the visual world of the magazines, no normativity about body size, no anxiety about looking. It is more that the magazines reference and signal to the readers that they know what they are doing. There is pleasure in those femininities constructed as beautiful and there is also anxiety. Commercial magazines cannot resolve these anxieties nor can they confront what lesbian desire would mean visually in the mainstream of the magazines' fashion and beauty pages, relegating this instead to the realms of readers' experiences. However, the new magazines can at least address their readers as able to resist what in the past might have been seen as a kind of fashion and beauty tyranny. Girls and women are now 'knowing' enough to recognize how they are persuaded to consume.

More! presents itself with a kind of youthful, cheeky impertinence. Its cover pokes fun at the way sex is used to pull the readers in. It is mocking itself. One cover reads as follow: 'Sex Scandal! Sordid Lies Could Wreck Your Career; Revealed: Claudia's Sexy Secrets; Sexy Hair Special; Party Styles to Pull a Cracker; "Trust Me I'm Celibate": The Dirty Tricks Men Use to Pull You' (7–20 December 1994). An earlier edition (13–26 April 1994) carried similarly sexual headlines: 'Bisexual Women: Double Trouble or Twice the Fun?; Nanny with Knobs On: Men Who Do Women's Work; Put the OOMph Back into Your Sex Life!; "I'm a Girl Who Really Likes the Boys!": Sharon Stone Gets Frisky,' and finally, 'I Read His Diary and Discovered His Dirty Secret'.

Alongside this kind of content *More!* gives over several pages to the semi-naked male body in every issue. These features are usually hooked on to a storyline, for example 'Do You Want to Live with a Male Model?'. This narrative structure allows 'at home' scenes (including in the bathroom) with a number of well-known male models. Likewise the 'men doing female jobs' feature also offers opportunities for the male body to be on display. Finally, in the same issue under the Mantalk section, there is an article titled 'Big Pecs Don't Mean Good Sex'. In this piece, where male body parts are also on display, a male journalist decries the male body being so much the object of attention. 'The bimboy has become a role model and as a muscle-free zone, I'm missing out.' The extensive coverage in *More!* of men and masculinity (a trend quickly pursued by its competitor *19*) responds, at one level, to readers wanting to know more about men and the male mind in order that they can 'feel more equal'. This at least was how an assistant editor at *More!* put it when asked (December 1994):

> We poll the readers regularly and what we discover is that they want to know everything they can about men because then they can make better decisions. Readers seem to enjoy the features we run where we ask ordinary guys to tell us exactly what they feel about this issue or that. It's a way of readers being able to plug into the things their boyfriends are more reluctant to talk about.

Following this kind of lead, *19* ran a lengthy feature on male masturbation. One of the *19* journalists explained (January 1995):

> Girls want to know why men masturbate, how often and what it means to them. This makes them feel more in control, they don't feel so threatened, even when they know their boyfriends are doing it when they are not around. It becomes a completely normal sort of thing.

These kinds of feature, along with those which provide first-hand accounts of female bisexuality, fit in with the informational grid of sexuality mentioned earlier. They simultaneously connect with AIDS awareness, as the following comment taken from the bisexual feature shows: 'As far as HIV and AIDS are concerned, we're seen as the ones in the middle, often as the people spreading the disease. I understand that argument but it just means you have to use condoms.' The article had attached to it contact addresses and numbers for further information and counselling services.

The two magazines which appear to foreground fashion and the body as the primary sites for the construction of female sexuality are *Elle* and the hugely successful *Looks*. In both magazines even more space is given over to visual imagery, with both fashion and beauty being presented as autonomous and erotic activities in their own right. Fashion photography has long been given over to showing models caught in states of oblivion, self-absorption and melancholic pleasure. *Elle* adds to this formula designer fashion as a source of heightened enjoyment. This creates its own distinctive image against the other magazines, for whom fashion sits alongside the features and the gossip. *Elle* is much more stylish than *More!*, *19* and *Marie Claire*, but it too finds space for the new sexuality topics. 'Sex addiction', for example (May 1994); 'Power Lesbians' (also May 1994); 'The World's 100 Sexiest Men' (December 1994); 'The Men Who Understand Women's Bodies' (August 1994); 'Same-Sex Affairs' (October 1994); 'Men in Crisis: Seducers or Sex Objects?' (also October 1994).

Looks is, as the title implies, almost wholly given over to fashion, beauty, health and the body; its tone, like *More!*'s, is heavily self-mocking, rude and humorous. Its covers include the promise of features on 'Boost Your Sex Appeal 100%' (October 1994); 'Yabba Dabba Drool! Men to Make Your Bed Rock' (August 1994); 'Bluffer's Guide to Sexual Confidence' (also August 1994); 'Scoff Horror! We Test Supermodel Diets' (August 1994); 'Fatten Up or Else! Supermodels in Weight Gain Scandal' (October 1994); ' "I Became a Man for a Day": One Cocky Girl's Story' (also October 1994); 'Sex Tips for Girls: Bring out the Goddess in You' (January 1995); 'Real Life Lovers' Secret Sex Diary; Up a Bit, Down a Bit ... Do Boys Know What Turns You On?; Snog-Proof Make-Up: We've Got It Licked; Bum's the Word! Hanging Out at the Mr UK Contest' (all in January 1995) and so on.

Finally, *Marie Claire* directs itself to the slightly older woman (25–35), and while this means that there is not the same kind of adolescent humour in its features, it is a magazine none the less largely concerned also with sexuality. Fashion and beauty are presented in terms of glamour, good sense and style, while features on jobs and travel also fit with *Marie Claire*'s formula for realism and fantasy, work and fun. All of these are, however, positioned around the much stronger headlines which the covers carry for their lead features, and these inevitably talk about sex. Once again, a sample from a pile of *Marie Claires* shows the following stories: 'Sex Stories: Affairs Within a Group of Friends'; 'Strippers at Weddings' (both in October 1994), or 'Orgasm School; How Many Lovers Have You Had?'; 'I Know He Has a Mistress' (all in December 1993). *Marie Claire* has also in the past taken the lead from the tabloid press and run articles on women sex tourists to Gambia, on incest ('My Brother is my Lover and We Have a Child'), on the 'Nun Who Became a Stripper', and also by Ruby Wax, 'Why We Need a School for Sex', all in November 1994.

Of all the magazines, *Marie Claire* has most carefully created an environment into which 'mature' feminine diversity can comfortably be placed. Unlike other women's magazines like *Cosmopolitan* it runs regular reportage features. *Marie Claire* also, within the language of barely disguised colonialist fantasies, publishes a regular tribal women slot, where non-white, non-Western women are simultaneously recognized as being 'just like us' and at the same time scrutinized for their otherness. In a 1995 TV advertisement for American Express, *Marie Claire* editor Glenda Bailey describes how the magazine reflects the intelligence of its readers, while in interview off-camera and in an editorial capacity she claims that women want as much sex as they can find in women's magazines (November 1994):

> We are not just about sex, we're the leading fashion magazine, but we also aim to inform our readers and they want to know about things that matter to them, even when it hurts. Everybody is interested in sex, we present it in a modern kind of way, we don't force it down our readers' throats. We manage to find the right kind of balance between the fascinating things that we might never think of doing but like to read about, and people's real-life sexual experiences. We are not the tabloid press, we don't go out looking for sordid stories and we never pay for people to tell their stories. Anybody who does one of our first-person features wants to share what has happened to them and does it voluntarily.

Drawing conclusions from this survey of the world of women's and girls' magazines presents various difficulties. One of the aims, however, has been to show how, across the spectrum of magazines, there is an increasing focus on strong, frank, and explicit sexual representations. The use of irony, humour and the assumed lack of innocence and naïvety on the part of the reader means that the sexual identities constructed through the pages of the magazine are more complex, more knowing, and 'equal' in their relationships with men. These features utilise a number of explanatory frames. One draws on the need for information, suggesting in a way that feminists have also done that knowledge means power. The second discourse, which is very visible in this new sexuality, emerges out of the public debates about safe sex in response to HIV and AIDS; and the third discursive element feeding into this field is more overtly commercial, even voyeuristic and based round the assumption that sex sells and that women want fantasy material in magazines as much as their male counterparts. Finally I have suggested that these magazine-specific sexual representations must also be considered in relation to the intertextual sexual meanings which connect diverse media forms. In this respect the image of Madonna occupies an important place. Taken together these seek to constitute a new form of sexual subjectivity, based round knowledge and self-reflexiveness. The widespread use of irony and humour allows a space for distance and detachment from what is being normatively advocated, i.e. lots of sex with male partners. If this is not to be taken too seriously, if magazines do not speak the whole truth, then it is up to the reader to consider what other truths there might be. The reader is actively invited to admit that magazines are escapist, fun and partial. She is encouraged to have an active rather than a passive relationship to the magazine form. All of this, as I have already suggested, could quite easily be understood as a means of creating an apparently more free, more diverse and more plural female sexual subjectivity, one which is, though, as fixed and stabilized in its new diversity as it once was in its homogeneity. The focus of the argument here, however, has been to explore another possibility. This has been to put on the agenda for future research the complex processes of magazine production, with particular attention being paid to the 'loop' of shared knowledge and commitment which can be traced between female magazine professionals, women working in similar capacities in the culture industries, feminist teachers, academics and researchers for whom the women's magazine has been an area for study and debate, and young women readers and consumers who themselves have grown up in a social environment where the politics of sexuality – though by no means resolved – are at least part of everyday life.

In conclusion, I have argued that magazines maintain their hold on women and girls as a privileged and pleasurable cultural space within which the female subject is actively produced while simultaneously being described and entertained. The magazines seek to further consolidate and fix an otherwise more unstable sense of both self and gender. While Butler would surely argue that this work is done largely on behalf of maintaining reproductive heterosexuality, the emphasis in this chapter has been to accept this as a broad critique but to suggest that, alongside and inside the matrices of exclusion, there are discernible shifts which serve to loosen the grip on normative femininity. Sexuality is the primary structure of meaning in these magazines, but it is a more nuanced, more knowing and less naïve sexuality than that of the liberated *Cosmopolitan* of the 1970s and 1980s.

While it is now commonplace to point to the prevalence of postmodern styles of presentation in the mass media, this article argues for the contextualizing of these styles through re-introducing to magazine scholarship a more sociological approach. Primarily this would mean paying more attention to the everyday practices of magazine producers. On the basis of current work of this type now being carried out in the field of girls' and women's magazines, I have argued that the ironic space in magazine discourse offers possibilities for critical reflection.

Notes

1 Circulation figures as of March 1995 for magazines referred to here are:

Marie Claire (monthly)	*430,000*
Cosmopolitan (monthly)	*460,582*
Elle (monthly)	*230,000*
19 (monthly)	*203,000*
More! (fortnightly)	*415,000*

2 This is taken from my current research on the fashion industry, to be published in 1996 as *Fashion and the Image Industries*. London: Routledge.

References

Althusser, L., 1971: 'Ideology and Ideological State Apparatuses', in *Lenin and Philosophy and Other Essays*. London: New Left Books.

Barthes, R., 1983: *The Fashion System*. New York: Hill and Wang.

Bourdieu, P., 1984: *Distinction: A Social Critique of the Judgement of Taste*. London: Routledge & Kegan Paul.

Beezer, A., Grimshaw, J. and Barker, M., 1986: 'Methods for Cultural Studies Students', in D. Punter (ed.) *Introduction to Contemporary Cultural Studies*: Longman.

Brunsdon, C., 1991: 'Pedagogies of the Feminine: Feminist Teaching and Women's Genres', *Screen* 32: pp. 364–82.

Butler, J., 1990: *Gender Trouble: Feminism and the Subversion of Identity*. New York: Routledge.

Butler, J., 1992: 'Contingent Foundations: Feminism and the Question of Postmodernism', in J. Butler and J.W. Scott (eds.) *Feminists Theorise the Political*. London: Routledge.

BUTLER, J., 1993: *Bodies That Matter: On the Discursive Limits of 'Sex'*. New York: Routledge.

COWARD, R., 1987: 'Sexual Violence and Sexuality', in Feminist Review (ed.) *Sexuality: A Reader*. London: Feminist Review/Virago.

DU GAY, P.,1993: 'Numbers and souls: retailing and the de-differentiation of economy and culture', *British Journal of Sociology*, 44(4), December: pp. 563–87.

DU GAY, P. and NEGUS, K., 1994: 'The Changing Sites of Sound: Music Retailing and the Composition of Consumers', *Media, Culture and Society*, 16: pp. 395–413.

FRITH, S. and SAVAGE, J., 1993: 'Pearls and Swine: Intellectuals and the Media', *New Left Review*, 198: pp. 107–17.

FRAZER, E., 1987: 'Teenage Girls Reading *Jackie*', *Media, Culture and Society*, 9(4): pp. 407–25.

FOUCAULT, M., 1983: *History of Sexuality*, vol. 1. London: Penguin.

GIDDENS, A., 1994: *Beyond Left and Right: The Future of Radical Politics*. Cambridge: Polity Press.

JAMESON, F., 1984: 'Postmodernism, or the Cultural Logic of Late Capitalism' *New Left Review*, 146: pp. 53–92.

LASH, S. and URRY, J., 1993: *An Economy of Signs and Spaces*. Cambridge: Polity Press.

MCROBBIE, A., 1991: *Feminism and Youth Culture: From* Jackie *to* Just Seventeen. London: Macmillan.

MERCER, K., 1990: 'Welcome to the Jungle: Identity and Diversity in Postmodern Politics', in J. Rutherford (ed.) *Identity: Community, Culture, Difference*. London: Lawrence & Wishart.

NIXON, S., 1993: 'Looking for the Holy Grail: Publishing and Advertising Strategies and Contemporary Men's Magazines', *Cultural Studies*, 7 (3): pp. 466–93.

RADWAY, J., 1984: *Reading the Romance: Women, Patriarchy and Popular Literature*. Chapel Hill, NC: University of North Carolina Press.

ROSE, J., 1987: 'Femininity and Its Discontents', in Feminist Review (ed.) *Sexuality: A Reader*. London: Feminist Review/Virago.

TAYLOR, H., 1989: *Scarlett's Women*. London: Virago.

STUART, A., 1990: 'Feminism: Dead or Alive?' in J. Rutherford (ed.) *Identity: Community, Culture, Difference*. London: Lawrence & Wishart.

WALKERDINE, V., 1990: *Schoolgirl Fictions*. London: Verso.

WILLIAMSON, J., 1978: *Decoding Advertisements*. London: Marion Boyars.

WINSHIP. J., 1987: *Inside Women's Magazines*. London: Pandora.

8

Rethinking Popular Music after Rock and Soul

David Hesmondhalgh

Academic writing on popular music provides the opportunity to think about the issues which emerge from the enormous amount of commentary surrounding music at greater length (and in hopefully greater depth) than in the frantic world of the cultural institutions where music is discussed and argued over: the music press, fanzines, record shops, live venues, clubs and so on. This does not mean that academic writing is better than music journalism, or better than what fans say about the music they like. But some of the best music scholarship has aimed at questioning some rash and simplistic ways of thinking about the production and consumption of musical texts.[1] In particular, recent criticism has raised doubts about notions of musical value associated with an era when rock and soul were at the centre of popular music myth and debate. The dominant paradigm behind a great deal, though not all, of the first generation of commentary on popular music was what we can call the ideology of rock and soul.[2] Fans who loved rock 'n' roll (and its roots in rhythm and blues) became critics and writers, institutionalizing and circulating a particular set of assumptions and value judgments. This writing is at its best in the early work of Greil Marcus (1975) and Peter Guralnick (1992). The thinking behind rock and soul ideology can be summarized – for the sake of clarity and convenience – as a set of oppositions, where the term on the left-hand side is assumed to be inferior to that on the right:

Mass	Community
Commerce	Creativity/Art
Artificiality	Authenticity
Large record companies	Small record companies

This system of values can be traced to conceptions of artistic activity formulated in nineteenth-century romanticism, though it also represents important transformations of them.[3] Developed as a set of ideas primarily in literature and philosophy, romantic thought saw the individual artist's ability to convey emotion as the goal of artistic activity, and art itself as a central component of human life. Applied to commercial popular music in a late twentieth-century context, it provided a powerful means for a clear division between, on one hand, rock and soul (associated with the qualities on the right) and, on the other, pop and various despised genres such as country (supposedly associated with those qualities listed on the left-hand side). This schema is still a powerful means of organizing the way people think about music around the world. In her book on rock culture in Liverpool, Cohen (1991: 134) identifies a series of oppositions, similar to those listed above, as the basis for the way local groups conceived of musical value. And beyond the Anglo-American heartland of rock and soul, Regev (1992) has traced the process by which 'authenticity' and 'artistry' were imported by Israeli cultural institutions as ways of evaluating music.

From the late 1950s on, rock and soul became the two dominant genres in global popular music. Associated with them were the value judgments outlined above. These provided audiences, musicians and record company workers with a set of conventions for understanding the production and consumption of records and performances. But by the 1980s, I will argue, there were signs of a marked shift in the way key sections of music comment and academic writing conceived of the oppositions listed above. In this survey, I want to examine these values and conventions in more detail, and to look at how writers on popular music have theorized the political and aesthetic value of music over the last few years, in the light of the decline of rock and soul and their concomitant ideologies.[4]

Rock and Soul Ideology

Much of the work of the leading academic writer on popular music, Simon Frith, has involved a sustained consideration of the problems and contradictions in the system of values I have outlined above. Frith's major full-length study of rock music, *Sound Effects* (1981), interrogates the belief in a continuing struggle between music and commerce in the main versions of rock ideology. Rock is a contradictory business, he argues: it is a commercially produced music for a mass audience, but it comes with a critique of commercialism and of mass culture (p. 11). Frith adopts a series of theoretical and empirical strategies for debunking rock myth.

Mass versus community. He does this first by criticizing the critiques of mass culture developed by F.R. Leavis in England and Theodor Adorno in Germany and the US. Both theories, he says, rely on a problematic distinction between true and false needs, and both fail to recognize the activity of popular audiences (pp. 42–5). Such attacks on mass culture approaches have become familiar, but more significant is Frith's assault on attempts by critics and fans to rescue rock from such criticisms. He suggests that the terms used by these groups to defend rock show that they share the mass culture critics' assumptions. He focuses on two particular versions of such defences. One type of rescue attempt is to claim that rock is a kind of folk music – the most basic appeal to a simplistic notion of community in writing on rock. The idea of folk music (which in itself is a bourgeois construct of what the culture of the peasantry or the Victorian working classes was supposed to be like – see Lloyd 1967) has relied on the key assumptions that there was and should be no distance between performers and audience; and that the music spontaneously expresses the nature of communal life, work and feeling. It has been enormously influential on the way of conceiving musical value represented above. But, says Frith, rock is certainly not a folk music of *teenagers*: it serves as popular culture for them, celebrating leisure rather than reflecting on work. Nor is it a folk music of *youth*: rock might have been some kind of expression for communities of oppositional youth groups in the late 1960s (for the hippies) and in the late 1970s (for punks) but these were brief moments, doomed to rapid co-optation.

Commerce versus creativity. Another way to rescue rock from the criticisms of cultural elitists and earnest Marxists was to claim that in fact it was a form of art, and here Frith opens up a deconstruction of the way rock ideology sets art against commerce. For Frith, the reality is that moments of artistic breakthrough, like moments of expression of community, are rare and fleeting, because of rock's continuing function as entertainment, and the basis of its production in a complex division of labour rather than in the kind of individual creativity usually associated with art (pp. 52–5).[5]

Artificiality versus authenticity. Other lines of attack follow on. Rock ideology, it is strongly implied by Frith, contains little to challenge prevailing economic, political and social structures. Folk values of sincerity and authenticity are easily adopted by the music industry for their own needs. Musicians may believe that they are bound to a community audience, but Frith suggests on the contrary that 'to be a rock musician is to be detached from a class background' (p. 75) and that the natural ideology of the musician is that of bohemianism and hedonism. Their very adoption of the romantic attributes of the artist is what sets them *apart* from the audience. Rock has, against the mass-culture-type criticisms of many insiders, achieved an unprecedented fusion of art and commerce, in that successful musicians have great freedom to produce what they want (p. 83).

Large versus small record companies. Frith then questions an associated orthodoxy, the assumption that independent record companies play a key role in the promotion of diversity and innovation. This, he says, is again to make an overdrawn distinction between art and commerce in what is essentially a commercial music. It romanticizes small businessmen who often exploit the musicians they employ:

> To reduce pop history to the struggles of musician (or small businessmen) heroes and corporate clowns is to ignore the critical issue: the music industry's strategies of market control (which certainly have their consequences for popular music) have been developed precisely because the market is one they can't control.
> (p. 91).

This emphasis on the difficulties of the industry in controlling a market determined by the volatile tastes of the youth audience looks forward to the last section of *Sound Effects*, where the gist of Frith's argument is that the power of rock lies in its use by youth audiences as a hedonistic, pleasurable leisure form. Frith is pessimistic in that he is prepared to recognize the limitations to claims for rock's power: the rapid taming of exciting moments (and the book was being revised[6] at a time when most people who were thinking seriously about music believed that punk was providing such a moment) into conventional marketing taste patterns; the individualization of consumption; its transfer from hedonistic leisure into safe background music (pp. 270–1). But he is more optimistic whenever he discusses the *uses* of such music, rather than the conditions of such production. Rock's vitality is contradictory, he says; it involves both escape and solidarity. With it, young people struggle over the meaning of pleasure.

Frith's book is still the most thorough and rigorous examination available of the politics of popular music, and it sets the agenda for academic popular music writing in the 1980s and 1990s in two related ways. First, its scepticism about the 'commonsense' assumptions of rock and soul ideology helped demolish a naïve politics of musical production based on mass culture criticism. Like Frith, Stratton (1983) challenges an overdrawn opposition of art and commerce, but goes beyond Frith by claiming that this very duality is fundamental to the maintenance of capitalist cultural production and consumption. The association of commercial structures with a predicted homogenization of music by many critics, he says, is a misguided attempt to reassert the romantic conception of the individual creator as the basis of the positive functions of art. In fact, because capitalism is a dynamic form, it needs ideologies like this in order to fuel innovation. In other words, criticisms of the standardization brought about by capitalist commercial production (such as those by Adorno) are merely versions of the very way of thinking which sustains capitalism in the first place.

Second, instead of locating (rock) music's political potential in unsustainable claims of 'authentic', links between performers and audiences, music and community, Frith's book drew attention to creative and active appropriations by audiences of the meanings and pleasures of popular music. Of course, Frith was not alone in advocating a concentration on audience appropriation as a way forward for understanding the politics of culture. As is well known, there was a marked shift in the 1980s towards the study of audiences in Europe and North America, in disciplines as diverse as mass communications, literature, film studies, media studies and sociology of culture (Morley 1989; Curran 1990). It is no surprise to find such a move occurring in popular music studies as well, though Frith's approach is subtle and complex.[7] But the study of popular music has its own version of this story of transformation.

Subcultures, Alliances and Scenes

Jim McGuigan (1992) has suggested that the necessary focus on practices of consumption in 1980s cultural studies has at times led to an 'uncritical cultural populism'. McGuigan scarcely deals with music, but popular music has often provided a privileged case for such cultural optimism. Yet it has also served as a focus for the most reductive mass-culture criticisms, whether from fans or critics. Some writers have connected music's proneness to utopian or dystopian conceptions of political possibility to its nature as abstract, non-referential sound (Attali 1985; Born 1993).[8]

Central to rock's implicit sociological understanding of youth culture was, in particular, the notion of *subculture*. The investment of energy and passion into musical consumption by groups of (usually) working-class young men served as a model for the idea that music could forge, or reinforce, communities. Sociological analysis of subcultures was pioneered by studies of 'deviance' by American interactionist sociology (e.g. Becker 1973) and by British sociologists influenced by them (Cohen and Taylor 1976). However, the most significant strand of work in the analysis of popular music and youth culture in the 1970s and 1980s was that of writers associated with the Birmingham Centre for Contemporary Cultural Studies (CCCS). Much of the CCCS's efforts were aimed at bringing a (neo-) Marxist understanding of class to bear on analysis of youth subcultures, but a more lasting legacy for the study of music audiences has been the impact of the CCCS's use of structuralism and semiology. These theoretical tools were used to develop theories of the potential for resistance to dominant ideology in clothing, hairstyles, modes of speech, dancing and leisure behaviour. The classic texts are those by Hall and Jefferson (1976), Willis (1978) and Hebdige (1979). Criticisms of the Birmingham/subculturalist approach are well known and need not be rehearsed in detail here. Briefly, its main limitations were: its focus on 'spectacular' forms of youth behaviour at the expense of the conformist (see Clarke 1990); its tendency to think of subcultures as being the property of young working-class men (McRobbie 1990); its universalizing of British social behaviour; and, as regards its usefulness for understanding music-related subcultures, its sidelining of musical meaning, as opposed to fashion and attitude (Laing 1985).[9]

The most important versions of the subculturalist approach as applied to the politics of musical culture are those of Hebdige (1979) and Chambers (1985). Both see the transgressive potential of *pleasure* as fundamental to the way that music can act as a focus for radical opposition. Although both books pay sophisticated homage to French post-structuralism (particularly the work of Roland Barthes (e.g. 1975) on '*plaisir*' and '*jouissance*') nevertheless the political operations of pleasure remain strangely undertheorized. Chambers and Hebdige are reacting strongly against a dour leftist critique of 'escapism'. Their elegant arguments for the presence of romance, imagination and pleasure in the lives of the consumers of popular culture are useful in counteracting blatantly generalized and inaccurate portrayals of the 'masses' in older criticism. But a powerful objection to a politics centred on transgression is that pleasure might well serve, in certain situations, as a means of obtaining or retaining power. Any ethical or political project that relies on pleasure (or the absence of pain) recalls hedonism – a largely discredited version of ethical philosophy which argues that pleasure is the aim of morally good action.

Ultimately, such vague appeals to pleasure and transgression meant that the subculturalist approach was not a significant challenge to the romantic ideology of rock. Even where, as in Hebdige's classic study (1979), there was emphasis on the artificiality and manufacture of style, a celebration of hedonism in the study of subcultures could easily be integrated into the assumption that music had most meaning when it emerged from a community of performers and audience, and when it was sustained by 'authentic', grassroots activity. British punk, at its height when Birmingham scholars were publishing their subcultural research in the late 1970s, no doubt seemed to confirm this idea.

An important move in recent research on popular music has been towards a more sophisticated understanding of the activities of music audiences than that embodied in the subculturalist approach, or in the related rockist assumptions of authenticity and community that Frith questions in *Sound Effects*. Thornton (1995), for example, has retained the notion of subculture, but against the Birmingham approach, distances herself from youth groups' own understandings of what they do, by assessing their criteria for judging musical-cultural activity. She analyses the changing ways in which youth groups accumulate 'subcultural capital' by struggling over patterns and conventions of taste within genres, rather than between strands of culture, as in the work of the French sociologist Bourdieu (1984). Rave culture's opposition of conformist mainstream clubs to hip underground ones is, she argues, a fiction, a means of distinction.

While writers like Thornton, and Redhead (1990) have attempted revisions of subculturalism, partially in the light of musical subcultural activity (such as the rave scene) in late 1980s and early 1990s Europe, others have attempted to move beyond the approach altogether. Straw (1991) is an important example. This is a difficult article which was aimed at a group of Straw's peers: it needs some explanation for newcomers to the kind of debate he is addressing. Straw examines the difference between two ways of accounting for the 'musical practices' within a geographical space (a country, a region, a city or a part of a town). He sets the rock notion of a stable community which engages with a heritage of geographically rooted forms (Straw refers to the very North American concept of 'heartland rock' to evoke such a link) against the idea of a *scene*, which has the advantage of taking account of 'processes of historical change occurring within a larger international music culture' (p. 373). For example, we could talk about the connections and differences between the alternative rock scene in an American college town, and that in a provincial French city. One of Straw's aims is to stress the importance of links across national and regional boundaries, partly in order to counter the simplifications that occur when critics talk of a 'national' music. Each music culture, he implies, is composed of scenes, and has its own 'logics': procedures for validating new and old music, for shifting boundaries of what is included and excluded as part of a genre, different rates of obsolescence, and processes of canonization. To illustrate his idea, Straw examines the cultures of alternative rock and of dance music.

Alternative rock is portrayed by Straw as a pluralist terrain: styles are rarely claimed as the future for alternative rock culture – they are absorbed into a diverse canon. Combining styles and genres seldom results in a synthesis; rather, such combinations are seen as adventures for a particular artist. For fans, there is great emphasis on apprenticeship in knowing the canon, and such 'connoisseurship' reinforces a masculine dominance amongst audiences. Also, says Straw, the aesthetic values of alternative rock are very stable from one cosmopolitan area to another. Straw suggests that this means that specific communities no longer emerge to lead the others, and that although the idea of local 'scenes' is still vital to alternative rock culture, success in a local community is no longer the main foundation for rock success.[10]

Straw's analysis of dance music culture points to its obsession with difference, with the marking of distinction. This is achieved not only via age, ethnicity and so on, but also through categories referring to the level of sexual interaction in clubs, whether DJs will play requests, and so on. Alternative rock incorporates its many canonical styles and combinations and fixes them within an ironic, bohemian display of prowess. Dance music culture, on the other hand, is portrayed as permanently in flux and movement (at least at the time that Straw was writing): its regional styles are nearly always at different stages in cycles of rising and falling influence. Straw's avowed aim is to seek the cultural politics of music neither in an optimistic examination of audience activity, nor in a pessimistic reading of the machinations of the industry. Instead, he locates the political power of music in its possibilities for forging alliances across racial and gender differences. So dance music's polycentrism and flux enables a number of different marginal groups attracted by such values to come together, leaving exposed 'the stable and canonical' roots of alternative culture and their connections to a white (male?) bohemianism.

Many issues emerge from this provocative piece. Straw shows a rare ability to fuse in-depth knowledge of specific cultural forms with theoretical insight. What concerns me here is not so much the accuracy or otherwise of his comments on these particular cultural formations, but rather his attempt to find a cultural politics for popular music in the aftermath of rock and soul's dominance, and his view that the political effectiveness of music is located in audience uses of music, specifically in the crucial notion of *alliance*.[11] This term is heavily laden with positive meanings, suggesting solidarity, and joint action for progressive social change. But this is a long way from the politics involved when people listen to the same radio stations, or even when they dance at the same clubs. This is not to say that the only significant political action takes place 'on the street' or in the workplace. I am simply pointing to the fact that how the two types of activity might be connected – how, for example, the international nature of such cultures might be connected to any kind of international solidarity when political activism is still very much based within national borders – is an issue that Straw opens up, but has not yet developed. There is also some ambiguity in the term 'scene': this is used by fans and critics to mean both the specific institutions of a particular musical culture in a particular place (e.g. the Manchester dance scene) and in a way where it is assumed to transcend the boundaries of a particular place (e.g. the acid jazz scene). In the latter case, the meaning is close to what Straw himself calls 'terrains' or 'cultures' in his article.

Straw's stress on the links between nodes in international networks of musical practice is the most serious attempt to apply the recent concern with space and place in social science and cultural studies (see Harvey 1989; Lash and Urry 1994) to popular music. His article is a welcome rejoinder to ethnomusicology (the anthropological study of music) and other forms of analysis (such as those influenced by the 'cultural imperialism' thesis) which too often have assumed that a musical culture is simply contained within a national or regional or city boundary. But potentially what might be lost in analyses which follow Straw's, suggesting the importance of cultural links between cosmopolitan centres, is a sense of an unequal distribution of power across different spaces (see also Frith 1991).[12]

Straw's theoretical language (articulation, scenes, alliances) recalls that of the project of another leading theorist of music as culture, Lawrence Grossberg, to apply neo-Marxist (the work of Gramsci, Lefebvre and Hall) and post-structuralist (Deleuze and Guattari) concepts to contemporary popular culture. Grossberg has developed a coherent and significant theory of the development of rock (see Grossberg 1992) but for anyone interested in popular music, his work is often frustratingly short on the kind of concrete analysis offered by Straw. And, as with Straw, the politics of music is located almost exclusively in audience activity. This can be seen in Grossberg (1994), the clearest outline of his theories yet available, and particularly interesting for its explicit attempt to theorize the politics of a new musical-ideological formation after rock.[13] Grossberg outlines three 'logics' of musical formations: those of production, consumption and effects/operational logics. It is this last category of operational logics which is given absolute priority in understanding rock, and in outlining what might be the features of a new formation (based around the music of house/dance and rap, but not confined to it). It is defined as 'the place of musical practices and relations in people's lived realities *understood socially . . . rather than psychologically*' (Grossberg 1994: 47, original emphasis).

Grossberg tries to counter the pessimistic view of the role of popular culture in fostering modern American conservatism outlined in his *We Gotta Get Out of This Place* (1992). He does so by suggesting that in this new musical-ideological formation there is greater potential for a 'polemological' understanding of everyday life. This is a term derived from the work of the French historian and theorist Michel de Certeau (e.g. 1984), and it denotes one of the forms that people's resistance to prevailing systems can take. In a well known article on de Certeau, Meaghan Morris sums up this attitude by borrowing a vernacular way of expressing opposition – 'they always fuck you over' (see Morris 1990: 23). The vagueness of the 'they' here is deliberate: it suggests the often unformulated conception people have of who is doing the oppressing, of where the power is. While such attempts to develop a politics of 'everyday life' may be valuable, to many activists they might look like a politics based on grumbling. But these limitations are not confined to Grossberg and Straw (who, in my opinion, are the most important North American contributors to debates on popular music) nor to theorists of the politics of popular culture influenced by similar intellectual sources. They are very real problems for anyone trying to understand the relationship between progressive political change and political consciousness.

Production and Aesthetics

In the 1980s, alongside the relocation of musical politics in the activity of audiences, came a questioning of some assumptions about the production of popular music held by a previous generation of countercultural theorists, such as Chapple and Garofalo (1977) and Harker (1980). Since the 1960s, there has been a long and thriving tradition of scholarship on the production of popular music. Much of this work has emerged from a branch of (mainly) US empirical sociology known as the 'production of culture' approach (Peterson 1982; Crane 1989). Scholars working within this field have often made attempts to draw connections between production factors and cultural outcomes. Peterson and Berger's (1990) article on cycles of innovation in popular music is a classic example. Focusing on the period 1948 to 1973, they claimed to find support for two hypotheses. The first was that there was a weak but inverse relationship between concentration and diversity in the US popular music industry. That is, the more US market share was concentrated in the hands of the major international record companies, the less was the diversity of performers in the US charts. The second hypothesis was that this inverse relationship formed a series of cycles, whereby relatively long periods of gradually increasing concentration and homogeneity were followed by brief bursts of competition and creativity.

There are serious problems with Peterson and Berger's conception of diversity, which is based on an analysis of lyrical content, and is confined to records in the Top 10.[14] Nevertheless, this was an important sociological version of one of rock and soul ideology's key ways of conceiving of the dynamics of production: the idea that small, independent companies were the means of sustaining any diversity, adventure and political or aesthetic opposition that music could provide. The corporations (the 'majors') were the villains of the piece, co-opting adventurous moments, and stifling innovation. Post-rock and -soul revisionism has increasingly challenged such a view. We have already seen that this was one of the strands of rock ideology that Simon Frith critiqued in *Sound Effects*. Keith Negus (1992: 16–18) has argued that such a simple binary opposition of majors and independents ignores the huge range of small companies who have no interest in providing any kind of challenge to the majors. Furthermore, says Negus, such small companies are now working with the majors in a web of complex relationships, involving financing, distribution and marketing (see also Frith 1988). Negus's examination of the industry concentrates almost entirely on the major corporations who dominate the production of popular music – the 'bad guys' of rock mythology. While early rock writing assumed that the links to multinational corporate finance inherently compromised the rebellious message of rock, Negus points to the way the large corporations are restructuring to achieve 'a large degree of autonomy' for workers (Negus 1992: 19). In order to counteract the conspiracy theory assumption that corporate staff tend to act as a unified whole (see Chapple and Garofalo 1977) Negus examines the conflicts and divergent goals within the major record companies.

Rock and soul ideology embraced small-scale capitalist production in the form of the independents, and attacked the corporations not for being capitalist, but for being corporate and bureaucratic. Once pop revisionism showed that such companies are becoming less corporate and bureaucratic, and that independents secretly wanted to be corporate capitalists anyway (if only they had the chance!) then a fundamental element of rock's production politics was in danger of dissolving. How then have more recent approaches to popular music conceptualized the politics of musical production? If musicians and small record companies could no longer be thought of as authentically expressing the desires and aspirations of communities, how have their activities been re-evaluated in contemporary academic work? In this final section, I want to suggest that some of the most fruitful directions in recent analysis have been those that have attempted to draw connections between production and aesthetic factors. A consideration of these factors could not possibly exhaust all the questions we would want to ask about consumption – there is no doubt that what audiences do with texts is an important area of investigation in its own right. But consumers are not sovereign. To enhance our understanding of processes of reception, we need to take account of the sociological and economic factors involved in the production and circulation of cultural goods.

The Importance of Production

A key area of development in understanding these factors has been the critical political economy of culture. Writers such as Nicholas Garnham (1990) and Bernard Miège (1989) have used the economic concept of use value to understand the nature of cultural goods as *commodities*. These are used as markers of difference and status by consumers; audiences are especially unpredictable in their cultural habits because artists, genres and styles can shift out of (and into) fashion. This makes capitalist cultural production a relatively risky business. Producers attempt to deal with this by spreading risk across a repertoire: one big hit can cancel out the cost of many failures. But this favours bigger firms, leading to oligopolistic control by small groups of massive producers. These firms also attempt to deal with the special nature of risk in the cultural industries by controlling the means of promotion and distribution (Garnham 1990: 161). Some goods are promoted and distributed much more heavily than others (Hirsch 1990). This means that some records, artists and styles are made more available than others, in terms of presence in the shops, and publicity and promotion in other media.

The issues of availability and diversity are central to a political economy of musical production. The marginalization of certain forms – or in the case of many African-American styles, their appropriation – is at the heart of much political debate about music (Garofalo 1993). Marginal musics can gain status by their exclusion and emerge from the wilderness to 'cross over' into the mainstream – and such a transition frequently triggers political and aesthetic debates about 'commercialisation' and 'selling out'.[15] Business control of the production and distribution of music, then, is not stable; but neither does the consumer have full power. In the analysis of this tussle, musical technologies have often taken pride of place, embraced by some as heralding a new age of control for small producers and consumers, condemned by others as the basis of a dystopian future, causing loss of traditional skills and the elimination of musicians' autonomy.

But here I want to examine two recent contributions to the study of new musical technologies (Goodwin 1991; Théberge 1989) which, while taking relatively optimistic and pessimistic positions respectively, avoid brash polarizations of the issues. I also want to point out that their discussions bring into focus important questions about the relationship between creative collaboration, commercial control and aesthetic strategies and outcomes. Théberge's article describes how sound engineers and independent producers[16] have arrived at a set of conventions for achieving the maximum technical manipulation of the individual instrument sounds that make up a record. This involves separating the musicians of a group within the studio, temporally (they lay down the track at different times) or spatially (they are kept in booths to avoid interference between tracks). The commercial demands of the star system also require a technology of overdubbing. This takes place after the group performs 'together' in the studio. In turn, for Théberge, the emphasis on the vocal in overdubbing reinforces the star system, which is clearly associated, in his view, with a dubious fetishization of the individual, rather than the desirable qualities of musical co-operation.[17] Drawing on Habermas's adaptation of Weber's theory of rationalization, Théberge emphasizes the way both processes diminish the interaction between musicians, and increase the technical rationality involved in contemporary musical production. Ironically, all this is aimed at a *simulation* of coherent group activity, reinforced in video and live performance.

Andrew Goodwin's article (1991) also notes the increasing artistic control of record producers, and outlines a number of ways in which technological developments such as the drum machine have helped to bring about rationalization: of the beat, by encouraging a rigid, 'industrial' notion of time; and of timbre, through the elimination of non-Western microtones on globally-distributed Western synthesizers. Goodwin's main emphasis, however, is on a number of potentially *progressive* developments associated with more recent, mainly digital, technology. One example he cites is the way that the enormous complexity of stereo imaging techniques, whereby the sound of the drums moves from speaker to speaker, ear to ear, serves to reveal the very constructedness of the recording. Here Goodwin adopts a typically postmodern aesthetic position (see below): popular forms achieve a kind of modernist (Brechtian) anti-realism almost by accident, subverting the popular from within. Other progressive developments, in Goodwin's view, are that pop production has been democratized by the 'historically cheap' (p. 90) availability of expensively produced sounds; and that interaction between parts is enabled by the way MIDI-linked sequencers and samplers allow experiments with sound variations, without the need for buying long hours of expensive studio time.

Goodwin is suitably cautious in his assertions about democratization. He is careful to point out that the skill involved in programming the new computers has resulted in further professionalization, and that a more general 'identification of technology with masculinity' (p. 92) may entail the exclusion of women. Other studies have also raised this key question of *access*. The view that 'talent will out' is one way in which record company workers tend to validate the status quo. Against this, Cohen (1991), for example, suggests the centralization involved in the British record industry, when she talks of the difficulties for any band of 'making it' if they stay in their home town of Liverpool, rather than moving to London. Frith and McRobbie (1990) and Gottlieb and Wald (1994) have written about the exclusion of women from different spheres of rock music; and the latter pair have looked at the Riot Grrrl movement as an attempt to open up space for women in independent/alternative rock. Like Bayton (1993) they draw attention to debates amongst feminist women on how best to negotiate between compromise and recognition, exclusion and appropriation (including Riot Grrrl's rejection of a longstanding feminist demand to be called 'women' rather than 'girls').

The Value of Aesthetics

Bayton and Gottlieb and Wald draw attention to the importance of alternative, independent networks in facilitating participation. A predominant focus on the ability of audiences to negotiate their own meanings from popular texts, alongside the rejection of romantic views of independence, has resulted in the scholarly marginalization of attempts to forge aesthetic and institutional alternatives in music. It is notable that Bayton and Gottlieb and Wald's accounts both pay due regard to debates over aesthetic strategies in discussing women as musicians: the level of aggression in the music, for example, and whether this represented a subversion of masculine (hardcore) musical codes, or a submission to them. Such aesthetic strategies are also discussed across a range of the activities that constitute musical culture, including live performance backdrops and stage behaviour. Music, it is implicitly recognized, is a multitextual affair, visual as well as aural, public and private, presented and represented in the full range of contemporary mass media (Born 1991).

For many years, there has been a strong tendency in cultural studies and the sociology of culture to dismiss such aesthetic debates. Students of empirical sociology distrusted the subjective basis of aesthetic experience. From a different perspective, Marxists and the radical Left have very effectively examined the way traditional aesthetics can serve as a weapon of prevailing systems of class power (see Bennett 1990). Wolff (1993b) provides a superb survey of sociological attitudes to the question of aesthetic value. Her main aim is to demonstrate, against a prevailing Marxist view, that aesthetic experience cannot be reduced to social and political issues. For Wolff, aesthetic experience has its own specific dynamics, and the recognition of this can lead to a more adequate analysis of traditional aesthetics. She argues too that the sociology of art necessarily involves critical judgements about cultural products, and that this should not force writers further towards aesthetic neutrality. Rather, she says, sociologists of art should be more upfront and reflexive about the critical values implicitly underlying their work, and implies that this might enable a richer investigation of the values attached, historically and contemporaneously, to 'works of art' (including popular products).

As Wolff observes, controversies over art works – particularly those associated with the 'political correctness' debate in the United States – suggest that debates taking place at the cusp of aesthetics and politics have the power to mobilize activism, whether of the Left or of the Right. An adequate analysis of musical culture needs to continue to address debates on aesthetics, rather than resorting to the presentation of data about the consumption and production of music, a phenomenon Wolff calls 'sociological imperialism' (Wolff 1993b: xiv). This necessitates in turn an examination of the agency and intentions of cultural producers, and the way they conceptualize (and internalize) such debates: be they musicians, film-makers, artists or any of the many other types of workers in cultural institutions. The neglect of these crucial issues in British cultural studies and in many recent approaches to musical culture in favour of active audience appropriations has helped to marginalize questions that radical cultural producers must face (Born 1993).[18]

The abundance of commentary surrounding contemporary popular music provides rich examples of aesthetic claims and strategies – and of the types of political values attached to them. One instance is the anonymity of techno and ambient music (reinforced by the frequent use of aliases and disguises in packaging and publicity) and its supposed refusal of the mainstream industry's star system. The severe repetition of techno, derived initially from its function as dance music, has become the basis of claims that the music provides a challenge to listeners. The ethereality of the ambient subgenre, on the other hand, is seen as a refusal of the blunt sensuousness of the mainstream of musical production, rooted in soulful voices and crisp guitars. In these cases, there is often a strong suggestion that a questioning of the musical mainstream has an intimate relationship with the interrogation of social and political power.

Meanwhile, in avant-garde rock and jazz, a key term remains *dissonance* (Durant 1984). Echoing the challenge to traditional jazz chord structures and timbres in the extraordinary period of jazz innovation from the late 1940s to the late 1960s, rock groups like Sonic Youth have experimented with unusual tuning systems and song structures. There is a strong implication in the discordant noise of various alternative rock mutations that 'conventional' harmony stands in some way for an acceptance of prevailing social conditions; and that dissonance is a challenge to it. On the other hand, rap and hip hop's early foregrounding of the bare, rhythmic elements of music has been portrayed as a self-reflexive deconstruction of music (e.g. Cross 1994: 17–18). The problem, as with any form of avant-garde experiment and innovation, is that the conventions of commercial entertainment forms are constantly shifting to incorporate new sounds, in order to provide new ways of stimulating emotion, interest and excitement.

Such vanguardist claims can be traced back to early twentieth-century modernism. These tactics play off against the popular: their aim is to negate it. A series of important debates amongst German Marxists in the 1920s and 1930s involving such thinkers as Adorno, Bloch, Benjamin, Lukacs and Brecht (see Laing 1978; Bloch et al. 1980) continues to be important and suggestive in analysing the connection between aesthetics and politics. Rather than in his often-cited dismissals of popular music, the significance of Adorno lies in his outline of the political value of such aesthetic strategies of complexity and difficulty in some modernist, avant-garde music, for example, that of Schoenberg (Adorno 1976). The other writers rarely addressed music, but their discussions have been enormously influential on how very many radical cultural producers conceive of their work, particularly in the debates over realism (often represented by Lukacs) and modernism (where Brecht's attempts to lay bare the bones of theatrical illusion are often invoked).

Postmodern aesthetics, in contrast to the avant-garde modernist project theorized by Adorno, tends to side with elements of the work of Brecht and Benjamin in placing greater emphasis on the necessity of engaging with the popular in a positive way, and in addition addresses issues of difference and cultural identity (Foster 1985). Here, recent claims for a radical aesthetic of popular culture have often been based on the potential of parody and pastiche (see Hutcheon 1985; Caughie 1991).[19] In the field of popular music, writers on MTV have made many such claims (e.g. Kaplan 1987) and have been challenged by Goodwin (1993) for being deaf to the aural aspects of the video clip, and blind to its economic context as a promotional tool. More broadly,

Jameson (1991) has criticized postmodern texts for engaging only in 'blank parody': parody that only refers to other forms, without criticism or analysis.

Conclusion: Aesthetics, Institutions and the Margins

The modernist/postmodernist split is only one way of conceptualizing the aesthetic strategies that producers may adopt, whether or not they might be familiar with the historical debates that precede them. My interest here is not to adjudicate in such debates, but to suggest the potential fruitfulness, in the next generation of popular music study, of attempts to combine analysis of structural-economic factors with acknowledgment of the agency and intentions of cultural producers. As I suggested earlier, this will reap most rewards where it makes full acknowledgment of the multitextual nature of musical production (see Laing 1985).

My main argument in this survey has been that in the 1980s, something of a vacuum developed in a critical understanding of the production of popular music, as a result of two developments which were positive in themselves: an increased focus on the popular music audience, and an examination of rock and soul ideology's own understanding of production politics. A shift took place in popular music studies (and in its siblings, media and cultural studies) in the late 1970s and early 1980s, from a focus on production and textual issues, to a concern with consumption. This was, in many cases, an understandable reaction against the elitism of some avant-garde aesthetic strategies of production. At its best, it recognized that much of the meaning of popular music derives from its popularity, its ability to suggest common patterns of feeling and response, and to this extent the shift to focusing on the 'demand side' of music was justified. But in its moment of excess, this has resulted in a validation of the stadium rock of self-congratulatory superstars, whether international or national (see some of the contributions to Garofalo 1992). The politics of music are also about the way activity on the fringes worries away at the centre. Being in the margins institutionally and industrially does not guarantee aesthetic challenge or innovation (Born 1993). The concept of the margins, of an 'outside' simplistically opposed to a mainstream centre, has rightly been probed and questioned by many writers (e.g. Thornton 1995). But at the moment it is this relationship between the fringes of institutional structures and aesthetic politics that needs to be reckoned with in studying popular music. An important future direction will be to address the musical margins as well as the mainstream, however tentative and careful we need to be about such distinctions.

Notes

1 The best journalism does so too. Simon Reynolds begins a collection of his critical writing with the following observation: 'This book is written in the conviction that what excites people in pop, and what they manage to articulate of those feelings are generally two very different things' (Reynolds 1990: 9).

2 This term, which I have borrowed from Marsh (1989), is not intended to elide the differences between the two forms, but to point to the importance of the relationships

between them. Soul music draws on many of the same discourses of authenticity/community as rock, and is probably as central to understanding the modern history of popular music. The term might also help to avoid overdrawn historical models of transition, for example, the idea that rock has given way to rap. See Nelson George's (1994) highly suggestive notion of 'post-soul black culture'.

3 See Pattison (1987) on music, and Wolff (1993a) on the sociology of art in general, for different considerations of the legacy of romanticism. Lawrence Grossberg (e.g. 1992) has devoted much attention to the historical context of the origins of rock ideology in the conservatism of 1950s America.

4 Because this is an introductory survey, I have tried to make reference, where possible, to Frith and Goodwin's very useful collection of classic scholarly work on popular music (1990). My thanks to Georgie Born, Dai Griffiths, Keith Negus, Sarah Thornton and especially Jason Toynbee for comments and advice.

5 For the sake of his argument, Frith accepts this prevalent notion of art. Where the focus is on high cultural formations (fine art, classical or art music) another way of demolishing the naïve art/commerce polarity might be to argue against the idea that 'art' is ever produced other than collaboratively. This is the approach taken by Wolff (1993a).

6 *Sound Effects* was a revised version of Frith's earlier book, *The Sociology of Rock* (1978).

7 Frith has always seemed keen to avoid orthodoxies. By 1988, he was arguing that production needed to be taken account of, as it largely determined patterns of consumption (Frith 1988).

8 This aspect of its character is perhaps what has led some commentators to try to locate the political power of music in lyrics. Griffiths (1992) provides an interesting musicological demonstration that music, rather than lyrics, can determine key aspects of political meaning in popular political song.

9 There is an excellent account in McGuigan (1992: Chapter 3) which carefully differentiates the work that emerged from Birmingham. McGuigan rightly points out that some key criticisms of the 'Birmingham' approach came from scholars trained at Birmingham; an example is McRobbie's famous criticisms of its exclusive focus on masculine subcultures (McRobbie 1990). Middleton (1990: 155–69) criticizes subcultural theory as it applies to popular music.

10 This echoes Frith's ideas about changes in breakthrough methods in popular music in an important earlier article (1988).

11 This remark should not be misconstrued as meaning that Straw is merely asserting that audiences are active in negotiating the *meaning* of texts. Anything but: Straw is sociologically examining the mediating role of cultural institutions. But his focus is on how this affects *consumption* practices.

12 Two theorists of space, Lash and Urry (1994) have argued for the retention of the ideas of 'core' and 'periphery' in order to maintain a focus on unequal access and distribution of economic and cultural power. But it remains to be seen whether this part of their analysis will be applied systematically to musical production and consumption.

13 Of all Grossberg's terms, I find 'formation' the most useful in the way it suggests the importance of understanding the relationships of the musical dimension of rock (or any other genre) with other social and cultural dimensions.

14 More recent contributions from the 'production of culture' approach have attempted to go beyond this conception of diversity. See, for example, Burnett (1990) and Christianen (1995).

15 At the time of writing, this seems to be happening with jungle (a subgenre of techno) in the UK, and already there are signs of a loss of prestige for this form amongst its fans as a result of this.

16 Here, for the only time in this chapter, I use the term in its usual musical sense to mean the worker who works with the group/singers, usually hired by the record company to achieve the 'sound' of the record. Elsewhere, I am using the more general meaning of 'people who make music'.
17 Negus (1992: 154–5) has argued that the star system provides the most productive way to examine musical-aesthetic strategies.
18 I have paid little attention in this chapter to the contribution of musicology to such debates. Musicology has been heavily criticized from within for its lack of attention to popular music, and to the attendant social relations of music as a whole. See Middleton (1990: Chapter 4) and McClary and Walser (1990). Nevertheless, a critical musicology that addresses music as culture (rather than as notated text) has much to offer the study of popular music.
19 Beadle (1993) is a romp through the history of twentieth-century music, which argues that pop music's infatuation with its own past in the 1980s was the equivalent of modernism's efforts to engage with the history of high cultural musical forms. It is a highly entertaining account, but its historical claims are glib, and are undermined by a lack of attention to the vastly differing institutional, economic and political circumstances of high modernism and pop.

References

ADORNO, T., 1976: *Philosophy of Modern Music*. New York: Seabury Press.
ATTALI, J., 1985: *Noise*. Manchester: Manchester University Press.
BARTHES, R., 1975: *The Pleasure of the Text*. London: Jonathan Cape.
BAYTON, M., 1993: 'Feminist Musical Practice: Problems and Contradictions', in T. Bennett, S. Frith, L. Grossberg, J. Shepherd and G. Turner (eds.) *Rock and Popular Music*. London: Routledge, pp. 177–92.
BEADLE, J.J., 1993: *Will Pop Eat Itself?* London: Faber & Faber.
BECKER, H., 1973: *Outsiders*. New York: Free Press. (First published 1963).
BENNETT, T., 1990: *Outside Literature*. London: Routledge.
BLOCH, E, LUKACS, G., BRECHT, B., BENJAMIN, W., and ADORNO, T., 1980: *Aesthetics and Politics*. London: Verso.
BORN, G., 1991: 'Music, Modernism and Signification', in A. Benjamin and P. Osborne (eds.) *Thinking Art: Beyond Traditional Aesthetics*. London: Institute of Contemporary Arts, pp. 157–76.
BORN, G., 1993: 'Afterword: Music Policy, Aesthetic and Social Difference', in T. Bennett, S. Frith, L. Grossberg, J. Shepherd and G. Turner (eds.) *Rock and Popular Music*. London: Routledge, pp. 266–92.
BOURDIEU, P., 1984: *Distinction*. London: Routledge.
BURNETT, R., 1990: 'Concentration and Diversity in the International Phonogram Industry', PhD dissertation. Gothenberg, Sweden.
CAUGHIE, J., 1991: 'Adorno's Reproach: Repetition, Difference and Television Genre', *Screen*, 32 (2): pp. 127–53.
CHAMBERS, I., 1985: *Urban Rhythms*. London: Methuen.
CHAPPLE, S. and GAROFALO, R., 1977: *Rock 'n' Roll is Here To Pay*. Chicago: Nelson-Hall.
CHRISTIANEN, M., 1995: 'Cycles in Symbol Production? A New Model to Explain Concentration, Diversity and Innovation in the music Industry', *Popular Music*, 14 (1): pp. 55–94.
CLARKE, G., 1990: 'Defending Ski-jumpers: A Critique of Theories of Youth Subcultures', in S. Frith and A. Goodwin (eds.) *On Record*. New York: Pantheon, pp. 81–96. (Written in 1981).
COHEN, S., 1991: *Rock Culture in Liverpool*. Oxford: Clarendon Press.

COHEN, S. and TAYLOR, L., 1976: *Escape Attempts*. London: Allen Lane.

CRANE, D., 1989: *The Production of Culture*. London: Sage.

CROSS, B., 1994: *It's Not About a Salary*. London: Verso.

CURRAN, J., 1990: 'The New Revisionism in Mass Communication Research: A Reappraisal', *European Journal of Communication*, 5: pp. 135–64.

DE CERTEAU, M., 1984: *The Practice of Everyday Life*. Berkeley, CA: University of California Press.

DURANT, A., 1984: *Conditions of Music*. London: Macmillan.

FOSTER, H. (ed.), 1985: *Postmodern Culture*. London: Pluto.

FRITH, S., 1978: *The Sociology of Rock*. London: Constable.

FRITH, S., 1981: *Sound Effects*. New York: Pantheon.

FRITH, S., 1988: 'Video Pop: Picking up the Pieces', in S. Frith (ed.) *Facing the Music*. New York: Pantheon, pp. 88–130.

FRITH, S., 1991: 'Anglo-America and Its Discontents', *Cultural Studies*, 5 (3): pp. 263–9.

FRITH, S. and GOODWIN, A. (eds.), 1990: *On Record*. New York: Pantheon.

FRITH, S. and MCROBBIE, A., 1990: 'Rock and Sexuality', in S. Frith and A. Goodwin (eds.) *On Record*. New York, Pantheon, pp. 371–89. (First published 1978).

GARNHAM, N., 1990: *Capitalism and Communication*. London: Sage.

GAROFALO, R. (ed.), 1992: *Rockin' the Boat*. Boston, MA: South End Press.

GAROFALO, R., 1993: 'Black Popular Music: Crossing Over or Going Under?', in T. Bennett, S. Frith, L. Grossberg, J. Shepherd and G. Turner (eds.) *Rock and Popular Music*. London: Routledge, pp. 31–48.

GEORGE, N., 1994: *Buppies, B-Boys, Baps and Bohos*. New York: Harper Collins.

GOODWIN, A., 1991: 'Rationalisation and Democratisation in the New Technologies of Popular Music', in James Lull (ed.) *Popular Music and Communication*, 2nd edition. London: Sage, pp. 75–100.

GOODWIN, A., 1993: *Dancing in the Distraction Factory*. London: Routledge.

GOTTLIEB, J. and WALD, G., 1994: 'Smells like Teen Spirit: Riot Grrrls, Revolution and Women in Independent Rock', in A. Ross and T. Rose (eds.) *Microphone Fiends*. London: Routledge, pp. 250–74.

GRIFFITHS, D., 1992: 'Talking about Popular Song (4): Politics', paper presented at a conference on 'Popular Music: The Primary Text'. Ealing, London, 4 July.

GROSSBERG, L., 1992: *We Gotta Get Out of This Place*. London: Routledge.

GROSSBERG, L., 1994: 'Is Anybody Listening? Does Anybody Care? On Talking About "the State of Rock" ', in A. Ross and T. Rose (eds.) *Microphone Fiends*. London: Routledge, pp. 41–58.

GURALNICK, P., 1992: *Feel Like Going Home*. London: Penguin. (First published 1971).

HALL, S. and JEFFERSON, T. (eds.), 1976: *Resistance Through Rituals*. London: Hutchinson.

HARKER, D., 1980: *One for the Money*. London: Hutchinson.

HARVEY, D., 1989: *The Condition of Postmodernity*. Oxford: Basil Blackwell.

HEBDIGE, D., 1979: *Subculture*. London: Methuen.

HIRSCH, P.M., 1990: 'Processing Fads and Fashions: An Organisation-set Analysis of Cultural Industry Systems', in S. Frith and A. Goodwin (eds.) *On Record*. New York: Pantheon, pp. 127–39.

HUTCHEON, L., 1985: *A Theory of Parody*. London: Methuen.

JAMESON, F., 1991: *Postmodernism, or the Cultural Logic of Late Capitalism*. London: Verso.

KAPLAN, E.A., 1987: *Rocking Around the Clock*. London: Methuen.

LAING, D., 1978: *The Marxist Theory of Art*. Hassocks, Sussex: The Harvester Press.

LAING, D., 1985: *One Chord Wonders*. Milton Keynes: Open University Press.

LASH, S. and URRY, J., 1994: *Economies of Signs and Spaces*. London: Sage.
LLOYD, A.L., 1967: *Folk Song in England*. London: Lawrence & Wishart.
MCCLARY, S. and WALSER, R., 1990: 'Start Making Sense! Musicology Wrestles with Rock', in S. Frith and A. Goodwin (eds.) *On Record*. New York: Pantheon, pp. 277–92. (First published 1988).
MCGUIGAN, J., 1992: *Cultural Populism*. London: Routledge.
MCROBBIE, A., 1990: 'Settling Accounts with Subcultures', in Simon Frith and Andrew Goodwin (eds.) *On Record*. New York: Pantheon, pp. 66–80. (First published 1980).
MARCUS, G., 1975: *Mystery Train*. New York: Dutton.
MARSH, D., 1989: *The Heart of Rock and Soul*. London: Penguin.
MIDDLETON, R., 1990: *Studying Popular Music*. Buckingham: Open University Press.
MIÈGE, B., 1989: *The Capitàlization of Cultural Production*. New York: International General.
MORLEY, D., 1989: 'Changing Paradigms in Audience Studies', in E. Seiter, H.Borchers, G. Kreutzner and E.-M. Warth (eds.) *Remote Control*. London: Routledge, pp. 16–43.
MORRIS, M., 1990: 'Banality in Cultural Studies', in P. Mellencamp (ed.) *Logics of Television*. London: British Film Institute, pp. 14–43.
NEGUS, K., 1992: *Producing Pop*. London: Edward Arnold.
PATTISON, R., 1987: *The Triumph of Vulgarity*. New York: Oxford University Press.
PETERSON, R.A., 1982: 'Five Constraints on the Production of Culture: Law, Technology, Market, Organizational Structure and Occupational Careers', *Journal of Popular Culture*, 16 (2): pp. 143–53.
PETERSON, R.A. and BERGER, D., 1990: 'Cycles in Symbol Production: The Case of Popular Music', in S. Frith and A. Goodwin (eds.) *On Record*. New York: Pantheon, pp. 140–59. (First published 1975).
REDHEAD, S., 1990: *The End of the Century Party*. Manchester: Manchester University Press.
REGEV, M., 1992: 'Israeli Rock, or a Study in the Politics of "Local Authenticity" ', *Popular Music*, 11 (1): pp. 1–14.
REYNOLDS, S., 1990: *Blissed Out*. London: Serpent's Tail.
STRATTON, J., 1983: 'Capitalism and Romantic Ideology in the Record Business', *Popular Music*, 3: pp. 143–56.
STRAW, W., 1991: 'Systems of Articulation, Logics of Change: Communities and Scenes in Popular Music', *Cultural Studies*, 5 (3): pp. 368–88.
THÉBERGE, P., 1989: 'The "Sound" of Music: Technological Rationalisation and the Production of Popular Music', *New Formations*, 8: pp. 99–111.
THORNTON, S., 1995: *Club Cultures*. Cambridge: Polity Press.
WILLIS, P., 1978: *Profane Culture*. London: Routledge.
WOLFF, J., 1993a: *The Social Production of Art*, 2nd edition. London: Macmillan.
WOLFF, J., 1993b: *Aesthetics and the Sociology of Art*, 2nd edition. London: Macmillan.

9

Approaches to the New Hollywood

Yvonne Tasker

Within film studies, the discussion of contemporary American cinema has frequently been overshadowed by a concern with the structures, directors, genres and individual films of 'classic Hollywood'. This picture has changed relatively recently, with the emergence of a variety of commentaries on, and a lively debate surrounding, the 'new Hollywood'. However a key question, which can be taken as symptomatic, has also been posed as to whether the new Hollywood actually exists. Or more specifically, to what extent is the new Hollywood 'new'? While it is clear that the American film industry has been transformed in a variety of ways in the postwar period – with significant shifts at the levels of production and exhibition – phrases such as the 'new Hollywood' or 'postclassical cinema' suggest rather more than an economic or industrial reorganization. They suggest developments in the American cinema industry far-reaching enough to mark a new period of production. This chapter addresses some of the arguments which have been advanced both for and against an economic and aesthetic transformation of the Hollywood cinema in recent years.

What then is the new Hollywood? At what level – formal, economic, in terms of patterns of consumption – does it make most sense to understand the decline of classic Hollywood and the emergence of something new? To what extent has there been a shift in commercial American cinema production, exhibition and distribution in the postwar period? Further, can specific changes in film style be located, as some have argued, during the 1970s? While the 1970s are often taken as the period in which certain trends in cinema production and film style become so explicit as to mark a definable shift, fixing a date for the emergence of new Hollywood has proved problematic. The level of economic reorganization that the industry has seen, the significance assigned to such changes, and shifts in film style all remain open to debate.

Since 'new Hollywood' is used to signify a range of changes by different critics in relation to different historical moments, this chapter offers an initial exploration of the term at two levels: first, an interrogation of the assumption that the end of the studio era marked a significant shift in the industry and that the decline of classic Hollywood was inevitably to follow. It is argued that a dramatic chronology of decline is inadequate to the task of mapping the postwar American film industry. Whilst the major names of the classic period remain with us, the development of media conglomerates with interests ranging across the leisure field has significant implications for an analysis of the industry today. One of the central components of change which might back up the idea of a new Hollywood is the development of the new multimedia corporations and new sites of exhibition and consumption. Whether the Hollywood film has changed formally or not, it exists within a transformed media landscape – that of the multimedia market-place. Hence the prominence assigned by many commentators to the high-profile film event characteristic of recent Hollywood cinema, with the increased importance of merchandising across a range of media forms. The existence of media conglomerates allows an industrial strategy in which one product or performer can be sold across a range of media and/or generate a series of other, associated products. In terms of film style, we can ask what impact such organizational structures might have on mainstream film productions.

The second level at which this chapter addresses the new Hollywood is to do with film style, examining the view that a more specific and formally 'new' Hollywood could be seen to emerge during the 1970s. This particular new Hollywood is associated with the prominence of a group of 'young' directors, the emergence of an American art cinema, and the use of new, 'disruptive' cinematic techniques such as zoom lenses, Steadicam or split screen. There also exists a different, though related, set of questions around the status of genre in the new Hollywood. The emergence of generic hybrids during the 1970s and 1980s has been singled out in particular as symptomatic of an evolution in film style in the commercial genre-based cinema. The extent to which phenomena such as the sequel, the genre pastiche and the proliferation of subgenres represent an erasure or an evolution of the generic system so typical of classic Hollywood is discussed in this context.

An analysis of new Hollywood reveals its evolving conglomerate structure and changes in film style to be closely related. It can be argued that formal shifts in film style represent an evolution or intensification of already existing trends, and to this extent they do not represent anything significantly new. The music video 'look' of a film like *Bad Girls* (1994) typifies a certain kind of new Hollywood. The dominance of music on the soundtrack, rapid montage and slow motion on the image is achieved at the expense of dialogue, character and even narrative. If the generic location is the Western, *Bad Girls* also draws on images and icons from a range of other forms: other Hollywood genres, television and music video. Whilst aspects of the film might be read as characteristic of an evolving video aesthetic in the cinema, it is also the case that this style draws on established cinema conventions such as the musical montage. The developing relationship between the production and marketing of popular film and music, particularly evident within media conglomerates, is not new either. Witness the use that the industry made in the classic period of popular successes in other media. We need to be aware of the complexities of classic Hollywood's history, before asserting the overwhelming newness of contemporary Hollywood. The industry has repeatedly responded and adjusted to economic pressures, changing technologies and changing markets.

The final part of this chapter explores the usefulness of the framework of postmodernism for understanding new Hollywood. The two terms are rarely brought together, but both positive and negative descriptions draw on a similar language – and both are equally often held not to exist at all. At a stylistic level the most obvious link comes through the much-cited generic 'recycling' of the cinematic past to be found in postwar Hollywood cinema. I have chosen this route through the material as offering a way of thinking about the relationship between changes in popular cinema and the substantial body of work developed around the concept of postmodernism – work which still tends to be applied to the popular cinema only in terms of selected films deemed to be, for one reason or another, 'postmodern'. I will argue that at some levels the framework of postmodernism has a purchase – for example, in the shift from the studio system to the package deal and the development of film as a component in the multimedia market-place. Similarly, elements associated with postmodern art, such as the erosion of distinctions between the spaces of the mainstream and the avant-garde may allow an interpretation of the American cinema's raiding of art cinema (which is also a reciprocal relationship). There are other important factors, however, that mitigate against an easy equation of 'new Hollywood' with postmodern cinema, and indeed against the assertion of the newness of new Hollywood itself.

The 'Decline' of the Studio System and the Move to Conglomeration

It has been convincingly argued that the decline of the studio system in the postwar period can be more accurately characterized as the reformulation of that system – the consequences can easily be both over- and understated (Gomery 1983; Bordwell et al. 1985; Hillier 1992). The starting point for this discussion, then, is to identify some of the different factors – historical, cultural and economic – which have been associated with the emergence of a redefined Hollywood film industry in the postwar period, before moving to look at the 1970s and 1980s more specifically. Some of these factors – such as the role played by television as a competitor – are themselves part of movie mythology. Running alongside film criticism, we find Hollywood's own discourse on itself and its history – indeed, the two may inform each other rather more than this distinction implies.

A significant break point, perhaps because it can be so definitely dated, identified by many histories of the American cinema, is the success of the antitrust suit initially brought by the US Federal government against the 'big five' companies in 1938. Ratified by the Supreme Court in 1949, studios were forced to divorce themselves from their theatres, though the impact was not felt until the 1950s. Supposedly shattering the comfortable oligopoly of the studio system, this move did not prevent the subsequent development of vast media conglomerates as the industry adapted to a changing environment. As Jim Hillier notes (1992: 8), factors such as the rapid decline in attendances at the end of the 1940s would have inevitably led to new strategies. Most standard film histories point to the confluence of a range of factors in offering a chronology of the decline of the studio system. Annette Kuhn in *The Cinema*

Book, for example, suggests 'the rise of television, the effects of the anti-communist scare within the film industry, and probably changing social trends in general' (in Cook 1985: 16). Her qualifications are indicative, including the reference to general social trends. While different historical accounts will emphasize particular factors over others (as does this chapter) all acknowledge that there is no simple cause-effect formulation which will enable us to understand changes in such large capitalist concerns.

In addition to those already cited, other elements that have been identified as significant in Hollywood's restructuring include: the impact of World War II; the emergence of the 'package' deal and moves to independent production; moves to fewer but more expensive productions on the part of the majors, exemplified by the phenomenon of the 'blockbuster'; the loss of a majority audience and the emergence of a variety of fragmented target audiences, most notably the youth market. The relative significance of these factors can be debated. World War II obviously had an important impact on international distribution and exhibition practices, for example, yet the war period is also repeatedly cited as the most profitable of the entire studio era, with profits peaking in 1946. If the crucial overseas market inevitably declined, the domestic market expanded to more than compensate. Douglas Gomery (1986: 23) notes how American urban centres with expanding industries generated by the war helped boost domestic profits to new levels. Gomery also indicates that while the revenues earned in Britain – which were double prewar levels – were difficult to get out of the country, they were invested in studio space and theatres. Such a flexible response can be seen to prefigure the co-productions characteristic of the postwar period, allowing companies to take advantage of tax and other incentives, as well as cheaper labour costs. With the escalation of production and promotional costs, the overseas market remains crucial to the profitability of a Hollywood film today.[1]

The limitations on production during the war years, and the sharp decline in audiences that followed in the postwar period can be seen to heighten the tendency towards the production of fewer, but more expensive, films by the major companies. Similarly, the anti-trust legislation, which meant the lack of a guaranteed space for exhibition, and the new competition from television exacerbated, rather than simply produced, this already existing tendency. Thus Thomas Schatz, while arguing that the blockbuster typifies new Hollywood, locates the phenomena with reference to earlier productions, citing specifically *The Best Years of Our Lives* and *Duel in the Sun* from 1946. The latter is seen as 'a prototype New Hollywood blockbuster: a 'pre-sold' spectacle (based on a popular historical novel) with top stars, an excessive budget, a sprawling story, and state-of-the-art production values' (in Collins et al. 1993: 11). Indeed Schatz makes the important point that the difficulty of both defining and periodizing the new Hollywood stems from the use of the term to 'mean something different from one period of adjustment to another' (p. 8).

Adjustment within the industry, rather than decline, is the key term. The one most commonly cited factor within both popular and academic histories of the American cinema in the postwar period is the emergence, establishment and impact of television as a competitor during the 1950s. Associated with this are a range of developments which form part of the evolution of a domestic leisure culture, including the boom in DIY, the development of other home-based technologies and leisure pursuits, and the significant population move away from urban centres. In the common-sense account of the impact of television, cinema responded with spectacular products such as cinerama, 3-D, wide screen and so on – offering pleasures not to be found on the monochrome TV screen. This account, whilst not false, emphasizes suspicion and hostility. By contrast, historians of the cinema have charted some of the variety of ways in which the cinema very early on came to terms with the new technology, as well as the different responses made by different companies. These include moves into television production with the evolution of the cheaper format of the made-for-TV movie, and the selling of back catalogues of films for television broadcast. Such moves, as with the later advent of widely available home video technology, still involve the product – movies – being sold and consumed. Television represented the development of a different, and lucrative, form of distribution and consumption. Today the two industries are difficult to separate.[2]

Any attempt to assess the impact of cinema's relationship with new technologies such as television and video will involve questions of film style. Television's rescreening of Hollywood's back catalogue of films is also a factor cited by those who champion the view that a new generation of cine-literate directors and cinema-goers emerged in the 1970s. Hence the increasing use during the period of rather self-conscious references to earlier films and cinematic moments. For some critics such referencing can be taken as sly acknowledgements of a shared past, partly produced through the screening of 'classic' films on television; for others this represents a characteristic lack of originality, plagiarism or empty nostalgia. Whatever view we take, the possibility of accessing films from the past through television and video represents one aspect of the proliferation of product in the contemporary media landscape.[3]

Just as the 'decline' of the studio system can be attributed to the confluence of a range of factors, those who have argued for the appearance of a new Hollywood in the 1970s also emphasize a range of elements. These include the emergence of an American 'art' cinema together with the expansion of independent production and the success of powerful director/producers such as Lucas and Spielberg; the use of new cinematic techniques fracturing the coherent narrative world of classic Hollywood narration; the rapid development of video and computer technologies; sophisticated merchandising around film 'events' as well as the exploitation of new marketing strategies. As is clear, claims made for a new Hollywood are functioning at a variety of registers. They speak of industrial change at the levels of production and exhibition, of changes at the level of consumption, and also, crucially, stylistic changes which it might be said moved the American cinema away from the well-established patterns of classic Hollywood.

The late 1960s and early 1970s represent a well-documented period of crisis for the industry, followed by a significant resurgence characterized by the blockbuster and its record-breaking box-office receipts, as well as a series of unexpected successes. *The Sound of Music* (1965) aside, the fact of the commercial success of such unusual films as *Bonnie and Clyde* (1967) and *Easy Rider* (1969) prompted a view amongst some journalists and critics – and in the context of considerable disarray, possibly some within the industry – that the future lay with a vaguely counter-cultural youth market. Taken together with the rapid expansion of independent and exploitation production, and the success of relatively young film-makers within Hollywood – notably Coppola, DePalma, Lucas, Spielberg – there emerges an exuberant rhetoric around ideas of independence, youth and innovation. The constriction, conservatism and formulaic patterns of the studio system are contrasted to the experimentation and youthful innovation of independent production. The title of Michael Pye and Linda Myles's study *The Movie Brats: How the Film Generation Took Over Hollywood* (1979) is symptomatic. Publicity around particular films, stars and directors during the 1970s drew on a rhetoric which suggested the emergence of something new and different within the cinema industry.[4]

In the wake of the decline of the studios, the industry did indeed see the emergence of independent production companies and the consolidation of the 'package' system of production in which the director is, at least potentially, a more important figure. However this may involve little more than the director taking over some of the role of the producer, whilst retaining the demarcation associated with the classical mode of film production (Bordwell et al. 1985: 372). In challenging the existence of a new Hollywood, Douglas Gomery argues that an emphasis on the position of directors such as Spielberg involves a distortion of underlying economic trends. Control is still in familiar hands, but we see the operation of a slightly enlarged oligopoly in which, in the long term, few films can fail to recoup their production costs since the 'majors' have access to international distribution networks and a variety of exhibition formats and technologies. Like Hillier, Gomery points to the absolute importance of securing a guaranteed distribution arrangement with one of the majors to achieve finance for a production at all. Hillier further notes not only the limited space and precarious finance available to independent production, but also the problematic definition of that category. After all, how independent is independent production? Technically, hugely expensive productions such as *Terminator 2* (1991) were independently produced (by Carolco). Bordwell, Staiger and Thompson also point out that although independent production came to characterize Hollywood after 1948, 'financing came primarily from the major producer-distributors which still controlled the industry' (p. 400). Independent production freed major companies from the cost of maintaining a huge staff. Studio space could be leased, with staff working freelance and distribution deals often ensuring a substantial return.[5]

Such commentaries qualify the rhetoric of youth and opportunity which has been generated, partly by the major corporations themselves, partly by journalism and by the personalities involved, around the newness and vitality of independent production as a challenge to the strictures of a formulaic past. None the less, the expansion of independent production and the search for new markets and products characteristic of the late 1960s and early 1970s did create opportunities, notably for the bigger-budget production, and crucially distribution, of work by black film-makers.[6]

The trend towards the blockbuster begins in the classic period, resulting from the conjunction of a variety of factors. For Bordwell, Staiger and Thompson, the profits generated by such films accelerated a move to conglomeration, rather than necessarily being simply a product of it, with companies 'diversifying into areas which might provide a stable growth income to counterbalance the more speculative film-finance operations' (p. 368). Diversification into other areas of entertainment and leisure in turn allowed the merchandising associated with a film to proliferate yet further. Bordwell and co-authors note a distinction between those firms which, through merger, became part of larger corporations and those which 'created their own conglomerate organizations through diversification' (p. 368). Their argument is directed towards the retention of the classic mode of film production within this structure, so that they suggest that 'the current major firms act primarily as financiers and distributors, allowing individual package units to operate on their own once a deal is set' (p. 368).

Whilst it is important to emphasize continuities in mode of production, the fact of conglomeration has a significance in other senses. The acquisition of the studios themselves, for example, signals that they represent in turn a form of diversification for larger corporate interests – the mergers and takeovers which have continued to take place over the last ten years underline this point. James Monaco's polemic survey *American Film Now* (Monaco 1984) emphasized the working of a particular corporate commercial logic in restricting what deals could be set up in the first place, rather than the mode of production once the deal was done.[7]

Within this developing conglomerate structure, the blockbuster, and the commercial logic which produced it, has been taken to represent the emergence of a definable new Hollywood from the mid-1970s. Thomas Schatz takes *Jaws* (1975) as an exemplar of new trends in Hollywood production, distribution and marketing, asserting that the success of the film 'recalibrated the profit potential of the Hollywood hit, and redefined its status as a marketable commodity and cultural phenomenon as well' (in Collins et al. 1993: 17). Schatz highlights a variety of factors in this context. The film was presold around a best-selling novel, had a huge promotional budget and was accompanied by the generation of media hype throughout production. Schatz also notes the expensive strategy of front-loading the film's theatrical release at hundreds of cinemas nationwide, and the way in which the film became a franchise in its own right with numerous tie-ins and spin-off merchandising, as marking a significant escalation of the blockbuster trend. In the generation of publicity and merchandising, and in the close relationship between the promotion of the book and the film as event, Schatz identifies the situation of the blockbuster as multimedia event as indicative of the new Hollywood.

The location of production and distribution within conglomerates with wider interests in the entertainment and leisure fields represents a reformulation of the industry. It is commonplace in contemporary Hollywood to find promotional budgets exceeding production budgets, since the value of a film results not only from cinema revenues, but from a range of associated events and products. Jim Hillier cites an interview in which a screenwriter uses this shift to characterize 'new Hollywood': an industry in which film represents only one aspect of 'multinational corporations that specialize in leisure-time products – books, records, magazines, theme parks and children's toys' (in Hillier 1992: 23). To some extent, then, the newness of new Hollywood stems from its existence within a changed media market-place in which diversification and conglomeration are essential to survival. Within this market-place new outlets for distribution and new products to market are essential. Video retail and rental represent, for example, both a new way to generate profit from old material, and a significant source of returns on new releases both domestically and overseas (Balio 1990: 333). On a grander scale, Schatz points to the generation of an extensive range of cultural products from blockbuster films in which the original film functions as a form of brand name. He notes that Disney, for example, earns more from theme parks than from films and television, though the theme parks must to some extent depend on continued visibility in those media (in Collins 1993: 29).

Film Style: Postclassical Cinema?

What then of new Hollywood and film style? Once again there exists a range of approaches to this question, and at least two contrasting ways in which the phrase 'new Hollywood' is used to indicate shifts in film style during the 1970s and since. Different periodizations and interpretations of new Hollywood can be understood in terms of the different historical moment in which the idea is invoked, and as associated with particular trends in film studies – from auteurism to an analysis of the market as a key determinant on production, to the political interpretation of the popular cinema. In discussing the phenomenal success of *Jaws*, Schatz points not only to its distribution and marketing as symptomatic of the new Hollywood, but to the (controlled) anarchy of its combination of a series of stories and genres. The film draws on and combines several generic precedents in a way similar to Lucas's *Star Wars* (1977) and other blockbuster successes of the period. Schatz cites Monaco's view of such films as 'machines of entertainment, precisely calculated to achieve their effect' (in Collins et al. 1993: 19); In this view, new Hollywood film style is perceived as a mechanical operation, in which films drawing on the styles and stories of the past demonstrate a cynical commercial sense combined with conservative values.

Many of the blockbusters of new Hollywood, such as the disaster movie cycle of the 1970s or *Raiders of the Lost Ark* (1981), have also been critically characterized as exciting experiences which are politically conservative and aesthetically bankrupt. *True Lies* (1994) similarly mobilizes a host of conservative conventions, with the casting of Art Malik as the leader of an incompetent group of 'Arab' fanatics, and the hysterical policing of women and children within the family by superdad/international spy Schwarzenegger. Spectacular action sequences and special effects, also typical of the blockbuster, are used extensively in the film. Its antecedents are openly drawn from the James Bond films. As in the earlier blockbusters an ironic (or nihilistic) humour is employed in, for example, a scene in which hero Arnold Schwarzenegger and heroine Jamie Lee Curtis are reconciled and embrace against the backdrop of a nuclear explosion. We can note here the refinement in the 1980s and 1990s of a style of blockbuster film-making in which character and narrative are subservient to spectacle and plot-driven action.[8]

If for some the new Hollywood is typified by the conservative values of the blockbuster, for many critics at the time the new Hollywood of the 1970s was epitomized by a type of American art cinema, associated with the work of directors like Robert Altman or Michael Cimino, seen as radically different from the Hollywood spectacle of the classic period. The new Hollywood of the

1970s encompasses the 'incoherent' text in both its most art-house version in films such as *Taxi-Driver* (1976) and in generic hybrids such as *Jaws* in the more avowedly mass-market sector. Largely discussed within the framework of auteurism, it is to the former that we now turn. An impression of stylistic change during the 1970s was partly generated by the use of non-classical cinematic techniques and new technologies, such as freeze frame or split screen, zoom lenses or Steadicam. Whether these techniques are seen as easily incorporated into the classic mode of production, or as challenging that system's conception of narrative and genre is a matter of some debate. Writing in 1976, Steve Neale provides the following summary of one perspective on the new Hollywood to be found in British film studies at the time:

> The use of devices such as the zoom and telephoto lenses, slow-motion and split-screen have destroyed the dramatic and spatio-temporal unity that founded classical *mise-en-scène* with its economy, density and 'subtlety' of signification; plot-linearity and its corollary, the goal-oriented hero, have been replaced by narrative fragmentation and troubled, introspective protagonists; genre conventions have to a large extent broken down, to be replaced by a 'realism' compromised by traditional dramatic values and the exigencies of narrative conventions or a use of older generic conventions invested with an empty nostalgia or a knowing cynicism or both.
>
> (Neale 1976: 118–19)

Neale's short discussion of a range of commentaries brings together, in a way characteristic of the times, an analysis of stylistic change with a recognition of economic change and a set of speculations on the political significance of such shifts in film style.[9] As is evident from Neale's description, for some critics, changes in film style were conceived as representing a dramatic break with the past. Films such as Coppola's *The Conversation* (1974) or Altman's *Nashville* (1975) fit more easily within this perspective on new Hollywood than, say, *Jaws*.

At stake in the claims made for a director such as Coppola during the 1970s was a new status as author-director, modelled on the European art cinema, for those working within the American cinema.[10] The work of such men can be understood as either the emergence of an American art cinema, or as indicating the incorporation of techniques and themes associated with European art cinema into American structures and modes of production. Bordwell, Staiger and Thompson offer a detailed analysis of *The Conversation* arguing that it 'exemplifies how the New Hollywood has absorbed narrational strategies of the art cinema while controlling them within a coherent genre framework' (1985: 377). They suggest that American film-makers such as Scorsese borrow European traditions made by American film-makers in relatively superficial ways. Thus 'in keeping with the definition of a non-Hollywood Hollywood, American films are imitating the look of European art films' (p. 375). But the authors go on to argue that there is a certain productive engagement between traditions here. Two aspects of the new Hollywood films save them from being mere pastiche. The 'almost complete conservatism of style', and a dependence on genre bind these films into the classic Hollywood tradition. Thus it is argued that 'Like the European art film, the new Hollywood film is sharply aware of its relation to the "old Hollywood"' (p. 375). Amongst other examples, 'DePalma's rehashes of Hitchcock, Lucas's use of Warner's war films and Universal serials as prototypes for *Star Wars*' (p. 375) are cited. Films from the new Hollywood which are avowedly popular are brought together with those contending for more serious status.[11] It is argued that a continued use of genre and an awareness of Hollywood's cinematic past tie the products of new Hollywood *to* that past. Yet the self-conscious, often self-indulgent repertoire of reference to the cinema of the past is one of the elements that marks out the new Hollywood as distinct, according to many accounts.

Reference to the cinematic past can be found in both the mass-market blockbuster as it developed in the 1980s, and in the American 'art cinema' products of the 1970s. Variously attributed to a pleasure in the forms of the past, a nostalgic yearning for times imagined as simple, or the industry's lack of imagination, the use of what Noel Carroll terms 'allusion' is a striking feature of popular cinema. Beginning from the *après noir* style and narrative of *Body Heat* (1981), Carroll's review of the 1970s and since locates a generation of film-makers and viewers engaged in 'a reward system based on reciprocal recognition' (1982: 55). The systematic use of allusion to other films, whether from Hollywood or Europe is, Carroll claims, producing 'a cinematic style that is subtly changing the nature of Hollywood symbol systems' (p. 55). The use of allusion may signal an association with a well-known or celebrated work, so that the film which makes the reference can be seen to aspire to similar status: DePalma's virtual remakes of Hitchcock films have been viewed in this way. The fact that such strategies may exclude large parts of the audience is also taken up by Carroll, who points to generic allusion as a more comprehensible route taken by some film-makers. Here the genre of which the film is part becomes the subject of commentary, and sometimes subversion.

While Carroll is partly critical of allusionism as an artistic strategy, in making sense of it he also draws heavily on an account, by now familiar, of the experiences and passions of a film-school generation. The 'rise of the new Hollywood and its allusionist auteurs' is situated within the economic context of industrial change and uncertainty at the end of the 1960s, but largely understood as allowing a space for the new auteurs to develop their concerns. The model of allusionism retains a sense of authorial control and vision, misguided or not, in which reference to the past is used productively. Yet this does not quite capture the tone of such 1970s blockbusters as *Star Wars*, which use a bewildering variety of references and genres apace, seemingly without logic. Monaco describes the film as 'a black-hole neutron star sucking everything in its wake. Whole genres of film disappear into it' (1984: 170). For Schatz the prevalence of plot-driven action and spectacle over character opens up the film, allowing its 'radical amalgamation of genre conventions and elaborate play of cinematic references' (in Collins 1993: 23). *Star Wars* is seen as an action-packed genre pastiche in which individual scenes, character types (or stereotypes) and the film as a whole draw from an extensive range of genres across different periods of film and television history. Drawing on recognizable genres and types reduces the need for characterization. The rationale that Schatz (and others) offers for such an incoherent use of reference is not authorial vision but the desire to maximize profit by appealing to different audiences with one film – an updated concept of the family audience. The quasi-family assembled in *Terminator 2* might also be understood in this way. Whilst Schwarzenegger was obviously the star and provided the focus for advertising images, the film also offered a strong female lead for Linda Hamilton as well as giving a central part to the character of a teenage boy, played by Edward Furlong.

Even if it is argued that the American art cinema of the 1970s new Hollywood was contained by the conventions of genre, the status of genre as a category is none the less one of the most problematic in contemporary cinema. The development of genre-based cinema is very much associated with the studio system of classic Hollywood, and functions as a form of standardization and differentiation of product within a streamlined production process. The advent of the package deal, independent production, freelance labour, the interrelations between different media forms and high concept productions: all contribute to challenging that streamlined process. It is not the case that genres were pure in classic Hollywood, but its status in new Hollywood is perhaps more uncertain and fragmented. The sequel, the genre pastiche and genre hybrid have already been mentioned.[12] The reworking of a variety of genres and styles, as parody or pastiche, raises the issue of whether these reworkings can themselves evolve, as classic genres did, over time. Clearly Carroll, writing at the start of the 1980s, did not view the formula as a valuable one for the future. He writes that allusion 'can deteriorate into mere affectation, nostalgia, and, at worst, self-deception' (1982: 80). So, has the development of new cinematic styles led to the evolution or the erasure of genre as a system?

In classifying films through genre, we tend increasingly to make reference to a variety of subgenres, and to combinations of generic elements. In the popular cinema of the 1980s and 1990s we find a range of popular films which do not sit easily within the familiar generic classifications of the classic period. Yet film critics are still concerned to think about such films in terms of genre since, while they clearly do not fit within established generic frameworks, they make explicit use of them. Hillier suggests that in some ways 'sequels could be said to take over the role that genres played in earlier production' (1992: 17). They certainly function within a similar commercial logic. Hillier notes that though sequels are generally more expensive and less successful than the original, they can be relied on to serve a particular market, cashing in on an already existing awareness and boosting sales of tie-in products. Ridley Scott's successful 1979 film *Alien* generated two sequels, *Aliens* (1986) and *Alien3* (1992). Though all make reference to science fiction and horror, and to the common core plot of Ripley (Sigourney Weaver) battling with the alien(s), the three films draw on a range of different generic elements. This serves to mark their difference from each other, and from the imitations that followed at least the first two films. *Aliens* draws in equal part on the codes of the war film, in particular the populist rhetoric and tough images of the 1980s cycle of films centred on Vietnam. *Alien3* takes the sadistic imagery of the prison film as its iconic centre. The codes of genre are still important to these films, which do not make excessive use of references to other films (with the possible exception of the second, directed by James Cameron). Both the retention of genres, and the combination of genres which redefines them, are typical of contemporary Hollywood.

It is perhaps indicative that one of the most frequently used generic combinations of the 1980s was that of comedy and horror. The comedy, often generated by parody and self-consciousness, is included within the genre piece itself, frequently appearing precisely at moments of greatest horror.[13] The widespread inclusion of parodic elements in mainstream films has generated discussion of the deployment of irony as a mode. Does the use of irony undermine the genres in which they appear, for example?[14] In his study of 'genericity in the 90s', Jim Collins returns us to the multimedia market-place, asking how the category of genre can function within a context in which 'popular entertainment is undergoing such a massive recategorization brought on by the ever-increasing number of entertainment options and the fragmentation of what was once thought to be a mass audience into a cluster of "target" audiences?' (Collins et al. 1993: 243). He begins his analysis with two opposing examples which draw on the images, icons and conventions of the Western – *Back to the Future III* and *Dances with Wolves* (both 1990). They represent two types of contemporary genre cinema, one 'founded on dissonance, on eclectic juxtapositions of elements that obviously don't belong together', the other 'obsessed with recovering some sort of missing harmony', a mode that he terms the 'new sincerity' (pp. 242–3). Collins insists that however different the uses that these two films make of the Western genre, they are both instances of a response to 'the same cultural milieu – namely, the media-saturated landscape of contemporary American culture' (p. 243). The argument refutes any idea that we see the continued existence of the Western genre as it is classically understood alongside newer, parodic versions. Both represent distinctive responses to the changed media landscape within which they are produced.

Collins' opposition between parody and sincerity is reminiscent of Noel Carroll's distinction between an often wearisome allusionism and 'annual excursions into deathly sincerity' represented by films such as *Kramer vs Kramer* (1979) in the cinema of the 1970s (1982: 56). *Bad Girls* provides a useful example in this context. Like *Maverick*, also released in 1994, the film uses the Western as its generic setting. Making use of a range of conventions and images drawn from the genre, the film parodies the Western without explicitly becoming comic. Elements of parody stem partly from the 'role reversal' involved in casting four women at the centre of the Western action, given the conventional roles typically assigned to women in the genre. Perhaps in an attempt to legitimate the central female roles, *Bad Girls* also looks to the women's film, and takes certain images of sexualized violence against women and their vengeance from the rape/revenge cycle. An incipient lesbian relationship is transmuted into a series of significant looks devoid of narrative significance, but which can be made sense of through the conventions of the buddy movie. Genre is neither played for laughs nor taken very seriously. The marketing of the film as a sexy feminist, Western appeals to a range of audiences. Within a classical understanding of the Western, it is an incoherent text. In Collins's formulation, *Bad Girls* incorporates elements of both parody and sincerity.[15]

Postmodernism and Contemporary Popular Cinema

Various aspects of new Hollywood suggest affinities with the critical framework of postmodernism. The irreverent recycling of genres, the prevalence of pastiche and nostalgia, as well as the reciprocal relationship between commercial and art cinemas: all strike chords with the characteristics of postmodern art. In turn, the reorganization of the American film industry as part of media conglomerates operating across a range of leisure fields, along with the use of independent production companies and freelance employees, clearly relates to some versions of economic/industrial change offered within postmodernism. The contemporary situation is very far from the factory system of the studio era. Yet Collins is rare in straightforwardly referring to contemporary cinema as part of a postmodern popular cinema. Different critics have cited a range of films as postmodern, or as of/about the experience of postmodernity. Using postmodernism as a framework within which to position the contemporary popular cinema, rather than particular examples of it, has proved problematic.[16]

It is useful to consider a specific example here. Ridley Scott's *Blade Runner* (1982) has repeatedly been cited as an example of postmodern cinema. The film has been written about extensively from a range of perspectives, partly because it is a rich source of imagery and narrative themes: it is in such senses an 'interesting' film. Many reasons have been given for reading the film as postmodern. Of these I have singled out five.[17] First, the setting and *mise-en-scène*, particularly the construction of a city space which brings together a diverse set of ethnicities and architectural styles in an alienated urban context dominated by advertising and other media images. This seems to conjure up the postmodern urban experience as a vision of the future. Second, the reference to and use of earlier moments of cinema history, particularly *film noir*, in the film's visual style and to some extent, its narrative. Though the femme fatale of *noir* is re-presented here as a form of compliant living doll, the characterization of the detective hero borrows rather self-consciously from this tradition. The conventions of the cinematic past are deployed to articulate the experience of a postmodern present. Third, the questioning of categories of identity around the distinction between human and non-human (replicant), which forms an important part of the narrative development. Fourth, the exploration of themes of time and space, particularly an experience of compressed time, and time/space as they are affected by the interaction of humans with different technologies. Fifth, the exploration of the role of the image (photographs in particular) in the constitution of identity and personal history. These briefly sketched points indicate that *Blade Runner* has been read both as a film that represents the experience of postmodernity, and, in its textual play with the conventions of the past, as an example of postmodern art itself. It is perhaps the way in which the two come together in Scott's film that results in it being so often referred to in the context of postmodernism. Yet if the framework of postmodernism does have a value for an analysis of contemporary cinema, it must also be involved in thinking beyond individual films as 'postmodern' or as symptoms of postmodernity.

Nostalgia, a defining term for both new Hollywood cinema and postmodernism, provides a point of entry to the possible relation between the two. James

Monaco's summation of the cinema of the 1970s retains a purchase here. 'The most powerful cultural force operating in the seventies was definitely nostalgia', he notes, going on to suggest that it will be 'impossible, twenty years hence, to revive the seventies; they have no style of their own' (1984: 283). Films do not need to be explicitly set in the 1950s to evoke nostalgically the images and/or values of that decade as Monaco indicates with reference to *American Graffiti* (1973), set in 1962 or *Rocky* (1976), set in the contemporary world. Yet the nostalgia film can also be seen as a sort of style. Fredric Jameson's comments on the nostalgia film as 'an elaborated symptom of the waning of our historicity' places this perception within the framework of postmodernism (Jameson 1984: 68). His well-known essay discusses new *film noir*, including *Body Heat*, along with films such as *American Graffiti* and *Rumble Fish* (1983). The language of the nostalgia film is not concerned with history as such, instead approaching ' "the past" through stylistic connotation, conveying "pastness" by the glossy quality of the image, and "1930-ness" or "1950-ness" by the attributes of fashion' (p. 67). And of course it is a cinematic past that is referred to. Accounts of both referentiality and the operation of nostalgia are overwhelmingly negative. These phenomena are taken to indicate, for example, an inability to articulate the present. Jim Collins's distinction between reference to the cinematic past in terms of parody or sincerity suggests, however, that such reference is not *necessarily* defined by nostalgia. Rather than focusing on the nostalgia film, Collins draws our attention to the operation of a *critical* nostalgia when confronted with the complexity of contemporary media. Negative judgements of our contemporary popular culture are set against the 'highly "mediated" nature of our contemporary cultural existences and the images needed to represent them' (Collins et al. 1993: 252). It is the attention to surface and to spectacle over character and narrative, the ahistoricism of contemporary cinema even when it seems most deeply engaged in references to history that is stressed in accounts of the new Hollywood. It is also such factors that suggest a link between new Hollywood and postmodernism. Yet the most significant factor to consider in this context is the radical transformation of the media market-place. The number of film images available and the different forms of entertainment and cultural commodities with which they interact propose a challenge to the consideration of film as a distinct medium.

Conclusion

As the studio system declined the American film industry transformed itself. Contemporary film production, distribution and exhibition form one part of vast media, communications and leisure corporations. Changes within the film industry and in the dominant style of the Hollywood film are both intimately bound up with the changes in the multimedia market-place as a whole. The interaction of film production and consumption with the institutions and technologies of television, video, cable and communications technologies is one part of this. The newness of new Hollywood stems from the rapidly changing entertainment world in which it exists. In this context an analysis of film style in the new Hollywood might be most usefully approached through an awareness of the interaction between film and other media and the proliferation of cultural commodities, rather than exclusively in terms of a relationship to the cinematic past.

Notes

1 Hillier discusses this factor. However he also points out that domestic box office is still taken as the most significant measure of the success of a Hollywood film (1992: 32–3). Austin's essay in Balio (1990) points to a similar picture in relation to video.

2 Essays in Balio (1990) address the relationship between film and television. Hillier notes the impact of Pay-TV and cable in, to some extent, reversing the dominance of television achieved during the uncertain period of the 1960s (1992: 37).

In Britain the difficulties of sustaining feature film production at all have produced a different relation of dependence between cinema and television.

3 I am not making any claims here that the proliferation of material is in any way equivalent to either diversity or choice. It is also worth noting though that, in the context of limited resources, the development of video technologies has had a significant impact on the field of film studies in Britain.

4 Of course control was passing into new hands at this time, but as Monaco points out, this did not impact particularly on the commercial logic in operation.

5 Some independent producers are able to secure a distribution deal on more favourable terms. Hillier cites Carolco and T2 as an example of this (1992: 18).

6 Both Hillier (1992) and Monaco (1984) pay attention to the part played by black film-makers in new Hollywood, though many other accounts neglect this aspect of the 1970s.

7 A good part of Monaco's book is given over to an emphasis on economics and the difficulty of setting up film productions. Here the trend towards the blockbuster is seen to push out smaller films, which are relegated to television. Thomas Schatz is more optimistic (in Collins et. al. 1993).

8 Such a judgement does not, of course, address what audiences might do with such product, or the themes and myths they invoke. This is an important area, though not covered directly in this chapter.

9 Neale's project is to assess the relevance of new Hollywood for the ideological interests of *Screen* as a political journal.

10 This is situated within a context in which European art films were more widely available through independent distribution (see Hillier 1992: 14).

11 One distinction might be whether the films look to European art or Hollywood traditions of the past.

12 Recent years have also seen a series of cinematic 'remakes' of television series. The first *Star Trek* film was released in 1979. More recent offerings have included two *Addams Family* films (1989 and 1993), *The Flintstones* (1994) and *Maverick* (1994). Whilst the entire *Star Trek* series of films (1979–94) can be logged under science fiction, and *Maverick* can be placed within the Western genre to an extent, a classic understanding of genre does little to help in placing such films with their almost parodic consciousness of the originals that they ape. That the transfer of works and characters from popular literature to film rarely seems to involve such a tongue-in-cheek response is worthy of note.

13 Stephen Neale's essay in Kuhn (1990) provides an interesting discussion of this phenomenon.

14 This irony has, as I have already noted, been read alternatively as nihilism.

15 I discuss the evolution of the Western in these terms in more detail in *Spectacular Bodies* (Tasker 1993).

16 Denzin (1991) relies on analyses of films which are taken largely to reflect postmodernity. Other studies invoke 'postmodern cinema', discussing a variety of examples without defining the limits of the category.
17 Obviously the readings of the readings presented here is rather summary. The primary sources were provided by a series of essays in Kuhn (1990), references in Sharrett (1993) and Harvey (1989).

References

BALIO, T. (ed.), 1990: *Hollywood in the Age of Television*. London: Unwin Hyman.

BORDWELL, D., STAIGER, J. and THOMPSON, K., 1985: *The Classical Hollywood Cinema: Film Style and Mode of Production to 1960*. London: Routledge.

CARROLL, N., 1982: 'The Future of Allusion: Hollywood in the Seventies (and Beyond)', *October*, 20.

COLLINS, J., RADNER, H. and PREACHER COLLINS, A. (eds.), 1993: *Film Theory Goes to the Movies*. London: Routledge.

COOK, P. (ed.), 1985: *The Cinema Book*. London: BFI.

DENZIN, N., 1991: *Images of Postmodern Society: Social Theory and Contemporary Cinema*. London: Sage.

GOMERY, D., 1983: 'The American Film Industry of the 1970s: Stasis in the "New Hollywood" ', *Wide Angle*, 5 (4).

GOMERY, D., 1986: *The Hollywood Studio System*. London: Macmillan.

HARVEY, D., 1989: *The Condition of Postmodernity*. Oxford: Blackwell.

HILLIER, J., 1992: *The New Hollywood*. London: Studio Vista.

JAMESON, F., 1984: 'Postmodernism, or the Cultural Logic of Late Capitalism', *New Left Review*, 146.

KUHN, A. (ed.), 1990: *Alien Zone: Cultural Theory and Contemporary Science-Fiction Cinema*. London: Verso.

MONACO, J., 1984: *American Film Now*. New York, New American Library. (First published 1979).

NEALE, S., 1976: 'New Hollywood Cinema', *Screen*, 17 (2).

PYE, M. and MYLES, L., 1979: *The Movie Brats*. London: Faber & Faber.

SHARRETT, C., (ed.), 1993: *Crisis Cinema: The Apocalyptic Idea in Postmodern Narrative Film*. Washington, DC: Maisonneuve.

TASKER, Y., 1993: *Spectacular Bodies: Gender, Genre and the Action Cinema*. London: Routledge.

10

Feminism, Technology and Representation

Sarah Kember

Introduction

> We might talk about the inscription within particular uses of language of structured and structuring potentialities, of alternative or even antithetical futures, hiding, waiting, in the same array of signifying elements, the same array of pent-up social forces, in a figural relationship *between* signifying elements and pent-up social forces, which is almost there, virtually there, waiting for syntactical articulation.
>
> (Hebdige 1993: 274)

This chapter examines feminist critiques of mainstream science and technology, and feminist attempts to structure alternative representations of the relationship between nature and culture. Although science and technology have been debated within feminism for at least 20 years, they represent a relatively new trajectory within cultural studies. Feminism has introduced cultural studies to debates on science and technology and it would seem that the uptake has been rapid. In 1991 Maureen McNeil and Sarah Franklin identified science and technology as one of the areas where there was a 'lack of overlap' between feminism and cultural studies (McNeil and Franklin 1991). They suggest that 'questions about science' began 'seeping into cultural studies' only in the 1980s and in response to 'theoretical shifts' and an 'altered constituency'.[1] Nevertheless, in an edited volume on cultural studies produced in 1992, Lawrence Grossberg et al. are able to include a section on 'Science, Culture and the Ecosystem' quite unproblematically. Where McNeil and Franklin discuss work on science and technology by feminists in the United States but refer mainly to the development of British cultural studies, Grossberg et al. include both British and American approaches but are concerned mainly with the development of cultural studies in the United States. The different theoretical and constituent traditions of British and American cultural studies may go some way towards explaining these attitudes towards the placement of science and technology.

It is probable that another explanation lies with the recent impact of Donna Haraway's work, which offers a feminist postmodernist account of science and technology and which extends its own constituency beyond that of gender to race and other aspects of identity, or more properly, difference. It therefore employs a theoretical and political framework which is in line with contemporary trends in cultural studies both in Britain and the United States. More specifically, Haraway's work relates to what Grossberg et al. (quoting Lata Mani) refer to as some of the more 'utopian moments' in cultural studies where it 'sometimes imagines "a location where the new politics of difference – racial, sexual, cultural, transnational – can combine and be articulated in all their dazzling plurality" ' (in Grossberg et al. 1992: 1). What is central for Haraway in the politics of difference is the relationship between humans and animals, and humans and machines. Where McNeil and Franklin discuss the importance of work leading up to *Primate Visions* (Haraway 1989) for a feminist analysis of science as a cultural phenomenon, this chapter focuses on *Simians, Cyborgs and Women* (Haraway 1991), and in particular on Haraway's utopian 'Manifesto for Cyborgs' which appears to have landed like a *Close Encounters* spaceship in the field of cultural studies and which, for the purposes of this essay, very usefully brings together feminist work on technology and representation with that on science and epistemology (or structures of thought and knowledge).

This chapter therefore aims to show how feminist debates on technology and representation have developed to incorporate a concern not only with the production of technologies in our society, but also with the production of scientific and cultural knowledges. This development involves a recognition that science and technology do not exist in the separate spheres of theory and practice where technology, as the appliance of science, appears to be unmarked by the culture in which it operates. Rather, science and technology are recognized as being jointly enmeshed in the material and symbolic practices of a society which is structured by economic, gender, racial and other divisions. Donna Haraway and others use the term 'technoscience' to describe the relationship between science and technology in contemporary society.

I will argue that contemporary feminist representations such as Haraway's cyborg stem from a critique of the structures of power and knowledge in technoscience, and that their transformation of those structures offers a blueprint for the future of technoscientific culture.

Feminist debates on technology and representation in the 1970s and 1980s were concerned primarily with how women were excluded from the production of technology and oppressed in their consumption of it. The debates drew on Marxist theories of the division of labour in capitalist society and were broadly sociological. In the feminist sociology of science and technology, capitalism and patriarchy are regarded as being the joint economies which regulate women's engagement with science, and with technologies in the home, in the workplace and in education. But what the feminist critique also revealed was that the ideology, or self-justification system, which supported these economies was based on some very suspect thinking. Namely, that women should not and do not take a leading role in the production of science and technology because they are not essentially suited to this area of work and enquiry. They are too weak or likely to be too emotionally involved and so on.

The ideology is supported by essentialist thinking which ties gender differences to biological or sex differences (women are emotional because they care for children) and is part of a generally hierarchical and binaristic Western philosophy.

The political task of the feminist debates on science and technology has always centred on a critique of the forms which dominate and oppress women, and on a demand for change. Bringing about change has involved and continues to involve documenting the hidden histories of women's production of technology and their resistance to oppression. It has also involved recognizing the role of essentialism in both scientific and feminist thought, and developing a critical and proactive engagement with epistemology. Within the framework of contemporary cultural theory, the concept of epistemology incorporates an awareness derived primarily from the work of post-structuralists such as Michel Foucault, that knowledge and power are intrinsically linked.

This chapter begins with 'The Critique of Essentialism', which looks at some of the feminist sociological debates on the gendered division of labour in science and technology and on the role of essentialist thinking in mainstream science. There is an increasing awareness in this work of the dangers of reproducing essentialism in a feminist critique of science, and it illustrates the need to unpack such categories as 'women' and 'technology' and to think carefully about which women and which technologies 'we' are talking about. Essentialism homogenizes the identity of women through a reference to biology, and there is a tendency for feminism to homogenize the experience of women through a reference to oppression. It is important for feminism to recognize the multiplicity of female identity and experience in order to provide an adequate critique of the dominant forms of science and technology and in order to bring about change.

Feminist sociological critiques have led to a demand for a feminist alternative or 'successor' science and technology which is considered in the next section 'Towards Embodiment'. The feminist successor science projects are attempts to turn the tables on mainstream science, which is regarded as being false or bad science because it incorporates capitalist and patriarchal values. A successor science would be a true or good science because it incorporates the values of feminism. The problem arises in defining feminist values without resorting to essentialism, and the projects tend to valorize qualities such as love and empathy which are marginalized or excluded from the production of mainstream science, and which are regarded as being the universal characteristics of female psychology (if not biology).

Successor science projects contain the idea of a feminist standpoint epistemology – thought and knowledge revised from a feminist standpoint. This may be better than a masculinist standpoint but it is still rather unitary and upholds the traditions of science in its claims to truth and universality. What moves the debate on significantly is the recognition by successor scientists such as Sandra Harding of the diversity within the category of 'women' and the possibility of a range of equally valid feminist standpoints. A range of feminist knowledges can be made valid by recognizing the status of black, working-class, lesbian and other forms of female experience and identity. Embodied knowledges are precisely those which incorporate and acknowledge the role of experience and identity in knowledge formation, and do not hide under the cloak of neutrality and universality. They signal a move towards the relativization of scientific truth, but are at the same time contextually grounded. For Donna Haraway, the production of embodied knowledges is crucial to the establishment of a more accountable and politically responsible science. For her it is necessary to see and know from another's standpoint as from one's own (whether that other is a woman, animal or machine) and this requires a degree of mobility across subject positions. She represents this epistemological positioning through the cyborg, and 'Cyborgs and Nomads' are discussed in the third section of this chapter.

Haraway's cyborg is not just any human/machine hybrid, but an embodiment of difference. It has no unitary identity but represents an epistemologically revised and transformed science. Crucially, it breaks down the hierarchical separation of male/female, mind/body, culture/nature, subject/object, self/other which characterizes Western knowledge in general. This cyborg, like Rosi Braidotti's nomadic subject (which may take the form of a cyborg with an unconscious and an identity) is a socialist-feminist political imaginary. It represents a way forward for feminist constructions of science, technology and subjectivity which is not pure science fiction but which is drawn from a sustained critique of dominant patriarchal science and culture. Haraway's cyborg and Braidotti's nomad have not forgotten where they came from. They may be hard to trace in the social realm but they have been created out of it, and are intended to be a force for change within it.

'Cyborgs and Nomads' also incorporates a critical review of cyberfeminism, which is defined by Sadie Plant as at attack on human agency by a feminized and autonomous information technology. In this account, technology itself is running the show, and it resists all forms of human intervention and control – patriarchal, capitalist, socialist or feminist. Cyberfeminism celebrates technological anarchy, the end of patriarchy and of socialist feminism, and the arrival of a dystopian future in which the distinction between social reality and science fiction has collapsed. My critique of this account is based on a desire to signal the importance of retaining a sociological framework which has established that science and technology are not autonomous or separate fields of theory and practice but are fully cultural processes and therefore embedded in the hierarchical structures of power and knowledge which disadvantage women (and other 'Others') and which must be changed through their agency. Change can be brought about by direct intervention in the production of science and technology, but also by intervening in the production of epistemology, which traditionally discriminates against women through its hierarchical structure and essentialist premiss. Essentialism seems to be reproduced in the cyberfeminist notion of information technology as a feminized, fluid, almost bodily attack.

The Critique of Essentialism

The critique of essentialism is therefore an important first step in the establishment of an effective feminist intervention. Sandra Harding, one of the leading feminist critics of science, notes that although feminist criticisms 'began by raising what appears to be politically contentious but theoretically innocuous questions about discrimination against women in the social structure of science, misuses of technology and androcentric bias in the social sciences and biology', they have gone on to 'question the most fundamental assumptions of modern, Western thought' (Harding 1987: 287). Harding argues that in order for feminism to find the 'alternative nonhierarchical images of the transformative science' it seeks, a critical engagement with epistemology is necessary:

> The destabilization of thought often has advanced understanding more effectively that restabilizations, and the feminist criticisms of science point to a particularly fruitful arena in which the categories of Western thought need destabilization'
>
> (p. 287).

One aspect of Western scientific thought which is destabilized in feminist criticism is the hierarchical and essentialist split between the mind and the body, thought and feeling. It is a split which was consolidated in the Enlightenment period and it aligns men with the capacity for rational thought and women (because of the biological function of reproduction) with less-valued physical and emotional capacities. This kind of essentialism has been used to explain (and by some to defend) the history of women's relative lack of involvement in science and technology, which themselves are characterized as being exclusively rational endeavours.

During the 1970s and 1980s feminist work in the sociology of science criticized the kinds of representation and material practices which essentialist thinking about the relation between gender and science produced. One of the central themes in this work is that science and technology perpetuate the sexual division of labour in our society and the oppression of women. Men have access to science and technology and women do not, so men have the power to define or represent and to control women through the kinds of science and technology they produce. The most frequently cited example here is the production of domestic technologies, which far from reducing the amount of time women spend doing housework, actually create new forms of housework for women to do. Judith Williamson (1987) gives the example of the 'three kinds of dirt' invented by the manufacturers, Hoover. In an essay designed to demonstrate the semiotic principle that 'the language of each culture does not so much name the world as define its possibilities', she reports that the *Hoover Book of Home Management* divides carpet dirt into three important categories: 'surface litter', 'light, clinging dust' and 'heavy dirt'. It then very helpfully outlines the 'three cleaning principles' which can remove them – and which correspond surprisingly enough with the various attachments of a Hoover. Williamson exposes the bogus scientificity of adverts for domestic products and shows how they legitimize their constructions of the world through a reference to nature. Ehrenreich, English (1979) and Friedan (1974) show how advertisements for domestic technologies in the 1950s constructed new categories of housework not only to sell products, but as part of a widespread postwar drive to remove women from the paid workforce and return them to the home. This was also done through a reference to 'natural' feminine desires for homemaking and child-rearing.

Other key sociological texts such as those by Faulkner and Arnold (1985) and the Brighton Women and Science Group (1980) concentrate not only on the exclusion of women from technology and the way in which they are defined and controlled in relation to work and domestic technologies, but also on how medical science and technology has a central role in the construction of essentialist ideas about gender. For example, in 'The Tyrannical Womb: Menstruation and Menopause', Lynda Birke and Sandy Best argue that because of the biological processes surrounding childbirth, medical science developed 'a view of women as sick, and hence inferior' but also as 'potentially dangerous, and therefore in need of control' (Brighton Women and Science Group 1980: 89). Alterations in women's physical and emotional states placed medical science in both 'fear and awe' of reproduction and the development of reproductive technologies, the increased medicalization of childbirth, has been seen to be as much a reaction to this anxiety as a desire to improve health care: 'I would argue that modern maternity care has been shaped *both* by the search for increased health and safety in and around birth and by the institutionalization of male control over women' (Evans in Faulkner and Arnold 1985: 117). Whereas the contributors to these early sociological debates advocated resistance to the medical control of women's bodies which took the form of renaturalizing childbirth, the development of self-help groups and so on, later work incorporates a different view of change which may be brought about by making a critical intervention in epistemology.

In *Feminism Confronts Technology*, Judy Wajcman discusses conflicting debates about reproductive technologies and the control of women's bodies, but she also points out that 'The strength of the feminist critique of professional medical care is not only its dissection of medical-technological treatment but its analysis of the way scientific and medical knowledge is itself gendered' (Wajcman 1991: 67). So whether such technology is seen as the key to women's liberation (freeing them from the tyranny of reproduction) or to patriarchal domination (reducing them to the status of living laboratories), the underlying point concerns the way in which women's bodies have been represented and constructed in medical knowledge. And whether the representations and constructions are of the body as a machine which is prone to breakdown and failure, or of the body as nature which is unpredictable and withholding, the point is that the female body is a problem in medical science, and one which therefore requires technological intervention.

Sexual difference is thus constructed hierarchically in medical knowledge and is one of the most significant binary structures which support it. To envision change involves a rethinking of these hierarchical binaries which are characteristic not only of Western medical science but of Western culture in general. Wajcman warns that an unthinking association between men and mind/culture is just as problematic as that between women and body/nature. Men are not given to rationality and control by any factor of biology but through the dictates and conventions of society: 'The enduring force of the identification between technology and manliness, therefore, is not inherent in biological sex difference. It is rather the result of the historical and cultural construction of gender' (Wajcman 1991: 137). What is more, there is a need to be specific about the forms of masculinity and the forms of technology in question. It may well be, as Wajcman suggests, that there is a dominant ideology of masculinity, conveyed through education, the family and the workplace, which encourages men to realize their identity through mastery and through the mastery of technology. But this doesn't apply to all men or all technologies, and she raises the interesting point that mastery can at times be seen to compensate for social inadequacy or a sense of powerlessness. Wajcman criticizes Sherry Turkle's psychoanalytic account of computer hackers as failures on the grounds that it 'is very individualistic and does not address the wider cultural context within which hackers operate'. For her, the question is

> whether for these men technical expertise is about the realization of power or their lack of it. That in different ways both things are true points to the complex relationship between knowledge, power and technology. An obsession with technology may well be an attempt by men who are social failures to compensate for their lack of power. On the other hand, mastery over this technology does bestow some power on these men; in relation to other men and women who lack this expertise, in terms of the material rewards this skill brings, and even in terms of their popular portrayal as 'heroes' at the frontiers of technological expertise.
> (Wajcman 1991: 144).

My own work has demonstrated the connection between mastery and compensation in relation to new forms of medical imaging technology which exceed the capabilities of the human eye, but give doctors an almost visionary status (Kember 1991, 1995). Wajcman's underlying point is that the gendering of technology is culturally constructed and therefore contestable. What is contested through the gendering of technology is power and the hierarchical division of labour in our society. With the transition from industrial to information technologies, Wajcman signals the danger that some feminists are falling into the kind of essentialist traps that others have taken such pains to clear:

> Traditionally, the significant discrepancy between the sexes in their ability to work with technology was attributed to physical strength or weakness and feminists spent the best part of the 1970s discrediting this doctrine of natural difference. I am prompted to wonder if it is merely an accident of history that, just as there is a major shift in the nature of technology from industrial to information technology, an increasing number of feminist accounts of women and computers are themselves emphasizing cognitive sex-differences.
> (Wajcman 1991: 155)

In other words, there is the suggestion that women engage differently with information technologies because of some essential psychological difference. They may be less competitive, more co-operative, more concerned with exploration than following rules. As Wajcman says, this is in danger of recalling the old sexual stereotypes of women as emotional and irrational – even if it is meant as a celebration rather than a condemnation.

Wajcman's awareness of the dangers of essentialism informs her call for continued work on the sociology of technology rather than a general feminist theory of technology. One of the strengths of her book lies in its reminder that the distribution of power in society, rather than just the demarcation of difference, is one of the most important factors in debates on gender and science. Another useful book by Kirkup and Smith Keller (1992) incorporates essays which demonstrate that a sociology of technology need not be at odds with a feminist theory which avoids the pitfalls of essentialism. Evelyn Fox Keller's contribution shows that this is perhaps one of the main challenges which faces the feminist alternative or 'successor' science and technology projects.

These concerns with essentialism form the background for current feminist debates on science and technology, and are central to the development of a non-discriminative epistemology. The development of a structure of knowledge which embraces experience and difference is, I would argue, a key stage in the political transformation of science and technology, and one which anchors and makes meaningful such future figurations as Haraway's cyborg.

Towards Embodiment

The demand which has come from within feminism for non-hierarchical images of difference and a transformative science and technology, stems from a materialist critique of mainstream science and technology. Judy Wajcman (1991) and Hilary Rose(1994) provide more detailed histories of the development of feminist critiques of science and technology than it is possible for me to do here, but in brief the materialist critique refuses to regard the production of science and technology as outside or somehow above the general system of production which characterizes Western society – capitalism. Science is no longer seen to be neutral and objective, but marked by inequalities of labour and ownership and by its own ideology or self-justification system. Just as for Marx, knowledge produced by the owners of the capitalist economy was false and that produced by those oppressed within the economy was true, so the radical critique of science called for an alternative, revolutionary, true science to emerge from the ranks of the oppressed. Reflecting on her own early contributions to the critique of science, Hilary Rose regrets 'the conceptual and political obliteration of gender' and recalls her realization that 'adding women to the marxist political economy of science and stirring was no longer enough' (Rose 1994: x). For her, giving due consideration to women's labour in the production of science and knowledge might actually 're-vision rationality itself, fostering representations of nature which were more pacific to women and nature alike' (p. x).

So a feminist materialist critique of science is based on an alignment of capitalism with patriarchy as joint systems of domination and oppression and as joint producers of bad science. In response, feminists produce a successor science based on different and better values (like love, empathy, collectivity) which serves as an alternative or true science. Along with the successor science comes the feminist standpoint epistemology – thought and knowledge revisioned from a feminist standpoint. Advocates include Hilary Rose, Evelyn Fox Keller and Sandra Harding. Critics warn of the essentialism which may underline the conception of gender maintained within feminist standpoints. Certainly, Evelyn Fox Keller (1985) offers a psychology of masculine science as marked by the tendency towards domination and control but she does not regard the workings of the unconscious as being entirely given and immune from social influence.

In a very useful chapter entitled 'Method, Methodology and Epistemology in Feminist Research Processes', Liz Stanley and Sue Wise chart the development of feminist critiques of science and social science, and highlight the work which has been done in challenging monolithic categories such as 'women', 'knowledge' and even 'feminism' itself (Stanley and Wise 1990). Their own feminist standpoint position, which advocates feminist research practice in the social sciences, is backed by an acknowledgement of the diversity within each of these categories, and it is the acknowledgement of diversity within feminist standpoint epistemologies which, in Harding's words, renders them 'transitional':

> once one standpoint is recognised, this then admits the possibility of a range of different but equally valid feminist standpoints. We are driven to recognise the existence of not only 'a' feminist standpoint but also those of black women, working-class women, lesbian women, and other 'minority' women ... Once we admit the existence of feminist stand*points* there can be no a priori reason for placing these in any kind of hierarchy; each has *epistemological* validity because each has *ontological* validity. Here we have contextually grounded *truths*
> (Stanley and Wise 1990: 28).

Once knowledge is relativized in this way, then the status and structure of science is problematized. A feminist standpoint 'still accepts the existence of "true reality" and the methods of science as the means to establish it' (p. 27). But to accept a plurality of standpoints involves adopting a degree of scepticism towards all universalizing claims, a position which, as Stanley and Wise point out, is characteristic of postmodernism. A feminist postmodernist epistemology is then constructed on the basis of relativist rather than universalist truth claims. It also incorporates the notion of difference in relation to experience and identity – a notion which it is fair to say is at least implicit in the work of all three of the standpoint feminists named above (see Fox Keller 1985; Harding 1987; Rose 1994).

Although feminist materialists and postmodernists are at odds over the question of universalism, postmodernists retain elements of materialism not least in their promotion of embodiment as an epistemological position. Embodied knowledge is that which incorporates and acknowledges the lived experience of the knower, and by doing so is better placed to recognize the separate integrity of the known. As Andrew Ross argues, embodiment is an epistemological position required of scientific culture as a whole if 'the demand for fresh futures that will be more radically democratic than our own present' is to be fulfilled (Ross 1991: 12).

Because embodied knowledge incorporates the experience, desires and politics of the self, it cannot make universalist truth claims – it cannot claim to speak for everybody. Donna Haraway is a particular advocate of embodiment as an epistemological position, and for her it is the only guarantee of any kind of objectivity at all: 'only partial perspective promises objective vision' (Haraway 1991: 190). This claim to objectivity is really more to a kind of accountability. Acknowledging the partiality and positioning of knowledge production is a way of being accountable for the kind of knowledge which is produced. It is the kind of knowledge in which you speak for yourself but ideally in a dialogue with others. With universalist knowledges there is no room for dialogue. Haraway claims that for her the lessons of partiality were learned through actually trying to see the world through another set of eyes: 'These are lessons which I learned in part walking with my dogs and wondering how the world looks without a fovea and very few retinal cells for colour vision, but with a huge neural processing and sensory area for smells' (p. 190). It is as possible to learn through the eyes of animals and machines as through those of other people:

> The 'eyes' made available in modern technological sciences shatter any idea of passive vision, these prosthetic devices show us that all eyes, including our own organic ones, are active perceptual systems, building in translations and specific *ways* of seeing, that is, ways of life.
>
> (p. 190)

This seeing from another's point of view, even if the other is a machine, is for Haraway a possible allegory for feminist versions of objectivity. Responding to the wider feminist debates on epistemology, Haraway aligns herself with the transitional feminist standpoints – or with the attempt to see from subordinated points of view. She argues that 'there is good reason to believe vision is better from below the brilliant space platforms of the powerful' but adds that the 'standpoints of the subjugated are not "innocent" positions' (p. 190). Rather, 'they are preferred because in principle they are least likely to allow denial of the critical and interpretative core of all knowledge' (p. 191). Although this is not entirely consistent with some of the claims to truth of standpoint feminists, Haraway is making clear that her standpoints position is not a way of buying in to what she would regard as an unaccountable relativism:

> Such preferred positioning is as hostile to various forms of relativism as to the most explicitly totalizing versions of claims to scientific authority ... The alternative to relativism is partial, locatable, critical knowledges sustaining the possibility of webs of connections called solidarity in politics and shared conversations in epistemology.
>
> (p. 191)

For Haraway giving up all claims to authority is as irresponsible as claiming absolute authority, and political agency is more likely to result from sharing limited amounts of power and knowledge – amongst the preferred. This is not so much a politics of identity as a politics of affinity – in other words, it is not based on a quest for sameness but rather on a quest for difference. The aim is to see from one's own viewpoint as from another's:

> A commitment to mobile positioning and to passionate detachment is dependent on the impossibility of innocent 'identity' politics and epistemologies as strategies for seeing from the standpoints of the subjugated in order to see well. One cannot 'be' either a cell or a molecule – or a woman, colonized person, labourer, and so on – if one intends to see and to see from these positions critically. 'Being' is much more problematic and contingent.
>
> (p. 192)

In the final section I will show how Haraway represents this ontological and epistemological positioning through the cyborg, and how her cyborg differs from the more familiar cyborgs of medical, military and mass culture. I will also examine the relationship between Haraway's cyborg and Rosi Braidotti's nomadic subject in order to indicate how the cyborg might be further developed.

Cyborgs and Nomads

According to Haraway, it is not a particular gender, racial or class identity which produces a transformative science, but rather a critical positioning, which she represents through the cyborg. The cyborg is a human/machine hybrid, or an embodiment of difference. It is not a subject but a subject position and its being is highly contingent. In fact, it isn't really an 'it' at all but precisely a non-hierarchical *image* of the transformative science that Haraway, Harding and other feminists are seeking. It is easier to occupy the subject position of the cyborg – a position which transgresses the boundary between subject and object, self and other – than it is finally and fully to 'be' a cyborg. Although it is easy to imagine that cyborgs are everywhere in the information and communication networks of contemporary society (and she does), ultimately there is an acknowledgement in Haraway's cyborg manifesto that cyborgs are Utopian. At the end of her manifesto she declares that the image of the cyborg is there to support her argument that science and technology need to be epistemologically revised but not written off:

> It is not just that science and technology are possible means of great human satisfaction, as well as a matrix of complex dominations. Cyborg imagery can suggest a way out of the maze of dualisms in which we have explained our bodies and our tools to ourselves.
>
> (Haraway 1991: 181)

The cyborg challenges what she calls 'the informatics of domination' not simply by resisting it but by dismantling the binaristic structure that holds it in place. It does not signal an alternative successor science, but a science transformed by the mobilization of subjugated subject positions. Getting to be a cyborg is no easy task. It involves a full and final renunciation of identity as the hierarchical separation between subject and object, self and other.

So what about the many forms of human/machine hybrids that exist both within institutional and popular culture? It would seem that there are cyborgs and there are cyborgs. From Robodoc to *Robocop*, the cyborgs of medical, military and mass culture seem rather to embody a fetishization of the unitary, differentiated self that a celebration of difference. Haraway is clear that the cyborg originated in military science as augmented man – simply a more efficient fighting machine. For her, cyborgs for earthly survival must be developed in response and in opposition to cyborgs for scientific progress – for increased efficiency and competitiveness in modern multinational capitalism. Certainly some of these mainstream cyborgs benefit humanity (this has always been the defence of progress), such as the Robodoc which assists surgeons in hip-replacement operations, or the body scanners which enable doctors to watch someone's insides functioning in real time without having to cut them open. But at the same time as offering immediate benefits to patients, such technologies shore up the power of the medical institution and perhaps even intensify the social hierarchies within it. I have argued elsewhere (Kember 1991, 1995) that medicine's new three-dimensional colour-enhanced computer imaging technologies may be seen to compensate for the declining status of doctors' optical and sensory expertise. New medical technologies are somehow extra-optical and extra-sensory. They see and feel better than humans alone do. In 'The Cyborg Cometh' (*Equinox*, Channel 4 1994), relying on Robodoc is seen to be better than relying on the art or the feel of the surgeon. But once technologically enhanced, the doctor is again visionary and healer – omnipotently powerful. Haraway describes infinite vision in medicine as an illusion, a 'god-trick'. a disembodied form of knowledge production. Feminist debates on new medical imaging and reproductive technologies have emphasized that gendered power relations have by no means been transformed, and the two volumes of *Camera Obscura* (Treichler and Cartwright 1992a and b) devoted to the subject demonstrate very clearly the need for feminists and other marginalized groups to produce their own representations and embodied knowledges.

In November 1994 medical science introduced its latest cyborg to the scientific community and to the general public. He is nicknamed Adam and he is the creation of a team of doctors in the United States who wanted to add a complete electronic visual archive of the human body to the National Library of Medicine's store of textbooks.

When Adam died he was submerged in gelatine and frozen to −70°C. He was then divided into four sections and put through an industrial planer. He was scanned, sliced and photographed at one-millimetre intervals from head to toe. The shavings were buried and the images were stored in a computer. Adam was thus recreated in cyberspace, and in November 1994 he became available on the internet. He is intended to represent the archetypal male form and will be used for medical research and training. He is expected to make a contribution to the development of virtual medicine and possibly to the elimination of the practice of dissection or anatomy in medical training.

So Adam (again) has quite a lot resting on him. There is also an Eve who (again) was done after Adam and in the interest of better image resolution has been sliced at one-third of a millimetre intervals. Eve's real identity will remain anonymous, but Adam's has been released (see Kember 1996).

For Donna Haraway the recreation of Adam and Eve would be part of, if not the epitome of medical science's god-trick – the fulfilment, perhaps, of its quest for bodily transcendence, immortality and omnipotence. It can be seen alongside developments in reproductive science and technology (from IVF to genetic engineering) to contribute to science's ability to 'father itself' (Franklin 1993), and for me it recalls the story of Frankenstein, based as it was on a woman's nightmare and a critique of scientific progress. Not only that, but one of the doctors is called Victor.

Above all, this project (called the Visible Human Project) illustrates the necessity of retaining a gendered account of power when exploring the wonders of cyberspace and considering the nature of cyborgs.

In general I would suggest that the relation between humans and machines in modern medicine may be more fetishistic than (ideally) cyborgian. The hierarchical relationship between the medical subject (self) and object (Other) is reinforced by new technology just at the point where it might have been threatened by it. If the reinforcement of power is illusory or fetishistic, it is none the less felt. It functions on both a material and ideological level. Similarly, Claudia Springer finds no ideal cyborgs in popular culture. Characters like Robocop and the Terminator may well be post-human but they are not post-patriarchal. Cyborg imagery, she argues, 'has not so far realized the ungendered ideal theorized by Donna Haraway' (Springer 1991: 309). These cyborgs are the most macho of macho men. They are not just hard but virtually indestructible. According to Springer it is as if integration with technology threatens the integrity and wholeness of the masculine subject, which reinforces itself with a vengeance. The violence which characterizes these cyborgs displaces their sexuality and enhances their autonomy. Pointing a weapon of science-fictional proportions at somebody and firing it is just the cyborg's way of saying I love you. The issue again is one of boundaries, but this time it is about the need to reinforce rather than redefine one's difference from the other. Springer draws on psychological research about fascist soldiers in order to argue that: 'the machine body becomes the ideal tool for ego maintenance'. Basically, violence is safer than sex when 'the sexual act evokes loss of self' (p. 317).

So cyborgs can be bad as well as good. The cyborgs we have are very much part of current economic and social relations which Haraway summarizes as the 'informatics of domination', and the ones we imagine point to two different kinds of future which Springer describes as 'either liberation or annihilation'. In any case, Springer argues 'What is really being debated in the discourses surrounding a cyborg future are contemporary disputes concerning gender and sexuality, with the future providing a clean slate, or a blank screen, onto which we can project our fascination and fears' (p. 322).

I would suggest that this is true of the discourses of popular culture, and of cyberpunk science fiction in particular. But whereas feminism and feminist political fiction acknowledges the importance of science fiction and its constructions of gendered and sexual identity, it is also concerned with the wider issues of ontology and epistemology which concern the construction of the self. So what feminism is debating through cyborg representations is the future of the self as a gendered and sexual, ontological and epistemological construct. It is a personal and political debate, in which concern for the self is at the same time a concern for the other. In an article entitled 'Technologizing the Self: A Future Anterior for Cultural Studies', Elspeth Probyn highlights the importance of these issues for cultural studies. She suggests that technologizing the self offers a way through the problematics of representation ('of who speaks for whom, and why') which are central to cultural studies and feminism. By technologizing the self she means finding a 'mode of speaking one's difference that does change matters both personal and social/theoretical' (Probyn 1992: 504). It is a position similar to that of embodiment and one which recalls Foucault's concept of technologies of the self: 'this language would be dependent on being able to care about another's difference; to go somehow from one's own experience to another's (p. 504). This going from one's own experience to another's signals a transformation in representation and epistemology and, for Probyn, relocates the necessity of caring within the theoretical tradition of cultural studies.

Like Haraway, Probyn is at pains to point out that she is not reaffirming a straightforward identity politics but rather a tactical construction of the self which is active on two levels: 'At an epistemological level, a self is used to reveal certain bases of knowledge, and at an ontological level selves reveal their affectivity of *being* in the world' (p. 506). This tactical employment of the self is at once serious and playful, political and pleasurable. It is the element of play which helps to prevent a reification of the self. This is a lesson, Probyn points out, that can be learned from the practices of 'camp':

> the resilience of its critical pleasures . . . can provide a starting-point for the left to consider how to enjoy the serious issue of establishing a politics of identity as a strategic form of empowerment, and yet not lapse into an essentializing rhetoric of authenticity.
>
> (p. 504).

So, in homage to campness, Probyn calls for a ' "wild" theory of the self' and 'a radical practice of enunciation where the truth of the I is indifferent but where difference is created in the tension, the movement, between a *she* and an I' (p. 505). She also recalls Rosi Braidotti's injunction to speak 'as if the subjectivity of all was at stake in the enunciative patterns of each one' (p. 509). For Braidotti, such a seriously playful subject position is figured not only in the image of the cyborg but also of the nomad.

Like the cyborg (and like Irigaray's image of the lips), the nomad is described by Braidotti as a 'figuration' for contemporary subjectivity (Braidotti 1994: 3). A figuration is at once an image and an epistemological and ontological position: 'The nomadic subject as a performative image allows me to weave together different levels of my experience: it reflects some autobiographical aspects, while also expressing my own conceptual preference for a postmetaphysical vision of subjectivity' (p. 7).

A postmetaphysical vision of subjectivity is 'one that develops the notion of corporeal materiality by emphasizing the embodied and therefore sexually differentiated structure of the speaking subject (p. 3). Unlike the cyborg, the nomad is a gendered subject, albeit a non-essentialized gendered subject which has not as yet been fully born:

> In feminist theory one speaks as a woman, although the subject 'woman' is not a monolithic essence defined once and for all but rather the site of multiple, complex, and potentially contradictory sets of experiences, defined by overlapping variables such as class, race, age, lifestyle, sexual preference, and others.
>
> (p. 4)

Still an embodiment of difference which may be 'a technological compound of human and post-human' the nomadic subject is a 's/he' and 'a cyborg, but equipped also with an unconscious' (p. 36). For Braidotti, the price to pay for retaining her identity and her sex is the realization that 'I am not new yet' (p. 39). The nomadic subject journeys across boundaries but hasn't yet arrived. Like the cyborg, s/he maps an elsewhere but one which is perhaps not so close, and one which certainly doesn't bear any resemblance to the available fictions of cyberspace. Cyberspace is where the hierarchies of social relations are intensified, and like Andrew Ross, Braidotti regards cyberpunk in particular as a fiction projected from male phantasies – specifically of a return to the matrix. As Springer points out, 'the word matrix, in fact, originates in the Latin *mater* (meaning both mother and womb)' (Springer 1991: 306). The phantasy of a return to the matrix involves both fear and fascination and is responsible for many of the most typical representations of the interface between bodies and technology: getting out of the 'meat' (floating disembodied in cyberspace) or reinforcing it (creating bionic bodies) in the face of adversity. This is not a phantasy or a set of images that Rosi Braidotti is happy with. She is more interested in seeing what might be symbolized from a female unconscious, or rather, from a negotiation between 'unconscious structures of desires and conscious political choices'. Braidotti reminds us of the case of psychoanalysis, which 'rests precisely on the demand that the pain involved in the processes of change and transformation be recognized and respected. In-depth transformations are as painful as they are slow' (Braidotti 1994: 31). To this end, she posits change as a kind of dance between the old and the new, and as a ritualized, repetitive, slow process of transition. New figurations of female subjectivity, such as the nomad, 'work through established forms of representation, consuming them from within' (p. 38). She refers to this process as a form of mimesis or parody which she calls 'as if' ('it is *as if* some experiences were reminiscent or evocative of others'), and she cites the work of Laurie Anderson as an example. Anderson's multimedia performance art is indeed parodic, and given her innovative experiments with technology and her willingness to play across the boundaries of identity in her work, she is a nomad who is perhaps as close to being a cyborg as anyone.

Cyborgs and nomads are feminist political imaginaries, 'performative images' constructed in the context of modern information and communication technologies. They are also imagined in opposition to an ongoing history of domination embedded in the structure of Western science and society. Both images may signal an epistemological shift in the structure of domination but they do not claim to render it obsolete. In 'Beyond the Screens: Film, Cyberpunk and Cyberfeminism', Sadie Plant also acknowledges the basis for a feminist critique of technology: 'There is no doubt that the wares of technology, hard and soft, old and new, are always intended as toys for the boys; technical development has always been a consequence of man's attempt to perpetuate and extend his dominion' (Plant 1993: 13).

But where she states that 'it is all true' that technology has been 'developed without and against women' and that new technologies such as virtual reality are 'the after-images of the weapons and surveillance systems', she also claims that 'it is these technologies, the pinnacles of man's supremacy, the high-tide of his speculations, that leave his world vulnerable to cyberfeminist infection' (p. 13). Plant defines cyberfeminism in terms of 'information technology as a fluid attack, an onslaught on human agency and the solidity of identity' (p. 12). She argues that just at the point where masculine agency and control is seen to be fulfilled in the matrix, the matrix fights back. And for Plant, this is the same as saying that nature and the feminine fight back:

> Hooked up to the screens and jacked into decks, man becomes the user, the addict, who can no longer insist on his sovereign autonomy and separation from nature. Increasingly integrated with the environment from which he always considered himself distinguished, he finds himself travelling on networks he didn't even know existed, and entering spaces in which his conceptions of reality and identity are destroyed. This is the return of the repressed, the return of the feminine, perhaps even the revenge of nature.
>
> (p.13)

Compelling as this concept is, what is at work within it is perhaps a rather problematic and essentialist association of femininity, nature and technology which seems only to transplant a phobic patriarchal phantasy into a feminist imaginary. Doesn't this concept of the matrix-mother revive the image of the *vagina dentata* but from the woman's point of view; as bite rather than fright?

For Plant, the matrix puts a sudden end to patriarchal domination and to human agency. Technology itself, albeit a feminised technology, is the key player in a dystopian future which holds no more promise for women than it does for men. The future in question is one which has been imagined in cyberpunk fiction, which in itself is seen to be inseparable from social reality. All that there is in this future is cybernetics; self-organizing technological systems which resist any form of external control. For Plant, even the muscular cyborgs of popular film are failed attempts to secure the boundaries of human identity: 'this is a mission they accomplish only by complicating control and proliferating chaos, disrupting security in the very process of reinforcing it' (p. 16). Plant's vision of cyberfeminism celebrates a future without human agency and one which marks not only the end of patriarchy but of socialist feminism: 'For all our good intentions, moral principles, and political vision, we are heading for a post-human world in which the intentions of the human species are no longer the guiding force of global development' (p. 16).

This would seem to me to be an unfortunate state of affairs, not least because it relinquishes the promise of monsters (such as Haraway's cyborg and Braidotti's nomad) to transform the future in their own non-unitary image. As Braidotti suggests, such a promise can only be fulfilled by monsters acknowledging their place in history (there can be no transformations with continuities) and in a social reality which is divisible from science fiction and neither Utopian nor dystopian but structured by unequal power relations.

Conclusion

This chapter has attempted to show how feminist work on epistemology has developed within and contributed to debates about the relation between gender and technology. These debates are multidisciplinary, drawing on sociology, women's studies, cultural studies, psychology, psychoanalysis, philosophy and the history of science. I have argued that the sociological input remains important in showing how the production of science, technology and epistemology is structured by the unequal distribution of power in society. The problem with cyberfeminism, as I see it, stems from the absence of this framework and its technological determinism.

I have suggested that Donna Haraway's representation of the cyborg signals an epistemological shift and constitutes one image of a transformative science and technology; that is, a science and technology no longer structured by domination. It is clear, however, that Haraway's cyborg is to a large extent Utopian and that the cyborgs in operation in the social realm tend, if anything, to reinforce the structure of domination. What then is the value of the cyborg as a feminist political imaginary? Haraway herself is candid about its limitations, but maintains its importance not only as a strategy for opposing dominant and dominating social formations, but as a way of describing the possibilities of some of the more 'creative and playful' uses of technology which are currently being made. She argues that even if a battle of/over the cyborgs is being lost to those in power, then that is no reason to give up: 'it's like refusing to leave in the hands of hostile social formations tools that we need for reinventing our own lives' (Penley and Ross 1991: 8). What is more:

> I know that there's a lot going on in technoscience discourses and practices that's not about the devil, that's a source of remarkable pleasure, that promises interesting kinds of human relationships, not just contestatory, not always oppositional, but something often more creative and playful and positive than that. And I want myself and others to learn how to describe those possibilities
>
> (p. 8)

So, as Constance Penley points out, Haraway's image of the cyborg is a 'suggestive and productive' paradox which describes a hybrid subject position which, to a limited extent, is being occupied, and one which might be more fully occupied in the future. This, as Penley suggests, is typical of most Utopian projects which 'hover somewhere in between the present and the future, attempting to figure the future as the present, the present as the future' – and is not in itself problematic. What is problematic is the possibility that her cyborg leaves no room 'for anything that could be called "subjectivity" ' (p. 8). Haraway's cyborg has no origin story, no unconscious and is not constituted through sexual difference. The advantage of this is that it is not defined within the dominant and hierarchical narrative of Oedipal subjectivity. But Haraway admits that in rejecting psychoanalysis she might, as it were, have thrown the baby out with the bath-water. She argues that 'the figures that we've used to structure our accounts of the unconscious so far are much too conservative, much too heterosexist, much too familial, much too exclusive', but in a retrospective view of the cyborg manifesto she calls for a psychoanalytic practice 'that recognizes the very local and partial quality of the Oedipal stories' (p. 9). More than that, and in the spirit of feminist successor science projects or, at least, feminist epistemological standpoints, she says that: 'At a certain point you ask if there isn't another set of stories you need to tell, another account of an unconscious. One that does a better job accounting for the subjects of history (p. 9).

It is clear that Braidotti's nomadic subject is constituted as much by a desire for a non-Oedipal as for a postmetaphysical account of subjectivity. She draws on the work of Luce Irigaray for this account, but makes the point that there is still a lot to do in the construction of new desiring subjects. Part of the task as she sees it involves a reconciliation of history and the unconscious:

> In my assessment, one of the central issues at stake in this project is how to reconcile historicity, and therefore agency, with the (unconscious) desire for change. The most difficult task is how to put the will to change together with the desire for the new that implies the construction of new desiring subjects.
>
> (Braidotti 1994: 31)

The task of reconciling history and the unconscious has been, and will continue to be undertaken within feminist debates on psychoanalysis. These will, I suggest, come to have an increasing importance in the development of those aspects of feminist work on science and technology which are concerned with subjectivity and with the politics of difference. What has been marked out so far is a crucial imaginary and epistemological shift in the terms of domination. What we have are figurations of the future, performative images of a better elsewhere. What we need, perhaps, is to elaborate more and better stories about how 'we' as desiring and historical subjects can get there. Another account of the unconscious might provide one such potent story. In the meantime I think it is important to signal what Dick Hebdige calls 'the virtual power of metaphor' (Hebdige 1993: 270) and figuration, or the capacity of language and representation to act – virtually.

Note

1 The theoretical shifts mentioned include those from structuralism to post-structuralism and from a Marxist concept of ideology to a Foucauldian account of power/knowledge. The altered constituency refers to a broadened range of political identifications, for example with struggles against sexism, racism and homophobia as well as against class oppression. According to McNeil and Franklin, scientific (specifically biological) arguments are used more often in defence of racism, sexism and homophobia than in defence of class prejudice.

References

Braidotti, R., 1994: *Nomadic Subjects: Embodiment and Sexual Difference in Contemporary Feminist Theory* New York: Columbia University Press.

Brighton Women and Science Group, 1980: *Alice Through the Microscope*. London: Virago.

Enrenreich, B. and English, D., 1979: *For Her Own Good*. London: Pluto Press.

Faulkner, W. and Arnold, E. (eds.), 1985: *Smothered by Invention*. London: Pluto Press.

Fox Keller, E., 1985: *Reflections on Gender and Science*. New Haven, CT: Yale University Press.

Franklin, S., 1993: 'Postmodern Procreation: Representing Reproductive Practice', *Science as Culture*, 3 (4) 522–61.

Friedan, B., 1974: *The Feminine Mystique*. New York: Norton.

Grossberg, L., Nelson, C. and Treichler, P.A., 1992: Cultural Studies: An Introduction. In L. Grossberg, C. Nelson and P.A. Treichler (eds.) *Cultural Studies*. London: Routledge.

Haraway, D.J., *Private Visions*. London: Verso.

Haraway, D.J., 1991: *Simians, Cyborgs and Women*. London: Free Association Books.

Harding, S., 1987: 'The Instability of the Analytical Categories of Feminist Theory', in S. Harding, and F. O'Barr (eds.) *Sex and Scientific Inquiry*. Chicago: University of Chicago Press.

Hebdige, D., 1993: 'Training Some Thoughts on the Future', in J. Bird, B. Curtis, T. Putnam, G. Robertson and L. Tickner (eds.) *Mapping the Futures*. London: Routledge.

Kember, S., 1991: 'Medical Diagnostic Imaging: The Geometry of Chaos', *New Formations*, 15.

Kember, S., 1995: 'Medicine's New Vision?', in M. Lister (ed.) *The Photographic Image in Digital Culture*. London: Routledge.

Kember, S., 1996: *Virtual Anxiety: Photography, New Technology and Subjectivity*. Manchester: Manchester University Press.

Kirkup, G. and Smith Keller, L. (eds.), 1992: *Inventing Women*. London: Polity Press/Open University Press.

McNeil, M. and Franklin, S., 1991: 'Science and Technology: Questions for Cultural Studies and Feminism, in S. Franklin, L. Lury and J. Stacey (eds.) *Off centre: Feminism and Cultural Studies*. London: Harper Collins.

Penley, C. and Ross, A., 1991: *Technoculture* Minneapolis, MN: University of Minnesota Press.

Plant, S., 1993: 'Beyond the Screens: Film, Cyberpunk and Cyberfeminism', *Variant*, 14.

Probyn, E., 1992: 'Technologizing the Self', in L. Grossberg, C. Nelson and P.A. Treichler (eds.) *Cultural Studies*. London: Routledge.

Rose, H., 1994: *Love, Power and Knowledge*. Cambridge: Polity Press.

Ross, A., 1991: *Strange Weather: Science and Technology in the Age of Limits*. London: Verso.

Springer, C., 1991: 'The Pleasure of the Interface', *Screen*, 32 (3).

Stanley, L. and Wise, S., 1990: 'Method, Methodology and Epistemology in Feminist Research Processes', in L. Stanley (ed.) *Feminist Praxis*. London: Routledge.

Treichler, P.A. and Cartwright, L. (eds.), 1992a: 'Imaging Technologies, Inscribing Science', *Camera Obscura*, 28.

Treichler, P.A. and Cartwright, L. (eds.), 1992b: 'Imaging Technologies, Inscribing Science 2', *Camera Obscura*, 29.

Wajcman, J., 1991: *Feminism Confronts Technology*. Cambridge: Polity Press.

Williamson, J., 1987: *Consuming Passions. The Dynamics of Popular Culture*. London: Marion Boyars.

SECTION III

Cultural Analysis and Consumption

Introduction

The first three of the chapters in this section can be read as an ongoing debate between James Curran and David Morley, focusing on the claims (and counterclaims) made for, and against, work within the field of cultural studies on the question of cultural consumption, during the 1980s and early 1990s.

The section begins with Curran's "The New Revisionism" in Mass Communication Research: A Reappraisal', first published in the *European Journal of Communication* in 1990. In this chapter Curran offers a critical review of what he calls the 'new revisionism' in cultural studies at large. The revisions at stake concern the critique which cultural studies work (and some work within mass communications) has offered to previously established models of media power within the 'critical' (and principally Marxist) approach to communication studies. Centrally, this 'revisionism' has taken the form of a critique both of any simplistic notion of the automatic or necessary determination of media production practices by structures of economic ownership and political regulation and also a critique of ideas of media audiences as passive zombies, or 'dupes', easily swayed by the power of the media. Partly under the influence of Foucault, much of this 'new revisionism', especially in its postmodern variants, has stressed both the dispersion of power across different fields of cultural activity and also the potential for media consumers to choose and manipulate media products actively, in the production of cultural meanings. While recognizing that some aspects of this 'revisionism' are valuable, in allowing us to develop more complex (and more adequate) models of the functioning of cultural power, Curran is also concerned to critique what he sees as the overblown claims made by some scholars, in respect of the creativity of media consumers – not least because of the consequent dangers of a 'romanticization' of 'consumer sovereignty'. Moreover, Curran argues that much of what has been presented as original in cultural studies work on media audiences, actually amounts to no more than a reinventing of the wheel, in so far as many of these 'new' approaches to media audiences were foreshadowed by earlier work in the mass communication tradition, of which most cultural studies scholars have displayed a culpable ignorance, in Curran's view.

Curran's chapter is then followed by David Morley's 'Populism, Revisionism and the "New" Audience Research', originally published in *Poetics* in 1992. In this article Morley offers an alternative overview of cultural studies work on media audiences and responds to some of Curran's criticisms of that work. Morley, like Curran, is dissatisfied with the burgeoning tendency, within some cultural studies work, to overemphasize both the 'polysemy' (or openness) of media texts and the cultural power of the 'reader', especially in analyses that fail to place the moment of 'reading' in its sociological context. In Morley's argument, it must always be recognized that 'readers' from different social positions have different types and amounts of 'cultural capital' at their disposal in making their 'uses' and 'interpretations' of media texts. None the less, Morley maintains that the project of understanding how audiences get pleasures and meanings from media materials remains central to the analysis of popular culture. He is thus critical of commentators such as Corner, whose own negative view of 'demand-side' research in cultural studies, especially in its largely ethnographic focus on micro-processes of consumption, seems to lead towards a position where the gains associated with much of cultural studies work (on what had previously been dismissed by many sociologists as merely the micro/trivial/domestic/private/feminine spheres) are in danger of being lost in the backlash against overblown accounts of our 'semiotic democracy'. In relation to Curran's criticisms, Morley avers that, in fact, the historical account which Curran offers, in which he claims that many of cultural studies' so-called new 'insights' are merely restatements of already well-established positions within mass communications, could only have been written with the benefit of hindsight. Thus Morley claims that, prior to the impact of the 'new revisionism', of which Curran is so critical, no one (Curran included) would have seen the importance of the historical work on media audiences which Curran now recounts as so self-evidently important.

Since the two essays were originally published in 1990 and 1992 respectively, and presented two sharply contrasting views, a retrospective 'Media Dialogue' has been added in which Curran and Morley reply briefly to each other's criticisms. This helps to clarify the nature of their agreements and disagreements.

Christine Geraghty's 'Feminism and Media Consumption', while maintaining the focus on audiences and the general issue of cultural consumption, also shifts the ground of attention in two ways: first, by contrasting the modes of television and film consumption (and their respective modes of theorization); and second, by focusing particularly on questions of gender, and on feminist perspectives in film and television theory. As Geraghty notes, the issue of 'spectatorship' has been rather differently theorized within film and television studies, with the former tending towards a tighter model of textual determinism, in its account of the film – spectator encounter. However, Geraghty is also concerned to draw out important differences of emphasis *within* film studies itself (see her comments on the debate between Williams and Kaplan, concerning the question of textual determination and, crucially, the possible readings of the position of the mother in Vidor's classic, *Stella Dallas*.). Geraghty goes on to explore the significance of the differential emphasis on textual analysis and empirical (and often ethnographic) work with actual audiences, within film and television studies, focusing also on the potential contributions (and difficulties) of psychoanalytic theories of gender, in a manner that foreshadows Valerie Walkerdine's contributions to this book (see Chapters 5 and 15). Geraghty also problematicizes any simple division between film studies work on 'woman as sign' and television studies work within a 'realist' problematic, insisting on the importance of more particular and nuanced questions of identification and audience address. In a similar vein (and again, in a way that can usefully be cross-referenced to Walkerdine's contributions), Geraghty's account of the female audience for Gainsborough Melodramas is careful to emphasize the necessity of situating our analyses within particular socio-historical conditions, rather than relying on decontextualized or generalized models of consumption. Here Geraghty's argument is also concerned to excavate an important and largely lost tradition of *non*-psychoanalytic work within film studies, against the usual characterization of the field, in which British film studies is reduced to the work of *Screen*, and the work of *Screen* itself is improperly reduced to a univocal psychoanalytic orthodoxy. In the final sections of the chapter Geraghty points to the irony of feminist scholars' apparent embrace of traditional concepts of femininity as a result of their engagement with women's genres such as melodrama and soap opera. In addition, she returns to the question of the 'extra-textual' and the complex problems (and insights) thrown up by the recent empirical work of Stacey and Gray. The question here, finally, is how we might critically understand audience work's 'apparent promise of the truth, emerging out of the mouths of real women'.

Valerie Walkerdine's 'Popular Culture and the Eroticization of Little Girls' addresses an area which she regards as having been badly neglected within cultural studies – the question of childhood and, more particularly, the question of working-class little girls' relation to sexuality, innocence and the erotic. These are clearly very powerfully charged areas of continuing debate and anxiety within contemporary society – witness the ongoing uncertainties about psychoanalysis, child abuse and 'false memory syndromes', to which Walkerdine refers. Walkerdine's analysis throws new light on questions of vulnerability and empowerment, in relation to feminine sexuality and gender identities, by means of an approach which offers us a model of 'feminity as the Other of rational childhood' (itself, in Walkerdine's view, always defined as intrinsically masculine). Part of the originality of Walkerdine's analysis rests in her complex invocation of popular culture as being, for working-class 'little girls' in particular, not simply the source of some regrettable 'corruption' of innocence but, rather, as also empowering, by virtue of its role in offering to the girl in that position an empowering possibility of 'badness' through sexuality. These matters clearly are both complex and contentious, but Walkerdine will not rest with any easy assignment of 'perversion' to a minority of 'bad apples': rather, she is concerned to identify the systematically contradictory nature of definitions of feminine sexuality at the heart of contemporary culture – for instance, in relation to the popular *Minipops* TV series, featuring heavily eroticized images of 'child stars'. In all of this, Walkerdine is also concerned to develop a mode of analysis which draws on psychoanalytic insights, but which is also sensitive to 'historically specific regimes of meaning and truth'. Thus, in focusing on the question of the psychic use of 'available cultural fantasies' within particular socio-historical settings (see also her comments, here and in

Chapter 5 on her own childhood) she attempts to avoid the limitations of universalist or overgeneralized psychoanalytically based modes of analysis.

While Walkerdine's chapter in this section focuses primarily on the question of gender, with the issue of class here remaining the subordinate theme, her earlier contribution (Chapter 5) was primarily concerned with the question of the 'masses' – in relation to their (problematic) irrationality, animality and 'badness'. Here Gareth Stanton offers a fascinating account of the contemporary significance of an earlier approach to the study of those selfsame 'masses' in Britain – the 'Mass-Observation' movement, launched by Tom Harrisson and Charles Madge, in the late 1930s. These days, 'Mass-Observation' usually gets little more than a passing nod of acknowledgement in histories of twentieth-century intellectual life in Britain. Stanton's point is that, in fact, this movement is not only much more important than is commonly recognized, as a precursor of contemporary cultural studies, but also that, with extraordinary precision, the history of 'Mass-Observation' foreshadows the very influential debates which have taken place over the last ten years, on the borderline between cultural studies and anthropology, concerning the possibilities of self-reflexive, 'postmodern' forms of ethnography (see also Clifford and Marcus 1986). As Stanton demonstrates, Harrisson's work as an anthropologist in the New Hebrides, during the 1930s, gave rise to texts (see his *Borneo Jungle* and *Savage Civilisation*) which, in their mobilization of a self-reflexive point of view, in their 'writerliness' and in their location of the procedure of a 'local ethnography' within the broader framework of the dynamics of the international economy of colonialism, pre-empt by nearly half a century the 'revolution' in contemporary anthropology wrought firstly by Asad's *Anthropology and the Colonial Encounter* (1973) and subsequently by the work of Clifford and Marcus (1986) and Marcus and Fischer (1986). This is no simple matter, of consequence only within the specialist history of the discipline of anthropology. These debates, concerning the relation of power and knowledge, the role (and responsibilities) of the observer/author – especially, as Stanton demonstrates, in the wake of the publication of Malinowski's's own *Diaries*, describing his procedures and feelings when conducting the study of the Trobriand Islands, that set the framework for anthropological fieldwork for half a century – have exploded in recent years, across the boundaries of the human and social sciences. What is so instructive, in Stanton's account, is the contextualization of Harrisson's work as a 'text out of time'. Stanton shows how this text now offers an extremely useful resource against which to triangulate contemporary debates in cultural studies. Much of this recent work seems bent on unknowingly replicating Harrisson and Madge's earlier attempts to turn the techniques of ethnography away from their original focuses on 'savages' and 'natives' (which can never transcend the tourist/colonial gazes, through which the Other is always constructed as an object of exotic fascination), and to attempt, instead, to develop that (still) most ambitious of cultural projects, 'an anthropology of ourselves'. This section thus ends, as it begins, with a call to scholars in these fields to attend more closely to the intellectual histories out of which contemporary debates can be seen to have emerged.

Note

Publications cited in this Introduction appear in the References to the appropriate chapters.

11

The New Revisionism in Mass Communication Research: A Reappraisal

James Curran

A new revisionist movement has emerged in media and cultural studies. Coming initially out of the radical tradition, it has devoted much of its creative energy to attacking the premisses and assumptions of that tradition. Indeed, in its fully fledged form, the new revisionism rejects the models of society, the ways of conceptualizing the role of the media, the explanatory frameworks and problematics of the principal radical paradigms in mass communication research.

This new revisionism often presents itself as original and innovative, as an emancipatory movement that is throwing off the shackles of tradition. It is none of these things. Part of the new thinking is revivalist rather than revisionist, a reversion to previous received wisdoms rather than a reconnaissance of the new. Another strand can be seen as a continuation of the 'radical' tradition but in a qualified form that incorporates pluralist and other insights.

During the same period, the liberal pluralist tradition of communications research has also adapted and changed. Some researchers within this tradition have modified their approach in response to attacks from radical critics: in effect, they have moved against the flow of traffic coming the other way.

In short, we are living through a genuine 'ferment in the field', in which numerous researchers have substantially revised their views. In an attempt to make sense of the current situation, I have tried to provide a selective 'reading' of trends in the field during the last fifteen years, concentrating mainly on research in the UK but with an occasional sideways glance at studies in continental Europe, Scandinavia and the United States. The term 'reading' – emblematic of the new revisionism – is perhaps too dignified a term for what follows. Notes would be a more accurate description.[1]

Polarization Between Pluralist and Radical Research Traditions c. 1975

Two readers, *Mass Communication and Society* and *Culture, Society and the Media*, published respectively in 1977 and 1982 but both mostly written in 1976, provide a useful starting point, since they crystallize a particular moment in the historical development of communications research (Curran et al. 1977; Gurevitch et al. 1982). They were constructed around the antinomy between pluralist and Marxist perspectives on the media, which were characterized in ideal-typical terms:

> The pluralists see society as a complex of competing groups and interests, one of them predominant all of the time. Media organizations are seen as bounded organizational systems, enjoying an important degree of autonomy from the state, political parties and institutionalized pressure groups. Control of the media is said to be in the hands of an autonomous managerial elite who allow a considerable degree of flexibility to media professionals. A basic symmetry is seen to exist between media institutions and their audiences, since in McQuail's words, the 'relationship is generally entered into voluntarily and on apparently equal terms' (McQuail 1977). Audiences are seen as capable of manipulating the media in an infinite variety of ways according to their prior needs and dispositions and as having access to what Halloran (1977) calls 'the plural values of society' enabling them to 'conform, accommodate or reject'.
>
> Marxists view capitalist society as being one of class domination; the media are seen as part of an ideological arena in which various class views are fought out, although within the context of the dominance of certain classes; ultimate control is increasingly concentrated in monopoly capital; media professionals, while enjoying the illusion of autonomy, are socialized into and internalize the norms of the dominant culture. The media, taken as a whole, relay interpretive frameworks consonant with the interests of the dominant classes, and media audiences, while sometimes negotiating and contesting these frameworks, lack ready access to alternative meaning systems that would enable them to reject the definitions offered by the media in favour of oppositional definitions.
>
> (Curran and Gurevitch 1977: 4–5)

The intention of most people involved in the production of these readers was to promote a polarized conflict between the two perspectives. This was partly a pedagogic device, since both books arose out of an Open University course and the aim was to encourage students to think for themselves and decide in favour of one or other tradition or to consider whether there might be a more convincing intermediate position. But the aim was also to assert as central to the debate an intellectual tradition – Marxism – that had been marginalized in British academic life for much of the postwar period. In particular, we wanted to resist the American domination of the field, with what seemed to many of us at the time as its sterile consensus, its endless flow of repetitive and inconclusive 'effects' studies situated in a largely 'taken-for-granted' pluralist model of society, and instead to generate a debate that reflected the diversity of European intellectual thought.

This phase of the field's development has been outlined elsewhere (Curran et al. 1982; Hall 1986) and does not need to be repeated. Arguably, the most original research during this period was in cultural studies and was preoccupied in one form or other with a debate about the determination of social practice. However, so far as journalism research is concerned, the most salient development was the Glasgow University Media Group's concerted assault on the pluralist conception of public service broadcasting as a disinterested channel of information and balanced forum of debate. They argued on the basis of a series of well-documented studies that much TV reporting was grounded on the assumptions of dominant groups in society (Glasgow University Media Group, 1976, 1980, 1982, 1985). Although provoking angry denunciations from broadcasters, this research was not subjected to detailed scholarly counter-attack from a pluralist perspective, with one notable exception (Harrison 1985).[2] The Glasgow Group's broadsides were accompanied by a fusillade of fire from other researchers who also argued that broadcasting coverage was structured in dominance (e.g. Hartmann 1975; Hall et al. 1976; Connell 1980; Morley 1981). Implicit in much of this research was the assumption – later to be questioned – that TV meanings were relatively unambiguous and that audience understanding of programmes was determined in a general sense by the meanings immanent in texts.

This attack was accompanied by a series of studies of 'moral panics'. Most of these studies argued that stereotypical and misleading portrayals of 'outsider' groups in the media helped to deflect wider social conflict and reinforce dominant social and political norms. This was illustrated by studies of media representation of political protest (Halloran et al. 1970; Hall 1973a), youth gangs (Cohen 1980), drug addicts (Young 1974), muggers (Hall et al. 1978), union militants (Beharrell and Philo 1977), football hooligans (Whannel 1979), 'scroungers' (Golding and Middleton 1982) and homosexuals (Watney 1987) among others (Cohen and Young 1981). Implicit or explicit in most of these studies were two key assumptions that were later to be challenged. The media's construction of reality was assumed to reflect the dominant culture; i.e. the media were portrayed either as offering a dominant ideological definition of reality that served dominant interests, or, in its stronger version, of misrepresenting what really happened in a way that promoted false consciousness. It was also assumed that the media were influential in terms of mapping society and furnishing conceptual categories and frames of reference through which people made sense of society. The media had, as Hall (1977) argued in an influential essay, an 'ideological effect'.

The stress on the 'effectivity' of the media was seemingly echoed by an influential group of film and TV analysts associated with the journal, *Screen*, which occupied a separatist and esoteric niche in the emergent radical tradition. They published a number of studies dissecting the textual strategies employed in films and programmes to generate supposedly 'subject' positions for the spectator. Thus, the optical point-of-view shot and the classic shot/reverse shot sequence were portrayed as 'suturing' devices for fostering audience identification and involvement (Heath 1976, 1977; see also Heath and Skirrow 1977). The general thrust of this research was that professional communicators are able to deploy compelling visual and narrative techniques which organize audience responses in certain prescribed ways.

This necessarily abridged account focuses on the common denominator of the critiques of the liberal perspective and pays little attention to the internal debates that took place between the divergent wings of the radical tradition. None the less, reference should be made to one family dispute among 'critical' researchers since this has a direct bearing on what happened later. This centred on explanations of why the media had a subaltern role in relation to dominant interests. One approach, associated with the Leicester Centre for Mass Communication Research, adopted a political economy interpretation which tended to emphasize the centrality of economic ownership, the indirect influences exerted by the state and the structures and logic of the market (Murdock and Golding 1977; Curran 1980, 1986; Hood 1980; Murdock 1982; Curtis 1984). An alternative, radical culturalist approach, associated with the Birmingham Centre for Contemporary Cultural Studies, attributed the media's subordination principally to ideological control, in particular to the unconscious internalization of the assumptions of the dominant culture by journalists, and their reliance on powerful groups and institutions as news sources (Chibnall 1977; Hall et al. 1978; Connell 1980). But despite their rather heavily accentuated differences, both approaches had a lot in common. Both worked within a neo-Marxist model of society; both perceived a connection, whether weak or strong, between economic interests and ideological representations; and both portrayed the media as serving dominant rather than universal societal interests.

Revisionist Models of Power and Ideological Representation

Support for this radical tradition was gradually eroded by growing disenchantment with the class-conflict model of society that framed much of its research output. One key influence promoting this disenchantment was the writing of Michel Foucault (1978, 1980, 1982). He offered a complex and multifaceted conspectus of society in which manifold relationships of power are said to be in play in different situations. These cannot be subsumed, according to Foucault, within a binary and all-encompassing opposition of class interests or traced to the mode of production and social formation. As he put it, with uncharacteristic succinctness:

> Power relations are rooted in the system of social networks. This is not to say, however, that there is a primary and fundamental principle of power which dominates society down to the smallest detail but taking as a point of departure the possibility of action upon the action of others (which is coextensive with every social relationship), multiple forms of individual disparity, of objectives, of the given application of power over ourselves or others, of, in varying degrees, partial or universal institutionalization, or more or less deliberate organization, one can define different forms of power.
>
> (Foucault 1982: 224)

The Foucauldian approach has been adapted by some researchers to construct studies of the media on a different axis from the Marxist approach but in a form that is similar. The role of the media is still considered in the wider context of social contestation but in relation to patriarchal rather than class exploitation. Arguably, some of the most interesting research to appear in recent years comes under this category.

The Foucauldian legacy is an ambivalent one. It has also promoted a decentring of cultural and media research. In some studies, the role of the media is reduced to a succession of reader-text encounters in the context of a society which is analytically disaggregated into a series of discrete instances (e.g. Bondebjerg 1989) or in which power external to discourse is wholly evacuated (e.g. Grodal 1989). In reality this is not very different from the American liberal tradition in which the media are typically analysed in isolation from power relationships or are situated within a model of society in which, it is assumed, power is widely diffused. Indeed, in the influential and prolific writing of John Fiske (1987, 1989a, 1989b, 1989c), the convergence is more or less explicit. His recent celebration of 'semiotic democracy', in which people drawn from 'a vast shifting range of subcultures and groups' construct their own meanings within an autonomous cultural economy, enthusiastically embraces the central themes of sovereign consumer pluralism.

To complicate matters still further, there has been to some extent a shift within the pluralist tradition away from discrete analyses of the media typified by investigations into media effects on violence, voting and the salience of political issues. Greater interest is now being shown by liberal researchers in the wider role of the media: its impact on the structures and functioning of the political system (Seymour-Ure 1989; Blumler 1990), its influence on socio-cultural integration (Graber 1988; McLeod 1988) and the formation of social identity (Reimer and Rosengren 1989) and, more broadly and crucially, the relationship between media and social change (Noelle-Neumann 1981; Rosengren 1981; McQuail 1987). At the same time, narrowly focused, discrete research, most notably, audience reception studies, is proliferating in what can still be termed loosely the 'radical' camp. The split between theorized and relatively untheorized research, between a holistic and discrete approach, between concern for macro and micro issues, that once characterized the radical and liberal research traditions has largely disappeared.

This is partly because the totalizing and systematic themes of Marxism have been rejected by a powerful revisionist movement within the radical tradition. As Stuart Hall writes:

> classical Marxism depended on an assumed correspondence between 'the economic' and 'the political': one could read off our political attitudes, interests and motivations from our class interests and position. This correspondence betweeen 'the political' and 'the economic' is exactly what has now disintegrated – practically and theoretically.
>
> (Hall 1988b: 25)

In retrospect Althusser, now often remembered ironically as an exponent of a crude Marxist functionalism, played a strategic role in promoting this revisionism by emphasizing the relative autonomy of social practice (Althusser 1971, 1976). Many post-Althusserians, following in his wake, rejected the notion of economic determinacy even in a weak, non-reductive form. This trend has been reinforced by the currently fashionable hypothesis that we are moving into a postmodernist era characterized by 'post-Fordist' production regimes, the pluralization of social and cultural life, and the rise of individualism and subjectivity in which the primacy of the economic has been dethroned (Baudrillard 1985; Gorz 1983; Lyotard 1984).[3]

Dissatisfaction with traditional Marxist formulations was also influentially expressed in a much-reprinted book by Abercrombie, Hill and Turner (1984). First, they argued that the concept of the 'dominant ideology' (a key concept, as we have seen, for media and cultural studies in the 1970s and early 1980s) was illusionary; on close inspection, it crumbles in almost every epoch into a miscellany of inconsistent and even contradictory ideas. Second, this miscellany of themes and ideas was not even 'dominant', since it was not widely accepted by the subordinate classes. Social cohesion, they argued, was to be explained in terms of resignation and routine rather than ideological incorporation. The second part of their argument was not fully or adequately documented for the modern period. However, it has since received powerful support in a major empirically based study (Marshall et al. 1989).

This attack was anticipated in a reformulated theory of the media and society influenced by Gramsci (1971, 1985). This reformulation entailed rethinking the earlier radical paradigm. The ruling class was reconceptualized as a shifting and often precarious alliance of different social strata. The dominant ideology was redefined as a 'field' of dominant discourses, an unstable constellation of ideas and themes which was liable to disaggregate at any point into its component elements. The media were portrayed as a site of contest between competing social forces rather than as a conduit for ruling-class ideas. Although the media were still viewed as skewed towards dominant interests, news organizations were implicitly assigned a more strategic role as a consequence of the new stress on the fragility of social alliances, the instability of ideological formations and the bubbling ferment of resistance from below. This reformulation was already gaining ground in the mid-1970s but in an uneven and partly assimilated form. For example, Hall's collaborative work, *Policing the Crisis*, was an uneasy synthesis of Althusserian and Gramscian perspectives, reflected in its interchangeable use of two differently nuanced concepts – 'control culture' and 'dominant field of the ruling ideologies' (Hall et al. 1978). His subsequent work (e.g. Hall 1988a) is grounded much more fully in a Gramscian analysis highlighting ideological competition, although it still overstates the influence of 'dominant' ideas and inflates, by implication, the power of the media (Crewe 1988; Curran 1990b). This reformulation can be seen as a persuasive attempt to hold the line against the revisionist tide and has many adherents. Ironically, Hall himself has recently shifted his position again, in effect conceding further ground (Hall 1988b).

Revisionist Accounts of Media Organizations

The development of 'critical' research into media organizations can also be viewed as a forced retreat from former positions, although radical researchers have recently shown signs of holding at least part of their crumbling Maginot line. The political economy approach represented the more conventional and traditional strand within radical approaches to the media, and was the first to buckle. Indeed, the emergence of the radical culturalist perspective associated with the Birmingham School was itself a compromise position which incorporated a pluralist critique. It tacitly acknowledged, in part at least, the validity of two key pluralist arguments: namely that economic ownership of the media has become increasingly separated from managerial control because of the growing dispersal of share ownership, and that journalists enjoy a considerable degree of independence from supervisory control. Its analysis was consequently grounded on the assumption that 'the day-to-day "relative autonomy" of the journalist and news producers' was a reality of most modern media organizations (Hall et al. 1978: 57).

During the 1980s, even researchers in the political economy tradition began to back off. Thus Peter Golding, a leading political economist, stressed the importance of ideological management and the individualist values of reporters rather than economic ownership of the press in accounting for the tabloid crusade against 'scrounging' welfare claimants (Golding and Middleton 1982). Similarly, Murdock – the other leading British political economist of the media – explained the pattern of media reporting of the 1981 race riots in terms of source availability and the discourses readily available to journalists. Again, little reference was made to capitalist economic ownership and managerial pressure in explaining why this reporting took such a conservative form (Murdock 1984). I also backtracked in revised editions of a textbook (Curran and Seaton 1985, 1988).

Yet, radical culturalist interpretations provide an uncertain refuge for disoriented political economists. In its classic British formulation, advanced by Hall and associates, it is claimed that powerful institutions and interests act as 'primary definers' for the media, and that journalists act as 'secondary definers' translating into a popular idiom the interpretive framework furnished to them by accredited sources (Hall et al. 1978). Philip Schlesinger (1990), however, has recently fired a devastating Exocet against this position. In brief, he argues that primary definers sometimes offer conflicting frames of reference to the media; that the concept of primary definer is simplistic in that it fails to acknowledge that some accredited sources are more influential than others; that it is implicitly atemporal in that it ignores the way in which changes in the balance of social forces alter the composition of primary definers; and, lastly, that it overstates the passivity of the media. These theoretical arguments are illustrated in concrete terms by recent case studies in Britain and in the United States (Hallin 1989; Curran 1990a). In effect, this critique is an extension of the reformulation noted earlier in which the view of society as dominated by the ruling class is challenged by an alternative model which stresses the fissures and tensions within the dominant power bloc, and the wider context of ideological competition and resistance from below.

This comes very close to conventional pluralist portrayals of the media as a forum of public debate. However, what differentiates it from classical pluralist accounts are two key arguments. One is that groups and classes within society have unequal access to the media and unequal resources with which to generalize their views and interests. Here, interestingly, there has been a shift within the pluralist tradition of media research. The stress on the individual autonomy of journalists in an organizational setting, exemplified by Tunstall's pioneering and illuminating research (Tunstall 1981), has given way to an increased attention to the interconnections between media organizations and power centres (e.g. Hess 1984; Sigal 1987; Ericson et al. 1987, 1989; Schudson 1989). In effect, some researchers within the liberal tradition have come round to the view that the organizational routines and values of most media institutions are skewed towards powerful interests.

The second argument is the claim that capitalist ownership can shape the norms and values of news organizations principally through control of senior editorial appointments, and that the market rarely functions in a way that is neutral between different interests in society. Here again, there are some signs of a shift in pluralist research, most notably in a recent study of the Canadian media, which documents the way in which changes in senior appointments can affect routine reporting (Ericson et al. 1987). It has also been argued that the ethnographic approach has a methodological blindspot that tends to obscure the way in which managerial pressures are brought to bear on journalists (Curran 1990a).

Whatever view one takes, the classic pluralist perspective of the media as an autonomous fourth estate has run into as much flak as the classic Marxist vision of the media as an ideological state apparatus. An intermediate perspective situated between these two positions has emerged as dominant, with reciprocal shifts on the part of researchers in both pluralist and radical camps. This said, continuing differences in the way in which economic and political power is conceptualized by different researchers will prevent a full convergence from taking place.

Revisionist Assessments of Audience Reception

However, it is around the issues raised by the production of meaning and audience reception that revisionist writing has had most public impact. The radical tradition of mass communication research was for the most part grounded in a relatively unproblematic analysis of meaning. But a new tradition of revisionist scholarship emerged that emphasized the inconsistencies, contradictions, gaps and even internal oppositions within texts. The shift is exemplified by a comparison between the pessimistic 'state-of-the-art' collection of essays on women and the media edited by Helen Baehr (1980) and more optimistic, redemptive readings of texts by revisionists like Cook and Johnston (1988)[4] and Modleski (1982) which emphasize internal points of resistance to patriarchal values or crucial ambivalences. This shift is expressed in its most extreme form in the claim that TV is a medium that often produces relatively open and ambiguous programmes, 'producerly texts' that 'delegate[s] the production of meaning to the viewer-producer' (Fiske 1989c). A similar argument has been advanced in relation to rock videos (Larsen 1989).

The second key shift was a reconceptualization of the audience as an active producer of meaning. This is an area of media research that has been extensively mythologized – a theme to which we shall return later. It is sufficient to note here that the assumption that audiences responded in prescribed ways to fixed, preconstituted meanings in texts – to be found in certain forms of formalist analysis – was challenged by the notion that meaning was constructed through the interaction of text and the social and discourse positions of audiences. This point was well made in a notable study of reactions to two *Nationwide* programmes by David Morley, one of the most distinguished and influential revisionist critics. He showed that divergent groups responded in very different ways to *Nationwide*, and that these differences reflected the different discourses and institutions in which they were situated. It was a particularly acute analysis, not least because of the way it illuminated the importance of different subcultural formations within the same class in generating different audience responses (Morley 1980).

The revisionist stress on audience autonomy has encouraged a more cautious assessment of media influence. Typical of this revisionist reorientation is a case study of a 'moral panic' that not only failed but backfired by creating increased sympathy for the intended victim (Curran 1987). Similarly, the failure of trans-European satellite TV to secure a mass audience has been explained in terms of audience autonomy rooted in linguistic and cultural differences (Collins 1989).

Finally, the implicit conclusion that the media had only limited influence encouraged some researchers to shift their focus of interest. The political aesthetic gave way to the popular aesthetic; the focus of investigation shifted from whether media representations advanced or retarded political and cultural struggle to the question of why the mass media were popular. This encouraged 'readings' of media content that sought to infer the nature of people's pleasure in them (e.g. Drotner 1989), and ethnographic studies of the audience that sought to probe the roots of their pleasure (e.g. Kippax 1988).

Rediscovering the Wheel?

This revisionism is often presented in assertive terms as an example of intellectual progress in which those hitherto mired in error have been confounded and enlightened. Thus, Morley (1989: 16–17) recounts how 'the whole tradition of effects studies' was dominated by 'a hypodermic model of influence' until the uses and gratifications approach advanced the concept of the active audience. This was an improvement, we are told, because 'from this perspective one can no longer talk about the "effects" of a message on a homogeneous mass audience who are expected to be affected in the same way'. However, even this improvement was 'severely limited', because it ultimately explained differential responses to the media in terms of 'individual differences of personality or psychology'. Only the new revisionism, we are informed, introduced a more satisfactory and rounded account.

This is a breathtaking, though often repeated,[5] caricature of the history of communications research that writes out a whole generation of researchers. It presents as innovation what is in reality a process of rediscovery. This mythologizing also has the effect of obscuring the multiple lines of intersection between past media research in the pluralist tradition and the new revisionism emerging out of the radical tradition. Effects research cannot be said in any meaningful sense to have been 'dominated' by the hypodermic model. On the contrary, its main thrust ever since the 1940s was to assert the independence and autonomy of media audiences and dispel the widespread notion that people are easily influenced by the media. It did this by developing many of the same insights that have been proclaimed afresh in the recent spate of 'reception' studies, albeit in a different technical language and sometimes with less subtlety.

Thus, effects researchers argued long ago that the predispositions that people bring to texts crucially influence their understanding of these texts, and that different predispositions generate different understandings. Thus, to cite one now-forgotten study almost at random, Hastorf and Cantril (1954) showed a film of a particularly dirty football match between Dartmouth and Princeton to two groups of students, one from each university and asked them among other things to log the number of infractions of the rules committed by each side. The Princeton students concluded that the Dartmouth team committed more than twice as many fouls as their side, whereas the majority of the

Dartmouth group concluded that both sides were about equally at fault. This prompted the authors to advance a 'transactional' perspective, in which 'it is inaccurate or misleading to say that different people have different attitudes to the same thing. For the thing is *not* the same for different people, whether the thing is a football game, a presidential candidate, communism, or spinach'. By implication, the apophthegm 'seeing is believing' should be recast as 'believing is seeing'.

This study was not unusual for this period in attributing differences of audience response to differences of shared disposition rather than, as Morley dismissively puts it, to 'individual differences of personality or psychology'. But it was also characteristic in offering a relatively simple, one-dimensional account of audience adaptation of meaning.

However, some effects researchers developed a much more complex model of audience interactions which anticipated revisionists' subsequent discovery of 'the interdiscursive processes of text-reader encounters'. An early example of this more sophisticated approach is provided by Patricia Kendall and Katherine Wolff's (1949) analysis of reactions to anti-racist cartoons. These featured Mr Biggott, an unattractive and cantankerous middle-aged man whose absurdity (highlighted by cobwebs coming out of his pin-point head) and extreme views were intended to discredit racist ideas. The study showed that 31 per cent failed to recognize either that Mr Biggott was racially prejudiced or that the cartoons were intended to satirize racism, and that in general there was a considerable diversity in the way in which audience members understood the cartoons. Some resisted their propagandistic intention by resorting to various means of disidentification; they viewed Mr Biggott negatively not because of his views (which they shared) but because he was judged to be intellectually or socially inferior. A few even found in the cartoons confirmation of their prejudices, completely subverting the cartoons' intention.[6]

But perhaps the most illuminating part of this study was its explanation of why respondents negotiated the cartoons' meanings in the way that they did, based on lengthy individual interviews. One group of respondents who were secure in their racist beliefs felt no need to distance themselves from Mr Biggott's racism and remained unaware that the cartoon was attacking their opinions. Another group of prejudiced respondents had a momentary understanding of the satirical purpose of the cartoon, experienced it as punishing, did a double-take by disidentifying with Mr Biggott (in one case identifying him as a Jew) and thus succeeded in obscuring from themselves the proselytizing intention of the cartoon. The key to understanding their complex reaction was their own feelings of guilt, uncertainty or embarrassment about their racist views. A third group of young prejudiced men imposed a different frame of reference that cut across the intended framework of meaning in the cartoon. Instead of seeing the cartoons as an attack on their own views, they viewed them as a satirical attack on the older generation in which Mr Biggott symbolized the weakness, powerlessness and absurdity of flawed authority figures (with one respondent referring overtly to his father). In some of the interviews with this group, one had a glimpse of the cartoons 'working' in the sense that they encouraged a reappraisal of prejudiced views within a discourse of modernity directed against the parental generation.

That audiences perceive mass-communicated meanings differently has thus been a central finding of media effects research for nearly half a century. Another aspect of the relative autonomy of the audience, documented by Lazarsfeld, Berelson and Gaudet as early as 1944, is the tendency of people to seek out media content that reinforces what they think and to avoid content that challenges their beliefs. But since the early 1950s, researchers have hotly contested the extent of selective audience exposure, and the evidence suggests that the rise of TV has reduced deliberate avoidance of media messages. However, defensive avoidance of dissonant messages persists to some degree, particularly when it is defined as inattention rather than as mere abstention.[7]

During the 1940s researchers also showed that subcultural formations within the audience influenced the extent to which media representations were *accepted* or not (e.g. Hyman and Sheatsley 1947). This has become a recurrent finding of 'effects' research, as can briefly be illustrated by a clutch of studies about *All in the Family*, the successful American TV series, that featured a bigoted, chauvinist, politically reactionary but 'lovable' working class protagonist, Archie Bunker, who had regular arguments with his liberal-minded son-in-law, Mike. Racially prejudiced adolescents in Canada and the US were much more inclined to think that bigoted Archie made sense and won in the end than young viewers with less prejudiced views (Vidmar and Rokeach 1974; cf. Brigham and Giesbrecht 1976). A comparable study in Holland revealed a more complex picture in which groups with different clusters of attitudes – whether ethnocentric, authoritarian or traditionalist – responded to the series in partially different ways (Wilhoit and de Bock 1976). However, the most interesting study, based on responses of six- to ten-year-olds to a single programme, produced a classic summation of some of the themes of the new revisionism: 'different types of children, bringing different beliefs, attitudes, and values to the viewing of the show as a result of different socialization processes, are affected in distinctly different ways' (Meyer 1976).

Brief reference should be made to two other strands of the 'effects' tradition, both of which are underdeveloped in 'reception' studies. The first is the stress on the dynamic processes of peer group mediation in blocking, reinforcing or modifying mass-communicated messages, following Katz and Lazarsfeld's landmark research (1955).[8] The other is the emphasis given in some studies to the selective retention of information. Levine and Murphy (1943) found that pro- and anti-communist groups tended to remember information which accorded with what they already believed, and to forget information which did not fit their world view; and that this selective forgetfulness increased over time. Subsequent research on retention has since substantially revised and refined understanding of the variables affecting selective memory.

The 'effects' tradition thus prefigures revisionist arguments by documenting the multiple meanings generated by texts, the active and creative role of audiences and the ways in which different social and discourse positions encourage different readings. In short, the research of the new revisionists is only startling and innovative from a foreshortened perspective of communications research in which the year AD begins with textual analyses of films and TV programmes in the journal *Screen*, and everything before that is shrouded in the eddying mists of time.

This said, the revisionist approach taken as a whole represents at one level an advance. It does focus more attention on the text, provides a much richer and fuller understanding of interdiscursive processes in audience reception and, above all, locates these in a more adequate sociological context. But it also represents at another level a backward step in its reluctance to quantify; its over-reliance on group discussions and consequent failure to probe adequately intra-group and individual differences;[9] and its invocation of the loose concept of 'decoding' which some researchers in the effects tradition have more usefully broken down analytically in a form that distinguishes between attention, comprehension, acceptance and retention.

This is also an appropriate point to consider parallels between revisionist, ethnographic studies of the audience and the uses and gratifications approach. It has become commonplace among revisionists to point to the shortcomings of uses and gratifications research as a preliminary to proclaiming the superiority of their own research. Thus, Ang (1985) argues that the revisionist approach is an improvement because, unlike the older tradition, it pays more attention to the mechanisms by which pleasure is aroused and it does not adopt an essentialist conception of need and gratification. There is some truth in her arguments, but the claim that the older tradition adopted an essentialist definition of need is only partly correct.

There are, in fact, considerable points of affinity between revisionist, ethnographic research and the earlier tradition that she attacks. This can be illustrated by comparing her own clever and illuminating study of Dutch reception of *Dallas* with a uses and gratifications study of radio serial listening in the US conducted by Herzog (1944) some four decades earlier. Both enquiries pointed to the way in which soap opera can relativize the problems of audience members and make them more bearable or indeed pleasurable. Both also indicated the way in which soap opera provides scope for idealized but playful identification. But while Herzog paid little attention to the actual content of soap operas, she did not resort to an essentialist definition of need and gratification. Indeed, she provided in some ways a more socially situated account of women's pleasure in soap opera than Ang because she drew upon interview material rather than, as in Ang's case, letters. This enabled Herzog to illustrate what Ang calls 'the tragic structure of feeling' in terms of the particular predicaments that women found themselves in, even if she did not generalize a feminist perspective.

Quite simply, uses and gratifications research does not always resemble the way in which it is represented by those asserting the novelty of the revisionist approach. There are similarities between the two traditions. Moreover, the inferences derived from reception analysis *as a whole* have not always pointed to new directions. In some cases, they have resulted in old pluralist dishes being reheated and presented as new cuisine.

Revisionist Models of Media Influence

The empirical demonstration of relative audience autonomy was a key building block in pluralist perspectives of the media. The 'findings' of empirical research were deployed to considerable effect to refute a model of the media as an agency of class control or as a means by which elites transmitted influence downwards. This refutation came to be anchored in a conception of society as a honeycomb of small groups in which power is widely diffused and public opinion – the indirect means by which the state is allegedly supervised and controlled – grows organically from below.

A somewhat similar argument is now being formulated by some revisionist critics within a different problematic. Reception studies documenting audience autonomy are being invoked to challenge the view of the media as the means by which dominant discourses are reproduced. This new revisionism is also linked to a view of society as a shifting range of subcultures and groups. By implication, the power to map and make sense of society in a form that serves and universalizes collective interests is widely diffused in society. There are no dominant discourses, merely a semiotic democracy of pluralist voices. But this new version of the pluralist argument overstates its case, not least because it exaggerates the impermeability of audiences to media influence. Just as the autonomy of media organizations from power blocs is overemphasized in classic pluralist formulations, so too is the autonomous status of audiences. In reality, the circuit of power is not totally disconnected at two points – the processes of encoding in media organizations and decoding by the audience.

In the first place, media texts are rarely wholly open but take the form of what Morley (1980) usefully calls 'structured polysemy'. That is to say, denotative symbols in texts cue, to a lesser or greater degree, audience understandings in certain preferred ways, even if these can be and sometimes are rejected. A simple illustration of this occurs in a recorded group discussion in which a respondent pointed to a TV still and challenged the interpretation that was being put on it by another member of the group, by saying simply and with visible effect 'they don't look like a mob' (Philo 1989). In effect, he invoked a widely shared understanding of denotative signs as 'evidence' to persuade others of the validity of his 'reading'. Second, audiences do not have an infinite repertoire of discourses to draw upon in adapting TV meanings. The location of individuals in the social structure will tend to determine which discourses they have ready access to. This influences in turn the range of 'readings' that they will derive from media content.

The combination of these two limitations on audience autonomy – the denotative 'steer' of preferred meanings and the uneven social distribution of discourse positions – has certain consequences. This is well brought out in Philo's study of audience reception of British TV news reporting of the miners' strike in 1984 to 1985 (Philo 1990). This shows that there was a clear correspondence between certain recurrent themes in TV reporting of the strike and what was understood, believed and remembered by the audience after a considerable lapse of time. The miners' strike was long drawn-out and very prominently reported. Perhaps partly due to the cumulative impact of constantly reiterated images and themes, TV meanings were not drowned out by the discourses that audiences brought to bear.

Indeed, the most revealing part of this important study is the double insight it provides into the dialogue that takes place between viewers and TV news. On one hand, it highlights the variety of resources that audience subjects drew upon in resisting or negotiating TV meanings – first-hand knowledge (and, even more important, word-of-mouth relaying of first-hand knowledge), class experiences, political cultures, other media accounts, sceptical dispositions towards the news media and internal processes of logic. Conversely, it also shows the way in which some people adjusted their opinions in the light of the information they received from TV, including, crucially, people who strongly identified with the striking National Union of Mineworkers (NUM) but who reluctantly came to accept certain anti-NUM themes in TV reporting (Philo 1990).

This study is consistent with a shift in mainstream effects research. The minimal effects model that dominated empirical American research for a generation has come under mounting attack from researchers in the pluralist tradition. They increasingly argue that the media do exert considerable influence, in certain circumstances, on audience beliefs, cognitions and opinions (McLeod and McDonald 1985; Iyengar and Kinder 1987; Kosicki and McLeod 1990). In doing so, they are qualifying a central tenet of pluralist canon. By a curious irony, revisionist celebrants of semiotic democracy are thus moving towards a position that pluralists are abandoning. They are engaged not so much in revisionism as an act of revivalism; they are reverting to the discredited received wisdom of the past.

Continuity and Discontinuity

However, revisionist reception studies are not homogeneous. There are two distinctive tendencies: one, a continuation of the radical tradition; and another which belongs to a less normative mode.

The radical tendency continues to situate cultural consumption in the broader context of social struggle. Janice Radway's celebrated study of American addicts of romantic novels exemplifies this approach. Her subjects were engaged in a symbolic reconstruction of masculinity; they were drawn to formulaic books in which hard, insensitive or unfeeling men are humanized by the love of a woman and are transformed into sensitive, nurturant and caring people (Radway 1987). There is a recognizable affinity between her report from the patriarchal front and Birmingham researchers' earlier reports from the class front, such as Hebdige's sympathetic portrayal of English 'teddy boys', 'mods' and 'rockers' (Hebdige 1979) and racist 'skinheads' (Hebdige 1981). Both seek to relate pleasure in cultural consumption to the social experience of audience subjects. But this experience is situated in a wider context of exploitative social relations in which audience subjects are seeking to find an imaginary solution to their position of subordination or are engaged in pleasurable forms of resistance.

Another strand of reception analysis has developed which is grounded in a less radical conception of society, and which frames cultural consumption in different terms. This approach is exemplified at its best by Fornas, Lindberg and Sernhede's (1988) ethnographic study of amateur teenage rock groups in Sweden.[10] The underlying assumption of this and similar research is that popular culture provides the raw material for experimenting with and exploring social identities in the context of a postmodernist society where the walls of tradition that support and confine them are crumbling. In this case, rock music is viewed as a laboratory for the intensive production of identity by adolescents seeking to define an independent self. The study is notable for the meticulous and close-grained observation that it brings to bear in a way that does not always have a counterpart in radical research. Thus, even Radway's (1987) *tour de force* offers an account of romance addicts' relationship to patriarchy but not to their flesh-and-blood husbands. Fornas et al.'s study, and others like it, are engaged in analysing cultural consumption and identity formation almost as an end in itself. It belongs to the literature on socialization within the pluralist tradition rather than to the radical tradition of cultural studies.

Revisionist Assessments of Cultural Value

The other notable contribution of revisionist thinking has been to reject the elitist pessimism about mass culture that was a significant strand within the radical tradition, represented by the Frankfurt school. A key formative influence in this shift was Pierre Bourdieu. He showed that there was a close correspondence in France between socio-economic position and patterns of taste in art and music. Cultural and aesthetic judgements, he concluded, had no absolute, universal validity but were merely ways of defining, fixing and legitimating social differences (Bourdieu 1986a, b). This insight has been developed by cultural historians who have shown that the boundary lines between high and low culture have shifted over time in response to strategies of exclusion pursued by elites seeking to maintain their social leadership (Dimaggio 1986) and in response to struggles over material rewards and prestige within the artistic community (Fyffe 1985).

A relativistic orientation was further reinforced by the growing recognition that meaning is created in the context of media consumption. This led logically to the conclusion that audiences can *create* quality in popular culture. For example, Hobson (1982) argued that the insights and understandings that audiences brought to their viewing of the widely despised British soap opera, *Crossroads*, reconstituted its cultural value. Similarly, Schrøder (1989) argued that Shakespeare's plays and *Dynasty* have a comparable cultural validity since they generated comparable audience experiences. Underlying this study, and many comparable works, is a key assumption succinctly stated by the American sociologist, Michael Schudson (1987: 59): 'the quality of art lies in how it is received, or how it is created within the context of reception, rather than in some quality intrinsic to the art object itself'. By implication, judgements about so-called popular or high culture are judgements about their audiences and their cultural competences. But these competences take different forms and are distributed in ways that do not correspond to conventional hierarchies of taste. Thus, as Brunsdon (1981) argued, soap opera requires a certain amount of cultural capital on the part of the audience, just as a Godard film does. These and similar arguments have led increasingly to the abandonment of literary norms in making judgements about the quality of popular culture and have encouraged instead a tacit system of valorization based on audience pleasure. Indeed, Ericson (1989) argues that this has become almost the defining characteristic of revisionist Scandinavian cultural studies.

In fact this reorientation within the radical tradition has not broken entirely new ground. Ironically, there was earlier a parallel, though less determined, tilt towards cultural relativism within the pluralist tradition. This too had an elitist strand, represented, for example, by T.S. Eliot (1948) and Dwight Macdonald (1957). This was challenged by a group of influential sociologists, most notably Shils (1961) and Gans (1974), who argued that the popular media diet included material of high quality relative to the cultural patterns of a large swath of the mass audience. This essentially defensive response took on a more aggressive form, however, when the revival of uses and gratifications research in the 1970s drew attention to the diversity and richness of people's pleasure in the media. This prompted researchers like McQuail, Blumler and Brown (1972) to attack the elitist assumption that mass consumption of 'common denominator' programmes is homogeneous, shallow and superficial. For example, they showed in an admirable study that, although TV quiz shows were viewed by some as relaxing entertainment, they were experienced by others, particularly those with limited schooling, as an enriching and testing educative experience.

To complete the symmetry of these two parallel developments, there are now indications of a general pulling back from cultural relativism. Within the revisionist radical camp, a cautioning voice is increasingly being heard. As Seiter et al. urge:

> the popularity of US television programmes on export around the world should not make us forget that other forms of television might also please (and, possibly, please better). In our concern for audiences' pleasures in such programmes, we run the risk of continually validating Hollywood's domination of the worldwide television market.
>
> (Seiter et al. 1989: 5)

They also argued that even the most 'creative' audiences can be confined – 'Soap operas allow women viewers to take pleasure in the character of the villainess, but they do not provide characters that radically challenge the ideology of femininity' (p. 5).

One reason, perhaps, for this rethinking is that the revisionists' popular aesthetic has been incorporated into neo-liberal rhetoric to justify the destruction of public service broadcasting in Europe. Deregulated market systems are now being advocated on the grounds that they will end elitist cultural distortion of TV and enthrone the sovereign consumer as the arbiter of what should be provided (Adam Smith Institute 1984; Gallagher 1989). This rhetoric has also encouraged a shift of emphasis within the pluralist tradition. Jay Blumler's former mild flirtation with cultural relativism, for example, is well and truly over. He has recently attacked the case for deregulation of TV on three broad counts. First, he argues that it is misleading even in its own terms; deregulation would narrow, as well as redefine, consumer choice and preclude certain forms of pleasure-giving programmes. Second, he invokes a series of totally unrelativistic arguments about programme 'quality', 'standards' and worthwhile categories of content like original drama that a market-driven TV system would endanger. Third, he makes normative judgements about the role of TV that go beyond the consumer-gratification model. TV should 'deepen the expression of experience about the human and social condition' and assist 'society in all its parts to bind, reconnect and commune with itself' (Blumler 1989: 87–8).[11]

Cultural relativism is also being challenged by a return of more politicized concerns across the field of media studies, prompted in part by the policy choices thrown into sharp relief by the New Right. This may be merely a local, British phenomenon. But the possibility that broadcasting could be remodelled along the free market lines of the capitalist press in Britain has prompted fresh thought on how this would affect relationships of power and struggle in society. The result has been a headlong revalorization of public service broadcasting in which earlier perceptions of British TV as an agency of the dominant order are now being heavily qualified by radical researchers. Thus, McNair (1988) argues that minority news and documentary programmes are more open to critical perspectives than mainstream programmes; whereas Schlesinger, Murdock and Elliott (1983) argue that drama is less ideologically closed than current affairs; and I go further in arguing that public service broadcasting is more open to popular opposition movements than the more 'closed' organizations of the popular press (Curran, 1990a). A somewhat similar shift of evaluation has taken place in the literature on the British welfare state, perhaps partly for the same reason. Both the welfare state and public service broadcasting have come under attack from the New Right, causing liberal and radical researchers to find more common ground with each other.

Retrospective

This account has deliberately emphasized the changes that have taken place during the last fifteen years, but it needs to be qualified in two ways. Some researchers concerned with the media, particularly historians and social psychologists, have remained unaffected by the intellectual ferment around them, and have continued doing the kind of research they have always done. There has also been an underlying continuity of thought, an evolutionary pace to some of the seemingly abrupt shifts of direction that have occurred. For example, recent empirical reception analysis owes a large debt to the theoretical formulations of Barthes (1975), Eco (1972) and Hall (1973b) in the early 1970s as well as having, as we have seen, points of affinity with empirical research pioneered in the 1940s. Similarly, the shift from an Althusserian to a Gramscian paradigm in the late 1970s was not as great a disjuncture as some have subsequently proclaimed.[12]

None the less, a major change has taken place. The most important and significant overall shift has been the steady advance of pluralist themes within the radical tradition: in particular, the repudiation of the totalizing, explanatory frameworks of Marxism, the reconceptualization of the audience as creative and active and the shift from the political to a popular aesthetic. Because this revisionism has evolved in response to an internal debate within the radical tradition rather than as a direct response to pluralist texts, the extent of the movement towards the pluralist tradition has been partly obscured. A sea change has occurred in the field, and this will reshape – for better or worse – the development of media and cultural studies in Europe.

Notes

1 This essay is in effect jottings designed to clarify what form a revised edition of *Mass Communication and Society* should take, and has benefited from conversations with my co-editor, Michael Gurevitch.
2 Philo (1987) replied to this attack on behalf of the Glasgow University Media Group.
3 Hebdige (1988) argues persuasively that one strand of postmodernist thought has rejected the teleological aspirations and rationalism that is a common intellectual heritage of *both* the Marxist and liberal, pluralist traditions.
4 In fact, Cook and Johnston's admirable essay was first published in 1974 in an obscure film festival publication, and has only recently been properly distributed. It was ahead of its time.
5 Ironically, Morley (1980) offered a more complex and slightly less misleading historical account nine years earlier.
6 This last point is only brought out fully in the analysis of the same data undertaken by Cooper and Jahoda (1947).
7 For further discussion of this, see Tan (1985).
8 For a useful, brief discussion of the ways in which Katz and Lazarsfeld's two-step flow model of mediation has been complexified, see McQuail and Windahl (1981).
9 There is a certain inherent implausibility in the relatively high degree of group consensus that Morley (1980) encountered in his fieldwork. Greater intra-group differences would probably have emerged if he had conducted individual interviews. For a recent example of research that highlights striking individual differences within groups in the processing of news, see Graber (1988).
10 My comments are based on a lengthy exposition and discussion of this research in English (Fornas 1989).
11 A first version of this influential research is available in published form in Blumler (1986). In its revised form, it is a powerful – all the more powerful for being qualified – indictment of the market-driven system in the US.
12 The extent of difference between Althusser and Gramsci has been overstated for defensive reasons. In fact, Althusser explicitly endorsed a number of key Gramscian themes, acknowledging for instance that the ruling class often takes the form of a social coalition; that the ruling ideology frequently contains contradictions; and 'that the struggle of the exploited classes may also be exercised in the forms of the ISAs [ideological state apparatuses] including the media, and thus turn the weapon of ideology against the classes in power' (Althusser 1984: 21 cf. 59).

References

ABERCROMBIE, N., HILL, S. and TURNER, B., 1984: *The Dominant Ideology Thesis.* London: Allen & Unwin.
ADAM SMITH INSTITUTE, 1984: *Omega Report: Communications Policy*. London: Alan Smith Institute.
ALTHUSSER, L., 1971: *Lenin and Philosophy*. London: New Left Books.
ALTHUSSER, L., 1976: *Essays in Self-Criticism*. London: New Left Books.
ALTHUSSER, L., 1984: *Essays in Ideology*. London: Verso.
ANG, I., 1985: *Watching Dallas*. London: Methuen.
BARTHES, R., 1975: *The Pleasure of the Text.* New York: Hill & Wang.
BAEHR, H. (ed.), 1980: *Women and the Media*. Oxford: Pergamon.
BAUDRILLARD, J., 1985: 'The Ecstasy of Communication', in H. Foster (ed.) *Postmodern Condition*. London: Pluto.

BEHARRELL, P. and PHILO, G. (eds.), 1977: *Trade Unions and the Media*. London: Macmillan.

BLUMLER, J.G., 1986: 'Television in the United States: Funding Sources and Programme Consequences', in *Research on the Range and Quality of Broadcasting Services*, Report for the Committee on Financing the BBC. London: HMSO.

BLUMLER, J.G., 1989: 'Multi-channel Television in the United States: Policy Lessons for Britain', Markle Foundation Report (mimeo).

BLUMLER, J.G., 1990: 'The Modern Publicity Process', in M. Ferguson (ed.) *Public Communication*. London: Sage.

BONDEBJERG, I., 1989: 'Popular Fiction, Narrative and the Melodramatic Epic of American Television', in M. Skovmand (ed.) *Media Fictions*. Åarhus: University of Åarhus Press.

BOURDIEU, P., 1986a: 'The Production of Belief: Contribution to an Economy of Symbolic Goods', in Richard Collins, James Curran, Nicholas Garnham, Paddy Scannell, Philip Schlesinger and Colin Sparks (eds.) *Media, Culture and Society: A Critical Reader*. London: Sage.

BOURDIEU, P., 1986b: 'The Aristocracy of Culture', in Richard Collins et al. (eds.) *Media, Culture and Society: A Critical Reader*. London: Sage.

BRIGHAM, J. and GIESBRECHT, L., 1976: ' "All in the Family": Racial Attitudes', *Journal of Communication*, 26 (3).

BRUNSDON, C., 1981: '*Crossroads*: Notes on Soap Opera', *Screen*, 22: pp. 32–7.

CHIBNALL, S., 1977: *Law-And-Order-News*. London: Tavistock.

COHEN, S., 1980: *Folk Devils and Moral Panics*, 2nd edition. Oxford: Martin Robertson.

COHEN, S. and YOUNG, J. (eds.), 1981: *Manufacture of News*, 2nd edition. London: Constable.

COLLINS, R., 1989: 'The Language of Advantage: Satellite Television in Western Europe', *Media, Culture and Society*, 11 (3): pp. 351–71.

CONNELL, I., 1989: 'Television News and the Social Contract', in Stuart Hall, Dorothy Hobson, Andrew Lowe and Paul Willis (eds.) *Culture, Media, Language*. London: Hutchinson.

COOK, P. and JOHNSTON, C., 1988: 'The Place of Woman in the Cinema of Raoul Walsh', in Constance Penley (ed.) *Feminism and Film Theory*. London: Routledge.

COOPER, E. and JAHODA, M., 1947: 'The Evasion of Propaganda: How Prejudiced People Respond to Anti-Prejudice Propaganda', *Journal of Psychology*, 23: 15–25.

CREWE, I., 1988: 'Has the Electorate Become Thatcherite?', in Robert Skidelsky (ed.) *Thatcherism*. London: Chatto & Windus.

CURRAN, J., 1980: 'Advertising as a Patronage System', in Harry Christian (ed.) *The Sociology of Journalism and the Press*, Sociological Review, Monograph 29. Keele: University of Keele Press.

CURRAN, J., 1986: 'The Impact of Advertising on the British Mass Media', in Richard Collins et al. (eds.) *Media, Culture and Society: A Critical Reader*. London: Sage.

CURRAN, J., 1987: 'The Boomerang Effect: The Press and the Battle for London, 1981–6', in James Curran, Anthony Smith and Pauline Wingate (eds.) *Impacts and Influences*. London: Methuen.

CURRAN, J., 1990a: 'Culturalist Perspectives of News Organizations: Reappraisal and a Case Study', in Marjorie Ferguson (ed.) *Public Communication*. London: Sage.

CURRAN, J., 1990b: 'The Crisis of Opposition: A Reappraisal', in Ben Pimlott and Anthony Wright (eds.) *The Alternative*. London: W.H. Allen.

CURRAN, J. and GUREVITCH, M., 1977: 'The Audience', *Mass Communication and Society Block 3*. Milton Keynes: Open University Press.

CURRAN, J., GUREVITCH, M. and WOOLLACOTT, J. (eds.), 1977: *Mass Communication and Society*. London: Edward Arnold.

CURRAN, J., GUREVITCH, M. and WOOLLACOTT, J., 1982: 'The Study of the Media', in Michael Gurevitch et al. (eds.) *Culture, Society and the Media*. London: Methuen.

CURRAN, J. and SEATON, J., 1985 and 1988: *Power Without Responsibility*, 2nd and 3rd editions. London: Routledge.

CURTIS, L., 1984: *Ireland: The Propaganda War*. London: Pluto.

DIMAGGIO, P., 1986: 'Cultural Entrepreneurship in Nineteenth Century Boston: The Creation of an Organizational Base for High Culture in America', in Richard Collins et al. (eds.) *Media, Culture and Society: A Critical Reader*. London: Sage.

DROTNER, K., 1989: 'Intensities of Feeling: Emotion, Reception and Gender in Popular Culture', in Michael Skovmand (ed.) *Media Fictions*. Åarhus: University of Åarhus Press.

ECO, U., 1972: 'Towards a Semiotic Enquiry into the TV Message', *Working Paper in Cultural Studies*, 3. Birmingham: Birmingham Centre for Contemporary Cultural Studies.

ELIOTT, T.S., 1948: *Notes Towards a Definition of Culture*. London: Faber & Faber.

ERICSON, R., BARANEK, P. and CHAN, J., 1987: *Visualizing Deviance*. Milton Keynes: Open University Press.

ERICSON, R., BARANEK, P. and CHAN, J., 1989: *Negotiating Control*. Milton Keynes: Open University Press.

ERICSON, S., 1989: 'Theorizing Popular Fiction', in Michael Skovmand (ed.) *Media Fictions*. Åarhus: Åarhus University Press.

FISKE, J., 1987: *Television Culture*. London: Methuen.

FISKE, J., 1989a: *Reading the Popular*. Boston, MA: Unwin Hyman.

FISKE, J., 1989b: *Understanding Popular Culture*. Boston, MA: Unwin Hyman.

FISKE, J., 1989c: 'Moments of Television: Neither the Text Nor the Audience', in Ellen Seiter et al. (eds.) *Remote Control*. London: Routledge.

FORNAS, J., 1989: 'Papers on Pop and Youth Culture', *University of Stockholm Centre for Mass Communication Research Working Papers*, 1.

FORNAS, J., LINDBERG, U. and SERNHEDE, O., 1988: *Under Rocken*. Stockholm: Symposion.

FOUCAULT, M., 1978: *The History of Sexuality*. Harmondsworth: Penguin.

FOUCAULT, M., 1980: *Power/Knowledge*. Brighton: Harvester.

FOUCAULT, M., 1982: 'Afterword: The Subject and Power', in Hubert Dreyfus and Paul Rabinow (eds.) *Michel Foucault: Beyond Structuralism and Hermeneutics*. Chicago: University of Chicago Press.

FYFFE, G., 1985: 'Art and Reproduction: Some Aspects of the Relations Between Painters and Engravers in London 1760–1850', *Media, Culture and Society*, 7 (4): 399–425.

GALLAGHER, R., 1989: 'American Television: Fact and Fantasy', in Cento Veljanovski (ed.) *Freedom in Broadcasting*. London: Institute of Economic Affairs.

GANS, H., 1974: *Popular Culture and High Culture*. New York: Basic Books.

GLASGOW UNIVERSITY MEDIA GROUP, 1976: *Bad News*. London: Routledge & Kegan Paul.

GLASGOW UNIVERSITY MEDIA GROUP, 1980: *More Bad News*. London: Routledge & Kegan Paul.

GLASGOW UNIVERSITY MEDIA GROUP, 1982: *Really Bad News*. London: Writers & Readers.

GLASGOW UNIVERSITY MEDIA GROUP, 1985: *War and Peace News*. Milton Keynes: Open University Press.

GOLDING, P. and Middleton, S., 1982: *Images of Welfare*. Oxford: Martin Robertson.

GORZ, A., 1983: *Farewell to the Working Class*, London: Pluto.

Graber, D., 1988: *Processing the News*, 2nd edition. White Plains, NY: Longman.
Gramsci, A., 1971: *Selections from Prison Notebooks*. London: Lawrence & Wishart.
Gramsci, A., 1985: *Selections from Cultural Writings*. London: Lawrence & Wishart.
Grodal, T., 1989: 'The Postmodern Melancholia of Miami Vice', in Michael Skovmand (ed.) *Media Fictions*. Åarhus: Åarhus University Press.
Gurevitch, M., Bennett, T., Curran, J. and Woollacott, J. (eds.), 1982: *Culture, Society and the Media*. London: Methuen.
Hall, S., 1973a: 'Deviancy, Politics and the Media', in Mary McIntosh and Paul Rock (eds.) *Deviancy and Social Control*. London: Tavistock.
Hall, S., 1973b: 'Encoding and Decoding the TV Message', Birmingham Centre for Contemporary Cultural Studies Paper (mimeo).
Hall, S., 1977: 'Culture, the Media and the "Ideological Effect" ', in James Curran, Michael Gurevitch and Janet Woollacott (eds.) *Mass Communication and Society*. London: Edward Arnold.
Hall, S., 1986: 'Cultural Studies: Two Paradigms', in Richard Collins et al. (eds.) *Media, Culture and Society: A Critical Reader*. London: Sage.
Hall, S., 1988a: *Hard Road to Renewal*. London: Verso.
Hall, S., 1988b: 'Brave New World', *Marxism Today*, October.
Hall, S., Connell, I. and Curti, L., 1976: 'The "Unity" of Current Affairs Television', *Working Papers in Cultural Studies*, 9.
Hall, S., Critcher, C., Jefferson, T. and Roberts, B., 1978: *Policing the Crisis*, London: Macmillan.
Hallin, D., 1989: *The 'Uncensored' War*. Berkeley, CA: University of California Press.
Halloran, J., 1977: 'Mass Media Effects: A Sociological Approach', *Mass Communication and Society Block 3*. Milton Keynes: Open University Press.
Halloran, J., Elliott, P. and Murdock, G. (eds.) *Demonstration and Communication*. Harmondsworth: Penguin.
Harrison, M., 1985: *TV News. Whose Bias?* London: Policy Journals.
Hartmann, P., 1975: 'Industrial Relations in the News Media', *Industrial Relations Journal*, 6 (4).
Hastorf, A. and Cantril, H., 1954: 'They Saw a Game: A Case Study', *Journal of Abnormal and Social Psychology*, 49: 129–34.
Heath, S., 1976: 'Narrative Space', *Screen*, 17 (3).
Heath, S., 1977: 'Notes on Suture', *Screen*, 18 (4).
Heath, S. and Skirrow, G., 1977: 'Television: A World in Action', *Screen*, 18 (2).
Hebdige, D., 1979: *Subculture*. London: Methuen.
Hebdige, D., 1981: 'Skinheads and the Search for White Working Class Identity', *New Socialist*, 1 (1).
Hebdige, D., 1988: *Hiding in the Light*. London: Routledge.
Herzog, H., 1944: 'What Do We Really Know About Daytime Serial Listeners?', in Paul Lazarsfeld and Frank Stanton (eds.) *Radio Research 1942–1943*. New York: Duell, Sloan & Pearce.
Hess, S., 1984: *The Government/Press Connection*. Washington, DC: Brookings Institute.
Hood, S., 1980: *On Television*. London: Pluto.
Hobson, D., 1982: *Crossroads*. London: Methuen.
Hyman, H. and Sheatsley, P., 1947: 'Some, Reasons Why Information Campaigns Fail', *Public Opinion Quarterly*, 9: 412– 23.
Iyengar, S. and Kinder, D., 1987: *News That Matters: Television and Public Opinion*. Chicago: University of Chicago Press.
Katz, E. and Lazarsfeld, P., 1955: *Personal Influence*. New York: Free Press.

KENDALL, P. and WOLFF, K., 1949: 'The Analysis of Deviant Case Studies in Communications Research', in Paul Lazarsfeld and Frank Stanton (eds.) *Communications Research 1948–1949*. New York: Harper.

KIPPAX, S., 1988: 'Women as Audience: The Experience of Unwaged Women of the Performing Arts', *Media, Culture & Society*, 10 (1): 5–21.

KOSICKI, G. and MCLEOD, J., 1990: 'Learning from Political News: Effects of Media Images and Information Processing Strategies', in Sidney Kraus (ed.) *Mass Communication and Political Information*. Hillsdale, NY: Lawrence Erlbaum.

LARSEN, P., 1989: 'Beyond the Narrative. Rock Videos and Modern Visual Fictions', in Michael Skovmand (ed.) *Media Functions*. Åarhus: Åarhus University Press.

LAZARSFELD, P., BERELSON, B. and GAUDET, H., 1944: *The People's Choice*. New York: Columbia University Press.

LEVINE, J. and MURPHY, G., 1943: 'The Learning and Forgetting of Controversial Material', *Journal of Abnormal and Social Psychology*, 38: 507–17.

LYOTARD, J.F., 1984: *Postmodern Condition*. Manchester: Manchester University Press.

MACDONALD, D., 1957: 'A Theory of Popular Culture', in B. Rosenberg and D. White (eds.) *Mass Culture: The Popular Arts in America*. New York: Free Press.

MCLEOD, J., 1988: 'The Mass Media and Citizenship', Stevenson Lecture, Department of Politics, University of Glasgow (mimeo).

MCLEOD, J. and MCDONALD, D., 1985: 'Beyond Simple Exposure: Media Orientations and Their Impact on Political Process', *Communication Research*, 12: 3–33.

MCNAIR, B., 1988: *Images of the Enemy*. London: Routledge.

MCQUAIL, D., 1977: 'The Influence and Effects of the Mass Media', in J. Curran, M. Gurevitch and J. Woollacott (eds.) *Mass Communication and Society*. London: Edward Arnold.

MCQUAIL, D., 1987: *Mass Communication Theory*. London: Sage.

MCQUAIL, D., BLUMLER, J.G. and BROWN, J.R., 1972: 'The Television Audience: A Revised Perspective', in Denis McQuail (ed.) *Sociology of Mass Communications*. Harmondsworth: Penguin.

MCQUAIL, D. and WINDAHL, S., 1981: *Communication Models*. New York: Longman.

MARSHALL, G., ROSE, D., NEWBY, H. and VOGLER, C., 1989: *Social Class in Modern Britain*. London: Unwin Hyman.

MEYER, T.P., 1976: 'The Impact of "All in the Family" on Children, *Journal of Broadcasting*, winter.

MODLESKI, T., 1982: *Loving With a Vengeance*. Hamden, CT: Archon Books.

MORLEY, D., 1980: *The 'Nationwide' Audience*. London: British Film Institute.

MORLEY, D., 1981: 'Industrial Conflict and the Mass Media', reprinted in Stan Cohen and Jock Young (eds.) *Manufacture of News*, 2nd edition. London: Constable.

MORLEY, D., 1989: 'Changing Paradigms in Audience Studies', in Ellen Seiter et al. (eds.) *Remote Control*. London: Routledge.

MURDOCK, G., 1982: Large Corporations and the Control of Communication Industries', in Michael Gurevitch et al. (eds.) *Culture, Society and the Media*. London: Methuen.

MURDOCK, G., 1984: 'Reporting the Riots: Images and Impacts', in John Benyon (eds.) *Scarman and After*. Oxford: Pergamon.

MURDOCK, G. and GOLDING, P., 1977: 'Capitalism, Communication and Class Relations', in J. Curran, M. Gurevitch and J. Woollacott (eds.) *Mass Communication and Society*. London: Edward Arnold.

NOELLE-NEUMANN, E., 1981: 'Mass Media and Social Change in Developed Countries', in Elihu Katz and Tamas Szecskö (eds.) *Mass Media and Social Change*. Beverly Hills, CA: Sage.

PHILO, G., 1987: 'Whose News?', *Media, Culture and Society*. 9 (4): 397–406.

PHILO, G., 1989: 'News Content and Audience Belief: A Case Study of the 1984–5 Miners Strike', PhD dissertation. Glasgow: Glasgow University.
PHILO, G., 1990: *Seeing and Believing*. London: Routledge.
RADWAY, J., 1987: *Reading the Romance*. London: Verso.
REIMER, B. and ROSENGREN, K.E., 1989: 'Cultivated Viewers and Readers: A Life Style Perspective', in Nancy Signorielli and Michael Morgan (eds.) *Advances in Cultivation Analysis*. Beverly Hills, CA: Sage.
ROSENGREN, K.E., 1981: 'Mass Media and Social Change', in Elihu Katz and Tamas Szecskö (eds.) *Mass Media and Social Change*. Beverly Hills, CA: Sage.
SCHLESINGER, P., 1990: 'Rethinking the Sociology of Journalism', in Margaret Ferguson (ed.) *Public Communication*. London: Sage.
SCHLESINGER, P., MURDOCK, G. and ELLIOTT, P., 1983: *Televising 'Terrorism'*. London: Pluto.
SCHRØDER, K., 1989: 'The Playful Audiencer: The Continuity of the Popular Cultural Tradition in America', in Michael Skovmand (ed.) *Media Fictions*. Åarhus: Åarhus University Press.
SCHUDSON, M., 1987: 'The New Validation of Popular Culture: Sense and Sentimentality in Academia', *Critical Studies in Mass Communication*, 4 (1).
SCHUDSON, M., 1989: 'The Sociology of News Production', *Media, Culture and Society*, 11 (3): 263–82.
SEITER, E., BORCHERS, H., KREUTZNER, G. and WARTH, E.-M. (eds.), 1989: *Remote Control*. London: Routledge.
SEYMOUR-URE, C., 1989: 'Prime Ministers' Reactions to Television: Britain, Australia and Canada', *Media, Culture and Society*, 11 (3): 307–25.
SHILS, E., 1961: 'Mass Society and its Culture', in N. Jacobs (ed.) *Culture for the Millions?* Princeton, NJ: Van Nostrand.
SIGAL, L., 1987: 'Sources Make the News', in Robert Manoff and Michael Schudson (eds.) *Reading the News*. New York: Pantheon.
TAN, A., 1985: *Mass Communication Theories and Society*, 2nd edition. New York: Wiley.
TUNSTALL, J., 1981: *Journalists at Work*. London: Constable.
VIDMAR, N. and ROKEACH, M., 1974: 'Archie Bunker's Bigotry: A Study in Selective Perception and Exposure', *Journal of Communication*, 24 (2): 36–47.
WATNEY, S., 1987: *Policing Desire*. London: Methuen.
WHANNEL, G., 1979: 'Football Crowd Behaviour and the Press', *Media, Culture and Society*, 2 (4): 327–43.
WILHOIT, G.C. and BOCK, H. DE, 1976: ' "All in the Family" in Holland', *Journal of Communicalion*, 26 (3).
YOUNG, J., 1974: 'Mass Media, Drugs and Deviances', in P. Rock and M. McIntosh (eds.) *Deviance and Social Control*. London: Tavistock.

12

Populism, Revisionism and the 'New' Audience Research

David Morley

1 The 'New Revisionism' in Audience Research

In his (1990) article, James Curran takes issue with the emphasis in current audience research on the active role of the reader in interpreting media texts, arguing that this approach, which he characterizes as representing a 'new revisionism' in the field, necessarily involves a denial of media power and an abandonment of any concern with the politics of communication.

It certainly seems that, over the last few years, things have changed in the world of media studies. As we all know, in the bad old days, TV audiences were considered as passive consumers, to whom things happened, as TV's miraculous powers affected them. According to choice, these (always other) people were turned into zombies, transfixed by bourgeois ideology or filled with consumerist desires. Happily, so the story goes, it was then discovered that this was an inaccurate picture because in fact, these people were out there, in front of the set, active in all kinds of ways – making critical/oppositional readings of dominant cultural forms, perceiving ideological messages selectively/subversively, etc., etc. So, it seems, we needn't worry – the passively consuming audience is a thing of the past. As Evans (1990) notes, recent audience work in media studies can be largely characterized by two assumptions: (a) that the audience is always active (in a non-trivial sense) and (b) that media content is 'polysemic' or open to interpretation. The question is, what these assumptions are taken to mean exactly, and what their theoretical and empirical consequences are.

2 From 'Active Audiences' to Sociological Quietism?

In an essay on the problems of the 'new audience research' Corner (1991) identifies a number of the key issues at stake in current arguments about the 'activity' of the media audience. He argues that, in recent years, the question of media power as a political issue has tended to slip off the research agenda of this burgeoning field of 'demand-side' research. In his analysis, this new research is seen largely to amount to 'a form of sociological quietism ... in which increasing emphasis on the micro-processes of viewing relations displaces ... an engagement with the macro-structures of media and society' (p. 269).

For my part, while in sympathy with much of Corner's argument, this particular formulation seems problematic, in so far as it mal-poses the relation between macro and micro, effectively equating the former with the 'real'. Corner's analysis fails to recognize, among other things, the articulation of the divisions macro/micro, real/trivial, public/private, masculine/feminine – which is what much of the work which he criticizes has, in various ways, been concerned with. More centrally, Corner seems to invoke a notion of the macro which is conceptualized in terms of pre-given structures, rather than (to use Giddens's (1979) phrase) 'structuration', and which fails to see that macro structures can only be reproduced through micro-processes. Unless one deals in a reified sense of 'structure', such an entity is, in fact, simply an analytical construct detailing the patterning of an infinite number of micro-processes and events (cf. de Saussure 1974, on the status of *langue*). It was precisely for this reason that the work of the media group at Birmingham University's Centre for Contemporary Cultural Studies in a formative period (see Hall et al. 1981) turned to an engagement with ethnomethodological perspectives: not in order to abandon the macro in favour of the micro (as many ethnomethodologists themselves seemed to do) but rather, the better to articulate the analysis of the one to that of the other.

In this connection, Gledhill (1988: 67) offers a useful formulation when she points to the central role of the concept of 'negotiation' of meanings, in allowing us to avoid 'an overly deterministic view of cultural production whether economic ... or cine-psychoanalytic'. Gledhill's central point concerns the homology between the substitution of the concept of 'negotiation' for that of 'effects' at the micro level, and the corresponding substitution of the concept of 'hegemony' (as a necessarily unstable and incomplete process) for that of the imposition of a 'dominant ideology' (as a given and guaranteed effect) at the macro level. The point precisely is that the general macro process can only operate through myriad micro performances of power, none of which can be guaranteed in advance, even if the general pattern of events is subject to the logic of probabilities. As Giddens (1979) argues, structures are not external to action, but are only reproduced through the concrete activities of daily life, and must be analysed as historical formations, subject to modification – as structures constituted through action, as much as action is constituted structurally.

In this connection Murdock (1989: 243) rightly points to the usefulness of Bourdieu's conception of the 'habitus', as a way of grasping the articulation of the two dimensions of structure and action – as a matrix of dispositions and competences capable of generating and underwriting a wide variety of specific practices but where, as Murdock puts, 'habituses are not habits. They do not entail the application of fixed rules and routines. Rather, they provide the basis for structured variations, in the same way that jazz musicians improvise around a ... theme.' At the same time, while Murdock stresses the positive aspects of

Bourdieu's overall theory, he is rightly critical of the exclusive stress that Bourdieu lays on early family socialization as the sole source of cultural capital and competences. As Murdock notes, while we must recognize that a person's initial socialization will play a key role in structuring their access to cultural codes, to see this process as necessarily irreversible is overly deterministic:

> clearly if, in later life, someone joins . . . a . . . political party or . . . religious cult, they will have access to additional discourses with the potential to restructure their interpretative activities in powerful ways. The 'prison house of language' may be a high-security installation, but escape is always possible.
>
> (p. 245)

Corner's critique, unfortunately, seems to conflate two different issues. On one hand, the conceptual shift from a model of dominant ideology as a given structure to a processual model of hegemony (and the consequent interest in the micro aspect of macro processes) and, on the other hand, the substantive reworking of the field under the impact of feminist theory and research, decentring the former principal concerns with class, in favour of a concern with the articulation of structures of gender and class, especially in relation to the media's role in articulating the public/private interface. This certainly is a research agenda with a transformed concept of media power (rather different to that of classical Marxism, for example) but it is hardly a research agenda from which power has slipped. In so far as it is a perspective, as Corner puts it, which has 'revised downwards' notions of media power, it is one which takes on board the critique made by Abercrombie et al. (1984) of the excesses of the 'dominant ideology thesis' (but see also my critical comments on this position below). This then is to follow neither the Parsonian reading of Durkheim (attributing all signs of social stability to the 'conscience collective' or the 'value-system' of society) nor the Frankfurt School reading of Marx (with its neglect of the role of the 'dull compulsion of the economic', in Marx's phrase, and the sheer facticity of economic interdependence, in any society with a complex division of labour). This is to avoid over-emphasizing the role of ideology or, more prosaically, in Connell's (1985) phrase, to avoid 'blaming the meeja' for everything.

None the less, I do share Corner's concern that much recent work in this field is marred by a facile insistence on the polysemy of media products and by an undocumented presumption that forms of oppositional decoding are more widespread than subordination or the reproduction of dominant meanings (cf. Condit 1989 on the unfortunate tendency towards an overdrawn 'emphasis on the polysemous qualities of texts' in media studies). To follow that path, as Corner correctly notes, is to underestimate the force of textual determinacy in the construction of meaning from media products, and not only to improperly romanticize the role of the reader, but to neglect all the evidence of the relatively *low* level of ambiguity, at some levels of meaning, of widespread systems of signification, such as those purveyed by the mass media. As Corner notes, to follow this primrose (and perhaps postmodern) path, in giving such emphasis to the polysemic qualities of media messages, is to risk falling into a 'complacement relativism, by which the interpretive contribution of the audience is perceived to be of such a scale and range as to render the very idea of media power naïve' (Corner 1991: 281).

Conversely, while taking many of the points raised by critics such as Corner with reference to the inherent problems and limitations of the 'preferred reading' model developed by Hall (1973), I remain convinced that the model, while needing developing and amending in various respects, still offers the best alternative to a conception of media texts as equally 'open' to any and all interpretations (usually derived from Barthes 1972) which readers wish to make of them. While I would agree that Hall's original model tends to blur together questions of recognition, comprehension, interpretation and responses, which may ultimately need to be separated analytically, there is a considerable body of work in the sociology of reading and literacy (see Hoyles 1977) which would argue that, given the context-dependent mode of understanding which readers ordinarily employ, too radical a separation of these issues will leave us with a neat but unrealistic model of what readers do when they read a text. Further, while it is true that the preferred reading model was originally developed for the analysis of news and current affairs journalism, and is easiest to employ directly in the analysis of material of that type, it is not as difficult as some critics (including Corner 1991) would seem to suggest to apply it to other materials. Thus, for example, given the hierarchies of discourse routinely offered by fictional texts, usually centring round the point of view of one or more privileged character(s), it is a relatively easy matter to transpose the model to the analysis of the classical realist text and its derivatives in the fictional realm.

The recent interventions of Brunsdon (1989) and Gripsrud (1989), cautioning against current tendencies to entirely dissolve the text into its readings can (with hindsight) be seen to have been foreshadowed by Counihan's (1973) critique of Chaney (1972), who decried the usefulness of any analysis of the message in itself – on the grounds that the 'content is not meaningful in itself . . . [but] is only meaningful in its interaction with an audience'. As Counihan remarks, in the context of Chaney's relentless dissolution of the message into the audiences' perceptions, uses and manipulations of it:

> It is as if the assertion of the necessity for a formal analysis of media 'texts' as a distinct region of communications research involved a radical denial of the inalienable rights of audiences to constitute all meanings
>
> (Counihan 1973: 43).

The analysis of the text or message remains, of course, a fundamental necessity, for the polysemy of the message is not without its own structure. Audiences do not see only what they want to see, since a message (or programme) is not simply a window on the world, but is a construction. While the message is not an object with one real meaning, there are, within it, signifying mechanisms which promote certain meanings, even one privileged meaning, and suppress others: these are the 'directive closures' encoded in the message. The message is capable of different interpretations depending on the context of association.

This was the point of the analytic procedure employed in the first part of the *Nationwide* project (see Brunsdon and Morley 1978), which was not designed to discover the 'real meaning' of the messages analysed, but simply to follow the 'directive closures' (in the form of headlines, high-status views etc.) so as to reproduce the reading of the message achieved by operating within the dominant decoding framework. This is not to imply that this is the *only* reading possible: the analysis is, of necessity, interpretive; its significance ultimately was to be investigated by the subsequent empirical work examining how messages were 'read' and which sections of the audience did make this kind of reading of the message, rather than a 'negotiated' or 'oppositional' reading.

3 The 'New Revisionism' and its Critics

In a similar vein to Corner, Curran (1990) offers a highly critical account of what he describes as the 'new revisionism' in mass communications research on media audiences. In brief, his charge is that while 'this ... "revisionism" ... presents itself as original and innovative, as an emancipatory movement that is throwing off the shackles of tradition ... [it] ... is none of these things' (p. 135), but rather amounts to 'old pluralist dishes being reheated and presented as new cuisine' (p. 151). In Curran's view, 'revisionists' (such as myself) are presenting 'as innovation what is in reality a process of rediscovery' (p. 146) and, as far as Curran is concerned, misrepresenting this 'revisionism' in 'assertive terms as an example of intellectual progress' in which 'those hitherto mired in error have been confounded and enlightened' (p. 146) when, in fact the 'revisionists' are actually 'engaged ... in an act of revivalism – reverting to the discredited wisdom of the past' (p. 153), in so far as most of the claimed 'advances' achieved by this new work are clearly predated and prefigured, according to Curran, by earlier work within both the 'effects' and 'uses and gratifications' traditions – of which the 'revisionists' are, in Curran's view naïvely ignorant. To some extent, Curran's argument is also supported by Evans (1990), who claims that authors within the 'interpretivist' tradition ('new revisionists', in Curran's terms) have tended to set up the faults of the earlier 'hypodermic effects' model of communications rather as a 'straw man' by contrast to which other positions would more easily seem sophisticated.

Curran's own principal tactic is to bolster his argument by quoting the work of hitherto neglected figures within the mainstream traditions of audience research, who argue against any simple hypodermic theory of 'effects', or who stress issues such as the social setting of media reception, thus demonstrating that recent emphasis on such issues is no more than old wine in new bottles. There are two key problems with this argument, one a matter of historiography, concerning the status of history as *histoire* (or story); the other concerning the status of 20/20 vision-in-hindsight.

In the first case, Curran fails to address the issue, which has been central to much recent historical debate, and which was placed on the agenda some years ago by Wright (1985) among others, concerning the role of (any) history in the present. As Wright argues, the past is no simple thing to be referred to: rather we must attend to the crucial role played by different constructed narratives and invocations of the past, in contemporary cultural, political (or academic) debates – as legitimating this or that opposing view or strategy in the present. While I am happy to regard Curran's own analysis as an intervention (and a very interesting one at that) in a contemporary debate about how the future trajectory of audience research should be conceptualized, its central (if unacknowledged) thrust is to mobilize his own version of history in support of a very particular set of claims as to how audience research should be conducted. This is simply to note that Curran's history is, inevitably, involved in doing something rather more than he claims; rather than simply 'setting the record straight' in the face of any 'breathtaking ... caricature of the history of communications research' (Curran 1990: 146) produced by the 'revisionism' Curran decries, it is advancing a particular (and partly unacknowledged) agenda of its own, which equally can be accused of 'writing out' particular problems and issues from the agenda of future research. I will return to the blind spots in Curran's analysis, below.

The second problem concerns hindsight. The history Curran offers is an informative one, alerting us to the achievements of scholars whose work has been unrecognized or neglected by many (myself included), thus far. However, my contention is that this is a particular history which could not have been written (by Curran or anyone else) fifteen years ago, before the impact of the 'new revisionism' (of which Curran is so critical) transformed our understanding of the field of audience research, and thus transformed our understanding of who and what was important in its history. I would argue that it is this transformation which has allowed a historian such as Curran to go back and re-read the history of communications research, in such a way as to give prominence to those whose work can now, with hindsight, be seen to have prefigured the work of these 'new revisionists'. The point is that it is only now, after the impact of 'revisionist' analyses, that the significance of this earlier work can be seen. Previously, much of it was perceived as marginal to the central trajectory of mainstream communications research. As Seiter et al. (1989: 14) note, if the 'academic pendulum swings along the fine line between re-seeing and revisionism' then the work of 're-visioning' (or reconceptualizing, and of always newly revising our perspectives) is central to the dynamic through which the field develops. In the nature of the case, it is difficult to accuse others of falsely imagining that history was simply that which led up to them, without, in the event, ending up in the unhappy position of making that claim (explicitly or implicitly) for one's own arguments.

According to Blumler et al. (1985: 257) the 'interpretivist focus on the role of the reader in the decoding process should be ringing bells with 'gratificationists' because ... they are the most experienced in dealing with a multiplicity of responses'. Similarly, Rosengren (1985: 278) claims that Radway's (1984) work 'indirectly offers strong validation of the general soundness of uses and gratifications research', and he goes on to claim that 'in her way, Radway has reinvented ... gratifications research'. As Evans (1990) notes, the first question, in this connection, is perhaps whether, rather than constituting evidence of a genuine unity between cultural studies and uses and gratifications perspectives, what we see here is, in fact, a misguided attempt to reduce interpretivist concepts to gratificationist terms. The second (and as Schroder 1987 notes, rather embarrassing) question is 'why has it required a cultural studies scholar to excavate a lost sociological tradition?' The answer that Schroder offers, and with which I, for one, incline to agree, is that in spite of the tributes now paid by Curran et al. to those who can, retrospectively, be identified as the forgotten 'pioneers' of qualitative media audience research 'the fact remains that, until the 1980s, their qualitative work ... [was] ... the victim of a spiral of silence, because they attempted to study what mainstream sociology regarded as unresearchable, i.e. cultural meanings and interpretations' (Schroder 1987: 14).

There are a number of further substantive problems with Curran's formulation of the issues at stake. In the first instance, in setting up a simple polarity between 'Marxist' and 'pluralist' perspectives, he unhelpfully blurs together the Gramscian and Althusserian perspectives within the Marxist tradition. In this respect his analysis replicates the confusions of Abercrombie et al.'s (1978 and 1984) critique of the 'dominant ideology thesis' (see my comments above on the importance of the distinctions between Athusser and Gramsci, with reference to the relationship between the analysis of micro and macro processes in media analyses). Further, Curran fails to grasp the significance of the encounter with semiology, within the cultural studies perspective, in transforming the concept of the message, away from a conveyor belt model of the transmission of content, towards one more fully informed by the insights of linguistics (notwithstanding the problems of formal semiotic models and the need to move beyond them to a social semiotics).

Some of the early work of the American mass communications researchers (see Merton 1946) was highly sophisticated in many respects, and did begin to open up questions about the actual processes of persuasion and the processes involved in resistance to persuasive arguments, which can now be seen to have foreshadowed the later contributions of semiology in the close analysis of these issues. Thus, Merton insisted on the need to interpret messages within the cultural contexts of their occurrence. However, subsequent work in that tradition largely failed to effectively develop Merton's insights. In this connection, Geertz has argued that the key problem for American communications researchers was that, despite their sophistication in other respects, they lacked anything more than the most rudimentary conception of the processes of symbolic communication. As a result, he argued:

> The links between the causes of ideology and its effects seem adventitious, because the connective element – the autonomous process of symbolic formulation – is passed over in virtual silence. Both interest theory and strain theory go directly from source analysis to consequence analysis without ever seriously examining ideologies as systems of interacting symbols, as patterns of interworking meanings. Themes are outlined, of course; among the content analysts they are even counted. But they are referred for elucidation not to other themes, not to any sort of semantic theory, but either backward to the effect they presumably mirror, or forward to the social reality they presumably distort. The problem of how ideologies transform sentiment into significance, and so make it socially available, is shortcircuited.
>
> (Geertz, quoted in Hall 1974: 278–9)

It was precisely this issue, I would contend, that the encounter with semiology enabled cultural studies researchers to open up, and thus, long afterwards, to begin to advance Merton's original insights, which had been largely neglected in mainstream research.

Finally, it seems necessary to distinguish between the different traditions which Curran lumps together under the rubric of the 'new revisionism'. It is hardly incidental that Curran and Gurevitch's *Mass Communication and Society* (1991) is structured around a set of arguments concerning the hypothetical 'convergence' (see also Schroder 1987; Jensen and Rosengren 1990) of radical and mainstream traditions in media research. In the context of that volume, the post-structuralist work of scholars such as Ang and Hermes (1991) is implicitly recruited in support of an argument that, to put it crudely, ultimately claims that Foucault's main significance was to demonstrate that liberal-pluralists were right (or, at least, more right than the Marxists) all along, about the 'dispersion' of power. In my view, and despite the problems of post-structuralist tendencies to regress towards a form of methodological individualism, to conflate these traditions is, in the end, unhelpful.

Curran is right to point to the ambivalence of the Foucauldian legacy in recent media studies, in so far as the predominant (and rather partial) reading of Foucault has promoted a decentring of media research in which, as Curran puts it, 'the role of the media is reduced to a succession of reader-text encounters in the context of a society which is analytically disaggregated into a series of concrete instances ... or in which power external to discourse is wholly evacuated' (Curran 1990: 140). As Curran rightly observes, such a perspective (in which power is seen as not so much diffused as defused) is, in reality, not very different from that of the American liberal-pluralist tradition. However, while Curran's proclaimed target is the rather broad (if undefined) one of the 'new revisionism', the proper focus of this critique seems to fall on a recent (and principally American) inflection of cultural studies, heavily influenced by the work of John Fiske (cf. also Schudson 1987).

4 Towards a 'Semiotic Democracy'?

While Fiske's work has undoubtedly had the great value of introducing cultural studies to a whole generation of (principally American) students, Curran is correct, in my view, in pointing to the problems attendant on this particular version of cultural studies (see Fiske 1987b in Allen 1987). Thus, as Curran notes, recent reception studies (both in America and Scandinavia) which document audience autonomy and offer optimistic/redemptive readings of mainstream media texts, have principally been invoked not simply as a challenge to a simple-minded effects model, but rather as, in themselves, documenting the total absence of media influence in the 'semiotic democracy' of postmodern pluralism. The implicit valorization of audience pleasure, in this work, leads easily into a cultural relativism which, as Curran notes, is readily incorporated into a populist neo-liberal rhetoric which would abandon any concern with cultural values – or 'quality' television (see Brunsdon 1990) – and functions to justify the positions of the deregulators who would destroy any version of public service broadcasting. As Seiter el al. (1989: 5) state pithily, 'in our concern for audiences' pleasures ... we run the risk of continually validating Hollywood's domination of the worldwide television market', which certainly would seem to be an odd destination to the trajectory of cultural studies media work.

As Curran observes (1990: 148), Fiske's celebration of a 'semiotic democracy', in which people drawn from a vast shifting range of subcultures and groups construct their own meanings within an autonomous cultural economy, is problematic in various respects, but not least because it is readily subsumable within a conservative ideology of sovereign consumer pluralism. To argue thus is by no means to deny the force of many of Fiske's insightful formulations into the complexities of the making and remaking of meanings in popular culture. As I have argued elsewhere (Morley 1989) alongside Fiske's works, the work of Bennett and Woollacot (1987) and Browne (1984) has usefully alerted us to the interdiscursive nature of textual meaning and to the difficulty of ever isolating, in any simply sense, a single text for analysis.

Larry Grossberg (1987: 33) has argued that 'not only is every media event mediated by other texts, but it's almost impossible to know what constitutes the bounded text which might be interpreted or which is actually consumed'. This is because the text does not occupy a fixed position, but is always mobilized, placed and articulated with other texts in different ways. However, it can be objected that this new emphasis upon intertextuality runs several risks, notably that contextual issues will overwhelm and overdetermine texts and their specificity. The question is whether, in following this route, we run the danger of arriving at a point in which the text is simply dissolved into its readings.

Fiske has called for a retheorization of the television text, which would allow us to investigate its openness, by mobilizing Barthes's distinction between 'work' and 'text'. Barthes argued that the work is the physical construct of signifiers, which becomes a text only when read. The text, in this formulation, is never a fixed or stable thing, but is continually being recreated out of the work. Fiske (1989: 56–7) argues that 'there's no such thing as "the television audience" [cf. Hartley 1987] defined as an empirically accessible object . . . we have now collapsed the distinction between "text" and "audience" . . . There is no text, there is no audience, there are only the processes of viewing.' None the less, curiously, in his analysis of TV quiz shows, Fiske (1984: 5) ends up reasserting the centrality of the text, explaining that he has found it necessary to make 'no empirical audience investigation' of the reasons for the popularity of such shows because 'my theory of popularity . . . is one that is best arrived at by a study of the text itself'.

In his discussion of the 'encoding/decoding' model Fiske (1987a: 63) suggests that the 'value of the theory lies . . . in its shift away from the text and towards the reader as the site of meaning' and argues that the principal value of ethnographic methods of study is that they 'enable us to account for diversity'. The problems here are (a) that this reading of the encoding/decoding model omits its central stress on strategies of textual closure ('preferred readings', etc.) and (b) that the object of ethnographic study is, in fact, the discovery of regularities and patterns of behaviour, decoding and responses, as much as it is the revelation (or celebration) of diversity. In this respect, I would agree with Ang (1990) that ethnography's critical edge does not reside in 'discovering and validating diversity and difference . . . it can work more ambitiously towards an unravelling of the intricate intersections of the diverse and the homogeneous' (p. 257).

Fiske tends to see the textual as the only site of closure, and to equate the social (the site of decoding) exclusively with flux and diversity. Again the problems are twofold. In the first instance, the social is also a site of closure – in so far as it is through social positioning that access to cultural codes (which can be mobilized in decodings) is regulated (cf. Corner 1991). In the second place, this attribution of negative (reactionary) values of fixing to the text, and the corresponding positive valuation of flux and diversity as the source of resistance ('the people still are uncomfortable, undisciplined, intransigent forces') is itself problematic. Behind this formulation lies a conceptual model which seems to be derived from a particular libertarian reading of Barthes's early essay on 'Myth Today' (1972) in which ideology is defined as the (bad) process of the fixing (and reification) of (dominant) meanings, while (good) resistance is seen to lie essentially in the unfixing and destabilizing of meanings. Curiously, despite their obvious substantive differences, there are interesting parallels here with the problem of psychoanalytic theories of spectatorship.

One central problem with what Gledhill (1988) describes as the cine-psychoanalytic critique of the effects of the classical realist text – in producing an ideological sense of fixed and stable identity for the spectator – is that in its (usually implicit) celebration of flux and instability, it naïvely abandons our necessary concern with the positive dimensions of the production of such identities. As Gledhill (1988: 72) puts it,

> social out-groups seeking to identify themselves against dominant representations . . . need clearly articulated, recognisable and self-respecting self-images. To adopt a political position is of necessity to assume, for the moment, a consistent and answerable identity. The object of attack should not be identity as such, but its dominant construction as total, non-contradictory and unchanging.

To argue thus is simply to recognize that the absence of a coherent sense of identity (whether at the individual level, as in the case of mental illness, or at the socio-cultural level, on the part of oppressed groups) is at least as problematic, in political terms, as is the ideological 'fixing' of such identities by dominant cultural forms. Many years ago sociologists routinely (if crudely) distinguished between social critics who could be described as 'integration-fearers' (clearly, the cine-psychoanalytic school is included here) and those better described as 'incoherence-fearers' (cf. Mann 1970). Any progressive cultural (or political) strategy must avoid the dangers of the Charybdis of incoherence as much as those of the Scylla of reification.

To return to the difficulties of Fiske's position, it is worth noting that Fiske extends his argument towards the idea of a 'readers liberation movement', involving a theory of audience reading which asserts the reader's right to make, out of the programme, the text that connects the discourses of the programme with the discourses through which he/she lives his/her social experience, and thus for programme, society and reading subject to come together in an active, creative living of culture in the moment of reading. While I sympathize with this concern with 'readers' rights', I would argue that the concept of 'rights' in this context is problematic, in so far as it is perhaps less a question of the readers' rights to make out of a programme whatever meaning they wish (which presumably involves a moral or philosophical discourse concerning rights in general) than a question of power – for example, the presence or absence of the power or cultural resources necessary in order to make certain types of meaning, which is, ultimately, an empirical question. (See also Gripsrud 1989, for a further critique of the dangers of any model of 'reader's liberation' which fails to deal with the social structuring of the distribution of cultural competences.)

In some of his later writing, Fiske has turned to the work of de Certeau (1984) and, in particular, de Certeau's concept of the tactics of the weak, in 'poaching' symbolic and material advantage in the interstices of dominant structures and institutions, controlled by the strategies of the powerful. While de Certeau's work is evidently of great interest, the dangers of a partial interpretation of that work, which over-stresses (if not romanticizes) the element of popular resistance, have been clearly identified by, among others, Frow (1991).

Evans (1990) rightly points to a crucial development in what he calls the 'interpretivist' tradition of audience research. Hall's original formulation of the encoding/decoding model contained, as one of its central features, the concept of the preferred reading (towards which the text attempts to direct its reader) while acknowledging the possibility of alternative, negotiated or oppositional readings. As Evans notes, this model has subsequently been quite transformed, to the point where it is often maintained that the majority of audience members *routinely* 'modify or deflect' any dominant ideology reflected in media content (cf. Fiske 1987a: 64)

5 Affirmative and 'Redemptive' Readings

Budd et al. (1990) argue that current audience research now routinely assumes that 'people habitually use the content of dominant media against itself, to empower themselves' so that, in their analysis, the crucial 'message' of much contemporary American cultural studies media work is an optimistic one: 'Whatever the message encoded, decoding comes to the rescue. Media domination is weak and ineffectual, since the people make their own meanings and pleasures; or, put another way, 'we don't need to worry about people watching several hours of TV a day, consuming its images, ads and values. People are already critical, active viewers and listeners, not cultural dopes manipulated by the media.' While I would certainly not wish to return to any model of the audience as 'cultural dopes', the point Budd et al, make is a serious one, not least because, as they note, this 'affirmative' model does tend to then justify the neglect of all questions concerning the economic, political and ideological forces acting on the construction of texts (cf. Brundson 1989), on the (unfounded) assumption that reception is, somehow, the only stage of the communications process that matters, in the end (cf. also Frith 1990). Apart from anything else, and at the risk of being whimsical, one might say that such an assumption does seem to be a curiously Christian one, in which the sins of the industry (or the message) are somehow seen to be redeemed in the 'after-life' of reception.

One crucial question concerns the significance that is subsequently given to often quite particular, ethnographic accounts of moments of cultural subversion, in the process of media consumption or decoding. Thus, Budd et al. note that, in his account of the ways in which Aboriginal Australian children have been shown to reconstruct TV narratives involving Blacks, in such a way as to fit with and bolster their own self-conceptions, Fiske (1986) shows a worrying tendency to generalize radically from this (very particular) instance, so that, in his account, this type of alternative response, in quite particular circumstances, is decontextualized and then offered as a model for 'decoding' in general, so that, as Budd et al. put it, 'the part becomes the whole and the exception the rule' (1990: 179; see also Schudson 1987).

It is in matters of this kind that some of Curran's (1976) earlier observations on the shortcomings of qualitative forms of media analysis are, in my view, borne out, in so far as the rejection of all forms of quantification (as a kind of methodological-ethical principle) precisely allow this kind of unguarded and unwarranted generalization. In a similar vein, Schroder (1987: 27) argues that

> one of the tasks ahead will consist in conceptualising a method which makes it possible to incorporate and preserve qualitative data through a process of quantification, enabling the researcher to discern the demographic patterning of viewing responses, for instance the proportions of 'preferred' or 'aberrant' responses within demographic groups and in the general population.

Along the way, Budd et al. raise a number of other problems about what they characterize as the 'affirmative trend in American cultural studies' and the burgeoning tendency to find (and celebrate) traces of 'opposition' everywhere. As they note, even if instances of such readings can be identified 'we still need to ask what difference [do they] make to relations of power? ... Surely ... watching television in itself can have an oppositional kick. But it does nothing outside itself' (Budd et al. 1990). In a similar vein Jensen (1990: 3) argues that

> oppositional decodings are not in themselves a manifestation of political power ... the wider ramifications of opposition at the textual level depend on the social and political uses to which opposition may be put, in contexts beyond the relative privacy of media reception.

The further problem here is that identified by Evans (1990), who notes that 'interpretivists' often make overblown claims that their perspective, in itself, involves an empowering of the audience, a privileging of the reader which is, in fact, quite illusory. As Evans puts it, such phrases seem to suggest that a given scholarly approach can empower or privilege 'the people' simply by dint of an analytic characterization whereas, in reality, 'as scholars, our own desire to have current ideological systems resisted may produce romanticized, even Utopian visions of the people we study, enacting our wishes' (p. 160). The point is well taken, and chimes with Frow's (1991) argument that we should beware of any tendency towards a kind of populist ventriloquism, in which there is an unacknowledged 'substitution of the voice of a middle-class intellectual for that of the users of popular culture' (p. 60) or in which the latter are invoked as bit-part players, only to speak the script constructed and shaped (implicitly) by the analyst. As Ang (1990) notes, in some versions of cultural studies the researcher is often presented as no longer a critical outsider, but rather a fellow participant, a conscious fan, giving voice to and celebrating consumer cultural democracy. The problem, as Ang goes on to argue, is that while 'audiences may be active, in myriad ways, in using and interpreting media ... it would be utterly out of perspective to cheerfully equate "active" with "powerful"' (Ang 1990: 247).

The equivalence that Newcomb and Hirsch (1984: 69) assert between the producer and consumer of messages, in so far as the television viewer 'matches the creator [of the programme] in the making of meanings' is, in effect, a facile one, which ignores de Certeau's (1984) distinction (see above) between the strategies of the powerful and the tactics of the weak (or as Silverstone and I have argued elsewhere (1990), the difference between having power over a text, and power over the agenda within which that text is constructed and presented). The power of viewers to reinterpret meanings is hardly equivalent to the discursive power of centralized media institutions to construct the texts which the viewer then interprets, and to imagine otherwise is simply foolish.

References

ABERCROMBIE, N. and TURNER, B., 1978: 'The Dominant Ideology Thesis', *British Journal of Sociology*, 29(2): pp. 149–70.

ABERCROMBIE, N., HILL, S. and TURNER, B., 1984: *The Dominant Ideology Thesis*. London: Allen & Unwin.

ALLEN, R. (ed.), 1987: *Channels of Discourse*. London: Routledge.

ANG, I., 1990: 'Culture and Communication', *European Journal of Communications*, 5 (2/3): pp. 239–61.

ANG, I. and J. HERMES, 1991: 'Gender and in media consumption', in J. Curran and M. Gurevitch (eds.) *Mass Media and Society*. London: Edward Arnold, pp. 307–28.

BARTHES, R., 1972: *Mythologies*. London: Paladin.

BENNETT, T. and WOOLLACOT, J. 1987: *Bond and beyond: The political career of a popular hero*. London: Macmillan.

BLUMLER, G., GUREVITCH, M. and KATZ, E., 1985: 'Reaching out: A future for gratifications research', in K. Rosengren et al. (eds.) *Media gratifications research*. Beverly Hills, CA: Sage.

BROWNE, N., 1984: 'The political economy of the television (super) text'. *Quarterly Review of Film Studies*, 9: pp. 174–82.

BRUNDSON, C., 1989: 'Text and audience', in E. Seiter et al. (eds.) *Remote Control*. London: Routledge, pp. 116–30.

BRUNDSON, C., 1990: 'Problems with quality'. *Screen*, 31 (1): pp. 67–90.

BRUNDSON, C. and MORLEY, D., 1978: *Everyday television: Nationwide*. London: British Film Institute.

BUDD, B., ENTMAN, R. and STEINMANN, C, 1990: 'The affirmative character of American Cultural Studies'. *Critical Studies in Mass Communication*, 7 (2), 169–84.

CERTEAU, M. DE, 1984: *The Practice of Everyday Life*. Berkeley, CA: University of California Press.

CHANEY, D., 1972: *Processes of Mass Communication*. London: Macmillan.

CONDIT, C., 1989: 'The rhetorical limits of polysemy'. *Critical Studies in Mass Communication* 6 (2) pp. 103-22.

CONNELL, I., 1985: 'Blaming the meeja', in: L. Masterman (ed.), *TV Mythologies*, pp. 88–94. London: Routledge.

CORNER, J., 1991: 'Meaning, genre and context: The problematics of "public knowledge" in the new audience studies', in: J. Curran and M. Gurevitch (eds.), *Mass Media and Society*, pp. 267–84. London: Edward Arnold.

COUNIHAN, M., 1973: 'Orthodoxy, Revisionism and Guerilla Warfare in Mass Communications Research'. University of Birmingham: (mimeo).

CURRAN, J. 1976: *Content and structuralist analysis of mass communication*, Open University Social Psychology Course, D305. Milton Keynes: Open University Press.

CURRAN, J., 1990: 'The "new revisionism" in mass communications research'. *European Journal of Communications* 5 (2/3), pp. 135–64.

CURRAN, J. and GUREVITCH, M. (eds.), 1991: *Mass Media and Society*, London: Edward Arnold.

EVANS, W., 1990: 'The interpretive turn in media research'. *Critical Studies in Mass Communication* 7 (2), pp. 145–68.

FISKE, J., 1984: 'TV quiz shows and the purchase of cultural capital'. *Australian Journal of Screen Theory* 13/14, pp. 5–20.

FISKE, J., 1986: 'Television: Polysemy and popularity', in *Critical Studies in Mass Communication*, 3: 391–408.

FISKE, J., 1987a: *Television Culture*. London: Methuen.

FISKE, J., 1987b: 'British cultural studies and television', in: R. Allen (ed.), *Channels of Discourse*, pp. 254–90. London: Methuen.

FISKE, J., 1989: 'Moments of television', in: E. Seiter et al. (eds.), *Remote Control*, pp. 56–78. London: Routledge.

FRITH, S., 1990: Review article. *Screen* 31 (2), pp. 231–36.

FROW, J., 1991: 'Michel de Certeau and the practice of representation'. *Cultural Studies* 5 (1), pp. 52–60.

GIDDENS, A., 1979: *Central Problems in Sociological Theory*. London: Hutchinson.

GLEDHILL, C., 1988: 'Pleasurable negotiations', in: E. Pribham (ed.), *Female Spectators*, pp. 64–89. London: Verso.

GRIPSRUD, J., 1989: 'High culture revisited'. *Cultural Studies* 3 (2), pp. 194–207.

GROSSBERG, L., 1987: 'The in-difference of television'. *Screen* 28 (2), pp. 28–45.

HALL, S., 1973: 'Encoding and decoding in TV discourse'. Reprinted (1981) in S. Hall et al. (eds.), *Culture, Media, Language*, pp. 128–38. London: Hutchinson.

HALL, S., 1974: 'Deviancy, politics and the media', in: P. Rock and M. McIntosh (eds.), *Deviance and Social Control*, pp. 272–90. London: Tavistock.

HALL, S., CONNELL, I. and CURTI, L., 1981: 'The unity of current affairs TV', in: T. Bennett et al. (eds.), *Popular Television and Film*, pp. 88–119. London: BFI/ Open University Press.

HARTLEY, J., 1987: 'Television audiences, paedocracy and pleasure'. *Textual Practice* 1 (2), pp. 121–38.

HOYLES, M. (ed.), 1977: *The Politics of Literacy*. London: Writers & Readers Publishing Collective.

JENSEN, K.B. and ROSENGREN, K., 1990: 'Five traditions in search of an audience'. *European Journal of Communication* 5 (2/3), pp. 207–38.

MANN, M., 1970: 'The social cohesion of liberal democracy'. *American Sociological Review* 35 (3), pp. 423– 39.

MERTON, R., 1946: *Mass Persuasion*. New York: Free Press.

MORLEY, D., 1989: 'Changing paradigms in audience research', in: E. Seiter et al. (eds.), *Remote Control*, pp. 16–43. London: Routledge.

MORLEY, D. and SILVERSTONE, R., 1990: 'Domestic communications'. *Media, Culture and Society* 12 (1), pp. 31– 55.

MURDOCK, G., 1989: 'Critical inquiry and audience activity', in: B. Dervin et al. (eds.), *Rethinking Communication* 2, pp. 226–49. Newbury Park, CA: Sage.

NEWCOMB, H. and HIRSCH, P., 1984: 'Television as a cultural forum', in: W. Rowland and B. Watkins (eds.), *Interpreting Television*, pp. 58–73. Newbury Park, CA: Sage.

RADWAY, J., 1984: *Reading the Romance* Chapel Hill, NC: University of North Carolina Press. (Published in Britain in a new edition 1987. London: Verso)

ROSENGREN, K., 1985: 'Growth of a research tradition', in: K. Rosengren et al. (eds.), *Media Gratifications Research*, pp. 275–84. Beverly Hills, CA: Sage.

SAUSSURE, F. DE, 1974: *Course in General Linguistics*. London: Fontana.

SCHUDSON, M., 1987: 'The new validation of popular culture: Sense and sentimentality in Academia'. *Critical Studies in Mass Communications* 4 (1), pp. 51–68.

SCHRODER, M., 1987: 'Convergence of antagonistic traditions?' *European Journal of Communications* 2, pp. 7– 31.

SEITER, E., BORCHERS, H., KREUTZNER, G. AND WARTH, E.M., 1989: 'Introduction' to E. Seiter et al. (eds.), *Remote Control*, pp. 1–15. London: Routledge.

WRIGHT, P., 1985: *On Living in an Old Country*. London: Verso.

13(i)
Media Dialogue: A Reply

James Curran

There are two seemingly different versions of recent trends in mass communications research. One is a discriminating account which distinguishes between different traditions of new audience research, corrects errors of analysis and offers an authoritative guide to the strengths and weaknesses of current work. The other conflates different traditions of research, suffers from intellectual blind spots and provides a selective reading of the past in order to promote a secret agenda. Which one is to be believed?

In fact, the disparity between the last two chapters is not as great as it might appear to be on first reading. One of the pleasures of working in an animated but harmonious university department is that it is possible to have sharply expressed intellectual differences without these fraying the threads of friendship. This also helps to see a half measure in a glass as being half full rather than half empty – to perceive areas of agreement rather than of disagreement. There seem to me to be four general points of affinity.

First, both chapters are critical of research which overstates the power of media audiences. Both point to the way in which audience autonomy is constrained potentially by two factors: signifying mechanisms in texts, and a variable degree of social access to ideas and meanings which facilitate contrary 'readings' of the media.

Second, the two chapters are critical of the inferences that have been derived from a romanticized view of audiences -- both in terms of exaggerating the 'bottom-up' power of subordinate groups, and in terms of validating a neo-liberal model of 'free market' media.

Third, both chapters adopt an equivocal tone in relation to new trends in the field, seeing these as representing an advance in some respects but not in others – though there is clearly a difference of emphasis.

Fourth, both chapters are implicitly committed to including a wide-screen view of media and audience processes: to examining the ways in which power relations in society and the political economy of the media influence media content and, indirectly, audience responses.[1] Both are also implicitly committed to making sense of audience responses in terms of the wider flow and contraflow of meaning contested in society. Micro analysis is not seen as an end in itself, as a postmodernist celebration of the irreducible complexity of audience responses to the richly textured meanings of the media, but rather as an aid to understanding the place of the media within an inegalitarian social order.

To this can be added a fifth area of agreement. David Morley argues in his reply that I understate the contribution that 'the encounter with semiology' has made in cultural studies audience research. In retrospect, I think that he is right.

Core Difference

This said, there is clearly a basic disagreement between the respective positions we adopt. I allege that cultural studies audience research has rediscovered some of the central insights unveiled by a previous generation of effects researchers. In particular, that audiences are active and selective; that dissimilar groups respond to the same communication in different ways; and that these differences arise from the different values, attitudes and orientations of individual audience members, influenced by their socialization and membership of social networks.

This, David Morley argues, is based on a selective view of past communications research based on 'a particular (and partly unacknowledged) agenda' informed by 'the blind spots in Curran's analysis (Morley 1992: 334). Above all, my historical review is informed by '20/20 vision-in-hindsight' (p. 334), by an understanding of what is important in past research based on the revelations of current work. David Morley spells this out:

> However, my contention is that this is a particular history which could not have been written (by Curran or anyone else) fifteen years ago, before the impact of the 'new revisionism' (of which Curran is so critical) transformed our understanding of the field of audience research, and thus transformed our understanding of who and what is important in its history. I would argue that it is this transformation which has allowed a historian such as Curran to go back and re-read the history of communications research, in such a way as to give prominence to those whose work can now, with hindsight, be seen to have prefigured the work of these 'new revisionists' ... *Previously much of it was perceived as marginal to the central trajectory of mainstream communications research.*
>
> (p. 335, emphasis added)

We will come to Curran's secret agenda and blind spots in a moment. The point that David Morley makes about the selective nature of all histories is in a sense correct. But this is not the same as saying that all historical views are partial and therefore equally valid or invalid. Histories are also subject to evidential scrutiny. To put Morley's argument to the test, it is necessary to find out whether the work I cite really 'was perceived as marginal to the central trajectory of mainstream communications research', whether, as he puts it, I am merely 'quoting the work of hitherto neglected figures within the mainstream traditions of audience research'. Put simply, were the studies I cite regarded as important fifteen or more years ago, or have they been plucked from obscurity?

In 1975, Charles R. Wright published the second edition of *Mass Communication*. The book was published by Random House, and its previous edition had been reprinted frequently, with translations into Italian, Spanish, Portuguese and Japanese. It is as mainstream a book, in the context of its time, as it is possible to find. Yet, a content analysis reveals that no less than 75 per cent of the early audience studies published before 1975 that I review are also discussed by Wright (1975). The pioneer audience research that seemed to me significant was also judged to be important in a mainstream textbook published twenty years ago. This is a genuine coincidence since I cannot recall reading the second edition of Wright's book before. In effect, both Wright and myself were drawing upon a conventional identification of past landmark research that reflects a stable consensus in the field about what is important. Furthermore, the studies that do not overlap are certainly not obscure. For example, Hastorf and Cantril's intriguing study (1954), ignored by Wright (1975), has been reprinted in at least two anthologies (Schramm and Roberts 1974; Corner and Hawthorne 1993).

Thus, the works I discuss have not been found in the obscure byways of past communications research, and are not authored by 'hitherto neglected researchers'. Indeed, when David Morley comments that 'the history Curran offers us is an informative one, alerting us to the achievements of scholars whose work has gone unrecognized or neglected by many (myself included), thus far' (Morley 1992: 335), he is confirming indirectly what I am saying. Their work has not gone unrecognized. It has merely been neglected by cultural studies scholars engaged in audience research.

Curran's Blind Spots

This dispute is part of a wider debate about the nature of the transformation that is taking place in media and cultural studies. I argue that a mythologizing of the past is obscuring the way in which one strand within new audience research is in fact moving towards a classical liberal position. It substitutes liberal pluralism with postmodernist pluralism, overstates the autonomy of the audience, and overestimates the bottom-up power of the people. Indeed, in its Panglossian perception of the capacity of audiences to manipulate the media, it is reviving a discredited, received wisdom of the past. But I was careful to emphasize that revisionist audience research is not monolithic. As I explained (Curran 1990: 153), 'revisionist reception studies are not homogeneous. There are two distinctive tendencies', one a continuation of the radical tradition and the other converging towards a mainstream liberal perspective.

However, this argument is played back quite differently by David Morley. My criticism is portrayed as a broad-brushed and indiscriminate assault on all revisionist audience research which I hold 'necessarily involves a denial of media power' (Morley 1992: 329). Three different sentences are quoted in which a key qualifying phrase – 'in some studies', 'in some cases' and the ironic 'celebrants of semiotic democracy' – are deleted by David Morley (pp. 337, 333, 334). Having buried the distinction that I make within the revisionist tradition, David Morley then complains: 'Finally, it seems necessary to distinguish between the different traditions which Curran lumps together under the rubric of the "new revisionism"' (p. 337). There is a key difference, he proposes, between Fiskean and non-Fiskean perspectives. To which my response is quite so. If ever further evidence is needed to confirm the potential power of the 'reader' to regulate the meaning of texts, to override textual closures and defy signifying mechanisms – I am being facetious not rude – it is to be found in David Morley's eloquent riposte.

Significantly, David Morley seems to think that his own work is under *general* attack, as is clear from his revealing phrase, 'in Curran's view, "revisionists" (such as myself) ... ' (pp. 333–4). This is a misapprehension. While David Morley's grasp of communications history seems to me shaky, I also think that he has made communications history. His audience research, combined with textual analysis, exemplifies what is new and exciting about new audience work. When I wrote that 'the revisionist approach taken as a whole ... does focus more attention on the text, provides a much richer and fuller understanding of interdiscursive processes in audience reception and, above all, locates these in a more adequate sociological context' (p. 150), I had him particularly in mind.

Another of Curran's blind spots, we are told, is the way he unhelpfully 'blurs' together the Gramscian and Althusserian perspectives within the Marxist tradition. What I argue was that there was an 'uneasy synthesis' in the assimilation of their perspectives; that they had some themes in common; and that Althusser, though now remembered as a crude functionalist, advanced a key theme that contributed subsequently to the erosion of radical functionalism. In other words, there was a process of evolutionary continuity in the radical rethink that took place, not the sharp break that is now remembered. For evidence of this, one needs to turn to actual 'historical' sources, such as a series of brilliant articles by Stuart Hall (1977, 1982 and 1985), not faulty memory.

The argument about how change occurred is different from an argument about what that change was. David Morley is wrong when he says my 'analysis replicates the confusions' (Morley 1992: 336) of Abercrombie et al.'s critique (1980). In fact, the very opposite is the case. Abercrombie and his colleagues assimilated both Althusser and Gramsci as part of a continuum of Marxist thought characterized, they argue, by a common allegiance to a spurious concept of a 'dominant ideology'. However, I point out that Abercrombie et al.'s 'attack was anticipated [i.e. pre-emptively answered] in a reformulated theory of the media and society influenced by Gramsci ... This reformulation entailed rethinking the earlier radical paradigm' (Curran 1990: 142). This involved conceptualizing the dominant ideology as 'a "field" of dominant discourses, an unstable constellation of ideas and themes' in a context of unresolved struggle in which the media are reconceived as 'a site of contest between competing social forces rather than as a conduit for ruling-class ideas' (p. 142). It was these key arguments that represented a decisive break with Marxist functionalism.

Lastly, there is Curran's secret 'agenda' (or, more prosaically, point of view). My reading of communications research is allegedly designed to promote the merging of radical and liberal perspectives. In support of this argument, David Morley writes 'it is hardly incidental' that I co-edited a book supposedly 'structured around a set of arguments concerning the hypothetical "convergence"' (Morley 1992: 337) of radical and liberal research or that it included an essay by Ang and Hermes (1991) with which I am assumed to agree. I don't as it happens (though this did not seem grounds for excluding a clever and provocative essay). And the book I co-edited described recent trends in media studies in terms not of convergence but of reconfiguration: as we argued in the book's introduction,

> the result is a redefinition of the field in which the traditional dichotomy between neo-marxist and liberal-pluralist perspectives have become less salient and also less sharply defined, while other perspectives – notably feminism, theories of subjectivity and particularistic versions of pluralism – have gained increased prominence.
>
> (Curran and Gurevitch 1991: 8)

Description should not be confused with prescription. That my account of the new revisionism in the chapter above was not entirely celebratory was perhaps implicit in my tone of voice. But let me be explicit where I was only implicit. The rise of the new revisionism strikes me as being double-edged. On one hand, some of its key themes – its break with functionalism, its stress on the complex configuration of power in society, its attention to news-source conflict, its focus on tensions and ambiguities in texts, and its rediscovery of audience power – are all important and useful advances. They can potentially invigorate a radical understanding of the media.

On the other hand, there are also tendencies within the new revisionism which threaten to inflate worthwhile qualifications of the radical tradition into a fundamental negation of it. These tend to deny class power, dissolve patterned media representations into ambiguity, grossly overstate the power of the audience, and detach 'culture' from the economic and political process. There is also a growing tendency to focus on the particular in a way that obscures rather than illuminates the general.

In the face of this miniaturization of research, it is desirable to retain an awareness of inequality and repressed conflicts of interest in society. It is still relevant to investigate how unequal power relations, both in society and in the organization of the media, influence media representations and, indirectly audience responses to these. Above all, it is important to investigate how these relate in turn to the processes affecting the allocation of rewards in society. Drinking from the well of revisionism, without falling in, will help us do that – a view that, I suspect, David Morley shares.

Note

1 Had I written this chapter now rather than five years ago, I would have emphasized more the continued centrality of a radical political economy perspective.

References

Abercrombie, N., Hill, S. and Turner, B., 1980: *The Dominant Ideology Thesis.* London: Allen & Unwin.

ANG, I. and HERMES, J., 1991: 'Gender and/in Media Consumption', in J. Curran and M. Gurevitch (eds.) *Mass Media and Society*. London: Edward Arnold.

CORNER, J. and HAWTHORN, J. (eds.), 1993: *Communications Studies*, 4th edition. London: Edward Arnold.

CURRAN, J., 1990: 'The New Revisionism in Mass Communication Research: A Reappraisal', *European Journal of Communication*, 5.

CURRAN, J. and GUREVITCH, M., 1991: 'Introduction', in J. Curran and M. Gurevitch (eds.) *Mass Media and Society*. London: Edward Arnold.

HALL, S., 1977: 'Culture, the Media and the "Ideological Effect" ', in J. Curran, M. Gurevitch and J. Woollacott (eds.) *Mass Communication and Society*. London: Edward Arnold.

HALL, S., 1982: 'The Rediscovery of "Ideology": Return of the Repressed in Media Studies' in M. Gurevitch, T. Bennett, J. Curran and J. Woollacott (eds.) *Culture, Society and the Media*. London: Methuen.

HALL, S., 1985: 'Signification, Representation, Ideology: Althusser and the Post-structuralist Debates', *Critical Studies in Mass Communication*, 2. (Reprinted in this book).

HASTORF, A. and CANTRIL, H., 1954: 'They Saw a Game: A Case Study', *Journal of Abnormal and Social Psychology*, 49.

MORLEY, D., 1992: 'Populism, Revisionism and the "New" Audience Research', *Poetics*, 21.

SCHRAMM, W. and ROBERTS, D. (eds.), 1974: *The Process and Effects of Mass Communication*, revised edition. Urbana, IL: University of Illinois Press.

WRIGHT, C., 1975: *Mass Communication*, 2nd edition. New York: Random House.

13(ii)

Media Dialogue: Reading the Readings of the Readings ...

David Morley

> The answer is simple enough, this definition ... is *false* (that's right: false, not true) and feeble: it supposes a bad (that's right, bad, not good) and feeble reading of numerous texts, first of all mine, which therefore must finally be read or re-read.
>
> (Jacques Derrida, quoted in Norris 1991: 158)

Derrida's comments, quoted above, come from his acrimonious debate with John Searle, about deconstruction in philosophy and, in their concern for an exactitude of reading, may come as a surprise to those who normally associate Derrida with the wilder shores of 'anything goes' philosophical/literary theory. In my comments here, in response to James Curran's preceding text, I shall hope to avoid any such acrimony of tone, as I do quite share James's conviction that 'sharply expressed intellectual differences' should not necessarily 'fray the threads of friendship'. I believe, with Clifford Geertz, that the point of intellectual debate is to allow its participants to vex each other with ever-greater precision, precisely in order to ensure some measure of overall intellectual advance. Moreover, I would agree with Charlotte Brunsdon's (1995) comments, in her account of the conflicts surrounding the emergence of feminism within the Centre for Contemporary Cultural Studies (in Birmingham, during the late 1970s) concerning the importance of recognizing the very real difficulties involved in 'the arguing of positions'. Stuart Hall (1992) has argued that we should resist the temptation to gloss over the extent to which theoretical paradigms often (and necessarily) grow out of 'argument, unstable anxieties and angry silences' (Hall 1992: 278) or even 'theoretical noise' (p. 228). My ambition here is not to enter an embattled polemic with my 'opponent'. The potential absurdities of that route are already apparent – they necessarily involve my querying James's reading of my reading of his reading of my reading of the history of mass communications research! However, some element of that complexity is inevitable in my enterprise, as I do believe that James's particular narrative (cf. White 1987) of this history is compelled to blur certain real historical divisions and differences. This blurring is necessary in order to support his overall argument that the 'new revisionism' is largely 'rediscovering the wheel', through ignorance of earlier work in mass communications, whose (apparently superseded) insights it is merely 'reheating'.

In his 'Reply', James makes much of the fact that Wright's *Mass Communication*, republished in New York in 1975, does contain a summary of some of the mass communications audience work which I hold to have been largely marginalized – until the 'new revisionist' work on audiences of the mid-1980s forced a retrospective reassessment of the importance of this earlier work. Given that Wright's book is considered by James to be 'as mainstream a book . . . as it is possible to find', that book is offered as counter-evidence to my claim that the study of audiences was no more than a marginal area within mass communications, at this time.

I will leave aside the dangers of mounting an argument on the basis of a sample of one case. However, there is one (relatively minor) question, as to whether what is or was marginal in mass communications in the USA correlates well with that which is or was marginal in the UK. In that connection, I would argue that audience studies were *less* marginal in the USA than in the UK, because, in the USA, the field was less dominated by the particular brand of fundamentalist Marxist political economy that was dominant in the UK – which was fairly committed to the proposition that all that mattered were institutional and political structures of ownership and control (as they were understood to be determining of audience effects, which could therefore safely be 'deduced', without needing to be researched in detail).

My own 'content analysis' of the significant works published in this field, in the UK, prior to the impact of the 'new revisionism', tells a different story than James's: a story primarily of the *absence* of attention to the audience. Thus, for example, Cohen and Young's highly influential *The Manufacture of News* (1973) contains one article out of twenty-six on audiences; Davis and Walton's *Language, Image and the Media* (1983) contains one article out of fourteen (by myself) about audiences; Collins et al.'s *Media, Culture and Society: A Critical Reader* (1986) contains one such article, out of sixteen; Curran et al.'s own *Bending Reality: The State of the Media* (1986) contains none. Curran, Gurevitch and Woollacott's (eds.) original *Mass Communication and Society* (1977) contains rather little on audiences (apart from the useful, though speculative, historical debate between Adorno, Horkheimer and Benjamin, and one 'summary' piece by McQuail). However, Curran and Gurevitch's (1991) collection, *Mass Media and Society*, devotes most of its last section to debates within audience research. Something, it seems to me, *has* changed here (and these are *not* books within 'cultural studies' – they are, quite definitely, mainstream 'communications' texts, published in the UK). What has changed, in my view is, as I originally argued, that the study of audiences has now been 'demarginalized' within mass communications. Within UK media/mass communications studies it was, I still contend, until relatively recently, a marginal field.

Now, one response could be that, as someone more associated with that field than me, given my personal identification as a 'cultural studies' scholar, James is in a better position than I to give an authoritative account of developments in communications. To which I would respond (a) that my own sociological training and inclination has always positioned me at least as much within that field as within cultural studies and (b) that audiences have long been my specialism, while James's has been in questions of institutions and ownership; in terms of subject areas, I therefore am, in that respect, more authoritatively positioned. All of which, of course, rapidly descends into a tedium of claim and counter-claim. I could put it more simply, perhaps more autobiographically. If, as James asserts, the field of mass communications and media studies has long been well irrigated with pre-existing wisdom, concerning audiences, and had no significant need of the contribution of this upstart 'new revisionism'; and if (as I have been doing) I have been attending conferences and reading in this field, since 1972, how come I never come across the people who were representing this wisdom? Where were they? Why were their books not in the shops that I visited? How come I was so hard-pressed to find *anyone* to talk to about audiences, until the mid-1980s? Because, I contend, up to that point, as I argued above, British (at least) media/mass communications scholarship was almost exclusively obsessed with questions of economics and political regulation, while most cultural studies scholars were (equally unhelpfully, from my point of view) almost entirely preoccupied with questions of textual analysis, as they inhabited a theoretical framework in which textual determination was, for them, every bit as overbearing as economic determination was for the fundamentalist Marxists.

However, ultimately, I am not so much concerned with the question of whether James or I is right about this or that point of detail (important as the 'evidential scrutiny' of detail is). I was motivated to make the criticisms which I did of James's (Curran 1990) article because I saw it as an important part of a burgeoning tendency for mass communications scholars to attempt to 'write off' the significance of much cultural studies work on audiences, on the basis of the perceived weaknesses of *some* such work, which does (as I would readily agree) tend towards a romanticization of 'consumer freedoms/creativity'. James's article was initially published as the lead piece in a special issue of the *European Journal of Communication* (1990) and presented at a plenary session of the International Communications Association Conference in Dublin, in that year. To that extent, it functioned to set a particular 'tone', which then served to legitimate subsequent pieces (e.g. Seaman 1992) which took a quite dismissive view of the whole field of 'active audience theory', as 'pointless populism' (in Seaman's terms). To this extent, I was perhaps less concerned than I might have been to respond to all the nuances of James's original argument and more concerned to combat what I saw as the potentially pernicious effects of its overall tone and thrust – in dislodging the hard-won gains of several years of audience work (of admittedly uneven quality) within cultural studies.

Of late, a number of scholars (see Garnham 1995, for one example) principally associated with the mass communications perspective on these issues, within the UK, have been heard to evince arguments that, of course, they have *always* recognized that there was more to life than questions of class and economic determination; and that questions of culture and meaning have always been important to them; that, of course, questions of race, gender and sexuality have always been prominent; that, naturally, the analysis of low-status forms of fictional media production is just as important as that of news and current affairs television; that, of course, they have *never* thought of audiences as passive dupes or zombies. Tell it to the marines, say I. A look back at some of the early debates between these scholars and those working in cultural studies (see Murdock and Golding 1977; Connell 1978, 1983; Garnham 1983) shows quite a different story, in which all these things that now, it seems, mass communications scholars have 'long recognized' had, in fact, to be fought for inch by inch, and forced on to the agenda by those primarily within the cultural studies tradition, against the background of much wailing and gnashing of teeth, on the part of the political economists.

Hall (1995) argues for the benefits of a kind of productive eclecticism in intellectual work – a mode of selective, syncretic inclusiveness in which one attempts to take what is best from various intellectual traditions and work with those elements, towards new syntheses. This he poses as an alternative to a kind of all-or-nothing approach, in which one orthodoxy supersedes another, as guarantor of Truth, and everything that went before always has to be junked, in favour of the newest paradigm. As a student of Hall's, I have always felt that this was the best thing I ever learnt from him. It is precisely for this reason that the first section of the first chapter of my book *The Nationwide Audience* (reprinted in Morley 1992) is given over to quite a detailed account of the work of the earlier mass communications scholars on whom Hall, Ian Connell and I had drawn, in developing the theoretical framework for the *Nationwide* project. Thus, that chapter details our debts to the early work of Katz and Lazarsfeld, Merton, Kendall, Berelson, Riley and Riley, Bandura and Berkowitz and, indeed, the very same Charles Wright of whom James supposes us to have been ignorant. In the summary account of that project (Morley 1981) there is a lengthy exposition of the attempt we were making to take on board and synthesize insights from a range of previously developed perspectives – from sociology as much as from semiotics – and an account of how and why we felt that this new synthesis did, none the less, constitute an important break with traditional mass communications research, in various respects. In the context of this way of proceeding (and presenting) our work, I find James's claim that we somehow pretended to have 'invented' a new approach, *ex nihilo*, quite unsustainable.

There are, of course, many more minor issues which could perhaps be debated. If we are to trade claims of mutual 'ignorance', then I find, for example James's claim that Schlesinger's (1989) article constitutes a 'devastating Exocet' fired against Hall's work on broadcasting, really rather puzzling, as a quick look at Hall's (1973) paper 'The Structured Communication of Events', would clearly show that Hall pre-empts each one of the supposedly 'telling criticisms' that James supposes Schlesinger to have made. As to any misrepresentation, on my part, of James's position in relation to the difference (or lack of it) between Althusser and Gramsci: while on p. 142 (of the 1990 essay) he does attempt to distinguish them, by pp. 157–8 we find that the shift from one to the other 'was not as great a disjuncture as some have subsequently claimed' and even that 'the extent of the difference has been overstated for defensive reasons'. In relation to my point about the function of the essay by Ang and Hermes (1991) in the context of *Mass Media and Society*. I could perhaps put it better than I originally did, by saying that, high as my regard is for both Ang and Hermes's work, I do feel (and here they would probably both disagree with me) that there is a kind of 'elective affinity' of a problematic kind, between certain forms of post-structuralism, liberalism and methodological individualism. Perhaps my complaint here is really that the editorial in the collection does not, in my view, satisfactorily address this issue, though lurking in the background, there may even be a point, in this connection, where James and I would tend to agree about the limitations of some Foucauldian forms of cultural studies, and thus both disagree with Ang and Hermes.

I am accused of misquoting James, by omitting key qualifying phrases in my rendition of his arguments. Guilty as charged. However, in mitigation I would maintain that, in the overall context of his article, the qualifying phrases which I omitted are no more than polite 'hedges', of an insubstantial kind, and that overall, my quotes *do* fairly represent the essential thrust of his argument. And people who live in glass houses should be careful of transposing a 'partly unacknowledged' agenda into a 'secret' one, which seems to me to be a rather different matter (though perhaps I should have said 'unconscious' rather than 'unacknowledged'). Finally, the reader must judge for him or herself. We are each involved in 'glossing', and 're-presenting' our positions, claiming to 'make explicit what was only implicit' and, most contentiously of all, perhaps, even trying to explicate what might have been implicit in a 'tone of voice'. There we might enter the thorny fields of semiology, but perhaps we should save that for another occasion. At least, in this instance, the reader has at his/her disposal a significant part of the 'evidence' – in so far as each of these pieces functions as commentary on the preceding one, and is thus subject to the check of 'evidential scrutiny'. You are the jury, as they say on TV.

PS: And if, minimally, all of this encourages more people to go back and read (or re-read, even with new eyes) the history of audience research, then so much the better for the field.

References

ANG, I. and HERMES, J., 1991: 'Gender and/in Media Consumption', in J. Curran and M. Gurevitch (eds.) *Mass Media and Society*. London: Edward Arnold.

BRUNSDON, C., 1995: 'A Thief in the Night: Stories of Feminism in the 1970s at CCCS', in D. Morley and K.H. Chen (eds.) *Stuart Hall: Critical Dialogues in Cultural Studies*. London: Routledge.

COHEN, S. and YOUNG, J. (eds.), 1973: *The Manufacture of News: Social Problems, Deviance and the Mass Media*. London: Constable.

COLLINS, R. et al. (eds.), 1986: *Media, Culture and Society: A Critical Reader*. London: Sage.

CONNELL, I., 1978: 'Monopoly Capitalism and the Media', in S. Hibbin (ed.) *Politics, Ideology and the State*. London: Lawrence & Wishart.

CONNELL, I., 1983: 'Commercial Broadcasting and the British Left', *Screen*, 24 (6).

CURRAN, J., 1990: 'The "New Revisionism" in Mass Communication Research: A Reappraisal', *European Journal of Communication*, 5.

CURRAN, J. et al. (eds.), 1986: *Bending Reality: The State of the Media*. London: Pluto Press.

CURRAN, J., GUREVITCH, M. and WOOLLACOTT, J. (eds.), 1977: *Mass Communication and Society*. London: Edward Arnold.

CURRAN, J. and GUREVITCH, M. (eds.), 1991: *Mass Media and Society*, London: Edward Arnold.

DAVIS, H. and WALTON, P., 1983: *Language, Image, Media*. Oxford: Blackwell.

GARNHAM, N., 1983: 'Public Service Versus the Market', *Screen*, 24 (1).

Garnham, N., 1995: 'Political Economy and Cultural Studies: Reconciliation or Divorce?', in M. Ferguson and P. Golding (eds.) *Beyond Cultural Studies*. London: Sage.

Hall, S., 1973: *The Structured Communication of Events*. Paris: UNESCO.

Hall, S., 1992: 'Cultural Studies and its Theoretical Legacies', in L. Grossberg et al. (eds.) *Cultural Studies*, London: Routledge.

Hall, S., 1995: 'Cultural Studies and the Politics of Internationalism', in D. Morley and K.H. Chen (eds.) *Stuart Hall: Critical Dialogues in Cultural Studies*. London: Routledge.

Morley, D., 1981: 'Interpreting Television', Open University *Popular Culture* Course U203 Block 3. Milton Keynes: Open University Press.

Morley, D., 1992: *Television Audiences and Cultural Studies*. London: Routledge.

Murdock, G. and Golding, P., 1977: 'Capitalism, Communications and Class Relations', in J. Curran, M. Gurevitch and J. Woollacott (eds.) *Mass Media and Society*. London: Edward Arnold.

Norris, C., 1991: *Deconstruction: Theory and Practice*. London: Routledge.

Schlesinger, P., 1989: 'Rethinking the Sociology of Journalism', in M. Ferguson (ed.) *Public Communication*. London: Sage.

Seaman, W., 1992: 'Active Audience Theory: Pointless Populism', *Media, Culture and Society*, 14.

White, H., 1987: *The Content of the Form: Narrative Discourse and Historical Representation*. Baltimore, MD: Johns Hopkins University Press.

14

Feminism and Media Consumption

Christine Geraghty

This essay suggests a framework for feminist work on female consumers of film and television fiction since the publication of Laura Mulvey's influential and powerful essay on visual pleasure and Hollywood cinema in 1975. The range of work on female audiences is now extensive and complex and cannot be contained within a single history; I have chosen, therefore, to focus on certain key debates which I hope will provide a framework for students when they go on to read material which is not directly referred to here. This essay is constructed around two axes. First, there are the different histories and disciplines of work on the female consumer in film theory and in television studies, differences which have led critics to trace out markedly different trajectories for the two areas of study. Second, there are the double connotations of the word 'consumption' itself, associated on one hand with fictions 'consuming' and inappropriately absorbing the female reader and, on the other, with the reader deliberately choosing her own fictions, despite the condescending or critical attitude of those around her. To make this study manageable, I have chosen to look first at the work done on one set of images – the concept of the mother in film and television studies – and to use that figure to examine what is at stake when feminist criticism focuses on the female consumer. With this as a base, I shall outline some of the key issues around representation and identification, before concluding with some comments about the way in which film and television theory has worked with the notion of femininity and the implications of constructing women as audience.

Work on the relationship between text and audience has tended to emphasize the difference between television/viewers and film/spectators. Such a distinction has hinged on film theory's attachment to the concept of a spectatorial position created by the text and understood through psychoanalytic discourses; and work in television studies on the social context in which viewing of a particular programme takes place. Shaun Moores, for instance, in comparing work on cinema and television audiences, points to the lack of 'qualitative empirical work on the public settings of cinema spectatorship' and suggests that the explanation lies in the 'continuing influence of textual semiotics and psychoanalytical perspectives in film studies' (Moores 1993: 33). Jackie Stacey, whose work on film fans itself challenges the model, characterizes the feminine spectator of film studies as 'passive', 'unconscious' and 'pessimistic' in contrast with the viewer presented by the cultural studies/ television tradition as 'active', 'conscious' and 'optimistic' (Stacey 1994: 24).

I want to explore this distinction and how it has developed in relation to the female consumer, but I also want to work with concepts of representation and identification which, while they might be deployed in different ways, provide common ground and a shared history for the two traditions. It is no accident, for instance, that the figure of the mother features so strongly in work on film melodrama on one hand and television soap opera on the other, providing, in both instances, studies of how the female consumer of stories of a mother's position might understand and enjoy the fictions being offered. Work done on the mother then provides a concrete example of the way in which feminist work on the consumer has developed.

The Figure of the Mother

In film studies, as we shall see, Mulvey's original article had raised the question of the female spectator in the cinema despite the way in which she ignored it. Mulvey posited a male gaze and yet films were not male-only zones like pin-ups or striptease; women went to the cinema and certain genres seemed to be made specifically for them. Work on 'the woman's film' and the 'maternal melodrama' offered the opportunity to examine the nature of women's pleasure in films which, characteristically for a women's genre, tended to be dismissed as 'weepies'. In many of these films such as *Mildred Pierce* (Curtiz, US, 1945), both versions of *Imitations of Life* (Stahl, US, 1934 and Sirk, US, 1959) and *All that Heaven Allows* (Sirk, US, 1955), the mother's role was central to the narrative.

The debate around the figure of the mother in such films can be usefully exemplified by the exchange between E. Ann Kaplan and Linda Williams around the film *Stella Dallas* (Vidor, US, 1937). In 'The Case of the Missing Mother: Maternal Issues in Vidor's *Stella Dallas*' (1990), first published in 1983, and a later article, 'Mothering, Feminism and Representation' (1987), Kaplan outlines the way in which motherhood had developed as a discursive category in nineteenth- and twentieth-century fiction and in sociological and psychological work on mothering and childcare. She identifies the prevalence of themes of sacrifice and devotion, the lack of interest in the needs of the mother as compared with the child and the polarity, developed in Freudian theory, of figures of the Good and Bad Mother. She traces a developing tendency from the 1930s to blame the mother for the child's problems and argues that by the 1940s and 1950s the mother has herself become the problem; 'aberrations in the grown-up child are her fault' (Kaplan, 1987: 130). It is in this context that Kaplan discusses the representation of Stella Dallas, a working-class mother bringing up her daughter, Laurel, on her own; at the end of the film, Stella separates herself from her daughter so that Laurel can marry into the upper-class milieu which is more 'appropriate' for her needs. Kaplan suggests that the film criticizes Stella as being a mother who over-identifies with her child, a mother who seeks her own pleasure from mothering. Laurel's welfare can only be secured when the mutuality between mother and daughter is broken and Stella has learned the 'proper construction' (Kaplan 1990: 131) of motherhood, the willingness to sacrifice, to watch from a distance. This lesson is summed up for Kaplan in the film's final image of Stella, standing in the snow to watch through an uncurtained window her daughter's wedding. Kaplan suggests that, as the film works through its narrative, the audience's identification with Stella's resilience and her resistance to traditional modes of mothering is gradually eroded; the source and control of the way we look at Stella, the gaze, is aligned firmly to the position of the upper-class family who 'adopt' Laurel. 'As a Mother, Stella is no longer permitted to control her actions, or be the camera's eye', Kaplan suggests; instead we are invited to look at her as a spectacle 'produced by the upper-class disapproving gaze (a gaze that the audience is made to share through camera work and editing)' (Kaplan 1987: 133). Thus the woman is punished in the narrative by being separated from her child and in the visual structure by becoming the object of the gaze. The sacrifice is literally of the self as the 'Mother-as-spectator' becomes the 'Mother as absent' (Kaplan 1990: 134) and the audience, far from being closely bound to Stella's position, is forced to be distanced from it.

Linda Williams took issue with Kaplan's 1983 reading in her article, 'Something Else Besides a Mother': *Stella Dallas* and the maternal melodrama' (1987), first published in 1984. Williams suggested that *Stella Dallas* was of particular interest because it textually demanded 'a female reading competence' which derived from 'the different way women take on their identities under patriarchy and is a direct result of the social fact of female mothering' (Williams 1987: 305). Stella's excessive femininity and her gradual realization of how her mothering appears to other eyes (those of Laurel, of the upper-class Morrisons) does not so much transfer the gaze as make the spectator conscious of the different roles which women are called on to play as wife and/or mother. Williams goes on to argue that the 'definitive closure' (p. 319) of the ending does not result in a fixed position for the spectator; the spectator is neither totally caught up in Stella's weeping nor distanced from her by the mechanisms outlined by Kaplan. Instead Williams argues that the female spectator shares the emotions generated by Stella's loss but recognizes precisely the patriarchal construction which equates motherhood with sacrifice; she suggests that possibilities for resistance can be glimpsed in the exchanges between mother and daughter and argues that these are not wiped out by the ending. Instead she proposes that

> female spectators do not consent to such eradicating solutions ... It is a terrible underestimation of the female viewer to presume that she is wholly seduced by a naive belief in these masochistic images, that she has allowed these images to put her in her place the way the films themselves put their women characters in their place.
>
> (p. 320)

This cursory summary cannot do justice to the complex arguments about the film or indeed the film itself, but from it we can tease out some of the concerns of psychoanalytic feminist film criticism during this period. Firstly, this exchange indicates that the text is not a stand-alone object from which meaning can be read; both Kaplan and Williams try to place *Stella Dallas* in the context of generic and historical arguments about melodrama and the woman's film. There is also, however, a characteristic debate about the text, about how far the formal resolution of the film's ending ties up or resolves the ideological problems that have been raised, with Kaplan placing much more emphasis on the effectiveness of this closure. Additionally, questions of the accurate representation of women's lives are invoked, though they are addressed somewhat obliquely. Kaplan and Williams both see women's experience of motherhood as a factor in their position as spectators. The position from which the film can best be understood, for which it demands identification, is linked to the gaze of the camera but the question for debate is how far the character of Stella can speak to and for women because her position of mother is recognized by women in the audience who are thereby appealed to as more competent readers. Interestingly also, both Kaplan and Williams, though they differ in other respects, are concerned with issues of over-identification and avoid positing a female spectator who is stereotypically absorbed in the emotional impact of Stella's plight. Kaplan's argument is based on a shifting of sympathy away from Stella while Williams's suggests that the female spectator is aware that she cannot choose a single, absorbing viewpoint but 'must alternate a number of conflicting points of view, none of which can be satisfactorily reconciled' (Williams 1987: 317). For Williams, at least, distance appears to be a political position offering a means of escape from male rhetoric and the imposition of a fixed viewpoint. I will return to some of these issues after we have looked at the way in which the mother was conceptualized in feminist television writing.

Here I shall focus on the literature on soap opera mothers which is extensive – again I can only pick out a very limited number of instances. One striking contrast centres on the nature of the audience's possible identification with the mother figure. On one hand, there is the work on British realist soaps in which, as I suggest in *Women and Soap Opera*, the weakness of the male characters means that the mother is a strong and forceful character who 'takes on the burden of being both the moral and practical support to the family' (Geraghty 1991: 75). In this model, the mother is the prop of the family, sustaining it through an endless series of emotional and practical crises which the other members of the family look to her to resolve. These soap opera mothers of programmes such as *Brookside* and *EastEnders* do complain about their role and sometimes try to resist it but are almost inevitably brought back into a 'structural role of selfless support' (p. 79) which ensures that the family survives. In her struggle, the soap opera mother is frequently supported by female friends with whom she can share her fond contempt for the men of the family and, while her daughters can be a source of further problems, as they grow up and become mothers in turn, they also become part of the female-dominated structure. For women in the audience, it is suggested, 'the matriarchal soap' (p. 74) creates a private space in which women's emotional work and 'competencies' (Brunsdon 1981: 36) in maintaining relationships within families and between friends and neighbours can be recognized and valued.

In contrast and in looking at the different format of US daytime soaps, Tania Modleski suggested that identification with the mother as the heroine of the programme creates a viewing position in which the viewer and character share certain traditionally feminine qualities. The spectator of soap opera

> is constituted as a sort of ideal mother: a person who possesses greater wisdom than all her children, whose sympathy is large enough to encompass the conflicting claims of her family (she identifies with them all) and who has no demands or claims of her own (she identifies with no one character exclusively).
>
> (Modleski 1984: p. 92)

The good mother understands that there are no rigid rights and wrongs in the emotional situations with which she is confronted and is understanding and sympathetic to 'both the sinner and the victim' (p. 93). Modleski related the text to the viewing situation by suggesting that the formal rhythms of soap opera, with its interrupted stories, its manifold strands and its various appeals for attention, matched the rhythms of the housework and childcare being undertaken by the mother while she watched. She emphasized the way in which both soap opera and housework are undervalued and suggested that reasons for this lay in their strong association with femininity.

In different ways, this work on soaps constructs pleasures for the female audience from the text; others have used interviews and questionnaires as the basis for analysis of the soap opera audience. One example of such work would be that of the Tubingen Soap Opera Project team which conducted twenty-six interviews with soap opera viewers in Oregon and particularly looked at whether Modleski's soap opera spectator – the passive and sympathetic 'ideal mother' – might be discovered among these viewers. This audience-based work, reported on by Seiter and others (1991) in ' "Don't Treat Us Like We're So Stupid and Naive": Towards an Ethnography of Soap Opera Viewers', found that far from responding sympathetically to such characters, working-class women viewers, in particular, express 'outrage, anger, criticism, or a refusal to accept a character's problems' (p. 238). The characters who conformed to traditionally feminine models of sympathy and kindness were derided by some of the interviewees as 'whiners' and a number of others commented on 'their preference of strong villainesses' (p. 239). It is not clear from the account whether any of these villainesses were also (less than ideal) mothers but the authors are confident that these women viewers find impossible 'the limitless sympathy that Modleski's textual position demands' (p. 241). There was, however, some evidence that part of the pleasure of soaps lay in their 'potential for reaching out into the real world of the viewers' and while pleasure in unreal fictions was strong, so also was the fiction's applicability 'to their own private situations and to the social roles they were involved in' (p. 236).

These examples of work on the soap opera mother can be used to point to a number of general issues. Soap opera, like melodrama for the film theorists cited above, is understood to be a female genre, providing a format which speaks specifically to women. The domestic space in which the female viewer is addressed is deemed important even to the text-based writers who are concerned with how soap opera representations might function in the context of the private space of the home. Soaps are described as being centrally about personal relationships and emotional dramas which are marked as fictional but which relate to the lived experience of the women watching them. Thus, central to the debate are arguments about what kinds of representations (the mother, the villainess) are the strongest source of identification, what power the mother figure wields in the programmes, and how far representations of the mother can empower or sustain the female viewer. The nature of the involvement in what is being watched is also important: Modleski stresses the viewer's overwhelming sympathy with the moral dilemmas presented; others such as Brunsdon stress the way in which soaps engage the audience in the traditionally feminine pleasures of exploring emotional options while the Tubingen group emphasize the way in which their viewers showed both involvement and distance by shouting insults at characters they disliked. What is also striking here is how questions of methodology are brought to the fore. Modleski's textually based, psychoanalytical model is specifically challenged by the Tubingen group on the basis of their work with real viewers, though the limitations of that work ('The "whiner' came up repeatedly in our interviews with a group of six women' (Seiter et al. 1991: 238)) are not much emphasized.

This example of the way in which the mother has been identified and used in film and television studies is inevitably limited; it indicates, however, some of the key issues which arise in work on female consumption: issues around representation, identification, the construction of femininity and the nature of a female audience. It is to these more general issues that I now turn.

Representation

The initial concern for women looking at both film and television was with how women were (or were not) represented. What image were women being offered of themselves? Christine Gledhill (1984), in a crucial summary essay first published in 1978, drew attention to the argument that ' "women as women" are not represented in cinema' (Gledhill 1984: 18) and quoted Sharon Smith, an early contributor to *Women and Film* magazine: 'women, in any fully human form, have been almost completely left out of film' (p. 19). This initial concern was important in that it drew attention, very early on, to the question of women's relationship with their own images on the screen rather than, for instance, their possible pleasures in male stars. However differently inflected over the years, this emphasis on women looking at themselves has remained of consistent interest to feminist writers.

In film theory, the question appeared to be answered by rejecting the assumption that the cinema could offer women the truth of their own position and experience. As Claire Johnston put it, in her highly influential pamphlet *Notes on Women's Cinema* (1973), 'What the camera in fact grasps is the "natural" world of the dominant ideology . . . ; the "truth" of our oppression cannot be captured on celluloid with the "innocence" of the camera' (p. 28). Laura Mulvey (1975) drew on this notion that representation involved construction rather than revelation when she asked not only how were women represented in Hollywood films but for whom? Woman in film for Mulvey, as for Johnston, operated not as a representation of reality but as a symbol. The woman's image was a sign, a sign not for women but for men, a sign which indicated a fearful absence or lack which had to be remedied for the male viewer. The woman's image was created to serve male defence mechanisms against castration; the threat the woman posed through her difference, her lack of a penis, had to be disavowed through her representation as a fetishized object or deflected through the sadistic voyeurism which led in the end to her punishment. The cinematic look is thus based on the defensive need for the male spectator to deal with the sign 'woman' which confronts him with his own inadequacies. The text itself can therefore be best understood by the male spectator, a figure which refers to no actual audience member but to the theoretical position from which it can be best enjoyed. Mulvey, using carefully chosen examples from Hitchcock, Von Sternburg and *film noir*, marked out the way in which the male spectator is allowed to look at the woman but has that look hidden by the movement of the camera and the looks of the characters so that the male gaze becomes Cinema itself. It was this totalizing vision which was to inform feminist film theory for the next decade. It fascinated and infuriated feminists who responded to the bleak assessment of what women represented in Hollywood but could not concur with Mulvey's call to pull down the whole edifice.

In work on the representation of women on television, there was less concern with woman as a sign of male desires and a greater interest in the way in which representation interacted with the social experience of women viewers. This was partly because feminist writers concentrated on 'women's programmes' in which characters, it was argued, were constructed at least in part around female rather than male needs. The interest of British writers in soaps, for instance, had been sparked by an engagement with the strong, independent women whom they featured; Lovell commented that *Coronation Street*'s strong, independent, sexually active women who very often worked outside the home represented 'an important extension of the range of imagery which is offered to women within popular forms' (Lovell 1981: 52). Other work built up around television fiction which seemed to be offering women something new and different, such as the British series *Widows* and the US series, *Cagney and Lacey*, both of which used the 'male' thriller/ detective format to appeal to women. Feminist writers responded enthusiastically, if critically, to both series. Julie D'Acci linked *Cagney and Lacey*'s notorious production difficulties[1] to questions of representation and suggested that the programme's difficult history 'points to an extreme discomfort on the part of the network with "woman" as represented as non-glamorous, feminist, sexually active *and* working class and single' (D'Acci 1987: 214). *Widows* too was taken to offer, in Gillian Skirrow's words, 'the achievement of more equal – ie at least a wider variety of – representations of women on mainstream television' (Skirrow 1985: 175). What was valued in both programmes were representations of female friendships in a male world, an emphasis on the domestic and the personal and a change in point of view, whereby the male values in the police/ crime series were 'made strange' and the women were recognizable rather than threatening.

It is tempting to make of these different routes into questions of representation a dichotomy between fantasy and realism in which film studies work focused on the woman as sign in a male-dominated fantasy and television studies worked with representations which had their roots in notions of women's reality. An important feature of both film and television theory, however, is a clear emphasis on the construction of women characters and a refusal, even in television studies, to appeal to an unproblematic realism. The difference in approach, therefore, is based not so much on questions of representation but on possibilities of identification and audience address.

Identification

Questions of identification are central to discussions about the nature of the female consumer's involvement with representations. Does she identify on the basis of gender, with female characters, with recognizable situations? Is she tearful and absorbed or critical and detached? Can women use the images offered to them or are they inevitably overcome, taken over by them?

It was over the question of identification that the logic of the psychoanalytic position in film theory began to break down. What Mulvey had proposed was not just a spectator's position constructed through the film text but a gendered position which seemed to deny a position for the female spectator except, as Mulvey later suggested, in so far as she could identify with the male protagonist and view herself as spectacle. For others, the position of the female spectator was central. At issue in the debate between Kaplan and Williams were questions of whether women in the audience could identify with Stella and, if so, whether they were identifying with their own negation. Was women's identification inevitably masochistic or were there identifications which supported and empowered women? It was under the pressure of this debate that different views began to emerge.

Some saw possibilities in the very negativity of women's signification in film. Mary Ann Doane, Patricia Mellencamp and Linda Williams, writing as editors of *Revision*, an important collection of essays in feminist film criticism, published in 1984, confirmed their understanding of the shift that had taken place in feminist film criticism. This involved a move away from the demand for positive representation which looked for 'an affirmation of female subjectivity'; instead, they acknowledged that women's images in film could be read 'as metaphors of absence, lack and negativity' but declared some optimism about the possibilities for women of taking up negative positions of absence and lack since they were after all 'valorised one(s) ... within modern theories of signification' (Doane et al. 1984: 11). 'Difference as oppressive' could, following French feminists, become 'difference as liberating' (p. 12), a way of evading the rigid boundaries of patriarchal systems of signification which Mulvey had delineated in the Hollywood narrative film.

Perhaps the most bleak position can be represented by Mary Ann Doane, who made an important contribution, developed across a number of books and essays, in which she suggested that, as the male spectatorial position was marked by voyeurism and fetishism in a response to fears of castration, so the female position was determined by her different relationship to castration. She argued that for the girl there had been no point in trying to deny the reality of her lack of a penis and so the distancing mechanisms of fetishism and the sadistic need to punish implicit in voyeurism are not in place. Instead, she suggested that 'the female spectator's desire can be described only in terms of a kind of narcissism' (Doane 1990: 45) and over-identification. The female spectator wants both to become the image and to weep in identification with the predicaments of the women in the narrative. Thus, Doane argued that what was often taken as the essence of femininity in relation to fiction, 'a closeness, a nearness, as present-to-itself' is in cinema the psychic 'delineation of a place culturally assigned to the woman'(p. 54). Here, *par excellence*, was the female spectator who was over-absorbed in the fiction, consumed by the vision of herself as the Other, rendered defenceless by the paranoia which being looked at induced.

For others, the way out of the dilemma was to deny gender-specific identification and emphasize the play of different positions which could be taken up. Elizabeth Cowie (1988), for instance, argued against the idea that gender in spectatorship was based on a social position (man/woman) taken up before the film started, which determined a response; instead, she proposed a play of look and identification in which masculinity and femininity are not oppositions which fix the spectator but possibilities open to any spectator. Cowie indeed envisages a spectator who appears to be no longer gendered, a gaze which is no longer male and argues that 'there is no single or dominant "view" or look in cinema ... but a continual construction of looks' (p. 137). To look for any understanding of identification in the content of the film, in the character of the heroine or her dilemma, is thus a mistake: 'identification in cinema is a question of continually shifting construction of subject position' (p. 37). When Constance Penley summarizes this approach, specifically male and female viewing positions for Hollywood cinema seem to be disappearing: 'the value of such a model', she suggests, 'is that it leaves open the question of production of sexual difference in the film rather than assuming in advance the sexuality of the character or the spectator' (Penley 1988: 11).

It is sometimes assumed that the psychoanalytic position which emphasized the positioning of the spectator by the film ('Screen theory' as it is sometimes referred to (Morley 1992: 64)) was monolithic in film theory in the late 1970s and early 1980s. But it is important to recognize other voices which were struggling to be heard. Such critics were by no means always hostile to psychoanalysis but – through work on narrative, context and the material formation of women's experience – at least raised questions about how far psychoanalytic accounts could provide answers to the problems posed about the female spectator. Mary Ann Doane might propose that feminist film theory was concerned with the spectator as 'a concept, not a person' (Doane 1989:142) but the importance of understanding what 'a person' might mean was a refrain during the period. Gledhill suggested as early as 1978 that the female audience was not necessarily compelled by the image of the fetishized woman and that women might identify in other ways with the female image offered to them: 'they pick up codes in the construction of characters and of the female discourse which signal contradictory aspects in the determination of women'. She cited extra-cinematic factors such as 'socioeconomic factors, psychological elements, cultural attributes' (Gledhill 1984: 38) and suggested that these extra-cinematic factors draw on other discourses which are at stake when women watch film. The material effectivity of such discourses, she proposed, was not necessarily wiped out by the dominance of the narrative nor the limits of the spectating position.

Tentatively, work began to emerge which did emphasize the importance of extra-cinematic factors. For some British writers, for instance, consideration of the way in which British cinema had been involved during the Second World War in the construction of national identity offered the opportunity to consider the question of female spectatorship in a specific context. The BFI dossier *Gainsborough Melodramas* provides one example of this kind of work.[2] Pam Cook (1983), in her essay on the woman's picture, argued that any 'discussion of the Gainsborough women's pictures ... should recognise the historical specificity of this female audience as British and wartime or immediately postwar' (p. 21). Sue Harper (1987) extended this to argue that the Gainsborough costume melodrama required 'a high degree of audience creativity' from this historically specific audience, which involved reading against narratives which tended to close down on the heroine's options and instead to understand the meaning of the film through the sensual pleasures of clothes and decor. What is important here is the way in which Harper tried to locate her argument in an understanding of the female audience as socially constructed in the 1940s by the contradictory demands of war work, separated families and the constraints of rationing. Some of this is based on supposition ('Such a view would be compelling to a female workforce resenting its dungarees' (p. 188)) while some is based on Mass-Observation material on, for instance, women's views on costumes and stars ('The film in this survey is favoured by six times as many women as men' (p. 189)). My argument is not whether this historical referencing was successful but that it was done at all and that the specificity of 'this' female audience allowed Harper to challenge more universalist notions of film spectatorship: 'the cardinal sin of male scopophilia does not obtain here.' She concludes her discussion of the fans' identification; 'the female stars ... function as the source of the female gaze both on screen and in the audience' (p. 190).

Other examples could be cited of work which sought to be specific about the particular pleasures certain films offered to women as audiences in specific circumstances – Maria La Place's (1987) essay on *Now Voyager*, for instance, or the interest of Charlotte Brunsdon and others in the new woman's film of the 1970s. I am not claiming that such work was of the same volume or, indeed, was of equal weight with psychoanalytic work on the female spectator. What I would suggest, though, is that it is evidence, in film studies, of continuing concern that work on the possibilities of identification for women spectators should address women as something other than a textual position.

Work on questions of identification for the female television viewer began, as we saw earlier, from a rather different position on representation. Women characters on television were not merely signs of male desires and fear; there was the possibility (by no means always realized) of characters representing women viewers' desires and fears. This is not to say that feminist writers on television continued to demand 'real women' while film criticism moved on to more sophisticated epistemological approaches, but that writers on television worked less problematically with the concept of female spectatorship; television viewing, unlike television production, was not constituted as dominated by the male viewer since certain programmes – soaps – and certain scheduling slots – daytime – seemed to be aimed at women. Work on the television text for the female viewer therefore was able to escape the film theorist's angst over the theoretical possibility of a viewing position for women and concentrated on the pleasures which might be available to the viewers of particular texts.

In this context, the concept of identification in television viewing was developed in two ways.[3] Firstly, there was identification with particular characters – with, as we have seen, the strong independent women of *Coronation Street* or with the feisty and intelligent Cagney and Lacey. Identification, however, was not so much with characters, it was argued, as with the situation they were in. Thus, Danae Clark argued that *Cagney and Lacey*'s capacity to inspire identification lay 'beyond its presentation of a new or "better" image of women', in Cagney and Lacey's capacity to control narrative events and thus challenge 'the boundaries of patriarchal construction' (Clark 1990: 118). The friendship between the characters, the support they gave each other and the way in which their personal lives intertwined with their work were all seen as positive sources of pleasure. Thus, D'Acci points to 'the representation of friendship' between Chris Cagney and Mary Beth Lacey and suggests that it 'opens on to spaces of women's culture and women's communities' (D'Acci 1987: 124). Clark also suggests that 'a woman's space' is created where 'Cagney and Lacey speak to each other without male intervention and are free to explore and affirm the dimensions of female partnership' (Clark: 130).

But as Ien Ang argued, in her work on *Dallas*, apparently very negative representations of women and their situations could also be 'a source of identification and pleasure' (Ang 1990: 77). Ang comments on the way in which the two key women characters, Sue Ellen and Pamela, 'personify two feminine subject-positions which are the result of being trapped in an all-embracing patriarchal structure' (p. 130). She goes on to argue that the pessimism of these two identificatory positions should not be understood as necessarily anti-feminist or 'politically bad' (p. 134). She suggests that the identification with Sue Ellen, in particular, has to be understood in terms of what is under the surface; identification is thus 'connected with a basic if not articulated, awareness of the weighty pressure of reality on one's subjectivity, one's wishes, one's desires' (p. 86). For the woman viewer, then, identification with Sue Ellen can involve the pleasures of letting go, of abandoning the work of constructing the female/feminine self in recognition of the forces which make the task so difficult. Ang thus interestingly combines the notion of being consumed or taken over by a fiction with the concept of choice, whereby the viewer, by turning on the programme and settling down with the box of tissues, is selecting 'a secure space in which one can be excessively melodramatic without suffering the consequences' (p. 87).

The second form of identification stressed by television theorists is not so much with characters and situations but with the process of viewing itself. This is particularly associated with soap opera where Brunsdon, for instance, had identified soap opera viewing as an active process which involved filling in the gaps of the programme by mapping out and judging the moral dilemmas at the heart of the stories. She associated this process with culturally constructed gender positions because it required the possession of 'traditionally feminine competencies associated with the responsibility for "managing" the sphere of personal life' (Brunsdon 1981: 36). The activity of viewing promoted 'informed speculation among the audience' (Geraghty 1981: 25) and the Tubingen Soap Opera Project team found 'in interviews over and over again ... that soap opera texts are products not of individual and isolated reading but of collective constructions – collaborative readings ... of small social groups' (Seiter et al. 1991: 233).

This kind of active, social identification was also seen as characteristic of women's viewing of programmes other than soaps. Clark suggested that 'the "fierce identification" experienced by [*Cagney and Lacey*]'s female viewers may derive from their participation in and empowerment by the show's discursive strategies' (Clark 1990: 118); Dorothy Hobson noted more generally the way in which, in a female-dominated workplace, 'discussion of television programmes ... completes the process of communication' (Hobson 1990: 62) and the tendency of women in the workplace she studied to 'extend the conversation to discuss what they would do if they were in the same circumstances' (p. 64).

In presenting her work, Hobson is concerned to reveal the importance and value of talk which might otherwise be dismissed as gossip or 'having a laugh' (p. 61). The account of the way in which they work and talk is intended to reveal 'the way that women bring their feminine characteristics to their work situation' (p. 62). This desire to represent women's activities and attributes which have been constructed as particularly feminine in a more positive light is a key characteristic of feminist writing on female consumption and it is to this I wish to turn in the final section.

Femininity and Consumption

I have traced out the different trajectories which have informed feminist work on film and television and which are now referred to, for instance, in the distinction between 'spectator' and 'viewer'. Nevertheless, this work of the 1970s and 1980s was being conducted in a common space defined by feminism, which meant that certain characteristics were shared even if, at some quite critical moments, these common features were somewhat submerged. This section will therefore look at some concepts which the different approaches to female consumption seem to share, concepts which offer possibilities and problems for both.

Perhaps the most striking feature of the debate on the meaning of women's consumption has been the turnabout in attitudes to traditional femininity and to texts which seem to call on femininity as the basis for pleasure. The developments in film theory which I have described above were crucial in shifting feminist theory away from a concern that Hollywood had presented only negative and demeaning stereotypes of women.[4] In both film and television studies, this break enabled a move away from 'images of women' to 'increased concentration on images for women' (Brunsdon 1991b: 365). In both cases, though in different ways, this allowed a shift from the notion that female characters operated as a model for women in the audience to a consideration of the broader processes through which femininity is constructed for and by women through such figures as the mother. This is not to say that the notion of a model disappeared. In some of the work on women's identification with female characters, concerns are at least implicitly expressed about the kind of example such characters were providing. On one hand, the model could be one which emphasized female virtues of strength and resilience, commitment to friendship and sensitivity to the feelings of others. This figure is of importance, as we have seen, in work on *Cagney and Lacey* and soap opera's independent women. As a model it also implied its opposite, the negative image of feminine vices such as an over-reliance on men, a propensity for self-sacrifice to family needs and an over-investment in personal relationships. This notion of a negative image is one factor in the debates over the meaning of the mother in *Stella Dallas*. The continuance of this strand remains an important link between theoretical work and broader feminist activity about, for instance, women's access to the media.

Nevertheless, much of the feminist work I have described in both film and television has been concerned to rework this split between good and bad models and rethink it in terms of the fictional expression of women's position as it is constructed through contradictory demands inside and outside the text. What has emerged is not so much a notion of a textual point of view in the film studies tradition but a woman's viewpoint constructed through the textual conventions of narrative, camera work and style, and also through the pressures of femininity on the consumer brought to bear by a much wider set of experiences. In film studies, this was developed with some difficulty, but it seems to me that the notion of a woman's viewpoint lies behind the speed with which the theory of the male gaze was transformed into a puzzle about what women's position could be, the desire almost that it should be there; and the possibility of female positions based, in part at least, on the social experience of being mothers and/or daughters is at stake in Williams's debate with Kaplan over *Stella Dallas*; it is also asserted by Harper in her defence of Gainsborough melodramas. In television studies, the possibility of a woman's viewpoint was often expressed more overtly in, for instance, Clark's claim that 'the knowledge and experience they [women viewers] do have as women allows them to identify with discussions' (Clark 1990: 122) which Cagney and Lacey have about what decisions they should make; it lies also behind Ang's assessment of Sue Ellen's appeal to her viewers based on the expression of feminine, or indeed feminist, feelings of frustration.

This shift from what an image did to women to what women could do with women's images allowed for a more complex attitude to femininity; in this approach, the traditional feminine sphere of the private and domestic was recognized as being both culturally constructed and lived by women in different ways. It was also recognized that women's work in maintaining the emotional and physical fabric of domestic life was widely disparaged. Part of the task in film and television studies during the 1980s was, therefore, to assert the importance of women's emotional work and recognize the way in which women's genres, pre-eminently melodrama and soap opera, could give voice to their experiences. These genres did not just provide models for identification; they also allowed for expression of complex feelings about the tasks demanded of women in their social positions as mothers, wives, daughters, friends.

This was accompanied by a growing emphasis on giving women a voice not just through the text but as audience, a factor which can be seen in some 'ethnographic' work. Dorothy Hobson bases her article, 'Women Audiences and the Workplace', on one woman's description of the viewing practices of women in her office. Hobson emphasizes her concern to let Jacqui's 'words predominate here because it is these women's experiences that she is relating – her narrative of their narratives within their working days' (Hobson 1990: 71). Jackie Stacey quotes extensively from the female film fans who responded to her questions and suggests that 'our understanding of female spectatorship' might 'be transformed by [their] accounts' (Stacey 1994: 9). In addition, feminist writers involved in such studies, while acknowledging their privileged position as academic researchers, have drawn on their own experiences of femininity to establish a level of 'identification' (Gray 1992: 34) with their women interviewees. Thus, Stacey begins her book *Star Gazing*, with an analysis of a photograph capturing her own teenage attempt to emulate Hollywood glamour. The Tubingen Soap Opera Project team, in reflecting on their interviews, felt that gender had provided a common ground which enabled their interviewees to share their experiences: 'If our identification as academics, foreigners and employers placed us in the category of "other", gender provided a position of "sameness" in relation to informants' (Seiter et al. 1991: 243). Ann Gray, discussing her working methods for interviewing women for *Video Playtime*, comments that she identified with some of the women whom she interviewed and considers that this 'shared position', based on similar experiences of being positioned through schooling, family and marriage as a feminine subject, was 'quite crucial to the quality of the conversations' she had (Gray 1992: 34).

This feminist approach of identifying in some way with female consumption, of seeking a shared position between audience and critic based on sharing the pressures and pleasures of 'we women' (Brunsdon 1991a: 124), has been important in the project of rescuing or, in Brunsdon's term, redeeming (p. 121) both feminine texts and the female audience. This has been reinforced by the emphasis on pleasure, on analysing but not condemning the pleasure available to female consumers of such texts. Mulvey's article was, it should be noted, about pleasure and it was precisely the question of women's pleasure (of what kind? in what? how?) which underpinned studies as different, for instance, as Doane's *The Desire to Desire* (1987) and Hobson's *Crossroads* (1982). As this work developed, the tendency has been to emphasize what is positive for women about their absorption in, for example, soap operas – as I do, for instance, in *Women and Soap Opera* (Geraghty 1991) – or in Hollywood melodramas – as Byars does in *All that Hollywood Allows* (1991). Absorption in consumption and the detachment implied by the act of choosing are thus presented not as opposites but as complex aspects of the pleasures of female consumption.

This emphasis on shared pleasures, on positive engagement by female consumers with texts and on the complexity of the female consumer's relationship with 'her' genres raises further questions, however, about how far it is possible in these postmodernist times to speak of positions and identities which are so strongly gendered. Throughout the writing I have described, one feels the tension between writing for and about the female consumer (as academic, as film lover, as soap opera fan) and maintaining an awareness of 'woman' as a constructed position. The editors of *Revision* warned that 'an attempt to delineate a feminine specificity' ran the risk of 'a recapitulation of patriarchal constructions and a naturalisation of "woman"' (Doane et al. 1984: 9) while Julie D'Acci precisely tries to denaturalize the relationship between *Cagney and Lacey* and its fans by stressing the way in which 'several discourses and discursive practices ... construct a variety of interpretations of the characters, a general discourse of multiple definitions of 'woman' and 'femininity' as well as a woman's audience for the series' (D'Acci 1987: 203–4). A further dimension has been added with the development of work with audiences, with its apparent promise of the truth emerging out of the mouths of real women, of the Oregon viewers refuting Modleski's textual claims by refusing to stand in position. Ien Ang and Joke Hermes (1991) have queried how far gender can still function as a stable mark of difference on which understanding and pleasure can be predicated. In some senses, this recalls Cowie's insistence that gender cannot be fixed nor positions gendered; and, as Ann Gray has argued, it also undermines the intellectual and political drive in much of the work I have discussed to show the way in which gender differences and commonalities can form 'the basis of social critique' (Gray 1992: 31).

There is evidence that the links between film and television studies are being made and that new work on gender and consumption will develop from this. Jackie Byars's *All that Hollywood Allows* (1991), for example, criticizes the dominant Lacanian psychoanalytic approach in film studies and asserts the possibility of a female look; Jane Gaines (1990) has pointed to the denial of race and class as factors in film theories of spectatorship; Charlotte Brunsdon (1991a) has questioned the shift from text to audience characteristic of television studies while Jackie Stacey's *Star Gazing* (1994) adopts an audience-based approach in order to pursue her analysis of women fans' identification with female Hollywood stars. The outline I have been able to give has been limited, and much recent work has explored avenues which I have not addressed – the interest in constructions of masculinity and the male body, for instance, or in women's involvement in non-female genres such as horror films. In addition, the feminism which underpinned the work I have described has been challenged for its tendency to assume commonalities on the basis of gender and thus override other factors which construct identity. So far as future work is concerned, however, I will make only two points in conclusion. First, it seems important that future work should be able to hold on to the possibilities of change for women and that work on femininity should not fall into the trap of accepting its limitations. Second, there is surely a gender split in current work on female consumption. Ann Gray (1992) asked the women in her study to label domestic technology in shades of pink and blue, depending on who used it or controlled it. Not surprisingly, the washing machine tended to be pink and the VCR blue. Should we be more surprised to find that in media theory issues of consumption, audience and pleasure are relatively pink but work on media ownership, control and regulation is deepest indigo? It may be that in order to understand women's consumption fully women need to overcome their feminine technophobia and wrestle these toys also off the boys.

Notes

1 These difficulties included two changes in actress for the character of Cagney and CBS's threat to cancel the show during its first series. For details, see D'Acci (1987) and (1994).

2 See Hurd (1984) for other essays on British films of the Second World War.

3 Psychoanalytically based work on television has of course continued. See, for instance, Mellencamp (1990) for examples of such work.

4 This is the approach adopted by Mollie Haskell (1975) and Marjorie Rosen (1973) in their discussion of Hollywood cinema.

References

Ang. I., 1990: 'Melodramatic Identifications: Television Fiction and Women's Fantasy', in M.E. Brown (ed.) *Television and Women's Culture*. London: Sage.

Ang, I. and Hermes, J., 1991: 'Gender and/in Media Consumption', in J. Curran and M. Gurevitch (eds.) *Mass Media and Society*. London: Edward Arnold.

Brunsdon, C., 1981: '*Crossroads*: Notes on Soap Opera', *Screen*, 22 (4).

Brunsdon, C., 1991a: 'Text and Audience', in E. Seiter, H. Borchers, G. Kreutzner and E. Warth (eds.) *Remote Control*. London: Routledge.

Brunsdon, C., 1991b: 'Pedagogies of the Feminine: Feminist Teaching and Women's Genres', *Screen*, 32 (4).

Byars, J., 1991: *All that Hollywood Allows*. London: Routledge.

Clark, D., 1990: '*Cagney and Lacey*: Feminist Strategies of Detection', in M.E. Brown (ed.) *Television and Women's Culture*. London: Sage.

Cook, P., 1983: 'Melodrama and the Woman's Picture', in S. Aspinall and R. Murphy (eds.) *Gainsborough Melodramas*. London: British Film Institute.

Cowie, E., 1988: 'The Popular Film as a Progressive Text: A Discussion of *Coma*', in C. Penley (ed.) *Feminism and Film Theory*. London: British Film Institute/ Routledge.

D'Acci, J., 1987: 'The Case of *Cagney and Lacey*', in H. Baher and G. Dyer (eds.) *Boxed In: Women and Television*. London: Pandora.

D'Acci, J., 1994: *Defining Women: Television and the Case of Cagney and Lacey*. Chapel Hill, NC: University of North Carolina Press.

Doane, M., 1987: *The Desire to Desire*. Bloomington, IN: Indiana University Press.

Doane, M., 1989: untitled entry. *Camera Obscura*, 20/21.

Doane, M., 1990: 'Film and the Masquerade', in P. Erens (ed.) *Issues in Feminist Film Theory*. Bloomington, IN: Indiana University Press.

Doane, M., Mellencamp, P. and Williams, L. (eds.), 1984: *Revision Essays in Feminist Film Criticism*. University Publications of America.

Gaines, J., 1990: 'White Privilege and Looking Relations: Race and Gender in Feminist Film Theory', in P. Erens (ed.) *Issues in Feminist Film Theory*, Bloomington, IN: Indiana University Press.

Geraghty, C., 1981 'The Continuous Serial – a Definition' in R. Dyer (ed.) *Coronation Street*. London: British Film Institute.

Geraghty, C., 1991: *Women and Soap Opera*. Cambridge: Polity Press.

Gledhill, C., 1984: 'Developments in Feminist Film Criticism', in M. Doane, P. Mellencamp and L. Williams (eds.) *Revision Essays in Feminist Film Criticism*. University Publications of America.

Gray, A., 1992: *Video Playtime*. London: Routledge.

Harper, S., 1987: 'Historical Pleasures: Gainsborough Costume Melodrama', in C. Gledhill (ed.) *Home is Where the Heart is*. London: British Film Institute.

HASKELL, M., 1975: *From Reverence to Rape: The treatment of women in the movies*. London: New English Library.
HOBSON, D., 1982: *'Crossroads': The Drama of a Soap Opera*. London: Methuen.
HOBSON, D., 1990: 'Women Audiences and the Workplace', in M.E. Brown, (ed.) *Television and Women's Culture*. London: Sage.
HURD, G. (ed.), 1984: *National Fictions*. London: British Film Institute.
JOHNSTON, C., 1973: 'Women's Cinema as Counter Cinema', in C. Johnston (ed.) *Notes on Women's Cinema*. London: Society for Education in Film and Television.
KAPLAN, E.A., 1987: 'Mothering, Feminism and Representation: The Maternal in Melodrama and the Woman's Film 1910–40', in C. Gledhill (ed.) *Home is Where the Heart is*. London: British Film Institute.
KAPLAN, E.A., 1990: 'The Case of the Missing Mother: Maternal Issues in Vidor's *Stella Dallas*', in P. Erens (ed.) *Issues in Feminist Film Theory*. Bloomington, IN: Indiana University Press.
LA PLACE, M., 1987: 'Producing and Consuming the Woman's Film', in C. Gledhill (ed.) *Home is Where the Heart is*. London: British Film Institute.
LOVELL, T., 1981: 'Ideology and *Coronation Street*', in R. Dyer (ed.) *Coronation Street*. London: British Film Institute.
MELLENCAMP, P. (ed.), 1990: *Logics of Television*. London: British Film Institute.
MODLESKI, T., 1984: *Loving with a Vengeance*. London: Methuen.
MOORES, S., 1993: *Interpreting Audiences*. London: Sage.
MORLEY, D., 1992: *Television, Audiences and Cultural Studies*. London: Routledge.
MULVEY, L., 1975: 'Visual Pleasure and Narrative Cinema', *Screen*, 16 (2).
PENLEY, C., 1988: *Feminism and Film Theory*. London: Routledge.
ROSEN, M., 1973: *Popcorn Venus: Women, Movies and the American Dream*. New York: Coward McCann & Geoghegan.
SEITER, E., BORCHERS, H., KREUTZNER, G. and WARTH, E., 1991: ' "Don't Treat Us Like We're so Stupid and Naive": Towards an Ethnography of Soap Opera Viewers', in E. Seiter, H. Brochers, G. Kreutzner and E. Warth (eds.) *Remote Control*. London: Routledge.
SKIRROW, G., 1985: '*Widows*', in M. Alvarado and J. Stewart (eds.) *Made for Television: Euston Films Limited*. London: British Film Institute.
STACEY, J., 1994: *Star Gazing*. London: Routledge.
WILLIAMS, L., 1987: ' "Something else besides a mother" *Stella Dallas* and the Maternal Melodrama', in C. Gledhill (ed.) *Home is Where the Heart is*. London: British Film Institute.

15

Popular Culture and the Eroticization of Little Girls

Valerie Walkerdine

If studies of popular culture have largely ignored young children and studies of girls are limited to teenagers, the topic of popular portrayals of little girls as eroticized – little girls and sexuality – is an issue which touches on a number of very difficult, and often taboo areas. Feminism has had little to say about little girls, except through studies of socialization and sex-role stereotyping. With regard to sexuality, almost all attention has been focused on adult women. Little girls enter debates about women's memories of their own girlhood in the main: discussions of little girls' fantasies of sex with their fathers or adult men; as in Freud's Dora case, the debate surrounding Masson's claim that Freud had suppressed the evidence that many of his female patients had been sexually abused as children; and of course, the discourse of abuse itself. The topic of little girls and sexuality has come to be seen, then, as being about the problem of the sexual abuse of innocent and vulnerable girls by bad adult men, or conversely, less politically correct but no less present, the idea of little girls as little seductresses, who in the words of one judge in a child abuse case are 'no angel[s]'. I want to open up a set of issues that I believe are occluded by such debates. That is, in short, the ubiquitous eroticization of little girls in the popular media and the just as ubiquitous ignorance and denial of this phenomenon.

Childhood Innocence and Little Lolitas

Janie is six. In the classroom she sits almost silently well behaved, the epitome of the hard-working girl, so often scorned as uninteresting in the educational literature on girls' attainment (Walkerdine 1989). She says very little and appears to be constantly aware of being watched and herself watches the model that she presents to her teacher and classmates, as well as to myself, seated in a corner of the classroom, making an audio recording. She always presents immaculate work and is used to getting very high marks. She asks to go to the toilet and leaves the classroom. As she is wearing a radio microphone

I hear her cross the hall in which a class is doing music and movement to a radio programme: the teacher tells them to pretend to be bunnies. She leaves the hall and enters the silence of the toilets and in there, alone, she sings loudly to herself. I imagine her swaying in front of the mirror. The song that she sings is one on the lips of many of the girls at the time I was making the recordings: Toni Basil's 'Oh Mickey'.

'Oh Mickey' is a song sung by a woman dressed as a teenager. In the promotional video for the song she wears a cheerleader's outfit, complete with very short skirt and is surrounded by large, butch-looking women cheerleaders who conspire to make her look both smaller and more feminine. 'Oh Mickey, you're so fine, you're so fine, you blow my mind', she sings. 'Give it to me, give it to me, any way you can, give it to me, give it to me, I'll take it like a man'. What does it mean for a six-year-old girl to sing these highly erotic lyrics? It could be argued that what we have here is the intrusion of adult sexuality into the innocent world of childhood. Or indeed, that because she is only six, such lyrics do not count because she is incapable of understanding them. I shall explore the issue of childhood innocence in more detail, and rather than attempting to dismiss the issue of the meaning of the lyrics as irrelevant, I shall try to place these meanings in the overall study of little girls and sexuality. In moving out of the public and highly supervised space of the classroom, where she is a 'good, well-behaved girl', to the private space of the toilets she enters a quite different discursive space, the space of the little Lolita, the sexual little girl, who cannot be revealed to the cosy sanitized classroom. She shifts in this move from innocent to sexual, from virgin to whore, from child to little woman, from good to bad. Is this one more place of the corruption of the young through imitation (*pace* the literature on children, television and violence for example)? Or do we have to try to tell a different kind of story, one that differs quite markedly from those previous stories of little girls and tries to intervene into the ponderous silence within feminism and cultural studies.

Children and the Popular

Cultural studies has had almost nothing to say about young children. Its agenda has been concerned primarily with male and later female youth. It is not surprising that this should have been so, given the concern of such work with the issue of resistance: if teenage girls had to struggle to gain a place (McRobbie 1980), tiny tots certainly come low in the resistance stakes! However, media studies by comparison, together with developmental and social psychology as well as education, have been fairly obsessed with children's viewing of television, especially with respect to sex and violence, though these disciplines have had nothing to say about children's consumption and engagement with other forms and aspects of popular culture. I shall return to the issue of television by examining the case of a moral panic in the 1980s about the Channel 4 series *Minipops*. But, I want to begin by examining some central issues about conceptions of childhood.

I want to explore some of the 'gazes' at the little girl, the ways that she is inscribed in a number of competing discourses. In this chapter I will concentrate on the figure of the little girl as an object of psycho-pedagogic discourse and as the eroticized child-woman of popular culture. I have written extensively elsewhere about psychology and education's production of 'the child' as what Foucault has termed a 'fiction functioning in truth' (Walkerdine 1984, 1988, 1989, 1992, 1993). I have argued that 'the nature of the child' is not discovered but produced in regimes of truth created in those very practices which proclaim the child in all his naturalness. I write 'his' advisedly, because a central plank of my argument has been that although this child is taken to be gender-neutral, actually he is always figured as a boy, a boy who is playful, creative, naughty, rule-breaking, rational. The figure of the girl, by contrast, suggests an unnatural pathology: she works to the child's play, she follows rules to his breaking of them, she is good, well behaved and irrational. Femininity becomes the Other of rational childhood. If she is everything that the child is not supposed to be, it follows that her presence, where it displays the above attributes may be considered to demonstrate a pathological development, an improper childhood, a danger or threat to what is normal and natural. However, attempts (and they are legion) to transform her into the model playful child often come up against a set of discursive barriers: a playful and assertive girl may be understood as forward, uppity, over-mature, too precocious (in one study a primary teacher called such a ten-year-old girl a 'madam': see Walkerdine 1989). Empirically then, 'girls' like 'children' are not discovered in a natural state. What is found to be the case by teachers, parents and others is the result of complex processes of subjectification (Henriques et al. 1984). Yet, while this model of girlhood is at once pathologized, it is also needed: the good and hard-working girl who follows the rules prefigures the nurturant mother figure, who uses her irrationality to safeguard rationality, to allow it to develop (Walkerdine and Lucey 1989). Consider then the threat to the natural child posed by the eroticized child, the little Lolita, the girl who presents as a little woman, but not of the nurturant kind, but the seductress, the unsanitized whore to the good girl's virgin. It is my contention that popular culture lets this figure into the sanitized space of natural childhood, a space from which it must be guarded and kept at all costs. What is being kept out and what safe inside this fictional space?

The discourses of natural childhood build upon a model of naturally occurring rationality, itself echoing the idea of childhood as an unsullied and innocent state, free from the interference of adults. The very cognitivism of most models of childhood as they have been incorporated into educational practices, leaves both emotionality and sexuality to one side. Although Freud posited a notion of childhood sexuality which has been very pervasive, it was rather concepts like repression and the problems of adult interference in development which became incorporated into educational practices rather than any notion of sexuality in children as a given or natural phenomenon. Indeed, it is precisely the idea that sexuality is an adult notion which sullies the safe innocence of a childhood free to emerge inside the primary classroom, which is most important. Adult sexuality interferes with the uniqueness of childhood, its stages of development. Popular culture then, in so far as it presents the intrusion of adult sexuality into the sanitized space of childhood, is understood as very harmful.

Visually these positions can be distinguished by a number of gazes at the little girl. Psychopedagogic images are presented in two ways: the fly-on-the-wall documentary photograph in which the young girl is seen always engaged in some educational activity and is never shown looking at the camera, and the cartoon-type book illustration in which she appears as a smiley-faced rounded (but certainly not curvy) unisex figure. If we begin to explore popular images of little girls they present a stark contrast. I do not have room in this piece to explore this issue in detail, but simply let me make reference to newspaper and magazine fashion shots, recent television advertisements, for example for Volkswagen cars, Yoplait yoghurt and Kodak Gold film. All present the highly eroticized alluring little girl, often (at least in all three TV ads) with fair hair and ringlets, usually made up and with a look which seductively returns the gaze of the camera. Indeed, such shots bear far more similarity with images taken from child pornography than they do with psychoeducational images. However, the popular advertisement and fashion images are ubiquitous: they are an everyday part of our culture and have certainly not been equated with child pornography.

It would not be difficult to make out a case that such images are the soft porn of child pornography and that they exploit childhood by introducing adult sexuality into childhood innocence. In that sense then, they could be understood as the precursor to child sexual abuse in the way that pornography has been understood by some feminists as the precursor to rape. However, I feel that such an interpretation is over-simplistic. The eroticization of little girls is a complex phenomenon, in which a certain aspect of feminine sexuality and childhood sexuality is understood as corrupting of an innocent state. The blame is laid both at the door of abusive and therefore pathological and bad men who enter and sully the terrain of childhood innocence; and of course conversely, with the little Lolitas who lead men on. But popular images of little girls as alluring and seductive, at once innocent and highly erotic, are contained in the most respectable and mundane of locations: broadsheet newspapers, women's magazines, television adverts. The phenomenon that we are talking about therefore has to be far more pervasive than a rotten apple, pathological and bad abusive men approach. This is not about a few perverts, but about the complex construction of the highly contradictory gaze at little girls, one which places them as at once threatening and sustaining rationality, little virgins that might be whores, to be protected yet to be constantly alluring. The complexity of this phenomenon, in terms of both the cultural production of little girls as these ambivalent objects and the way in which little girls themselves as well as adults live this complexity, how it produces their subjectivity, has not begun to be explored.

I want to point to a number of ways in which this issue can be fruitfully examined (all of which are developed in Walkerdine, in press).

Eroticized Femininity and the Working-Class Girl

Let us return to Janie and her clandestine singing. I have been at some pains to point out that Janie presents to the public world of the classroom the face of hard-working diligent femininity, which, while pathologized, is still desired. She reserves the less acceptable face of femininity for more private spaces. I imagine her dancing as she sings in front of the mirror: this act can be understood as an acting out, a fantasizing of the possibility of being someone or something else. I want to draw attention to the contradictions in the way in which the eroticized child-woman is a position presented publicly for the little girl to enter, but which is simultaneously treated as a position which removes childhood innocence, allows entry of the whore and makes the girl vulnerable to abuse. The entry of popular culture into the educational and family life of the little girl is therefore to be viewed with suspicion, as a threat posed by the lowering of standards, of the intrusion of the low against the superior high culture. It is the consumption of popular culture which is taken as making the little working-class girl understood as potentially more at risk of being victim and perpetrator (as has similarly been propounded in relation to young boys and violence, *pace* the James Bulger murder). Janie's fantasy dirties the sanitary space of the classroom. But what is Janie's fantasy, and at the intersection of which complex fantasies is she inscribed? I want to explore some of the popular fictions about the little working-class girl and to present the way in which the eroticization presents for her the possibility of a different and better life, of which she is often presented as the carrier. The keeping at bay of sexuality as intruding upon innocent childhood is in sharp contrast to this.

There have been a number of cinematic depictions of young girls as capable of producing a transformation in their own and others' lives, from Judy Garland in *The Wizard of Oz*, through Shirley Temple, *Gigi, My Fair Lady* to (orphan) *Annie.* I described these briefly in Chapter 5, Section I. In the majority of these films the transformation effected relates to class and to money through the intervention of a lovable little girl. Charles Eckert (1991) argued that Shirley Temple was often portrayed as an orphan in the Depression whose role was to soften the hearts of the wealthy so that they would identify her as one of the poor, not dirty and radical, but lovable, to become the object of charity through their donations. In a similar way, Annie is presented as an orphan for whom being working class is the isolation of a poor little girl, with no home, no parents, no community. She too has to soften the heart of the armaments millionaire, Daddy Warbucks, making him soften at the edges, as well as finding herself happiness through dint of her own lovable personality. It is by this means that she secures for herself a future in a wealthy family, which she creates, by bringing Daddy Warbucks and his secretary Grace together. By concentrating on these two characters alone it is possible to envisage that the little working-class girl is the object of massive projections. She is a figure of immense transformative power, who can make the rich love, thereby solving huge social and political problems; and she can immeasurably improve her own life in the process.[1] At the same time she presents the face of a class turned underclass, ragged, disorganized, orphaned, for whom there is only one way out: embourgeoisement. Thus, she becomes the epitome of the feminized, and therefore emasculated, less threatening, proletariat. In addition to this, Graham Greene pointed to something unmentioned in the tales of innocent allure: the sexual coquettishness of Shirley Temple. His pointing to her paedophilic eroticization led to the closure of the magazine *Night and Day* of which he was editor, after it was sued for libel in 1936.

What does the current figure of the eroticized little girl hold? What fantasies are projected on to her and how do these fantasies interact with the fantasy scenarios little working-class girls create for themselves and their lives? I have explored aspects of the life of one such little girl elsewhere (Walkerdine 1993 and forthcoming).

If she is simultaneously holding so much that is understood as both good and bad, no wonder actual little girls might find their situation overwhelming. It would be easy to classify Janie and other girls' private eroticization as resistance to the position accorded to her at school and in high culture, but I hope that I have demonstrated that this would be hopelessly simplistic.

Fantasies of Seduction

Let us see then what psychoanalysis has had to say about seduction and the eroticization of little girls. It is easy to pinpoint Freud's seduction theory and his account of an auto-erotic childhood sexuality. We might also point to the place of the critiques of the seduction theory in the accusation that psychoanalysis had ignored child abuse; the raising of the spectre of abuse as a widespread phenomenon; and the recent attacks on therapists for producing 'false memories' of abuses that never happened in their clients. In this sense then, the issue of little girls and sexuality can be seen to be a minefield of claim and counter-claim focusing on the issue of fantasy, memory and reality. If one wants, therefore, to examine sexuality and little girls as a cultural phenomenon, one is confronted by a denial of cultural processes: either little girls have a sexuality which is derived from their fantasies of seduction by their fathers or they are innocent of sexuality, which is imposed upon them from the outside by pathological or evil men who seduce, abuse and rape them. Culturally, we are left with a stark choice: sexuality in little girls is natural, universal and inevitable; or, a kind of Laura Mulvey-type male gaze is at work in which the little girl is produced as object of an adult male gaze. She has no phantasies of her own and in the Lacanian sense, we could say that 'the little girl does not exist except as symptom and myth of the masculine imaginary'. Or, in the mould of the Women Against Violence Against Women approach of 'porn is the theory, rape is the practice', we might conclude that 'popular representations of eroticized little girls is the theory and child sexual abuse is the practice'. Girls' fantasies prove a problem in all these accounts, because only Freud credited them with any of their own, although Freud made it clear that, like others working on psychopathology at the time, feminine sexuality was the central enigma. Indeed his main question was 'what does the woman, the little girl, want?' A question to which Jacqueline Rose in her introduction to Lacanian writing on feminine sexuality (1985) asserts that 'all answers, including the mother are false: she simply wants'. So little girls have a desire without an object, a desire that must float in space, unable to find an object, indeed to be colonized by masculine fantasies, which create female desire in its own image. Of course, Laura Mulvey's original 1974 work on the male cinematic gaze has been much revised and criticized (e.g. *Screen* 1992). But the position has somewhat polarized, with critics for and against psychoanalysis, with those opposing psychoanalysis pointing to its universalizing tendencies and dredging up the concept of 'social fantasy'. However, what is not clear in these criticisms is how the critics would engage with the intersection of the social and the psychic. It is all very well to oppose psychoanalysis but cultural processes do not all happen in a rational, conscious world. How then to do justice to the psychological aspects of this issue without reductionism?

Let us return to the psychoanalytic arguments about sexuality. Laplanche and Pontalis (1985) discuss seduction in terms of 'seduction into the fantasies of the parents'. Those fantasies can be understood in terms of the complex intertwining of parental histories and the regimes of truth, the cultural fantasies which circulate in the social. This may sound like a theory of socialization, but socialization implies the learning of roles and the taking on of stereotypes. What we have here is a complex interweaving of the many kinds of fantasy, both 'social' in the terms of Geraghty (1991) and others; and psychic, as phantasy in the classic psychoanalytic sense. Lacan, of course, argued that the symbolic system carried social fantasies which were psychic in origin, an argument he made by recourse to structuralist principles, from de Saussure and Levi-Strauss. However, it is possible to understand the complexity in terms which conceive of the psychic/social relation as produced not in ahistorical and universal categories, but in historically specific regimes of meaning and truth (Henriques et al. 1984).

However, what Freud did argue for was what he called a 'childhood sexuality'. What he meant was that the bodily sensations experienced by the baby could be very pleasurable, but this pleasure was, of course, always cross-cut by pain, a presence marked by the absence of the care-giver, usually the mother. In this context little children could learn in an omnipotent way that they too could give these pleasurable sensations to themselves, just as they learnt, according to Freud's famous example of the cotton-reel game, that in fantasy they could control the presence and absence of the mother. So, for Freud there is no *tabula rasa*, no innocent child. The child's first senses of pleasure are already marked by the phantasies inherent in the presence and absence of the Other. However, as Laplanche and Pontalis point out, the infantile sexuality, marked by an 'infantile language of tenderness', is cross-cut by the introduction of an adult 'language', the language of passion. 'This is the language of desire, necessarily marked by prohibition, a language of guilt and hatred, including the sense of orgastic pleasure' (Laplanche and Pontalis 1985: 15). How far does this view take us down the road of sorting out the problems associated with childhood innocence etc. models?

The model suggests that there are two kinds of sexuality: an infant one about bodily pleasures and an adult one which imposes a series of other meanings upon those pleasures. We should note here, therefore, that Laplanche and Pontalis do go as far as implying that not all of the fantasy is on the side of the child, but that the parents impose some of their own. The sexuality would then develop in terms of the admixture of the two, in all its psychic complexity. Let me illustrate that briefly by making reference to a previous study of mine (Walkerdine 1985) in which I discussed my own father's nickname for me, Tinky, short for Tinkerbell, which I was reminded of by a father, Mr Cole's nickname for his six-year-old daughter, Joanne, as Dodo. I argued that Tinky and Dodo were fathers' fantasies about their daughters: a fairy with diminutive size but incredible powers on the one hand and a preserved baby name (Dodo, as a childish mispronunciation of JoJo) on the other. But a dodo is also an extinct bird, or for Mr Cole, that aspect of extinction which is preserved in his fantasy relationship with his daughter: a baby. Joanne is no longer a baby; babyhood, like the dodo has gone, but it is preserved in the fantasy of Mr Cole's special nickname for his daughter, and in so designating her, he structures the relationship between them: she remains his baby. In the case of my own father's fantasy, Tinky signified for me the most potent aspect of my specialness for him. I associated it with a photograph of myself aged three winning a local fancy-dress competition, dressed as a bluebell fairy. This is where I won and 'won him over': my fairy charms reciprocated his fantasy of me, designating me 'his girl' and fuelling my Oedipal fantasies.

I am trying to demonstrate that those fantasies are not one-sided, neither on the side of the parent, nor the little girl, but, as the Tinky example illustrates, the 'language of adult desire' is entirely cultural. Tinkerbell and bluebell fairies are cultural phenomena which can be examined in terms of their semiotics and their historical emergence, as well as their production and consumption. My father did not *invent* Tinkerbell or the Bluebell Fairy. Rather he used what were available cultural fantasies to name something about his deep and complex feelings for his daughter. In return, I, his daughter, took those fantasies to my heart and my unconscious, making them my own. Now, of course it could be argued that this sails very close to Laura Mulvey's original position, following Lacan, that woman (the little girl) does not exist (or have fantasies which originate with her) except as symptom and myth of male fantasy. But I am attempting to demonstrate that a position which suggests that fantasies come only from the adult male is far too simplistic. My father might have imposed Tinkerbell on me but my own feelings for my father had their own role to play.

I want to argue that the culture carries these adult fantasies, creates vehicles for them. It carries the transformation of this into a projection on to children of the adult language of desire. In this view the little seductress is a complex phenomenon, which carries adult sexual desire but which hooks into the equally complex fantasies carried by the little girl herself. The idea of a sanitized natural childhood in which such things are kept at bay, having no place in childhood in this model, becomes not the guarantor of the safety of children from the perversity of adult desires for them, but a huge defence against the acknowledgement of those, dangerous, desires on the part of adults. In this analysis, 'child protection' begins to look more like adult protection.

It is here then that I want to make a distinction between seduction and abuse. Fantasies of Tinky and Dodo were enticing, seductive, but they were not abuse. To argue that they were is to make something very simplistic out of something immensely complex.

As long as seduction is subsumed under a discourse of abuse, issues of 'seduction into the fantasies of the parents' are hidden under a view which suggests that adult sexual fantasies about children are held only by perverts, who can be kept at bay by keeping children safe and childhood innocent. But if childhood innocence is really an adult defence, adult fantasies about children and the eroticization of little girls is not a problem about a minority of perverts from whom the normal general public should be protected. It is about massive fantasies carried in the culture, which are equally massively defended against by other cultural practices, in the form of the psychopedagogic and social welfare practices incorporating discourses of childhood innocence. This is not to suggest that children are not to be protected. Far from it. Rather, my argument is that a central issue of adult sexual projections on to children is not being addressed.

Ann Scott (1989) sees seductiveness as a form of parental intrusion, in which children are seduced into the fantasies of their parents. We could add here, and into the fantasies of the culture. Such fantasies in this model are about unresolved adult sexuality and eroticism, for example, desire for the mother marked by prohibition, projected on to little girls: doubly prohibited and therefore doubly exciting. The popular cultural place which admits the possibility that little girls can be sexual little women provides a place where adult projections meet the possibility for little girls of being Other than the rational child or the nurturant quasi-mother, where they can be bad. It can then be a space of immense power for little girls and certainly a space in which they can be exploited, but it is not abuse.

So the issue of fantasy and the eroticization of little girls within popular culture becomes a complex phenomenon in which cultural fantasies, fantasies of the parents and little girls' Oedipal fantasies mix and are given a cultural form which shapes them. Laplanche and Pontalis (1985) argue that fantasy is the setting for desire, 'but as for knowing who is responsible for the setting, it is not enough for the psychoanalyst to rely on the resources of his (*sic*) science, nor on the support of myth. He (*sic*) must become a philosopher!' (p. 17).

In post-structuralist terms this would take us into the domain of the production of knowledges about children and the production of the ethical subject. I want to explore lastly this latter connection by suggesting several courses of action and to examine the issue (briefly) through a specific example of a 'moral panic' about popular culture and the eroticization of children.

Minipops

I want to end this chapter by looking at the case of *Minipops*, a series transmitted on Channel 4 television in 1983. The series presented young children, boys and girls, white and black, singing current pop songs, dressed up and heavily made up. This series became the object of what was described as a moral panic. The stated intention of the director was to present a showcase of new talent, the idea having come from his daughter, who liked to dress up and sing pop songs at home. The furore caused by the programmes was entirely voiced by the middle classes. The broadsheet papers demanded the axing of the series on the grounds that it presented a sexuality which spoiled and intruded into an innocent childhood. One critic wrote of 'lashings of lipstick on mini mouths'. By contrast, the tabloids loved the series. For them, the programmes represented a chance for young children to be talent-spotted, to find fame. There was no mention of the erosion of innocence. Why this difference? It would be easy to imagine that the tabloids were more exploitative, less concerned with issues of sexual exploitation so rampant in their own pages, with the broadsheets as upholders of everything that is morally good. However, I think that this conclusion would be erroneous. While I deal with this argument in more detail elsewhere (Walkerdine, in press), let me point out here that I have argued that the eroticized little girl presents a fantasy of otherness to the little working-class girl. She is inscribed as one who can make a transformation, which is also a self-transformation, which is also a seductive allure. It is not surprising, therefore, that the tabloid discourse is about talent, discovery, fame: all the elements of the necessary transformation from rags to riches, from flower-girl to princess, so to speak. Such a transformation is necessarily no part of middle-class discourse, fantasy and aspiration. Rather, childhood for the middle class is a state to be preserved free from economic intrusion, producing the possibility of the rational and playful child who will become a rational, educated professional, a member of the 'new middle class'.

I would argue, then, that the examination of the complex cultural phenomenon which I have outlined would require analyses at all of the levels that I have signalled. Each without the other would be reductive.

Seduction and the eroticization of little girls are complex cultural phenomena. I have tried to demonstrate that the place of the little working-class girl is important because her seductiveness has an important role to play in terms of both a social and personal transformation, a transformation which is glimpsed in the fantasies of fame embodied in series like *Minipops*. The figure of the little working-class girl then simultaneously 'holds' the transformation of an emasculated working class into both lovable citizens and the fear against which the fantasy defends. This is the little Lolita: the whore, the contagion of the masses which will endanger the safety of the bourgeois order. On the other hand, child protection – as the outlawing of perversion and a keeping of a safe space of innocent childhood – can also be viewed as class-specific, and indeed the fantasy of the safe space which has not been invaded by the evil masses.

I have tried to place an understanding of unconscious processes inside of all of this. Because, as I hope that I have demonstrated, psychic processes form a central component of how social and cultural fantasies work. Some may argue that my recourse to psychoanalysis presents such psychic processes as universal and inevitable, but I have tried to show how the social and the psychic merge together to form particular fantasies at a specific moment. This is only a very small beginning that may help to sort out how we might approach a hugely important topic which has been badly neglected in cultural and feminist theory.

Note

1 My previous work on girls' comics (Walkerdine 1985) pointed to very similar fictions occurring in comic stories directed at young working-class girls.

References

ECKERT, C., 1991: 'Shirley Temple and the House of Rockefeller', in C. Gledhill (ed.) *Stardom*. London: Routledge.

GERAGHTY, C., 1991: *Women and Soap Opera*. Oxford: Polity Press.

HENRIQUES, J., HOLLWAY, W., URWIN, C., VENN, C. and WALKERDINE, V., 1984: *Changing the Subject: Psychology, Social Regulation and Subjectivity*. London: Methuen.

LAPLANCHE, J. and PONTALIS, J.-B., 1985: 'Fantasy and the Origins of Sexuality', in V. Burgin, J. Donald and C. Kaplan (eds.) *Formations of Fantasy*. London: Routledge.

McROBBIE, A., 1980: 'Settling accounts with subcultures', *Screen Education*, 34: pp. 37–50.

ROSE, J., 1985: 'Introduction', in J. Lacan and the Ecole Freudienne *Feminine Sexuality*, London: Macmillan.

SCOTT, A., 1989: 'Seduction and Child Abuse', *Feminist Review*, 31: pp. 6–16.

SCREEN, 1992: *The Sexual Subject*, London: Routledge.

WALKERDINE, V., 1984: 'Developmental Psychology and the Child Centred Pedagogy', in J. Henriques et al. *Changing the Subject: Psychology, Social Regulation and Subjectivity*. London: Methuen.

WALKERDINE, V., 1985: 'Video Replay', in V. Burgin, J. Donald and C. Kaplan (eds.) *Formations of Fantasy*. London: Routledge.

WALKERDINE, V., 1988: *The Mastery of Reason*, London: Routledge.

WALKERDINE, V., 1989: *Counting Girls Out*, London: Virago.

WALKERDINE, V., 1992: 'Reasoning in a Post-modern Age', paper presented at Fifth International Conference on Thinking. Australia: Townsville.

WALKERDINE, V., 1993: 'Beyond Developmentalism', *Theory and Psychology*, 3 (4): pp. 451–69.

WALKERDINE, V., in press: *Daddy's Girl: Young Girls and Popular Culture*. London: Macmillan.

WALKERDINE, V. and LUCEY, H., 1989: *Democracy in the Kitchen: Regulating Mothers and Socialising Daughters*. London: Virago.

16

Ethnography, Anthropology and Cultural Studies: Links and Connections

Gareth Stanton

> The anthropology of ourselves is still only a dream.
>
> (Harrisson and Madge 1937: 10)

Introduction

Students of cultural studies, on occasion, have very little understanding of disciplines which might have had a direct influence on their own area of interest. Indeed, it is often the case that such connections have been largely lost or ignored as cultural studies has come to take on an increasingly strong identity of its own. Exploration of these links, however, can help us to shed fresh light on contemporary developments. Here I wish to attempt such an exploration. More specifically, in this paper I shall examine a number of potential links between British social anthropology (and its major methodological tool, ethnography, which usually takes the form of 'participant observation') and cultural studies. It is necessary from the outset to make the nature of these links clear, because the argument which follows is both many stranded and, in places, contentious. In the first instance I shall outline the view of anthropology's development which is usually served up for anthropology students in Britain, that is to establish the founding moment of modern British social anthropology – an event generally associated with the work of the Polish *emigré* Bronislaw Malinowski. He has generally been regarded as the person who laid down the rules of modern anthropology as a discipline which required of its practitioners a spell of intensive fieldwork in close contact with the people under study. This new discipline with its new methods became the dominant mode of British anthropology for many decades.

However, for a variety of reasons, the Malinowskian citadel has recently been stormed. A new spirit of doubt stalks anthropology, a new spirit which demands new ways of accounting for itself, new forms of self-expression. Such recent strategies as have appeared can be seen as a new movement within anthropology (although with nothing, as yet, approaching the dominance

Malinowski's own brand of functionalism once possessed). How this movement relates to such trends as modernism, postmodernism or the realist tradition in literature remains an area of intense debate. It is becoming clear to some, however, that anthropology is, in some senses, increasingly drawing closer to cultural studies. For some (Knauft 1994) this is regarded as a matter of some concern. In this chapter, however, I shall attempt to trace the development of a historical moment that was both influenced by anthropology and that can be seen as a pioneering venture in academic cultural studies. This was the Mass-Observation movement. The bridge between the two academic disciplines is a single text. *Savage Civilisation* appeared in 1937, and yet it has many of the distinctive qualities sought after by some of the practitioners of the new forms of anthropology in the post-Malinowskian era. The author of this book, Tom Harrisson, was one of the co-founders of the Mass-Observation movement, the first movement in Britain to set out with the objective of documenting British cultural life in the broad sense implied by T.S. Eliot (1947) in his *Notes Towards a Definition of Culture*. One of the methods used in order to achieve this objective was modelled on participant observation – quasi-Malinowskian principles were to be used in order to arrive at an 'anthropology of ourselves'. The Mass-Observation movement itself became part of the cultural landscape and for a short period was the butt of jokes about snooping and prying. However, Malinowski himself lent the movement his support. I will argue that the history of the movement is a demonstration of the shared heredity of anthropology and cultural studies. This link has long been suppressed by both disciplines, but it needs, once more, to be recovered and recognized.

A Revolution in British Social Anthropology?[1]

In Anglo-Saxon circles the story of the development of modern anthropology is a fairly simple one, or at least it had been until the publication of Bronislaw Malinowski's field note personal diary in 1967, *A Diary in the Strict Sense of the Term*. Up until this point it was generally held that the foundation myth of British social anthropology was beyond doubt. A young Polish scholar had, as a result of illness, taken to reading works of anthropology on his sickbed. These included a book which was to have widespread influence in the twentieth century, J.G. Frazer's *The Golden Bough*.[2] This of course was the book which was to be pillaged by the American poet T.S. Eliot on his way to composing what has been proclaimed a flagship of the modernist movement in the world of poetry, his poem *The Waste Land*. Malinowski's acquaintance with the anthropology of the time, runs a version of the hero legend, led the Pole to give up his studies in chemistry and physics and head for the London School of Economics to study with scholars such as Westermarck and Seligman. The brand of ethnography these men practised was one which involved fieldwork, that is to say, prolonged periods of time spent in the world of the ethnographic 'other', but the time spent was not usually restricted to a single localized region and bore, if anything, a close relationship to the nineteenth-century explorer/traveller tradition and the work of men such as the now much reviled (in 'post-colonial' circles) British explorer and diplomat, Richard Burton (Said 1979;

Kabbani 1986). The so-called 'armchair' anthropologists such as Frazer simply corresponded with people in the field: missionaries, colonial officials and so forth, creating their theories on the basis of such information combined with their knowledge of ancient mythology and folklore. Westermarck, himself also an *emigré* but from Finland, serves as a paradigm of the model of research which is close to the explorer type, but which is approaching a model of fieldwork which would have been recognizable to the classic functionalist ethnographers. He travelled extensively in one country, Morocco, and worked in the vernacular, using 'native' informants.

By contrast to earlier anthropologists, at least Seligman and Westermarck actually endeavoured to learn languages and make contact with the peoples that they were interested in. Malinowski himself then went several more steps forward, so the myth has it. He insisted that this was the proper and only way to proceed and laid down rules for the conduct of anthropological fieldwork, based on his own work in the Trobriands. For anthropologists this is well-trodden territory, but here it is worth repeating Young's description of Malinowski's innovations:

> First of all they comprised the necessary conditions for intensive work ... the anthropologist must spend a long time in one place and remain in close contact with the people throughout, and he must communicate with them in their own language. Second, there were actual strategies and techniques of data collection, to which Malinowski attached somewhat cumbersome labels: (1) The method of 'statistical documentation of concrete evidence', which involved the recordings of maps, censuses, genealogies, statements of norms and the observation of actual cases. (2) Another set of materials which Malinowski called 'the imponderabilia of everyday life', should be collected 'through minute, detailed observations'. Finally, the fieldworker must accumulate a *corpus inscriptionum*, consisting of 'ethnographic statements', characteristic narratives, typical utterences, items of folklore and magical formulae.
>
> (Young 1979: 7–8)

The goal is to grasp the way in which the 'native' views the world, his (for this tended to be the case) understanding of his reality.[3] To sum up his attitude, Malinowski urged that:

> The anthropologist must relinquish his comfortable position in the long chair on the veranda of the missionary compound, Goverment station, or planters bungalow, where, armed with pencil and notebook and at times with a whiskey and soda, he has been accustomed to collect statements from informants, write down stories, and fill out sheets of paper with savage texts.
>
> (Quoted from Malinowski's 1925 Frazer Memorial Lecture by Kuklick 1991: 287)

It has been suggested that this attitude fostered by Malinowski – and his own personal self-aggrandizement during his own life – leads to a vision of the anthropologist as hero.[4] But, as the American historian of anthropology, George Stocking has suggested, the role of Malinowski is more complicated than simple versions of this myth might run:

> The emergence of fieldwork was a multifaceted process to which many individuals before and after Malinowski contributed. But Malinowski's deliberate archetypification of the role of 'the Ethnographer' offered, both to prospective anthropologists and to various publics at the boundaries of the developing

> discipline, a powerfully condensed (yet expansive) image of the anthropologist as the procuror of exotic esoteric knowledge of potentially great value.
>
> (Stocking 1989: 209)

Despite such nuanced appreciations of the development of anthropology it was certainly the case that, by the early 1950s, the students of the functionalist founders of modern British social anthropology could reel off its purpose and objectives with some degree of clarity. The social anthropologist, Evans-Pritchard explained in 1951 that it

> studies primitive societies directly, living among them for months or years, whereas sociological research is usually from documents and is largely statistical. The social anthropologist studies societies as wholes – he studies their oecologies, their economics, their legal and political institutions, their family and kinship organisations, their religions, their technologies, their arts, etc., as parts of general social systems.
>
> (Quoted by Asad 1973: 11–12)

Strong on method, Malinowski was often, however, regarded as weak in respect of general theory (e.g. Jarvie (1964) has argued that anthropology is rendered trivial by a fieldwork technique which concentrates on the simple recording and cataloguing of facts). In fact, later commentators, such as the anthropologist Maurice Bloch, argue that British anthropology, although in theoretical disarray and almost entirely ignorant of intellectual currents such as Marxism, actually had its 'glory days' in the years 1920–60. British anthropology was unique, he argues, 'for its detailed studies of actual societies in operation, and for relating whole varieties of phenomena to create a synthesis' (Bloch 1983: 145). This can only be understood as a reference to the methodological innovations introduced by Malinowski. That is not to suggest that certain problems with his prescriptions had not appeared. Malinowski himself recognized that the accumulation of data simply led to there being lots of data and that it needs interpretation to arrive at 'laws and generalisations' (in fact, he included a final section of autocritique in his final Trobriand monograph, *Coral Gardens and their Magic*, 1935).

Although much of this is somewhat simplified, the consequences for the development of British social anthropology were as follows. One man, Malinowski, pronounced a revolution in method for the subject. He denounced all previous efforts as flawed and set out to produce a rationale for anthropology that was both scientific and humanist. By establishing a secure foothold within British academe (and because of his charismatic personality) he was able to recruit and maintain a group of devoted acolytes who went forth and propagated his vision of anthropology. Some authors felt that there were problems with the general tenor of Malinowski's pronouncements. A.H. Hocart, a respected ethnographer, for example, argued in the early 1930s that anthropologists could never understand alien cultures as well as they did their own and that if they wished to be engaged in social reform that they should stay at home (Kuklick 1991: 187). Most, though, accepted Malinowski at face value and were prepared to follow the methodological path on which they thought he had embarked. In any case, Malinowski's net was of the 'large drift' variety and he was prepared, later in his careeer, to acknowledge that there were problems which he had not been able to deal with in his work, such as the colonial context of his work. He was prepared also to get involved with developments in the arena recommended by Hocart to anthropologists should they want to get involved in matters practical, i.e. on the home front. It is this latter issue which I shall develop in some depth by examining the work of a group of writers and investigators who, on the basis of Malinowskian principles, set out to generate an 'anthropology of ourselves' for the British context – the Mass-Observation movement.

Before that, however, I shall examine briefly Malinowski's contemporary legacy. His confident view of anthropology and its aims and objectives, it would seem, is now in tatters. Grimshaw and Hart, for example, recently alleged that he is responsible for much that is actually wrong with modern anthropology. In their view he has 'come to be seen as a purveyor of fiction and a fraudulent self-publicist whose fieldwork diaries posthumously revealed the strain between his professional and private personalities' (Grimshaw and Hart 1994: 235). For them, the real father of British social anthropology is not Malinowski, but Rivers, the 'Lenin' of British social anthropology to Malinowski's 'Stalin', so Grimshaw and Hart suggest. Far from being an innovator, they continue, Malinowski smuggled nineteenth-century scholarship and pseudoscience in through the back door. In fact, their reading of anthropology as it developed during the interwar period is similar, in some senses, to the picture painted famously by Perry Anderson, who figured Malinowski as one of the white wave of migrant intellectuals whose innate conservatism made, in Anderson's opinion, British intellectual life in the twentieth century so unlike that in continental Europe (Anderson 1969). Grimshaw and Hart's comments come close to Anderson's points concerning the failure of Britain to develop anything resembling a 'sociology' along continental lines (i.e. a radical vision of society constructed upon notions of conflict and contradiction rather than consent). The reaction against Malinowski, in recent years, can be addressed in three loose but related areas which I shall now discuss.

The Revolution Undermined

The Colonial Critique

With the end of colonialism, in most parts of the world, the discipline of anthropology has been forced to reconsider its own position in relation to the whole colonial enterprise. Implicit in discussions of the relationship between the two are what I would call a 'strong' critique and a 'weaker' version (as well as those who deny the importance of the link).

In a detailed discussion of a version of the 'weak' critique, Kuklick makes a number of interesting observations regarding the Malinowskian 'anthropologist as hero' approach to doing fieldwork. Discussing the career of a typical colonial officer, she points out that careers were likely to start in rural areas often distanced from other colonial officials. In some respects, she suggests, it was a romanticized view which they held that, in some senses, facilitated the triumph of functionalist anthropology.[5] The descriptions functionalist anthropologists offered of their research methods 'were very like political officers' accounts of their administrative procedures' (Kuklick 1991: 189). Anthropologists could now be seen as 'kindred spirits' (p. 189). The colonial rural officer

> believed that a thorough understanding of his subjects was as much intuitive as intellectual, and that it allowed him to recognise their special character. He often proclaimed (erroneously) that his administrative decisions had no analogues elsewhere, that they were formulated to suit the unique needs of his people. The functionalist anthropologist also claimed to reach understanding of his or her research subjects through a process of near mystical communion with them with (at least supposedly) none of the distractions that other Europeans might provide. And like the colonial official, the functionalist anthropologist emphasized that each people were at least to some degree unique, and could be understood only in their own terms.
>
> (p. 190)

Kuklick's discussion of the compatibility between the 'hero' anthropologist (although this is to bend Susan Sontag's original application of this expression to Claude Levi-Strauss slightly, see Sontag 1961) and the colonial officer – and by extension the whole endeavour of colonialism – is an interesting one. However, it is impossible to dispute that with the collapse of the colonial regimes, a certain animosity towards the figure of the anthropologist became evident. While an older nationalist leader such as Jomo Kenyatta actually sat in Malinowski's seminar at the LSE and himself wrote an exemplary monograph, *Facing Mount Kenya*,[6] others such as Nkrumah now viewed anthropologists with deep suspicion (Kuper 1983: 99). Kuklick's discussion, however, puts an interesting spin on Adam Kuper's contention that there was, in fact, very little effective link-up between colonial finance and anthropological fieldwork, colonial administrators being more likely to regard anthropologists with disdain than anything else (Kuper 1983: Chapter 4). In another context, Kuklick argues that the work of Malinowski-influenced functionalists 'may perhaps be better appreciated as a paean to the merits of egalitarian democracy than as an apology for colonialism' (Kuklick 1984: 76). This is clearest in Evans-Pritchard's work on the Nuer. As Renato Rosaldo has noted, the Nuer, in Evans-Pritchard's account, 'represent an ideal of human liberty, even in the midst of colonial domination' (Rosaldo 1986: 96). The Nuer, in this sense, were simply portrayed as an idealized version of ourselves.

These 'weak' critiques of the relationship between anthropology and colonialism do not necessarily destroy the Malinowskian imperative, but critiques developed in the early 1970s were to take a much stronger position on the relationship. Anthropology came to be viewed in some sense as the handmaiden of colonialism or imperialism, or, indeed, both. In the British context, the work which stated the line of argument most forcibly was Asad's *Anthropology and the Colonial Encounter* (1973). It was this work which laid much of the ground, within anthropology in Britain, for the latter's own encounter with political economy and French structural Marxism. This admission of anthropology's role within the colonial system was to be joined in later years by a number of formulations coming initially out of comparative literary studies and utilizing the post-structualist rhetoric of French philosopher Michel Foucault, trends which merged into a more general 'crisis of representation'. Much of all this was made possible within anthropology by the collapse of faith in the original Malinowskian formulation. This was a process which had been, in no small part, induced by the publication of Malinowski's own fieldwork diaries in 1967. It is these to which I shall now turn.

The Diary

Clifford Geertz's somewhat maverick assessment of the career of Malinowski hints that his revolution in anthropological methodology was suspect:

> The breakdown of epistemological (and moral) confidence that, for all his outward bluster, began with him – as we can now see from his more lately published *Diary* – has issued now in a similar breakdown in expositive confidence and produced a flood of remedies, more or less desperate.
>
> (Geertz 1988: 23)

At the time of the diary's publication, in 1967, Geertz described its author, in a review in the *New York Review of Books*, as a 'crabbed, self-preoccupied, hypochondriacal narcissist, whose fellow feeling for the people he lived with was limited in the extreme' (quoted by Young 1979: 12) As Young comments, rather than anthropologist-as-hero we now have anthropologist as anti-hero, a fittingly dialectical progression. In what ways then had Malinowski transgressed? As Young suggests, expressions such as the following, 'As for ethnology: I see the life of the natives as utterly devoid of interest or importance, something as remote as the life of a dog' (Malinowski quoted by Young 1979: 12), were likely to cause alarm amongst those who had taken his methodological prescriptions at their face value. Indeed, the whole tone of the diary could be interpreted as suggesting a degree of disdain wholly unfitting for one who built his career on championing rational 'Trobriand man' as a corrective to the naïve formulations and speculations of earlier generations of anthropologists concerning the form and nature of 'savage' thought and mental processes. Certainly, his repeated references to the Trobrianders as 'niggers' were bound to create a stir (though it should be noted that Edmund Leach, in an early review in the *Guardian*, stressed the absurdity of translating *nigrami* as niggers rather than blacks, deemed a more acceptable usage by Leach (see Firth 1988: xxiii)).This point aside, and given the outbursts which no 'mistranslation' argument can dismiss, Raymond Firth noted, in his original 1967 introduction, that such moments reveal 'a darker side of the relation of an anthropologist to his human material' (Firth 1988: xvi). This very discussion of 'human material' might cause a shudder now, but Firth forgave Malinowski his lapses. Writing in a new introduction, in 1988, Firth reviews the debate stimulated by the publication of the diary. Here he is prepared to grant that the publication of the diary destroyed the aura of 'Olympian detachment' which is given by the classic functionalist ethnographies, the view suggesting that 'the anthropologist came, saw, recorded and retired to write up the material, apparantly untouched by his or her experiences' (Firth 1988: xxviii). For Firth then, it is this element of detachment, rather than the hero anthropologist, that the diary destroyed. This, however, is one view: as Stocking had remarked in 1986, 'reaction to the diary has not got much beyond the disillusioning references to the Trobriand "niggers" ' (Stocking 1986: 23). Stocking himself was to attempt to probe the diaries in relation to Malinowski's encounter with

Freudian psychoanalysis, but other writers were to take a somewhat different approach to the humanity of fieldworkers in general and attempted to transform the anthropological enterprise into a more reflexive, literary form.

A clue to this transition is given in Firth's 'review' of the reviews, provided in the second edition of Malinowski's diary. One figure who looms large is the American anthropologist and cultural critic James Clifford, who, Firth remarks, in his approach to ethnographic writings 'has become fascinated by the notion of fiction and tends to treat any text with an element of personal subjectivity' (Firth 1988: xxx) as 'fiction'. It is with the writings of Clifford and a number of his colleagues that we see the coalescence of a number of voices into something approaching a coherent movement in anthropology. If we were to put a finger on one moment in this process it would be the publication of the Clifford and Marcus edited collection *Writing Culture* in 1986.[7]

Writing Culture

Clifford, basing himself on the literary critic Steven Greenblatt, himself a writer who leans on anthropology on occasion, and his notion of Renaissance self-fashioning (Greenblatt 1980), discusses the Malinowski conundrum under the rubric of 'ethnographic self-fashioning'. The world in which we now live he describes as a 'syncretic', 'postcultural' one (Clifford 1988: 94). Beginning with an epigram from Joseph Conrad's novel *Victory*, Clifford develops an extended comparison of the two Poles refashioning their identities in relation to the world around them. *Argonauts of the Western Pacific* (1922), Malinowski's first Trobriand book, Clifford argues, was part of this refashioning process, a text in which the diary is excluded and written over 'in the process of giving wholeness to a culture (Trobriand) and a self (the scientific ethnographer)' (Clifford 1988: 112). This quintessential anthropologist of the ethnography would disintegrate with the appearance of the revelations of the diary which, 'once entered into the public record of anthropological science, shook the fiction of cultural relativism as a stable subjectivity, a standpoint for a self that understands and represents a cultural other' (p. 112). For Clifford, the appearance of the diary made it possible for the late 1970s and 1980s to witness the appearance of new forms of ethnographic realism, both more dialogical than in the past and more resistant to closure; tendencies collected in the 1986 collection. Such works, he suggests, teeter precariously between realism and modernism. This suggestion, however, leads us into murky definitional waters.

For Geertz (1988), the writing of Evans-Pritchard constitutes 'ethnographic realism', a form which is rigorously constructed to give the impression of reality. Geertz's discussion of the Malinowski diary, however, leads him to muse on what he terms 'I-witnessing' ethnographies of more recent vintage, writings which do not aspire to forms of realism used by such writers as Evans-Pritchard. He mentions a trio of American ethnographers who have worked in Morocco, Paul Rabinow, Kevin Dwyer, and Vincent Crapanzano, whose work has frequently been cited in the context of new experimental ethnography or even under the rubric 'postmodern' ethnography. As one of its alleged proponents, Crapanzano is slightly sceptical concerning such developments. 'In the last few years', he writes, 'there has been much talk – salvationist talk – about developing experimental modes of writing ethnography' (Crapanzano 1992: 1). Marcus and Fisher announced in 1986 that what is happening 'seems to us to be a pregnant moment in which every human project of ethnographic research and writing is potentially an experiment' (Marcus and Fisher 1986: ix). In more general terms and following Rabinow, Fardon notes that the work of Clifford and his followers has meant that anthropological texts are being produced by means of texts rather than by fieldwork (Fardon 1990: 5).

Such a description of the challenge to older versions of 'doing anthropology' does have some hint of the dispute which postmodernism has with forms of realism and rehearses Baudrillard's endless regression of meaning. For this 'new' anthropology, however, there do appear to be some problems. Indeed there seems to be some confusion over what is modern or postmodern, as Robert Pool (1991) has demonstrated. A critic such as Scott can describe the collection *Writing Culture* as 'meta-anthropological' and postmodernist in atmosphere, claiming that postmodern anthropology proposes that culture is mobile, that it is unbounded and conjunctural (Scott 1992). Tyler, himself a contributor to the *Writing Culture* volume, writes that the collection is 'not postmodern, its authors neither invert the relationship between aesthetics and epistemology nor revolutionize the three-fold hierarchy of epistemology, politics and aesthetics' (Tyler 1987: 50).

Scholte (1987) argues that the recent history of 'Anglo-American cultural studies' is largely defined by three movements: a 'critical anthropology' of which he cites Hymes (1974) as an early variety, though doubtless he would also include Asad (1973), and Wolf (1982) as a more recent example; a feminist anthropology, producing Shostak's *Nisa!* (1983), a recent classic; and finally, symbolic anthropology, with which he lumps the developments surrounding the *Writing Culture* collection and the journal *Cultural Anthropology*. The core of this collection for Scholte, however, is a postmodern transition 'from a single idea of ethnographic authority to a multiplicity of descriptive experiments and interpretive paradigms' (Scholte 1987: 37).

To add to all this apparent confusion, Webster has suggested that there are two major forms of the 'new ethnography':

> While consciously experimental ethnography was being explicated in terms of reflexivity and interpretative theory, another ethnographic form was tacitly taking shape in departures from the previously established theories of anthropological structuralism rewritten in terms of a semiology of culture history.
>
> (Webster: 267)

While it would be wrong to suggest somehow that 'experimental' ethnography (or whatever we choose to call it) has a total grip on the throat of anthropology in general, the denials of its importance in certain quarters[8] suggest that there is something worth examining. As Bruce Knauft has remarked, 'There is a palpable if somewhat reactionary feeling among anthropologists that the intense development of cultural studies has usurped the anthropological notion of "culture".' (Knauft 1994: 133). Indeed, as the anthropologist Nicholas Thomas argues in an assessment of the current state of academic flux, recent work has 'almost created a postdisciplinary humanities field, in which histories, cultural studies, cultural politics, narratives and ethnographies all intersect and are all open to being challenged' (Thomas 1994: 19).

This sentiment is reflected in the remarks of Marc Manganaro who points to a similar 'coalescence of anthropology and current studies on discourse emerging from literary and other cultural studies' (Manganaro 1990: 3).

It is from within the predicament of such mergers and doubts that I shall examine the growth in Britain of the Mass-Observation movement. My starting point is a text which shares some features in common with the new experimental ethnographies. It is a work which takes a highly critical view of colonialism and cultural contact with the West and integrates, to some degree, the voice of the author into the body of the text and, yet, was published in 1937. As I noted in my introduction, the author of the book, Tom Harrisson, was also one of the founders of the Mass-Observation movement itself.

A Text out of Time? Tom Harrisson's *Savage Civilisation*[9]

> Already most places are passing out of the Iron Age into the age of aluminium. The age of electric hell is here.
>
> (Harrisson 1938: 11)

The book itself commences with a short series of epigrams entitled 'Seasaw', beginning with a quotation from Aldous Huxley, 'In every tropic land the poorest people are always the inhabitants' (a statement the validity of which he denies in the actual text, see Harrisson 1937: 290). Other authors quoted include T.S. Eliot, Nietzsche and Paul Robeson. What are, in effect, the acknowledgements are entitled 'Jigsaw' and here he describes how the book came about. He had been with the Oxford University Expedition to the New Hebrides and had stayed on in Malekula. When his return fare home was spent he 'went native', becoming a 'wandering unwhite whiteman' (p. 12). Of the book itself he writes, 'This is not a story of decadence or despair but of inevitability; with oases in chaos' (p. 6). There is then a short geographical interlude followed by a section entitled 'Persons', which deals with what would then have been described as 'natives'. Much of the material would certainly make its way into a 'classic' functionalist monograph dealing with the region. He talks at length of the peoples' attitudes to pigs (and their teeth) and the process behind the accumulation of these animals, which lies behind competitive feasting.[10] The real difference, however, lies clearly in the fashion in which he has presented his material. It is written in the first person, as if Harrisson had indeed 'gone native': 'To us the great moments are those of the Na-Leng dances; the greatest interest is in our pigs, they come before food and sleeping' (p. 20). While this style might seem crude and naïve in some respects now, at the time it represented a significant break with functionalist forms of presentation. This may well be a reflection of the fact that Harrisson was not linked into the seminar system of Malinowski at the LSE and therefore avoided the pressures to conform to certain modes of presentation imposed by academic convention (although he had been a student at Cambridge, he did no formal postgraduate work). However, there are several other points which make his work, in feel at least, closely resemble some of the recent efforts at a more 'literary' anthropology.

Appended to the section 'Persons' is a short commentary on the the text. He discusses his attraction to the place, Matanavat, in which he stayed, and the 'balanced system of classless capitalism, typical of the New Hebrides, [that] came easy to me' (p. 70). Before attempting to reconstruct a picture of that life before the arrival of the whites, however, he suggests that 'Now it is time to welcome the advent of another type of culture that was peculiar particularly in morals and deaths' (p. 71). Here, and this is a crucial break with the anthropology of the time, Harrisson goes on to talk about the history of the conquest of the New Hebrides. Weaving together various accounts, including that of Pedro Francisco de Quiros (the last of the 'great' Spanish navigators), he attempts to recreate, in ironic style, the early incidents of contact.[11] From here he goes on to document the navigational virtuosity of the Polynesians and Melanesians in relation to the great navigators of the Western tradition, establishing the superiority of the former. With the explorations of the last European navigators Harrisson suggests:

> The initiation of the native is now complete. A white man had been to all the main islands. He had fired off his stickshining and smoke after, with my brother crying out there on the sand shore as we took him and ran in our fear . . . to the hut where the in him went out, went without meaning, with no hate or pigs – he had made no preparation.
>
> (p. 121)

The book continues with a historical exploration of a number of aspects of the complex imperial/colonial nexus in this part of the Pacific: the sandalwood trade and the atrocities and deceits associated with it; the ravages caused by whalers in the region; the influence of the various competing missionaries, on village life and on matters such as dress – the appearance of 'Western' clothing styles (what Harrisson termed 'shirtism'); the development of pidgin in the region and a number of other items excluded from the functionalist accounts. An important subject in this respect is the nineteenth- and twentieth-century use of Melanesian 'native labour' both in Fiji and on the plantations of Queensland – the process of transhipment which came to be known as 'blackbirding'. These movements Harrisson documents particularly for the nineteenth century, describing some of their effects on the men's home communities. He discusses the politics of 'White Australia' and Queensland's sugar industry. Indeed, he discusses the implications of the mass repatriation of blackbird labour which resulted from political pressures for a 'white Australia'. He notes the words of Rivers in 1913:

> At the present moment there exists in Melanesia an influence far more likely to produce disintegration of native institutions than the work of the missionaries. I refer to the repatriation of labourers from Queensland which was the result of the movement for a white Australia.
>
> (Quoted p. 250)

He outlines the spread of white settlement, the decline in the region's native population. He applauds the good sense of kava drinking (the missionaries opposed it). He exposes the land grabbing associated with the development of plantation agriculture and the copra trade. This latter he describes as a phase in the region's history which saw the 'native' 'irrevocably harnessed to the wheel of making things which were to him pointless, things to be manufactured in other lands into stuff for which he had no use, things of our progress, the unessentials that build this staggering civilisation' (p. 284).

The general tenor of the writing should be established by now and, indeed, its relationship to our foregoing discussion of Malinowskian brands of functionalism. The main point is that, in this last example, Harrisson actually draws the local actor, the native, into the nexus of the world capitalist economy, a connection which anthropologists were not to make for several decades, and one which advocates of the current American cultural anthropology (such as George Marcus) have only recently begun to pursue, in their efforts to generate an anthropology which can deal with the micro process of the local and integrate it into the global macro, without ironing out all forms of local difference.

Worth mentioning are the specific remarks which Harrisson makes with regard to anthropology. In his discussion of native decline in population he is dismissive of certain of Rivers's ideas concerning the Melanesian psychological 'will to live' being demolished by the onslaught of contact with the West. For Harrisson, the absence of immunological resistance to imported pathogens and the general depredations of the whites was perfectly adequate to explain the decline in population. More than this, however, he specifically criticizes Rivers's *History of Melanesian Society*, published in 1914:

> This has been regarded as a great scientific work. That is a mistake. It is only great prose. It is a brilliant piece of circular subjective reasoning and creative literature. It is the result of a short study, mostly among mission natives on board a mission yacht.
>
> (Harrisson 1937: 339).

Warming to his task, he suggests that it is the 'anthropologist's custom to detach his daily life from the people among whom he is working, to eat his own foods' (p. 343). It is, he suggests, an 'adolescent science'.

His period in Malekula made Harrisson wonder why it was that people had been financed to do work in exotic regions, but not at home among 'ourselves'. As far as he was concerned the crude contrast of 'savage' and 'civilized', which he had attempted to make in *Savage Civilisation*, was intended to undermine the very contrast itself, but the consequences of this need to be pursued. What was there, he asked himself,

> of Western civilisation which impacted into the tremendously independent and self-contained culture of those cannibal people on their Melanesian mountain? Only one thing, significantly in the mid-thirties: the Unilever Combine … Thus it happened that the trail led from the Western Pacific to the south of Lancashire. William Lever was born in Park Street, Worktown.
>
> (Harrisson 1961: 25–6)[12]

Worktown was in fact Bolton, where Harrisson was to initiate a study into British social and cultural life. Initially he was alone, but soon he was to become one of the intellectual movers behind a populist experiment in the social sciences – the Mass-Observation movement.

An Anthropology of Ourselves?

Underlying much of this discussion is the comparison which I wish to draw with the development of cultural studies in the British context. The founding moment of cultural studies is usually given as being the late 1950s (McGuigan 1992). I want to look back to the late 1930s and examine the development of the Mass-Observation (M-O) project as a little-recognized precursor to the development of academic cultural studies in Britain.

All too often, M-O is reduced in recent accounts of cultural studies to a couple of sentences, if mention of it is made at all. McGuigan serves as an example of such treatment, largely ignoring the work M-O conducted. There are a number of reasons why this might be. In the first case, much of the work done by M-O never reached print and remained in archive form (the main archive is currently based at the University of Sussex). Second, M-O was never formulated in explicitly political terms (although at the time of its founding, Charles Madge was a communist) so, from the distance of the 1990s (and in the light of Foucauldian perspectives on the 'panopticon') it takes on the veneer of having been just another ruse of the powerful – total surveillance, every dictator's dream. Indeed, it is possible to detect something sinister in the concept of the M-O project, as originally conceived by its founders Charles Madge and Tom Harrisson. This is understandable, as the two, in an early pamphlet (Harrison and Madge 1937) argued that M-O intended to work by a new method: 'Ideally, it is the observation by everyone of everyone, including themselves' (p. 10) – as the popular Penguin edition of the first results of the study, *Britain*, trumpeted on the front cover: 'The Science of Ourselves' (Mass-Observation 1939). But it is possible to look beyond this essentially Orwellian reading of M-O. This is not *1984*. This fact was understood by many commentators at the time. Malinowski, who was to become a member of the M-O advisory board, was to suggest that M-O was inconceivable in a totalitarian environment. Evidently he did not see a process of total control reminiscent of a police state in the objectives of M-O. The pursuit and availability of the information being sifted by M-O was, in his reading, essential to the workings of a healthy democracy. Malinowski clarifies this issue:

> Mass Observation is invaluable in these days when power is in the hands of the masses who may remain free and allowed to express their own opinion, within limits, or else have to be gagged, dominated by gangs and pedagogues, who also have to work through the masses, but mass indoctrinated as well as intimidated.
>
> (Malinowski in Harrison and Madge 1938: 120)

This view is endorsed by a more recent commentator on M-O, Tom Jeffery (1978). M-O, he suggests, 'was a political challenge of the man in the street, of us against them; it was a populist demand, that democracy should mean what it says, rule by the people, appraised of the facts' (Jeffery 1978: 4).

At the time of its founding, M-O attracted a great deal of publicity and much of this was of a hysterical variety. Indeed, the publicity it attracted was itself analysed by M-O. Ironically that work was carried out by a young man who later in life was to have a hysterical voice all of his own in a British tabloid, Woodrow Wyatt. The terms of abuse heaped on M-O, which he lists, are extensive: 'maniacs, organisers of a cult, cranky, beastly, Groupey, Beaver players, inferior to Holman Hunt's "Light of the World", mass-mystics, spies ...' (Harrisson and Madge 1938: 63). Such attitudes surfaced in various places. Graham Greene, for example, caricatures an observer, the Indian, Muckerji, in his novel, *The Confidential Agent.*[13] It is necessary, however, to look beyond such limited appreciations of the intentions of Harrisson and the rest of M-O. As I have indicated in my discussion of his Melanesian book, Harrisson's personal project was essentially anthropological in scope. Writing almost thirty years later, Harrisson summed up the objectives of M-O as seeking

> ... to supply accurate observations of everyday life and *real* (not just published) public moods, an anthropology and a mass-documentation for a vast sector of normal life which did not, at that time, seem to be adequately considered by the media, the arts, the social scientists, even by the political leaders.
>
> (Harrisson 1976: 13)

On this occasion he describes the method as being two-pronged, one a self-documentary method, coupled with a more observational approach. Here he likens the study of Britons to bird-watching, which was one of his particular interests. Mass-Observation was to be a 'scientific study of human social behaviour, beginning at home' (p. 13). As he and Madge stated early on, M-O was to be an 'anthropology of ourselves'.

The structure of feeling of the time, if we can so describe it, is also revealed in the pamphlet where they made this announcement, *Mass-Observation* (Harrisson and Madge 1937). In some respects it indicates that the general mood of doubt at that time was similar to that evoked by certain brands of postmodernism. The pamphlet, its authors assure the reader, 'assumes that the contemporary attitude of doubt is not the end of the epoch of science, but the beginnings of a new epoch of science (p. 11).

Calder and Sheridan (1984) explain the original impulse behind the formation of M-O. A letter to the *New Statesman* from a schoolteacher called Geoffrey Pyke in 1936 called for an anthropological study of the 'primitive' reactions to the abdication of King Edward VIII. The journal received a reply from Madge outlining that a group had already been formed for just that purpose. Madge thought that fieldwork would have to proceed in a more roundabout fashion than it did in such places as Africa. This was because British society was seen to be 'ultra-repressed' in the Freudian sense. Clues to unravelling all this might only be arrived at indirectly through the workings of coincidence. In this sense nothing could be ignored by prospective investigators, everything must be recorded – a necessity which could produce surrealistic lists of projects for investigation worthy of a Borges, ranging from such objects of study as the aspidistra cult, through the private lives of midwives to the objects on people's mantelpieces. This apparent surrealism was no coincidence. Both Madge and the film-maker Humphrey Jennings, who was also involved in M-O at this stage, were interested in surrealism.[14] Jennings, in fact, was a member of the organizing committee of the International Surrealist Exhibition which opened at the New Burlington Galleries, London, in June 1936.

In the vast amount of material which was generated by Mass-Observation, in contrast with some of the aspirants to a 'postmodern' anthropology, it is rare for the paid investigators to reveal themselves as subjective actors (volunteers, however, would allow the intrusion of personal opinion and feeling into their diaries and contributions), but the accounts do often introduce the presence of the observer. There was definitely the realist notion of the eye as a camera, albeit one with a particular slant, depending on the nature of the observer. As Madge and Harrisson wrote in *First Year's Work*, 'Mass-Observation has always assumed that its untrained observers would be subjective cameras, each with his or her own distortion. They tell us not what society is like but what it looks like to them' (quoted by Calder and Sheridan, 1984: 4–5). Harrisson wrote that 'from the beginning film was of the highest interest to us. We were film minded' (quoted in Richards and Sheridan 1987: 1). Much of the Bolton work had concentrated on cinema and film-going, but the research that was conducted was not collected and published until 1987. This is, perhaps, one reason why cultural studies has paid so little attention to M-O. Of initiatives such as M-O and the documentary movement (Humphrey Jennings is something of a lynchpin here, having been involved in both) Iain Chambers has observed: 'Optics, and the pragmatic limits of a liberal empiricist culture – the world is simply "there", to be observed, filmed and reproduced – are combined in a diffused "naturalism" (Chambers 1986: 89). This reading reflects Stuart Hall's (1972) comments on M-O which, while sympathetic, ignore the more complex presentation of self given by some of the founders of M-O. While Chambers's view has a superficial validity, we need to probe more deeply. Certainly in the case of Jennings, the very writer who at first glance might be taken to give most support to the sort of view held by Chambers, this is becoming very clear. As Kevin Jackson has underlined in his introduction to a collection of Jennings's letters, poems and published works:

> Jennings was never much interested in statistics and averages, and it does not take a very penetrating gaze to see that beneath its would-be scientific prose, Mass-Observation – at least conducted by Jennings – was really a kind of first cousin to surrealism.
>
> (Jackson 1993: xiv)

There is clear evidence from his letters that Jennings saw himself as distinct from other members of the documentary movement. Writing to his wife Cicely, for example, he complains about criticisms he has received over the soundtrack for his film *This is England*. The comments, he writes, come 'of course from Rotha and other of Grierson's little boys who are still talking as loudly as possible about "pure documentary" and "realism" and other such states of self-advertisement' (quoted in Jackson 1993: 16).

The judgement of M-O normally held within cultural studies then obscures some of the factors motivating the work of M-O but as the 'visionary' period for M-O was effectively the early war period the whole emphasis drifted away from the 'visionary' and into the area of commissioned market research as many of the staff, including Harrisson, were gradually lost to the war effort. In 1947 Harrisson, the ornithologist and explorer returned east to Sarawak, where he worked as curator of the island's museum.[15] Madge meanwhile had split from the organization in 1940 because of his disagreements with Harrisson over M-O and its wartime links with the Ministry of Information.

After the war, M-O continued to operate but increasingly it turned to more straightforward market research. In 1961, however, the energetic Harrisson was back with the outfit for a period to co-ordinate a restudy of some of the areas which M-O had been extensively working on in the late 1930s and early 1940s. This work resulted in the publication *Britain Revisited* (Harrisson 1961). The absence of such restudies in classical anthropology was, of course, one of the criticisms which Madge and Harrison had levelled at the discipline – a criticism which Malinowski had refuted, citing various studies of American Indian groups (which he claimed, in effect, had been continuously under anthropological scrutiny since the Spanish conquest, in Harrisson and Madge 1938). If anything, by this time, Harrisson's own views on anthropology had hardened into a bizarre doctrine, far distant from anything remotely innovative in contemporary terms. 'Observing' had indeed become the fetish that 1930s critics made it out to be in the caricatures such as that penned by Graham Greene. The original intention of M-O, Harrisson notes here, was 'to *observe* – to observe the *mass* and seek to have the mass observe itself' (Harrisson 1961: 17). He has gone a long way from the original debate with Malinowski when he proposes that 'The nearer social anthropology gets to the anthropologist in life and the language of his own experience, the more difficult he finds it to achieve anything acceptable as social *science*' (p. 19).

Here Harrisson does fall foul of the critique put forward by Chambers, but the position represents an extreme rejection of any evidence other than the purely visual. Linguistic evidence is deemed inadmissible if the enquiry is to be dignified with the title 'science'. In line with this proposition, he suggests that the best piece of technical equipment for the anthropologist is the earplug! Few anthropologists, from any epoch, are likely to endorse such a position, and here his suggestion might well be termed 'dotty'. But his claim that such events as the St Bartholomew's Day 'Cow Head Festival' were only now being considered as suitable and worthy objects of scientific interest – traces of the event were sought out in the restudy – the original material was reported initially in *Britain* – was true. The orientation of M-O laid the groundwork for the publication of books such as Hoggart's *Uses of Literacy* (1957) with its 'anthropological approach to the "ordinary cultures" of "everyday life"', a seminal text for all students of cultural studies. Charles Madge is more straightforward in a postscript to the restudy. As he remarks, the original objective of the group was to 'understand "ordinary people" in relation to the great issues of politics' (Harrisson 1961: 277). His modest proposal that the importance of M-O was that it assumed 'that a wide range of human phenomena had serious significance' (p. 280) could easily stand as a motto for more recent developments within academic cultural studies and in doing so resurrects cultural studies' links with anthropology. This, indeed, is the sense of culture as 'a whole way of life' which Raymond Williams found so laudable in T.S. Eliot's definition of culture (Williams 1958: 233). Hoggart prefaces his *Uses of Literacy* with a quotation from the American literary and social critic, Ludwig Lewisohn: 'The men of our age of critical realism, goaded by mass-stupidity and mass-tyranny, have protested against the common people to the point of having lost all direct knowledge and vision of it' (Hoggart 1957: 10). This was precisely the sentiment which lay behind the formation of M-O.

Conclusion

What then happened to the impulse behind Mass-Observation? What became of its mission to borrow from surrealism and psychoanalysis and, using methods modelled on aspects of functionalist anthropology, generate an anthropology of ourselves? It did not live up to its promise.

By definition academics arrive after the event when owls have flown. In the area of cultural studies, or the anthropology of selves, the appearance of the academic lends *gravitas* and dignity to manifestations of the popular. At its inception, cultural studies in Britain sought, first, to bring to light the integrity and wholeness of working-class culture and community in Britain across several centuries and, second, to defend the space which had thus been created both against detractors at home (elitists of varying complexions) and against the arrival of mass-produced entertainments from across the Atlantic – Hoggart's 'shiny barbarism'. The quest for 'holism' that this implies, the existence of cultural wholes to be demarcated and delineated, was something British functionalist anthropology shared with the Mass-Observation movement in a very particular sense. For social anthropology in Britain, if we agree with Maurice Bloch, this 'holistic' approach was its very genius; its appreciation of the fact that societies were structured wholes. In this sense M-O shared similar impulses – simply it took on too much. The whole it took as its unit of study, as Harrisson's intellectual trajectory informs us, encompassed, to all intents and purposes, the world. The only theory that it had was (and this is perhaps hard to grasp in retrospect) the brilliant insight that these seemingly banal, everyday matters were, in fact, of importance and deserved, demanded even, intense study and analysis; and that this could be achieved as a populist movement, involving the very people under study. Here is a link to some of the strands of the postmodern impulse in recent anthropology, the Geertzian 'natives point of view', from which emerge the dialogic ethnographies such as that of Dwyer's *Moroccan Dialogues* (1982) or Dumont's *The Headman and I* (1978). However, the anthropological honesty, reflexivity and so forth, that we find in such accounts does not, sadly, remove the causes of economic inequality which set off the play of power in the modern world. We need to transcend a position which views societies as totalities, we need to think of systems and of process on a global scale, just as Harrisson attempted.

McGuigan is correct in suggesting that M-O did not outline a credible theoretical synthesis of its data,[16] but given the short span of its most intensive activity and the fact that a war was going on, the achievements of the group stand out as being remarkable. Doubtless there are many criticisms which we might wish to level at M-O.[17] A straightforward class breakdown, for example, demonstrates that many of the active Observers in Worktown appear to have been Oxbridge graduates (Harrisson 1961: 25); Harrisson himself was a product of the British public school system (Harrow), but it is correct to connect him, as Godfrey Smith does (Smith 1987), with the name of George Orwell (Eton). Harrisson's installing himself in Bolton for the 'Worktown' studies was motivated by similar reasons as Orwell's stays in Wigan, which led to *The Road to Wigan Pier* (1937). Indeed, Harrisson's version of cultural populism might have shared some of the flaws ascribed to Orwell by Raymond Williams (Williams 1971).[18] In this sense the M-O project lies closer to the roots of cultural studies in Britain than McGuigan suggests. Both Brantlinger and Turner, in their studies of British cultural studies, 'locate its beginnings in the post-war breakdown of the consensus about the direction and value of British cultural life' (quoted in Barker and Beezer 1992: 3). Of course, this had been precisely the motivation behind the establishment of M-O, some years earlier (the spirit of doubt associated now with postmodernism – which, seen in this light, starts to look like a cyclical disorder). The strained integration of what appears the 'holistic' account of the section 'Persons' in Harrisson's ethnographic account is based on the author's attempt to confront the so-called 'lowest amongst these low' (Harrisson 1937: 19) Melanesians (the inhabitants of Malekula) with the savage civilization of the West. His 'outline of tribal life' was attempted as the 'necessary foundation' (p. 15) of the story of 'savage civilization'. But the admission to the account of these other forces, the traders, missionaries, blackbirders and so forth, denied by the Malinowskian account, hint at what anthropologists were saying under their breath[19] and demonstrates the profound novelty of the book, both in its construction and its efforts to confront real historical forces.

Why, however, the ultimate failure of M-O? Was it simply a failure to raise adequate funds, the fervour finally blunted and recruited to the aims of market research? There may not have been much money for the anthropology of the colonial 'other', but outside the popular front of the war there was even less funding for the sort of research conducted by M-O, and it increasingly had to restrict itself to the tasks it was commisioned to perform, becoming, by degrees, a market-research company.

Interestingly it was after reading the work of the anthropologist Rivers, in 1914, and his observations that colonialism and the onslaught of the Europeans were destroying Melanesian will to live, that T.S. Eliot noted that modern materialism was having a similar effect upon British culture. If present trends were to continue, he wrote then, 'it will not be surprising if the population of the entire civilized world rapidly follows the fate of the Melanesians' (from his essay 'Marie Lloyd', quoted by Kuklick 1991: 294). Rivers had been dead for over a decade by the time Harrisson arrived in Malekula. Harrisson was there when his friend from college days, Malcom Lowry, was composing his modernist classic *Under the Volcano* in 'exotic' Mexican exile, noting the eerie intrusion of Peter Lorre's hand into the Mexican Day of the Dead (see Bowker 1993). Certainly Harrisson's life shares something with that of a novelist such as Lowry. Perhaps, too, as Manganaro suggests, anthropology also holds a place in the modernist movement. Perhaps too, anthropology and cultural studies can use these joint facilities to explore the consequences of late-modernity, and see, as Harrisson did so clearly, the roots of the modern world in the past; to see clearly the false boundaries that have often been placed on research in the name of totalities. This is the new world of migrancy and diaspora, the centre no longer holds, the homeless are all we have. The tired voice of Theodor Adorno rings across the years: 'Dwelling, in the proper sense, is now impossible. Today, we should have to add: it is part of morality not to be at home in one's home' (Adorno 1978: 38–9). The brute force of the transnational is all, propelling various migrant actors around the world, faster and faster. 'For a man who no longer has a homeland, writing becomes a place to live. In it he inevitably produces . . . refuse and lumber. In the end, the writer is not even allowed to live in his writing' (Adorno, quoted in Daniel 1992: 33–4). Is it that this refuse and lumber is also the wreckage at the feet of Walter Benjamin's angel of history (Benjamin 1968) as it is propelled backwards into the future by the storm of progress? In a BBC broadcast made in 1938, Humphrey Jennings discussed the subject of poetry and national life. He began with a discussion of the 'poets' of the Trobriand Islands, cultivating their crops and reciting their garden magic. Towards the end of the talk he mentions the French surrealist poet Apollinaire and his vision of the poet – another source, it could be argued, for Benjamin's vision. Our relation to the past is best understood, Jennings suggests, in relation to Apollinaire,

> who said that unlike other men he didn't stand with his back to the past and face the future; on the contrary, he stood with his back to the future, because he was unable to see it, and with his face to the past, because it was in the past that he could discover who he was and how he had come to be him.
>
> (Jennings, quoted Jackson 1993: 281–2)

Notes

I would like to express a debt of gratitude to David Morley for his extremely detailed and helpful comments on several evolving drafts of this paper.

1 This is a reference to the work of philosopher I.C. Jarvie and his book *The Revolution in Anthropology* (1964).

2 The sales of the book were by all accounts exceptional. Kuklick provides a plausible explanation for this, in the era of the First World War she suggests 'disillusioned intellectuals found the objective correlatives to their feelings of despair in his eternal images of dying kings and parched fields' (Kuklick 1991: 9). For more detail see Ackerman's (1987) biography of Frazer, *J.G. Frazer: His Life and Work*.

3 Just to introduce a comparative perspective of sorts, it is only in his personal diaries that Malinowski's frustration with his 'native' informants really comes through. The method he outlined, participant observation, does not really deal with questions of duplicity or plain concealment. In a different context, that of collecting folktales from the black population in the southern states of America, 'deeply ingrained attitudes and stategies remained long after slavery to plague white folklorists attempting to collect slave lore' (Levine 1977: 100). Such a statement demonstrates that there is a large area itself concealed by the questions of 'natives' and lies. See Bhabha (1993) for an interesting exploration of the topic from the perspective of the post-colonial critic. The folklorists often spent many years before they were made aware of certain observances or aspects of communal behaviour. In this light it could be charged that Malinowskian-type fieldwork is too limited in time to provide the anthropological omnipotence demonstrated by most textual versions of the anthropologist's practice. The ability to be deceived is at the root of another great anthropological scandal, the Freeman/Mead controversy (Freeman 1983). Finally I would like to return to Lawrence Levine's book for a refreshing perspective on the knowledge and power implications of social research. Levine tells of the efforts of sociologist and song-collector, Howard Odum, to record the lyrics of a song being sung by a road gang outside his Georgia home. As Levine has it, 'When he finally made out the words, they were: "White man settin' on wall/White man settin' on wall/White man settin' on wall all day long,/Wastin' his time, wastin' his time." ' (quoted in Levine 1977: 205).

Still, Malinowski was an advance on some. An early field anthropologist, appointed to the government of what was then called Southern Nigeria in 1907, Northcote

Thomas, apparently proposed to ingratiate himself with his subjects by 'donning false teeth filed in African fashion' (Kuklick 1991: 201).

4 This image of the anthropologist as hero was famously used by Susan Sontag (1961) in a review of the work of Levi-Strauss, whose own fieldwork was not, in fact, in the Malinowskian mould. A much closer reading of the anthropological developments up until 1922 and the publication of *Argonauts*, reveal that Malinowski was simply pulling together a number of strategies which had already been developed (Urry 1993). Malinowski is slowly being revealed to be a more complex figure than my simplified account suggests. It has recently been suggested, for example, that he was heavily influenced by the writings of Nietzsche (Thornton and Skalnik 1993).

5 For a discussion of competing paradigms such as diffusionism or evolutionism within anthropology, see Kuper (1983). A chief rival of Malinowski, the diffusionist Elliot Smith (based at University College London) was of the opinion that 'to sit on a Melanesian Island for a couple of years and listen to the gossip of villagers' required no scientific skills (Kuklick 1991: 211).

6 Kenyatta's book is a fascinating one on a number of counts. It marks the first in a variety of studies which have come to be described as 'anthropology at home' to use the expression in its new incarnation (Jackson 1987). The latter movement is necessitated by the fact that much of the world is too violent for innocent anthropologists, many of whom are no longer very heroic, so they are forced to conduct research at home and do battle with sociologists and their ilk over questions such as primacy of methods and so forth. Kenyatta's case was wholly different and can be better viewed as an early example of indigenous anthropology. Of interest to my concerns in this chapter is Malinowski's introduction to Kenyatta's book. 'Anthropology begins at home', he writes, 'has become the watchword of modern social science' (Malinowski, in Kenyatta 1938: vii). This was written at the time in which Malinowski was himself involved with M-O.

7 Although an earlier expression of the position is contained in Marcus and Cushman (1982).

8 The position adopted by Adam Kuper (1994) makes this rejection of such new forms clear from a British perspective.

9 Although this chapter owes much to Henrika Kuklick's patient research, she wrongly gives the impression, perhaps unintentionally, that Harrisson's work represents part of a genre of travellers' accounts which 'offered thrilling reports of explorers' physical heroism in the wilds of Empire' (Kuklick 1991: 13). In her account, this is to be distinguished from the anthropologists who forwent their armchairs in pursuit of scientific regularities, rather than the merely exotic or curious. In fact Harrisson had consulted a number of ethnographic 'authorities' and had read the account of Malekula written by Bernard Deacon, who had died of blackwater fever in the field. Deacon, in turn, had gone to the field with a large number of the field notes of John Layard, a maverick figure in the history of British anthropology. When Deacon's notes were prepared for publication after his death, large sections of Layard's notes were incorporated into the text without acknowledgement. Some might find cause here to talk of intertextuality (see MacClancey 1986).

10 Judging from the ethnographic accounts of the region, a common interest. An often cited account is Strathern's *The Rope of Moka* (1971).

11 Such accounts are of course more common now. Classic examples include the work of historian Dee Brown, notably *Bury My Heart at Wounded Knee* (1970) and, more relevant here perhaps, Moorehead's unjustly ignored account (1966) of the conquest of the Pacific zones, *The Fatal Impact* (although Obeysekere (1989) does draw attention to this work). More recent examples include the work of John Hemming, for example his book *The Conquest of the Incas* (1983) or Kirkpatrick Sale's *The Conquest of Paradise* (1992). The use of such materials as navigators' diaries in the reconstruction of various

aspects of the moment of conquest has been much in evidence in literary studies of late. Two of the most well-known accounts in this respect are Todorov (1984) and Greenblatt (1991). The first of the modern world's 'spaces of terror' (Taussig 1987), the destruction of the Guanches (the indigenous inhabitants of the Canary Islands) is described in Crosby (1986). It is ironic that Malinowski completed *Argonauts* in the Canaries.

12 On two occasions in *Savage Civilisation* Harrison refers to projects dealing with 'copra and combines' (p. 298) and in a note in the bibliography he claims that he is working, with Oliver Bell, on a study of Leverhulme and Unilever (p. 439). On Harrisson's life, see Green (1970).

It is perhaps worth noting that one of the 'cardinal figures' (Gates 1988: 180) in the twentieth-century Afro-American literary canon, Zora Neale Hurston did graduate work in anthropology at Columbia University in 1927 under Franz Boaz. Already by that date she reported to Boaz that in parts of the American south 'The bulk of the population now spends its leisure in the motion picture theatres or with the phonograph' (quoted in Levine 1977: 227). Her work *Tell My Horse*, based on work in Jamaica and Haiti bears comparison with Harrisson's *Savage Civilisation* in its form and flagrant disregard for the norms of 'ethnographic authority' (Clifford 1983). For a brief survey of Hurston's ethnographic work see Gordon (1990).

13 Asked about the information he collects, Muckerji announces that:

> 'I type it out on my little Corona and send it to the organisers – we call it Mass Observation.'
> 'Do they print it?'
> 'They file it for reference. Perhaps one day in a big book – without my name. We work,' he said regretfully, 'for science.'
>
> (Greene 1971: 142)

I would like to thank Josep Llobera for putting me on the trail of this reference, originally published in 1939.

14 In France the links between ethnography and surrealism were, on the whole, stronger: see Clifford (1981), Webster (1990) and Richardson (1993) for recent anthropological appreciations of these connections. Jennings's posthumously published work, *Pandaemonium* (1985), lives up to Walter Benjamin's surrealist-inspired desire to produce a book made up entirely of quotations. It is a compilation of quotations from works dealing with the coming of the industrial revolution.

15 By a very strange quirk of fate it was a meeting with Harrisson in Sarawak which led Derek Freeman to what Freeman described as a 'Road to Damascus' experience in his notions about human behaviour and which ultimately led him to build his attack on the ethnographic *oeuvre* of Margaret Mead – a cause almost as celebrated as the Malinowski diaries themselves (see Stocking 1989: 255).

16 This is no more than Harrisson and Madge claimed for some of their earlier work anyway. As they wrote in *First Year's Work*, 'The original purpose of the Day surveys was to collect a mass of data without any selective principle, as a preliminary to detailed studies of carefully chosen topics' (quoted by Calder and Sheridan 1994: 5).

17 Gender and M-O, for example, is an interesting area. The early study *The Pub and the People*, Mass Observation (1987) could be said to have a 'masculine attitude', but then in all probability so did Bolton pubs in the 1930s. One of the observers makes enquiries about joining the Royal and Antediluvian Order of Buffaloes. A drinker told him 'We're good company . . . You get four pound when your wife dies' (p. 275).

18 At times it is evident that Harrisson did not view the masses as a homogeneous entity. Writing about national morale during the Second World War, he criticized those who did take such an attitide. Harrisson argued that it was not possible to talk of a single 'national morale' as there were 45 million national morales (see Richards and Sheridan 1987).

19 Such accounts also fall in line with other versions of pre-lapsarian humanity which abound in the literature. For a good account of such writings, see Pagden (1982). On civilizational contacts in general, see Bitterli (1989). Bitterli's work resonates strongly with the sentiments underlying that classic of French anthropological prose, Levi-Strauss's *Triste Tropiques* (1973). If we are to believe Levi-Strauss, this book was to mark his swan-song as an anthropologist, hence the liberties he took with the 'genre' (Eribon 1991).

References

ACKERMAN, R., 1987: *J.G. Frazer: His Life and Work*. Cambridge: Cambridge University Press.

ADORNO, T., 1978: *Minima Moralia*. London: New Left Books.

ANDERSON, P., 1969: 'Components of the National Culture', in R. Blackburn and A. Cockburn (eds.) *Student Power*. Harmondsworth: Penguin.

ASAD, T., 1973: *Anthropology and the Colonial Encounter*. London: Ithaca Press.

BARKER, M. and BEEZER, A. (eds.), 1992: *Reading into Cultural Studies*. London: Routledge.

BENJAMIN, W., 1968: *Illuminations*. New York: Schocken Books.

BHABHA, H., 1993: *The Location of Culture*. London: Routledge.

BITTERLI, U., 1989: *Cultures in Conflict*. Cambridge: Polity Press.

BLOCH, M., 1983: *Marxism and Anthropology*. Oxford: Oxford University Press.

BOWKER, G., 1993: *Pursued by Furies: A Life of Malcolm Lowry*. London: Harper Collins.

BRANTLINGER, P., 1990: *Crusoe's Footprints: Cultural Studies in Britain and America*. London: Routledge.

BROWN, D., 1970: *Bury My Heart at Wounded Knee*. London: Holt, Reinhart & Winston.

BULMER, M. (ed.), 1985: *Essays on the History of British Sociological Research*. Cambridge: Cambridge University Press.

CALDER, A., 1985: 'Mass-Observation 1937–1949', in M. Bulmer, (ed.) *Essays on the History of British Sociological Research*. Cambridge: Cambridge University Press.

CALDER, A. and SHERIDAN, D., 1984: *Speak for Yourself*. London: Jonathan Cape.

CHAMBERS, I., 1986: *Popular Culture: The Metropolitan Experience*. London: Methuen.

CLIFFORD, J., 1981: 'On Ethnographic Surrealism', *Comparative Studies in Society and History*, 23: pp. 539–64.

CLIFFORD, J., 1983: 'On Ethnographic Authority', *Representations*, 1: pp. 118–46.

CLIFFORD, J., 1988: 'On Ethnographic Self-Fashioning: Conrad and Malinowski', in J. Clifford *The Predicament of Culture: Twentieth Century Ethnography, Literature and Art*. Cambridge, MA: Harvard University Press.

CLIFFORD, J. and MARCUS, G. (eds.), 1986: *Writing Culture*. Berkeley, CA: University of California Press.

CRAPANZANO, V., 1992: *Hermes' Dilemma and Hamlet's Desire: On the Epistemology of Interpretation*. Cambridge, MA: Harvard University Press.

CROSBY, A., 1986: *Ecological Imperialism*. Cambridge: Cambridge University Press.

DANIEL, J.O., 1992: 'Temporary Shelter: Adorno's Exile and the Language of Home', *New Formations*, 17.

DUMONT, J.P., 1978: *The Headman and I*. Austin, TX: University of Texas Press.

DWYER, K., 1982: *Moroccan Dialogues*. Baltimore, MD: Johns Hopkins University Press.

ELIOT, T.S., 1947: *Notes Towards a Definition of Culture*. London: Faber & Faber.

ERIBON, D., 1991: *Conversations with Claude Levi-Strauss*. Chicago: University of Chicago Press.

FARDON, R. (ed.), 1990: *Localising Strategies*. Edinburgh: Scottish Academic Press.
FIRTH, R., 1988: 'Introduction', in B. Malinowski *A Diary in the Strict Sense of the Term*. London: Athlone.
FREEMAN, D., 1983: *Margaret Mead and Samoa: The Making and Unmaking of an Anthropologist*. Cambridge, MA: Harvard University Press.
GATES, JR, H.L., 1988: The Signifying Monkey: A Theory of African American Literary Criticism. Oxford: Oxford University Press.
GEERTZ, C., 1988: *Works and Lives: The Anthropologist as Author*. Oxford: Polity Press.
GORDON, D., 1990: 'The Politics of Ethnographic Authority: Race and Writing in the Ethnography of Margaret Mead and Zora Neale Hurston', in M. Manganaro (ed.) *Modernist Anthropology: From Fieldwork to Text*. Princeton, NJ: Princeton University Press.
GREEN, T., 1970: *The Adventurers*. London: Michael Joseph.
GREENBLATT, S., 1980: *Renaissance Self-fashioning*. Chicago: University of Chicago Press.
GREENBLATT, S., 1991: *Marvellous Possessions*. Oxford: Oxford University Press.
GREENE, G., 1971: *The Confidential Agent*. London: Heinemann. (First published 1939).
GRIMSHAW, A. and HART, K., 1994: 'Anthropology and the Crisis of the Intellectuals', *Critique of Anthropology*, 14 (3).
HALL, S., 1972: 'The Social Eye of Picture Post', in *Working Papers in Cultural Studies*, 2. University of Birmingham.
HARRISSON, T., 1937: *Savage Civilisation*. London: Victor Gollancz.
HARRISSON, T., 1938: *Borneo Jungle*. London: Lindsey Drummond.
HARRISSON, T., 1961: *Britain Revisited*. London: Victor Gollancz.
HARRISSON, T., 1976: *Living Through the Blitz*. Harmondsworth: Penguin.
HARRISSON, T. and MADGE, C., 1937: *Mass-Observation*. London: Frederick Muller.
HARRISSON, T. and MADGE, C., 1938: *First Year's Work 1937–38*, with an essay by Bronislaw Malinowski. London: Lindsey Drummond.
HEMMING, J., 1983: *The Conquest of the Incas*, revised edition. Harmondsworth: Penguin.
HOGGART, R., 1957: *The Uses of Literacy*. London: Chatto & Windus.
HYMES, D., 1974: *Reinventing Anthropology*. New York: Vintage.
JACKSON, A., 1987: *The Humphrey Jennings Film Reader*. Manchester: Carcanet.
JARVIE, I.C., 1964: *The Revolution in Anthropology*. London: Routledge & Kegan Paul.
JEFFERY, T., 1978: *Mass-Observation: A Short History*. University of Birmingham: Centre for Contemporary Cultural Studies.
JENNINGS, H., 1985: *Pandaemonium*. London: Pan.
KABBANI, R., 1986: *Europe's Myths of Orient*. London: Macmillan.
KENYATTA, J., 1938: *Facing Mount Kenya: The Tribal Life of The Gikuyu*. London: Secker & Warburg.
KNAUFT, B., 1994: 'Pushing Anthropology Past the Posts: Critical Notes on Cultural Anthropology and Cultural Studies', *Critique of Anthropology*, 14 (2).
KUKLICK, H., 1984: 'Tribal Exemplars: Images of Political Authority in British Anthropology, 1885–1945', in G. Stocking (ed.).
KUPER, A., 1983: *Anthropologists and Anthropology: The British School 1922–72*. Harmondsworth: Penguin.
KUPER, A., 1994: 'Culture, Identity and the Project of a Cosmopolitan Anthropology', *Man*, 29 (3).
LEVINE, L.W., 1977: *Black Culture and Black Consciousness: Afro-American Folk Thought from Slavery to Freedom*. New York: Oxford University Press.

LEVI-STRAUSS, C., 1973: *Tristes Tropiques*. London: Cape.
MACCLANCEY, J., 1986: 'Unconventional Character and Disciplinary Convention', in G. Stocking (ed.).
MCGUIGAN, J., 1992: *Cultural Populism*. London: Routledge.
MALINOWSKI, B., 1922: *Argonauts of the Western Pacific*. London: Routledge.
MALINOWSKI, B., 1935: *Coral Gardens and their Magic*. New York: American Book Co.
MALINOWSKI, B., 1935: *A Scientific Theory of Culture and Other Essays*. London: Allen & Unwin.
MALINOWSKI, B., 1988: *A Diary in the Strict Sense of the Term*. London: Athlone. (First published in 1967).
MANGANARO, M. (ed.), 1990: *Modernist Anthropology*. Princeton, NJ: Princeton University Press.
MARCUS, G. and CUSHMAN, D., 1982: 'Ethnographies as Texts', in B. Siegal (ed.) *Annual Review of Anthropology*, vol. II. Palo Alto, CA: Annual Review.
MARCUS, G. and FISHER, M., 1986: *Anthropology as Cultural Critique*. Chicago: University of Chicago Press.
MASS-OBSERVATION, 1939: *Britain*. Harmondsworth: Penguin.
MASS OBSERVATION, 1987: *The Pub and the People*. London: Century Hutchinson. (First published 1943).
MOOREHEAD, A., 1966: *The Fatal Impact: The Invasion of the South Pacific*. London: Hamilton.
OBEYSEKERE, G., 1989: *The Apotheosis of Captain Cook: European Mythmaking in the Pacific*. Princeton, NJ: Princeton University Press.
ORWELL, G., 1937: *The Road to Wigan Pier*. London: Gollancz.
PAGDEN, A., 1982: *The Fall of Natural Man: The American Indian and the Origins of Comparative Ethnology*. Cambridge: Cambridge University Press.
POOL, R., 1991: 'Postmodern Ethnography?', *Critique of Anthropology*, 11 (4).
RICHARDS, J. and SHERIDAN, D. (eds.), 1987: *Mass-Observation at the Movies*. London: Routledge & Kegan Paul.
RICHARDSON, M., 1993: 'An Encounter of Wise Men and Cyclops Women', *Critique of Anthropology*, 13 (1).
RIVERS, W.H.R., 1914: *The History of Melanesian Society*, 2 volumes. Cambridge: Cambridge University Press.
ROSALDO, R., 1986: 'From the Door of His Tent: The Fieldworker and the Inquisitor', in J. Clifford and G. Marcus (eds.) 1986: *Anthropology as Cultural Critique*. Chicago: University of Chicago Press.
SAID, E., 1978: *Orientalism*. London: Routledge & Kegan Paul.
SALE, K., 1992: *The Conquest of Paradise*. London: Macmillan.
SCHOLTE, R., 1987: 'The Literary Turn in Anthropology', *Critique of Anthropology*, 7 (1).
SCOTT, D., 1992: 'Criticism and Culture: Theory and Post-Colonial Claims on Anthropological Disciplinarity', *Critique of Anthropology*, 12 (4).
SHOSTAK, M., 1983: *Nisa!*. Cambridge, MA: Harvard University Press.
SMITH, G., 1987: 'Introduction', in Mass-Observation *The Pub and the People*. London: Century Hutchinson. (First published 1943).
SONTAG, S., 1961: 'The Anthropologist as Hero', in S. Sontag *Against Interpretation*. New York: Dell Publishing.
STOCKING, G. (ed.), 1986: *Malinowski, Rivers, Benedict and Others: Essays on Culture and Personality*. Madison, WI: University of Wisconsin Press.
STOCKING, G., 1989: *Romantic Motives: Essays on Anthropological Sensibility*. Madison, WI: University of Wisconsin Press.
STRATHERN, A., 1971: *The Rope of Moka*. Cambridge: Cambridge University Press.

TAUSSIG, M., 1987: *Shamanism, Colonialism, and the Wildman: A Study in Terror and Healing*. Chicago: University of Chicago Press.
THOMAS, N., 1994: *Colonialism's Culture*. Cambridge: Polity Press.
THORNTON, R. and SKALNIK, P., 1993: *The Early Writings of Bronislaw Malinowski*. Cambridge: Cambridge University Press.
TODOROV, T., 1984: *The Conquest of America: The Question of the Other*. New York: Harper Row.
TURNER, G., 1990: *British Cultural Studies*. Boston, MA: Unwin Hyman.
TYLER, S., 1987: 'Still Rayting', *Critique of Anthropology*, 7 (1).
URRY, J., 1993: *Before Social Anthropology: Essays on the History of British Anthropology*. Chur, Switzerland: Harwood Academic Publishers.
WEBSTER, S., 1990: 'The Historical Materialist Critique of Surrealism and Postmodernist Ethnography' in M. Manganaro (ed.) 1990: *Modernist Anthropology*. Princeton, NJ: Princeton University Press.
WILLIAMS, R., 1958: *Culture and Society*. London: Chatto & Windus.
WILLIAMS, R., 1971: *Orwell*. London: Fontana.
WOLF, E., 1982: *Europe and the People Without History*. Berkeley, CA: University of California Press.
YOUNG, M. (ed.), 1979: *The Ethnography of Malinowski: The Trobriand Islands 1915–18*. London: Routledge & Kegan Paul.

Index